CNE 4 Short C

Dorothy Cady

Drew Heywood

Debra Niedermiller-Chaffins

New Riders

New Riders Publishing, Indianapolis, IN

CNE 4 Short Course

By Dorothy Cady

Published by:
New Riders Publishing
201 West 103rd Street
Indianapolis, IN 46290 USA

Printed in the United States of America 1 2 3 4 5 6 7 8 9 0

CIP data available upon request

Warning and Disclaimer

This book is designed to provide information about the NetWare computer program. Every effort has been made to make this book as complete and as accurate as possible, but no warranty or fitness is implied.

The information is provided on an "as is" basis. The author and New Riders Publishing shall have neither liability nor responsibility to any person or entity with respect to any loss or damages arising from the information contained in this book or from the use of the disks or programs that may accompany it.

Publisher Don Fowley
Publishing Manager Emmett Dulaney
Marketing Manager Ray Robinson
Managing Editor Tad Ringo

Acquisitions Editor
Alicia Buckley

Software Specialist
Steve Weiss

Production Editor
John Sleeva

Copy Editors
Nancy Albright
Gail Burlakoff
Lillian Yates

Technical Editors
Robert King
Tim Petru

Associate Marketing Manager
Tamara Apple

Acquisitions Coordinator
Tracy Turgeson

Publisher's Assistant
Karen Opal

Cover Designer
Jay Corpus

Book Designer
Sandra Schroeder

Production Team Supervisor
Laurie Casey

Graphics Image Specialists
Jason Hand, Clint Lahnen, Laura Robbins, Craig Small, Todd Wente

Production Analysts
Angela D. Bannan
Bobbi Satterfield

Production Team
Heather Butler, Angela Calvert, Kim Cofer, Kevin Foltz, David Garratt, Aleata Howard, Joe Millay, Erika Millen, Gina Rexrode, Erich J. Richter, Christine Tyner, Karen Walsh

Indexer
Bront Davis

About the Authors

Dorothy L. Cady is a former senior technical writer for Novell, Inc. in Provo, Utah. Ms. Cady started with Novell in 1990 as a team leader for the Software Testing Department's Documentation Testing Team, helping to ensure the quality of the documentation that ships with NetWare 2, 3, and 4, NetWare Lite, and Personal NetWare products.

Ms. Cady is a Certified Novell Instructor (CNI), a Certified Novell Engineer (CNE), a Certified Novell Administrator (CNA), and an Enterprise CNE (ECNE).

Dorothy is now a freelance writer and instructor with over twenty years experience in the computer industry, both in private and public service. She also is the author of *CNA Study Guide* and *New Riders' Guide to NetWare Certification*, as well as co-author of other New Riders books. She is also the author of *Bulletproof Documentation: Creating Quality Through Testing.*

Drew Heywood has been involved in the micro-computer industry since he purchased an Apple IIe in 1979. For the past nine years, he has focused on networking. From 1991 through February 1995, Drew was a product line manager at NRP, where he launched NRP's network book line and expanded the line to include some of the most successful book titles in the industry. Drew and his wife, Blythe, have most recently founded InfoWorks, Inc. to support his dual interest as a computer book author and a consultant. Drew was the author of NRP's *Inside Windows NT Server, Inside NetWare, Fourth Edition,* and has contributed to several NRP books, including *Networking Technologies* and *CNE Short Course*, both of which are members of NRP's CNE Training Guide series.

Debra Niedermiller-Chaffins is Training Manager for MicroAge of Southeast Michigan in Novi, Michigan. Ms. Niedermiller-Chaffins has been working since 1988 to help organizations develop autonomy and self-sufficiency in training future Certified NetWare Engineers operations. She is a Certified NetWare Instructor and a CNE, specializing in training future CNEs. In addition to teaching, Ms. Niedermiller-Chaffins also supports a small client base, which provides her with a background of real-world networking scenarios. She is the author of *Inside Novell NetWare, Special Edition, NetWare Training Guide: Managing NetWare Systems, NetWare Training Guide: Networking Technologies,* and *Inside NetWare Lite,* also published by New Riders Publishing.

Trademark Acknowledgments

Acknowledgments

I would like to thank Emmett Dulaney for always looking out for my best interests—a rare quality in a Publishing Manager. I would also like to thank Robert King and Tim Petru for their help and expertise in this book. A special thanks to the staff at New Riders, especially John Sleeva who was patient, tolerant, and dedicated to the task at hand.

Contents at a Glance

Table of Contents

Part III: Networking Technologies

Part VI: NetWare 4.1 Installation

Introduction

The staff of New Riders Publishing is committed to bringing you the very best in computer reference material. Each New Riders book is the result of months of work by authors and staff who research and refine the information contained within its covers.

As part of this commitment to you, the NRP reader, New Riders invites your input. Please let us know if you enjoy this book, if you have trouble with the information and examples presented, or if you have a suggestion for the next edition.

Please note, though: New Riders staff cannot serve as a technical resource for NetWare or for related questions about software- or hardware-related problems. Please refer to the documentation that accompanies NetWare or to the applications' Help systems.

If you have a question or comment about any New Riders book, there are several ways to contact New Riders Publishing. We will respond to as many readers as we can. Your name, address, or phone number will never become part of a mailing list or be used for any purpose other than to help us continue to bring you the best books possible. You can write to us at the following address:

New Riders Publishing
Attn: Publisher
201 W. 103rd Street
Indianapolis, IN 46290

If you prefer, you can fax New Riders Publishing at (317) 581-4670.

You can send electronic mail to New Riders at the following Internet address:

`edulaney@newriders.mcp.com`

NRP is an imprint of Macmillan Computer Publishing. To obtain a catalog or information, or to purchase any Macmillan Computer Publishing book, call (800) 428-5331.

Thank you for selecting *CNE 4 Short Course*!

PART PART PART PART PART PART PART PART PART PART PART PART

I

NetWare 4.1 Administration

CHAPTER 1

Understanding NetWare 4.x

Those of you already familiar with NetWare 3 networks will find several differences, as well as several similarities, in the way NetWare 3 and NetWare 4 provide basic network services. The purpose of this chapter is to lay the foundation for a more complete understanding of how to administer a NetWare 4 network. To accomplish that goal, this chapter provides information about the following topics:

- *Basic network components and function*
- *NetWare Directory Services and the Directory tree*

Basic Network Function and Components

When discussing a network in the context of Novell networks, the type of network being discussed is a *client-server* network (one in which at least one computer functions as a network file server, providing services to other network computers called clients).

Basic Network Function

The basic function of a network is to enable users to share resources, as well as to access resources through other networks or remote hosts. This capability is provided by software (called the *operating system*) that controls the access to network resources. NetWare 4 is a network operating system.

Network Components

A network consists of two or more computers connected in a manner that enables them to share resources, as well as to access resources through other networks or remote hosts. The definition of a network generally includes the physical components associated with a network. At a minimum, those components include the following:

- File server
- Workstation
- Network board (one for each file server and workstation)
- Communications media

NetWare 4 networks include computers running the NetWare 4 operating system. These computers are called *network servers.*

A *client* is any device that requests services or resources from a server. The most common type of client is a computer, commonly called a *workstation,* used to access network resources. NetWare 4 supports computers running the following computer operating systems:

- DOS
- Microsoft Windows
- OS/2
- Macintosh
- Unix

A *network board* is a circuit board that provides communication between computers.

Communications media is the connection (link) between network boards. Two of the most commonly used communications media are coaxial cable and twisted-pair.

Another basic component of a network includes peripheral devices (such as printers or modems). Although not a required minimum component, peripherals usually are considered part of a network's basic hardware components.

NetWare Directory Services and the Directory Tree

You already may be familiar with the term *directory services.* In general, the term refers to the directory and file structure associated with a network file server's storage of programs and user data. In NetWare 4, as in other NetWare and competing network products, directory services remain the same. In NetWare 4; however, the term *NetWare Directory Services* (NDS) refers to something other than the NetWare directory and file structure. NDS refers to the directory or naming service for the database of network resources that NetWare 4 maintains. An understanding of NDS, what it is and how it differs from the network's general directory services, is key to understanding and administering a NetWare 4 network.

Understanding NDS

Unlike the directory services provided by the network, NDS does not provide directory and file services. Instead, NDS provides information about and access to all the network's logical resources.

For example, general directory services would provide you with information about and access to a specific user data file. NDS, however, provides information about and access to such things as the user's network account, rather than a particular file the user has stored on the network. This means that, through NDS, you can find out information about the user's account, such as the user's full name, login identification, telephone number, and other related information.

Networks provide access to a wide variety of network services, including the following:

- Printing
- Security
- Electronic messaging

NetWare Directory Services (NDS) is another type of network service. NDS, like other network services, is provided by file servers on the network. Only NetWare 4 file servers (as opposed to NetWare 3 or NetWare 2) can provide NDS.

The primary responsibility of NDS is to provide information about and access to network services. All network client requests for network services must use NDS. When a network client requests information about network resources, services from the network, or access to network services, NDS locates the necessary information and then provides the requested information, service, or access.

NDS is a replicatable, partitionable, distributed database containing information about network resources. Because it can be *replicated* (copied), *partitioned* (divided), and distributed, all or any specified portion or copy of the database can be stored on any NetWare 4 file server in the network. This means that, although entire copies or copies of portions or divisions (*partitions*) of the database may be stored on different servers in the network, the information contained within NDS can be made accessible from any client on the network. This is what gives NetWare 4 its global design.

Understanding the NDS Database

The NDS database is made up of the following three named items:

- Objects
- Properties
- Values

Objects

Every resource available on the network is represented in the NDS database as an object. An *object* is simply a record of information about that particular network resource. The network resource itself—whether a physical resource, such as a printer, or a logical resource, such as a group of users—is represented in the NDS database as an object.

The following three *object classes,* or types of objects, are allowed in the NDS database (see fig. 1.1):

- [Root]
- Container
- Leaf

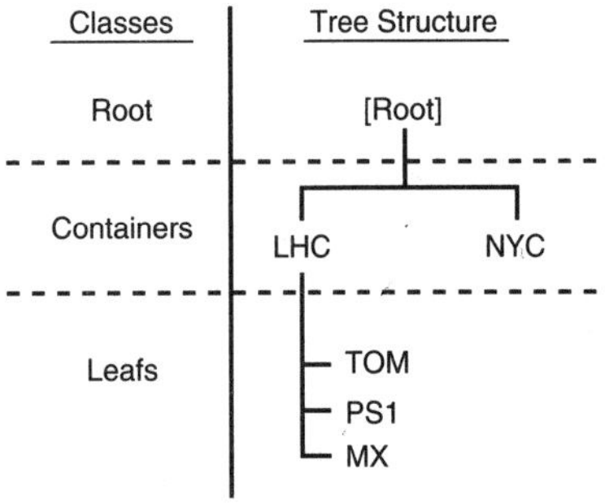

Figure 1.1
NDS object classes.

As with the general directory structure, the NDS directory structure is referred to as a *tree structure.* This description is appropriate because the NDS directory structure is arranged hierarchically, much as directories, subdirectories, and files are arranged in a hierarchical order resembling an upside-down tree in the general directory structure. In addition, as the DOS-based general directory structure has a top, represented by a drive letter and referred to as the *root,* the NDS structure begins with a top level, also called the root. In NDS, the root is referred to as the *Root object,* and is referenced as [Root] or [Treename].

> **Note:** There can be only one Root per NDS database. That root can contain only Country, Organization, and Alias objects.

In the general Directory tree structure, directories and files exist. In the NDS tree structure, container objects and leaf objects exist.

A *container object* is any NDS object that can contain or hold other objects. Container objects are similar to directories in the general directory structure, because directories can contain other directories or files.

> **Note:** Although sometimes referred to as a container object, [Root] is not a true container object for the following reasons:
>
> - It is created by NetWare 4 when the first NetWare 4 server is installed on the network.
> - You cannot move, delete, or rename it.

Following are the three defined classes of container objects:

- **Country (C).** Used to provide a logical division of the tree into countries, using two-character abbreviations (such as US for United States of America)

> **Note:** This class of container objects is optional. If used, it must be placed immediately below [Root]. You can only place Organization and Alias objects beneath the Country container.

- **Organization (O).** Used to provide a logical grouping of network resources, such as entire companies or only departments within a company.

Note: This class of container objects is required. Organization objects can be placed in Country or in other Organization objects, but cannot be placed in Organizational Unit objects. All objects (except an Alias object that points to [Root], Country, or Organization) can be placed in an Organization container.

- **Organizational Unit (OU).** Used to provide additional logical grouping of network resources into subgroups, such as company departments or teams.

Note: This class of container objects is optional. It can contain other OUs, and all objects except [Root], Country, and Organization. In addition, although it can contain Alias objects, it cannot contain any Alias objects that point to [Root], Country, or Organization.

A *leaf object* is any NDS object that cannot contain or hold other objects. Leaf objects are similar to files in the general directory structure, because files cannot contain or hold other files or directories.

Of the variety of leaf objects that exist, the following are some that are frequently referenced:

- **Alias.** A pointer to another object in the database
- **Computer.** Print server or other computer that does not provide file storage and retrieval services (such as a router)
- **Directory Map.** Path pointer, usually directed at a frequently used path such as an application directory
- **Group.** List of users in need of common access rights
- **NetWare Server.** Network file server
- **Organizational Role.** A position or responsibility to which different users can be assigned at different times
- **Print Server.** Network print server
- **Printer.** Printer physically connected to the network
- **Profile.** Login script for multiple users
- **Print Queue.** Queue into which print jobs can be placed to be processed
- **User.** Network user
- **Volume.** Physical volume on a NetWare file server

Properties

For each object on the network, the NDS database can store certain types of information. The types of information about any given object (that can be stored in the NDS database) are called that object's *properties.*

For example, the NDS database can store various types of information about the User object, including the user's name, address, telephone number, and so on. These types of information constitute some of the properties of the User object.

Although some properties are the same for different object classes, some object classes may have properties that are more specific to that object class.

For example, every object class contains the Access Control List (ACL) property. Only leaf objects, such as Directory Map, User, and so on, can have a Common Name (CN) property, however.

Values

The information stored in each of an object's properties is called that property's *value.*

For example, the value of the ACL property for a given object is the list of other objects that can access this object. This is true regardless of the class of object with which the ACL property is associated. In other words, the ACL property of a User object and the ACL property of a Printer object contain the same type of information (a list of users with access to the object), even though the actual content (value) of the list may differ (see fig. 1.2).

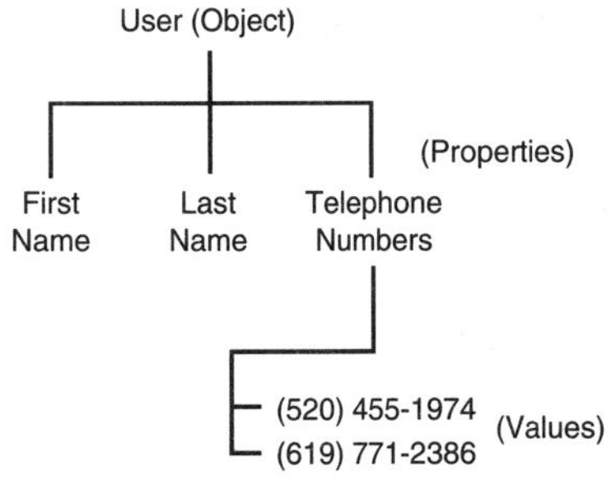

Figure 1.2
Property values.

Questions

1. The software that controls the access to network resources is called the ______ software.

   ○ A. operating system

   ○ B. workstation

   ○ C. client

   ○ D. peripheral

2. The basic function of a network is to ______, as well as to ______.

   ☐ A. print documents

   ☐ B. allow users to share resources

   ☐ C. provide access to remote resources

   ☐ D. save money

3. The ______ operating system is *not* supported by NetWare 4.

   ○ A. Unix

   ○ B. DOS

   ○ C. Macintosh

   ○ D. LSL

4. A ______ is any device that requests services or resources from a server.

   ○ A. media

   ○ B. peripheral

   ○ C. server

   ○ D. client

5. Although not required minimum components, ______are usually considered part of the basic hardware components of a network.

   ○ A. media

   ○ B. peripherals

   ○ C. servers

   ○ D. clients

6. Country, Organization, and Organizational Unit are all ______ objects?

   ○ A. leaf

   ○ B. container

   ○ C. ACL

   ○ D. [Root]

7. Of the following, which *three* are named items in the NDS database?

   ☐ A. object

   ☐ B. property

   ☐ C. leaf

   ☐ D. value

8. A list of objects with access to another object is called the ______ of this object's ACL.

   ○ A. property

   ○ B. value

   ○ C. object

   ○ D. information

9. To make it easy to assign different users to a specific position or job responsibility, you can create a(n) ______ leaf object.

   ○ A. Alias

   ○ B. Printer

   ○ C. Organizational Role

   ○ D. User

10. If you want to see whether user Mary has access rights to a printer object, you must see the ______ of the printer's ACL.
    - ○ A. value
    - ○ B. property
    - ○ C. object
    - ○ D. purpose

Answers

1. A
2. B, C
3. D
4. D
5. B
6. B
7. A, B, D
8. B
9. C
10. A

CHAPTER 2

Setting Up and Securing the Network File System

Chapter 1, "Understanding NetWare 4.x," introduced you to the aspect of NetWare 4 that constitutes the most significant change from earlier versions of NetWare—NetWare Directory Services. This chapter explains how to set up and secure the network and its associated file system, one main aspect of NetWare that has remained relatively consistent throughout various versions.

One major network file-system difference between NetWare versions is related to how you perform the actual setup and security. In NetWare 4, the two main utilities used to set up and secure the NetWare network file system are the Graphical User Interface (GUI) utility called NetWare Administrator, along with NETADMIN, its DOS-based equivalent.

This chapter discusses setting up and securing the network file system under NetWare 4, and provides information about the following topics:

- Designing, planning, and creating the network file system
- Understanding and planning basic file system security
- Implementing basic file system security

Designing, Planning, and Creating the Network File System

NetWare uses volumes and directories to organize files and data. *Volumes*, created during the installation of NetWare file servers, are the basic building blocks of the network's file system structure. The volume called SYS contains the NetWare operating system and associated files.

Other volumes can be created to do the following tasks:

- Hold applications
- Store user data
- Accommodate different operating systems (particularly if they use non-DOS file-naming conventions, such as Macintosh and OS/2)
- Increase system fault tolerance
- Any other logical use

Because volumes are the basic building blocks, they should be carefully planned before implementation. Careful planning makes it easier to back up and restore data on the network, implement security, make efficient use of disk space, and administer the network. NetWare 4's installation software starts the planning process by creating the first volume for you, and placing required directories and NetWare operating system files on that volume.

The volume and directories created during installation are shown in figure 2.1.

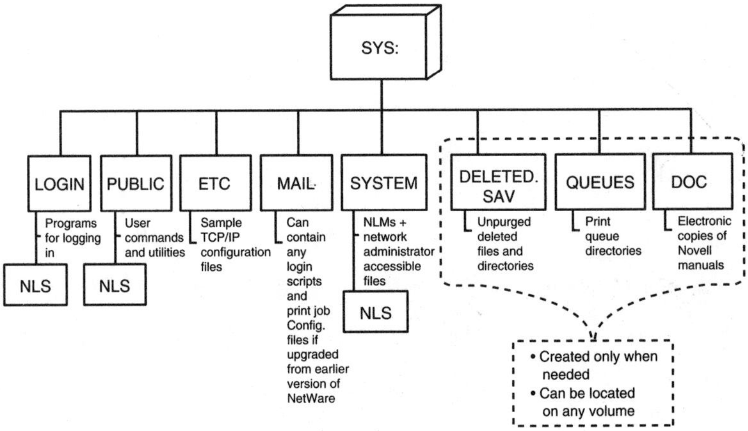

Figure 2.1
NetWare 4 installed volume and directories.

Additional directories, which network administrators may add in order to create an efficient directory structure, can include the following:

- **User data.** To provide an area where users can place their files
- **Applications.** To install various network applications, making it simpler to update and maintain application programs

Note With a separate applications directory, you can separate the program files (EXE, BAT, and COM files) from user-created data files. This separation contributes to the logical structure of your network file system design, and makes it easier to add new applications to the network, as well as to update to newer versions.

- **Configuration.** To store configuration files for various network applications
- **DOS.** To make it easy for users to access DOS commands for various versions of DOS

Note If you establish a DOS network directory, set the COMSPEC command for each workstation to point to the network DOS directory containing that workstation's version of DOS. This helps to ensure that the workstation can find the correct version of COMMAND.COM when exiting network applications.

- **Shared data.** To let groups of users with common data needs share a common directory

Understanding and Planning Basic File System Security

When planning and implementing network file system security, you should understand the following basic concepts related to file system security:

- Directory and file rights
- Trustee assignments
- Inheritance
- Reassignment of rights
- IRF (Inherited Rights Filter)
- Security equivalence
- Effective rights

To implement file system security, you must first understand each of these basic security concepts. This section describes each of these concepts and relates them to NetWare 4 file system security.

Directory and File Rights

Before you can access any file or directory, you must have the right to access it. Just as there are different ways to manage or manipulate a file or directory, there are different types of rights you can have. For example, if you want to read a file, you need the right to read the file. In NetWare 4, the right you need in order to read a file is called the Read right. NetWare 4 file and directory rights are shown in table 2.1.

Table 2.1
NetWare 4 File and Directory Rights

Right	*Abbreviation*	*What You Can Do with This Right*
File Scan	F	See files and directories
Erase	E	Delete files and directories
Write	W	Open and modify a file
Supervisor	S	Everything all other rights enable you to do
Create	C	Make new files or directories
Read	R	Open and read or run files
Access Control	A	Change trustee assignments and IRF
Modify	M	Change attributes or name

Trustee Assignments

In NetWare 4, rights are assigned to objects in the NDS tree. A *trustee* is an object (such as a user, group, or container) that has been assigned rights to another object. Before an object can have rights to a directory or file, that object must be defined as a trustee of the volume on which the directory or file is stored (placed on the Volume object's trustee list). The trustee can then be given rights to the directory or file as previously listed in table 2.1. Giving rights to a trustee is also known as *making a trustee assignment.*

Inheritance

You assign rights to a trustee for a directory or file at a specific level in the directory structure. The rights you assign to that trustee then flow down through the directory structure to other directories and files contained at and below the level at which you made the assignment. When a right is granted in a *parent directory* (a directory immediately above any subdirectory), that right is granted also to all *children* (subdirectories and files) contained below the parent directory. This flow of rights is called *inheritance.* The rights received by other directories and files as a result of this process are said to have *inherited* those rights.

Note: Container objects can also be called parent or child objects. *Parent* container objects are those which hold other container or leaf objects. *Child* objects are the container or leaf objects contained within a container object.

Reassignment of Rights

After you have made a rights assignment, you can change an object's rights at a lower level in the directory structure in either of two ways: by granting the object different rights at a lower level in the directory structure, or by using the IRF.

Granting a specific set of rights to a trustee at a level in the tree below the level at which you first granted rights is called a *reassignment of rights.* You can reassign rights whenever you need to change a trustee's access to the file system or to NDS objects. The drawback to reassigning rights is that you then need to keep track of which rights you assigned and where you assigned or reassigned those rights. When assigning or reassigning rights to multiple trustees for multiple objects, you can easily lose track of exactly which rights any given trustee may have been assigned. Using an IRF may be a better option.

IRF

The IRF is a list of all available rights at any given point in the tree. Its function is to control the flow of rights through the tree. Using the IRF, you can prevent one or more rights from being inherited. The IRF applies to all trustees and can permit or prevent any or all available rights from flowing down.

Note: In NetWare 4, unlike NetWare 3, the Supervisor property and Supervisor object rights can be blocked by using an IRF.

The only rights the IRF cannot filter out are those rights granted to a trustee at the same level on which the IRF is implemented. That is, the IRF cannot filter out a trustee assignment made at the same level as the IRF.

Security Equivalence

Objects (such as users, groups, and containers) are made trustees of directories, files, or other objects. The trustee is then given various rights, which determine the access the trustee has to the directory, file, or object. To simplify the assignment of rights, you can make an object *security equivalent* to another object. By doing so, any rights the first trustee has then also become rights of the object assigned security equivalence.

For example, every User object has a Security Equal To property, the value of which is a list of other objects. The objects included in that list have all the same rights to other objects, directories, and files that the original User object has.

Effective Rights

A User, Group, or Organizational Role object can obtain rights to the NetWare file system in several ways. Objects can obtain rights through the following methods:

- Trustee assignments
- Security equivalence
- Inheritance
- Parent containers
- The [Public] trustee
- Default rights assignments

The first two methods only grant rights to objects if a user with sufficient rights plans and implements security to make use of trustee assignments and security equivalence. These two methods have already been discussed.

The next two methods—inheritance and parent containers—grant rights based on other aspects of security, such as the trustee assignments and security equivalence that have been granted. These methods also have already been discussed.

The last two methods in the list—the [Public] trustee, and default rights assignments—are discussed next to help you better understand effective rights.

The [Public] Trustee

The [Public] trustee is a unique trustee, which is part of NDS when the first NetWare 4 file server is created. This trustee can be used to give the Read and File Scan right to anything *connected* (NetWare DOS Requester is loaded but the user has not yet logged in to the network) to the network by simply making [Public] a trustee of an object, directory, or file.

Note Granting rights to the [Public] trustee enables you to give all users and objects Read and File Scan rights without requiring that they first be logged in to the network. The Read and File Scan rights are granted to the [Public] trustee by default.

The Read and File Scan rights granted to [Public] by default are not the only default rights in NetWare 4. The other default rights assignments are discussed next.

Default Rights Assignments

If you choose to create a user directory when the User object is created in NDS, the User object is given all file system rights, except Supervisor, to its user directory. In addition, the following objects are given Supervisor rights in the file system:

- Objects with NDS Supervisor object rights to the Server object
- Bindery Services Supervisor object

The user who created the NDS file server object is also given all rights to that object, including the file system Supervisor right.

Regardless of the method through which a User, Group, or Organizational Role object obtains rights to the NetWare file system, the rights obtained at any given point in the file system are called *effective rights.* The NetWare operating system calculates the object's effective rights at any point in the file system to determine what access the object will be given. To ensure network security, the network administrator must also be able to ascertain effective rights for specific users.

(1) Introduction to network

(2) Understanding NDS

(3) NETWARE File System

(4) NETWARE Security

(5) NETWARE CONFIGURATION } Read well in this area

(6) PRINTING.

Teacher TEL NO

Victor → 0958 605 644

→ 0181 221 0879

A ✓
BC ✓
D ✓
D ✓
B ✓
B
ABD ✓
C ✓
B/A ✓

To determine effective rights, you must first know which rights have been granted through various objects. To find this information, check trustee assignments for the User object itself. Next, see whether the User object has been given any security equivalencies, or whether it is part of a Group. Also, check rights assigned to the User object's parent container, as well as any containers above it from which the User object can inherit rights. This means that you need to know which rights these container objects have, and whether those rights were specifically granted to the container, assigned by default, or assigned to [Public].

When you know which rights the User object has been granted or inherited, follow the flow of those rights through the tree. Remember to take into account any IRFs that may filter out any or all of those rights.

Implementing Basic File System Security

When planning file system security, you must consider the following two main factors:

- Rights flow down from the top and, therefore, should be planned from the top down.
- Trustee assignments also should be planned.

When planning and designing for top-down file system security, including trustee assignments, consider the following:

- Design from limited access to greater access, from the highest level of the tree to the lowest level (top-down).
- Give each trustee only the rights needed at each level.
- Use inheritance to simplify rights flow, as necessary, and use the IRF to eliminate rights flow when specific rights are no longer needed.
- Plan rights, starting at [Root], to flow down to the directories, subdirectories, and files.
- Grant rights only as high in the file system structure as necessary.
- Plan and make rights assignments to groups first, individual users next, and security equivalencies last.

One more issue to consider when planning file system security is the attributes that can be assigned to individual files and directories. Table 2.2 shows the available file and directory attributes.

Note The Archive Needed, Hidden, Read Only, Read Write, and System attributes are DOS attributes. The Copy Inhibit, Delete Inhibit, and Rename Inhibit attributes are applied to Macintosh files only.

To implement file system security, use the network administration tools provided by NetWare. The two primary tools you use are the NetWare Administrator and NETADMIN utilities.

Using the NetWare Administrator and NETADMIN utilities you can accomplish several tasks, many of which are security-related, including:

- Grant, revoke, and reassign rights
- View effective rights
- Set IRFs
- Manage directory and file attributes
- Manage directory and file trustee lists
- Manage Group, User, and other objects

Table 2.2
File and Directory Attributes

Attribute	*Abbreviation*	*Apply To*
Archive Needed	A	Files
Can't Compress	Cc	Files
Compresses	Co	Files
Copy Inhibit	Ci	Files
Delete Inhibit	Di	Files and directories
Don't Compress	Do	Files and directories
Don't Migrate	Dm	Directories
Don't Suballocate	Ds	Files
Execute Only	X	Files
Hidden	H	Files and directories
Immediate Compress	Ic	Files and directories
Migrate	M	Files
Normal	N	Files and directories
Purge	P	Files and directories
Read Only	Ro	Files
Read Write	Rw	Files
Rename Inhibit	R	Files
Rename Inhibit	Ri	Directories
Shareable	Sh	Files
System	S	Files and directories
Transactional	T	Files

Note To use the NetWare Administrator and NETADMIN utilities, as described in the following sections, you must have the utility running and be pointed to the correct location in the directory tree.

Granting, Revoking, and Reassigning Rights

You can use both the NetWare Administrator and the NETADMIN utilities to grant, revoke, and reassign rights.

Using NetWare Administrator to Grant, Revoke, and Reassign Rights

To grant rights by using the NetWare Administrator utility, first choose the object from the main NetWare Administrator window, then choose Rights to Files and Directories. Next, choose the Add button. When the Select Object window opens, select the files and directories to which the object is to be granted rights (see fig. 2.2).

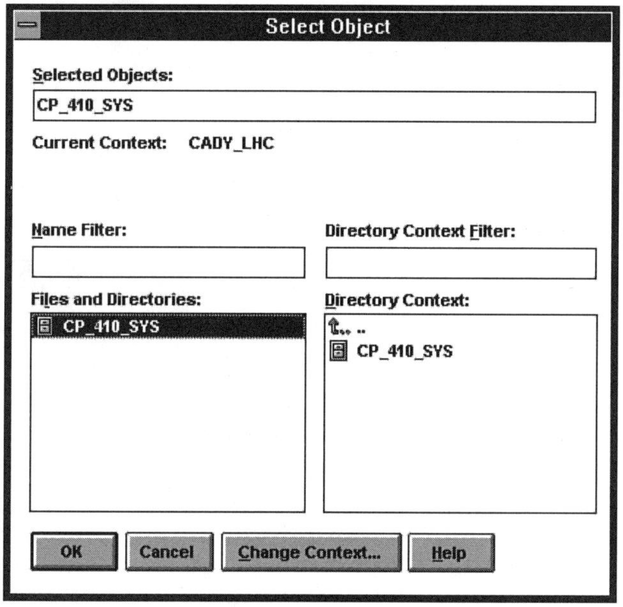

Figure 2.2
The Select Object window.

After an object has been granted rights to directories and files in a volume, those rights can be reassigned (modified) or deleted. To reassign or delete rights, choose Rights to Files and Directories from the main NetWare Administration window, and then from the Rights to Files and Directories User window (see fig. 2.3), mark or unmark the rights to be granted or revoked, or remove the user as a trustee by choosing the Delete button.

Using NETADMIN to Grant, Revoke, and Reassign Rights

To grant, revoke, or reassign rights by using the NETADMIN utility, first choose the object from the Object menu's Class list. Then, from the Actions for user: *username* screen, choose the View or edit rights to files and directories option.

Next, provide the Volume Object name and the beginning path, to specify where the object will be granted rights. Also choose whether rights will be granted only for directories at the defined path, only for files, or for both directories and files, and whether subdirectories will be included.

Now press F10 to display the list of trustee rights. If no rights have been assigned to this object, the list is blank. To assign (add) rights, press Insert and specify the Directory in which trustee should be added. Default rights are granted. To modify those rights, press Enter, then add to the list of available rights by pressing Insert and marking or choosing the additional rights to be assigned.

Follow this same process to revoke (or reassign) rights, modifying the list of rights assigned to this object as necessary.

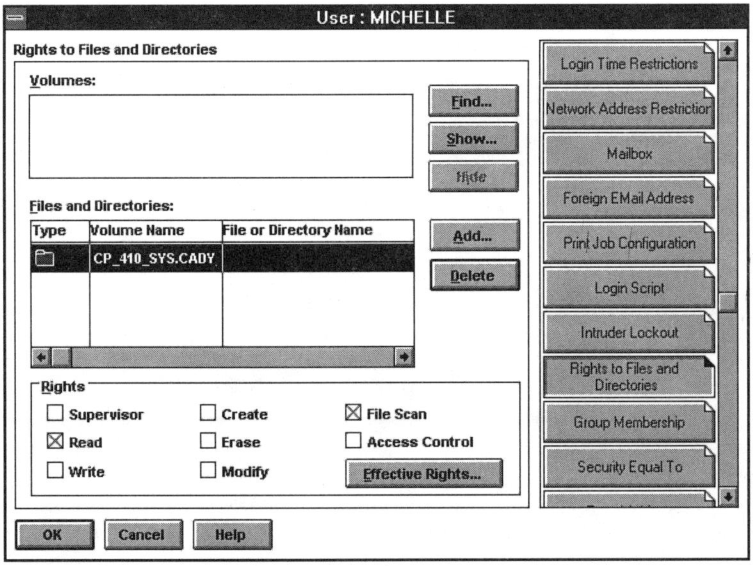

Figure 2.3
The Rights to Files and Directories window for user Michelle.

View Effective Rights

Whether you are running the NetWare Administrator or the NETADMIN utility, you can view effective rights by following the same basic procedure used to grant, reassign, or revoke rights. The main difference, of course, is that you view the rights but do not modify them.

Note You can also use the RIGHTS command to see effective rights.

Setting IRFs

IRFs can be set anywhere in the file system structure. Before setting an IRF, make sure that you are pointed to the exact location in the file system structure where you want to set or modify the IRF. Then, using either NetWare Administrator or NETADMIN, you can set or modify the IRF.

Using NetWare Administrator to Set IRFs

To set an IRF by using NetWare Administrator, complete the following steps:

1. Select the directory or file from the NetWare Administrator window.
2. Choose Details from the Object pull-down menu.
3. Choose either the Trustees of this File or Trustees of this Directory button, depending on whether you originally selected a file or directory.
4. Mark, unmark, or leave unchanged the box next to each right listed in the Inheritance Filter portion of the Trustees of this File or Directory window (see fig. 2.4).

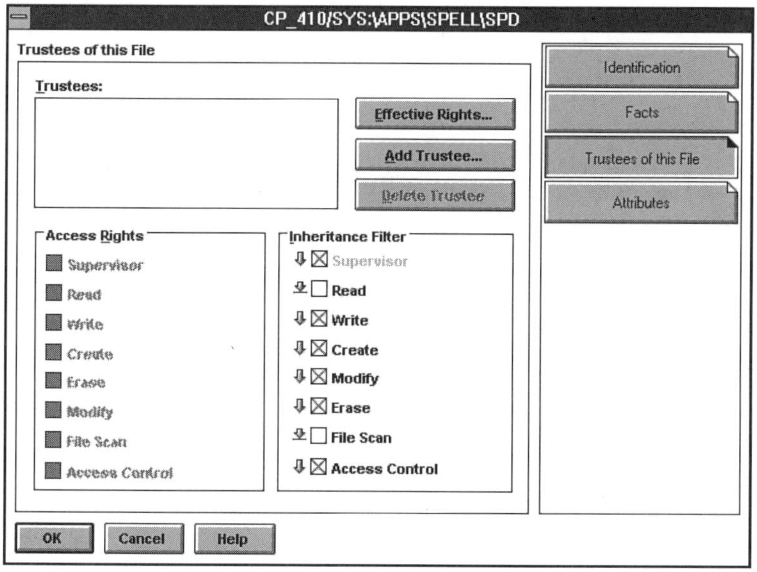

Figure 2.4
The Trustees of this File window.

Note: If a right is grayed out, or shown in gray instead of black ink, that right is unavailable. A mark (X) in the box next to a right indicates that the right can be inherited. To prevent inheritance of a right, unmark the box next to that right.

Using NETADMIN to Set Volume Object IRFs

To set IRFs by using the NETADMIN utility, complete the following steps:

1. Choose the Volume object from the **O**bject, Class list.
2. Choose View or edit the trustees of this object from the Actions for volume: *volume_name* menu.
3. Choose Inherited Rights Filters from the Trustees of this object menu.
4. Press Insert to see a list of properties that can be filtered.
5. Choose the properties to be filtered.

   For example, to restrict the Object Rights property, choose [Object Rights] from the Properties menu. The [Object Rights] property is then listed on the Inherited Rights Filters screen.
6. Choose an item from those listed on the Inherited Rights Filters screen. A list of the rights that are allowed (not currently screened out by the IRF) is displayed.

   For example, choose [Object Rights]. The Entry rights allowed screen opens, displaying the object rights currently not screened out by the IRF.
7. Modify rights to be allowed by pressing Insert to see a list of rights from which to choose to add. Or delete rights from the list of rights currently not screened out by the IRF.

Managing Directory and File Attributes

Directory and file attributes can be managed by using the NetWare Administrator utility. You cannot use the DOS-based NETADMIN utility to change directory or file attributes. To change directory or file attributes from DOS, use FILER.

To manage directory and file attributes by using NetWare Administrator, first choose the volume and then expand the directory structure until you find the directory or file whose attributes you want to manage.

Next, choose the directory or file itself. When the Identification window for this directory or file opens (see fig. 2.5), choose the Attributes button.

In the Attributes window (see fig. 2.6), mark or unmark attributes as necessary, then choose OK to display the previous window.

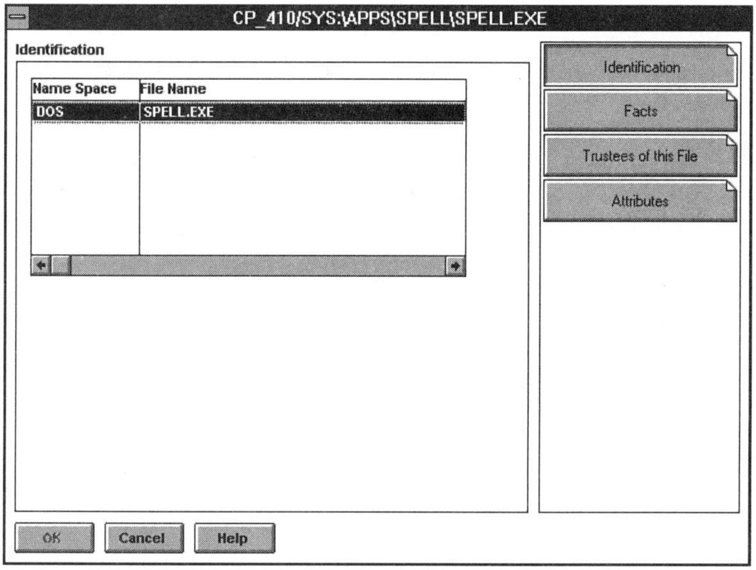

Figure 2.5
The Identification window.

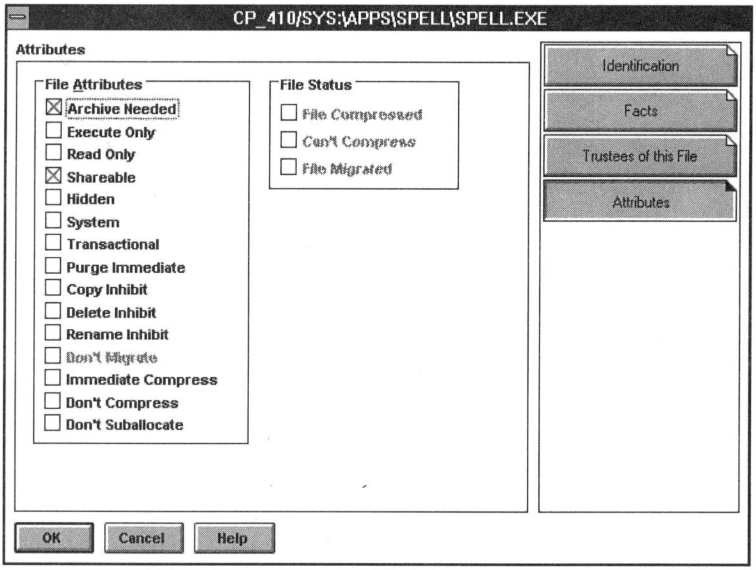

Figure 2.6
The Attributes window.

Managing Directory and File Trustee Lists

To manage directory and file trustee lists, select the object from the list of objects in NetWare Administrator. Then choose Trustees of this object from the Objects pull-down menu. In the Trustees window (see fig. 2.7), you can see which other objects are currently included on this object's list of trustees. By using the buttons in this window you can perform the following tasks:

- Add trustees
- Delete trustees
- Modify a trustee's object and property rights
- View a trustee's effective rights
- Modify the IRF

Managing Group, User, and Other Objects

Before you can manage an object, it must exist. If the object does not already exist, you can create it by using the NetWare Administrator or NETADMIN utilities.

Using NetWare Administrator to Create and Manage Group, User, and Other Objects

To use the NetWare Administrator utility to create an object, first select (from the NetWare Administrator window) the container where the object is to be added, then choose Create from the Object pull-down menu (see fig. 2.8).

Using NETADMIN to Create and Manage Group, User, and Other Objects

To use the NETADMIN utility to create an object, press Insert at the Class, Object screen, select the type of object to be created from the Select an object class screen, then provide the requested information.

When creating a Group object, for example, you provide a name and mailbox location.

When objects exist in the NDS tree, you can manage those objects. Various management tasks can be performed on an object.

You can use NETADMIN to delete objects, for example, by selecting the object from the list of objects, pressing Delete, and confirming the deletion.

You can use NETADMIN to perform the following management tasks as well:

- Viewing or editing properties of the object
- Renaming the object
- Moving the object
- Viewing or editing rights to files and directories
- Viewing or editing the trustees of the object

Each of these management tasks is performed by choosing the appropriate option from the Actions for *Object: Object_name* menu, and then providing requested information.

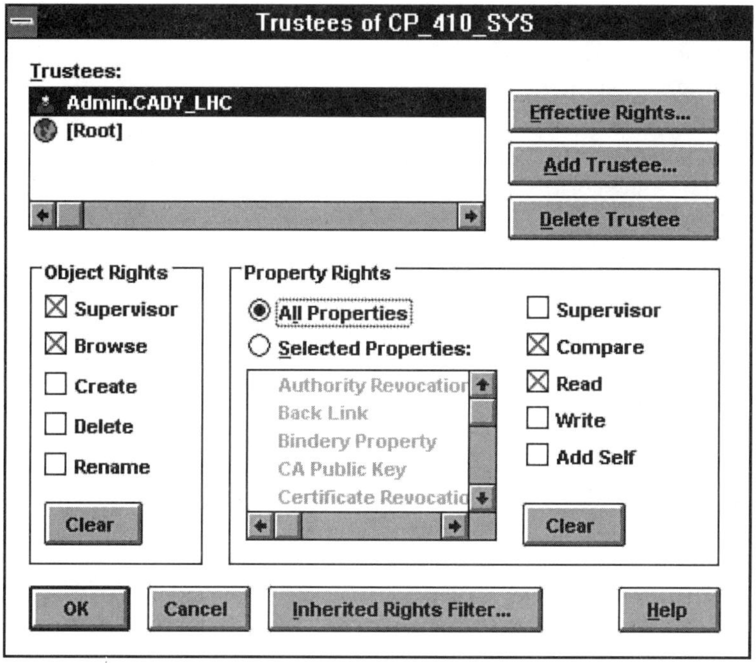

Figure 2.7
The Trustees window.

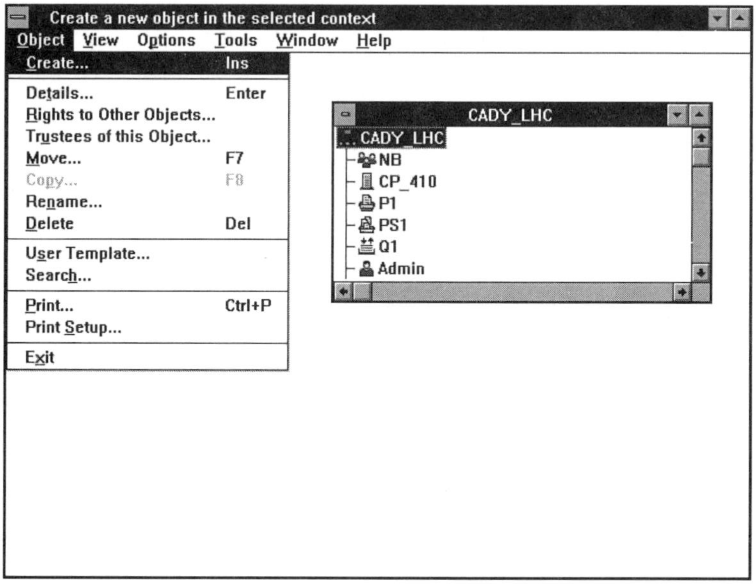

Figure 2.8
The NetWare Administrator window, with Object submenu open.

In addition to using the NetWare Administrator and NETADMIN utilities, you can also use the RIGHTS command to grant, revoke, and view information about rights from the DOS prompt.

Note: The RIGHTS command is frequently used for the following reasons:

- To view trustees (RIGHTS /T)
- To see your effective rights (RIGHTS)

In addition, you can use the NDIR command to view information about files and directories.

Note: Following are two lesser-know but useful NDIR options:

- **/VOL.** Enables you to view volume information
- **/SPA.** Enables you to view space information

In addition to RIGHTS and NDIR, you can use the menu utility FILER to perform various file and directory tasks.

Questions

1. The basic building blocks of the NetWare file system structure are ______.
   - ○ A. volumes
   - ○ B. directories
   - ○ C. files
   - ○ D. databases
2. Which *two* are created during installation?
   - ☐ A. USER
   - ☐ B. SYS
   - ☐ C. DELETED.SAV
   - ☐ D. ETC
3. The ______ does *not* have to be considered when you plan and implement network file system security.
   - ○ A. physical location of user ADMIN
   - ○ B. rights inheritance
   - ○ C. IRF
   - ○ D. directory and file rights
4. Which of the following correctly lists the hot keys for NetWare 4 file and directory rights?
   - ○ A. NOMFILES
   - ○ B. RUNFASTR
   - ○ C. FEWSCRAM
   - ○ D. SUPERMAN
5. A/an ______ is a/an ______ assigned rights to a directory or file.
   - ○ A. reassignment of rights, object's
   - ○ B. IRF, object's
   - ○ C. object, inheritance
   - ○ D. trustee, object
6. Which of the following is *not* one of the ways a User, Group, or Organizational Role object can obtain file system rights?
   - ○ A. Trustee assignment
   - ○ B. Security equivalent
   - ○ C. Parent container
   - ○ D. Child container
7. Of the following, which *two* are default rights assigned to [Public]?
   - ☐ A. Read
   - ☐ B. Write
   - ☐ C. Access control
   - ☐ D. File scan
8. Migrate, Normal, and Purge are all known as ______.
   - ○ A. Trustee assignments
   - ○ B. Object rights
   - ○ C. File attributes
   - ○ D. Default [Public] rights
9. To view effective rights, you *cannot* use the ______ utility/command.
   - ○ A. NETADMIN
   - ○ B. NetWare Administrator
   - ○ C. RIGHTS
   - ○ D. REVOKE

10. When a right is grayed out, what does it mean?
    - ○ A. The right has been revoked.
    - ○ B. The right is unavailable.
    - ○ C. The right can only be granted to ADMIN.
    - ○ D. The right can only be granted to leaf objects.

Answers

1. A
2. B, D
3. A
4. C
5. D
6. D
7. A, D
8. C
9. D
10. B

CHAPTER 3

Setting Up Network Printing and Mail Services

Shared printing and electronic mail are two particularly useful features of a network. NetWare 4 provides both of these services. This chapter discusses network printing and electronic mail within a NetWare 4 network, and provides information about the following topics:

- *Setting up print services*
- *Customizing and managing print jobs*
- *Controlling access to and management of printing*
- *Installing and configuring messaging services*

Setting Up Print Services

The process of setting up NetWare 4 print services includes setting up both hardware and software components. Hardware components include the following:

- Printers
- Servers
- DOS workstations
- Cabling

NetWare 4 printing software components include the following:

- PSERVER.NLM
- NPRINTER.NLM
- NPRINTER.EXE

In addition to setting up these hardware and software components, when you set up NetWare 4 printing you must also create the following three NDS objects:

- Print Servers
- Print Queues
- Printers

Setting Up Printing Hardware and Running Related Software

The first step in making shared printing available is to set up the hardware associated with printing on a NetWare 4 network, and to run the related software. You must consider the following hardware-related printing setup issues:

- Connecting a printer to a NetWare server
- Connecting a printer to a DOS workstation
- Bringing up a print server

Connecting a Printer to a NetWare Server

In order to have print services on a NetWare 4 network, at least one of the NetWare 4 file servers must also be functioning as a NetWare 4 print server. In NetWare 4, printers can be attached to any of the file servers, regardless of whether the file server is also functioning as a print server.

Note For more information about print servers, see the "Bringing Up a Print Server" section, later in this chapter.

To physically connect a printer to a NetWare server, attach the printer cable to a printer port on the file server.

Note If an NDS Printer object has not yet been created for this printer, you must create one before this printer is accessible to the network. (Instructions for creating NDS Printer objects are provided later in this chapter.) In addition, a network print server must be up and running, instructions for which are also discussed later in this chapter.

Note When the printer is attached to a NetWare 4 file server that is not also a print server, you must configure the Printer object for this printer to be Manual Load.

Connecting a Printer to a DOS Workstation

As long as the NetWare print server software is loaded on at least one NetWare file server, you can attach printers to DOS workstations as well as to file servers.

Connect printers to workstations the same way you connect them to file servers—by cabling them to the computer's printer port. Then, activate workstation-related printing software by running NPRINTER.EXE on the workstation. To run NPRINTER.EXE, type **NPRINTER *[printer|print_server printer_number]*** at the workstation keyboard, and press Enter. Replace *printer* with the name of the Printer object created for this printer, or replace *print_server* with the print server name assigned to this printer. If you chose to provide a print server name instead of a Printer object, you must also provide a printer number, replacing *printer_number* with the logical printer number assigned to this printer.

Note As with printers attached to file servers, a print server must exist somewhere on the network. In addition, an NDS Printer object for this printer must be created before you load NPRINTER.EXE. Furthermore, when the printer is attached to a workstation, you must configure the Printer object to be Manual Load.

Bringing Up a Print Server

A *print server* is a NetWare file server on which PSERVER.NLM and NPRINTER.NLM have been loaded to provide printing services. A print server is responsible for sending print job requests to assigned printers.

In NetWare 4, you bring up a print server by loading PSERVER.NLM on a NetWare 4 file server, which automatically loads NPRINTER.NLM.

Note When the printer is attached to a print server, you must configure the Printer object to be Auto Load (also called *Local*).

To load the print server software on a NetWare 4 file server, type the following command at the file server console, and press Enter:

```
LOAD PSERVER .cn=print_server.ou=name.o=name
```

Replace *.cn=print_server.ou=name.o=name* with the specific context and common name assigned to the print server.

Note To ensure that the print server is loaded each time the file server is loaded, add the preceding command to the AUTOEXEC.NCF file.

When a print server is up, it can service up to 255 printers and any number of assigned print queues.

Table 3.1 summarizes NetWare 4 printing services. It shows where printers can be connected, and how their printing services are made available on a NetWare 4 network.

Table 3.1
Summary of Printing Options in NetWare 4

Printer Connected to	*Software to be Loaded/Run*	*Printer Object Load Configuration*
File Server	NPRINTER.NLM	Manual Load
Print Server	PSERVER.NLM NPRINTER.NLM	Auto Load
Workstation	NPRINTER.EXE	Manual Load

Creating NDS Print Objects

The second major task associated with setting up network printing is to create necessary related NDS printing objects, of which there are the following three types:

- Print servers
- Print queues
- Printers

You can create these objects manually, or you can run the Quick Setup option provided in PCONSOLE to automatically create one of each of these objects. When you use PCONSOLE to set up printing services, only one of each type of object is created. You must create additional objects manually if you need more than one Print server, Print queue, and Printer object on your network.

To run the Quick Setup option in PCONSOLE, complete the following steps:

1. Run PCONSOLE from the DOS prompt by typing **PCONSOLE** and pressing Enter.
2. Choose Quick Setup (see fig. 3.1).
3. Modify any default fields that need to be changed, and provide appropriate printer values as necessary.
4. Press F10.

You can also create Print server objects, Print queue objects, and Printer objects by using the NetWare Administrator utility. To create any of these objects, run the NetWare Administrator utility, and set the current context (location in the tree) to the location in the NDS tree where you want the object to reside. Then choose Create from the Object pull-down menu, and continue creating the object, depending on its type, as described in the following sections.

Creating Print Server Objects

To create a Print Server object, complete the following steps:

1. Choose Print Server from the list of object classes.
2. Provide a name for the Print Server.

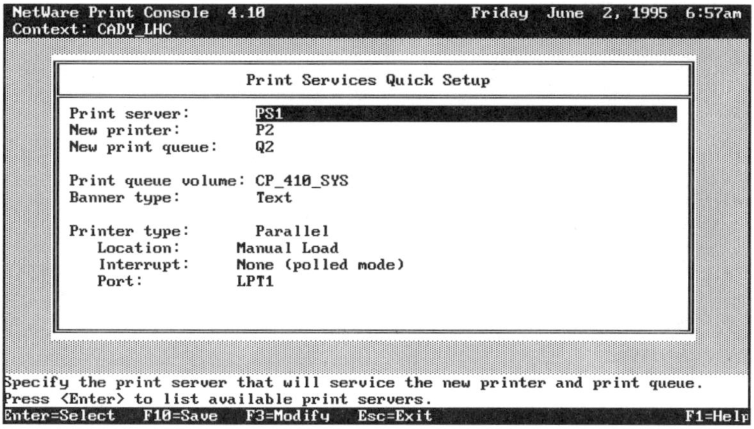

Figure 3.1
The PCONSOLE Quick Setup screen.

3. Mark the Define Additional Properties box (see fig. 3.2).

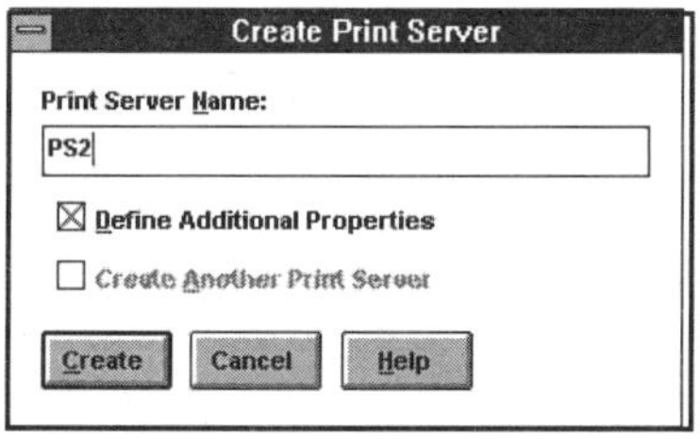

Figure 3.2
The Create Print Server window.

4. Choose Create.
5. Fill in at least the minimum information necessary (the Print Server object name and Printer objects to be managed by this Print Server object).
6. Choose OK.

Note When a Print Server object is created, default rights and assignments are created for the Print Queue Operator, Print Queue User, and the Print Server Operator List.

Creating Print Queue Objects

To create a Print queue object, complete the following steps:

1. Choose Print Queue from the list of object classes.
2. Choose the type of Print Queue object (Directory Service Queue or Reference a Bindery Queue).
3. Provide at least the minimum information necessary for a Print Queue object (a name for the print queue, and the name of the volume where the print queue is to be placed).

4. Mark the Define Additional Properties box (see fig. 3.3) if additional information (such as a description, location, operator flags, and so on) is to be provided.

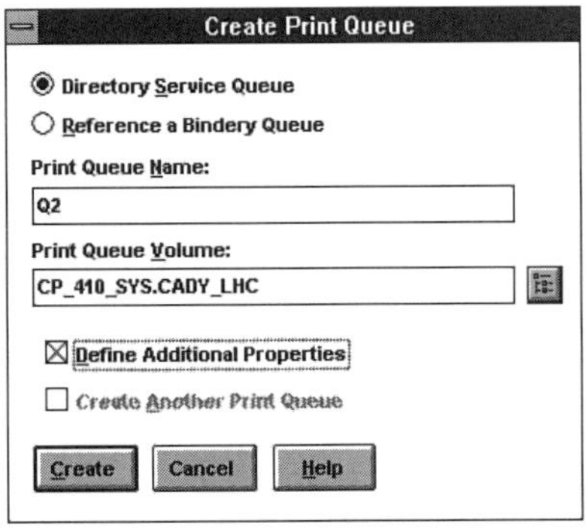

Figure 3.3
The Create Print Queue window.

Note: If you chose to define additional properties, fill in the information you want to provide on the form that opens (Print Queue Identification), then choose OK on this form.

5. Choose OK.

Creating Printer Objects

To create Printer objects, complete the following steps:

1. Choose Printer from the list of object classes.
2. Provide a name for the printer.
3. Mark the Define Additional Properties box (if necessary).

Note: Fill in additional information, as necessary, if you chose to define additional properties, then choose OK.

4. Choose Create.

Customizing and Managing Print Jobs

Some aspects of a network print job can be customized. With NetWare 4, you can choose what to customize, and then create custom print jobs.

You can, for example, choose whether to have a banner page printed before each print job, or whether a special form should be used with a particular print job. In addition, NetWare 4 enables you to manage various aspects of print jobs (such as which print queue a print job can use).

In addition to customizing print jobs, you can manage print jobs. Print job management includes management of print queues, print servers, and printers.

Customizing Print Jobs

To create customized print jobs, use the NetWare Administrator or PRINTCON utilities. You can then use these customized print jobs when you use the CAPTURE or NPRINT *Job* option.

To create print job configurations by using NetWare Administrator, first choose the level at which you want the print job configuration to be placed.

> **Note** If you create the print job configuration at the container level, all user objects in that container have access to the print job configuration by default. To ensure that only a specific user has access to the print job configuration, create it at the user object level.

After you select the level, choose Details from the Object pull-down menu. Next, choose Print Job Configuration from the list of available objects. Choose the New button, then fill in the necessary fields in the Print Job Configuration window (see fig. 3.4).

When you create a print job configuration, you must include at least a name for the print job configuration (Print Job Name) and choose a printer or print queue object for the print job configuration to use (Printer/Queue). Other fields can be left at their default settings, or can be modified as necessary. Table 3.2 lists the fields in the Print Job Configuration window, and briefly explains their function.

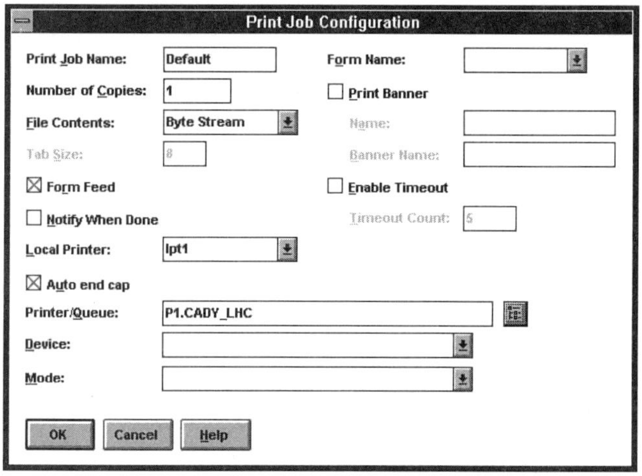

Figure 3.4
The Print Job Configuration window.

Table 3.2
Print Job Configuration Fields

Field Name	*Hot Key*	*Function*
Print Job Name	J	Provides name to be used when choosing a print job
Form Name	O	Chooses form used when this print job configuration is chosen
Number of Copies	C	Number of copies (1 to 65,000) to be printed when this print job configuration is used
Print Banner	P	Specifies whether banner page should be printed at beginning of each job that uses this configuration
Name	A	Any name that identifies owner of print job; placed on the banner page (default is user's login name)
Banner Name	B	Name that identifies the print job itself; default is either the file name (NPRINT commands) or the port number (CAPTURE commands)
File Contents	F	Text (tab commands are understood and their size can be set), or Byte stream (no tabs)
Tab Size	S	Number of spaces to be used between tab stops
Form Feed	R	Specifies whether form should be ejected from printer after print job is complete
Enable Timeout	E	Specifies whether print job should be considered complete after specified amount of time has elapsed since last command was sent to printer
Timeout Count	T	Specifies how much time can elapse before job is considered complete when Enable Timeout option is used
Notify When Done	N	Determines whether print job's originator (workstation) should receive notification when job has been printed
Local Printer	L	Indicates which printer port (LPT1 through LPT9) printer is attached to
Auto end cap	U	Automatically closes print queue file when print job has been printed
Printer/Queue	Q	Specifies printer or queue this print job configuration should use
Device	D	Specifies print device to be used for jobs that use this configuration
Mode	M	Enables you to choose a print mode, as determined by print device you chose

Managing Print Jobs

Print servers, print queues, and printers periodically require administrator intervention. Intervention may include such tasks as preventing new print servers from adding jobs to print queues, deleting print jobs from a print queue, or pausing, stopping, and restarting the printer. These tasks, as well as many other print job management tasks, can be accomplished by using either of the following utilities:

- PCONSOLE
- NetWare Administrator

Managing Print Jobs with PCONSOLE

You can accomplish several print job management tasks by running PCONSOLE at a workstation, then choosing one of the following from the PCONSOLE Available Options menu:

- Print Queues
- Printers
- Print Servers

To manage print queues, choose Print Queue from the Available Options menu, choose the print queue to be managed, then choose what you want to manage from the Print Queue Information menu (see fig. 3.5).

You can choose to perform various print queue management tasks by choosing any of the following from the Print Queue Information menu:

- **Print Jobs.** Enables you to add (press Ins) print jobs to the queue, cancel (press Del) print jobs, or change fields on a print job's information screen (choose the print job).
- **Status.** Enables you to view information about the print queue. This information includes the number of jobs currently in the queue, the number of active print servers for this queue, and the status (YES/NO) of operator flags.
- **Attached print servers.** Enables you to see which print servers can service this print queue.
- **Information.** Enables you to see the Object ID assigned to this print queue, the name of the file server associated with this print queue, and the volume in which this queue is located.

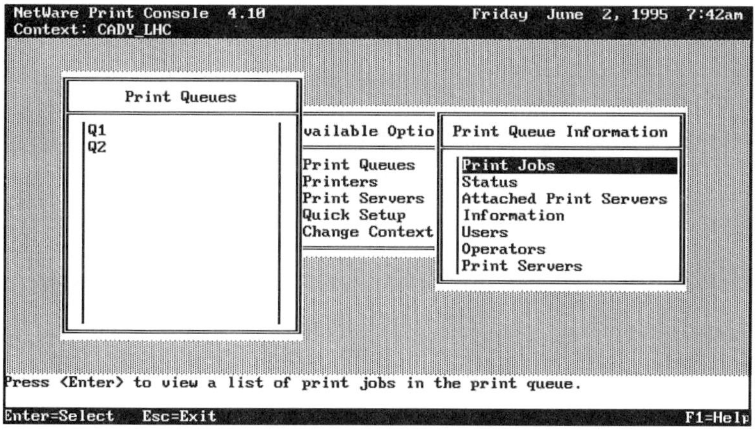

Figure 3.5
The Print Queue Information menu.

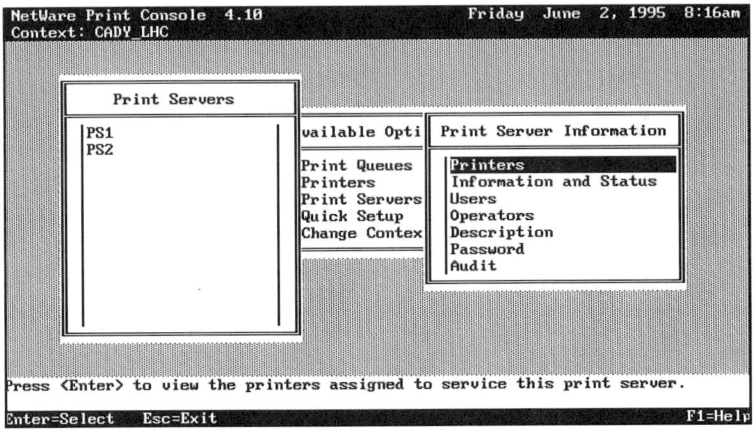

Figure 3.6
The Print Server Information menu.

- **Users.** Enables you to add or remove users from the list of authorized users.
- **Operators.** Enables you to add or remove operators from the list of authorized print queue operators.
- **Print Servers.** Enables you to add or remove print servers from the list of authorized print servers.

You can choose to perform various print server management tasks by choosing any of the following from the Print Server Information menu (see fig. 3.6):

- **Printers.** Enables you to add, Delete, rename (press F3), or modify the configuration of a printer (choose the printer)
- **Information and Status.** Enables you to shut down the print server, or change its name
- **Users.** Enables you to add or Delete users authorized to send jobs to this print server
- **Operators.** Enables you to add or Delete objects that can manage this print server
- **Description.** Enables you to edit the description associated with this print server
- **Password.** Enables you to change this print server's password
- **Audit.** Enables you to turn auditing for the print server on or off, set the maximum allowable size for the audit file, and view and delete the audit file

You can modify various items of printer-related information as well, by first choosing Printers from the Available Options menu, then choosing a specific printer. Figure 3.7 shows the Printer Configuration screen for the printer named PS1.

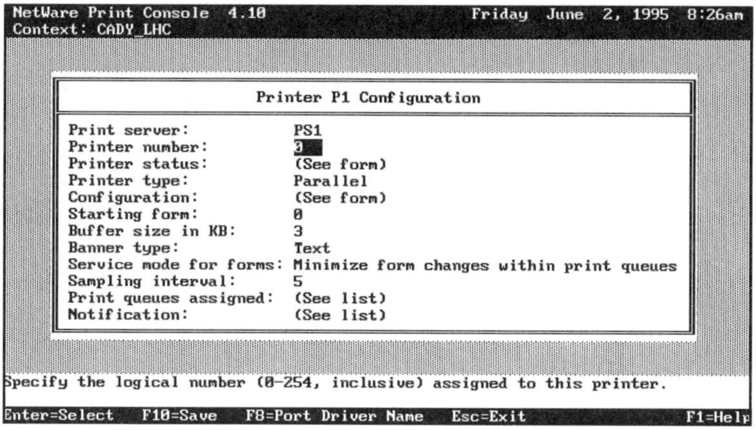

Figure 3.7
The Printer Configuration screen.

You can modify information for the printer by choosing any of the following fields from the Printer Configuration screen:

- Printer number
- Printer status
- Printer type
- Configuration (of the printer itself)
- Starting form
- Buffer size in KB
- Banner type
- Service mode for forms
- Sampling interval
- Print queues assigned
- Notification (list of objects to be notified)

Managing Print Jobs with NetWare Administrator

To manage print jobs by using the NetWare Administrator utility, select the print object (Print Server, Printer, or Print Queue) you want to manage from the NetWare Administrator, then choose Details from the Object pull-down menu. Then, depending on the type of printing object you chose, either fill in or modify the fields on the forms associated with each type of print object.

The following forms are associated with the Print Queue object:

- Identification
- Assignments
- Operators
- Users
- Job list

Forms associated with the Print Server object include the following:

- Identification
- Assignments
- Users
- Operator
- Auditing log
- Print layout

These forms are associated with the Printer object:

- Identification
- Assignments
- Configuration
- Notification
- Features
- See also
- Printer status

Controlling Access to and Management of Printing

To spread out the responsibility for managing network printing, various types of users can be assigned to perform various tasks. Different types of users have different rights and responsibilities for managing printing. Table 3.3 shows the types of users who can manage printing services, and the management duties they are given by default.

Table 3.3
Default Network Printing Management User Capabilities

User Type	*Default Tasks That Can Be Performed*
Container Supervisor	Create and delete Printer objects Create and delete Print Server objects Create and delete Print Queue objects Change print queue list of users Change print queue list of operators Change assignment of print queues Change Notify list Monitor print servers
Printer Notify List	Receive error messages from a printer
Print Queue Operator	Manage print jobs in print queue for self and others Change print queue operator flags
Print Server Operator	Change assignment of print queues Change Notify list Change status of printer Bring down a print server (unload print server files)
Print Queue User	Submit, modify, and remove own jobs in print queue
Print Server User	Monitor print servers Receive error messages from a printer

Installing and Configuring Messaging Services

Messaging services are concerned primarily with active communication between network users. Messaging services are responsible for storing, retrieving, and delivering communications in many forms (binary data, text, graphics, and video and audio data).

To accomplish network communication, NetWare's messaging services provide a *messaging engine* (technology that has been integrated with NDS to accommodate the transportation, storage, and retrieval of network communications), *mailboxes* (electronic storage locations for individual network users), and *messaging applications* (utilities to simplify access to and use of network messaging services).

Note Although various NetWare-compatible applications can be used to access and use messaging services, NetWare 4 includes a basic NDS-aware electronic mail application called FirstMail, the use of which is discussed in Chapter 8, "Accessing and Using Network Resources."

Before you can use NetWare's Message Handling Services (MHS), it must be installed. You can install MHS when you install the NetWare 4 file server, or you can install it later. To install MHS when you install NetWare 4, you must choose the Customized installation option. Otherwise, you install MHS by using INSTALL.NLM.

Before you can install MHS, your file server must meet the following minimum requirements:

- 500 KB of RAM available
- 2.5 MB of hard disk space to store MHS programs, plus additional disk space for user mailboxes
- A CD-ROM drive

Note To handle 10 network users who need no more than 100 messages per day, the file server must meet the following minimum requirements:

- 80386 microprocessor
- 12 MB file server RAM
- 65 MB hard disk space

To install MHS, either load INSTALL.NLM after the NetWare 4 file server has been installed, or choose the customized installation path during the NetWare 4 file server installation. Then complete the following steps:

1. Choose Product options.
2. From the Other Installation Actions menu, choose the Choose an item or product listed above option.
3. From the Other Installation Items/Products menu, choose Install NetWare MHS.
4. Choose the path.

Note If the current path does not point to the location of the NETMAIN.ILS file, press F3 and change the path.

5. When the Postmaster General Authentication window opens, enter (in the Name field) the name of the user responsible for administration of MHS, making certain to provide the

user's complete context; then (in the Password field) enter the user's password, and press Enter.

6. Choose the volume on which the MHS database is to be installed (if the NetWare 4 server has multiple volumes), and press Enter.

7. Modify the AUTOEXEC.NCF file to include the LOAD MHS command.

> **Note** Choose NCF file options from the Installation Options menu to modify the AUTOEXEC.NCF file. Remember, the server must be taken down and reloaded before any changes made to the AUTOEXEC.NCF file will become effective.

During the basic installation of NetWare 4, the Messaging Services object is created. When the Messaging Services object exists, mailboxes must be assigned to NDS objects. Assign mailboxes to any of the following NDS objects:

- Users

> **Note** To assign a mailbox to a user, use the Messaging Server object and choose the Users property.

- Groups
- Organizational Role
- Organizational Unit

In addition, you can create distribution lists by choosing Create from the NetWare Administrator Objects pull-down menu, then choosing Distribution List. Provide a name for the distribution list, then add users, groups, and other NDS objects as appropriate.

> **Note** If your network contains a gateway, you can add the External Entity object so that messages can be sent to users not included in the list of NDS users.

Questions

1. Of the following, which one *cannot* be used to provide printing services to the network?
   - ○ A. Print server
   - ○ B. File server
   - ○ C. Workstation
   - ○ D. Stand-alone computer

2. Which *two* commands load the print server software on a NetWare 4 file server?
   - ☐ A. LOAD NPRINTER.NLM
   - ☐ B. LOAD PSERVER.NLM
   - ☐ C. INSTALL PSERVER.NLM
   - ☐ D. INSTALL PSERVER.EXE

3. The ______ PCONSOLE option automatically sets up printing services.
   - ○ A. Automatic Setup
   - ○ B. Print Install
   - ○ C. Basic Setup
   - ○ D. Quick Setup

4. Of the following, which one allows you to create Print Server objects, Print Queue objects, and Printer objects?
   - ○ A. NETADMIN
   - ○ B. PSERVER
   - ○ C. NetWare Administrator
   - ○ D. CAPTURE

5. The minimum information required when creating a Print Queue object is ______.
   - ○ A. a print queue name only
   - ○ B. a print queue name and volume
   - ○ C. a volume only
   - ○ D. a print queue name, volume, and print server

6. Which of the following is *not* a true statement?
   - ○ A. If you create a print job configuration at the container level, all user objects in that container have access to it by default.
   - ○ B. You can create a print job by choosing the Details option from the NetWare Administrator Object pull-down menu.
   - ○ C. The minimum information you must provide when creating a print job configuration is the volume on which it is to be stored.
   - ○ D. When managing printing on a NetWare 4 server, you must consider management of print queues, print servers, and printers.

7. Of the following, which *two* are fields you can fill in when you create a print job configuration?
   - ☐ A. File Server Name
   - ☐ B. No End Cap
   - ☐ C. File Contents
   - ☐ D. Timeout Count

8. The ______ option on the Print Queue Information menu enables you to view information about the print queue, such as the current number of jobs in the queue.

   ○ A. Print jobs

   ○ B. Status

   ○ C. Information

   ○ D. Print Servers

9. To delete the print server's audit log, choose the ______ option from the Print Server Information menu.

   ○ A. Information and Status

   ○ B. Description

   ○ C. Operators

   ○ D. Audit

10. When you want to give another network user the responsibility for downing a print server, you can create a ______ object.

   ○ A. Print Server Operator

   ○ B. Print Server User

   ○ C. Container Supervisor

   ○ D. Print Server Supervisor

Answers

1. D
2. A, B
3. D
4. C
5. B
6. C
7. C, D
8. B
9. D
10. A

CHAPTER 4

Setting Up Secure User Access

Network security is both a software and a hardware issue. Hardware security may include such issues as controlling physical access to network file servers and providing protection against power surges and losses.

NetWare software security includes both file system and NDS (Network Directory Services) security. Although security issues between the two are often similar—file system security controls access to files and directories, and NDS security controls access to NDS objects—NDS and file system security are separate issues. In this chapter, only issues related to NDS security (and not to file system or hardware security) are discussed.

This chapter, because it focuses on providing secure access to the network for network users, discusses the following security and network access issues:

- Understanding and implementing security
- Ensuring secure network access through user objects
- Automating network access through a DOS workstation

Understanding and Implementing Security

In NetWare 4, all network resources such as users, groups, and so on are recorded as objects in the NDS database. Just as access by users to network directories and the files they contain is regulated by file system security, access to the network and the resources it provides is regulated by NDS security. NDS security controls who can access NDS objects and the properties associated with them.

To gain access to the network, users must first have a User object created by the network administrator. (See the "Ensuring Secure Network Access through User Objects" section of this chapter for information about how to create User objects.)

NDS User objects must be assigned, at a minimum, a Login Name property value, and a Last Name property value. This information, along with other property values (including password requirements and values) is then stored in the NDS database. The user then logs in to the network, using the Login Name and Password property values. Login security compares these two values, checks for any restrictions that may have been set up for this User object, verifies that a valid User object and Password combination were used, and if not, tracks login attempts based on any set Intruder Limits. Then, if everything is correct, login security authenticates the login request and grants the User object access to NDS network resources.

To access NDS resources on the network, the user seeking access must first have been given the necessary NDS rights. Before rights can be granted to a User or other NDS object, however, that object must be made a trustee of the NDS resource. Then various rights such as Browse, Create, and so on can be assigned.

Note

An object is made a trustee of another object by adding the first object to the Object Trustees ACL (Access Control List) of another object. To simplify this process, using the NetWare Administrator utility, you can drag one object on top of another object and drop it there. This process automatically makes the dragged object a trustee of the receiving object.

For example, to give user object SAM the right to see all objects in container PAYROLL, user object SAM must be added to the Object Trustees (ACL) property for the PAYROLL container. Using the NetWare Administrator utility, User object SAM can be dragged on top of the PAYROLL container object and dropped. Then user object SAM must be given the Browse object right.

Note also that every object in the NDS tree has an Object Trustees (ACL) property.

Unlike the file system, which has only one set of rights, NDS has two sets of rights that can be assigned—object rights and property rights. *Object rights* are used to control what access an object has to another object. *Property rights* are used to control what access an object has to the information contained in an object's different properties.

For example, if you give user object SAM the Browse object right to container PAYROLL, user SAM will be able to see all objects within and below that container. If you then also give user object SAM the Read property right to the PAYROLL container, user object SAM will be able to see the values contained in each of this container's properties.

Table 4.1 lists all object and property rights, provides a brief description of each, and lists the type of right (object or property).

Table 4.1
List of Object and Property Rights

Type of Right	*Name of Right*	*Description*
Object	Browse	See objects in the tree
Object	Create	Create new objects
Object	Delete	Delete objects in the tree
Object	Rename	Change an object's name
Property	Add Self	Add or remove self as a value
Property	Compare	Compare any value to itself
Property	Read	Read a property's values
Property	Write	Add/change/delete values
Object	Supervisor	Access all properties of the object
Property	Supervisor	See and manipulate all values

Note When assigning property rights, you can choose between assigning all property rights for the object (choose the All Properties option when assigning property rights for the object), or assigning only specific property rights (choose the Selected Properties option, then choose which rights to assign to which properties).

Another similarity between NDS and the file system is that of inheritance. The file system and NDS both have a structure of rights inheritance. Both object and property rights flow down through the NDS tree structure to containers and subcontainers in much the same way that rights flow down through the file system structure from directories to subdirectories and files.

As with file system rights, the flow of object and property rights can be stopped or blocked at any lower level in the tree. To block rights at lower levels in the NDS tree, either make a new trustee assignment, or implement the IRF (Inherited Rights Filter) at the level in the tree where you want to block the flow of rights.

Note Rights assigned individually by using the Selected Properties option overwrite any rights assigned by using the All Properties option. This NDS feature makes it possible to make new trustee assignments at lower levels in the tree without having to first make specific or selected assignments at each higher level in the tree. Because rights assigned through the Selected Properties option cannot be inherited, selected assignments at each level in the tree would be necessary if the All Properties option were not first chosen at some higher level in the tree.

In the file system, users can be made security equivalent to another user in order to gain the same access as another user. In NDS, objects can also be made security equivalent to other objects. By default, each User object within a container of the tree is made security equivalent to the container in which it resides.

For example, when the container object HOME is made a trustee of another NDS object, such as the server object LHC_CADY, all user objects residing in the HOME container are also made trustees of the LHC_CADY server object.

There are several methods whereby an object can receive various object and property rights. Some of them have already been mentioned, including being made a trustee of an object and given object and property rights to that object, or being made security equivalent to a container. Because, as with the file system, there are several ways a user object can receive rights or have them modified or revoked, the term *effective rights* applies to both file system security and NDS security.

To determine the effective rights of an NDS object, you must consider all of the following:

- All explicit trustee assignments given to that User object
- Any Group objects to which the User object has been added
- The rights of the container in which the User object resides
- Whether the User object is also an occupant of an Organizational Role object
- All security equivalencies to other User objects granted to this User object
- Rights granted by default, such as those given to the [Public] trustee, which apply universally to all User objects

In addition, you must also consider where in the NDS tree you are located (current context) when determining effective rights, and whether the IRF has prevented any of the User object's rights from flowing down to this level in the tree.

Note Unlike file system security, the Supervisor right can be blocked with the IRF in NDS security. This must also be taken into consideration when calculating effective rights.

When NDS is installed, a NetWare 4 file server is added to (installed in) the network, or a User object is created, certain default rights are assigned at various locations in the NDS tree. Table 4.2 lists the associated rights assigned by default to various trustees when each of these three actions occur on the network.

Default rights assignments are designed to take care of common rights needs. Sometimes, however, default assignments are not sufficient; additional rights are necessary to enable users to access other network resources, or to manage NDS objects and properties. When additional rights assignments are needed, consider the following:

- Grant the Read right to the Path property or to the All Properties option to enable a user to access a Directory Map object
- Grant the Read right to the Login Script property of the All Properties option to enable a user to access and use a Profile Login Script object

Also, consider the following as guidelines for assigning additional NDS rights:

- Verify the current default assignments before making changes

- Use the Selected Properties option instead of the All Properties option whenever feasible, to help protect network information and assign specific rights rather than general rights
- Grant the Write property right to the Object Trustees (ACL) property of an object only when truly necessary, to avoid giving the trustee the ability to grant all rights (including Supervisor) to any trustee
- Exercise caution when granting the Supervisor object right to a Server object, or the Write property right to the Object Trustees (ACL) property of the Server object, because both actions grant Supervisor file system rights to all associated file server volumes
- Filter out the Supervisor right with an IRF only after making certain that another object with the Supervisor right has been assigned to the container so as to prevent a total lockout of the ADMIN and, subsequently, no management capabilities in that branch of the tree

Table 4.2
NDS Default Rights Assignments

Action	*Trustee*	*Right Assigned*
[Root] is created	[Public] User object ADMIN	Browse right to [Root] Supervisor object right to [Root]
Server object added	Server object Object's creator [Public]	Supervisor object right to itself Supervisor object right to the server object Read right to Messaging Server property
User object created	User object	Read to All Property Rights, and Read and Write to Login Script and Print Job Configuration properties
	[Root]	Read to Network Address and Group Membership properties
	[Public]	Read to Default Server property

Ensuring Secure Network Access through User Objects

Before a user can access network resources, the user must have a User object in the NDS database. The NetWare 4.1 installation software creates the ADMIN User object, and gives that User object all rights to the NDS tree. The network Administrator (ADMIN User object) then creates other User objects. How to create and manage User objects is the focus of this section.

Two NDS utilities—NetWare Administrator and NETADMIN—enable you to create and manage NDS User objects. Using either of these two utilities, you can do the following:

- Create and use a User_Template
- Create User objects
- Manage User objects

Creating and Using a User_Template

A User_Template lets you set up a master from which all property values can be copied to a User object each time you create a new User object. This can greatly reduce the amount of setup work you must perform for each new User object. You can create a User_Template in any of three ways, all of which involve the NetWare Administrator utility. You cannot create a User_Template with NETADMIN. You can create a User_Template in the following three ways:

- By using the User_Template option from the Object pull-down menu
- By choosing to create a User object, and calling it User_Template
- By choosing to create a User_Template when you create an Organization object or an Organizational Unit object

To create a User_Template with the NetWare Administrator utility, log in to the network as a user with Supervisor rights, open the NetWare Administrator utility, change your current context to point to the container where you want to create the User_Template, and then, depending on the method you chose to create a User_Template, complete the appropriate set of steps.

If you want to use the User_Template option from the Object pull-down menu, complete the following steps:

1. Choose User_Template from the Object pull-down menu.
2. Provide a Given Name, at a minimum.
3. Fill in other fields on this Identification page as necessary (see fig. 4.1).
4. Choose other pages such as Environment, Login Restrictions, and so on, and fill in fields as necessary.
5. When you have filled in all appropriate fields on all necessary pages, choose OK to save your changes.

If you want to create a User object and call it User_Template, complete the following steps:

1. Choose Create from the Object pull-down menu, then choose User.
2. Type **User_Template** in the Login Name field, then type **Template** in the Last Name field. (Both fields must be filled in to create a User object, with User_Template in the Login Name field indicating to the operating system that this User object is a User_Template.)
3. Expand the tree, if necessary, until you can see the User_Template object, then choose that object (see fig. 4.2).
4. Choose the User_Template object to open the User: User_Template Identification window.
5. Provide a Given Name, at a minimum.
6. Fill in other fields on this Identification page, as necessary.

7. Choose other pages such as Environment, Login Restrictions, and so on, and fill in fields as needed.

8. When you have filled in all appropriate fields on all necessary pages, choose OK to save your changes.

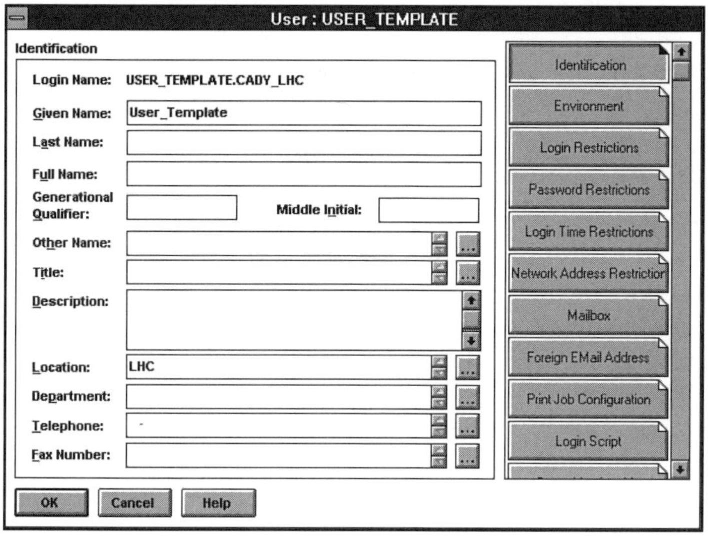

Figure 4.1
The User_Template Identification page.

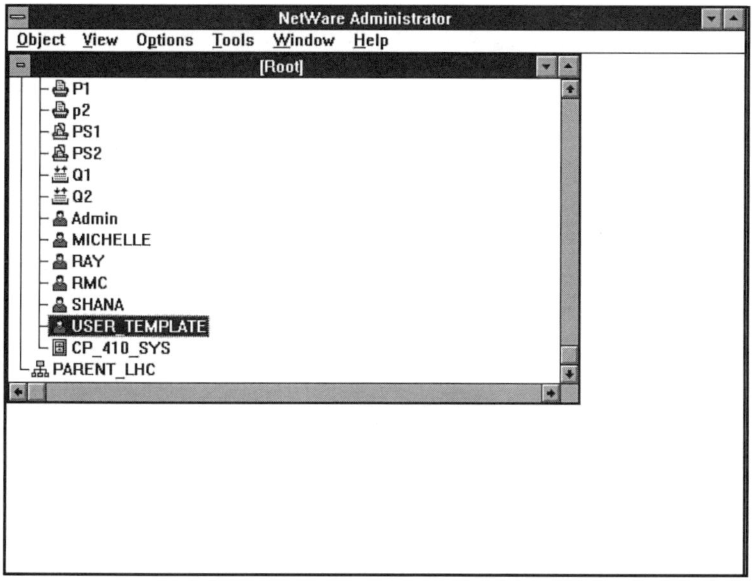

Figure 4.2
The expanded tree, showing User_Template.

If you want to create a User_Template when you create an Organization object or an Organizational Unit object, then complete the following steps:

1. Choose **C**reate from the **O**bject pull-down menu, then choose either Organization (if your context is [Root]) or Organizational Unit (see fig. 4.3).

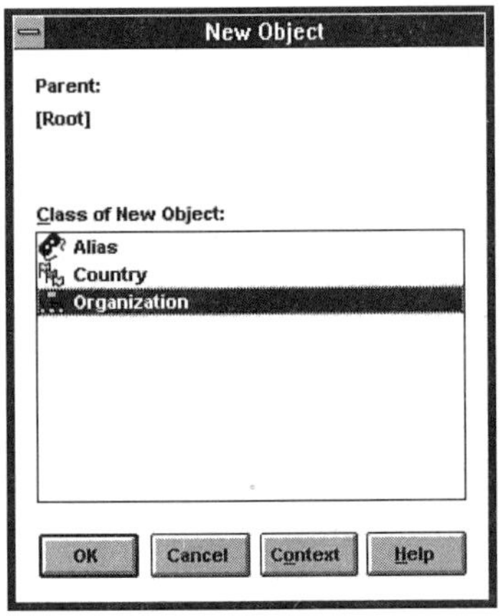

Figure 4.3
The New Object window.

> **Note** Because you will create Organizational Unit objects far more often than Organization objects, the balance of the numbered steps explain only how to create a User_Template when you create an Organizational Unit object. This note explains the remaining steps for creating a User_Template when you create an Organization object:
>
> - Choose Organization from the New Object menu.
> - Provide a name for the object.
> - Mark the Define User Defaults box.
> - Choose Create. The User_Template is created.
> - To see and modify this User_Template, expand the tree until you can see the User_Default object, then choose the User_Default object and provide the necessary information.

2. When the Create Organizational Unit window opens, type **User_Template** in the Organizational Unit **N**ame field.

3. Mark the Define **U**ser Defaults box, and choose Create.

4. To see and modify this User_Template, expand the tree until you can see the User_Template object, then choose the User_Template object and provide the necessary information.

After you create the User_Template, you can choose to apply it to each User object you subsequently create. In addition, you can edit the User_Template, changing what is applied to new users when they are created. You change the User_Template by running the NetWare Administrator utility, expanding the tree, choosing the User_Template object, then modifying information on the various screens. When all information is satisfactory, choose OK.

You can also modify a User_Template, using the NETADMIN utility, by following these steps:

1. Choose Manage objects from the NetAdmin Options menu.

2. Choose the User_Template object.

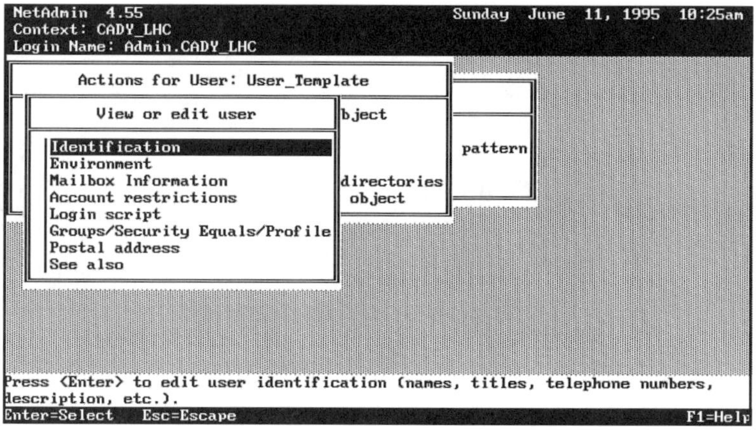

Figure 4.4
The View or edit user screen.

3. Choose View or edit properties of this object from the Actions for *object: object_name* menu.
4. Choose the page (Identification, Environment, Mailbox information, and so on) whose contents you want to edit (see fig. 4.4).
5. Make the necessary changes, then press F10 to save those changes.

After you create a User_Template and modify it to suit your network's particular needs, you can apply that User_Template each time you create a User object.

You can create User objects using either the NetWare Administrator or NETADMIN utilities. When using the NetWare Administrator utility, mark the Use User Template box in the Create User box to apply the User_Template when creating a user (see fig. 4.5).

When using the NETADMIN utility, set the Copy the User Template Object? to Yes (the default) in the Create User Object screen.

The following section explains how to create User objects, using the NetWare Administrator and NETADMIN utilities.

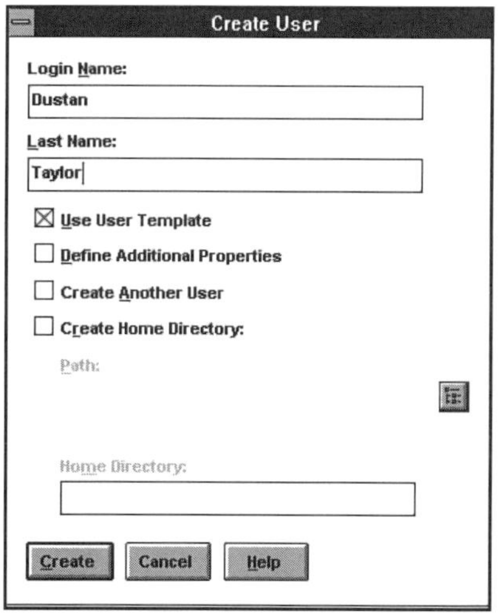

Figure 4.5
The Create User box.

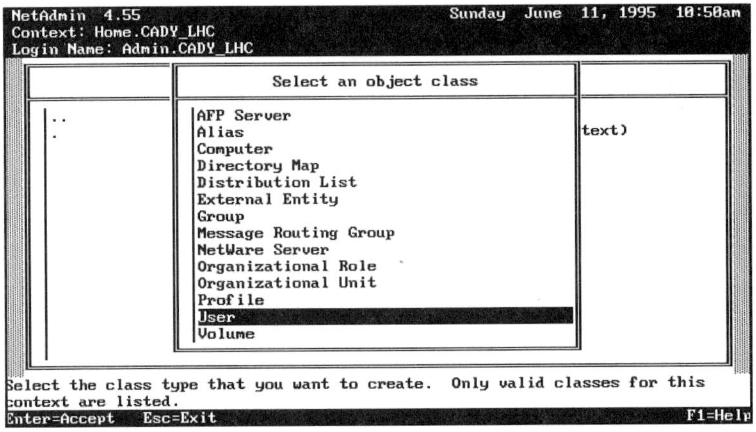

Figure 4.6
The Select an object class screen.

Creating User Objects

To create a User object by using the NetWare Administrator utility, complete the following steps:

1. Choose Create from the Object pull-down menu, then choose User.
2. Type, in the Login Name field, the name the user is to use when logging in to the network.
3. Type the user's last name in the Last Name field, if you choose to provide this information; then mark any of the appropriate boxes (such as Use User Template), providing any additional information as requested (such as the path to the user's home directory if creation of a home directory was chosen as an option).
4. Choose Create.

To create a User object by using the NETADMIN utility, complete the following steps:

1. Change your current context to the context where the User object is to be created.
2. Press the Ins key, and choose User from the Select an object class screen (see fig. 4.6).
3. Type, in the Login Name field, the name the user is to use when logging in to the network.
4. Type the user's last name in the Last Name field, then provide any additional related information, as necessary.
5. Press F10 to save this information and create the User object.

Managing User Objects

User objects in particular require regular maintenance. New User objects need to be added, whereas others need to be deleted or modified. Security issues such as login restrictions must also be dealt with. The following common User object management tasks are discussed in this section:

- Adding and changing User object property values
- Setting account restrictions
- Implementing and resetting intruder detection

Note: To pass the NetWare 4.1 Administration CNE test, you must be able to perform each task in the preceding list, using the NetWare Administrator utility. Therefore, only the steps to be followed for performing these tasks by using the NetWare Administrator utility are discussed here (even though both the NetWare Administrator and NETADMIN utilities can be used to perform these tasks).

Adding and Changing User Object Property Values

To add or change a User object's property values, log in to the network as a user with Supervisor rights, start the NetWare Administrator utility, and complete the following steps:

1. Expand the directory tree, then choose the User object whose property values you want to add or change.
2. From the User Identification page, choose the property or choose another page containing properties whose values are to be added or changed. (See table 4.3 for a list of pages and some of the more frequently referenced property values you can add or change on each page.)
3. When you have made all necessary additions or changes, choose OK to save all changes.

Note: If you choose Cancel instead of OK, all changes on all pages are lost. You must choose OK to save all changes.

Table 4.3
Some User Object Pages and Their Common Properties

Page Name	*Property*	*Description*
Identification	Login Name	Name used by user to identify him/herself to the network and gain access to its resources
	Given Name	User's first name
	Last Name	User's last name
	Title	Job function or responsibility
	Department	Department or division in which user works
	Telephone	User's telephone numbers
	Fax Number	User's FAX number
Environment	Default Server	Complete context for user's default file server, as set in Preferred Server statement of workstation NET.CFG file
	Home Directory	Location (volume and path) of user's home directory

continues

Table 4.3, Continued
Some User Object Pages and Their Common Properties

Page Name	*Property*	*Description*
Mailbox	Mailbox Location	Name of messaging server where user's mailbox is stored
	Mailbox ID	Unique name for this user's mailbox, as stored in NDS database
Print Job Configuration	Print Job Configurations	Enables you to add, modify, or delete an existing configuration, or change the default print job configuration for this user
Login Script	Login Script	Holds login script commands specific to this user
	Profile	Enables you to specify a profile login script to be activated when this user logs in to the network
Intruder Lockout	Account Locked	Enables you to unlock a locked user account
Rights to Files and Directories	Volumes	Enables you to find, show, or hide names of any volumes on which the user has File or Directory rights
	Files and Directories	Enables you to see all files or directories to which this user has a trustee assignment
	Rights	Displays user's Trustee rights assignment for specified file or directory
	Effective Rights	Enables you to see the \ effective rights for this object
Group Memberships	Memberships	Displays groups of which this user is a member, and enables you to Add this user to a group, or Delete this user from a group
Security Equal To	Security Equals	Displays list of objects to which this User is security equal, and enables you to Add objects to and Delete objects from the list

Setting Account Restrictions

Set account restrictions by using the following pages from the NetWare Administrator utility:

- Login Restrictions
- Password Restrictions
- Login Time Restrictions

Table 4.4 shows a list of user account-restriction-related pages, and several of their more frequently used user properties.

Table 4.4
List of User Account-Restriction Pages and Common User Properties

Page Name	*Property*	*Description*
Login Restrictions	Account Disabled	Enables you to prevent user from logging in to network
	Account has Expiration Date	Sets date and time on which user's account will expire
	Limit Concurrent Connections	Enables you to limit number of workstations from which user can be simultaneously logged in to the network
Password Restrictions	Allow User to Change Password	Enables you to specify whether user can change his or her own password
	Require a Password	Enables you to force user to have a password for his or her user account
	Minimum Password Length	Indicates minimum number of characters required for a password, if one is required
	Force Periodic Password Changes	Enables you to require that users change their passwords at specified regular intervals
Login Time Restrictions	Reset	Use to reset segments of time you blacked out to prevent this user from accessing the network during those time segments

Implementing and Resetting Intruder Detection

To implement intruder detection, complete the following steps:

1. Select the level of the tree where you want to implement intruder detection.
2. Choose Details from the Object pull-down menu.
3. Choose the Intruder Detection page button to open the window shown in figure 4.7.
4. Mark the Detect Intruders and Lock Account After Detection boxes.
5. Accept the default values for the associated properties, or change the values as necessary.
6. Choose OK to save the changes.

To reset intruder detection on a user's account, using the NetWare Administrator utility, expand the tree to display objects, choose the User object, then choose the Intruder Lockout page from the NetWare Administrator utility. From this page you can set or change various Intruder Lockout properties. Table 4.5 shows a list of user Intruder Lockout properties that you can set or change.

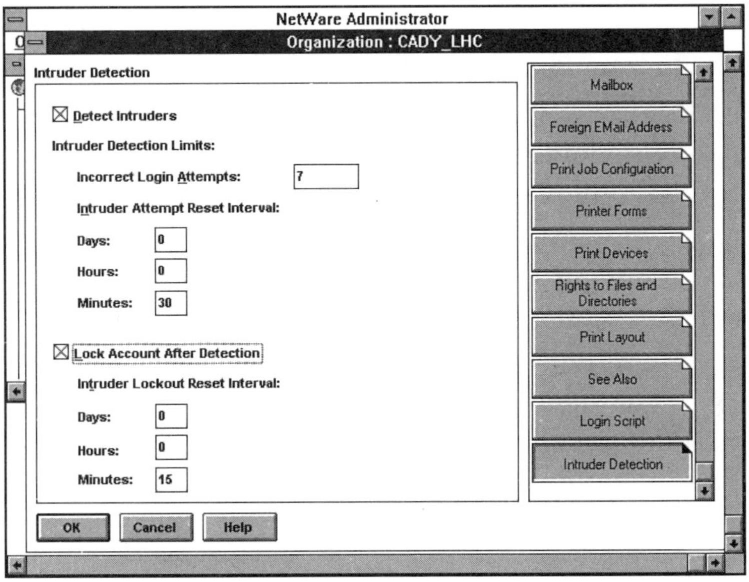

Figure 4.7
The Intruder Detection window.

Table 4.5
Intruder Lockout Properties

Property Name	*Description*
Account Locked	When marked, indicates that an attempt to log in to network using this user's login name and an incorrect password occurred, unsuccessfully, several times
Incorrect Login Count	Indicates number of attempts made to log in, using the incorrect password
Account Reset Time	Indicates at what time account will be unlocked, if currently locked, or at what time Incorrect Login Count will be reset
Last Intruder Address	Displays workstation network address from which last incorrect login attempt was made

Automating Network Access through a DOS Workstation

After security and access for users is set up and configured at the NDS database and file server level, the user's workstation must be set up to enable the user to access the network. In addition, after basic workstation installation has been accomplished, workstations should have their configuration files set up so as to automate the process of loading files and preparing for logging in to the network.

Setting up a user's workstation and automating the process of loading files in preparation for network log in involves the following two procedures, both of which are discussed in this section:

- Installing NetWare Client for DOS and MS Windows
- Modifying workstation files to automate network connection

Installing NetWare Client for DOS and MS Windows

A workstation that is to be connected to a NetWare 4 network must meet the following minimum requirements:

- IBM (or compatible) XT, AT, 8088 (or higher) microprocessor
- 4 MB hard disk space for a DOS or MS Windows Client

Note: If less than 5 MB of disk space is available when you install the NetWare Client for DOS and MS Windows software, you receive an `Insufficient disk space` error message.

The NetWare Client for DOS and MS Windows software can be installed from disk, or across the network from the SYS:PUBLIC\CLIENT \DOSWIN directory. Set up for installation by placing the WSDOS_1 disk in a disk drive, or by logging in to a NetWare 4 file server and mapping a drive to the SYS:PUBLIC\CLIENT\DOSWIN directory. Then install the NetWare Client for DOS and MS Windows software by completing the following steps:

1. Type **Install** and press Enter.
2. Accept C:\NWCLIENT as the default directory where the client files will be stored, or change this field on the NetWare Client Install screen (shown as step 1 in fig. 4.8) to reflect a different location.
3. If you prefer to modify the client's AUTOEXEC.BAT and CONFIG.SYS files manually, change the YES default in step 2 to NO when you are prompted to `Allow changes? (Y/N)`.
4. If the client has MS Windows installed, change the NO default in step 3 to YES when you are prompted to `Install support for MS Windows? (Y/N)`.

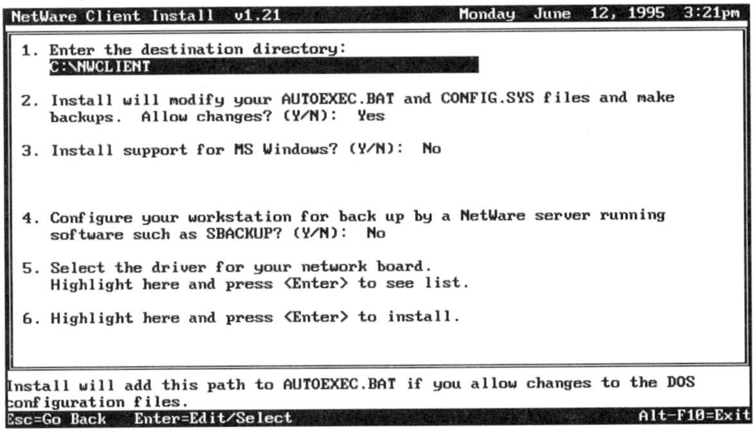

Figure 4.8
The NetWare Client Install screen.

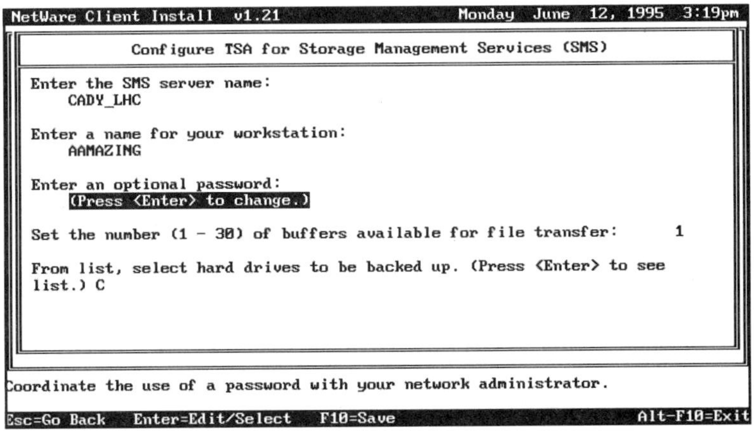

Figure 4.9
The screen for configuring client backup.

5. If you want this client to have its hard disk backed up from the file server, change the NO default in step 4 to YES when you are prompted to `Configure your workstation for back up by a NetWare server running software such as SBACKUP (Y/N)`.

   If you choose to allow this client to be backed up, you are prompted with a screen that enables you to Configure TSA for Storage Management Services (SMS). Figure 4.9 shows this screen with entries for a client on the CADY_LHC file server.

6. Choose a network board driver for the network board installed in this client from step 5 on the NetWare Client Install screen, by choosing Highlight here and press <Enter> to see list (step 5).

   If a network board and driver are already installed when you run the NetWare Client for DOS and MS Windows install program, and the install program can recognize the board, a message window indicating that the board has been recognized is displayed (see fig. 4.10). Press Enter to continue.

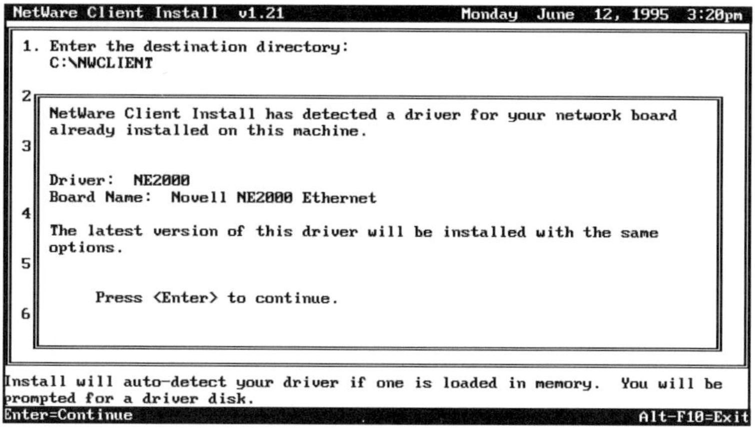

Figure 4.10
The Network Board Driver Detected message screen.

If no board is detected, or you want to change the selected board, you can choose from a list of network boards.

7. Select step 6 (Highlight here and press <Enter> to install), then press Enter to install the NetWare Client for DOS and MS Windows software.

Modifying Workstation Files to Automate Network Connection

If you chose not to let the client installation software modify the AUTOEXEC.BAT and CONFIG.SYS configuration files, you must modify them yourself. In addition to the AUTOEXEC.BAT and CONFIG.SYS files, you will have to work with the NET.CFG file, and possibly with the STARTNET.BAT file.

The CONFIG.SYS file must contain the following line for workstations you want to make NetWare 4 clients (or from which you want to access NetWare 4 resources):

```
LASTDRIVE = Z
```

The AUTOEXEC.BAT file must contain either a call to the STARTNET.BAT file (@CALL C:\NWCLIENT\STARTNET.BAT), or the lines that are part of the STARTNET.BAT file, as shown in the following paragraph.

If used, the STARTNET.BAT file contains the following lines:

```
C:
CD \NWCLIENT (or replace with the directory
where the NetWare Client for DOS and MS
Windows files are stored)
LSL.COM
NE2000 (replace with the driver file used by
this client)
IPXODI
VLM
F:
LOGIN user_login_id (replace user_login_id
with this user's login name)
```

The NET.CFG file provides configuration information for the workstation's connection software. This file must contain at least a Link Driver driver_name command with parameters, and a NetWare DOS Requester heading with two additional entries, as shown in the following example of a NET.CFG file:

```
Link Drive NE3200
     INT 5
     PORT 300
NetWare DOS Requester
     FIRST NETWORK DRIVE = F
     PREFERRED SERVER = CADY_LHC
```

Questions

1. The first step you must perform before granting the Browse object right to a specific user is to ______ .
   - ○ A. move the User object to the other object's container
   - ○ B. grant the Browse object right to a group to which the user presently belongs
   - ○ C. create a group and add the User object to it
   - ○ D. make the User object a trustee (add it to the object's ACL)
2. The ______ and ______ property rights enable you to read a property's values.
   - ☐ A. Add Self
   - ☐ B. Read
   - ☐ C. Supervisor
   - ☐ D. Browse
3. Which of the following is *not* a true statement?
   - ○ A. Rights assigned individually, using the Selected Properties option, overwrite any rights assigned by using the All Properties option.
   - ○ B. Both the file system and NDS have a structure of rights inheritance.
   - ○ C. You can block the Supervisor right in both the file system and NDS.
   - ○ D. When the [Root] object is created, only [Public] and ADMIN are assigned default rights to [Root].
4. A ______ can be used to simplify creation of User objects.
   - ○ A. User_Template
   - ○ B. User_Map
   - ○ C. User_Object
   - ○ D. User_Container
5. The field you must fill in on the User_Template Identification page when creating a User_Template object is ______ .
   - ○ A. Last Name
   - ○ B. Given Name
   - ○ C. Login Name
   - ○ D. Other Name
6. To create a User object with the NetWare Administrator utility, what option do you choose from the Object pull-down menu?
   - ○ A. User
   - ○ B. Details
   - ○ C. Add
   - ○ D. Create
7. Of the following, which *three* are true statements:
   - ☐ A. The Identification page of a User object contains the user's Given name.
   - ☐ B. The Environment page of a User object contains the user's Home Directory.
   - ☐ C. To specify a Profile login script to be used, open the Login Restrictions page for the user.
   - ☐ D. To unlock a user's account, use the Intruder Lockout page for that user.

8. To set a date and time when a user's account will expire, you must open the ______ page for that User object.
   - A. Identification
   - B. Login Restrictions
   - C. Password Restrictions
   - D. Intruder Lockout

9. Which of the following is *not* a property of a user's Intruder Lockout page?
   - A. Incorrect Login Count
   - B. Reset
   - C. Account Locked
   - D. Last Intruder Address

10. To specify drive Z as the last network drive, place the ______ statement into the ______ client configuration file.
    - A. LAST DRIVE = Z, AUTOEXEC.BAT
    - B. LASTDRIVE = Z, STARTNET.BAT
    - C. LASTDRIVE = Z, CONFIG.SYS
    - D. LAST DRIVE = Z, NET.CFG

Answers

1. D
2. B, C
3. C
4. A
5. B
6. D
7. A, B, D
8. B
9. B
10. C

CHAPTER 5

Customizing User Access

To some extent, setting up a user's workstation for network access customizes that user's access to the network. In reality, however, the setup process customizes the client's access more than the user's access. Other options for customizing user access exist. This chapter provides information about the following two options:

- *Login scripts*
- *Menus*

Creating Login Scripts

NetWare 4 has four types of login scripts: container, default, profile, and user. The NetWare administrator can create all of them except the default login script.

> **Note** The default login script is part of the LOGIN.EXE file, and cannot be created or modified by network users. It runs only if no user login script exists. To prevent it from running when no user login script exists, place the NO_DEFAULT command in a container or profile login script.

Container Login Script

The *container* login script is the first login script run when a user logs in, if such a login script exists in the user's parent container. Used primarily to establish the general environment for the user, the container login script may include commands to perform such tasks as the following:

- Establish global network assignments
- Provide actions, associated with the user's login, that are relatively unique to users in the parent container (such as mapping drives and starting menus or applications)
- Set up access to various network files and printers

Figure 5.1 shows a sample container login script for the Organization: CADY_LHC container.

To create a container login script, complete the following steps:

1. Log in to the network as a user with Supervisor rights, then start the NetWare Administration utility.
2. Expand the NDS tree to display the container where you want to create the login script, then highlight (select) that container.
3. Choose **D**etails from the Object pull-down menu.
4. Choose the Login Script page button.
5. Type the login script commands you want to place in this container login script (refer to fig. 5.1).
6. Choose OK.

Profile Login Script

The *profile* login script executes after the container login script, if a container login script exists. Frequently, a profile login script is used to provide (to users whose User objects are in a different parent container) the same types of conditional operations that the container login script provides for this container's users.

You can, for example, set up the profile login script to do the following:

- Map network drives
- Send messages
- Provide access to printers

The profile login script is a property of the Profile object (see fig. 5.2).

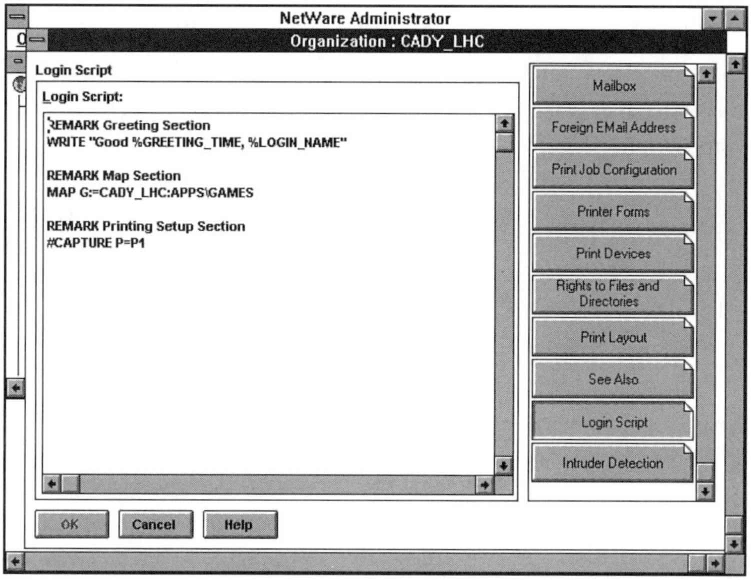

Figure 5.1
A sample container login script.

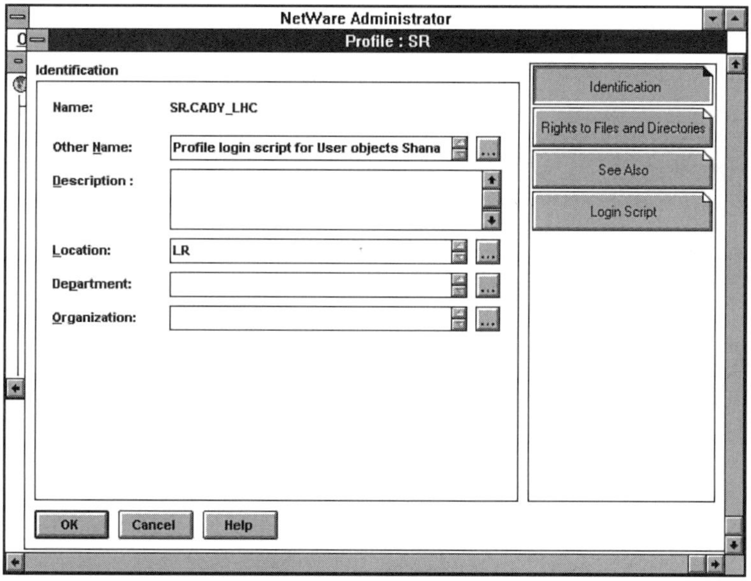

Figure 5.2
The Profile object SR Identification page.

To create a profile login script, complete the following steps:

1. Log in to the network as a user with Supervisor rights, then start the NetWare Administration utility.
2. Expand the NDS tree to display the container where you want to create the profile login script.
3. Choose **C**reate from the Object pull-down menu.
4. Type a name for the profile login script, then mark the **D**efine Additional Properties box, and choose **C**reate (see fig. 5.3).
5. When the Profile: *profile_name* Identification page opens, choose the Login Script page button.
6. Type the login script commands you want to place in this login script.
7. Choose OK.

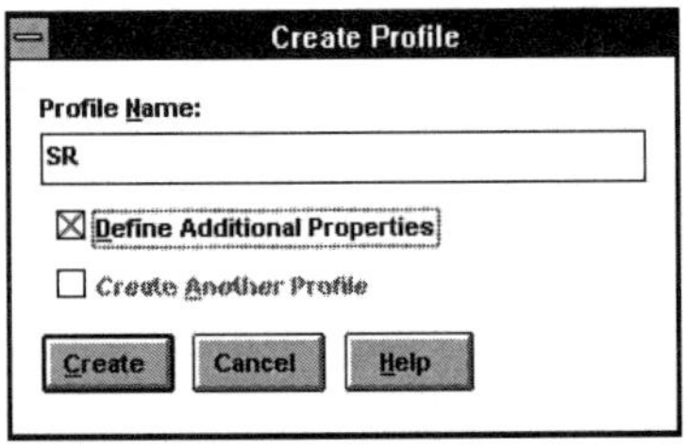

Figure 5.3
The Create Profile dialog box.

User Login Script

The *user* login script runs after the container and profile login scripts (if applicable) have run. If a user login script exists, the default login script will not run. Therefore, the user login script should contain at least basic system mappings (if such mappings have not been provided in one of the other types of login scripts). Following are other common uses for a user login script:

- Running commands that apply only to this user
- Setting up connection to printers commonly accessed by this user
- Sending to the user notices or reminders based on specific days of the week
- Starting, at the time the user logs in to the network, any menus and applications used frequently by this user

The user login script is a property of the User object (see fig. 5.4).

To create a user login script, complete the following steps:

1. Log in to the network as a user with Supervisor rights, then start the NetWare Administration utility.
2. Expand the NDS tree to display the User object for whom you want to create a user login script, then select that User object.
3. Choose **D**etails from the Object pull-down menu.
4. Choose the Login Script page button.
5. Type the login script commands you want to place in this user's login script.
6. Choose OK.

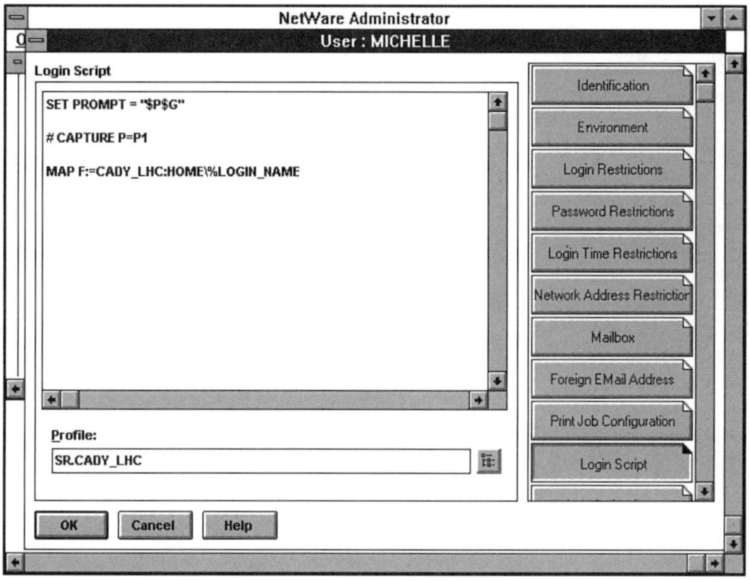

Figure 5.4
The User object MICHELLE login script page.

Note You can also specify a profile login script to be run for this user when he or she logs in to the network. To specify a profile login script, choose the **Profile** field and enter the complete name of a profile login script. If you choose to run a profile login script for this user, the profile login script is executed before the user login script.

When you create a login script of any type, you must use specific commands in the proper context. In addition, you must apply the following rules:

- Only one command can be entered on each line.
- Blank lines can be inserted with no effect.
- When using variables in a command, they must be preceded by the percent (%) sign.

Note A *variable* is a term that tells the computer to replace the term with its equivalent value. For example, the variable %LOGIN_NAME tells the computer to use the user's actual login name, rather than the term %LOGIN_NAME.

- Variables should be written in uppercase letters.

Table 5.1 lists several of the most commonly used login script commands available for NetWare 4 login scripts.

Table 5.1
NetWare 4.1 Login Script Commands

Command	*Description*	*Example*
#	Executes an external command	#CAPTURE P=P1
CLS	Clears the monitor	CLS
COMSPEC	Tells the PC where to find the COMMAND.COM file	COMSPEC=S3:COMMAND.COM
DISPLAY *file*	Prints a text file to the screen	DISPLAY AUTOEXEC.BAT
DRIVE	Specifies the default drive letter	DRIVE G
EXIT *file*	Ends the login script and runs a file	EXIT TODAY1.BAT
FIRE PHASERS	Causes the computer to beep	FIRE PHASERS 2 times
MAP	Sets a drive mapping or displays current settings	MAP G:=CADY_LHC:APPS
REMARK	Indicates that anything that follows is not to be run	REMARK This login script was last changed on 6/95
WRITE	Displays a message on the screen	WRITE "Remember your daily report!"

Creating Menus

When a user logs in to the network, you can simplify the user's access to resources by providing a menu of items from which to choose. Generally, if the user always accesses only one utility and rarely accesses any other network resources, a menu is unnecessary. If the user must access three different application programs, for example, then a menu from which to choose may be very useful. To enable the user to access a menu, you can use the EXIT *file* command in the user's login script, replacing *file* with the name of the menu.

Before a user can access a menu, that menu must be created. To create a menu, type the menu commands in a file, using the correct order and terminology. Use any DOS text editor to create the file. Save the file with an SRC extension.

For example, if you want to create a menu file for a group of users to access various applications in the Accounts Payable department, you might create a DOS text file called AP.SRC.

After you create the basic source file, you compile that source file, the result of which is a usable menu file with a DAT extension. This file can then be run for user access. To compile the source file, you use the MENUMAKE command followed by the name of the source file.

For example, to compile the AP.SRC file, type **MENUMAKE AP** and press Enter. The result, if your efforts are successful, is a usable menu file called MENUMAKE.DAT.

Note If you chose to name the source file with an extension other than SRC, specify the complete file name (including the extension) when you compile the file. If, in the preceding example, you had named the menu source file AP.TXT instead of AP.SRC, you would have to type **MENUMAKE AP.TXT** when compiling the source file.

If the source file does not compile successfully, you probably have made some mistakes in specifying the commands in the menu source file. (Commands specify such things as what the menu is to look like when it runs, and how the menu is to process information and execute commands.) To successfully compile the source menu, you must correct the errors. To correct the errors, you need to understand not only the commands themselves, but also the requirements for using commands.

NetWare menu source files can contain only two types of menu script file commands—organizational and control commands.

Organizational commands specify what the menu will look like when it displays on-screen. The following are the two organizational commands:

- MENU
- ITEM

Control commands specify which commands to execute and how to process information provided. There are four basic control commands, one of which has three alternative uses. The following are the four control commands:

- EXEC
- LOAD
- SHOW
- GET*X*

Note When you use any of the commands in a menu source file, the commands must be typed in uppercase letters.

In addition to the commands, the menu source file contains options that can be used with each command. For example, when you use the ITEM command, you can also use its associated BATCH option. Doing so enables you to remove the otherwise memory-resident menu from the workstation's memory, thereby freeing up room in which to load application programs and files.

Table 5.2 shows each of the organizational and control commands, as well as the options that can be used with each command. The table also provides the format to be followed when you use the command, a list of options that can be used with each command, and a brief description of those options.

Table 5.2
NetWare 4.1 Menu Commands and Options

Command	*Command Description and Format*	*Options and Descriptions*
MENU	Specifies start of each menu screen, along with number and name of menu **Format:** `MENU` *`menu_number, menu_name`*	No options available
ITEM	Defines menu options **Format:** `ITEM` *`item_name {options}`*	BATCH—removes menu from memory CHDIR—returns to default directory after a menu option is chosen PAUSE—displays "Press any key to continue" message and pauses until a key is pressed SHOW—displays name of a DOS command being run when one has been requested
EXEC	Runs a specified command **Format:** `EXEC` *`{option}`*	EXIT—closes menu and exits to the DOS prompt DOS—shells out to DOS requiring the user to type **EXIT** to return to the menu. LOGOUT—closes menu and logs user out of network, returning user to DOS prompt
LOAD	Runs another menu from within this menu, when the other menu was created as a separate menu file **Format:** `LOAD` *`menu_name.DAT`*	No options available
SHOW	Runs submenus created as part of this menu; can be used to display up to 255 submenus **Format:** `SHOW` *`menu_number`*	No options available
GET*X*	Prompts for user input. If *X* is replaced with the letter O, input is *optional*. If *X* is replaced with the letter R, input is *required* before additional processing can be done. If *X* is replaced with the letter P, input provided by the user is stored for later use. **Format:** `GETX` *`instruction{prepend}`* ➥*`length,prefill[append]`*	No options available

Note: When the GET*X* command is used, the user must press F10 before processing will continue. In addition, the following rules apply to the use of GET*X* in menus:

- GET*X* must be placed between the ITEM command and any EXEC command associated with it.
- You may use no more than 100 GET*X* commands per ITEM.
- You can prompt the user for a response no more than 10 times per dialog box, or you can use the caret (^) symbol to place each prompt in its own dialog box.
- Each prompt must be on a separate line in the menu file.

The following sample menu source file is named TEST.SRC:

```
MENU 01,Menu Options
  ITEM ^BNetWare Commands
    Show 10
  ITEM ^AApplications
    Show 20
  ITEM ^DLogout
    EXEC LOGOUT
  ITEM ^CClose Menu
    EXEC EXIT

MENU 10,NetWare Commands
  ITEM NLIST
    GETO Class Name and Option:{}25,,{}
    EXEC NLIST
  ITEM DIR {PAUSE}
    GETO Drive letter:{}25,,{}
    EXEC DIR

MENU 20,Applications
  ITEM Word Processor
    EXEC C:\WP\WP.EXE
  ITEM Screen Shots
    EXEC C:\COLLAGE\SNAP C:\BOOKS
```

After running the MENUMAKE utility to compile this source file, the menu file called TEST.DAT is created. The user can then run this menu by typing **NMENU** followed by the name of the menu. For example, when the user types **NMENU TEST.DAT** at the prompt and presses the Enter key, the result is the menu shown in figure 5.5.

Note: The user must have Read and File Scan rights to the directory containing the menu file, and Read, File Scan, and Write rights to the user's directory.

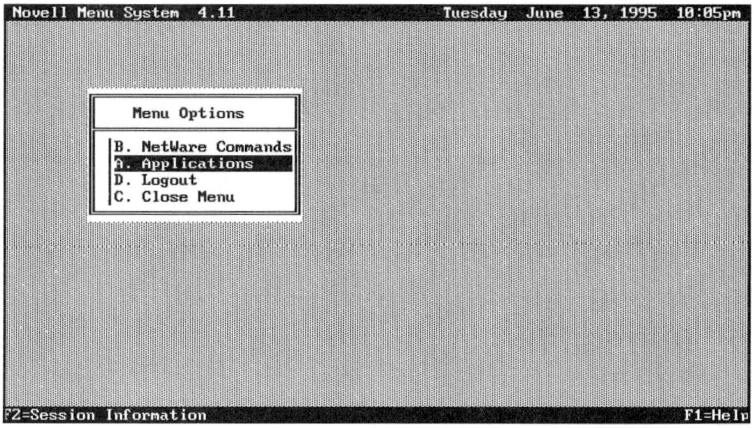

Figure 5.5
Menu displayed from running the TEST.DAT file.

Questions

1. Which of the following is *not* a type of login script?
   - ○ A. Container
   - ○ B. Profile
   - ○ C. Optional
   - ○ D. User

2. The ______ and ______ login scripts can be selected from inside the User object's Login Script page.
   - □ A. container
   - □ B. profile
   - □ C. optional
   - □ D. user

3. The ______ login script is *not* run for a user whose parent container is not the same as that of this login script.
   - ○ A. container
   - ○ B. profile
   - ○ C. optional
   - ○ D. user

4. Which of the following is *not* a true statement?
   - ○ A. The user login script is used to run commands that apply only to the user.
   - ○ B. A profile login script must be given a name.
   - ○ C. The user login script is a property of the User object.
   - ○ D. None of the preceding statements is true.

5. Which rule relates to creating login scripts?
   - ○ A. Variables must be preceded by a percent (%) sign.
   - ○ B. Multiple commands can be entered on the same line, if separated with commas.
   - ○ C. Only Organizational and Control commands are used when you create login scripts.
   - ○ D. All of the preceding rules relate to creating login scripts.

6. If both types of login scripts are run, the ______ login script executes before the user login script.
   - ○ A. container
   - ○ B. default
   - ○ C. profile
   - ○ D. optional

7. Of the following, which *three* are valid login script commands?
   - □ A. CLS
   - □ B. #
   - □ C. PLAY SOUND
   - □ D. WRITE

8. A file with a ______ extension is a menu source file.
   - ○ A. DAT
   - ○ B. SOU
   - ○ C. SRC
   - ○ D. EXE

9. To start an application from a menu, you must use the ______ control command.

   ○ A. EXEC

   ○ B. LOAD

   ○ C. SHOW

   ○ D. GET*X*

10. The user must have ______ and ______ security rights to access a menu file.

    ○ A. File Scan, Write

    ○ B. Write, Read

    ○ C. File Scan, Write

    ○ D. Read, File Scan

Answers

1. C
2. B, D
3. A
4. D
5. A
6. C
7. A, B, D
8. C
9. A
10. D

CHAPTER 6

Using NetWare Console Commands

NetWare 4 file servers enable you to store, access, and manage files and the NDS database, and to provide services that network users request. The ability to access, manage, and protect NetWare 4 file servers is, therefore, of paramount importance. Access to NetWare servers is provided through console commands. The basic design of the NetWare 4 operating system (the Core OS) and its associated NLMs (NetWare Loadable Modules) also provides access.

This chapter discusses the NetWare console commands and NLMs commonly used to protect and access NetWare 4 file servers. Also included here is information about the use of console commands, NLMs, remote console access, and SBACKUP. The chapter addresses the following topics:

- Understanding and securing the NetWare 4 file server
- Implementing and using remote console management
- Enhancing file server security by using SBACKUP

Understanding and Securing the NetWare 4 File Server

The NetWare 4 file server provides access to resources on the network, and provides services requested by users. To provide access to resources and services, the NetWare 4 file server interface provides console commands and NLMs. NLMs are also one portion of the NetWare operating system. The other portion is called the *NetWare Core OS.*

NLMs provide added functionality. By loading different NLMs on the file server, you can pick and choose what functionality you implement. NLMs that provide services such as linking disk and LAN drivers are always loaded on every NetWare 4 file server. NLMs that provide services such as management utilities may be loaded only when they are needed.

NetWare 4 provides the following four types of NLMs:

- **Disk drivers.** These NLMs are responsible for controlling communication between the NetWare 4 operating system and the computer's hard disk drives. Standard NetWare disk driver NLM files use a DSK extension. The newer NPA (NetWare Peripheral Architecture) files have CDM and HAM extensions.
- **Name space modules.** Thanks to these NLMs, files whose names are not based on DOS file-naming conventions can be stored in the NetWare 4 file system. Name space files have a NAM extension.
- **Network board (LAN) drivers.** These NLMs are responsible for controlling communication between the NetWare 4 operating system and the network board. LAN driver files have a LAN extension.
- **NLM utilities.** These NLMs are utilities that are run from the file server console or from a workstation running the remote console software. The NLM utilities provide access to monitor and configure file server software. The NLM utility modules have a NLM extension.

To load an NLM, type the following command at the file server console, and press Enter:

LOAD *NLM_name [parameters]*

Replace *NLM_name* with the name of the NLM to be loaded. If the NLM is not currently found in the SYS:SYSTEM directory, which is the default location for NLMs, you can also specify the path to the NLM before providing the name of the NLM to be loaded.

Replace *[parameters]* with any parameters to be used when loading this specific NLM. For example, to change the keyboard type at the file server, type **LOAD KEYB *keyboard_type***, replacing *keyboard_type* with the type of keyboard. The type of keyboard you enter in place of the *keyboard_type* command is a parameter of the LOAD KEYB command.

Table 6.1 shows a list of some of the more commonly used NLMs.

The NetWare Core OS runs on every NetWare 4 file server. Without it, a NetWare 4 file server is not a file server, but just another computer physically attached to the network. The NetWare Core OS provides the following five basic services:

- Authentication of network users
- File system services
- NetWare Directory Services
- Network security
- Routing services

Table 6.1
Commonly Used NLMs

NLM	*NLM Type*	*Function*
ISADISK.DSK	Disk driver	Controls ISA hard disks
INSTALL.NLM	NLM utility	Installs and configures NetWare
MAC.NAM	Name space	Allows files using Macintosh naming conventions to be stored on and retrieved from a NetWare file server
MONITOR.NLM	NLM utility	Displays NetWare OS statistics
OS2.NAM	Name space	Allows files using OS/2 naming conventions to be stored on and retrieved from a NetWare file server
RSPX.NLM	NLM utility	Permits remote access to the file server console
NE2000.LAN	LAN driver	Controls NetWare 4 OS communication with the network board
PSERVER.NLM	NLM utility	Loads NetWare print server software on a file server

NLMs provide network services, and a means of controlling and configuring those services. The Core OS also provides a means of accessing and controlling the NetWare operating system. It provides utilities, called *console commands*, which can be run from the NetWare OS system prompt. Just as NLMs can be compared to external DOS commands, NetWare console commands are similar to internal DOS commands. Following are several of the more commonly used NetWare console commands:

- **BROADCAST.** Use to send a message to workstations with current network connections
- **CLS.** Use to clear the console screen displaying only the system prompt
- **CONFIG.** Use to view the file server's name and its network (LAN) configuration information
- **DOWN.** Use to unload the operating system software
- **EXIT.** Use to return to the DOS prompt after using the DOWN console command
- **HELP.** Use to view information about NLMs and console commands (see fig. 6.1)
- **LOAD.** Use to run NLMs by placing them into file server memory
- **MODULES.** Use to view a list of currently loaded NLMs
- **UNLOAD.** Use to remove NLMs from file server memory

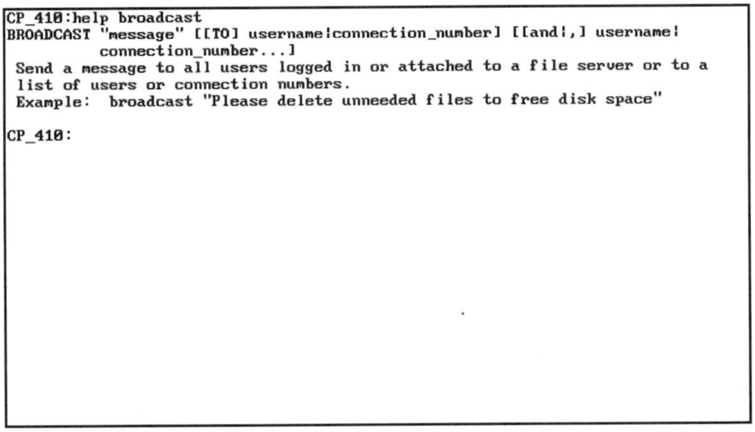

```
CP_410:help broadcast
BROADCAST "message" [[TO] username|connection_number] [[and|,] username|
          connection_number...]
 Send a message to all users logged in or attached to a file server or to a
 list of users or connection numbers.
 Example:  broadcast "Please delete unneeded files to free disk space"

CP_410:
```

Figure 6.1
Display of the Help BROADCAST console command.

Implementing and Using Remote Console Management

Loading NLMs and entering console commands while sitting at the network file server is not always convenient, or even possible. NetWare provides remote console management NLMs and a utility to enable you to access the file server console from a workstation just as easily as if you were sitting at the file server console.

To use the remote console utility, you need to load the associated NLMs at the file server (REMOTE.NLM and RSPX.NLM or RS232.NLM), then log in to the file server and run the RCONSOLE utility.

Note Add the command to load the remote console management NLMs to the file server's AUTOEXEC.NCF file to ensure that remote console management is always available.

Connection to a file server can be made from a workstation attached directly to the network, or from a workstation attached to the network through a modem. The first type of connection is referred to as an *SPX connection.* The second type of connection is referred to as an *asynchronous connection.* With both types of connection, the REMOTE.NLM must be loaded when you implement remote management on a file server. If the type of connection you will be using is an SPX connection, you must also have the RSPX.NLM loaded. If the type of connection you will be using is asynchronous, you must also have the RS232.NLM loaded. Then, when you run the RCONSOLE utility, you choose the type of connection from the first RCONSOLE screen, as shown in figure 6.2.

If you choose the SPX connection type, choose the file server whose console you want to work with, then provide the remote console password when prompted. In addition to loading and unloading NLMs and issuing file server console commands, you can press Alt+F1 to activate the RCONSOLE Available Options menu (see fig. 6.3), and then choose to perform any of the following tasks:

- Change from one screen to another (Select a Screen to View)
- See directories and files on the DOS partition of the file server's hard disk (Directory Scan)
- Copy files from the workstation to the file server (Transfer Files To Server)
- Temporarily change to the workstation's DOS prompt, then return by typing **EXIT** (Invoke Operating System Shell)
- Quit RCONSOLE (End Remote Session With Server)
- Close the Available Options menu and redisplay the console (Resume Remote Session With Server)
- See the network address of this workstation (Workstation Address)
- Manipulate when typing done at the keyboard will be processed (Configure Keystroke Buffering)

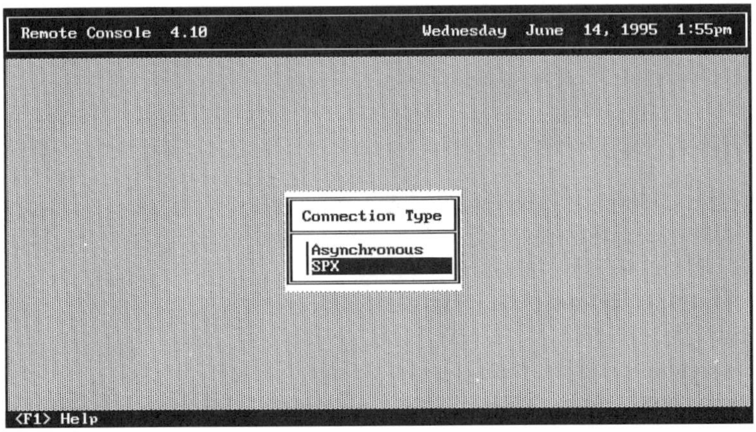

Figure 6.2
RCONSOLE's Connection Type screen.

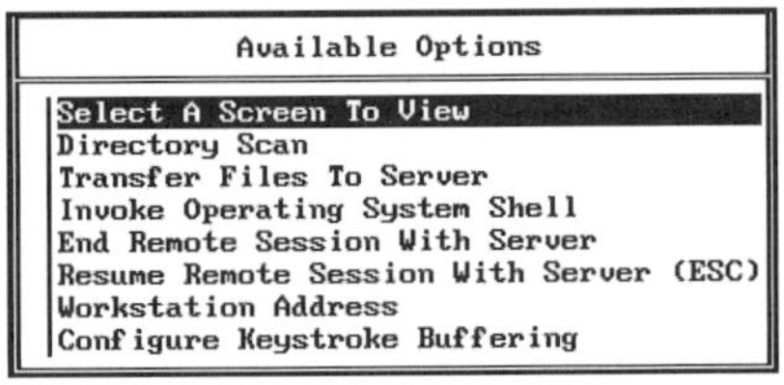

Figure 6.3
RCONSOLE's Available Options menu.

Some keystroke combinations also enable you to perform tasks. By pressing Alt+F3, you can move forward through server console screens; press Alt+F4 to move backward through server console screens. You can exit RCONSOLE by pressing Alt+F2, or close the Available Options menu and resume the remote session with the server by pressing the Esc key.

If you chose the asynchronous connection type, both the workstation and the file server must have an attached modem. After you choose Asynchronous, you can choose to Connect To Remote Location; then choose the location, or configure location information by choosing the Configuration menu option.

One way to secure your network file server is to require a password on the RCONSOLE utility. Other methods include locking up the server itself, using the console password feature available in MONITOR.NLM, or the SECURE CONSOLE command. Another way to help secure your file server is to back up the files and programs stored on it.

Enhancing File Server Security Using SBACKUP

Many compatible backup utilities are available for backing up and restoring NetWare files and programs. Because not everyone wants to spend the additional money to purchase this software, however, NetWare 4 includes the SBACKUP utility.

Regardless of which backup software you use, it can provide sufficient security only if it is used regularly. To ensure regular use of the backup software, you should assign the responsibility for routine backup to a specific network user. In addition, you should decide which backup strategy is most appropriate for your network.

Note When you assign the responsibility for network backup, you must also assign the following rights:

- To back up the NetWare server's file systems, the user must have Read and File Scan rights.
- To back up NDS, the user must have the Browse object right and the Read property right.
- The user must also know the password for each workstation to be backed up, as well as for the file servers being backed up (Target) or running the backup software (Host).

You can choose from the following three basic backup strategies:

- **Full.** Backs up all files and clears the Modify bit
- **Incremental.** Backs up all files created or changed since the last full or incremental backup, and clears the Modify bit
- **Differential.** Backs up all files created or changed since the last full backup, and clears the Modify bit

Note You can combine the full backup with either the incremental or differential backup strategies, but you should not combine incremental and differential backup strategies.

Before you can back up file servers and workstations, certain files must be loaded on the file server or the workstation. To back up a file server, a driver for the backup device must be loaded on the Host file server. The appropriate TSA file must be loaded also. Then SBACKUP must be loaded.

For example, to backup a NetWare 4.1 file server, including the NDS database, load TSA410.NLM and TSANDS. To back up a NetWare 3.12 server, load TSA312.NLM. To back up a NetWare 3.11 server, load TSA311.NLM. To backup a NetWare 2.2 server, load TSA22.NLM. After you have loaded the TSAs for each type of server you will be backing up, then load the SBACKUP.NLM.

Note If you are going to back up a workstation's hard disk, you must load the TSADOS.NLM at the file server, and the TSASMS.COM file at the workstation.

To back up a network file server, load the previously indicated files (TSA*xxx*.NLM and SBACKUP.NLM), then complete the following steps:

1. From the SBACKUP Main menu, choose Change Target to Backup From or Restore To.
2. Choose a *server_name*. NetWare File System to back up.
3. Provide a user name and password when prompted.

Note The user name should be either the network administrator's name, or the name of another user who has been granted the necessary rights to run backups and restores.

Figure 6.4
SBACKUP's Main Menu.

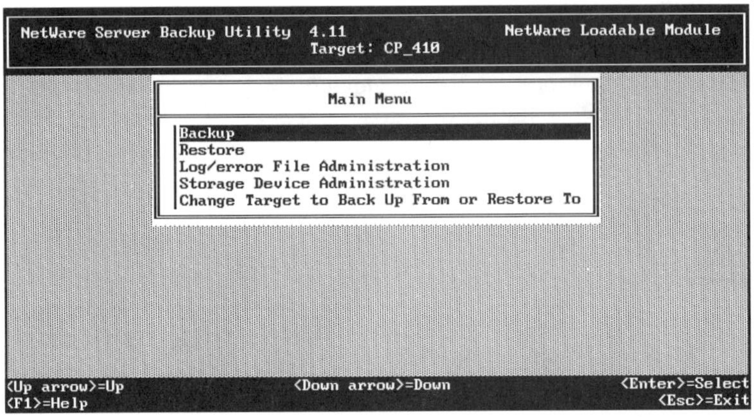

4. Choose Backup from the Main Menu (see fig. 6.4).
5. Choose a backup device if more than one is available and the option to choose is provided.
6. Provide a location for the session log file and error file.
7. Choose the type of backup to be performed.
8. Provide a description for this backup.
9. Choose to proceed now.
10. Insert the tape or other media being used and provide a label for the media, then continue with the backup, swapping out new tapes as necessary.

Note You can also back up a network workstation by loading the previously indicated files (TSADOS.NLM and SBACKUP.NLM at the server, TSASMS.COM at the workstation), choosing Change Target to Backup From or Restore To from the Main menu, then choosing a *server_name.DOS Workstation TSA* to back up, and following the basic procedure used to back up a file server.

Restore backups by choosing Restore instead of Backup from the SBACKUP Main menu. As prompted, provide the same restore-related information you provided for the original backup, such as the location of the session files and the device to restore from. In addition, when you restore, you must specify the type of restore—one file or directory, an entire session, or a custom restore. Then proceed with the restore, swapping in tapes as necessary.

Questions

1. Access to the network and other basic resources is provided through ______.
   - ○ A. NLMs
   - ○ B. the Core OS
   - ○ C. RCONSOLE
   - ○ D. name space modules

2. The NLMs responsible for controlling communication between the OS and the hard disk drives are ______.
   - ○ A disk drivers
   - ○ B. name space modules
   - ○ C. network board (LAN) drivers
   - ○ D. NLM utilities

3. The ISADISK.DSK is *not* ______.
   - ○ A. an NLM
   - ○ B. responsible for controlling ISA hard disks
   - ○ C. a disk driver
   - ○ D. a console command

4. NLMs are stored in ______ by default.
   - ○ A. SYS:PUBLIC
   - ○ B. SYS:LOGIN
   - ○ C. SYS:ETC
   - ○ D. SYS:SYSTEM

5. Which is *not* a basic service provided by the NetWare core OS?
   - ○ A. Authentication
   - ○ B. NDS
   - ○ C. OS Statistics
   - ○ D. Routing

6. Of the following, which is *not* a remote-console-related NLM?
   - ○ A. REMOTE.NLM
   - ○ B. RSPX.NLM
   - ○ C. MODULE.NLM
   - ○ D. RS232.NLM

7. Of the following, which *three* are NetWare console commands?
   - □ A. CLS
   - □ B. BROADCAST
   - □ C. NLIST
   - □ D. UNLOAD

8. A ______ backup backs up all files created or changed since the last full backup, and doesn't clear the modify bit.
   - ○ A. Custom
   - ○ B. Incremental
   - ○ C. Differential
   - ○ D. Full

Answers

1. B
2. A
3. D
4. D
5. C
6. C
7. A, B, D
8. C

CHAPTER 7

Managing the Directory Tree and File System

As a NetWare 4 network administrator, your responsibilities may include such tasks as planning NDS, setting up resources and making them accessible, automating the user's environment, organizing and managing the directory structure, and managing and keeping the entire network running. The simplicity or difficulty of this last task—managing and keeping the entire network running—depends on the success of each of the other tasks, particularly that of planning, organizing, and setting up the network.

This chapter is designed to provide you with the basic information you need to know in order to successfully manage NetWare Directory Services, as well as the directory structures, files, and volume space used by NetWare 4 file servers. To that end, this chapter provides information on the following topics:

- Managing the file system
- Naming Directory tree objects
- Accessing objects in the Directory tree
- Automating user access to the Directory tree

Managing the File System

To successfully manage the file system, you must be able to manage directories, files, and space on the NetWare volume. Many of the DOS utilities you use for managing DOS directories and files can be used also to manage NetWare directories and files. In addition, NetWare provides the following utilities for file system and volume management:

- FILER
- FLAG
- NDIR
- NCOPY
- NETADMIN
- NetWare Administrator
- RENDIR

As a network administrator, you probably have had experience with most of these utilities, using them to perform file system management tasks. Because the NetWare Administrator is a relatively new utility and is specific to NetWare 4, your experience with this utility may be limited. Detailed knowledge of this utility is important to passing the NetWare 4 Administration CNE exam. Therefore, the NetWare Administrator utility is used in most of the tasks explained in this section.

The following file, directory, and volume management tasks are discussed:

- Creating directories
- Viewing and modifying directory information
- Renaming directories
- Deleting directories and their contents
- Copying and moving directory structures
- Copying and moving files
- Viewing and modifying file information
- Deleting, purging, and salvaging files
- Managing volume space

Note

You are assumed to have the necessary rights to perform all the tasks discussed in this section. In addition, the instructions are based on the assumption that you already have the Network Administrator utility running, and that you have expanded the Directory tree to display the volume where you will be managing directories and files.

Creating Directories

To create a directory, select (highlight) the location where you want the directory to be created, then complete the following steps:

1. Choose Create from the Object pull-down menu (or press Insert).
2. In the Create Directory dialog box, type a name for the Directory Object.

3. Mark Define Additional Properties if you want to define properties specific to this directory.
4. Choose Create.
5. When the Identification page for this directory opens, choose the Facts, Trustees of this Directory, or Attributes page button to further define properties for this directory.

Viewing and Modifying Directory Information

To view or modify information related to a specific directory, select the directory from the Directory tree, then complete the following steps:

1. Choose Details from the Object pull-down menu.
2. Choose the Facts, Trustees of this Directory, or Attributes page button to open subsequent pages where you can view or modify directory properties.
3. If applicable, when you have made all necessary modifications, choose OK.

Renaming Directories

To rename an existing directory, select the directory from the Directory tree, then complete the following steps:

1. Choose Rename from the Object pull-down menu.
2. In the Rename dialog box, type a new directory name (see fig.7.1).
3. Choose OK.

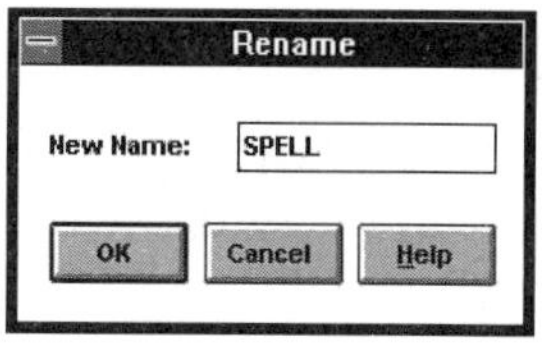

Figure 7.1
The Rename dialog box.

Deleting Directories and Their Contents

To delete a directory and its contents, expand the directory so that its files and subdirectories are displayed, then complete the following steps:

1. Mark the directory and any files and subdirectories to be deleted by pressing the Shift key while you move and click the mouse.
2. Choose Delete from the Object pull-down menu (or press Delete).
3. Choose Yes at the Do you really want to delete the objects? prompt.

Copying and Moving Directory Structures

To copy or move a complete directory structure, complete the following steps:

1. Mark the directory to be copied or moved, by pressing the Shift key while you move and click the mouse.
2. Choose Copy from the Object pull-down menu.
3. Type a Destination for the directory and its structure, or choose the Browse button next to the Destination field and browse the tree.
4. Choose OK.

Copying and Moving Files

To copy one or more files, expand the directory where the files are located so that you can see the file names, then complete the following steps:

1. Mark files to be copied, using the Shift key and mouse button.
2. Choose Copy from the Object pull-down menu.

Note: You can also use the mouse to drag and drop the file from one directory to another.

3. In the Move/Copy dialog box, type a Destination for the files (see fig. 7.2), or choose the Browse button next to the Destination field and browse the tree.
4. Choose OK.

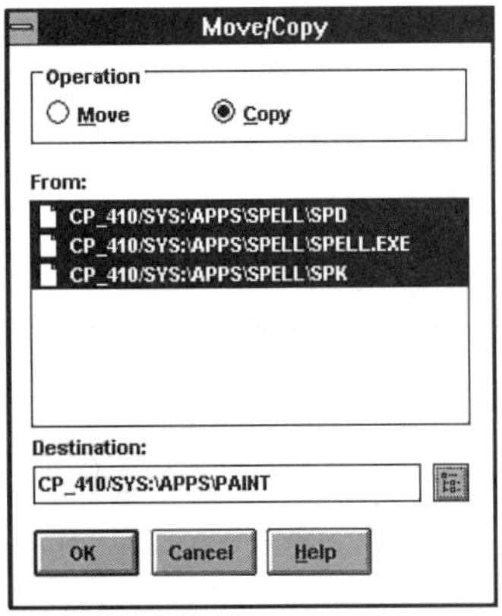

Figure 7.2
The Move/Copy dialog box.

Note: You use this same process to move files from one directory to another. The difference is that you mark Move instead of Copy at the top of the Move/Copy dialog box.

Viewing and Modifying File Information

To view or modify information related to a specific file, select the file, then complete the following steps:

1. Choose Details from the Object pull-down menu.
2. Choose the Facts, Trustees of this Directory, or Attributes page button to open subsequent pages where you can view or modify file properties.
3. If you made modifications to a file's properties, choose OK to save those changes.

Deleting, Purging, and Salvaging Files

You delete a file the same way you delete a directory, except that you select the file to be deleted (instead of the directory). You can automatically *purge* (make unrecoverable) a file—either when you delete it or later—or you can choose to not purge the file and make it possible to *salvage* (recover) the file at a later time.

To automatically purge a file when you delete it, set the Purge Immediate attribute for the file (see fig. 7.3).

To purge files that have been deleted but are not yet purged, complete the following steps:

1. Choose Salvage from the Tools pull-down menu.
2. Choose where you want the salvageable files to be listed from (Current Directory or Deleted Directory), as well as how you want the files sorted (by Deletion date, File name, and so on).

3. Choose List to see a list of salvageable files (see fig. 7.4).
4. Choose Purge.
5. Answer Yes when prompted with either Purge all files from deleted directories? or with Purge all files from this directory?
6. Choose Close.

To salvage files, complete the following steps:

1. Choose Salvage from the Tools pull-down menu.
2. Choose where you want the salvageable files to be listed from (Current Directory or Deleted Directory), as well as how you want the files sorted (by Deletion date, File name, and so on).

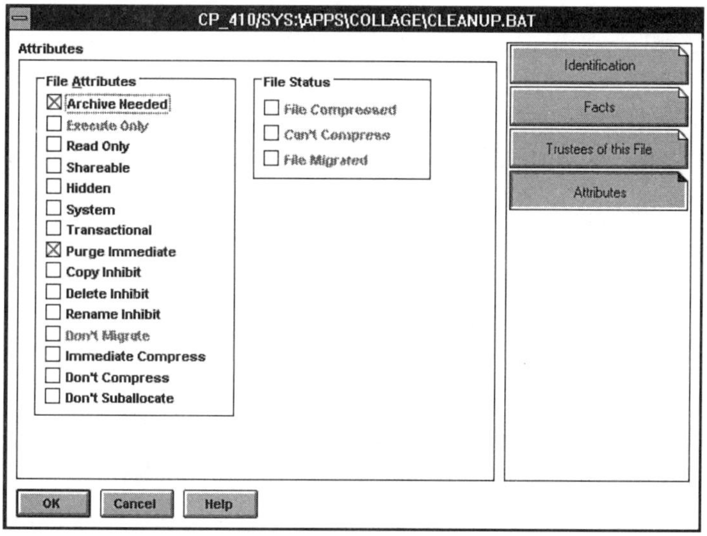

Figure 7.3
The CLEANUP.BAT File Attribute page, with Purge Immediate marked.

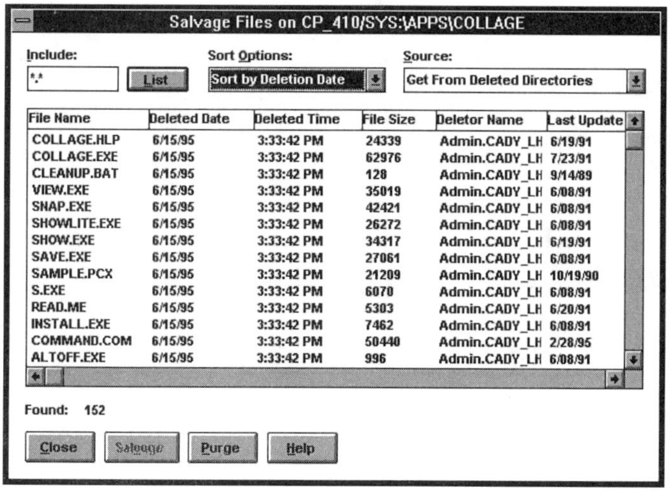

Figure 7.4
The Salvage Files window.

> **Note:** If the Salvageable files will be restored to the DELETED.SAV directory at the root of the *volume_name* volume message is displayed, choose OK.

3. Choose List to see a list of salvageable files.
4. Mark files to be salvaged, then choose Salvage.
5. Choose Close.

Managing Volume Space

Volume space usage information is a property of the Volume object. To view information about volume space usage, restrict volume space usage, and change file and directory ownership, use the NetWare Administrator utility, (or the NETADMIN utility), and the NDIR utility.

To view information about volume space usage, complete the following steps:

1. Select the Volume from the NetWare Administrator.
2. Choose Details from the Object pull-down menu.
3. Open the Statistics page to view volume information (see fig.7.5).

The Volume Statistics page contains the following areas of information:

- **Disk Space.** Shows both the total available disk space and the amount of disk space currently being used
- **Directory Entries.** Shows both the total number of directory entries available and the number currently being used
- **Deleted Files.** Shows the number of deleted files and those not yet purged

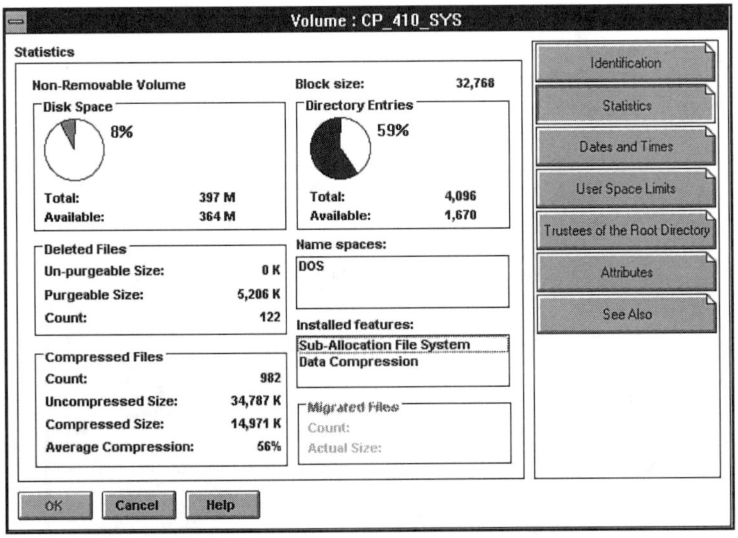

Figure 7.5
The Volume Statistics page.

- **Name Spaces.** Shows which name space NLMs are loaded on the volume
- **Installed Features.** Shows what features (such as suballocation and data compression) are active on the volume
- **Compressed Files.** Shows how many files on the volume are stored as compressed files, what the total size of those files is, and the average percentage of file compression

Note File compression reduces the storage space required for a file, saving as much as 63 percent of storage space. File compression attributes can be set (by using NetWare Administrator, NETADMIN, or FLAG) to indicate whether a file should be compressed as soon as it is closed (Immediately Compress), or not compressed at all (Not Compress). Then, using INSTALL.NLM, you can turn compression on, and all files with the IC attribute will be compressed.

- **Migrated Files.** Shows how many files have been migrated, and the size of those migrated files

Note Data migration is used to free up active storage space by transferring inactive files from hard disk to optical storage devices. If HCSS is installed, NDIR, FILER, NETADMIN, or NetWare Administrator can be used to view data migration statistics. Migration is an attribute of directories and files. If data migration is active, you can prevent inactive files and directories from being migrated by applying the Don't Migrate (DM) attribute.

To restrict volume space usage for a user, complete the following steps:

1. Select the volume from the tree, using the NetWare Administrator.
2. Choose Details from the Object pull-down menu.
3. Open the User Space Limit page to view volume information, and browse through the tree until a list of network users is displayed.
4. Select the user whose volume space usage you want to restrict.
5. Choose Modify.
6. In the Volume Space Restriction dialog box, mark the Limited Volume Space box, and type (in the Volume Space Limit (Kb): area) the amount of volume space to be allotted to this user (see fig. 7.6).

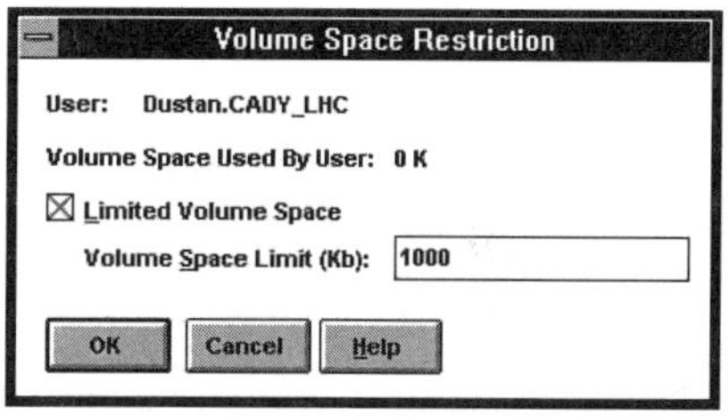

Figure 7.6
The Volume Space Restriction dialog box.

Note You can also limit the amount of space available to a directory by selecting the directory, choosing Details from the Object pull-down menu, opening the Facts page, and typing (in the Limit field) the number of kilobytes to be allowed.

When space usage becomes a problem, one way around that problem is to change the owner of one or more of the directories or files. Changing ownership is particularly helpful also when one user copies files or directories to another user; because these copies now have a new owner, the properties should reflect that fact.

To change file and directory ownership, choose the directory or file, then choose Details from the Object pull-down menu. Next, open the Facts page, and change the Owner field.

Naming Directory Tree Objects

If the Directory tree has only one container, accessing objects in that container is relatively simple. When there is more than one container in the tree, however, accessing objects in containers that are not the user's parent container becomes more difficult. When a user is accessing an object in a different container, NetWare often needs to be told exactly where to look for that object. When looking in the DOS directory structure for a file that is not in the current directory, you provide the exact path. When looking in NDS for an object that is not in the user's current context, you provide an exact object name—either a distinguished name or a relative distinguished name.

Note: A *common name* (CN) is the name of a leaf object. *Context* is an object's location in the Directory tree. *Current context* is the user's current location (area to which the user is currently pointing, much like the current path in DOS) in the Directory tree.

A *distinguished name* is the object's common name and its context. A distinguished name is identified with a beginning (leading) period, and all objects in a distinguished name are separated with a period. No two objects can have the same distinguished name.

A *relative distinguished name* lists the path to an object, does not contain a leading period, can contain an ending period, separates objects with a period, and uses the user's current context as a starting point.

To illustrate, using a Directory tree structure for a small business (see fig. 7.7), you would enter a distinguished name for user MICHELLE as follows:

```
.CN=MICHELLE.OU=NOBUS.O=LHC_PARENT
```

If user MICHELLE's current context (in fig. 7.9) is .O=LHC_PARENT, you would enter the relative distinguished name for user MICHELLE as follows:

```
CN=MICHELLE.OU=NOBUS
```

NDS has other object names that can be applied to describe an object in the NDS tree. The first—*CONTEXT*—refers to an object's location in the NDS Directory tree. It is written from the [Root] of the tree to the actual location or container of the object within the tree. Referring again to figure 7.9, user MICHELLE's context is stated as follows:

```
O=LHC_PARENT.OU=NOBUS
```

A user can be defined by specifying its context.

In addition, users can be defined by their common name. All leaf objects in the Directory tree have a common name (CN) associated with them. The common name, which is given to the object when it is created, is the name you see next to the icon for the leaf object when you display the Directory tree

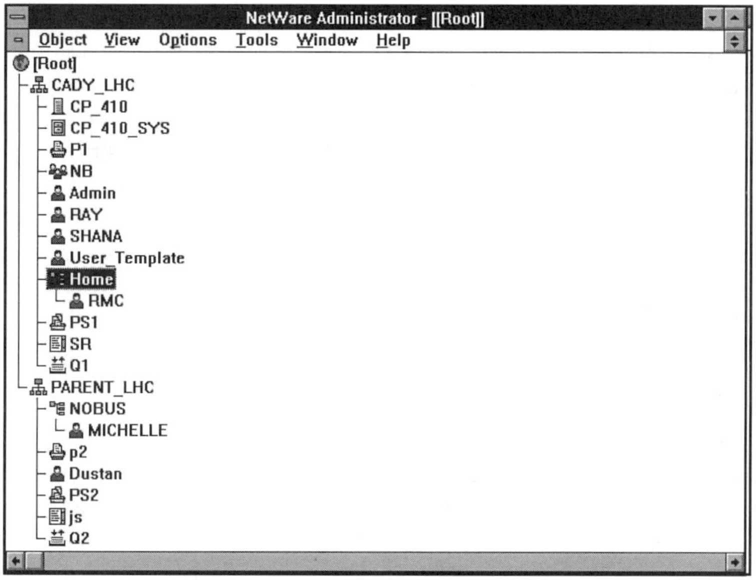

Figure 7.7
The Directory tree structure.

A user's name is also its common name. For example, user MICHELLE's common name is MICHELLE. It is written as CN=MICHELLE.

Note You can reference an object by its common name only, if your current context is the same as that of the leaf object. If, for example, your current context is O=LHC_PARENT.OU=NOBUS, you can access the print queue named Q1 by referring to its common name of Q1.

Accessing Objects in the Directory Tree

The NetWare Directory tree is structured to be functional as well as organizational. This structure lets you design and organize your network's Directory tree so that it follows the use of resources on your network. You can base your Directory tree design on a logical use of resources rather than on just a physical organization. You can also organize your Directory tree by your company's organizational structure, its geographical distribution, by job responsibility, or by any combination of these.

How you design your Directory tree affects how objects in the Directory tree are accessed. For example, if the Directory tree is designed around geographical distribution, but users in different locations with similar job responsibilities must share data, access for some users may be different than for other users. Some users may need to access only resources in their parent container. Others may need to access resources in additional containers.

Before users access resources, however, they need to understand not only how the design of the Directory tree affects their access to network resources, but also where their *current context* (the object's current location in the directory structure) is set, and how to change that context.

To change context, you can specify the context by using either typeful naming or typeless naming. In *typeful naming*, you use the abbreviations associated with containers in the tree. To specify an Organization, for example, you use O. When changing context, you specify a typeful name by using the abbreviation, followed by the equal sign (=) and then the name of the object. In addition, typeful names require that you use a period (.) between each object included in the name. User MICHELLE's typeful name would be shown as:

```
.CN=MICHELLE.OU=NOBUS.O=LHC_PARENT
```

In *typeless naming*, you do not use container name abbreviations or the equal sign. User MICHELLE would be shown as:

```
MICHELLE.NOBUS.LHC_PARENT
```

To change your current context as well as to view objects in the Directory tree, you can use the NetWare CX command. To view your current context, type **CX** and press Enter. To view the Directory tree structure from below your current context, type **CX /T**. To see see all objects in your current context, type **CX /ALL /T**. To change to [Root], type **CX /R**, or change your context up one level by typing CX followed by a period (**CX.**). You can also type any distinguished name after the CX command, such as CX .OU=NOBUS.O=LHC_PARENT, and change your context to that context.

Although moving about the Directory tree by using the CX command is possible, it can be cumbersome for network users. To make the process of moving through the Directory tree structure easier for users, you can set up in the tree objects designed specifically to enable users to access objects in contexts other than their current context. Objects you can create in the tree for this purpose are Alias, Directory map, and Group objects, which are explained in table 7.1.

Table 7.1
Objects that Enable Easy Access to Different Contexts

Object	*Description*	*Purpose*
Alias	Object that points to another object in the Directory tree	Provides access to an object located in another context and which must be shared
Directory Map	Object that points to a directory on a volume	Makes access to an executable program easier for the user
Group	Object that enables multiple users to have the same rights on the network	Regulates access to network resources for more than one user

Automating User Access to the Directory Tree

You can simplify access to the Directory tree for network users by following two guidelines. First, set the users' current context for them when they log in to the network. Second, when you set up mappings in login scripts for users, be certain to use correct naming.

To set the user's current context, place the following command in the NET.CFG file on the user's workstation:

```
NAME CONTEXT="distinguished name"
```

Replace *distinguished name* with the distinguished name that points to the user's parent container. For example, for user MICHELLE (refer to fig. 7.9), replace *distinguished name* with OU=NOBUS.O=LHC_PARENT.

Note Users who log in to the network from a workstation other than their own will not have the correct context set for them. The NAME CONTEXT command is workstation-specific, because it is part of the NET.CFG file of each workstation.

To set up mappings in login scripts for users, use the MAP command. When specifying the path, provide the complete path, using a distinguished name instead of a relative distinguished name.

For example, to map a search drive to the NOBUS container, place the following command in the user's login script:

```
.CP_410_SYS.CADY_LHC
```

The CX command, a variety of utilities (FLAG, NDIR, NetWare Administrator), and so on, are all provided by NetWare to help you successfully manage the Directory tree and file system.

Questions

1. Of the following, which task *cannot* be performed by using the NetWare Administrator utility?

   ○ A. Manage volume space

   ○ B. Move files

   ○ C. Create directories

   ○ D. Create volumes

2. Salvage files by choosing ______ from the ______ pull-down menu.

   ☐ A. Delete

   ☐ B. Tools

   ☐ C. Salvage

   ☐ D. Object

3. Which area of the volume statistics window contains information about NetWare Loadable Modules that make it possible for Macintosh or OS/2 files to be saved on the network?

   ○ A. Directory Entries

   ○ B. Name Spaces

   ○ C. Installed Features

   ○ D. Compressed Files

4. Which *three* utilities can you use to set file compression attributes?

   ☐ A. NetWare Administrator

   ☐ B. NETADMIN

   ☐ C. FILER

   ☐ D. FLAG

5. One way to get around a space usage problem is to ______.

   ○ A. turn compression on and flag all files as NC

   ○ B. create groups and assign all users to a group

   ○ C. change the owner of some files or directories

   ○ D. apply the DM flag to files and directories

6. All leaf objects have a ______ name.

   ○ A. common

   ○ B. disguised

   ○ C. unique

   ○ D. relative

7. Based on figure 7.7, which of the following is a correctly written distinguished name for user DUSTAN?

   ○ A. .CN=DUSTAN.OU=NOBUS.O =PARENT_LHC

   ○ B. .CN=DUSTAN.O=PARENT_LHC

   ○ C. CN=DUSTAN.OU=PARENT_ LHC.O=[Root]

   ○ D. CN=DUSTAN.O=PARENT_LHC

8. The term ______ refers to an object's location in the NDS Directory tree.

   ○ A. context

   ○ B. common name

   ○ C. organization

   ○ D. distinguished name

9. A ______ is the object's common name plus its context.
   - A. context
   - B. common name
   - C. organization
   - D. distinguished name

10. If you want to make it easy for a user to access a directory on a volume that contains an executable program, create a ______ object.
   - A. Group
   - B. Profile Script
   - C. Directory Map
   - D. Alias

Answers

1. D
2. C, B
3. B
4. A, B, D
5. C
6. A
7. B
8. A
9. D
10. C

CHAPTER 8

Accessing and Using Network Resources

Most of a network administrator's work involves providing authorized users access to network resources, and preventing unauthorized users from gaining access to the network. After everything is set up and organized on the network, the user must connect to and log in to the network, and use the available resources.

This chapter provides information about how users perform the following tasks:

- *Connect to the network*
- *Log in to the network*
- *Access network data*
- *Access and use applications*
- *Print on the network*

Connecting to the Network

To connect to the network, a user must first have a PC. This PC, with the proper hardware and software, becomes a workstation on the network. For a stand-alone computer to become a workstation, it must have a network board installed and connected to the network cable (see fig. 8.1).

After the physical connection is made, a software connection to the network must also be made. A software connection requires several software files. Each of these files must be loaded into the workstation's memory in the required order. The software files needed to establish network communication are:

- Link Support Layer (LSL.COM)
- Network board driver (such as NE2000.COM)
- Communications protocol (IPXODI.COM)
- NetWare DOS Requester (VLM.EXE and associated VLM files)

Figure 8.1
Hardware necessary for network communication.

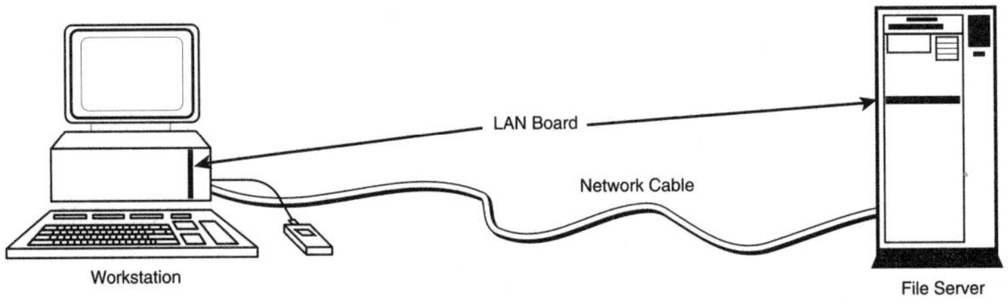

Link Support Layer

The LSL.COM file, which loads the Link Support Layer, implements the ODI specification (see the "Communications Protocol" section, a little later in the chapter). Its function is to route network information from various protocols to the network board driver as well as to the related communications software. Because of its function, the Link Support Layer is often called the *switchboard.*

After you load the workstation's operating system (DOS), load the LSL.COM file to provide protocol routing.

Network Board Driver

The *network board driver* is the software that is compatible with the network board installed in your workstation. Its function is to activate the network board and then control its actions. It is the go-between (connection software) for the workstation's software and the physical components that constitute the network hardware.

NetWare 4 requires that network board drivers be of a specific type, known as MLID (*Multiple Link Interface Driver*), which support ODI specifications. The communications protocol software used by DOS workstations (see the following "Communications Protocol" section) supports multiple protocols on the same cabling system. MLID network board drivers also support multiple protocols by making it possible for the network board to accept data from various protocols.

Load the board driver by loading the file associated with the network board installed in your workstation. For example, if your workstation has an NE2000 network board installed, load the NE2000.COM file, or the network board file that came with your network board. Load the network board driver file after loading the LSL.COM file.

Communications Protocol

The communications protocol used by DOS workstations is a version of the NetWare IPX communications protocol. The file that loads the communications protocol is called IPXODI.COM because it provides communication based on the ODI (Open Data-Link Interface) specification. By following the ODI specification, users can take advantage of multiple protocols on the same cabling system, even using the same network board.

Load the communications protocol file for DOS workstations by loading the IPXODI.COM file. Load IPXODI.COM after you load the network board file.

NetWare DOS Requester

The NetWare DOS Requester is a series of files, the manager of which is the VLM.EXE file. This file and its associated files are the connection point between the workstation's DOS-based files (the DOS operating system and DOS applications) and the network.

The NetWare DOS Requester enables the DOS operating system and DOS application programs to communicate across the network and to make requests for network services. It also stores information related to the workstation's network connection, information that is deleted when the user logs out of the network and breaks the logical network connection.

To load the NetWare DOS Requester into workstation memory, type **VLM** at the DOS prompt, and press Enter. By default, this loads the NetWare DOS Requester into extended memory. If extended memory is unavailable, or if you prefer to load the NetWare DOS Requester into a location other than extended memory, you can issue this command followed by the /M switch, and your choice of memory locations.

To load the NetWare DOS Requester into conventional memory, for example, follow the /M with a C. That is, type **VLM /MC** and press Enter. Use **X** instead of **C** to load the files into extended memory, or **E** instead of **C** to load the files into expanded memory.

Load the NetWare DOS Requester last, after you load the IPXODI.COM file. The NetWare DOS Requester is the last connection software to be loaded. After all connection software files have been loaded into workstation memory, you can log in to the network.

Note All workstation connection software can be unloaded from workstation memory if you follow two rules.

First, the order in which you must unload the software is opposite the order in which you loaded it. In other words, you must unload the NetWare DOS Requester before you unload the IPXODI.COM file; the IPXODI.COM file must be unloaded before you unload the network board driver file (such as NE2000.COM); and the network board driver file must be unloaded before you unload the Link Support Layer software (LSL.COM).

Second, unload each file by issuing the same command you used to load the file, but following that command with a space, a slash, and the letter U. For example, unload the LSL.COM file by typing **LSL /U** and pressing Enter.

Logging In to the Network

After the physical connection has been made (network board installed in the workstation and connected to the network cable) and all connection software has been loaded into the workstation, you can log in to the network. Before logging in, however, change to the first network drive. (In most cases this is drive F, but the actual drive letter depends on what you specified as the first network drive under the NetWare DOS Requester heading in the NET.CFG file on the workstation.)

After you change to the first available network drive, type **LOGIN** and press Enter. When prompted, provide your login name and password.

Note If your Name Context was set properly in the workstation's NET.CFG file, you do not have to specify your distinguished name when you log in—you simply specify your login name. Otherwise, specify your distinguished name as your login name when prompted, or as part of the first login command, as shown in the following example:

```
LOGIN .CN=MICHELLE.OU=NOBUS.O=LHC_PARENT
```

Typing **LOGIN** runs the LOGIN.EXE file found in the LOGIN directory on a NetWare 4.1 file server. After you run the LOGIN.EXE file and are successfully logged in to the network, no additional login information is necessary for access to network services.

You can automate the connection and login process by putting the necessary files in your workstation's AUTOEXEC.BAT file, or in a separate file (such as STARTNET.BAT) to be called from the AUTOEXEC.BAT file. The following listing shows a sample STARTNET.BAT file for a network workstation:

```
C:\COLLAGE>TYPE C:\NWCLIENT/STARTNET.BAT
@ECHO OFF
CD C:\NWCLIENT
C:\QEMM\LOADHI /R:2 /LO NWCACHE 1024 1024 /
➥LEND=ON /DELAY=OFF
SET NWLANGUAGE=ENGLISH
LH C:\NWCLIENT\LSL.COM
C:\QEMM\LOADHI /R:2 C:\NWCLIENT\NE2000.COM
C:\QEMM\LOADHI /R:2 C:\NWCLIENT\IPXODI.COM
rem c:\QEMM\LOADHI /R:2 SERVER
rem c:\QEMM\LOADHI /R:0 /LO VLM /ME
rem VLM /ME
rem End of remarked-out section.
CD \
rem C:\NWCLIENT\NET LOGIN
C:\NWCLIENT\VLM.EXE
C:\NWCLIENT\TSASMS.COM

C:\COLLAGE>\
```

Accessing Network Data

After you are granted access to the network file system, you can take advantage of the variety of services it provides—storage space for your data files, application software, shared network printing services, and so on. Before you can store and retrieve data on the network, however, you need a basic understanding of the network file system and how to access and manage it.

The network file system is designed to function in much the same way the DOS file system functions. In DOS, the drive itself is the root of the file system. In NetWare, the volume is the root of the file system. A NetWare *volume* is a logical division (an amount of physical storage space) of the file server's storage area, most commonly the hard disk. A NetWare 4 file server can have as many as 64 volumes, but must have at least one (called SYS). The following are additional facts about NetWare volumes:

- Maximum storage space is 32 terabytes (TB)
- Maximum volume space is 32 TB
- Maximum segments per volume is 32
- Minimum size for the SYS volume is 2.5 megabytes (MB)

In NetWare 4, volumes have both a physical name and a volume object name. The *physical name* is the name assigned to the volume when you create it. The *volume object name*, which is assigned by NetWare 4 when the volume object is created, consists of the name of the file server and the volume name, with the two being separated by the underscore (_) character. The network administrator can change the volume object name.

Below the NetWare root (volume), directories and files can be added in much the same way that directories and files are added to the DOS root. For example, you can use the DOS MakeDir (MD) command to create directories. You can also use the NetWare Administrator utility to create directories.

Regardless of how you create network directories, after the directories have been created, users can store program and data files in those directories. Users must be able to access the network directories, however. Users can use a variety of NetWare utilities and DOS utilities to access network data.

To access data on the network, the most important NetWare utility users need is the MAP utility. This utility is similar to DOS commands, in that it is entered at the command line, with or without various options. The purpose of the MAP utility is to provide access to data on the network by establishing paths that point to areas in the network file structure where the data can be found. Just as DOS uses drive letters (A, B, C, and so on) to point to the physical resource, NetWare uses letters to point to the logical resource. These letters, and the location of the NetWare directory structure to which they point, are called *drive mappings*. The two types of drive mappings are *network* and *search*. You map network drives to access data on the network, and you map search drives to access executable programs on the network (see the "Accessing and Using Applications" section of this chapter).

Any drive letters not being used by physical DOS devices can be used to map network drives or search drives. Most commonly, the letters F through K are used to map network drives; the letters Z through

L are used to map search drives. Table 8.1 shows the MAP command and the options used to MAP network drive letters.

Note A *Directory Map object* is an object on a NetWare 4 network, which acts as a pointer to a specific directory on the network. It is created primarily to provide users with quick access to the exact directory that contains an application program.

Table 8.1
Using MAP to Create Network Drives

Command	*Description, Example, and Result*
MAP	Displays current mappings (see fig. 8.2) Example: MAP Result: *a list of your current mappings*
MAP N *path*	Maps next available network drive letter to specified path Example: MAP N CP_410\SYS:APPS Result: H: = CP_410\SYS:APPS (*assuming that the last mapped drive was drive G)*
MAP G:=*path*	Maps specified drive letter to specified path Example: MAP G:=CP_410\SYS:APPS\WP Result: G: = CP_410\SYS:APPS\WP
MAP ROOT I:=*path*	Maps specified drive letter to specified path, making drive appear as though it is mapped to the root Example: MAP ROOT I:=CP_410\SYS:APPS Result: I:=CP_410\SYS:APPS \ (*If you type I: at the prompt, it displays as* `I:\>`)
MAP P K:=*volume:*	Maps specified drive letter to a physical volume Example: MAP P K:=SYS: Result: K:=CP_410\SYS: (*assuming that the file server name is CP_410*)
MAP L:=*name*	Maps specified drive letter to a Directory Map object Example: MAP L:=WORD Result: L:\CP_410\SYS:APPS\WP

```
C:\COLLAGE>map

Drives A,B,C,D,E map to a local disk.
Drive F: = CP_410_SYS: \MEDICAL
Drive G: = CP_410_SYS: \APPS\WP
Drive H: = CP_410_SYS: \APPS
Drive I: = CP_410_SYS:PUBLIC \
Drive K: = CP_410_SYS: \
Drive L: = CP_410_SYS: \APPS\WP
     -----    Search Drives    -----
S1: = Z:. [CP_410_SYS: \PUBLIC]
S2: = Y:. [CP_410_SYS: \]
S3: = C:\NWCLIENT
S4: = C:\DOS

C:\COLLAGE>\
```

Figure 8.2
MAP display.

You can also use the NetWare User Tools utility to map network drives. With the NetWare User Tools utility open, press Alt+D to choose the Drive Connections screen. Choose the exact path to be mapped from the Resources side of the NetWare Drive Connections window, and drag it to the drive letter to which you want to map to that path (see fig. 8.3).

In addition to the MAP command, you can use several other NetWare commands to view and manage the network file system. Table 8.2 lists and describes those commands.

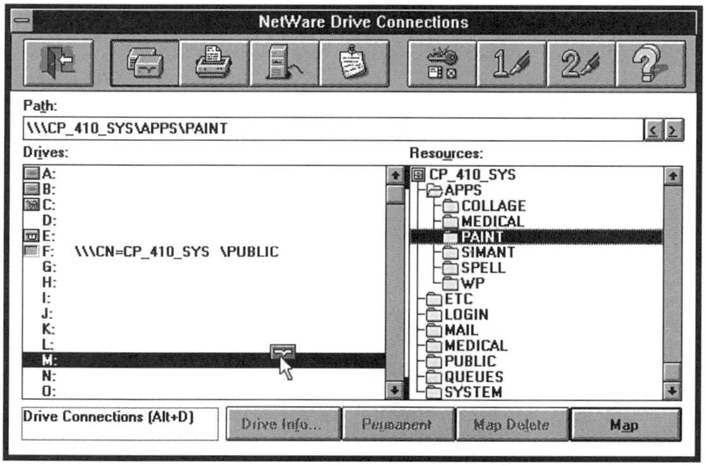

Figure 8.3
Mapping a drive, using the NetWare User Tools utility.

Table 8.2
NetWare File-Management Commands

Command	*Description*
NDIR	Displays file name, size, last update, and attributes of network files in current context
NDIR /DO	Displays a list of directories in the current context only, as well as the date and time they were created
NDIR /DO /SUB	Displays a list of directories (and their subdirectories) in the current context, as well as the date and time they were created
NDIR /FO	Displays a list of files only (in the current context), with their last update, size, and attributes
NDIR /FO /SO option	Displays a list of files in the current context, with date of their last update, size, and attributes; list is displayed in specific sort order by replacing option with any of the following sort options: **AC** Last accessed date **AR** Last archived date **CR** Created or copied date **OW** Owner **SI** File size **UP** Last updated date **UN** Not (Un-) sorted
NDIR /FO /REV SORT *option*	Displays list of files in current context in reverse sort order, replacing *option* with any of the sort options shown with the preceding command
NDIR /?	Displays help information for the NDIR command
NLIST VOLUME	Lists information about volumes in current context
NLIST VOLUME /N	Lists only names of volumes in current context
NLIST VOLUME /D	Lists detailed information about all volumes in current context
NLIST /?	Displays help information for the NLIST command

Accessing and Using Applications

You map network drives to access *data* on the network. You map search drives to access *applications* on the network. After a search drive is mapped to the directory containing an application, you can run the application by typing the name of its executable file. Because you have a search drive mapped, the executable file is located and run. NetWare uses search drive mappings in much the same way that DOS uses the PATH statement.

When DOS uses the PATH to find an executable file, it searches specified directories in the order in which they appear in the PATH statement. When NetWare uses search drives to find an executable file, it searches in numeric order, beginning with search drive 1 (which is drive letter Z, by default), unless reordered (using the MAP INS command) by the user.

To create a search drive, use the MAP command. Table 8.3 shows different search drive commands and provides information about their use.

Table 8.3
Search Drive Mappings

Command	*Description, Example, and Result*
MAP S16:=*path*	Maps next available search drive to specified directory for running an executable file Example: MAP S16:=CP_410/SYS:APPS/WP Result: X: CP_410/SYS:APPS/WP (*assuming that next available search drive letter was drive X*)
MAP INS S1:=*path*	Maps next available search drive letter into first search position, moving all other search drive mappings down one level Example: MAP INS S1:=CP_410/SYS:PUBLIC Result: W: CP_410/SYS:PUBLIC (*assuming that next available search drive letter was drive W, because three other letters —Z, Y, and X—have already been used*)
MAP S2:=*path*	Maps next available search drive letter as search drive 2, replacing any mapping that may currently exist for search drive 2 Example: MAP S2:=SYS:SYSTEM Result: X: CP_410\SYS:SYSTEM (*assuming that current context is set to the CP_410 file server, and drive letter X was next available search drive letter*)

> **Note:** As was explained earlier, you can also map a network drive to a Directory Map object in order to access an application on the network.

After network search drives have been set up, you can access and run applications on the network. One of the applications that you can run is FirstMail, the electronic mail application provided by NetWare. With Basic MHS installed (refer to Chapter 3, "Setting Up Network Printing and Mail Services"), you can run the FirstMail utility to send and receive e-mail. FirstMail is installed in SYS:PUBLIC, to which a search drive should be mapped from the SYSTEM login script.

Printing on the Network

You can also take advantage of print services provided by print queues, print servers, and printers on a network.

Print queues hold (store) the print jobs you send, until a print server can take the job and route it to the appropriate printer. Print queues—directories in the QUEUES directory on a NetWare volume—can be created on any physical volume. For a print queue to be accessible, however, a corresponding NetWare 4 Print Queue object must exist. The Print Queue object is used to locate the actual print queue directory, and then regulate who can access the printer (by controlling who is allowed to send print jobs to the print queue).

Print servers monitor print queues and printers (up to 256 printers per print server), and pass print jobs from print queues to printers. As with print queues, a corresponding Print Server object must exist on the network.

Printers are the devices that print documents. As with print queues and print servers, a corresponding Printer object must exist on the network. Printers can be physically connected to the following hardware:

- NetWare file servers with the print server software loaded (combination file server and print server)
- Regular NetWare file servers
- Workstations
- Network cable system

Print jobs can be sent to print queues or, if the application from which the print job is being sent is network-aware, directly to a printer on the network. Print jobs that would otherwise be sent directly to the workstation's printer port (such as LPT1 or LPT2) can instead be redirected to a network printer.

To redirect a non-network-aware print job, use the CAPTURE command or the NetWare User Tools for Windows or DOS (also called NETUSER) utilities. Then, from within the application, set up printing by choosing a print driver and then printing jobs to the chosen printer or to a file. From the DOS prompt, use NPRINT or PCONSOLE to send the print job to a printer.

To redirect a print job to a printer by using CAPTURE, place the CAPTURE command in a login script or inside a menu. Use any of the commands associated with the CAPTURE command, the most commonly used of which are shown in table 8.4.

Table 8.4
Commonly Used CAPTURE Commands

Command	*Abbreviation*	*Purpose*
Autoendcap	AU	Automatically sends print job when application is closed
Local	L	Specifies local port number
Notify	NOTI	Informs user when print job is finished
Printer	P	Specifies which printer is to receive the print job
Server	S	Specifies NetWare server to which print job should be directed (if server is not the default server)
Show	SH	Displays current status of CAPTURE command
Timeout	TI	Specifies number of seconds that must elapse between receipt of material for printing and indication that the print job is complete

Note: You can also issue the CAPTURE command without any parameters, if a default print job configuration exists (was created using the PCONSOLE utility).

To redirect a print job by using the NetWare User Tools utility, choose Printer Connections, then drag-and-drop a print queue or printer from the Resources list to a port in the Port list.

To send a job to a network printer from the DOS prompt (instead of from an application), use the NPRINT utility. To use NPRINT, type **NPRINT *filename options*** and press Enter. Replace *filename* with the name of the file to be printed. Replace *options* with any of the options you can use with the NetWare command. (Refer to table 8.4 for a list of the more common options.)

To use PCONSOLE to send a print job to a printer, start the PCONSOLE utility, then choose Print Queues from the Available Options menu. Next, choose a print queue from the list of Print Queues, and choose Print Job. Press Insert, choose the path where the file is located, choose the file, then choose a print job configuration (if prompted). Press F10 to place the print job in the print queue.

Questions

1. The proper load order for network communication software is ______.
   - ○ A. LSL, LAN driver, IPXODI, VLM
   - ○ B. IPXODI, LSL, LAN driver, VLM
   - ○ C. VLM, IPXODI, LAN driver, LSL
   - ○ D. LSL, LAN driver, VLM, IPXODI

2. The ______ file routes information from various protocols to the network board driver.
   - ○ A. LSL
   - ○ B. IPXODI
   - ○ C. LAN driver
   - ○ D. VLM

3. The file used to activate the network board is called ______.
   - ○ A. LSL
   - ○ B. IPXODI
   - ○ C. LAN driver
   - ○ D. VLM

4. Which of the following files is responsible for managing the related NetWare DOS Requester files?
   - ○ A. LSL
   - ○ B. IPXODI
   - ○ C. LAN driver
   - ○ D. VLM

5. The maximum NetWare 4 volume space is ______.
   - ○ A. 64 KB
   - ○ B. 2.5 MB
   - ○ C. 32 KB
   - ○ D. 32 TB

6. To map the next available network drive to a given path, use the ______ command.
   - ○ A. MAP N:=*path*
   - ○ B. MAP N *path*
   - ○ C. MAP INS N:=*path*
   - ○ D. MAP ROOT N *path*

7. Of the following, which *two* can be used to automate the connection and login process?
   - □ A. CONFIG.BAT
   - □ B. AUTOEXEC.BAT
   - □ C. STARTNET.BAT
   - □ D. NET.BAT

8. A ______ command can be used to trick an application program into believing that it is being installed and run from root.
   - ○ A. MAP ROOT
   - ○ B. MAP INS ROOT
   - ○ C. ROOT MAP
   - ○ D. ROOT INS MAP

9. To see a list of directories only within the current context, type ______ and press Enter.
   - A. NDIR
   - B. NDIR /SO
   - C. NDIR /DO
   - D. NDIR /FO

10. To see what the current status of your CAPTURE statement is, use the ______ command.
    - A. CAPTURE SH
    - B. CAPTURE NOTI
    - C. CAPTURE P
    - D. CAPTURE TI

Answers

1. A
2. A
3. C
4. D
5. D
6. B
7. B, C
8. A
9. C
10. A

PART II

NetWare 4.1 Advanced Administration

CHAPTER 9

Setting Up and Managing a NetWare 4.x Network

The availability of sophisticated network operating systems, such as NetWare 4, has helped to change relatively simple networks, with a few NetWare servers spread out over a limited geographic location, into complex systems capable of encompassing the following features:

- *Multiple versions of NetWare networking systems and computer operating systems*
- *A variety of hardware (including peripherals)*
- *Geographically extensive locations*
- *A variety of topologies*

Administrators of these newer, more complex networks must have a greater variety of skills and networking knowledge.

This chapter addresses the issues of a complex network, and the responsibilities of a network administrator who manages a complex network. The chapter examines the following four topics:

- Managing complex networks
- Planning and creating the NDS tree
- Using UIMPORT to create User objects
- Accommodating pre-NetWare 4 applications with bindery emulation

Managing Complex Networks

Although *complex networks*—local area networks (LANs) combined into wide area networks (WANs)—are substantially more complex to set up and manage than NetWare networks have been in the past, there are many benefits to implementing and managing these complex networks. The most important benefit is the resources such a network provides to its users. Among these resources is the ability to log in once to the network and be authenticated to all areas of the network to which you have been given rights. In addition, resources are easier to locate and use, and a greater variety of resources can be made available because a few can be purchased and shared. Communication across wide geographic boundaries is also important in today's business environment. This capability (or lack of it) can make the difference between succeeding in today's geographically dispersed business environment, or not succeeding.

As the administrator of a complex NetWare 4 network, you are presented with a variety of challenges and responsibilities. Those challenges and responsibilities generally include the following:

- Planning NetWare Directory Services (NDS)
- Installing, setting up, and managing the network hardware and software
- Dividing, distributing, and replicating the NDS database
- Providing for and enhancing NDS and general network security, including setting up an auditing account
- Setting up and maintaining network print services, using a variety of print devices to meet a variety of network user needs
- Ensuring network reliability through regular backup (and restoration, if necessary) of the NDS database and the network file system information
- Understanding, implementing, and integrating varied operating systems and networking protocols
- Managing system data, network features, and optimum network performance

Planning and Creating the NDS Tree

One of the first responsibilities of a network administrator is to plan, and then create, the NDS tree.

Note Sometimes a network administrator's first responsibility is that of installing one or more NetWare 4 file servers. This is not always the case, however, because many companies either hire consultants or have an existing network that has grown big enough to necessitate hiring a full-time network administrator.

The NDS tree can become increasingly difficult to administer if not carefully planned to meet the organization's needs and requirements. Because of NDS's hierarchical nature, the planning and design of the tree can follow the organizational structure of an organization, provided that it meets the organization's needs. The flexibility of NDS enables administrators to design a network for optimum resource sharing, minimum user impact, and highest security (through distribution of parts of the NDS database across multiple NetWare 4 file servers). To take advantage of this flexibility, however, network administrators need a basic understanding of NDS.

NDS is a database of information, which can be divided (partitioned) and copied (replicated) across multiple NetWare 4 file servers. The database consists of the following types of objects:

- [Root]
- Container
- Leaf

Each NDS tree can have only one [Root] object. The [Root] object represents the top of the NDS tree, and can hold only two types of container objects—Country or Organization—and only one type of leaf object—Alias. The [Root] object is created automatically when the first NetWare 4 file server of the NDS tree is installed. The user ADMIN also is created at that time, and is given full rights to the NDS tree, from the [Root] on down through the tree. The [Root] object cannot be deleted.

Container objects are objects that hold other objects—both container and leaf objects. There are three types of container objects: Country, Organization, and Organizational Unit. As its name implies, the *Country object* is intended to divide the NDS tree into units by country. The *Organization object* provides a somewhat less broad division, being used to represent such things as corporations, universities, divisions, and so on. The *Organizational Unit object* is used to further divide the NDS tree into smaller divisions, such as the departments, business units, or geographical divisions that may also be represented in a company or government agency.

Some types of container objects are limited as to what type of objects they can *hold* (have placed beneath them in the NDS tree hierarchy), as well as to where they themselves can be located in the NDS tree. For example, the Country container object can hold only Organizational objects or Alias objects, and can be placed only below [Root]. The Organization object can hold only Organizational Unit objects or leaf objects, and can be placed either below [Root], or below the Country object. Organizational Unit objects can contain only other Organizational Unit objects or leaf objects, and cannot be located directly beneath [Root].

Country container objects have other restrictions, as well. They can only be placed immediately below the [Root] object, and they can only be named by using a two-character X.500-compliant country abbreviation (such as *US* for the United States of America). The names of other objects can be up to 64 characters long. Finally, the Country container object is optional on NetWare 4 networks (whereas at least one Organization object is mandatory).

Leaf objects represent network resources, and are the outermost portion of the NDS tree, much as leaves themselves are located on the outermost portion of a tree that grows outdoors. Leaf objects cannot hold other objects. No Organization objects or Organizational Unit objects can be placed below a leaf object in the NDS tree (see fig. 9.1).

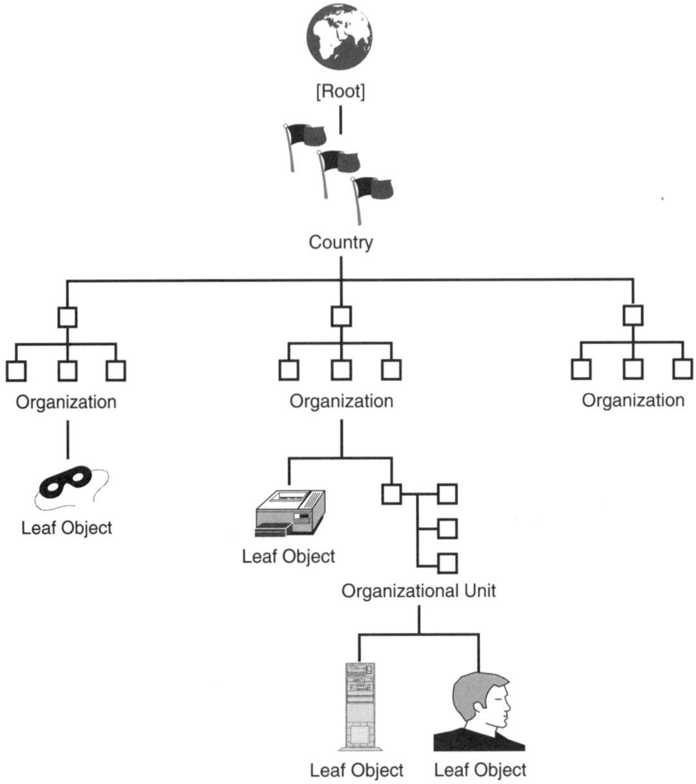

Figure 9.1
The NDS tree structure.

Many of the 16 types of leaf objects are shown in figure 9.2. A brief description of each of the 16 follows:

- **AFP Server.** An AppleTalk Filing Protocol (AFP) server, sharing files and programs
- **Alias.** An object used to point to a different object located elsewhere in the NDS tree
- **Bindery.** A NetWare 2.*x* or 3.*x* object, added to the NDS tree as the result of a NetWare 4 upgrade, and accessible only through bindery emulation
- **Bindery Queue.** A NetWare 2.*x* or 3.*x* print queue object, added to the NDS tree as the result of a NetWare 4 upgrade; provides backward compatibility for bindery-based utilities
- **Computer.** A record of information about a network computer, such as its brand, serial number, and so on
- **Directory Map.** A path (similar to a mapped network drive) that points to a specific directory on a network volume

Note This object is particularly useful to accommodate users who traditionally travel between an organization's offices. By creating Directory Map objects to local resources that the traveling user can then access through that user's Container login script or Profile login script, the user can log in to the NDS database from any location by using his or her standard login, and then access Directory Map objects to access local resources.

In addition, use of the DOS SET LOCATION command in the user's login script helps to ensure that local drive mappings are provided for this user.

- **Group.** A list of network users who require the same rights assignment
- **NetWare Server.** A NetWare 2.1*x*, 3.1*x*, or 4.*x* file server
- **Organizational Role.** A job responsibility that can be assigned to different people in succession
- **Print Server.** A network print server
- **Printer.** A printer on the network
- **Print Queue.** A network print queue
- **Profile.** A common login script that can be assigned to one or more network users who need common actions or access to network resources
- **User.** A network user with an assigned user name and rights
- **Volume.** A physical network volume, as represented by this object
- **Unknown.** An unidentifiable object, usually the result of an NDS replication change or corrupted object

One important responsibility of a network administrator is to plan the network design before implementing it. As you plan and design the NDS tree, be sure to consider the following three things:

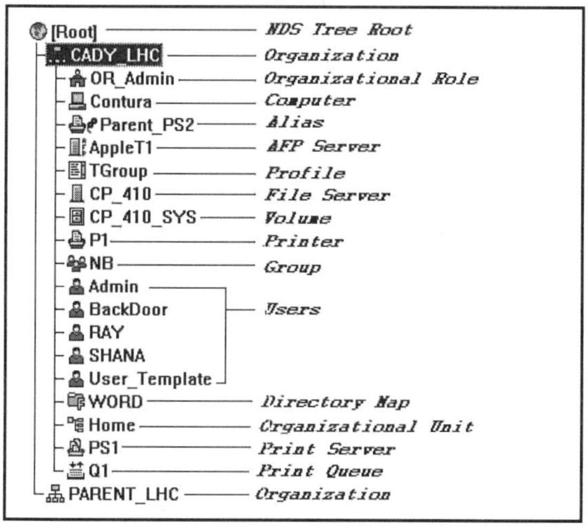

Figure 9.2
NDS leaf objects, as displayed in the NetWare Administrator.

- **Naming conventions.** Establish and follow guidelines for naming container and leaf objects, making certain that names do not exceed 64 characters; are unique when stated as complete names; use only the 00 (English) code page; and do not use characters that are not compatible with bindery, such as the slash (/), backslash (\), and so on.

Note Because of bindery limitations, the names of container and leaf objects can be no more than 47 characters long.

- **Top-level design.** When designing the NDS tree, start at the top and work down, remembering that the top level is the most difficult to restructure later. Also bear in mind that the structure of the NDS tree can be designed to match the organization's structure, and that three to five levels is often sufficient for implementing the NDS tree. The fewer levels, the shorter the complete name for any given object will be.

- **Placing objects for logical access.** In addition to the object-placement limitations of NDS (the Country object can be placed only below [Root]; only the Alias and Organization objects can be placed under the Country object; and so on), consider the logical arrangement of objects in the NDS tree.

  For example, set up groups and logical groupings whenever possible, creating container objects to hold the groups and simplify navigation of the NDS tree by network users. Also, note that although ADMIN User objects can be created at various locations in the NDS tree, the first ADMIN User object is created in the first Organization (by default) when NetWare 4 is installed and the NDS tree is created.

Use the NetWare Administrator utility to create objects and establish the NDS tree structure. When using the NetWare Administrator utility, begin at the top-level of the tree by choosing **B**rowse from the **T**ools pull-down menu (see fig. 9.3), and selecting [Root]. Then create the highest level of the tree, creating one or more Country or Organization objects, and place additional objects at lower levels in the NDS tree.

Using UIMPORT to Create User Objects

Most objects must be created by hand, but if a database of information about your network's current users exists, you can use this database and the UIMPORT utility to automate the object-creation process.

First, check the database file for any special characters (quotation marks, commas, and so on). Second, convert the database file from whatever format it currently exists in (word processing, dBASE, and so on) to a delimited ASCII text file. Third, determine what special character you will use to delineate fields within the file. (Do not use any special character—such as a comma—that already exists in the database file, although the comma is frequently used as a delineator.) Fourth, create the import control file. Finally, run the UIMPORT utility.

The import control file specifies several factors that the UIMPORT utility needs in order to function. First, it specifies which character is used as the field separator in the text file. Next, it indicates whether the NDS user template should be applied when creating each User object from the database file. Finally, it indicates which fields to include when creating each User object.

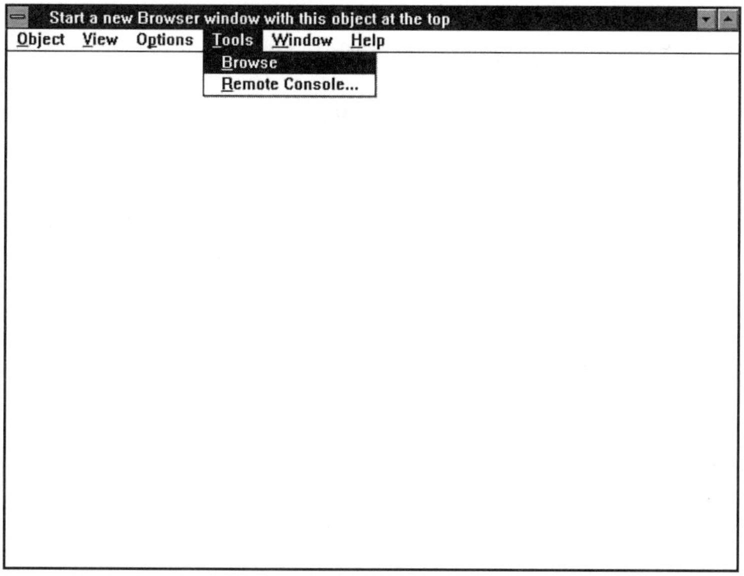

Figure 9.3
The Tools pull-down menu, showing the Browse option.

Note Name and Last Name fields are mandatory, unless you are running UIMPORT an additional time to update User object information for existing users, instead of running it to create new User objects. If you are simply updating information, you do not need to include the Last Name.

Two headers—Import Control and Fields—also are mandatory in the import control file. The following shows a sample import control file.

```
Import Control
    Separator=,
    User template=y
Fields
    Name
    Last name
    Postal (ZIP) code
    Post office box
    City
    State or province
    Telephone
```

A typical data file entry might look similar to the following:

> Johnson, MaryBeth, 92054, P.O. Box 718, Vista, CA, (619) 439-0001

With the data and import control files prepared for use, log in to the network, and make sure that your User object has at least the Create or the Supervisor right to the container object where the User objects are to be created (as well as to the file system, if user home directories will be created). Then type the following command at the DOS prompt, and press Enter:

UIMPORT *[control_filename] [data_filename]* ➥*[/C]*

Replace *[control_filename]* with the name of the import control file. Include the path if this and the data file are not located in the same directory.

Replace [*data_filename*] with the name of the file you created when you copied the database file into a delimited ASCII text file.

Use the /C option if you want the output from the UIMPORT utility to provide a continuous display instead of stopping at each screen for a response (pressing the Enter key).

Note: You can also request that a list of all errors that occurred during the running of the UIMPORT utility be placed in a log file. To make this request, include a log file name (it must end with a LOG extension) at the end of the UIMPORT command, before you press Enter.

The ASCII text file will now create User objects. You can verify their creation by using the NetWare Administration or the NETADMIN utility.

Using Bindery Services to Accommodate Pre-NetWare 4 Applications

The purpose of bindery services is to provide backward compatibility with the NetWare bindery and with applications that function based on the bindery. Using bindery emulation, the context for the pre-NetWare 4 file server will be set to the NDS tree container in which the pre-NetWare 4 file server is located.

Keep in mind the following information about bindery emulation:

- Bindery emulation is transitional and will be phased out by Novell at some time in the future.
- If bindery emulation is turned on during the installation process, the context for the NetWare server will be set to the context in which the NetWare server was installed.
- NetWare bindery-based clients can only log in to a NetWare 4 server that has bindery emulation loaded.
- The context for bindery emulation must be set only to the Organization (O) or Organizational Unit (OU) level, no matter which level of the NDS tree that O or OU exists in.
- To set the bindery context, use the SET BINDERY CONTEXT = *context* command at the NetWare 4 file server console, or in the server's AUTOEXEC.NCF file.

Note: If you set the bindery context in the AUTOEXEC.NCF file, you must unload and then reload the server for the change to take place.

Questions

1. Which of the following best describes a complex network?
   - ○ A. File servers and workstations, all located in a small geographical area
   - ○ B. Multiple workstations sharing limited resources
   - ○ C. LANs combined into WANs
   - ○ D. WANs combined into LANs

2. Which *two* objects can contain other objects?
   - □ A. Group
   - □ B. Organization
   - □ C. Organizational Unit
   - □ D. Organizational Role

3. Which of the following is *not* always a network administrator's responsibility?
   - ○ A. Dividing, distributing, and replicating the NDS database
   - ○ B. Providing for and enhancing NDS
   - ○ C. Setting up and maintaining print services
   - ○ D. Installing NetWare 4.1 file servers

4. A ______ is an object in which no other objects can be contained.
   - ○ A. [Root]
   - ○ B. Organizational Unit
   - ○ C. Country
   - ○ D. Leaf

5. Of the following, which is *not* a restriction of Country objects?
   - ○ A. They can hold only the [Root]
   - ○ B. Only two characters can be used to name them
   - ○ C. They can hold no leaf objects except Alias
   - ○ D. They can hold Organization objects, but not Organizational Unit objects

6. Which of the following is used to record information such as serial number, brand, and so on?
   - ○ A. Directory Map object
   - ○ B. Computer object
   - ○ C. Alias object
   - ○ D. NetWare Server object

7. Of the following, which *three* are types of NDS objects?
   - □ A. [Root]
   - □ B. Container
   - □ C. UIMPORT
   - □ D. Leaf

8. A ______ is an object used to point to a path on a network volume.
   - ○ A. Alias
   - ○ B. Bindery
   - ○ C. Directory Map
   - ○ D. Volume

9. To assign the same rights to more than one network User object, create a ______ object.

   ○ A. Group

   ○ B. Alias

   ○ C. Volume

   ○ D. Unknown

10. If you want to convert a standard database of user information to NDS User objects, you do *not* have to ______.

   ○ A. convert the database to an ASCII text file

   ○ B. create a batch file that incorporates the information in the database

   ○ C. prepare an import control file

   ○ D. run the UIMPORT utility

Answers

1. C
2. B, C
3. D
4. D
5. A
6. B
7. A, B, D
8. C
9. A
10. B

CHAPTER 10

Partitioning and Replicating NDS

One of the greatest assets of NetWare 4 is the global database, which can be divided and copied across the entire NetWare Directory Services (NDS) tree. Understanding what partitioning and replicating of the NDS tree can do to protect the NDS tree, and the process involved in partitioning and replicating the tree, is one of the network administrator's most important tasks.

In this chapter you learn about the following topics:

- *Planning partitions and replicas*
- *Creating and managing partitions and replicas*

Planning Partitions and Replicas

A *partition* is a section of the NDS tree that has been logically (but not physically) divided from the rest of the NDS tree. A *replica* is a copy of an NDS tree partition.

Because a partition is a logical division of the NDS tree (a portion of the NDS database), it contains information only about the objects contained in the NDS tree, not about the file system (or any of the directories or files it may contain).

Following are the four types of replicas:

- **Master.** The first copy created when a partition is created; can be used for login purposes, and is stored on the file server on which the partition resides
- **Read/Write.** Additional copies of the partition (default type of replica); can be modified, or if necessary, can replace the Master partition should it become corrupted; and can be used for login purposes, but cannot be used to merge or split a partition
- **Read-Only.** Additional copies of the partition, which cannot be used in the same manner as a Read/Write or Master replica; can be used only for searching purposes, not for login purposes
- **Subordinate Reference.** A pointer to a replica, rather than an actual copy of a partition.

> **Note** The list of all servers that have a replica of a specific partition is known as the *replica ring*. A replica ring is maintained by each file server, and can communicate with other servers in the ring to update each other when changes occur to that specific partition. When merging or splitting partitions, be certain that all file servers included in the replica ring for that specific partition are online.

When the NDS tree is created and partitioning is done, certain default configurations occur for replications. The [Root] and first Organization are created as a partition and replicated in the following way: The first file server in this replica ring receives the Master replica of this partition. The second and third file servers in the replica ring receive Read/Write replicas of this partition.

When the second partition is created, the file server on which it resides receives the Master replica of this second partition, and Read/Write replicas of this second partition are placed on the other two file servers.

If a third partition is created, the file server on which it resides receives the Master replica, and a Read/Write copy is placed on another file server in the ring.

To be effective, replicas of the NDS database must be synchronized with each other. This is a background process in which all changes to the NDS database (creating User objects, updating User object rights, moving objects, and so on) must be copied to all affected replicas. This process is automatic; because it is based on the time stamp associated with each transaction, changes are made to the NDS database and each affected replica in the correct order.

Most replica information is collected and sent out at 10-second intervals. The exception is the changes associated with user logins. To help reduce network traffic, particularly when multiple users are logging in at about the same time, that information is only collected and sent out every 5 minutes.

Creating and Managing Partitions and Replicas

Partitions and replicas (except those created automatically when a server is installed) are created, as well as managed, by using the NetWare Administrator utility. When determining which partitions and replicas to create, consider the defaults.

Be sure to design the partitions and replicas to achieve the most effective level of fault tolerance and to make access to NDS information as efficient as possible. In addition, be sure to consider the following factors in your planning:

- Physical location of file servers.
- WAN versus LAN implementation, and related considerations.
- Number of replicas to be created and maintained.
- Size of each replica. (To simplify administration, Novell recommends limiting the number of objects within partitions to a maximum of 5,000.)

With these goals and factors in mind, your design should be as effective as possible. You can then proceed to create partitions, manage replicas, and so on.

Creating Partitions

Before creating partitions, make sure that you have the Supervisor right to the parent container, so that you will be able to merge or split a partition.

To create partitions, first choose Partition Manager from the Tools pull-down menu in the NetWare Administrator utility (see fig. 10.1).

Next, select the container you want to make a new partition, then choose Create as new partition. When prompted with the Confirmation dialog box, choose Yes. Note that the Confirmation dialog box indicates that creating a new partition can take 10 minutes or longer. Be sure to include this time in your plans when you create new partitions.

Creating Replicas

As mentioned previously, several replicas are created automatically when a NetWare 4 file server is installed. You can create additional replicas if you have the proper rights—you need Supervisor right to the server object which is to hold the replica.

To create a replica, complete the following steps:

1. Choose Partition Manager from the NetWare Administrator Tools pull-down menu.
2. Move through the tree structure until you are situated at the root of the partition.

3. Select (highlight) a server to hold the replica.
4. Double-click on icons, as necessary, until the container for which you will be creating a replica appears.
5. Select that container object.
6. Choose Replicas and provide information about the name of the partition for which a replica is being created, the context of the Master replica, and the server name where the Master replica is stored.
7. Choose Add Replica and double-click on objects in the Server box until the proper context for the server on which the replica is to be stored appears.

   In NetWare 4.1, you can choose the type of replica to create (see fig. 10.2).

8. Select the server.
9. Choose OK.

In addition to creating partitions and replicas, several other tasks are associated with managing partitions and replicas. The most important ones include adding NetWare 4 file servers to or removing NetWare 4 servers from the NDS tree, removing NetWare 4 volumes from the NDS tree, redefining partitions, repairing replicas, and so on.

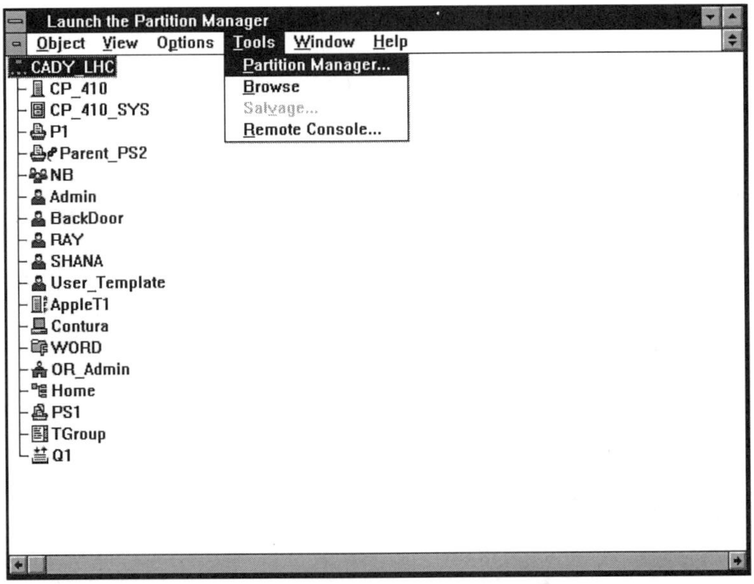

Figure 10.1
The Tools pull-down menu.

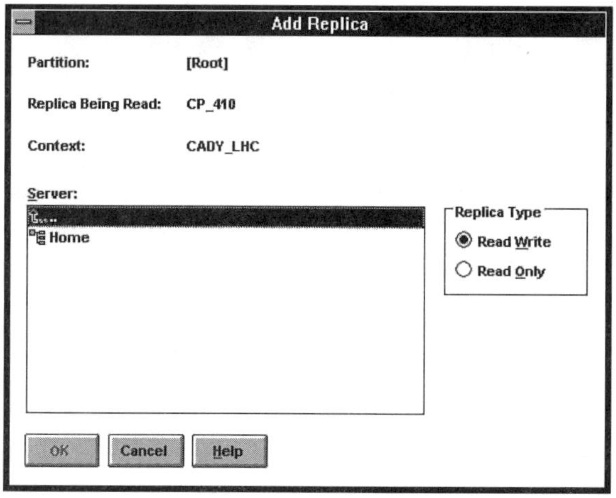

Figure 10.2
The Add Replica dialog box.

Adding NetWare 4 File Servers to the NDS Tree

When a new NetWare 4 file server is added to the NDS tree, the following rules apply:

1. The first 3 servers in partitions receive replicas (Master and two Read/Write).
2. If a new context is created when installing a server, it is made part of the existing partition.
3. If upgrade is performed from 3.*x* to 4.*x*, a Read/Write replica is put on the server to support bindery services.

Note If the new server had simply been added to an existing Organization or Organizational Unit, the partitions would not have changed, and the new server could then be given a Read/Write replica of the existing partition.

Removing NetWare 4 File Servers from the NDS Tree

You can remove NetWare 4 file servers by using either the NetWare Administrator Partition Manager, or the DOS PARTMGR utility. (Although, technically, you can also use the NETADMIN utility to remove NetWare 4 file servers, doing so may result in serious and unpredictable behavior.

To use the NetWare Administrator Partition Manager, choose Partition Manager from the Tools pull-down menu. Choose the server you want to remove from the partition, choose Server partitions, change the Master partition to a Read/Write partition, and wait a reasonable period of time for this change to take effect. Then delete all partitions on this server, and finally, choose Delete Server.

To use the PARTMGR utility to delete a server, type **PARTMGR** at the DOS prompt (after logging in to the network as a user with Supervisor rights), and press Enter. Move through the NDS tree until you select the server to be removed (see fig. 10.3).

Figure 10.3
The PARTMGR Object, Class screen.

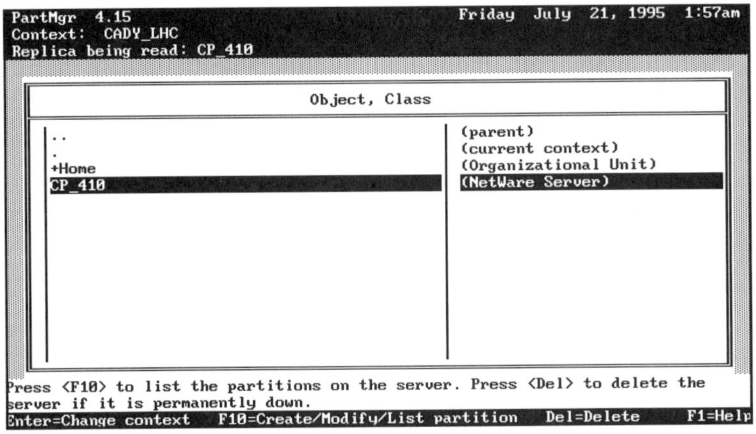

Next, choose the replicas on this server and remove them. After waiting a reasonable period of time (24 hours is not unreasonable), select the server object and press Delete. When prompted to confirm the deletion of this server, choose Yes.

Note Before you bring down this file server, wait until enough time has passed for all servers in the same replica ring as this server to be notified that this server has been removed from the replica ring.

Removing NetWare 4 Volumes from the NDS Tree

To remove a NetWare 4 volume from the NDS tree, you must first remove the file server from the tree. The volume objects are then displayed in the tree as Unknown objects. Use the NETADMIN or NetWare Administrator utility to choose and delete these Unknown objects from the NDS tree.

Redefining NDS Partitions

If the existing partitioning scheme is not meeting all your network needs as originally planned, you can redefine one or more partitions. When redefining a partition, keep the following in mind:

- To redefine a partition, you must have access to the Master replica.
- All file servers in the replica ring must be up and running.
- Other replicas will be updated with changes made to the Master replica.
- Redefine replicas when network traffic is minimal, because synchronization increases network traffic; objects cannot be created, deleted, or moved until the synchronization is complete (which may take anywhere from 20 minutes to an hour, or longer).

Modifying Replicas

In addition to redefining partitions, you can change the type of a replica. For example, if a Master replica becomes corrupted or for some reason is unusable, you can change one of the partition's Read/Write replicas to a Master replica. This automatically changes the Master replica to a Read/Write replica, as there can be only one Master replica per NDS partition.

To replace a corrupted Master replica by changing a Read/Write replica to the Master, load the DSREPAIR.NLM server utility at the file server, then complete the following steps for a NetWare 4.0 file server:

1. Choose Select Options.
2. Choose Do not check consistency of local replicas (if running NetWare 4.01), or Do not repair replica rings (if running NetWare 4.02).
3. Return to the Select Options menu and choose Begin repair.
4. When the repair is complete, choose Exit.

If you are running DSREPAIR.NLM on a NetWare 4.1 file server, the utility looks much different. To access the same functionality as is found in the NetWare 4.01 and 4.02 DSREPAIR.NLM, choose the Replica and partition operations option from the Advanced Options menu (see fig. 10.4).

Viewing Partitions

You can use the Partition Manager option in the Tools pull-down menu of NetWare Administrator to view partitions. Simply choose icons until you locate the server containing the replica for which you want to view partition information. Then, choose Server Partitions to display a list of the partitions this server holds.

Merging Partitions

You can also use the NetWare Administrator's Partition Manager tool to merge partitions. Choose the partition you want to merge (double-click on the icons until you locate the partition). Next, choose the container object, and then choose Merge partition.

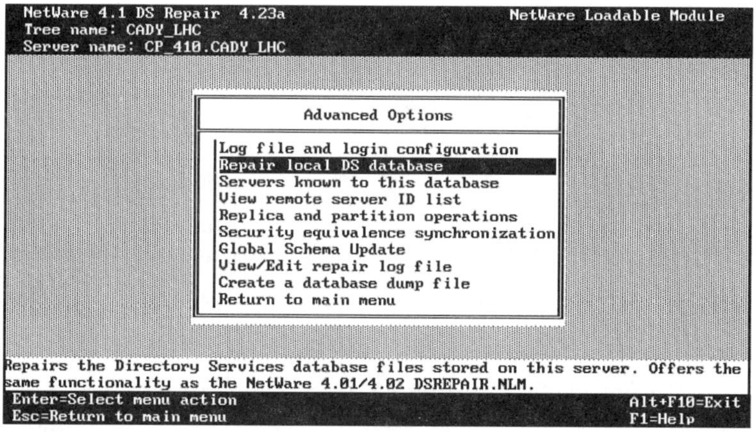

Figure 10.4
The DSREPAIR.NLM Advanced Options menu.

Changing Replica Types

Using the NetWare Administrator's Partition Manager tool, you can also change a replica's type. From the Partitions screen, double-click on icons until you locate the file server containing the partition to be changed, then choose that partition. Next, choose Replicas. Select (highlight) the replica whose type you want to change, then choose Change Type. Select the type of replica you want this replica to become, and choose OK.

Deleting Replicas

You can also delete a replica by using the NetWare Administrator's Partition Manager tool. Double-click on icons until you locate the file server containing the partition to be deleted, then choose Replicas. Next, select (highlight) the replica to be deleted, and choose Delete Replica.

Questions

1. Replicas can be defined as ______.
   - ○ A. division of the NetWare file system
   - ○ B. logical grouping of NetWare objects
   - ○ C. copies of NDS partitions
   - ○ D. backups of NDS object rights
2. The *four* types of replicas are ______.
   - ☐ A. Master
   - ☐ B. Read/Write
   - ☐ C. Read-Only
   - ☐ D. Read-Once
   - ☐ E. Subordinate Reference
3. The ______ replica type *cannot* be used for login.
   - ○ A. Master
   - ○ B. Read/Write
   - ○ C. Read-Only
   - ○ D. None of the above
4. A ______ replica is the first one created when a partition is created.
   - ○ A. Master
   - ○ B. Read/Write
   - ○ C. Read-Only
   - ○ D. None of the above
5. The ______ is a list of servers that have a replica of a specific partition.
   - ○ A. Master replica
   - ○ B. Replica order
   - ○ C. Master order ring
   - ○ D. Replica ring
6. Most replica information is collected and sent out at ______ intervals, but login information is collected every ______.
   - ○ A. 5-minute, 10 seconds
   - ○ B. 10-second, 5 minutes
   - ○ C. 10-second, 10 minutes
   - ○ D. 5-second, 5 minutes
7. Of the following, which *three* are true statements?
   - ☐ A. The first file server in a new partition receives the Master copy of the replica.
   - ☐ B. The second file server in a new partition receives a Read/Write replica.
   - ☐ C. Replication is a foreground process, and should be conducted after regular business hours to improve network traffic.
   - ☐ D. To be effective, replicas of the NDS database must be synchronized with each other, a process over which the network user has no control.

8. To create a partition, you must have ______.
   - A. the Supervisor right to the file server
   - B. the Supervisor right to the parent partition
   - C. the Supervisor right to the container object
   - D. the Supervisor right to the parent container

9. The topmost container of a new partition is called the ______.
   - A. parent container
   - B. parent partition
   - C. parent organization
   - D. parent [Root]

10. If you want to remove a replica, you can use the NetWare Administrator or ______.
    - A. Tools
    - B. PARTMGR
    - C. NETADMIN
    - D. Partition Manager

Answers

1. C
2. A, B, C, E
3. C
4. A
5. D
6. B
7. A, B, D
8. B
9. A
10. B

CHAPTER 11

Securing and Backing Up a NetWare 4.x Network

There are two levels of logical security provided by the NetWare 4 operating system—NDS security, and file system security—both of which are independent of one another. Although file system security in NetWare 4 is very much like file system security in NetWare 3, the basics of NetWare 4 file system security are discussed here, along with NDS security.

In addition to NDS and file system security, one additional method of providing security to your network is that of backing up the NDS database, the NetWare operating system files, and the file system by using the SBACKUP utility, which supports the storage management services (SMS) architecture.

This chapter discusses the following network security topics:

- NDS security
- File system security
- SMS and SBACKUP

NDS Security

In NetWare 4, NDS security can be administered completely separately from file system security. *NDS security* deals only with the NDS database and the objects it contains. *File system security* deals with the file system itself. The two are completely separate, with one exception. The user who installs a NetWare 4 file server into the NDS tree (usually the network Administrator) is given the Supervisor object right to the File Server object. This right automatically makes the user a trustee of the file system, and gives him or her the Supervisor right to the file system.

Note To make NDS and file system security completely separate, first make a different administrative user the trustee with the Supervisor right to the complete file system. Then reduce the rights to the File Server object of the user who installed the file server (to all property and all object rights, except Supervisor). After you make these changes, the network Administrator will still be able to manage the File Server object, but will have no specific rights to the file system. Another administrative user will have all rights to the file system, but no administrative or Supervisor rights to the NDS tree, including this File Server object.

To give any user, group, container, or other object rights to any object in the NDS tree, the object being given rights must first be made a trustee of the other object. The trustee can then be given object and property rights.

Object rights are rights that enable a trustee to manage the object for which the rights have been given. Following are the five object rights:

- **Supervisor.** Gives to the trustee all access privileges for all properties of the object, but can be blocked by the *inherited rights filter* (IRF)
- **Browse.** Gives the object's trustee the right to view the object in the NDS tree
- **Create.** Gives the object's trustee the right to create new objects below this container object in the NDS tree
- **Delete.** Gives the object's trustee the right to remove the object from the NDS tree
- **Rename.** Gives the object's trustee the right to modify the name of the object

Note Be careful when you give a trustee the Supervisor object right, because this right also gives the trustee the Supervisor property right for all properties of this object.

Property rights specify how a user can access information related to an object. The Browse property right, for example, enables the user to see the object in the NDS tree, whereas the Read property right enables the user to read the value assigned either to All Properties of this object (if assigned that way), or to one or more specific properties of this object (such as the name, telephone number, address, and so on).

The following Property rights, of which there are five, can be assigned:

- **Supervisor.** Gives the user all rights to a specified property, or to all properties, if so designated
- **Compare.** Gives the user the right to compare a given value to the values assigned to a specific property, in order to determine whether there is a match (such as whether a User object has been included as a value in the electronic mailing list of another User object)
- **Read.** Gives the user the right to read the values associated with a property (also includes the Compare right)
- **Write.** Gives the user the right to add, change, or modify the values associated with a specific property (also includes the Add Self right)
- **Add Self.** Gives the user the right to add or remove itself as a value of the specified property, such as adding or removing itself to or from the list of users assigned to a group

Note When giving property rights to an object in the NDS tree, you can give property rights to individual properties of an object, or you can give rights to All Properties of the object. For example, you can give User object TOM the Supervisor object right to only one (or more) properties (such as telephone number) of User object JOSEPH, or you can give User object TOM the Supervisor object right to All Properties of User object Joseph.

All NDS trustee assignments are values of (stored in) the ACL (*Access Control List*) property of the NDS object. The *values* (lists of trustees and their assigned rights) of the ACL property for any given object control who has access (rights) to that object. Be careful, therefore, when assigning the Write property right to the ACL of an object; users assigned this right may change their property right to Supervisor for their own User objects.

In the NetWare file system, rights assignments made at one level in the file system structure flow down to directories and files at lower points in the file system. This is true also in the NDS tree. Trustee assignments made at one container level of the NDS tree can flow down to other, lower (child) container levels. The effective rights of an object in the NDS tree, therefore, must take into account the flow of rights (inherited rights) from upper (parent) container levels in the NDS tree to lower (child) container levels. In addition, the following points must be considered:

- Explicit trustee assignments made to any parent containers, whether through the use of security equivalencies, membership in a group, direct assignment, and so on will flow down to the child objects.
- Explicit trustee assignments made at a specific container level must be considered in conjunction with any rights inherited from any parent container.
- The IRF can block out any rights flowing from a parent container to a child container, including the Supervisor right.

An NDS object can receive rights from several sources. Rights can flow from [Public], which is located at the top of the NDS tree and capable of granting rights to the NDS tree to users (even before they log in to the network). Rights can be given through trustee assignments made to containers, group objects, and objects to which the user has been made security equivalent. Certain rights are assigned by default to the user when that User object is created. (Such rights include the Browse object right to its own User object, the Read property right to all its own properties, and the

Read and Write property rights to the User object's Login Script and Print Job Config properties). In addition, rights granted to objects in the NDS tree can be removed with the IRF.

To calculate a user's effective rights, apply the following formula:

Explicit trustee assignments granted at the current container level (ETACC), plus explicit trustee assignments granted at any parent containers (whether made through assignment to a group, security equivalencies, or assignment as a trustee to other objects, when those objects also have trustee assignments), and those rights granted by the PUBLIC trustee and the [Root] object (ETAPC), less any rights filtered out through the application of an IRF at either the current or any parent containers (IRF) equal the user's effective rights.

Note The PUBLIC trustee is not an actual NDS object. Rather, it is a trustee assignment received by everyone attempting to connect to the network, even before that connection and login process are complete. By default, the PUBLIC trustee has the Browse property rights; therefore, all users can view the NDS tree, even before they connect and log in to NDS.

In other words, to calculate effective rights in NDS, use this formula:

ETACC + ETAPC - IRF = Effective rights

Note The fact that containers also have rights to other objects in the NDS tree is a concept new to NetWare 4.*x*. In a sense, container objects act like natural groups because objects, including User objects, are contained in container objects. Because of that containment, User objects inherit the rights assigned to the container object itself. This concept is similar to the concept of inheriting rights to other objects because you have been made a member of a group. The association is referred to as an *implied security equivalence.*

If users seem to be receiving unauthorized access to the NDS tree, check the following to find the problem:

- Explicit trustee assignments for the User object; Groups and Organizational Roles the user may be a member of; security equivalencies; all the user's containers, from its parent container to the [Root]; and any inherited rights resulting from explicit trustee assignments made in parent containers
- Inherited rights as a result of any trustee assignments, memberships, security equivalencies, parent containers, [PUBLIC], and [Root]

If users are not able to access network resources for which they are supposed to have rights, you can use the same process to determine where rights that should have been granted have not been granted.

In addition, you can use the NETADMIN or NetWare Administrator utilities to check trustees of this object at the container level, the RIGHTS command at the DOS prompt, or the FILER utility to determine an object's rights.

The rights a User object receives are based on the default rights it was given when it was created, the rights it receives as an object in its parent container, and so on. These rights are often sufficient for a user. There may be times; however, assigning additional rights is necessary. You should consider assigning additional rights if any of the following conditions are present:

- A need exists to divide up the responsibility for administering the NDS tree. (Make an explicit trustee assignment of all object and all property rights, including Supervisor, at the container level to the secondary administrators.)
- You need to create and assign profile login scripts. (If the user is not in the same container where the profile login script resides, make the user a trustee of the profile login script with the Browse object right and the Read property right to the login script.)
- Directory Map objects have been created. (Assign the Read All Property right to users who need access to the Directory Map object.)
- Some users have been given special assignments related to properties of objects in the NDS tree, such as updating mailing list information. (Assign the Read and Write property rights to each property that the user is responsible for updating.)
- An Alias object has been created for a user on the network. (Assign the Alias object the Read object right to the Login Script property of the container in which the Alias object resides.)
- Additional rights are needed to ensure adequate access to printers throughout the NDS tree. (Assign the Browse property right for the user to the container in which the Printer or Print Queue object resides, if the User object resides in a different container; or specifically make the user a print server or print queue operator if you want him or her to manage a Print Queue or Print Server object.)

File System Security

File system security and NDS security differ in certain aspects.

As mentioned before, the user responsible for installing the NetWare 4 server into the NDS tree receives the Supervisor right to the File Server object. This Supervisor right then flows down the directory structure as the Supervisory directory right to all directories and files in the file system. Although the Supervisor right in the NDS tree can be blocked by the IRF, the Supervisory file system right cannot be blocked by the IRF.

In addition, although you combine trustee assignments and then subtract the results of an IRF to determine effective rights in the NDS tree, any explicit trustee assignments made to a file in the file system are the effective rights.

User objects contained in the same container in which the file server was installed receive (by default) the Read and File Scan rights to SYS:PUBLIC. If the User object is contained within a separate container, these rights must be assigned to that User object. One of the simplest ways to accomplish that is to give these rights to the other container object. These rights will then be inherited by all objects within this other container, or, if all users in the network need to access all files in SYS:PUBLIC, these rights can be assigned at the [Root] object.

Rights to access applications and home directories on NetWare 4 servers must also be assigned to User objects. At a minimum, users need the Read and File Scan rights to applications, and all rights (except, perhaps, Supervisory and Access Control) to their home directories.

SMS and SBACKUP

NetWare's storage management services (SMS) provide backup and restore capabilities by using the SMS-compliant utility SBACKUP, or any other third-party backup and restore software that is SMS-compliant. Using SBACKUP, you can backup the file system information from *target* devices (including DOS workstations, OS/2 workstations, and NetWare file servers), as well as NDS and BTRIEVE databases, to the *host* device (a NetWare file server with backup software and a backup device installed).

To enable SMS to accommodate various backup devices and software, it was designed using an open, modular architecture implemented primarily through the use of NLMs (NetWare Loadable Modules). The NLMs are loaded on the host file server, as well as on any target file servers. In addition, special workstation software is loaded on the target workstations whose file system is to be backed up.

Modules loaded on the host server include the following:

- Device drivers that manage the physical operations of the storage devices and media
- Storage Device Interface (SDI), which acts as an intermediary between the SBACKUP utility and the backup device via the device drivers
- Storage Management Data Requester (SMDR), which acts as the communication mediator between SBACKUP and the Target Service Agents (TSA) and SDI
- Target Service Agents for the NDS database, the NetWare server, and the workstations act as transfer agents passing commands, requests, and data between the SMDR and the NDS database, NetWare server, or workstation
- Workstation Manager, which acts as the workstation message receiver, taking announcement messages indicating the workstation's availability on the network, and keeping an internal list of workstations available for backup
- SBACKUP, the utility used to perform backup and restore operations when a separate third-party (non-Novell) backup utility is not used

To ensure consistent backup, you can use the following four types of backup:

- **Full.** All data is backed up and the archive bit is cleared. Full backups can be very time consuming and may use a great deal of backup medium, such as tape or disk space. Full backups have the advantage, however, of requiring only one day's backup to complete a restore. When combined with differential backups, the restore process is slower than when combined with incremental backups.
- **Incremental.** Only files that have been added or modified since the last backup was performed are backed up, and the archive bit is cleared. Because only the new or modified files are backed up by each incremental backup, several tapes or disks may have to be used to complete a full backup or restore, particularly when incremental backups are combined with regular full backups. The main advantage of an incremental backup is that it keeps a sequential history of file modifications and additions.
- **Differential.** All files that have been added or modified since the last full backup are backed up, and the archive bit is *not* cleared. Only the latest of the tapes or disks will have to be used to restore, because these latest ones contain all new and modified files since the last full backup. This type of backup takes longer than an incremental backup, but you can restore with

minimal effort by restoring the last full backup and the latest differential backup. When differential backups are combined with full backups, more space will be used on the backup media, so fewer media will be used than with the full and incremental combination.

Note: Differential and incremental backups should never be combined, because some files probably will be lost if a restore is necessary.

- **Custom.** You specify which files are to be backed up, and whether you want the archive bit to be cleared. Custom backups give you flexibility (through the use of the Include and Exclude options) in your choice of what to back up, and may reduce the overall time required to complete a backup. Should a restoration become necessary, however, the custom backups you have performed may not be sufficient to properly and fully restore your network files. In this case, some network files may be lost, incomplete, or too old to be useful.

Regardless of which backup type you choose, determine how you will rotate the use of your backup media (weekly, monthly, and so on); how you can implement a backup strategy to simplify the restoration process if it becomes necessary; how much network downtime you can afford, while performing backups; as well as which network files you will back up, and how frequently you will back them up.

Although the SMS architecture makes it possible for you to choose alternative backup software, if you choose to run the SBACKUP utility, consider the following:

- Sufficient disk space on the SYS volume of the host server must be available to house temporary files created by SBACKUP during the backup process.
- The backup media should have sufficient capacity to permit completion of the backup without changing the media, particularly if you will be conducting unattended backups.
- Delayed backups should not begin until at least two hours have passed since NetWare compressed the last file.
- Name spaces must be properly supported, and correct name case formats must be used when specifying paths and file names for backup purposes.
- During backups, volumes cannot be mounted or dismounted, and drivers cannot be unloaded, without causing files to become corrupted, or worse, the file server to abend (abruptly end).

You can use SBACKUP to back up files by following these steps:

1. Load device drivers for your backup device: the TAPEDAI.DSK general device driver shipped with NetWare 4, if you are using a SCSI tape drive for your backups; TSAs for the target servers; and then SBACKUP.
2. From the SBACKUP Main Menu (see fig. 11.1), choose Backup.

Note: If necessary, first choose the Change Target to Back Up From or Restore To option from the SBACKUP Main Menu, then choose a different target.

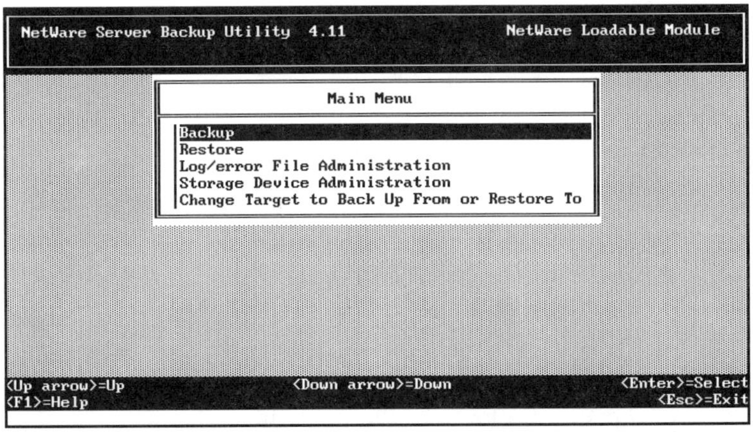

Figure 11.1
The SBACKUP Main Menu.

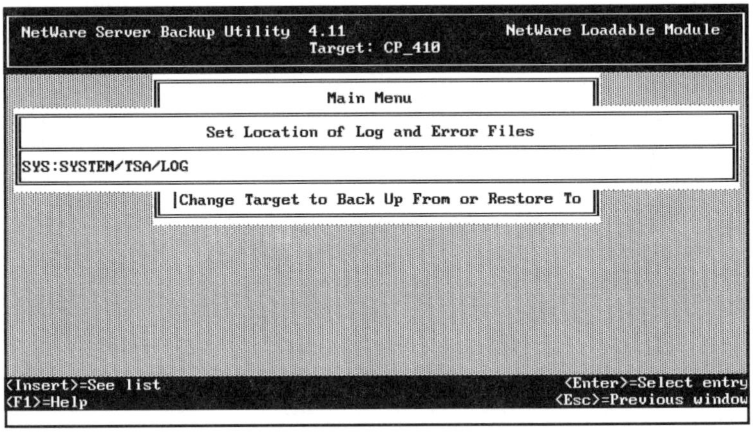

Figure 11.2
The Set Location of Log and Error Files prompt.

3. Choose, from a list of targets, the target from which to conduct the backup. Then, if prompted, provide the name of the user conducting the backup (generally that user is the Admin User object, or one assigned to conduct backups and given the proper rights), and the User object's password. If the user is authenticated, you receive a message indicating that you are connected to the chosen target.

4. Choose a TSA to use. If only one type of media is available for backup, it will be selected for you by default. Otherwise, you must choose the backup media to use.

5. Specify where the log and error files are to be stored, if prompted with Set the Location of Log and Error Files (see fig. 11.2).

6. From the Type of Backup menu (see fig. 11.3), choose a backup type—Full, Differential, Incremental, or Custom.

7. Provide additional information as prompted, depending on the type of backup you chose.

   If you choose a full, differential, or incremental backup, you are prompted to provide a Description of what you are backing up.

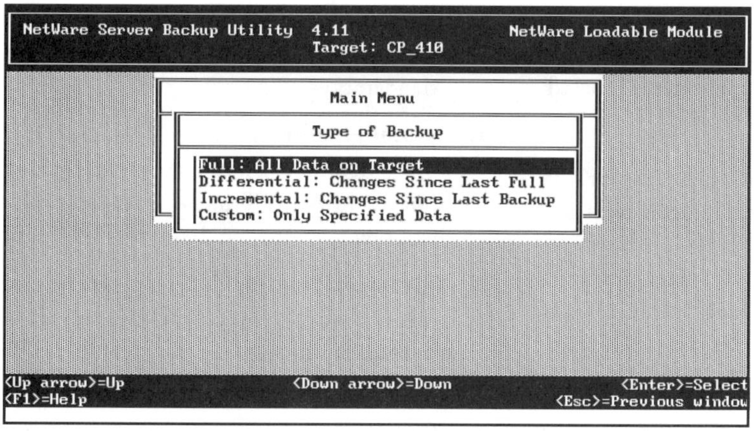

Figure 11.3
The Type of Backup menu.

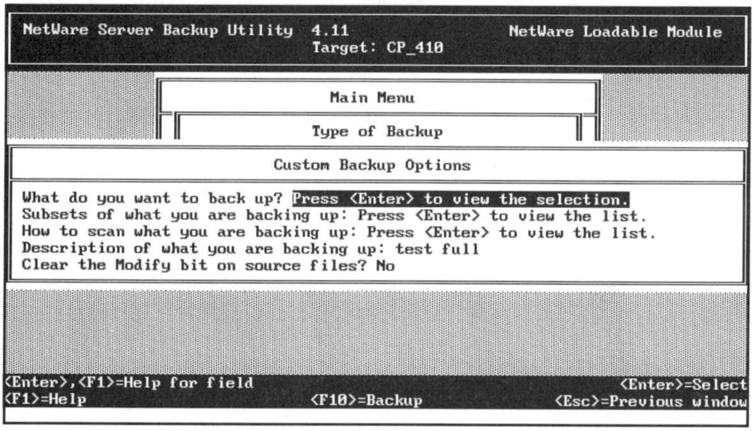

Figure 11.4
The Custom Backup Options screen.

Provide a brief description, press Enter to accept that description, then press F10 to begin the backup.

If you choose a custom backup, you see the prompts on the Custom Backup Options screen (see fig. 11.4).

From the Custom Backup Options screen, choose what you want to back up, as well as any subsets you want to specifically include, exclude, or be scanned for when the backup is run. Also, provide a description for this backup, and indicate whether you want the Modify bit to be cleared. Then, press F10.

8. From the Proceed with the backup? menu, choose to Start the Backup Now, or to Start the Backup Later.

   If you choose to start the backup now, provide the media label information at the Enter a label for the media set prompt, and continue with the backup.

   If you choose to begin the backup later, fill in the Start date, Start time, and if necessary, the System Time fields on the Start the Backup at menu. Press F10, then verify the start time.

If for some reason you prefer not to run the backup at all, you can choose the No, Return to the Options Form option from the Proceed with the backup? menu.

To restore a backup made using the SBACKUP utility, follow the same initial process used for backing up the data, but choose Restore from the SBACKUP Main menu instead of choosing Backup. Then, from the Restore Session menu, choose either Choose a Session to Restore, or Restore Without Session Files.

> **Note** If you choose to restore from a specific session, you are prompted to specify where the session files are located, and then choose the specific session to be restored from a list of sessions.

The next step is to choose the media, as was the case with the original backup. Then, from the Restoring From menu, choose what is to be restored. Finally, mount the media to restore from, and begin the restore process.

If you choose to back up or restore a DOS workstation, you must load the DOS TSA (TSA_SMS.EXE) at the workstation, and choose the DOS TSA from the SBACKUP menu, as well as an available drive or DOS workstation.

If you want to customize the workstation backup, you can include various options when loading the DOS TSA. Some of these options must be used; they are designated as (Mandatory) in the following list:

- **/B[uffers]=n.** To specify the number of 1 KB buffers the DOS TSA can use during backup
- **/D[rives]=x.** To indicate by drive letter which drives can be backed up for this workstation (Mandatory)
- **/N[ame]=name.** To assign a name to this workstation, so that it can be chosen by name from the SBACKUP menu (Mandatory the first time)
- **/P[assword]=word.** To set a password that must be used when backing up this workstation's files (Mandatory, unless you're using the /T option)
- **/T[rust].** To enable this workstation's files to be backed up without requiring a password (Mandatory, unless you're using the /P option)
- **/SE[rver]=name.** To specify the name of the host file server (Mandatory)
- **/ST[ack]=number.** To increase the stack size from the default of 2,048 bytes, if you receive Stack Overflow error messages
- **/U[nload].** To remove the TSA from workstation memory

You also have the option to manage the backup session files (the backup log files, and the backup and restore error log files), using the SBACKUP utility. This is particularly useful if you need to troubleshoot backup session problems.

These logs provide information about the date and time, as well as a brief description of the session; the target that was backed up; media set identification; names of volumes, files, and directories that were backed up; and where on the storage media the backup data can be found.

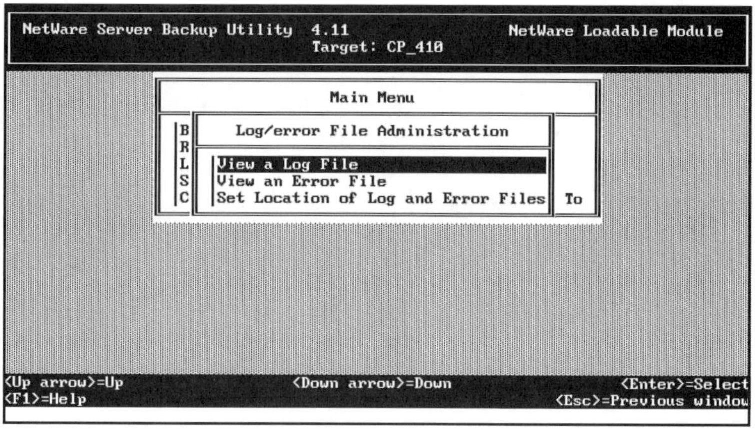

Figure 11.5
The Log/error File Administration menu.

To view session information, choose the Log/error File Administration option from the SBACKUP Main menu, then choose either View a Log File or View an Error File from the Log/error File Administration menu (see fig. 11.5). To help maintain the validity of session files, delete any session-related logs that are no longer valid or needed.

Questions

1. NDS security deals only with ______.
   - ○ A. the NDS database
   - ○ B. NDS User objects
   - ○ C. the NDS database and file system
   - ○ D. the file system

2. The *two* types of NDS rights are:
   - □ A. Object
   - □ B. User
   - □ C. File
   - □ D. Property

3. The ______ right includes the Add Self right.
   - ○ A. Compare
   - ○ B. Read
   - ○ C. Write
   - ○ D. Browse

4. The ______ is *not* an actual NDS object.
   - ○ A. [Root]
   - ○ B. PUBLIC trustee
   - ○ C. Alias
   - ○ D. OU

5. Users who need access to a Directory Map object must have the ______ right.
   - ○ A. File Scan
   - ○ B. Browse
   - ○ C. Supervisor
   - ○ D. Write

6. By default, the ______ receives the Supervisor right to the file system on a file server.
   - ○ A. user who installed the NetWare 4 server
   - ○ B. Supervisor user
   - ○ C. network administrator
   - ○ D. PUBLIC trustee

7. Of the following, which *three* can be used to troubleshoot rights problems?
   - □ A. NETADMIN
   - □ B. NetWare Administrator
   - □ C. Rights
   - □ D. NETUSER

8. The ______ acts as the communication mediator between SBACKUP and the Target Service Agents.
   - ○ A. device driver
   - ○ B. TSA for the NDS database
   - ○ C. SMDR
   - ○ D. SDI

9. Which *two* types of backups should never be used together?
   - □ A. Full
   - □ B. Incremental
   - □ C. Differential
   - □ D. Custom

10. If you want to back up or restore a DOS workstation, you must load the ______ file at the workstation.

    ○ A. SMS_TSA

    ○ B. DOS_TSA

    ○ C. TSA_SMS

    ○ D. SMS_DOS

Answers

1. A
2. A, D
3. C
4. B
5. B
6. A
7. A, B, C
8. C
9. B, C
10. C

CHAPTER 12

Auditing a NetWare 4.x Network

Although earlier versions of NetWare let you perform minor auditing tasks—you could establish accounting charge rates for various network uses, and then track the charges—that was not true auditing. NetWare 4 provides an auditing feature that goes well beyond simply setting and tracking accounting charge rates. NetWare 4 enables the network administrator to establish a separate user account for an auditor, then turn that account over to another user. That user then decides what will be tracked, for how long it will be tracked, how large the auditing file can become, and so on, all without any input or further assistance from the network administrator. NetWare 4's auditing software provides true independent auditing capabilities, thanks to the AUDITCON utility.

Auditing is a useful and functional feature of NetWare for the following tasks:

- To help decentralize control of the network and spread out some of the responsibility for network security.
- To ensure that users are following proper security procedures while accessing the file system (creating files and then setting the appropriate security; granting access to other users only when such access should be granted; changing both file ownership and trustee rights when necessary, and so on).
- To ensure that network administrators are following the proper security procedures, such as making the correct user and group trustee rights changes when job responsibilities or assignments change, revoking temporary network access when the need for such access is no longer valid, and updating application and other network software on a timely basis.
- To track network resource usage to ensure that access to resources and the availability of a variety of network resources are adequate.
- To enhance system fault tolerance by using the auditing information to pinpoint areas of weakness in network security.
- To troubleshoot network problems (major ones, such as a crash, or minor ones), using the logs to reconstruct what occurred before the problem.

This chapter discusses the AUDITCON utility, and explains how an auditor sets up and follows NDS and file system auditing.

Using AUDITCON to Audit a NetWare 4 Network

Network auditing is not enabled by default on NetWare 4 file servers. The network administrator must make auditing available by performing the following three basic steps:

- Setting up the auditor's environment
- Enabling auditing
- Telling auditor users their temporary passwords

To set up the auditor's environment, the network administrator must create a User object for the auditor, if not assigning the auditing responsibility to an existing user. Next, the administrator must assign rights to the User object, create a directory and assign the auditor user the necessary rights to access it so that audit files can be stored and retrieved, and automate the login process, particularly the establishment of drive mappings that enable the auditor to function effectively on the network.

To enable auditing on the network, the network administrator logs in to the network with Supervisor rights, and runs the AUDITCON utility. (To run the AUDITCON utility, type **AUDITCON** at the workstation's DOS prompt, and press Enter.) Then, the network administrator completes the following steps:

1. If the current server is not the server for which auditing is to be enabled, choose Change current server from the Available audit options menu (see fig. 12.1), and choose the correct server.
2. Choose Audit directory services from the Available audit options menu.
3. Choose Audit directory tree from the Audit directory services menu.
4. When the Audit directory tree screen opens (see fig. 12.2), select (highlight) the level of the tree at which auditing should begin (such as [Root]), then press F10 to open the Available audit options menu.
5. Choose Enable container auditing.
6. Provide a password, then retype the password when prompted.

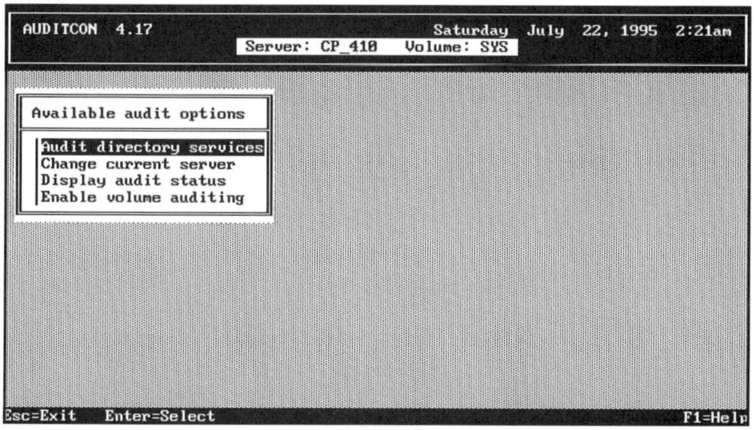

Figure 12.1
The Available audit options menu.

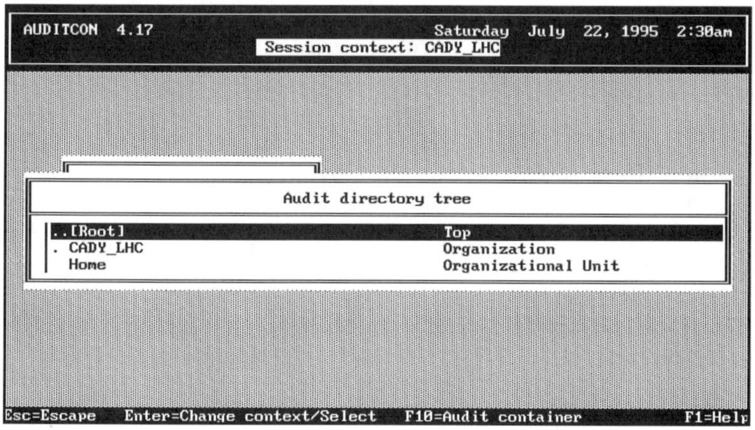

Figure 12.2
The Audit directory tree screen.

7. Choose Audit container login to open the expanded Available audit options menu (see fig. 12.3).

With auditing enabled, the auditor's environment set up, and the auditor notified about the temporary password, the auditor can now perform the following basic auditing tasks:

- Change the auditor's temporary password
- Implement auditing parameters

To perform basic auditing tasks, the auditor also uses the AUDITCON utility. To run AUDITCON, the auditor logs in to the network, then types **AUDITCON** and presses Enter. With the AUDITCON utility running, the auditor's first responsibility is to change the temporary password set for the auditor's user account by the network administrator.

To change the temporary password, the auditor completes the following steps:

1. Choose Auditor Volume Login from the Available audit options menu.
2. When prompted, type the temporary password into the opened dialog box.
3. From the Available audit options menu, choose Auditing configuration.
4. From the Auditing Configuration menu, choose Change audit password.
5. When prompted, type the temporary audit password and press Enter, type the new password and press Enter, then retype the new password and press Enter to verify that it was typed correctly the first time.

Note

It is very important that you not forget the auditor's password because, if you do, the only cure is to reinstall the audited container.

After the password has been changed, the auditor can establish auditing parameters. This task also is accomplished by using the AUDITCON utility. With AUDITCON running, the auditor can perform the following tasks:

- Enable other auditors to log in simultaneously to a container or volume
- Broadcast warnings to network users or to the console
- Set parameters related to event recording, including file sizes, and warning conditions and usage

To enable other auditors to log in simultaneously to a container or volume, the auditor completes the following steps:

1. Choose Auditing configuration from the Available audit options menu.
2. Choose Audit options configuration from the Auditing configuration menu.
3. Toggle the Allow concurrent auditor logins field to read Yes instead of No (see fig. 12.4), and then press Enter.
4. Press Esc to close this screen. Then answer Yes when prompted with Save Changes.

To broadcast warnings to network users or to the file server console, the auditor completes the following steps:

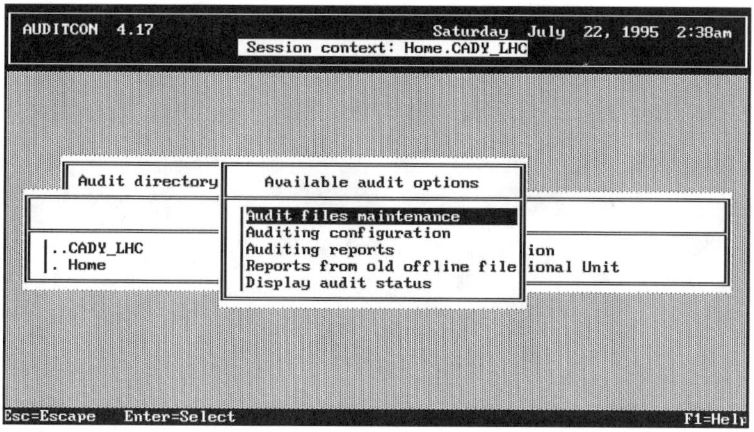

Figure 12.3
The expanded Available audit options menu.

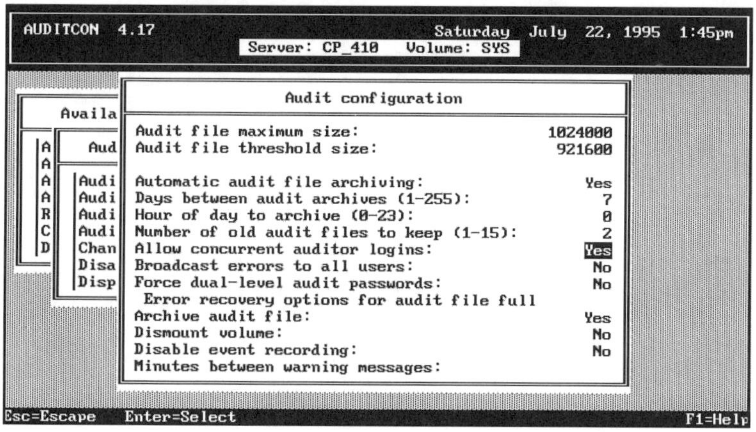

Figure 12.4
The Audit configuration screen.

1. Choose Auditing configuration from the Available audit options menu.
2. Choose Audit options configuration from the Auditing configuration menu.
3. Toggle the Broadcast errors to all users field to read Yes instead of No, if you want all network users, the file server console, and the error log to receive the errors that indicate the Audit data file is reaching its maximum size.

Note Novell recommends that you leave this option set to No so that users do not receive this message (see fig. 12.5). It interrupts their work—and they can do nothing about it, anyway.

4. Press Esc to close this screen. Then answer Yes when prompted with Save Changes.

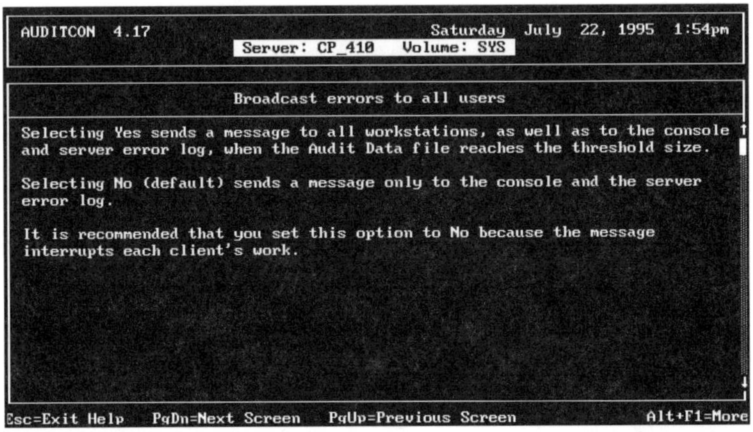

Figure 12.5
The Broadcast errors to all users screen.

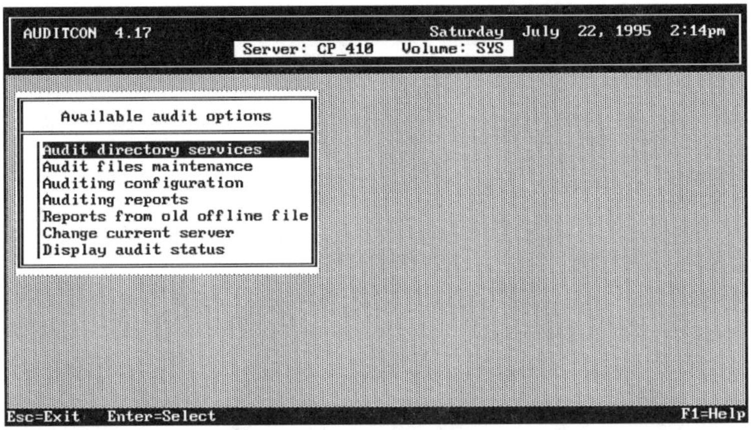

Figure 12.6
The Available audit options menu after auditor volume login.

To set parameters related to event recording—such as file sizes, warning conditions, what events should be audited, and so on—the auditor again uses the AUDITCON utility. With AUDITCON running, the auditor can choose to define auditing event recording for the container level, the volume level, or both. When you set parameters at the NDS container level, events can be set for auditing based on the NDS event, or based on a network user. When you set parameters at the volume level, events can be set for auditing based on the NDS event, the file or directory, or the user.

To audit by container, the auditor first logs in to the volume by choosing Auditor volume login from the Available audit options menu (and supplying the password when prompted). Depending on which event-recording parameters are to be set or changed, the auditor next chooses one of the following options from the Available audit options menu (see fig. 12.6).

Note: Most of these options lead to another menu from which to choose a task.

- **Audit directory services.** To audit an NDS container (display status of or enable auditing on) or change your current context
- **Audit files maintenance.** To close, delete, or copy an old audit file; to reset the audit event files; or to display audit status (see fig. 12.7)
- **Auditing configuration.** To define which events related to the volume should be audited (see fig. 12.8)
- **Auditing reports.** To choose data to be accessed from the audit files

Table 12.1 describes the options on the first three menus; these options comprise most of the tasks a network auditor is responsible for performing.

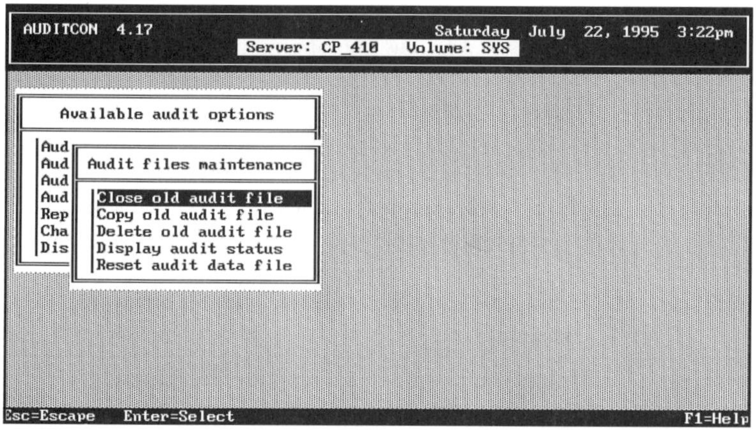

Figure 12.7
The Audit files maintenance menu.

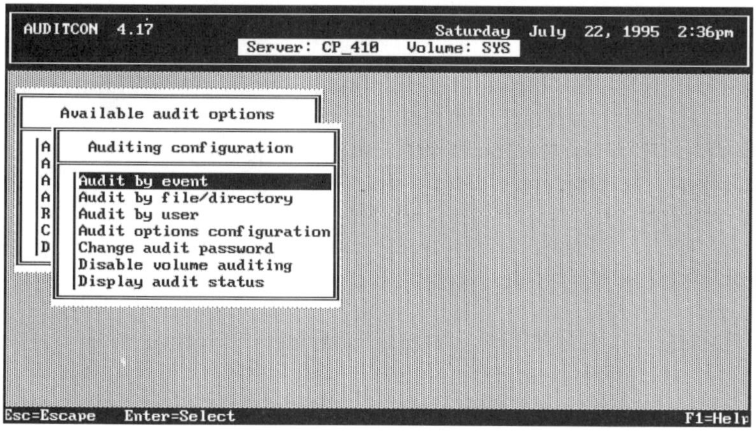

Figure 12.8
The Auditing configuration menu.

Table 12.1
Auditor Menu Options

Menu	*Option*	*Description*
Audit Directory Services	Audit Directory Tree	Displays list of NDS containers to choose from, in order to audit them
	Change Session Context	Enables you to change current NDS tree context
Audit Files Maintenance	Close Old Audit File	Enables you to close out a pre-NetWare 4.10 audit file, kept open to provide security for the file
	Copy Old Audit File	Enables you to copy an audit file to a location in the file system, simultaneously compressing and encrypting it
	Delete Old Audit File	Deletes old audit file
	Display Audit Status	Displays information about auditing, such as file size, record count, whether auditing is turned on, and so on
	Reset Audit Data File	Archives old audit file while still available online, to a maximum of 15 files
Auditing Configuration	Audit by Events	Enables you to turn on auditing for file, queue, server,and user events
	Audit by File/ Directory	Enables you to turn auditing on/off for specific directories or files
	Audit by User	Enables you to turn auditing on or off for individual users
	Audit Options Configuration	Enables you to set file size, error recovery, auditor login requirement, and so on
	Change Audit Password	Enables you to change auditor's password
	Disable Volume Auditing	Enables you to turn off auditing for a specific volume
	Display Audit Status	Displays status information, such as file size, record count, and so on

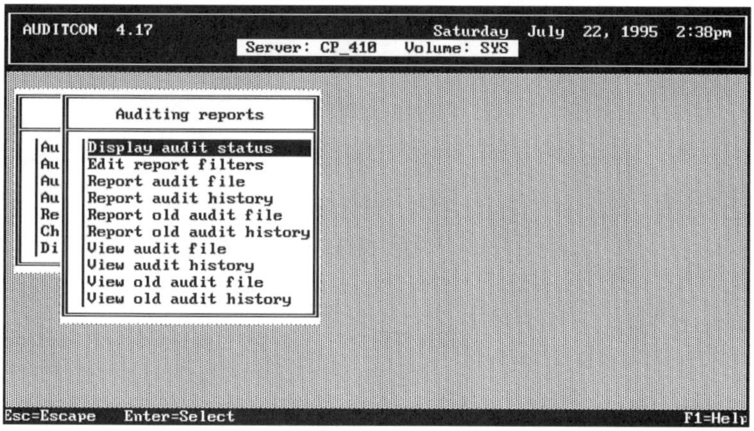

Figure 12.9
The Auditing reports menu.

Network auditors are responsible also for determining which events should be audited, when they should be audited, and for producing reports that display the result of auditing. As a general guideline, Novell recommends the following:

- To justify the use of network resources, audit frequency of writes to application files and print queue usage.
- To troubleshoot network performance problems, audit number of times application file is opened.
- To see whether network security has any holes, audit changes made to the ACL (Access Control List) of NDS objects, as well as whether any sensitive files have been opened on the network.
- To find out whether a specific user has access to the network (but shouldn't), audit files opened and written in areas you want to watch, as well as any files opened by this user.
- To find out whether the NetWare server is properly secured, audit user logins, the mounting and dismounting of volumes, and NetWare server events.
- To determine whether file security is adequate, audit file reads, writes, creates, and deletes.

To create auditing reports, the network auditor uses the Auditing reports option in the Available audit options menu, and works with the following types of report-related options found in the Auditing reports menu (see fig. 12.9):

- **Edit report filters.** Enables you to create or edit filters to determine how you want report information to be formatted and displayed
- **Report audit file/history; Report old audit file/history.** Enables you to transfer report information from the current or previous versions of the audit file to another file in the file system
- **View audit file/history; View old audit file/history.** Enables you to see the current and previous versions of the audit file on your screen; note, however, that history information applies only to volumes

Questions

1. The network administrator uses AUDITCON primarily to______.
   - ○ A. enable auditing
   - ○ B. establish an auditor user
   - ○ C. create a home directory for the auditor
   - ○ D. all of the above
2. Auditing is a useful tool because it ______ (choose *three*).
   - ☐ A. ensures that users follow proper procedures
   - ☐ B. decentralizes network control
   - ☐ C. gives network administrator greater network power
   - ☐ D. tracks network resource usage
3. To enable auditing, choose the Enable container auditing option from the______menu.
   - ○ A. Auditor password
   - ○ B. Auditing configuration
   - ○ C. Auditor volume login
   - ○ D. Available audit options
4. A/An ______ determines whether multiple auditors can log in simultaneously to a container or volume.
   - ○ A. network administrator
   - ○ B. auditor user
   - ○ C. system manager
   - ○ D. authorized user
5. The______option is *not* part of the Available audit options menu.
   - ○ A. Audit directory services
   - ○ B. Change auditor password
   - ○ C. Display audit status
   - ○ D. Enable volume auditing
6. Which option does Novell recommend you leave set to No, so that users will not be interrupted when working?
   - ○ A. Minutes between warning messages
   - ○ B. Automatic audit file archiving
   - ○ C. Broadcast errors to all users
   - ○ D. Archive audit file
7. Of the following, which *three* are found on the Audit configuration screen?
   - ☐ A. Audit file maximum size
   - ☐ B. Mount SYS volume
   - ☐ C. Force dual-level audit passwords
   - ☐ D. Disable event recording
8. The Auditing reports option is found on the ______ menu.
   - ○ A. Available audit options
   - ○ B. Audit directory services
   - ○ C. Change current server
   - ○ D. Display audit status

9. The ______ menu option enables you to shut down pre-NetWare 4.10 audit files that were previously kept open for security reasons.
   - A. Audit directory tree
   - B. Copy old audit file
   - C. Close old audit file
   - D. Reset audit data file

10. The ______ menu option archives the old audit file but keeps it available online.
    - A. Audit directory tree
    - B. Copy old audit file
    - C. Close old audit file
    - D. Reset audit data file

Answers

1. A
2. A, B, D
3. D
4. B
5. B
6. C
7. A, C, D
8. A
9. C
10. D

CHAPTER

13

Planning, Customizing, and Troubleshooting Printing

In simple networks, printing design and implementation can be simple. In complex networks, printing can become very complicated as the result of several major planning, monitoring, and customizing issues. This chapter discusses the following issues associated with printing in a complex network:

- *Planning*
- *Monitoring*
- *Customizing*
- *Managing*
- *Troubleshooting*

Planning Issues

Complex networks often require complex printing environments, which may include the following:

- Multiple printers
- Multiple print queues
- Multiple print servers
- A variety of print job configurations
- A variety of printer definitions
- A variety of printer languages

To accommodate the quantity and variety of printing environment variables, NetWare 4.1 provides two software components—PSERVER.NLM, and NPRINTER (in both an EXE and NLM version). The PSERVER NLM adds the print server function to a NetWare 4 file server, enabling the server to handle up to 256 network printers. The NPRINTER NLM provides the capability to attach printers to network servers, regardless of whether they are also print servers (running the PSERVER NLM). The NPRINTER executable (EXE) software enables you to make printers attached to workstations available to other network users.

When planning network printing services, you must consider how many print servers you will need (PSERVER.NLM and/or NPRINTER.NLM), which file servers you will also use as print servers, whether you will attach printers to workstations (NPRINTER.EXE), how many print queues you will need (and to which print servers you will attach them), where network printers will be located, and so on.

If you choose, you can assign multiple print queues to a single printer. How many print queues you assign to a printer, what types of queue you assign, the volume of printing to be handled, and the priority assigned to each print queue will affect printing throughput and time. You can manage printing throughput by assigning different priorities to different print queues, as well as by assigning different print queues to different types of printers.

You can increase printing throughput by assigning multiple printers of the same type to a single print queue. In this way, all print jobs sent to that queue can be serviced by the next available printer.

You can also use print job configurations to provide efficient printing services to network users who are using applications that are not network aware, or which require a print driver. Several printer definition files are provided by NetWare 4.

One other issue that must be considered when dealing with a mixed printer-language environment—AppleTalk, Unix, and so on—is that you may need to purchase separate software, and load additional NLMs on NetWare file and print servers.

Monitoring Issues

Even good planning does not always meet all network needs. As time goes by, therefore, network administrators must monitor overall network printing performance. In particular, print queues (because they contain information about both print servers and printers) and printers themselves should be monitored.

To monitor print queues, you can use the PCONSOLE utility. To run this utility, log in to the network as a user with Supervisor rights, then type **PCONSOLE** at the workstation and press Enter. When the PCONSOLE Available Options menu opens (see fig. 13.1), complete the following steps to check print queue status:

1. If necessary, use the Change Context option and set the context to the container in which the print queue is located.
2. Choose Print Queues from the Available Options menu.
3. Choose a print queue from the Print Queues list.
4. Choose Status from the Print Queue Information menu to open the Print Queue Status screen (see fig. 13.2).
5. View the following items of information in the Print Queue Status screen:

   Current number of print jobs

   Current number of active print servers
6. View or modify the following operator flags:

   Allow users to submit print jobs

   Allow service by current print servers

   Allow new print servers to attach

To monitor printers, you also use the PCONSOLE utility. From the PCONSOLE Available Options menu, choose Printers, then complete the following steps:

1. Choose the printer from the Printers list.
2. View the items of information provided on the Printer *printer_name* Configuration screen (see fig. 13.3), as explained in table 13.1.

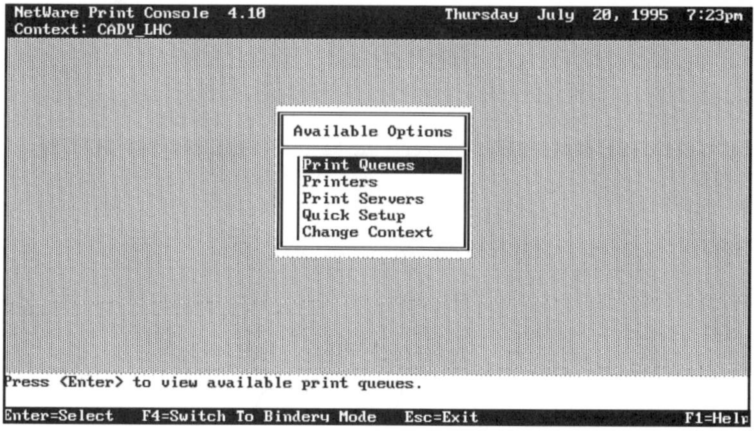

Figure 13.1
The PCONSOLE Available Options menu.

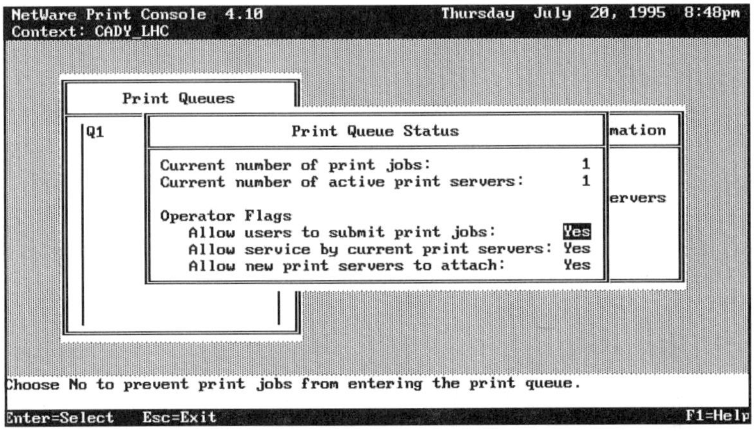

Figure 13.2
The PCONSOLE Print Queue Status screen.

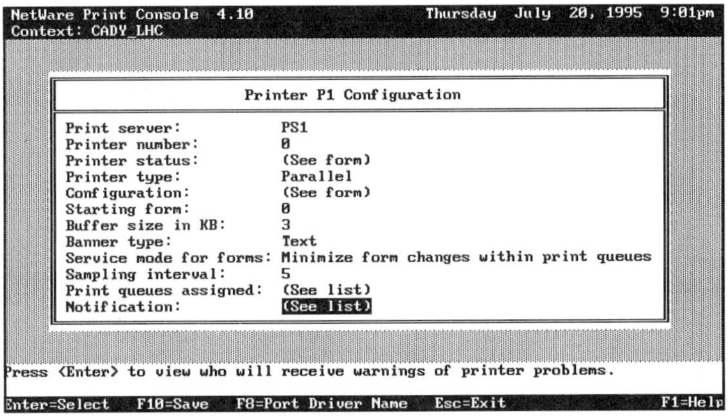

Figure 13.3
PCONSOLE Printer Configuration screen.

Table 13.1
Printer Configuration Screen Information

Field Name	*Sample Entry*	*Description*
Print server	PS1	Print server servicing this printer
Printer number	0	Unique number for this printer configuration
Printer status	(See form)	Displays printer status and active print job, and enables mode and form changes
Printer type	Parallel	Displays and enables change of printer type (Parallel, Serial, Unix, and so on)

Field Name	*Sample Entry*	*Description*
Configuration	(See form)	Displays printer configuration information on separate form
Starting form	0	Specifies form number to use with this configuration
Buffer size in KB	3	Size of printer server's internal buffer
Banner type	Text	Banner type, Text or PostScript
Service mode for forms	Minimize form changes within print queues	Specifies which print form is to be used with this print configuration
Sampling interval	5	States number of seconds between times that print server checks print queue for print jobs
Print queues assigned	(See list)	Shows queues serviced by this printer
Notification	(See list)	Lists users and groups notified when printer has problems

Customizing Issues

There are four actions that you can perform to customize printing for your network environment, as follows:

- Designating printer forms
- Mounting forms
- Building or importing printer definitions
- Using print job configurations

To designate printer forms, use the PRINTDEF utility or the NetWare Administrator. Define forms to be mounted or dismounted by using the Change forms as needed, Minimize form changes across queues, Minimize form changes within queues, and Service only mounted form service mode options.

To mount forms, choose the Printer object from the Browser in the NetWare Administrator utility, choose the Identification page, then choose Mount Form, and choose a form to mount.

To build printer definitions, choose the Print Devices page from the appropriate Organization or Organizational Unit in the NetWare Administrator utility. Next, choose the Create button, type a name for this new printer definition (see fig. 13.4), then choose OK.

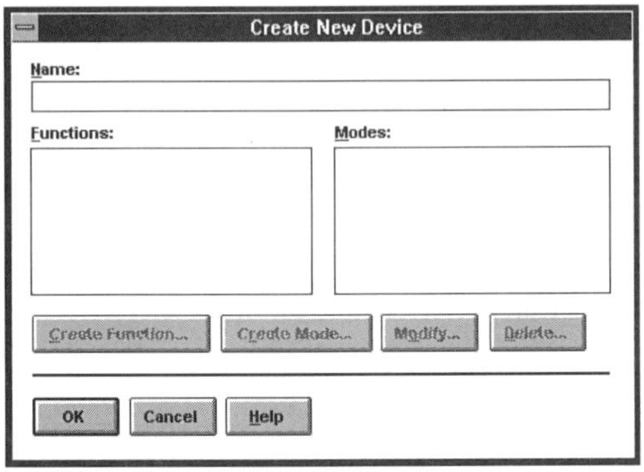

Figure 13.4
The Create New Device dialog box.

After the name has been assigned, select the printer definition name you just created, choose Modify, choose Create Function, then add function calls for this printer (see fig. 13.5).

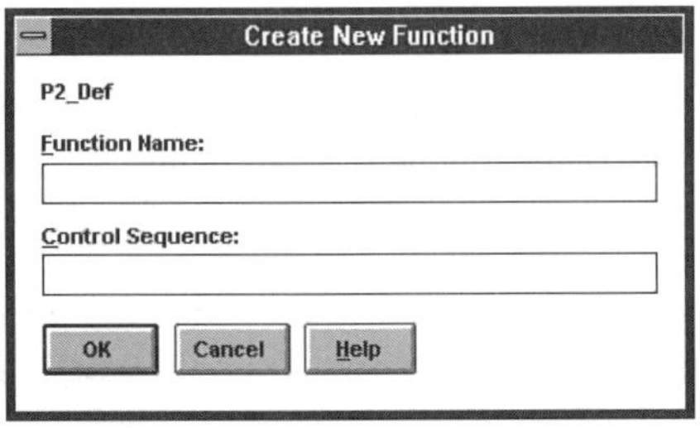

Figure 13.5
The Create New Function dialog box.

To import printer definitions, choose the Print Devices page from the appropriate Organization or Organizational Unit in the NetWare Administrator utility. Next, choose Import, and choose the printer definition to be imported.

To use print job configurations, call them with the CAPTURE command, choose a device and mode from a list of defined Print Devices in the PRINTDEF utility, or choose no device or mode. To configure print jobs, use the PRINTCON utility, and after choosing the Organization or Organizational Unit object, choose the Print Job Configuration page, then choose the print job configuration used most to make it the default print job.

Managing Issues

To manage printing, you need to understand printing in a complex NetWare 4 network. You must understand three key issues: print jobs sent to NetWare servers or print servers, print jobs sent to AppleTalk printers, and how to use NPRINTER.EXE with MS Windows.

Print Jobs Sent to NetWare Servers or Print Server Printers

Print jobs sent to NetWare servers or print server printers are directed by the configuration of the NetWare DOS Requester. The NetWare DOS Requester can be configured either for local printing or for network printing.

If set to send print jobs to a local printer, the NetWare DOS Requester turns control of the job over to DOS, after which the NetWare DOS Requester is no longer responsible for the print job.

If set to send print jobs to a network printer, the NetWare DOS Requester sends the print job to a logical printer port, which it has created to correspond to local printers. Next, it converts the print job to a NetWare Core Protocol (NCP) and sends it to the NetWare server holding the related queue. The NetWare server creates a file handle and temporary file for this print job. The NetWare DOS Requester continues sending the print job until the entire print job has been sent. The print job is then marked as Ready to print. After the print server locates the print job in the print queue, the print job's configuration is evaluated, and it is sent to the appropriate printer.

Print Jobs Sent to AppleTalk Printers

NetWare 4 workstations send print jobs to AppleTalk printers through print servers that use the ATXRP.NLM (AppleTalk Printer Access Protocol). ATXRP.NLM functions as an AppleTalk driver for the print server, using the AppleTalk Printer Access Protocol (PAP). Figure 13.6 shows the NetWare-to-AppleTalk printing process.

Using NPRINTER.EXE with MS Windows

The NPRINTER.EXE program is a terminate-and-stay-resident (TSR) program loaded into workstation memory. It can be loaded into memory seven separate times. Each time you load NPRINTER.EXE, however, it uses 4 KB of workstation memory.

NPRINTER.EXE can be loaded from the DOS prompt or from a menu. If you are using NPRINTER with MS Windows, load NPRINTER before you start MS Windows, and either configure the printer to use polled mode, or modify the SYSTEM.INI file under the [386Enh] heading to include the following two lines (replacing *n* in the second line with the actual IRQ number):

```
[port]AutoAssign=0
[port]IRQ=n
```

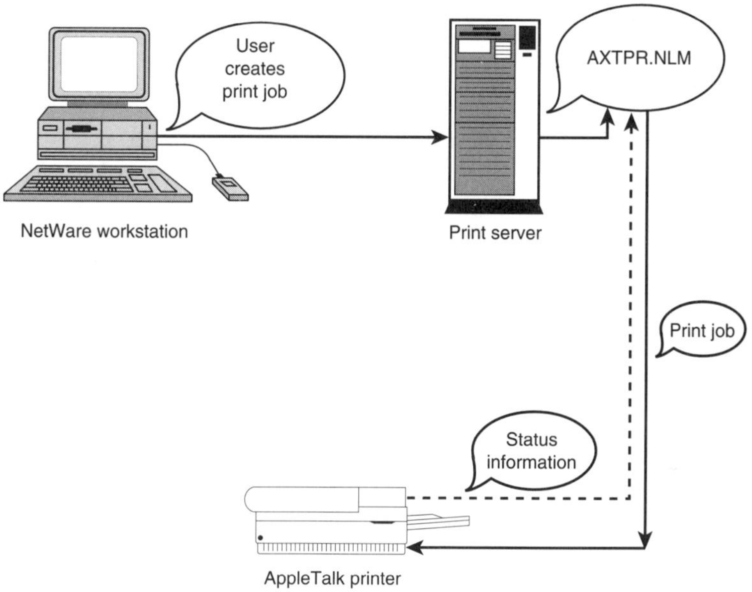

Figure 13.6
The NetWare-to-AppleTalk printing process.

Troubleshooting Issues

When printing problems occur, troubleshooting can be done at three levels: Physical, Logical, and Procedural.

Problems at the Physical level, which involves the hardware, are the most common. Examples include loose cables, printer paper jams, empty paper trays, broken parts, bad interface boards, and so on. Because some physical problems are easier to locate than others, a good approach is to begin by examining the easier problems first, proceeding to the more difficult problems as each easier problem is ruled out.

The Logical level involves software, and is most often associated with such issues as incorrect object configuration, improper network address, incorrect forms, corrupted driver or communication software, and so on. As with Physical-level problems, check the easiest possibilities first, progressing to the hardest. If necessary, correct configurations or network addresses, and reinitialize or reinstall software.

The Procedural level involves incorrect commands, or print jobs sent to the wrong printer. This level of problem, which is associated with users themselves, can be corrected or avoided by making certain that network users understand the proper use of printing services provided on the network. To correct these types of problems, you usually educate the users, or customize their environment (placing commands in workstation configuration files, and so on) so that they are less likely to repeat the mistake.

The following steps are recommended for solving printing problems:

1. Obtain background information about the problem.
2. Investigate the problem.
3. Isolate or narrow down the problem.
4. Repair the problem.
5. Return all printing and related systems to normal operating conditions.
6. Document errors or malfunctions associated with and identified with the problem.

Some common printing problems you may encounter include the following:

- Characters in print job that do not belong there, often caused by a timeout value which is too short
- Printer off-line indications, when printer is not off-line, may indicate electrical interference
- Print jobs sent to a context other than the user's default do not print; may indicate that the user's CAPTURE or NPRINT commands need the full context specified
- Print jobs or print queues with errors may require that the Print Queue and Print Server objects be deleted and re-created
- Print jobs printing in the wrong language (or not printing at all) may have been sent to a printer with a different printer language installed, and should be rerouted to the correct printer

Planning, monitoring, and customizing printing in a complex network can be a bit complicated. Once done, however, it simplifies printing for the network users.

Questions

1. Which of the following is *not* generally found in a complex printing environment?
   - ○ A. Several print queues assigned to the same print server
   - ○ B. Multiple print queues
   - ○ C. One print server and one printer
   - ○ D. A variety of languages

2. You can increase printing throughput by ______.
   - ○ A. creating only one print server to handle all print queues
   - ○ B. assigning multiple printers of the same type to a single print queue
   - ○ C. monitoring print servers
   - ○ D. mixing the printer language environment

3. Monitor print queues by using the ______ utility.
   - ○ A. PCONSOLE
   - ○ B. PRINTDEF
   - ○ C. MONITOR
   - ○ D. PSERVER

4. A ______ is a printer configuration field that specifies the number of seconds between print server and print queue polling.
   - ○ A. Printer status
   - ○ B. Printer number
   - ○ C. Notification
   - ○ D. Sampling interval

5. The printer configuration field that specifies either Text or PostScript is the ______ field.
   - ○ A. Printer type
   - ○ B. Configuration
   - ○ C. Banner type
   - ○ D. Notification

6. Customizing printing involves all but *one* of the following:
   - ○ A. Importing printer definitions
   - ○ B. Monitoring print queue status
   - ○ C. Designing printer forms
   - ○ D. Mounting forms

7. Of the following, which *three* are print queue operator flags?
   - □ A. Allow users to submit print jobs
   - □ B. Allow administrators to change languages
   - □ C. Allow service by current print servers
   - □ D. Allow new print servers to attach

8. Which of the following statements regarding NPRINTER.EXE is *not* true?
   - ○ A. It can be loaded into memory up to eight times.
   - ○ B. It must be loaded before MS Windows.
   - ○ C. It can be loaded from a DOS prompt or from a menu.
   - ○ D. It may require that the SYSTEM.INI file be modified.

9. To designate printer forms, use the ______ or ______ utilities.

   ☐ A. NetWare Administrator

   ☐ B. PCONSOLE

   ☐ C. PRINTDEF

   ☐ D. PRINTCON

10. If you want to troubleshoot printing problems, you must consider three levels of potential problems. Of the following, which one is *not* a level of printing problems?

    ○ A. Physical

    ○ B. Logical

    ○ C. Emotional

    ○ D. Procedural

Answers

1. C
2. B
3. A
4. D
5. C
6. B
7. A, C, D
8. A
9. A, C
10. C

CHAPTER 14

Administering a NetWare 4.x Network

NDS administration concentrates on the setup and management of the NDS tree and database. Network administration centers around the file server, the workstation, and the services provided and used by these two aspects of a NetWare 4 network. This chapter discusses how the network Administrator manages network clients, and examines the following important features of the NetWare 4 file server:

- *Preparing workstations to access network resources*
- *Understanding and managing memory and data storage features of NetWare 4*
- *Using the MONITOR, SET, and SERVMAN console utilities*

- Providing support for non-DOS client operating systems, multiple protocols, and multiple languages

Preparing Workstations to Access Network Resources

Although Unix, Macintosh, and OS/2 workstations can access the NetWare 4 network services, DOS-based computers are the primary type of computer used to access the NetWare network. Before they can access the network, however, they must be prepared to do so. To prepare a DOS-based computer to access the network, the necessary hardware must be installed and configured, the workstation must be connected to the network, and the proper software must be set up. Setting up the proper software is the focus of this section.

Setting up a workstation to access the network requires the following:

- Installing and configuring the DOS-based workstation (client) connection software
- Creating or modifying the NET.CFG file
- Providing support for MS Windows, OS/2, Macintosh, and Unix workstations
- Maintaining client software by using the WSUPGRD and WSUPDATE utilities

Installing and Configuring Client Connection Software

Several software files, known collectively as the *client connection software,* make it possible for a PC to become a workstation (client) on the network. The following two groups of files make up the client connection software:

- DOS Requester
- ODI (Open Data-Link Interface) software

The DOS Requester

The DOS Requester provides the architecture surrounding DOS. It is responsible for performing a variety of tasks—sharing drive table information with DOS, handling the redirection of file and print requests, maintaining connections to the network, and handling network packets. Unlike the NETX workstation software that shipped with earlier versions of NetWare, the DOS Requester also includes the following features:

- Ability to handle as many as 50 network connections
- Background authentication
- Multiple language support
- A modular design
- Memory swapping
- Elimination of duplication of effort between DOS and the network shell
- Backward compatibility (NETX.VLM)

The DOS Requester consists of several files, all of which end with the VLM extension, that are managed by the VLM.EXE file. The VLM.EXE file loads all the necessary VLM files in the correct order, then manages various tasks associated with the VLMs, such as routing application requests to the proper VLM; managing communications between multiplexor VLMs and their associated child VLMs; and controlling memory allocation, management, and services.

To implement the DOS Requester at the workstation, type **VLM /M*x*** and press Enter, replacing ***x*** with one of the following three options to specify where in workstation memory the DOS Requester should be loaded:

c = Conventional

x = Extended (XMS memory)

e = Expanded (EMS memory)

Each DOS Requester file is responsible for its own function on the network. For example, the PRINT.VLM file is responsible for managing various printing functions.

All DOS Requester files fit into one of three categories, based on the type of service they perform. Those three categories are redirection, transport, and service.

The DOS redirection VLM (REDIR.VLM) is responsible for making a network drive appear (to the computer) as though it were a DOS drive. Without this redirection capability, the computer would not be able to recognize network drives.

The transport protocol VLM (TRAN.VLM) is primarily responsible for handling workstation-to-server connections and the transmission of packets between the workstation and the file server.

The three service protocol VLMs—NWP.VLM, FIO.VLM, and PRINT.VLM—handle a variety of network service functions, as follows:

- The NWP.VLM is a multiplexor VLM. It is responsible for handling network connections, logins and logouts, broadcasts, and different implementations of the NetWare operating system—bindery (BIND.VLM), NetWare directory services (NDS.VLM), and NetWare Lite peer-to-peer (LITE.VLM). The RSA.VLM is responsible for NDS encryption, and is also associated with the NWP.VLM.

Note: VLMs associated with a multiplexor VLM are called *Child VLMs,* whereas the multiplexor VLM is referred to as the *Parent VLM.*

- The FIO.VLM is responsible for implementing basic file transfers, including cached or noncached, and burst mode reads and writes.
- The PRINT.VLM is the print redirector.

Most of these VLMs are required; that is, they must be loaded. Four of the VLMs are optional: PRINT.VLM, NETX.VLM (which provides backward compatibility to the NetWare shell), AUTO.VLM (which provides automatic reconnection when a file server connection is lost), and NMR.VLM (which makes the NetWare Management Responder available).

The ODI Software

The ODI software implements the *Open System Interconnection* (OSI) model, which enables multiple protocols and multiple LAN drivers to function on a single workstation or single file server. ODI provides support for AppleTalk, TCP/IP, and IPX/SPX protocols.

ODI has three layers—the LAN board and Multiple Link Interface Driver (MLID), the Link Support Layer (LSL), and the protocol stack layer (see fig. 14.1).

The LAN board and MLID enable different types of network packets to be transmitted to and accepted by the workstation. Various LAN driver files, such as NE3200.COM, are responsible for communication to their related LAN boards.

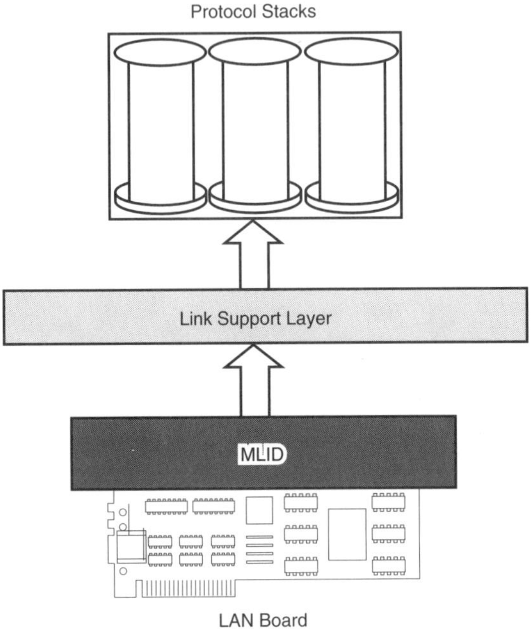

Figure 14.1
ODI layers.

The LSL routes packets between the LAN boards and the protocol stacks. The LSL is often referred to as the *switchboard,* because it performs this routing function. It enables DOS workstations to use various protocols, including TCP/IP, IPX, and AppleTalk. It is implemented by loading the LSL.COM file at the workstation.

The protocol stack layer holds the protocol stacks for protocols such as AppleTalk, IPX, and TCP/IP. It accepts packets passed to it from the Link Support Layer. The packets are then sent either to the NetWare operating system or to another network, as necessary. The protocol stack files include files such as IPXODI.COM and TCPIP.EXE. The one commonly loaded on NetWare networks is the IPXODI.COM file, but the one appropriate for the communications in your network is the one that should be loaded.

Creating or Modifying the NET.CFG File

The NET.CFG file provides startup information for networking, much as the CONFIG.SYS file provides startup information for the computer. To be effective, the NET.CFG file must contain certain parameters. Those parameters must be located in specified sections, indented beneath the section headings.

The modifications that must be made fall into the following three sections:

- Link Driver
- Link Support
- NetWare DOS Requester

The Link Driver section provides information about the LAN driver. It specifies the LAN driver's name, and various hardware and software settings. The settings you choose to include depend on the network board you are using.

For example, the workstation may have an NE2000 LAN board installed, with an interrupt set to 5, and the port set to 320. In this case, the Link Driver section of the NET.CFG file would be similar to the following example:

```
Link Driver NE2000.COM
     INT 5
     PORT 320
```

The Link Support section contains information related to configuring the receive buffers, memory pool buffers, and other related information.

For example, the Link Support section may be similar to the following:

```
Link Support
     BUFFERS 8
```

The NetWare DOS Requester section can contain settings that specify which file server should be used for login when possible (PREFERRED SERVER), which drive letter is to be used as the first available network drive (FIRST NETWORK DRIVE), and a variety of other parameters. Figure 14.2 shows a sample NET.CFG file.

Following are some of the more commonly used NET.CFG parameters:

- **USE DEFAULTS = ON** (Used by VLM.EXE to specify the use of defaults when loading VLMs)
- **CONNECTIONS = #** (To set how many network connections can be used, ranging from 2 to 50; used by CONN.VLM)
- **PREFERRED TREE = *<tree_name>*** (To specify which NDS tree to authenticate to; used by the NDS.VLM)
- **NAME CONTEXT = *<name_context>*** (To set the name context for the workstation; used by the NDS.VLM)
- **LOCAL PRINTERS = <none>** (To specify phantom ports, so the user can set up more logical ports for printing different types of jobs than DOS can normally access; used by PRINT.VLM)

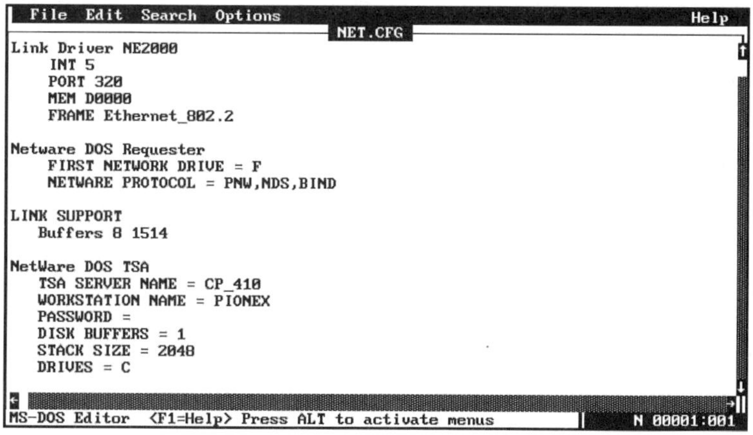

```
 File  Edit  Search  Options                                    Help
                                NET.CFG
Link Driver NE2000
    INT 5
    PORT 320
    MEM D0000
    FRAME Ethernet_802.2

Netware DOS Requester
    FIRST NETWORK DRIVE = F
    NETWARE PROTOCOL = PNW,NDS,BIND

LINK SUPPORT
   Buffers 8 1514

NetWare DOS TSA
   TSA SERVER NAME = CP_410
   WORKSTATION NAME = PIONEX
   PASSWORD =
   DISK BUFFERS = 1
   STACK SIZE = 2048
   DRIVES = C

MS-DOS Editor  <F1=Help> Press ALT to activate menus        N 00001:001
```

Figure 14.2
Sample NET.CFG file.

- **LARGE INTERNET PACKETS = ON** (To turn on LIP; used by IPXNCP.VLM)
- **CACHE BUFFERS = #** (To specify the number of cache buffers to use; used by FIO.VLM)
- **CACHE BUFFER SIZE = 512** (To set the size of a cache buffer; used by FIO.VLM)
- **PB BUFFERS = #** (To turn Packet Burst buffers off, use zero. Any number other than zero—up to 10—turns Packet Burst buffers on. Used by FIO.VLM)

Providing Support for MS Windows, OS/2, Macintosh, and Unix Workstations

For a workstation running MS Windows to take advantage of NetWare 4's MS Windows-based utilities, certain files must be modified. These files are modified when you install the workstation software that includes the NetWare DOS Requester. Table 14.1 displays information about the files to be modified.

Table 14.1
MS Windows Workstation Files to be Changed

File Name	*Location*	*Function of File*
NETWARE.DRV	\WINDOWS\SYSTEM	Allows network access from within an MS Windows application
VIPX.386	\WINDOWS\SYSTEM	Provides task-switching capabilities, which enable DOS applications being run in MS Windows to use Enhanced Mode
VNETWARE.386	\WINDOWS\SYSTEM	Coordinates receipt and dialog display of broadcast messages in conjunction with the NETWARE.DRV and NWPOPUP.EXE files
NWADMIN.INI	\WINDOWS	Specifies options for MS Windows-based user tools
NETWARE.INI	\WINDOWS	Contains customization information for the MS Windows driver
ET.INI	\WINDOWS	Provides information for initializing the Novell ElectroText online documentation set

File Name	*Location*	*Function of File*
SYSTEM.INI	\WINDOWS	Contains configuration information that is modified to load NetWare User Tools, specify the NetWare device version and type of network being used, and set timing to ensure that network traffic runs smoothly
WIN.INI	\WINDOWS	Contains configuration information that is modified to ensure that the NetWare User Tools icon is displayed when Windows is loaded
PROGMAN.INI	\WINDOWS	Contains configuration information that is modified to add NWUSER.EXE (executable file for NetWare UserTools utility) to the list of groups

Note During workstation setup, all the files in table 14.1, except the SYSTEM.INI, WIN.INI, and PROGMAN.INI files, are copied to their respective directories. These three files already exist and need only be updated.

If your workstation is an OS/2 workstation (instead of a DOS-only or DOS and MS Windows workstation), installing the client software installs the OS/2 Requester. As with the installation of the NetWare DOS Requester on a workstation running MS Windows, installing the OS/2 Requester installs the necessary files, icons, and so on to place the NetWare Tools in a Novell group window on the desktop.

Like the NetWare User Tool for Windows, the NetWare Tools utility for OS/2 enables you to perform several tasks, including tasks related to the following:

- Setting your context
- Making network drive connections, and connecting to servers and printers
- Establishing the message receipt environment, and sending messages to network users and groups
- Managing print jobs
- Working with passwords
- Viewing information about file servers

NetWare also provides a series of NetWare Loadable Modules (NLMs) to support Unix systems (TCP/IP support). These NLMs are installed into the SYS:SYSTEM directory, and related database files are stored in the SYS:ETC directory. This feature is provided as an optional product, called NetWare NFS (Network File System). NetWare NFS makes it possible for packets to be routed from NetWare servers to Unix hosts and clients, and for users to access NetWare print queues by using Unix commands.

Using the WSUPGRD and WSUPDATE Utilities to Maintain Client Software

The WSUPGRD and WSUPDATE utilities simplify the process of updating the same files on multiple workstations. WSUPGRD updates the current IPX LAN driver to one that is ODI compliant. WSUPDATE updates any workstation files from the network.

To use the WSUPGRD utility, type **WSUPGRD [*path*] [/*options*]**, at the command line, and press Enter, or place it into a login script. Replace [*path*] with the path pointing to the complete driver name, and replace [/*option*] with any of the following available options, as necessary:

- **/C** To cause the utility to exit with an error code of level 1 instead of 0 if the upgrade is not completed
- **/E0 or /E1 or /E2** To specifiy whether no changes should be made to the AUTOEXEC.BAT file (E0); or whether the IPX driver command in the AUTOEXEC.BAT file should be replaced with the commands to load the ODI driver (E1); or whether the IPX driver command in the AUTOEXEC.BAT file should be removed and a call added to the NWSTART file, which is then created and will be called to load the ODI drivers
- **/I** To show the hardware ID in the master configuration table for the ODI driver (an option that cannot be used with other options when running this utility)
- **/N** To keep the old copy of the IPX driver, instead of deleting it when the ODI driver is upgraded
- **/S** To keep the NET.CFG file from being generated with the information contained in the original IPX driver's configuration table

To use the WSUPDATE utility, type the following command at the command line:

WSUPDATE [*network_path*] [*drive.\volume:*] [*client_path\filename*] [/*options*]

Then press Enter. Or place the entire command into a login script. Replace [*network_path*] with the path pointing to the location of the new file. Replace [*drive.\volume:*] with the mapped drive letter to search for the old file, the NDS Volume object name, or use the /ALL option instead of specifying a drive letter. Replace [*client_path\filename*] with the name of the old file being replaced by the new file. Replace [/*option*] with any of the following available options, as necessary:

- **/ALL** To search all currently mapped drives
- **/C** To copy the new file over the old, without first making a backup copy of the old file
- **/E** To erase the existing file so that a new one can be created, using the /L option

- **/F=***[path\file]* To tell this command to ignore any other options issued with this command, and to look instead in the *[path\file]* area to find a file containing options for this utility
- **/LOCAL** To search all local drives on the workstation
- **/L=***[path\file]* To specify the log file for this utility to use
- **/P** To prompt the user to proceed with or abort the update in the case where no files should be updated on that user's workstation
- **/O** To update all files, including those flagged as Read Only
- **/R** To keep the old version of the file as a file renamed with a OLD extension
- **/S** To search for any copies of the file to be updated, including any that may be stored in subdirectories on the specified path
- **/?** To view online help information about this utility

Understanding and Managing Memory and NetWare 4's Data Storage Features

You can use the MONITOR, SET, and SERVMAN utilities (discussed in the following section) to monitor memory usage and set or configure various system parameters so as to customize or fine-tune your network system. Most of the success of this fine-tuning is a result of the way NetWare manages memory and optimizes disk space. As a network Administrator, having a basic understanding of NetWare's memory-management architecture and disk-space optimization methods makes it possible for you to monitor the success of your network, and manipulate it to further fine-tune it, if you choose to do so.

To understand NetWare's memory-management architecture and disk-optimization method, you must have a basic knowledge of the following:

- Memory allocation and deallocation
- Memory protection
- Block suballocation
- File compression
- Data migration

Memory Allocation and Deallocation

Software requires memory in order to function. Some software may even require specific locations in memory. For NetWare to provide memory to software, it needs some method by which it can divide and assign (allocate) memory. NetWare uses a memory allocation technique known as *paging.* Paging is a process that divides RAM into specified block sizes—4 KB, in NetWare's case. Memory allocation sets aside a certain area in RAM and then makes that area available in pools of memory to processes, instructions, data, and so on, as necessary. Whenever memory is needed, such as to load an NLM, memory is made available from a pool of memory. When the memory is no longer needed, the memory is *deallocated* (released, using an application programming interface called FREE).

Garbage collection helps to prevent memory fragmentation, It combines smaller blocks of memory into bigger blocks. Memory can be used after a free and before garbage collection.

Garbage collection occurs in the background, so as not to interfere with regular network activity. It can be controlled, even interrupted if necessary. Controlling garbage collection involves the use of the following three NetWare SET commands:

- Garbage Collection Interval
- Number of Frees for Garbage Collection
- Minimum Free Memory for Garbage Collection

The Garbage Collection Interval enables you to specify how frequently memory should be recovered. Although the default setting is every 15 minutes, you can change this setting to range from every 1 minute to every 60 minutes.

The Number of Frees for Garbage Collection setting enables you to specify how many calls made by each NLM must occur before garbage collection begins. Although the default is 5,000, you can set this number as low as 100 or as high as 100,000.

The Minimum Free Memory for Garbage Collection setting enables you to specify how low the number of bytes in the alloc memory pool must be before garbage collection begins. Although the default is 8,000, you can make the setting as low as 1,000 or as high as 1,000,000.

Memory Protection

Because all processes share the same maximum quantity of available memory, some processes can accidentally overflow onto the memory areas being used by other processes, resulting in memory corruption. To prevent that from happening, NetWare has a memory protection scheme. This scheme effectively divides memory into two groups, or *domains*—OS and OSP. The OS domain is the *operating system* domain. The OSP domain is the *operating system protected* domain.

As the network administrator, you can decide where to load NLMs that are not part of the NetWare product (referred to as *third-party* NLMs). The NetWare OS and related NLMs are loaded into the OS domain on NetWare file servers. Other NLMs can be loaded into this domain as well, but until they have proven themselves to be stable on the network, you may prefer to place them into the OSP domain. The OS domain and OSP domain do not access the same areas of memory. Consequently, the NetWare OS and accompanying NLMs will not experience memory overwrite problems from NLMs that are loaded into the OSP domain.

Setting up where a NLM is to be loaded (the OS or OSP domain), is a simple process. To perform this process, place the LOAD DOMAIN command in the file server's STARTNUP.NCF file. You can then use commands to set the domain to OSP, load additional NLMs, and reset the domain to OS.

> **Note** You have to unload the server and reload it to have the LOAD DOMAIN command take effect.

For example, if you are testing a new NLM, called SEEME.NLM, on your server, type **SET DOMAIN=OSP**, and press Enter. Next, type **LOAD *<path>*SEEME**, and press Enter. Finally, type **SET DOMAIN OS**, and press Enter.

This memory protection scheme is based on the ring protection memory model, which divides memory into four logical, concentric rings numbered 0, 1, 2, and 3. Ring 0 (OS Domain) is where the NetWare operating system files are loaded and run. NetWare actually implements only two rings of the ring protection model. Ring 0 is still treated as ring 0, but ring 3 is treated as the second ring. Ring 3 is where modules are loaded when you choose OSP Domain.

In addition to protection of processes by rings, processes loaded into the same ring are protected from each other through a procedure known as *segmentation.* Segmentation specifies which memory a process can use inside a ring by limiting the size of memory a process can use. In effect, segmentation walls off one process from another inside a ring.

Figure 14.3 shows the ring memory protection scheme applied in NetWare 4, including the use of segmentation.

NetWare 4 memory protection also implements the Intel 386/486 paging architecture. NetWare covers, uncovers, and maps sections of memory by using paging. This enables NetWare to assign various areas in memory, which may or may not be contiguous, to function as though they were contiguous.

Block Suballocation

Block suballocation is one of three features NetWare uses to optimize disk space. The other two are file compression and data migration.

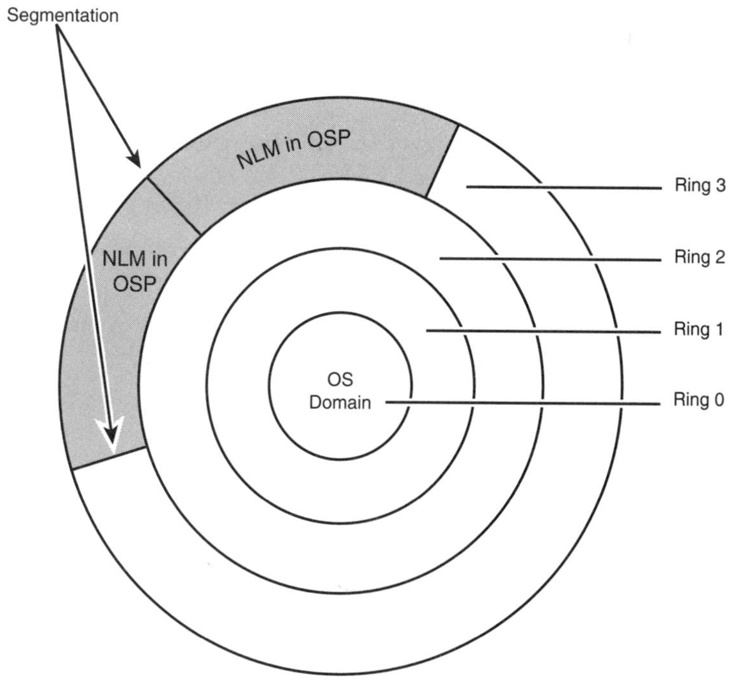

Figure 14.3
Ring memory protection scheme.

In block suballocation, the available hard disk space is divided into sections called *allocation blocks.* A typical allocation block size may be 4 KB. When a file is saved to the hard disk, that file is saved starting at the beginning of a block. As long as all files are the same size as any combination of blocks, such as a 4 KB file, an 8 KB file, a 12 KB file, and so on, all accessed blocks are filled. If the files to be saved are not increments of 4 KB, however, but are of various sizes (such as 2 KB, 1 KB, and 3 KB), each of these files is still saved into its own 4 KB block because each new file to be saved must start at the beginning of a block. In the case of 2 KB, 1 KB, and 3 KB files, 12 KB of total disk space is now allocated, even though only a total of 6 KB of files is being stored. The other 6 KB of space is unusable.

This is where suballocation comes in. NetWare can divide (suballocate) each of the blocks into 512-byte sections. Now, when a 2 KB is saved, the file is stored in the first 2 KB of the block. The other 2 KB is now available, in 512-byte sections, for use by other files. If the next file to be saved is 5 KB in size, the first 4 KBs are saved in an available 4 KB block, and the leftover 1 KB can be broken into 512 bytes and stored in suballocation blocks.

For suballocation to function, it must be enabled. You must enable suballocation when you install the volume on which it will be enabled. To install a volume, you load the INSTALL.NLM. To enable suballocation, choose Volume Options from the INSTALL.NLM's Available Options menu. Next, choose Block Suballocation, then press Enter to toggle suballocation on or off.

File Compression

In file compression, files to be stored on the network are read, analyzed, described in a temporary file, checked to determine whether compressing the file will save the minimum amount of disk space required (2 percent is the minimum, by default), copied to a compressed file if the minimum amount of disk space will be saved but not compressed if the minimum is not met, checked for errors, and then saved to the hard disk in place of the original uncompressed file.

One drawback with file compression is that it has performance overhead. Saving files to disk takes longer when disk compression is turned on. This is true even if all files are not compressed, because the process up to the point of compression must still occur. Because compression can be run during the hours when the network is not very active, however, and because only files that have not been accessed for a certain period of time are compressed, there is no noticeable performance decrease on the network.

On the other hand, file compression has a major benefit. File compression statistics indicate that the average compression ratio for a volume is 63 percent. That means that on a 100 MB volume, data can be compressed to take up only about 37 MB.

If you choose to use file compression, you first enable compression by using the INSTALL utility (NLM). As with block suballocation, file compression is enabled by volume. You can choose to enable suballocation on some volumes, but not on others. Or you can enable it on all volumes, or disable it on all volumes.

At installation, file compression is enabled, by default, for each volume. If you do not want it enabled, you must disable file compression when you install the server. You can always turn it on later if you choose to do so, but because you cannot turn it off at the volume level after it has been enabled during the installation process, you may choose to always set file compression off when you install file servers.

To enable or disable file compression, using the INSTALL utility, choose Volume Options from the Available Options menu, choose the volume, select File Compression, then toggle it on and off by pressing the Enter key.

> **Note** You can disable file compression at the directory and file level, or for the entire file server, if you choose. Even if you enabled file compression at the volume level when you installed the server, and later change your mind, you can later disable it for the entire file server by using the ENABLE FILE COMPRESSION SET command.

You can elect several file compression settings by using either the SET command or the SERVMAN utility. These settings, which apply to all files and directories on a volume, are the following:

- **Compression Daily Check Stop Hour.** Sets the time of day compression should stop searching for compressible files
- **Compression Daily Check Starting Hour.** Sets the time of day the system should start searching for compressible files
- **Convert Compressed to Uncompressed Option=#.** Specifies how to restore a decompressed file (0 = do not recompress the file, 1 = leave compressed if only one access until the Days Untouched Before Compression time is met, and 2 = always leave uncompressed)
- **Days Untouched Before Compression.** Sets the length of time (7 days, by default) a file must remain untouched before it is compressed
- **Deleted File Compression Option.** Specifies whether deleted but not purged files should be handled (0 = do not compress, 1 = compress next day, and 2 = compress immediately)
- **Enable File Compression.** Sets compression to OFF (still enabled but no files on server will be compressed) or ON for the file server
- **Maximum Concurrent Compressions.** Specifies the number of volumes that can run compression on files at the same time (2 is the default)
- **Minimum Compression Percentage Gain.** Specifies how much smaller (by percentage) the file must be after compression before this file becomes a candidate for file compression
- **Uncompress Free Space Warning Interval=# minutes # seconds.** Sets, in minutes and seconds, how much time should pass between warnings when the amount of available disk space becomes too low (0 prevents any warnings from being sent)
- **Uncompress Percent Disk Space Free To Allow Commit=%** Specifies how much disk space (in percentages) must still be available before decompressing files

You can also use FLAG, FILER, or NetWare Administrator to set compression-related attributes on files and directories. Two attributes apply. They are *Immediate Compress* (IC), and *Don't Compress* (DC). Setting the IC attribute causes the file to be compressed immediately after it is saved by the user, instead of when the regular time for compressing files arrives. Setting the DC attribute enables you to exempt certain files or directories from being compressed, even when you have set compression on the other files and directories.

In addition to enabling and configuring compression, you can view statistics related to compression by using the NDIR, FILER, and NetWare Administrator utilities, as follows:

- **NDIR.** Type **NDIR [*volume_name:*]/VOL** and press Enter to see statistics for an entire volume, or type **NDIR [*path*]/COMP** and press Enter to see statistics for a specified ([**path**]) file or directory.
- **FILER.** Type **FILER** and press Enter. Next, choose View Volume Information, then choose Statistics.
- **NetWare Administrator.** Change your context to that of the volume's parent container. (You can use the View menu option, or open the Browser and walk the tree.) If you have not already done so, open the Browser window and choose the Volume object. Next, highlight the Volume object and press the right mouse button. Choose Details. Then choose the Statistics page button to view related statistics.

Data Migration

In data migration, you can optimize online disk space by storing infrequently accessed files on *high-capacity storage systems* (HCSS), such as optical drives. This frees online disk storage space for those files used most frequently. The least-used files are migrated first, followed by the next least used, and so on. This is known as the *least recently used* (LRU) algorithm.

Note One typical HCSS is called the Jukebox. The Jukebox can store multiple optical disks, changing them as needed to access the required file.

Data migration is implemented through the real-time data migrator NLM (RTDM.NLM), and the device driver that accompanies the HCSS device being used for migration. Files that have been migrated are readily accessed by network users, provided that sufficient hard disk space is available. Files migrated to HCSS devices must be transferred back (demigrated) to the hard disk before users can actually access them.

As with file compression and suballocation, you install and configure data migration by using the INSTALL.NLM, after physically connecting and installing the HCSS device. To set up data migration, complete the following steps:

1. Load the HCSS' device driver and the NetWare-supplied HPCHGR driver (if using a Jukebox) at the file server console. (Type **LOAD *device_driver***, and press Enter, then type **LOAD HPCHGR**, and press Enter at the file server console.)
2. Type **SCAN FOR NEW DEVICES** at the file server prompt, to add (register) these device drivers to the list of devices currently recognized by this file server, and press Enter.
3. Create an HCSS Volume object in the NDS database, making certain that the HCSS volume is *not* part of the SYS: volume.
4. Type **LOAD HCSS** on the file server console, and press Enter.
5. Modify the NWADMIN.INI file on the workstation you will be using to manage HCSS, so that the following lines appear under the [Snapin Object DLLs] section heading:

```
Vis HCSSDecider=hdecsnap.dll
Vis HCSSObject=hobjsnap.dll
Vis HCSSMedia=hmedsnap.dll
```

6. Using NetWare Administrator, choose the HCSS volume and create the HCSS domain directory, which should then display two options in the Tools menu—HCSS Parameters and HCSS Create.
7. Choose HCSS Create, provide a required unique name for the HCSS domain directory, then choose Create.
8. Choose HCSS Media from the NetWare Administrator Tools menu, then choose Import Media.
9. Prepare the media, then choose either Format, Assign, or Cancel from the HCSS Media Management dialog box.
10. Depending on your choice in step 9, format, assign to a domain, or eject (cancel) the media.
11. After an optical disk has been assigned and the media has been formatted (if necessary), you can set HCSS file storage limits on the server's hard disk.

Using the MONITOR, SET, and SERVMAN Console Utilities

You use the MONITOR, SET, and SERVMAN utilities to monitor memory usage in NetWare 4 file servers, and to set or configure various system parameters in order to customize or fine-tune your network system.

Using MONITOR

To use the MONITOR utility, type **MONITOR** at the file server console, and press Enter. The MONITOR menu opens, along with the General Information screen (see fig. 14.4).

You use the MONITOR utility to perform a variety of tasks, including the following:

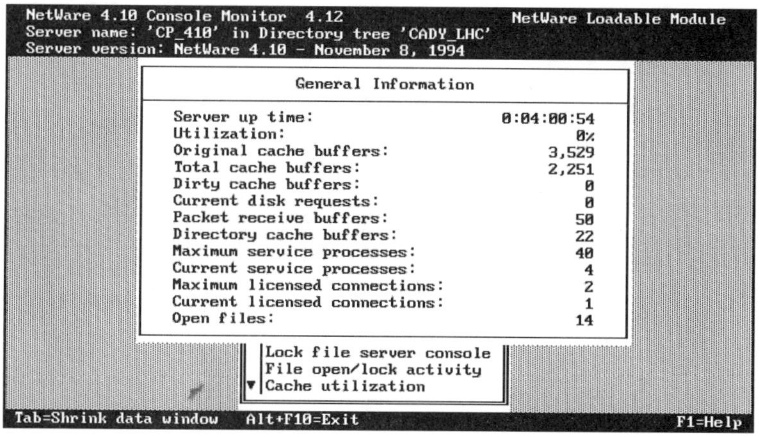

Figure 14.4
MONITOR General Information screen.

- **Viewing activity on and statistics related to the file server.** The MONITOR General Information screen displays a variety of information about the NetWare file server. This information includes the length of time the server has been running, the percentage of the server's ability currently being used, and statistics related to cache buffers (original, total, and dirty). Also displayed is information about the current number of disk requests, packet receive and directory cache buffers, service processes (maximum and current), current licensed connections, and number of open files.
- **Locking the file server console.** To lock the file server console, use the /L option when you load MONITOR. For example, type **LOAD MONITOR /L**, and press Enter.
- **Viewing information related to file server memory (RAM) and processor (CPU) utilization.** Memory utilization information includes information about how memory has been allocated, the percent of allocated memory currently in use, the number of memory blocks and bytes in use, and the number of free blocks. You can use the Resource Utilization option in the MONITOR Available Options menu to see allocated memory in the memory pools.
- **Optimizing memory.** From a module's Allocated Memory Information screen, you can perform a task known as garbage collection to again make available for use areas in memory that were allocated and then released, but were not returned to the pool of memory and made available for use by other modules.
- **Viewing information about and managing the system's hard disks.** The Disk Information option on the MONITOR's Available Options menu shows you disk-related information. Among other things, this option lets you change the Read After Write Verify status of the hard disk, activate or deactivate a hard disk, and mount, dismount, lock, or unlock a removable media device.

Using SET

Use the SET utility to adjust operating system parameters and change the AUTOEXEC.NCF and STARTUP.NCF files, and to view information about adapters, partitions, mounted volumes, and network statistics. You can type **SET** at the file server console, press Enter, and view a list of Settable configuration parameter categories from which to choose (see fig. 14.5).

```
CP_410:set
Settable configuration parameter categories
    1. Communications
    2. Memory
    3. File caching
    4. Directory caching
    5. File system
    6. Locks
    7. Transaction tracking
    8. Disk
    9. Time
    10. NCP
    11. Miscellaneous
    12. Error Handling
    13. Directory Services
Which category do you want to view:
```

Figure 14.5
Settable configuration parameter categories.

You can also type the SET command, followed by a parameter, and see what the existing settings are for that parameter. In addition, you can type the SET command, followed by a parameter and a value for that parameter, to change that parameter's value.

> **Note:** Some SET parameters must be entered into one of the file server's startup files (STARTUP.NCF or AUTOEXEC.NCF). For example, the Minimum Packet Receive Buffers parameter must be placed in the STARTUP.NCF file. You cannot change this parameter at the file server console, because these buffers are allocated when the server boots.

Using SERVMAN

The SERVMAN utility has the same functionality as the SET command, as well as some of the functionality of the MONITOR command. The SERVMAN utility presents the information in menu format. It also has a screen which provides Server General Information, including such information as the length of time the file server has been up and running, the percentage of processor utilization, the processor's speed, the number of NLMs currently loaded, the number of volumes currently mounted, the number of active queues and logged-in users, and the number of name space NLMs loaded on the server.

In addition, the SERVMAN utility provides an Available Options menu from which to set various parameters (see fig. 14.6).

The SERVMAN Available Options menu offers the following four options:

- Server parameters
- Storage information
- Volume information
- Network information

The Server parameters option enables you to see or change various operating system parameters, including changing their values in the AUTOEXEC.NCF and STARTNET.NCF files. The Storage information option enables you to see information about adapters, devices, and partitions. The Volume information option enables you to view information about currently mounted volumes. The Network information option enables you to see a variety of network information.

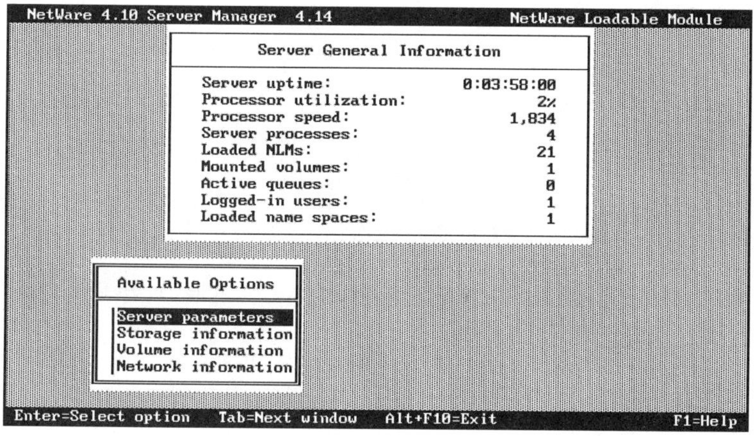

Figure 14.6
SERVMAN utility main screen.

Providing Support for Non-DOS Client Operating Systems, Multiple Protocols, and Multiple Languages

NetWare uses various NLMs to provide support for non-DOS client operating systems and multiple protocols, and to configure and manage communication protocols. The following NLMs—some of which are part of the NetWare 4 product; others, separate products—provide these kinds of support, configuration, and management capabilities:

- MAC, OS/2, and Unix name space NLMs
- PROTOCOL, SPXCONFG, STREAMS, and associated NLMs
- CONLOG and INETCFG NLMs

MAC, OS/2, and Unix Name Space NLMs

The MAC.NAM, OS2.NAM, and NFS.NAM are NLMs that provide name space support, respectively, for Macintosh, OS/2, and Unix operating systems. With these NLMs, files named using these operating systems can be saved on NetWare volumes, even though the file names do not follow the eight-dot-three (8.3) DOS naming convention.

By adding name space support to a NetWare volume, you not only make it possible to store these files with long names on a NetWare volume (OS/2 file names can be up to 255 bytes long), but doing so also increases the space provided in the Directory Entry Table (DET). Because volumes with name space loaded require twice as many directory entries per volume, space requirements increase whenever you load a name space NLM on a volume. Be sure to consider this fact when you try to load a name space NLM on a NetWare volume that is already quite full.

After you add name space to a volume, using the **ADD NAME SPACE *NLM_name* TO *volume_name*** command at the file server console, you must load the related NLM (such as MAC.NAM, for example, if you replace ***NLM_name*** with **MAC**. The volume will not load if the associated **LOAD *name_space*** command is not also run at the file server console. The name space NLMs are stored in the DOS partition.

Note: The ADD NAME SPACE command has to be loaded on a volume once for each name-space type NLM you want to add to that volume. For example, you use the ADD NAME SPACE command once to load Macintosh name spacing, and once to load OS/2 name spacing. After that, the associated LOAD command must be run each time you boot the file server. The LOAD *NLM_name* command should be added to the STARTUP.NCF file to ensure that it is run each time the file server is booted.

PROTOCOL, SPXCONFIG, STREAMS, and Associated NLMs

Several NLMs are responsible for ensuring that various communication protocols can be used in the NetWare environment. Those NLMs are shown in table 14.2.

Table 14.2
Communication Protocol NLMs

NLM	*Associated NLM*	*Function*
CLIB	STREAMS and others	To provide routines and functions required by other NLMs
IPXS	STREAMS and CLIB	To provide the IPXS protocol stack
SPXS	STREAMS, CLIB, and sometimes TLI	To provide the SPXS protocol stack
STREAMS	CLIB, TLI, IPXS and SPXS	To provide an interface between NetWare and various transport protocols, including IPX/SPX, TCP/IP, and OSI
TLI	STREAMS and CLIB	To provide an interface between STREAMS and application programs

Although these NLMs support the different communication protocols that can be used in the NetWare environment, two utilities provide configuration capabilities and protocol information. These utilities are SPXCONFG and PROTOCOL.

The SPXCONFG utility enables you to configure watchdog and timeout information, retry count, maximum concurrent SPX sessions, and maximum open IPX sockets (see fig. 14.7).

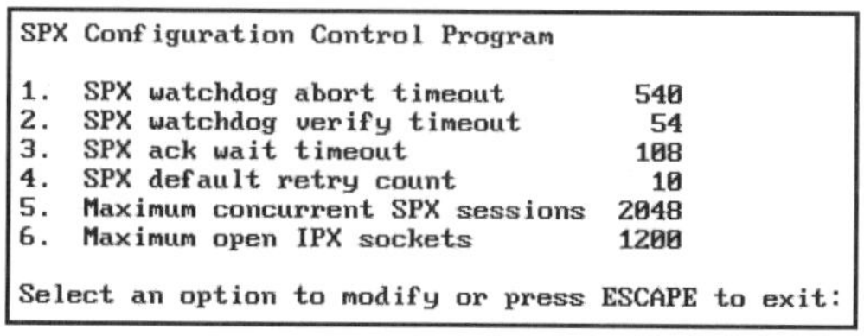

Figure 14.7
SPX Configuration Control program.

The PROTOCOL command provides a list of all protocols currently registered with the file server. It also enables you to register additional protocols (see fig. 14.8).

CONLOG and INETCFG NLMs

The CONLOG NLM is used to trap information when the system is initialized. To use this utility, place the following lines in the AUTOEXEC.NCF file:

```
LOAD CONLOG
LOAD SNMP
INITIALIZE SYSTEM
UNLOAD CONLOG
```

You can configure LAN driver, protocol, and remote access commands by using the INETCFG utility. When you type **LOAD INETCFG** at the

Figure 14.8
List of registered protocols.

```
CP_410:protocol
The following protocols are registered:
  Protocol: IPX  Frame type: VIRTUAL_LAN  Protocol ID: 0
  Protocol: IPX  Frame type: ETHERNET_802.3  Protocol ID: 0
  Protocol: IPX  Frame type: ETHERNET_802.2  Protocol ID: E0
CP_410:
```

file server console, and press Enter the first time, you are prompted to Transfer LAN driver, protocol, and remote access commands. By responding Yes, you open the Internetworking Configuration menu (see fig. 14.9) from which you can manage configuration and view information about boards, network interfaces, WAN call directory, protocols, and bindings.

After CONLOG is loaded, you can use the INETCFG console command to view the configuration information CONLOG collects in the SYS:ETC\CONSOLE.LOG file (see fig. 14.10). To view the CONSOLE.LOG file, choose View Configuration from the Internetworking Configuration menu, then choose Console Messages.

Figure 14.9
Internetworking Configuration menu.

```
Internetworking Configuration  3.10a              NetWare Loadable Module

 Internetworking Configuration

 Boards
 Network Interfaces
 WAN Call Directory
 Protocols
 Bindings
 Manage Configuration
 View Configuration

Add, delete, and configure interface boards.
ENTER=Select ESC=Exit Menu                                        F1=Help
```

Figure 14.10
CONSOLE.LOG file, viewed through INETCFG.

```
Internetworking Configuration  3.10a              NetWare Loadable Module

                    View (Read-Only) Console Messages

CONLOG-1.02-10: System console logging started Fri Jul 28 15:05:37 1995.
CONLOG-1.02-9: Logging system console to sys:etc\console.log.
CP_410:load inetcfg
Loading module INETCFG.NLM
  Internetworking Configuration
  Version 3.10a   November 4, 1994
  Copyright (C) 1992-1994 Novell, Inc.  All rights reserved.
  Auto-loading module TUI.NLM
  Textual User Interface
  Version 1.04    October 19, 1994
  Copyright 1992-1994 Novell, Inc.  All rights reserved.
  Auto-loading module SNMP.NLM
  SNMP Agent
  Version 3.01    October 19, 1994
  Copyright 1992-1994 Novell, Inc.  All rights reserved.
  Auto-loading module TLI.NLM

View the console messages generated by loaded modules.
ESC=Exit Viewing                                                  F1=Help
```

Questions

1. The VLM responsible for making a network drive appear as though it were a DOS drive is ______.

   ○ A. AUTO.VLM

   ○ B. FIO.VLM

   ○ C. NWP.VLM

   ○ D. REDIR.VLM

2. The ______ and ______ are responsible for enabling different types of network packets to be transmitted to and accepted by the workstation.

   □ A. LAN board

   □ B. IPXODI

   □ C. LSL

   □ D. MLID

3. To specify more ports than DOS can normally address, place the ______ command in the NET.CFG file.

   ○ A. LOCAL PRINTERS = <none>

   ○ B. PB BUFFERS = #

   ○ C. CONNECTIONS = #

   ○ D. NAME CONTEXT = <name_context>

4. The ______ file is responsible for providing task-switching capabilities, allowing DOS applications being run in MS Windows to use Enhanced Mode.

   ○ A. NETWARE.DRV

   ○ B. VIPX.386

   ○ C. VNETWARE.386

   ○ D. NWADMIN.INI

5. The ______ option, used with the WSUPDATE command, causes the old version of the file to be renamed with a .OLD extension instead of deleted.

   ○ A. /C

   ○ B. /E

   ○ C. /R

   ○ D. /O

6. To place questionable NLMs into an area of memory where they cannot interfere with the normal functioning of the NetWare OS, type LOAD ______ at the file server console.

   ○ A. DOMAIN

   ○ B. SEEME

   ○ C. OS

   ○ D. OSP

7. Of the following, which *three* are memory-management features of NetWare?

   □ A. Block suballocation

   □ B. Ring deallocation

   □ C. File compression

   □ D. Data migration

8. The average compression ratio for a disk with file compression turned on is ______.

   ○ A. 48%

   ○ B. 63%

   ○ C. 72%

   ○ D. 80%

9. The command that registers device drivers to the list of devices currently recognized by this file server is ______.

   ○ A. LOAD HPCHGR

   ○ B. LOAD DEVICE DRIVER

   ○ C. SCAN FOR NEW DEVICES

   ○ D. LIST DEVICES

10. Which of the following is *not* a name space NLM?

   ○ A. MAC.NAM

   ○ B. OS/2.NAM

   ○ C. NFS.NAM

   ○ D. UNIX.NAM

Answers

1. D
2. A, D
3. A
4. B
5. C
6. A
7. A, C, D
8. B
9. C
10. D

CHAPTER 15

Optimizing a NetWare 4.x Network

There are two circumstances under which you should examine the efficiency of your network. The first comes when your network is experiencing performance problems. The second is when everything seems to be functioning just fine, but the growing needs of your network dictate improved network performance.

You can use the MONITOR utility to view statistics related to your network's performance, and the SERVMAN utility to adjust network performance. You can also use two other utilities—DSREPAIR and VREPAIR—to correct problems with the NDS database and network volumes.

This chapter discusses these four utilities, network performance, and related items of information under the following topics:

- Using MONITOR to track network performance
- Understanding and tracking SAP and RIP traffic
- Understanding Packet Burst and LIP
- Repairing the NDS database and NetWare volumes

Using MONITOR to Track Network Performance

The MONITOR utility provides information and statistics about a wide variety of network performance-related issues, such as the following:

- Cache and packet receive buffer usage
- Memory usage
- Processor usage
- Resource usage

It also provides a variety of more general information, available on the first screen (General Information) of the MONITOR utility (see fig. 15.1).

The MONITOR General Information screen provides information about the following items:

- **Server Up Time.** Total days, hours, minutes, and seconds (dd:hh:mm:ss) since the last time SERVER.EXE was run to start the server
- **Utilization.** Percentage of total available processing time during which the processor is being used
- **Original Cache Buffers.** Total number of memory blocks assigned to caching when the server was first brought up
- **Total Cache Buffers.** Number of remaining memory blocks assigned to caching after NLMs and other programs requiring cache buffers have been loaded
- **Dirty Cache Buffers.** Total number of cache memory blocks currently open and unwritten to disk
- **Current Disk Requests.** Total disk requests currently unfulfilled for this server
- **Packet Receive Buffers.** Number of buffers set aside to receive requests for service from network clients
- **Maximum Service Processes.** Total number of task handlers set aside for processing client requests
- **Current Service Processes.** Number of task handlers currently processing client requests

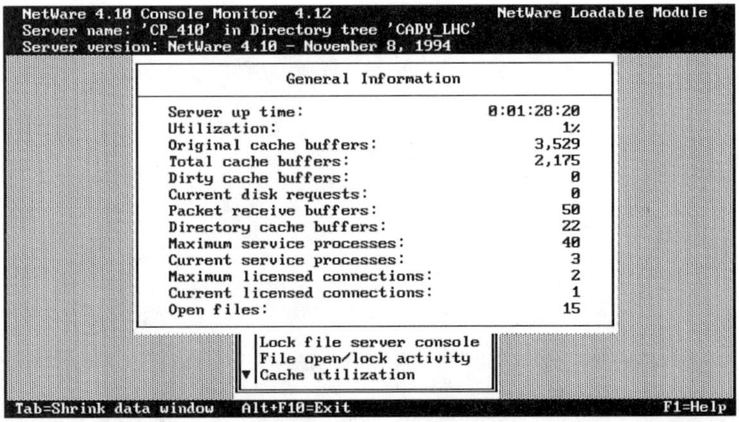

Figure 15.1
MONITOR's General Information screen.

- **Maximum Licensed Connections.** Total number of connections available for accessing file and print services on this file server (called *Connections in Use* on earlier versions of NetWare 4)
- **Current Licensed Connections.** Number of connections to this server currently being used for accessing file and print services
- **Open files.** Number of files currently in use by all network clients and the file server

Note

Earlier versions of NetWare 4 also showed Directory Cache Buffers. This statistic reflected the number of buffers set aside specifically for directory caching.

The MONITOR utility also provides an Available Options menu from which submenus can be opened, so that you can view a variety of information and statistics related to this NetWare file server. In order to monitor and optimize the network, the network administrator should pay close attention to the following four main categories of information:

- Cache buffer and packet receive buffer usage
- Memory usage
- Processor usage
- Resource usage

Cache Buffer and Packet Receive Buffer Usage

A *buffer* is an area of memory set aside to be used as temporary storage. NetWare uses two types of buffers—cache and packet receive buffers. NetWare sets aside a certain amount of memory to use for caching files, the *File Allocation Table* (FAT), Turbo FAT indexes (for files with more than 64 regular entries), the *Directory Entry Table* (DET), user files, and the *directory hash table,* which stores directory names. This memory is referred to as the *cache buffer pool.* In addition, NetWare sets aside areas of memory where requests for service from network clients are received and temporarily stored until they can be processed.

You can view information about two types of buffer usage—cache buffers and packet receive buffers—on the MONITOR utility's General Information screen, which displays the following related statistics:

- **Original Cache Buffers.** Displays the total number of memory blocks assigned to caching when the server was first brought up. This figure is based on the number and size (4 KB is the default) of memory blocks provided during installation, minus those used for the NetWare core operating system and DOS.
- **Total Cache Buffers.** Shows the number of remaining memory blocks assigned to caching after NLMs and other programs requiring cache buffers have been loaded. If this statistic falls to 20 percent or less of the original cache buffers statistic, your file server is likely to crash. This figure should realistically be at least 50 percent.
- **Dirty Cache Buffers.** Displays the total number of cache memory blocks currently open and unwritten to disk. This statistic should generally read 0%, or exceed that percentage for only very short periods of time. Prolonged percentages above 0% may indicate a disk channel problem.
- **Packet Receive Buffers.** Shows the number of buffers set aside to receive requests for service from network workstations. The default is 10. The number is determined by the topology of your network.

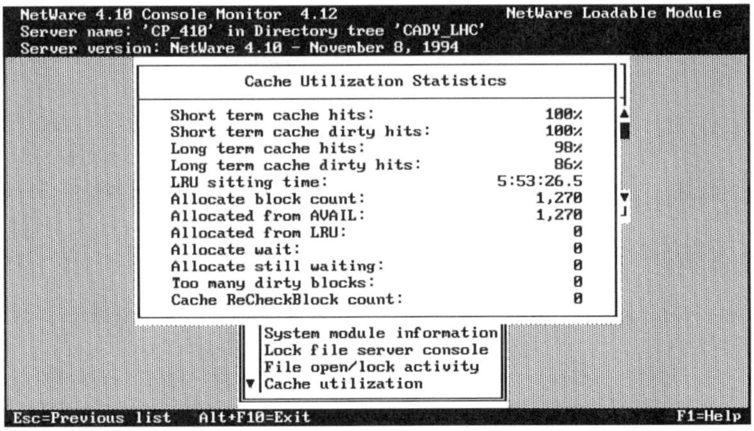

Figure 15.2
The Cache Utilization Statistics window.

By choosing the Cache utilization option from the Available Options menu, you can see additional information (see fig. 15.2), the most important figure of which is the Long Term Cache Hits statistic. If this statistic is less than 98 percent, add more memory to the file server.

Additional cache utilization fields in this window are explained in table 15.1.

Packets are sections of data sent across a network. The allowable size for a packet is negotiated between the server and workstation. The allowed range is dependent upon the LAN driver, but ranges from 576 to 6,500 bytes. The following are the default maximum packet sizes for various topologies:

Topology	*Size*
Token Ring at 4 or 16 Mbps	4,202 bytes
Ethernet	1,518 bytes
ARCnet	576 bytes

The largest possible packet size both the server and client can handle should be the setting used for packet size. The Maximum Physical Receive Packet Size parameter can be set by using the SERVMAN utility.

The network administrator can modify the following three specific packet receiving-related parameters:

- **Maximum packet receive buffers.** Enables you to set the number of packet receive buffers the operating system can allocate. The default setting is 100, but a range of 300 to 500 is more appropriate for an active file server.
- **Maximum service processes.** Enables you to specify how many service processes (task handlers) can be allocated for servicing client requests. Increasing this parameter reduces the need for packet receive buffers after the maximum number of service processes has been reached.
- **Minimum packet receive buffers.** Enables you to specify how many packet receive buffers should be allocated when the file server starts up. The default is 10. You can only set this parameter in the STARTUP.NCF file. It cannot be entered at the file server console, because the setting must be available to the file server at startup.

Table 15.1
Cache Utilization Information

Field Name	*Example*	*Function*
Short-term cache hits	100%	Percentage of time in last second that a disk cache read was successful
Short-term cache dirty hits	100%	Percentage of time in last second that a disk cache read was successful, and the information was in dirty cache buffers
Long-term cache hits	98%	Disk blocks already in cache; if it falls below 98%, add more memory
Long-term cache dirty hits	86%	Disk blocks in dirty cache (waiting to be stored)
LRU sitting time	5:53:26.5	Length of time elapsed since least-used item in list was accessed
Allocate block count	1,270	Disk cache block requests issued since server was started
Allocated from Avail	1,270	Disk cache blocks not already being used when located
Allocated from LRU	0	Disk cache blocks found in Least Recently Used list
Allocate wait	0	Number of times a disk cache request had to wait for a block of LRU to be made available; a high number indicates need for additional file server memory
Allocate still waiting	0	Length of time a disk cache had to wait for an LRU block to be cleared; if less than 7 to 10 minutes, indicates need for additional memory
Too many dirty blocks	0	Number of times a write request was delayed because of a busy disk channel or a large number of competing write requests
Cache ReCheckBlock count	0	Number of retries for a disk cache request, due to a busy target block

Memory Usage

You can view memory usage information for each module loaded on the file server. To view related information, you can use the System module information and Memory Utilization options in the MONITOR utility.

To use the System module information option, choose System module information from the MONITOR Available Options menu. Then, choose the system module whose memory usage information you want to view. When the list of Resource Tags opens for this module (see fig. 15.3), choose a resource tag.

For example, if you choose the Alloc memory resource tag for the NetWare 4.10 Console Monitor system module, you can view the following information (see fig. 15.4):

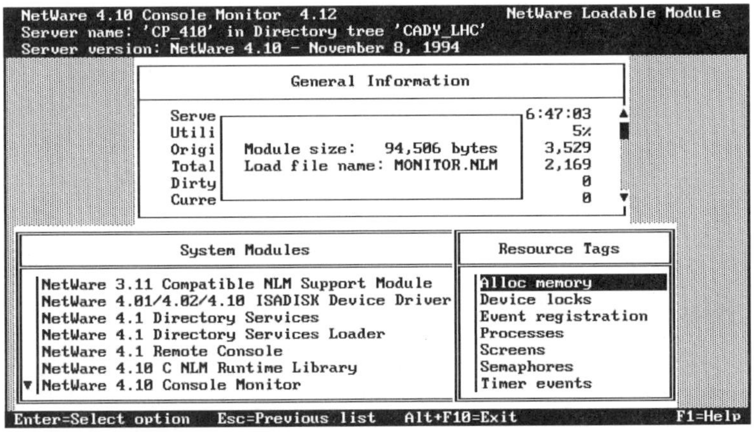

Figure 15.3
NetWare 4.10 Console Monitor resource tags.

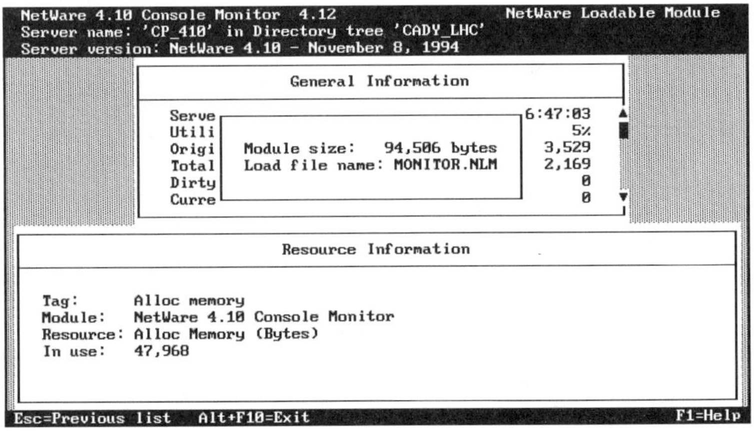

Figure 15.4
NetWare 4.10 Console Monitor Resource Information screen for Alloc memory tag.

- **Module size—size of the chosen module.** In this example, the module is the NetWare 4.10 Console Monitor, and the size is 94,506 bytes.
- **Load file name—name of the module.** In this example, the module is called MONITOR.NLM.
- **Tag—name of the chosen resource tag.** In this example, the chosen resource tag is Alloc memory.
- **Module—the module responsible for allocating the resource.** In this example, the module allocating the resource is the NetWare 4.10 Console Monitor.
- **Resource—the resource currently being tracked.** In this example, the tracked resource is Alloc memory.
- **In use—the amount of this resource currently being used.** In this example, the resource amount is 47,968 bytes.

To use the Memory Utilization option, choose this option from the MONITOR Available Options menu. Next, choose a module from the list of System Modules. When you choose the NetWare 4.10 Console Monitor system module, for example, the information screen shown in figure 15.5 is displayed. The following types of information are made available for the chosen module:

- **4 KB cache pages.** Number of 4 KB cache pages that have been allocated from memory for this module
- **Cache page blocks.** Number of 4 KB cache pages being used by this module
- **Percent in use.** The percentage of allocated memory being used by this module
- **Percent free.** Percentage of memory allocated to this module that is not currently being used
- **Memory blocks in use.** Number of KB blocks of memory being used by this module
- **Memory bytes in use.** Number of bytes of memory currently being used by this module
- **Memory blocks free.** Number of KB blocks of memory currently free for use by this module
- **Memory bytes free.** Number of bytes of allocated memory that remain available to this module

Processor Usage

You can view processor usage information by choosing the Processor utilization option from the MONITOR Available Options menu, then choosing from the list of Available Processes and Interrupts. Figure 15.6 displays the processor utilization screen for the Console Command. The following information is presented for each item:

- **Process Name.** The name of the process or interrupt chosen from the list of Available Processes and Interrupts
- **Time.** How long the processor took to run the program, or how long the processor spent inside the routine
- **Count.** Number of times the process ran or the interrupt was serviced during the sampling time
- **Load.** Percentage of time the processor took to run the process or service the interrupt
- **Total sample time.** Length of time the total sample process took

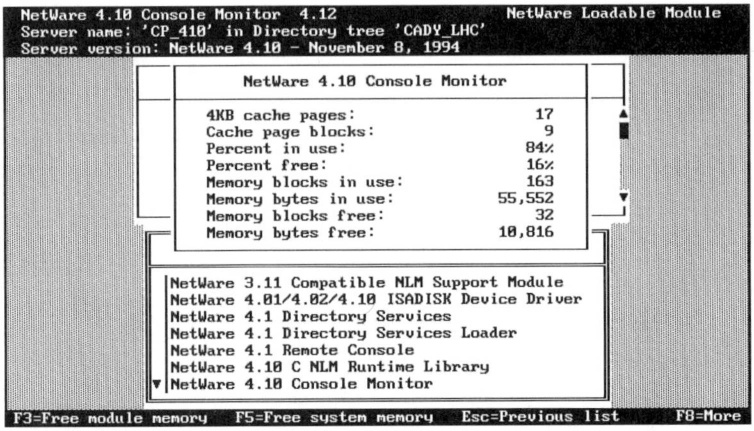

Figure 15.5
NetWare 4.10 Console Monitor memory utilization information.

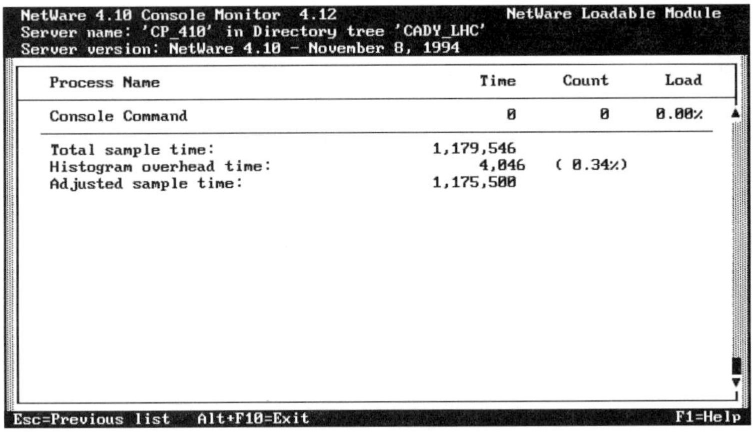

Figure 15.6
Console Command processor utilization information.

- **Histogram overhead time.** How long the processor spent providing the statistics resulting from this sampling
- **Adjusted sample time.** The difference between the total sampling time and the histogram overhead time—result is the length of time the process or service actually ran

Note To see this information for all processes, press F3 after choosing the Processor utilization option from the MONITOR Available Options menu.

Resource Usage

You can view resource usage information by choosing Resource utilization from the MONITOR Available Options menu. Next, from the list of Tracked Resources, choose the resource whose usage you want to view, and then choose a resource from the Resource Tags list. The resulting screen (see fig. 15.7) provides the following resource information:

- **Tag.** Name of the chosen resource. The chosen resource tag is REMOTE Console Commands.

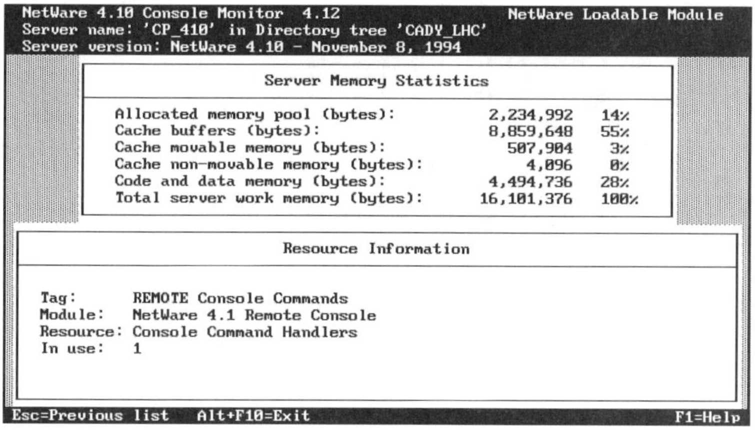

Figure 15.7
Remote Console Commands Resource Information.

- **Module.** Module for which this resource information is being provided. The module allocating the resource is the NetWare 4.1 Remote Console.
- **Resource.** Resource currently being tracked. The tracked resource is Console Command Handlers.
- **In use.** Number of resources currently being used. The number is 1.

Understanding and Tracking SAP and RIP Traffic

Service Advertising Protocol (SAP) is the convention NetWare servers, gateways, and so on use to send packets across the network announcing their availability to network clients. In addition, network routers use SAP to exchange information about servers. Each SAP packet can contain a maximum of seven advertised items. SAP packets are sent out every 60 seconds, captured by network clients, and stored in a table for future use. The problem with SAP packets on the network (SAP traffic) is that, without some filtering applied, SAP traffic can have a great impact on network throughput. By adding a filter to limit the number of SAP packets sent, however, you can not only reduce SAP traffic but also enhance network security by hiding servers that should not be generally available on the network.

Router Information Protocol (RIP) is a convention routers use to exchange information within a NetWare network. By exchanging information, routers can create and maintain a table of information that clients can use to determine the shortest route to take to reach a distant network. Clients accomplish this by sending out a RIP request packet, to which the router responds. In addition to responding to RIP request packets, routers also send out RIP broadcast packets every 60 seconds to let all other routers on the network know the same routing information.

You can track the SAP and RIP traffic on the network by using the TRACK ON and TRACK OFF commands. By typing **TRACK ON** at the file server console, and pressing Enter, you display a variety of messages, such as those shown in figure 15.8.

Figure 15.8
The TRACK ON screen.

```
Router Tracking Screen
IN     [2F965EDC:000000000001]  7:36:46 pm   CP_410        1
OUT    [2F965EDC:FFFFFFFFFFFF]  7:37:02 pm   PS1           1    CP_410        1
          CADY_LHC____  1   CADY_LHC____  1  CP_410        1
OUT    [2D699C8D:FFFFFFFFFFFF]  7:37:02 pm   PS1           1    CP_410        1
          CADY_LHC____  1   CADY_LHC____  1  CP_410        1
OUT    [3E9F33A4:FFFFFFFFFFFF]  7:37:02 pm   PS1           1    CP_410        1
          CADY_LHC____  1   CADY_LHC____  1  CP_410        1
IN     [2F965EDC:000000000001]  7:37:13 pm   CP_410        1
IN     [2F965EDC:000000000001]  7:37:13 pm   CP_410        1
IN     [2F965EDC:000000000001]  7:37:14 pm   PS1           1
<Use ALT-ESC or CTRL-ESC to switch screens, or any other key to pause>
```

Note: Use the TRACK OFF command to discontinue tracking SAP and RIP packets.

Different fields displayed by the TRACK ON command include the following information:

- **IN/OUT.** A reference to whether the packet is being received by (IN) the network device (server, router, and so on), or being sent (OUT) across the network by the device. (In fig. 15.8, the first line below the screen title—Router Tracking Screen— is for an incoming packet. The information in the second line is for an outgoing packet.)
- **Network number.** Indicates the internal or cabling number of the network server sending the packet, or the network number of a network known to this server for an incoming packet. (In fig. 15.8, the first IN line displays a network number of 2F965EDC.)
- **Hops.** Displays a single number that indicates how many servers and routers a packet has to pass through before it reaches its destination. (The third line in fig. 15.8 shows 1 hop.)
- **Server name.** Name of the NetWare server. (The third line in fig. 15.8 shows a file server name of CADY_LHC.)
- **Ticks.** Specifies how many 1/18ths of a second it would take a packet to reach its destination from the file server that sent it; generally displayed with the number of hops, separated by a slash (/). (Fig. 15.8 does not show the travel time for a packet.)

Understanding Packet Burst and LIP

Both Packet Burst and Large Internet Packets (LIP) are concerned with the distribution of network packets across the network media. Packet Burst controls the number of packets sent across the media at one time, whereas LIP controls the size of each packet sent.

Packet Burst

Earlier versions of networks sent all network packets across the network one packet at a time. NetWare 4 (and some earlier versions of NetWare 3), allow *packet bursting*—the transmission of multiple packets across the network without requiring a response for each packet. Packet Burst can increase network performance by 10 to 300 percent. The range depends on a variety of factors, including memory, bandwidth, and the size of each file. Packet Burst uses two techniques—burst gap time and burst window size—to decide how much data is sent in each burst.

Burst gap time indicates how much time should pass before packets are grouped and sent across the media. The purpose of burst gap time is to prevent overfilling a client's available buffer space.

Burst window size specifies how many packets can be sent per burst. In theory, as many as 128 512-byte packets can be sent per burst. The reality is determined, however, by the number and size of buffers the client has available, as well as by how consistently the packets are reaching their destination. If buffers are already full when a packet burst is received, resulting in one or more packets being lost, the number of packets sent per burst is negotiated and reduced.

Both the file server and client must be capable of handling packets in burst mode. If the client is not capable of handling burst mode, packets are still sent out one packet at a time. By default, packet burst is turned on at the workstation, and connections are negotiated through the NetWare DOS Requester when the workstation attaches to or logs in to the network.

Note Although applications make read and write requests, the most common requests serviced by using Packet Burst, applications do not need to be Packet Burst-aware. The negotiation is done by the NetWare DOS Requester, based on available workstation buffers/memory.

You can disable Packet Burst at a workstation, but you cannot disable it at the file server. To disable Packet Burst at a workstation, enter the following line into the workstation's NET.CFG file:

```
PB Buffers=0
```

You can set Packet Burst buffers anywhere from 0 to 10 (0 turns off Packet Burst). To regulate the amount of workstation memory dedicated to Packet Burst, set the number at 2 or 3.

LIP

Large Internet Packets (LIP) enable file servers and workstations to negotiate the size of packets they will exchange across the network. The one confining element is that packets larger than 512 bytes can only be sent when the router is capable of handling larger packet sizes. If the router can only handle 512-byte packets, the server and workstation will ultimately negotiate a packet size no greater than that which the router can handle.

In those cases where no router is involved, or where a router is capable of handling larger packet sizes, a larger packet size can be negotiated by telling LIP to ignore the router check during packet negotiation.

To enable LIP at the file server, you can either type **SET ALLOW LIP PACKETS = ON**, and press Enter at the file server console, or add the command to the file server's STARTUP.NCF file. You can use this command for all network topologies except ARCnet.

To enable LIP at a workstation, place the following line in the workstation's NET.CFG file:

```
LARGE INTERNET PACKETS = ON
```

If network routers can handle the larger packet sizes, enable the routers by using the following command on all network routers:

```
SET MAXIMUM PHYSICAL RECEIVE PACKET SIZE =
➥packet_size
```

Repairing the NDS Database and NetWare Volumes

Occasionally your network will experience corruption problems in the NDS database, or on a NetWare volume. NetWare provides two utilities to automatically identify and correct NDS database and NetWare volume corruption problems. These two utilities are DSREPAIR and VREPAIR.

DSREPAIR

Use DSREPAIR by loading this NLM on the file server. (Type **LOAD DSREPAIR**, and press Enter.) On NetWare 4 networks that are pre-NetWare 4.10, after loading the DSREPAIR utility NLM, type **1** to access the list of options, specify a pause after each error is found (type **1**) or send error messages to a file (type **2**), then type **2** to begin the repair. When prompted, save changes and exit DSREPAIR (type **3**).

Note DSREPAIR should not be run until sufficient time has passed to enable any partition changes to be properly replicated across the network. In addition, after you load the DSREPAIR NLM, the NDS database is locked and can only be unlocked by unloading (exiting) the DSREPAIR NLM.

In NetWare 4.10 networks, DSREPAIR presents a different menu (see fig. 15.9).

To use DSREPAIR on a NetWare 4.10 network, load the DSREPAIR NLM, then choose Unattended full repair from the Available Options menu. The repair is performed (see fig. 15.10).

This option automatically repairs any NDS database errors it finds that it can fix without operator assistance, and records all transactions in the log file. The log file is automatically displayed for you when the repair is complete. In addition, you can later choose the View/Edit repair log file option to view the recorded transactions (see fig. 15.11).

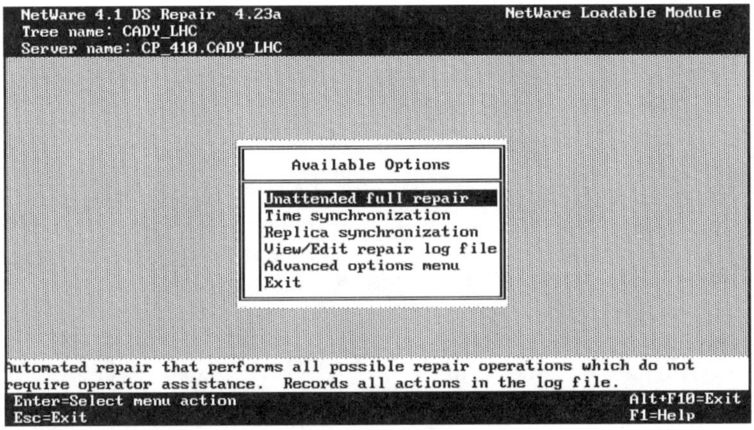

Figure 15.9
DSREPAIR's Available Options menu.

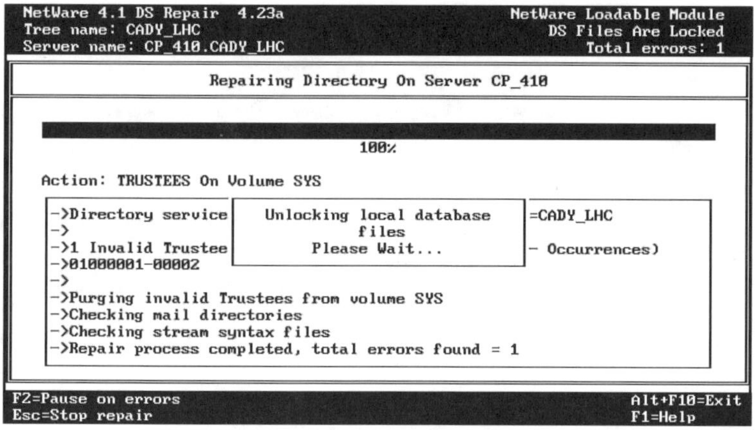

Figure 15.10
The Repairing Directory on Server CP_410 Sample DSREPAIR screen.

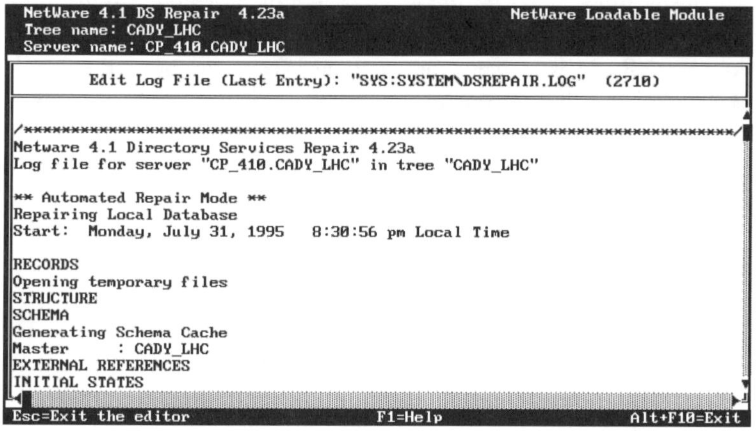

Figure 15.11
DSREPAIR's Edit Log File screen.

VREPAIR

The VREPAIR utility can be used to repair minor problems with a NetWare volume, if the volume is still mountable. Problems that may cause volume corruption without making it impossible to mount the volume include power failures or fluctuations that corrupt the volume, disk read errors, disk hardware failures, and so on.

To run VREPAIR, type **LOAD VREPAIR** at the file server console, and press Enter. Next, type **DISMOUNT *volume_name*** to dismount the volume to be repaired. Then type **2** to set VREPAIR options (see fig. 15.12). Choose Repair a Volume, and if necessary, choose the volume to be repaired (when more than one exists). You can also specify what is to occur when VREPAIR finds a large number of errors. Choose 1 to have it pause after each error, 2 to have the errors written to a text file, or 3 to cause the process to stop before repairs are made, and allow you to answer the prompt to repair the volume.

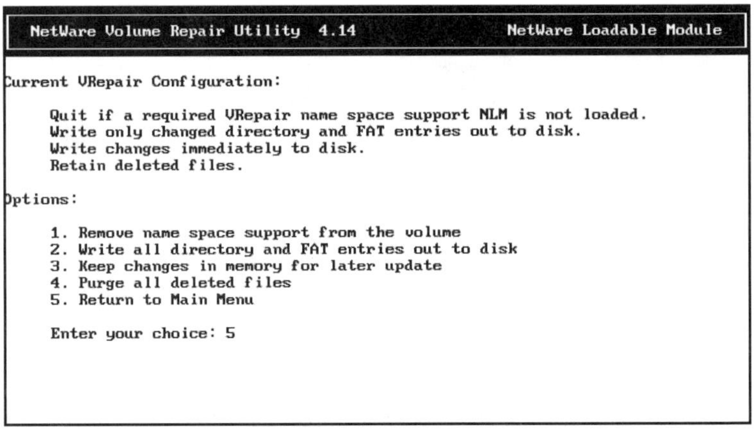

Figure 15.12
VREPAIR's Options menu.

You should rerun VREPAIR as many times as necessary to eliminate all volume errors. When VREPAIR finds no more errors, exit VREPAIR and remount the volume. If the volume cannot be repaired and remounted, you must load the INSTALL.NLM and re-create the volume, using your most current backup to restore the data it contained.

Questions

1. The short-term cache hits found in the MONITOR utility should not be allowed to fall below ______ before adding more memory.
   - ○ A. 80 percent
   - ○ B. 82 percent
   - ○ C. 92 percent
   - ○ D. 98 percent

2. The MONITOR cache statistic which, if displaying a number less than 7 to 10 minutes, indicates the need for additional memory, is called ______.
   - ○ A. Cache ReCheckBlock count
   - ○ B. Allocate wait
   - ○ C. Allocate still waiting
   - ○ D. Too many dirty blocks

3. The default maximum packet size for Token Ring is ______.
   - ○ A. 5,760 bytes
   - ○ B. 4,202 bytes
   - ○ C. 1,518 bytes
   - ○ D. 576 bytes

4. To see how many 4 KB cache pages have been allocated from memory for a specific module, ______.
   - ○ A. choose the Memory utilization option in MONITOR
   - ○ B. choose the Processor utilization option in MONITOR
   - ○ C. choose the Resource utilization option in MONITOR
   - ○ D. choose the Cache utilization option in MONITOR

5. The term used to indicate how long the processor spends providing statistics resulting from a processor sampling procedure is called the ______.
   - ○ A. histogram
   - ○ B. count
   - ○ C. adjusted sample time
   - ○ D. time

6. The convention used by NetWare servers and gateways to send packets across the network announcing their availability of service is called ______.
   - ○ A. SAP
   - ○ B. RIP
   - ○ C. TAG
   - ○ D. NDS

7. Of the following, which *three* are related to packet receiving?
   - ☐ A. Maximum packet receive buffers
   - ☐ B. Maximum service processes
   - ☐ C. Minimum packet receive buffers
   - ☐ D. Minimum service processes

8. The ______ command is used to view packet traffic on a NetWare file server.
   - ○ A. DSREPAIR
   - ○ B. TRACK ON
   - ○ C. MONITOR
   - ○ D. SERVMAN

9. To repair a corrupted NDS database, use ______.
   - ○ A. DSREPAIR
   - ○ B. TRACK ON
   - ○ C. MONITOR
   - ○ D. SERVMAN

10. If you want to ______, use the VREPAIR utility.
    - ○ A. repair the NDS database
    - ○ B. change the cache settings
    - ○ C. correct problems on a volume that do not prevent the volume from mounting
    - ○ D. replace the NetWare DOS Requester settings to allow LIP exchange

Answers

1. D
2. C
3. B
4. A
5. A
6. A
7. A, B, C
8. B
9. A
10. C

PART PART PART PART PART PART PART PART PART

III

Networking Technologies

CHAPTER 16

Computer Network Concepts

Computer networks enable computers to communicate directly in order to exchange information and services. Because computers are all different, are used in different ways, and might be located at different distances from each other, the task of enabling them to communicate can get quite involved, drawing on a wide variety of technologies.

As you study for the Networking Technologies test, you will be delving into some fundamental networking concepts. This chapter will ensure that you have a basic understanding of those concepts before you plunge into the details. Here you will learn a working definition of a computer network, along with definitions of the types of networks and their components.

Upon completing this chapter, you will be able to do the following:

- Define computer networking
- Describe the following models of network computing: centralized, distributed, and collaborative
- Describe the characteristics of local, metropolitan, and wide area networks
- Describe the essential elements of a computer network
- Describe servers, clients, and peers as they relate to computer networking

These skills will prepare you to understand the technologies that are examined in greater detail later in this section.

Models of Network Computing

Novell defines *networking* as the sharing of information and services. By this definition, people are networking when they are exchanging information. This course, however, is specifically concerned with computer networking, which has evolved under several different models to respond to different needs. These models are centralized, distributed, and collaborative.

Centralized Computing

The earliest computers were large, difficult to manage, and expensive. Originally, these large *mainframe* computers were not networked in the sense you are familiar with today. Jobs were entered into the system by reading commands from card decks. The computer would execute one job at a time and generate a printout when the job was complete. Terminals, which enabled users to interact with the centralized computer, were a much later development.

In the computing environment of the mainframe world, all the processing and data storage are centralized in the mainframe computer. *Terminals* are simple devices that display characters on screens and accept typed input. Because terminals are simply input/output devices and do not process or store data, by Novell's definition of networking, no sharing of information is involved and no networking is taking place in a terminal-host environment. Networks developed when it became necessary for mainframe computers to share information and services.

In summary, the *centralized computing* model involves the following:

- All processing in the central, mainframe computer
- Terminals are connected to the central computer as input/output devices
- Networks may be employed to interconnect two or more mainframe computers

Distributed Computing

As personal computers were introduced to organizations, a new model of distributed computing emerged. Instead of concentrating computing in a central device, PCs made it possible to give each worker an individual computer. Each PC can process and store data independently.

Under the distributed computing model, networking has evolved to enable the many distributed computers to exchange data and share resources and services.

In summary, *distributed computing* involves the following:

- Multiple computers capable of operating independently
- Tasks that are split up among the various computers
- Networks that enable the computers to exchange data and services

Collaborative Computing

Also called cooperative computing, collaborative computing enables computers in a distributed computing environment to share processing power in addition to data, resources, and services. In a collaborative computing environment, computers might "borrow" processing power by running programs on other computers on the network, or processes might be designed so they will run on two or more computers. Obviously, collaborative computing cannot take place without a network to enable the various computers to communicate.

In summary, *collaborative computing* involves the following:

- Multiple computers
- Networks that enable the computers to exchange data and services
- Multiple computers that may cooperate to perform a task

Local, Metropolitan, and Wide Area Networks

Computer networks may be classified according to their size characteristics. The most commonly used categories are the following:

- **Local area networks** (LANs), which are confined to a relatively small area, typically limited to a few tens of kilometers in size. LANs typically employ a single transmission medium and are generally defined within a particular building or campus of buildings.
- **Metropolitan area networks** (MANs) may grow in size to that of a metropolitan area, up to about 100 kilometers in scope. To be able to transmit data longer distances, MANs typically require different transmission media and network hardware.
- **Wide area networks** (WANs) can cross the boundaries of states, countries, or even continents, and can be truly world-wide in scope.

An organization with computer operations at several widely separated sites may employ an *enterprise* WAN to interconnect the sites. An enterprise WAN can use a combination of private and commercial network services, but is dedicated to the needs of a particular organization.

Some WANs can be considered *global* in scope because they cross continental boundaries. An example is the Internet, which interconnects thousands of computers on all continents.

Of the three categories of network sizes, LANs and WANs are most frequently encountered.

Components of Computer Networks

Until now, the definition of a computer network has been simply "something" that enables computers to exchange information. The time has come for a more thorough definition. Novell's definition of a network includes three components, as follows:

- Two entities that have information to share. On a computer network, computers share *network services.*
- A pathway by which the entities can contact each other. The pathway through which computers contact each other is called the *transmission media.*
- Rules that establish orderly procedures for communication. The rules that govern computer communication are called *protocols.*

Each of these three components is discussed later in further detail.

Note: Merely having a transmission pathway does not produce communication. When two entities communicate, they do not merely exchange data, but they understand the data they receive from each other. The goal of computer networking is not merely to exchange data, but to be able to understand and use data received from other entities on the network.

Network Services

Networks enable computers to share their resources by offering *services* to other computers. Novell uses the term *service providers* to describe computers (or other entities) that share their capabilities with others. A service provider consists of the hardware and software that provides a specific network service.

Service providers share their capabilities with other entities on the network. A waiter in a restaurant is an example of a human service provider. Examples of network services include the following:

- File services
- Print services
- Communication services
- Electronic mail

Service requesters are entities that utilize network services. A customer ordering lunch in a restaurant is a human example of a service requester.

Service providers will advertise the services they can make available. Service requesters examine the lists of services and request the services they require.

Note: Service providers offer services to service requesters.

In this course, remember that the definition of networking is extremely generic. Any entities (human or machine) that are exchanging information are networking. Any entity (human or machine) on a network can become a service provider or a service requester.

Computer networks consist of three types of service providers and service requesters, as follows:

- *Servers* function only as service providers.
- *Clients* function only as service requesters and do not provide services for other computers.

- *Peers* may concurrently provide and request services. In a peer network, a given computer might be requesting file services from one computer, while at the same time providing print services to another.

Whether a computer functions as a server, client, or peer depends on the software the computer is running. Examples from the NetWare world include the following:

- NetWare 3.12, which turns a PC into a file and print server
- NetWare client software (the NetWare Shell or Requester), which turns a PC into a client
- Personal NetWare, which enables a computer to function as a peer, both requesting and providing services

Networks that enable any computer to both provide and request network services (any entity can function as a peer) are frequently called *peer-to-peer* networks.

Many networks are configured so a given computer will function as either a service provider or a service requester, but not both. With this approach, a server is at the logical center of the network and provides all network services. Therefore, this is frequently called a *server-centric approach.* NetWare 3.12 and 4.1 are the most popular software for configuring server-centric networks.

You will learn more about network services in Chapter 17, "Network Services."

Transmission Media

Entities on networks communicate through some media. Human entities may communicate through telephone wires or sound waves in the air. Computers can communicate through cables, light, and radio waves.

Transmission media enable computers to send and receive messages, but do not guarantee that the messages will be understood.

You will learn more about transmission media in Chapter 19, "Transmission Media" and in Chapter 20, "Transmission Media Connections."

Protocols

Rules are necessary to ensure that messages are understood. The rules of English enable two English-speaking people to understand each other's messages.

The rules that govern computer communication are called protocols. A *protocol* is one or more standards that enable two devices to communicate.

Protocols of many types are utilized on networks. Chapter 19 will introduce you to the model that you can use to organize your understanding of protocols. The majority of this section, starting in Chapter 21, "OSI Physical Layer Concepts," will be devoted to expanding your knowledge of network protocols.

Questions

1. Which model of network computing does *not* take advantage of the processing capability of a user's desktop computer?
   - A. Centralized
   - B. Distributed
   - C. Collaborative
   - D. All of the above utilize the processing capabilities of personal PCs

2. In which model do users' personal computers process information independently from each other?
   - A. Centralized
   - B. Distributed
   - C. Collaborative
   - D. None of the above

3. In which model of network computing do computers share each other's processing capabilities?
   - A. Centralized
   - B. Distributed
   - C. Collaborative
   - D. Departmental

4. Which type of network is most likely confined to a building or a campus?
   - A. LAN
   - B. MAN
   - C. WAN
   - D. Departmental

5. What is the size limit of a wide area network?
   - A. 100 kilometers
   - B. 1,000 kilometers
   - C. 10,000 kilometers
   - D. Worldwide

6. Which *two* entities can share services on a network?
   - A. Servers
   - B. Clients
   - C. Peers
   - D. Requesters

7. Which *two* entities can utilize services on a network?
   - A. Servers
   - B. Clients
   - C. Peers
   - D. Communicators

Answers

1. A
2. B
3. C
4. A
5. D
6. A, D
7. B, C

CHAPTER 17

Network Services

Network services are the first components of the network model. Network services are the resources that servers share with clients, enabling clients to leverage the computing power of other computers on the network.

An operating system *(OS) is the computer program that directly manages the resources in a computer, including memory, disk drives, printing, and input/output functions. This course regards DOS, OS/2, and Unix as* local *or* desktop *operating systems—operating systems that are confined to a single computer. A* network operating system *(NOS) such as NetWare can be distributed on several computers on a network.*

It is possible to build network services as add-ons to local operating systems. Although DOS PCs can be made to network with some add-on programs, the result seldom has the robust, high-level of performance of an operating system that is made for networking. Network operating systems generally include built-in support for file, printing, and other services. Building networking into the NOS improves both performance and reliability, and has the added benefit of being easier to manage than a lot of add-ons.

Services such as file and printer sharing were the earliest incentives for networking computers, but many new network services are now becoming commonplace. In this chapter, you will learn about many network services and how they are managed on NetWare LANs.

When you complete this chapter, you will be able to do the following:

- Describe a variety of network services
- Identify appropriate network services to match organizational needs
- Determine how network services are implemented in centralized and distributed computing environments

In addition, you will examine how the following services function on a network:

- File services
- Print services
- Message services
- Application services
- Database services

File Services

File services enable networked computers to share each others' files. This capability was perhaps the primary reason it became so desirable to network personal computers. Users needed to exchange files, a problem that could be solved, if inconveniently, simply by trading files on disks. More importantly, users needed to share data in common database files, something that can only be done with a network.

The working definition for this course is that file services consist of all network applications that store, retrieve, or move data files. A feature of file services is access control. File services enable users to read, write, and manage files and data, but they should also restrict users to authorized file operations so that files are not accidentally overwritten or deleted.

This section examines the following file services:

- File transfer
- File storage
- File archiving
- Data migration
- File update synchronization

File Transfer

Without a network, the options for transferring files between computers are limited. You can, of course, exchange files on floppy disks, a process that came to be called "sneaker-net" because it consisted of networking by actually running around. Or you could use communication software to dial another computer and transfer files via a modem or a direct serial connection.

Note Although Novell course materials mention this file service first, NetWare 3.*x* and 4.*x* do not excel at file transfer between workstations. It is possible to copy files directly from one server to another, but not directly from one client to another. File transfer with NetWare 3.*x* and 4.*x* is most easily achieved by storing files to be shared on the NetWare server.

It is possible to add file transfer capability to clients using products, such as Novell's Personal NetWare, which enable clients to transfer files directly using peer-to-peer networking techniques.

NetWare 3.*x* and 4.*x* do support file transfer between servers and between clients and servers, but not directly from client to client.

When users are transferring files, the need for security arises. It might be necessary to limit file transfers to authorized users using password-controlled security systems, to assign file attributes that restrict the operations that may be performed with a file, or to encrypt files so they may be read only by authorized users.

File Storage

Most networks have at least some centralized file storage. All NetWare file servers are capable of storing vast amounts of data, sharing it with users, and controlling access to a high degree of precision.

For many years, most storage consisted of *online* storage—storage on hard disks that was always accessible immediately on demand. The files that could be accessed on a server were limited to the amount of hard drive space that was available. Hard drives are fast, but the cost to store a megabyte of data is fairly high. Hard drives have another disadvantage: Generally speaking, they cannot be removed for off-site storage, exchange, or simply to build a library of files that is seldom required, but must be fairly readily available.

Almost all companies have large amounts of data that is used infrequently. There is no need to keep all of the financial reports available from the previous year, for example, but they had better be available in case of an audit.

One approach is *offline* storage, which consists of removable media that are managed manually. The most popular media used are data tapes or optical disks. Once data is written to a tape or optical disk, the disk can be removed from the server and shelved. Users who require offline data might need to know which tape or optical disk to request. Some systems provide indexes or other aids that make requesting the proper offline storage element automatic. A system operator still has to retrieve the tape or disk and mount it on the server, however.

When the slow response of offline storage is unacceptable, a near-line storage approach may be selected. *Near-line* storage employs a machine, often called a *jukebox*, to manage large numbers of tapes or optical disks automatically. The proper tape or disk is retrieved and mounted by the jukebox without the need for human intervention. With near-line storage, huge amounts of data can be available with only slight delays, but at a much lower cost than would be required to store the data on hard drives.

Data migration is a technology that automatically moves less-used data from online storage to near-line or offline storage. The criteria for moving files can depend on when the files were last used, the owner of the files, file size, or a variety of other criteria. An efficient data migration facility makes it easy for users to locate migrated files. Figure 17.1 illustrates one approach to data migration.

Figure 17.1
Data migration.

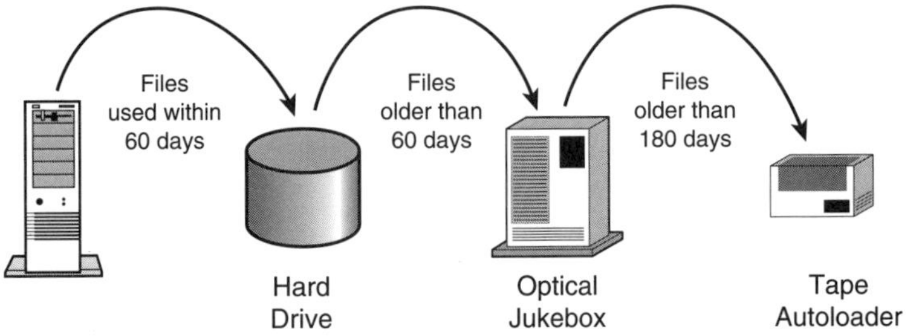

Novell supports the following standards for file storage and migration:

- *Real-Time Data Migration* (RTDM)
- *High Capacity Storage System* (HCSS) provides support for optical jukeboxes
- *Mass Storage Services* (MSS) schedules and maintains distributed hierarchical storage

File Archiving

File archiving (or backup) is basically offline storage that is primarily geared to creating duplicate copies of online files. These backup copies serve as insurance against minor or major system failures.

Networks enable file archiving to be centralized. It is possible, for example, for a single site to back up all the servers on a network. Many current backup systems also have the capability of backing up various client workstations, making it feasible to archive all files on the network to a central facility, whether the files are located on network servers or clients

File-Update Synchronization

In its simplest form, *file-update synchronization* is a means of ensuring that all users have the latest copy of a file. File-update synchronization services can manage files by monitoring the date and time stamps on files to determine which were saved most recently. By tracking the users who access the file, along with the data and time stamps, the service can update all the copies of the file with the most recent version.

File-update synchronization, however, can be considerably more involved. In a modern computing environment, it is not always feasible for all users to access all files in real time. A salesman, for example, might be carrying a notebook computer on which to enter orders. It would be impractical to dial the central LAN every time an order was to be entered, so the salesman would enter orders offline (while disconnected from the network) and store them in the laptop. That evening, he would call the central LAN, log in, and transmit all of the day's orders at one time.

During this process, files on the LAN must be updated to reflect new data in the salesman's portable computer. In addition, the salesman's PC might need some updating, with order confirmations or new pricing information, for example. The process of bringing the local and remote files into agreement is known as file-update synchronization.

File-update synchronization becomes considerably more challenging when additional users are sharing the data files simultaneously. Complex mechanisms must be in place to ensure that users do not accidentally overwrite each others' data. In some cases, the system simply flags files that have multiple, conflicting updates and requires a human to reconcile the differences.

Print Services

Network printing was the second big incentive to install LANs. Among the advantages of printing on a network are the following:

- Many users can share the same printers, which is especially useful with expensive devices, such as color printers and plotters.
- Printers can be located anywhere, not just next to a user's PC.
- Queue-based network printing is more efficient than direct printing because the workstation can get back to work as soon as a job is queued to the network.
- Modern printing services are available that enable users to send facsimile (fax) transmissions through the network to a fax server.

In this course, *print services* are defined as network applications that control and manage access to printers, network fax, and other similar devices. The print service functions discussed in this course are as follows:

- Providing multiple access
- Servicing simultaneous print requests
- Operating without distance limitations
- Managing specialized equipment types
- Providing facsimile (fax) service

Providing Multiple Access

A typical printer has a limited number of available connecting points, such as parallel or serial interface ports. In fact, many printers can have only a single active port, which means that a limited number of users' PCs can be connected to ports on a given printer. Without a network, this might mean that a printer is required for each PC.

Networks break the relationship of one PC to a port. Any user on the network can print to any network printer simply by printing through the network print service. In most organizations, this means that the number of printers can be reduced, even to a single printer for a department.

Servicing Simultaneous Print Requests

When each printer is servicing several users, print services must have an organized means of achieving two goals, as follows:

- Enabling any user to print at any time
- Printing all of the users' jobs in an orderly fashion

Print services manage these complex tasks by employing a technique known as *queuing*. A queue is a line where things wait to be serviced—theater patrons wait in a queue until a ticket clerk can service their ticket requests, for example.

Network print queuing works as shown in figure 17.2. In the figure, you can see how print jobs from several users are collected in the queue. While printing to a queue, the users' PCs are fooled into thinking that they are printing to a directly attached printer. Network printing services reroute printed data to the queue instead of to the PC's printer port.

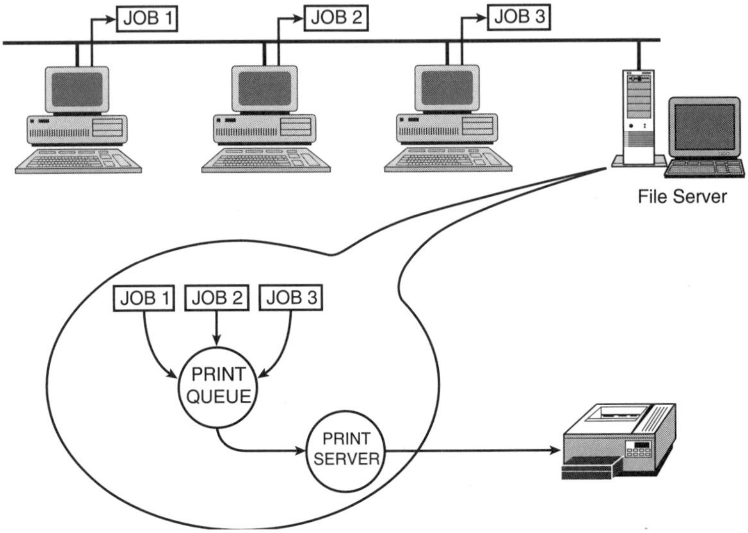

Figure 17.2
How print services use print queues.

Once the jobs are in queues, the print jobs are sent one-by-one to a printer. Even though a printer can print only one thing at a time, the appearance to the users is that they can print freely, even when the printer is busy.

Interestingly, print queuing usually services print requests more rapidly than printers that are connected directly to users' PCs. A network queue can collect print data at network speeds, which are generally much faster than printers can actually put the data on paper. After the print data is safely stored in a queue, the user can go on about his or her work knowing that the job will be printed as soon as the printer becomes available.

Operating without Distance Limitations

When a printer is connected directly to a PC, it can never be very far from the PC itself. Fifteen to fifty feet is the extreme limit of most printer cables.

Printers on a network, however, can be located anywhere. Any user can use any printer, whether the printer is nearby, in the next building, or across the country. This enables organizations to place printers where they are needed, not just where a user's PC is found.

Managing Specialized Equipment Types

Although many printer types have decreased in cost considerably, some types of printers remain so expensive that they must be shared if owning them is to make sense. Some examples are the following:

- **High-speed printers.** Do you really want to print that 1,000 page report to your personal four-page-per-minute laser?
- **Quality color.** The best color printers, such as thermal transfer, cost many thousands of dollars.
- **Large format printers and plotters.** When 8 1/2×11 is not large enough, it might be nice to have an 11×17 printer or a plotter available.

Providing Facsimile (Fax) Service

A standard fax machine uses a scanner to read the image on a printed form, render that image in electronic signals, and transmit the signals to another fax machine where the original paper image is reconstructed. Fax machines have become so popular that long lines are often encountered by users and much paper is wasted.

A new class of print service directs printed images to a device that can transmit the images as facsimiles. A network fax service enables any user to send a fax directly from a network application, such as a word processor, without needing to print the document and hand-carry it to the public fax machine. The fax service uses queuing so that many users can generate faxes simultaneously. Then the fax service takes care of transmitting the images in an orderly manner.

Moreover, a network fax server can receive faxes and route them electronically to users without generating a printout. Users can view faxes on their PCs, print them if desired, or store them as data files for future use.

Message Services

File services can pass data between users when the data comes in file form. Today, however, many new types of data are available, including audio, video, and graphics. Text data can be simple text, or it can come in exotic forms such as hypertext, which contains electronic links to other text, documents, images, sounds, or other types of data.

Message services consist of a wide variety of services that go beyond simple file sharing to store, transfer, and access text, binary, graphic, video, and audio data.

This course examines four types of message services, as follows:

- Electronic mail
- Integrated electronic mail and voice mail
- Object-oriented applications
- Workgroup applications

Electronic Mail

E-mail is the new reason to install a LAN. In fact, a LAN is an excellent platform for electronic mail because it provides reliable, high-speed service and is low in cost. E-mail is a technology for electronically transferring messages between networked computers.

E-mail systems can service anything from a local workgroup, to a corporation, to the world. By installing e-mail routing devices, mail can be transferred smoothly and efficiently among several LANs. Perhaps the most gargantuan e-mail system is found on the Internet, which enables users in dozens of countries throughout the world to exchange electronic messages more easily than mailing a paper letter.

Early text-based e-mail has given way to elaborate systems that supported embedded sound, graphics, and even video data. Modern e-mail systems also enable traveling clients to "call in" to send and receive mail.

Integrated Electronic Mail and Voice Mail

New messaging technologies are leading to closer interoperation of e-mail and voice mail systems. Voice mail can be more than a simple telephone answering system. Because voice-mail systems are themselves based on computers, they can be connected to networks, and voice data can be managed by messaging services. Eventually, this will enable various voice and e-mail systems to interoperate and freely exchange data.

A traveling user might direct that her e-mail messages should be forwarded to her voice mail. She then could call in and have the messages read electronically by a text-recognition system. Alternatively, speech recognition devices might be used to read a user's voice mail and convert it to a text-based e-mail message.

Note: Novell's Groupware division has produced a product called GroupWise that has some of these features.

Object-Oriented Applications

Objects are building blocks (consisting of abstract data types and program code) that can be combined to construct large, more complex, object-oriented applications.

Messaging services can be used as intermediaries that enable objects on the network to communicate. Messaging service applications achieve this by acting as agents for the objects. The object simply delivers data to an agent, which is then responsible for delivering the data to the destination object. This eliminates the need for objects to have the capability of communicating with all other objects on the network.

Workgroup Applications

Workgroup applications use network services to improve communication in workgroups. Two types of workgroup applications are discussed in this course: workflow management and linked-object documents.

Workflow Management Applications

Workflow management applications route electronic forms and documents among workgroup users. When reliable electronic signatures are added to the process, it becomes possible to replace numerous processes that are traditionally paper-bound. An electronic purchase order system might function like this:

1. The requester fills in an electronic form.
2. The form is routed to the requesters supervisor for an approval signature which is added electronically.
3. The signed form is routed to a budget manager who ensures that funds are available. Funding verification might even take place automatically before the form is brought to the budget manager's attention.
4. The approved purchase request is used to generate a paper purchase order that can be faxed to the vendor.

You can see how users along the way can add information to the form. The pioneering example of a workflow management application is Lotus Notes. Novell provides an automated forms management package called InForms.

Linked-Object Documents

Documents need no longer be regarded simply as files containing text. Modern documents can consist of many different types of objects, including text, graphics, sound, voice, spreadsheet data, and video. Various types of objects can be assembled to build documents.

Objects are more than just data. An object also has a degree of "intelligence" that enables it to pass messages to documents where they are integrated. Some sense of this operation can be had by experimenting with OLE in Microsoft Windows.

Directory Services

Until recently, most services on a network were operated fairly independently. Suppose that a network consisted of two file servers and an e-mail server. The network administrator would need to manage user accounts on all three servers independently. The larger the network, the more difficult network administration becomes.

Directory services can greatly simplify other network tasks as well. A *directory service* integrates all the information about objects on the network into an overall directory structure. Objects on the network can consult the directory to identify other objects and to enable objects to exchange messages. The objects themselves do not need to know the address, location, or messaging formats required to communicate—all of this information is provided by the directory service.

The directory structure hides the physical structure of the network from applications and from users. A print server is simply a part of the network—it is not a service being offered by a particular computer.

The actual directory, however, is stored in files that physically reside on one or more server. When information in the directory is duplicated on several servers, a *directory synchronization* process is needed to keep all copies of the directory up-to-date.

NetWare Directory Services is a directory service that has been integrated into NetWare 4.*x*.

Application Services

Application services enable applications to leverage the computing power and specialized capabilities of other computers on the network.

For example, business applications often must perform complex statistical calculations that are beyond the scope of most desktop PCs. Statistical software with the required capabilities might need to run on a mainframe computer or on a Unix minicomputer. The statistical package, however, can make its capabilities available to applications on users' PCs by providing an application service.

The client PC would send the request for a calculation to the statistics application server. After the results become available, they would be returned to the client. In this way, only one computer in an organization requires the expensive software license and processing power required to produce the statistics, but all client PCs can benefit.

Application services enable organizations to install servers that are specialized for specific functions. The most common application servers currently are database servers, discussed in the next section. Other application services, however, are beginning to emerge.

Application servers are an effective strategy for making a network more scaleable. New application servers can be added as new types of application needs emerge. If more power is needed for the application, only the application server needs to be upgraded. A database server, for example, might grow from a PC to a multiprocessor RISC system running Unix without requiring many or even any changes to the client PCs.

Note: Each application service does not necessarily need to be hosted on a separate computer. Along with file and print services, NetWare servers can provide e-mail, database, and communication services.

If demand for services loads the server down and hurts performance, it is easy to move an application service to its own computer. This scaleability is one of the advantages of a LAN architecture.

Database Services

Database services are the most common examples of application servers. Because database servers enable applications to be designed in separate client and server components, they are frequently called *client-server databases.*

With a client-server database, the client and server applications are designed to take advantage of specialized capabilities of the client and database systems, as follows:

- The client application manages data input from the user, generation of screen displays, some of the reporting, and generating data retrieval requests that are sent to the database server.
- The database server manages the database files; adds, deletes, and modifies records in the database; queries the database and generates the result required by the client; and transmits results back to the client. The database server can service requests for multiple clients more or less at the same time.

Database services relieve clients of most responsibilities for managing data. A modern database server is a sophisticated piece of software that can do the following:

- Provide database security
- Optimize the performance of database operations
- Determine optimal locations for storing data without requiring clients to know where the data is located
- Service large numbers of clients by reducing the time any one client is accessing the database
- Distribute data across multiple database servers

Distributed databases are becoming increasingly popular. They enable portions of databases to be stored on separate server computers, which may be in different geographic locations. This technique, known as *distributed data,* looks like a single logical database to users, but places the data users need in the most accessible location. East Coast sales data, for example, might be located on a database server in Boston, while West Coast sales data is on a server in San Diego. Special database mechanisms must be in place to keep the data in the copies of the database synchronized.

More simply, databases can simply be replicated; complete copies of the database can be stored in various locations. This provides a redundancy factor because disaster is unlikely to strike all copies at once. Additionally, database replication improves application response time because users can access the database locally rather than through a relatively slow wide area network.

As shown in figure 17.3, the most popular strategies for replication databases are the following:

- Master server updates, where a single master server receives all updates and, in turn, updates all replicas
- Locally driven updates, where any local server can receive an update and is responsible for distributing the change to other replicas

Implementing Services in Centralized and Distributed Environments

Just as networks may be organized according to centralized or distributed models, the services offered on networks can be centralized or distributed.

A *centralized* service may be located entirely on a mainframe computer or on a LAN server that uses a server-centric NOS. On networks that employ a peer-to-peer NOS, services may be centralized or may be *distributed* on two or more computers.

Note A server-centric NOS does not imply a client-server relationship between workstations and the server. When a workstation is configured to function only by requesting services from the network server, network services then are centralized, but do not adhere to a client-server model.

A client-server model implies that the client is an intelligent device that cooperates with the server to manage data.

The remainder of this section discusses issues related to implementing network services.

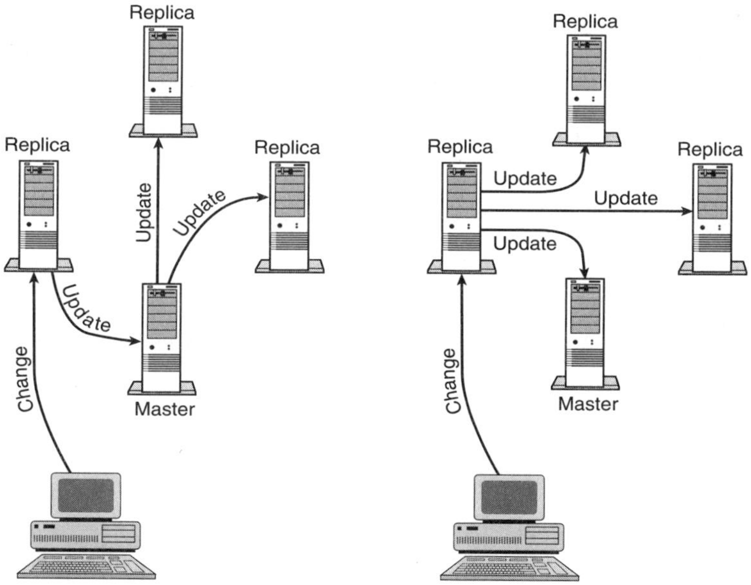

Figure 17.3
Master-driven and locally driven database replication.

Control of Resources

The centralized approach follows the adage "Put all your eggs in one basket and watch that basket very carefully." When hardware and software are concentrated, they can be maintained by experts and closely monitored with management tools. This does not necessarily mean that all devices are physically located in the same area, only that they are grouped for efficient and effective management.

The centralized approach is also logically simpler, and fewer disruptive events are likely to jeopardize data. When resources are distributed through a network, it can be difficult to isolate the causes of problems.

The most important resources that are being controlled on any network are *files* which contain the organization's critical data. In most cases, organizations will choose to store the most critical files on a centralized file server from which all users will access and share the files. This approach is called *server-centric*, *client-server*, or *dedicated server file service*. It is important to understand the advantages and disadvantages of the centralized and distributed approaches.

Centralized File Services

Dedicated file servers have the following benefits:

- Files are in a specific place where they can be reliably archived.
- Central file servers can be managed more efficiently.
- Central file servers can contain expensive, high-performance hardware that expedites file services and makes the file servers more reliable.
- The cost of specialized file server technology is shared by a large number of users.

A few issues, however, should be considered with regard to central file services, as follows:

- When all data is stored on a single server, a single point of failure exists. If the server fails, all data becomes unavailable. This makes proper design and management of the server essential.
- Because all clients are contending for file services from a single source, average file access times might be slower with a centralized file server than when files are stored on individual, local hard drives.

Centralized file services are generally chosen for organizations that want to achieve the highest levels of protection for their data files.

Distributed File Services

In a peer-to-peer environment, any computer can share its files and applications with any other computer. The sharing of services must be established for each individual computer, and each user must have the skills required to manage the networking services on his or her PC. Because services are provided by many different computers, users must become aware of which computers are providing which services. Clearly, the skills and responsibility required of users is higher than for centralized file services.

Some advantages of distributed file storage include the following:

- No single point of failure. When a computer fails, only the files stored on that computer become unavailable.
- Individuals typically experience faster access for files located on local hard drives than for files on centralized file servers.
- No specialized server hardware is required. File services can be provided with standard PCs.

Some issues related to distributed file storage include the following:

- It is more difficult to manage the file service and to protect the integrity of files. File backup is more difficult when files are distributed across many PCs.
- Individual PCs generally do not have high-reliability hardware, including uninterruptible power supplies, disk mirroring, and so forth.
- However, file services provided by peers are typically not as fast as file services provided by a central file server that is specifically designed for the purpose.
- When higher performance is required, rather than upgrading one central file server, each computer must be upgraded.

Organizations tend to choose peer-to-peer networking for two primary reasons. One is a desire to network with their current stock of PCs without the expense of a centralized server. Another is that peer-to-peer is an informal networking approach that fits the working style of many organizations.

Server Specialization

Humans often specialize so that they become very good at one type of task. This approach has benefits for network servers as well. By dedicating each server computer to providing a specific set of services, it becomes possible to carefully tailor the computer to the requirements for that service. This results in optimal performance, simpler troubleshooting, and enhanced scaleability. Server specialization implies that the network is being organized using a centralized approach.

Selecting Network Operating Systems (NOS)

When vendors develop network operating systems, designers will choose whether to use a centralized or a distributed model. Some network operating systems are clearly designed to implement LANs based on centralized models, including the following:

- Novell NetWare
- Banyan VINES
- OpenVMS
- IBM OS/2 LAN Server
- Microsoft Windows NT Server

On the other hand, many products are designed to implement peer-to-peer networking models, including the following:

- Novell Personal NetWare
- Microsoft Windows for Workgroups and Windows NT
- AppleTalk (the networking system for Apple Macintosh computers)
- Artisoft LANtastic

Many peer-to-peer products can be added to networks that are primarily managed by centralized servers. You can, for example, install Personal NetWare on networked PCs, enabling them to interact with each either using a peer-to-peer approach. The PCs, however, retain the capability of accessing the main NetWare servers to utilize centralized services.

Questions

1. Which of the following is a network operating systems?

   ○ A. OS/2

   ○ B. NetWare

   ○ C. Unix

   ○ D. MS-DOS

2. Which *two* of the following are offline file storage media?

   ☐ A. Tape data cartridges

   ☐ B. Removable disks

   ☐ C. Hard disk drives

   ☐ D. Optical jukebox

3. Which of the following is a near-line file storage media?

   ○ A. Optical jukebox

   ○ B. Hard disk drive

   ○ C. Floppy disks

   ○ D. Removable hard drives

4. Which file service is responsible for creating duplicate copies of files to protect against file damage?

   ○ A File transfer

   ○ B. File-update synchronization

   ○ C. File archiving

   ○ D. Remote file access

5. Which *two* of the following are file services?

   ☐ A. Archiving

   ☐ B. Remote file access

   ☐ C. Update synchronization

   ☐ D. Data integrity

6. What is the most important feature that enables networks to support printing from many users?

   ○ A. Networkable printers

   ○ B. Printer priorities

   ○ C. Queuing

   ○ D. Print servers

7. Which *three* types of information can be processed by a message service?

   ☐ A. Text

   ☐ B. Audio

   ☐ C. Interactive

   ☐ D. Video

8. Which *three* statements are true regarding directory services?

   ☐ A. Directory services enable users to determine physical locations of services.

   ☐ B. Directory services manage resources on multiple servers from a central point.

   ☐ C. Directory services enable users to access network services on multiple servers.

   ☐ D. The directory may be stored on more than one server.

9. Which *three* statements are true regarding application services?
   - ☐ A. Clients request services.
   - ☐ B. Application services lack scaleability.
   - ☐ C. Application servers can be optimized to specialize in a service.
   - ☐ D. Multiple services can be offered by the same server PC.

10. Which *three* statements are true regarding database services?
    - ☐ A. A database server improves data security.
    - ☐ B. All data must be located on the main database server.
    - ☐ C. Database performance may be optimized.
    - ☐ D. Database services enable multiple clients to share a database.

11. Which *three* are advantages of a centralized approach to providing file services?
    - ☐ A. Centralized files may be readily archived.
    - ☐ B. It provides the best possible performance.
    - ☐ C. Management is efficient.
    - ☐ D. The cost of high-performance, high-reliability servers can be spread across many users.

12. Which *two* are advantages of a distributed approach to providing file services?
    - ☐ A. There is no central point of failure.
    - ☐ B. It is less difficult to manage than a complex, centralized server.
    - ☐ C. It is easily scaled to improve performance for all users.
    - ☐ D. Specialized equipment is not required.

Answers

1. B
2. A, B
3. A
4. C
5. A, C
6. C
7. A, B, D
8. B, C, D
9. A, C, D
10. A, C, D
11. A, C, D
12. A, D

CHAPTER 18

The OSI Layered Protocol Model

If servers are to provide services to clients, the two parties must be able to communicate. Besides the cables that you see, numerous processes run behind the scenes to keep things running smoothly. These processes are called protocols. As Chapter 16 explains, protocols, along with services and transmission media, make up the three components of a network according to the course model.

After reading this chapter, you will be able to perform the following tasks:

- *Explain the place of rules in the communication process*
- *Describe the seven-layer OSI Reference Model*
- *Discuss how network protocols form protocol stacks*
- *Explain how protocols at given layers interact with peer layers in the protocol stacks of other devices*

Rules and the Communication Process

Networks rely on a great many rules to manage information interchange. Some of the problems that must be solved include the following:

- The procedures used to initiate and end an interaction
- The signals used to represent data on the media
- How to direct a message to the intended destination
- Procedures used to control the rate of data flow
- Methods that enable different computer types to communicate
- How to ensure that messages are received correctly

The process of enabling computers to communicate is an extremely complex one, often too complex to solve all at once with just one set of rules. Instead, the industry has chosen to solve parts of the problem so that the solutions can be put together like pieces of a puzzle. This puzzle comes together a different way each time to build a complete communication approach for any given situation.

The OSI Reference Model

To best understand how the pieces fit together, it is useful to have a model in mind. The most commonly used model is the *Open Systems Interconnection* (OSI) Reference Model, defined by the *International Organization for Standardization* (ISO).

The OSI model organizes communication protocols into seven layers. Each layer addresses a narrow portion of the communication process. The layers of the OSI model are shown in figure 18.1.

Each of these layers are examined in detail, starting with Chapter 21, "OSI Physical Layer Concepts." This chapter, however, introduces only the general characteristics of the model.

Layer 1, the physical layer, consists of protocols that control communication on the network media. Layer 7, the application layer, interfaces the network services with the applications in use on the computer. Between are five other layers that perform intermediate communication tasks.

Note You need to know the names and order of the seven layers. Two phrases follow that will help you remember the first letters of the layers:

All **P**eople **S**eem **T**o **N**eed **D**ata **P**rocessing

Please **D**o **N**ot **T**hrow **S**ausage **P**izza **A**way

Choose one, depending on whether you are most comfortable working from the top of the model down or from the bottom up.

Note The network media itself is not part of the model, which only deals with protocols. Protocols represent software constructions, whereas cabling is hardware. Networking cannot exist, however, without communication media. Sometimes, you will hear the medium referred to informally as "Layer Zero" of the OSI model.

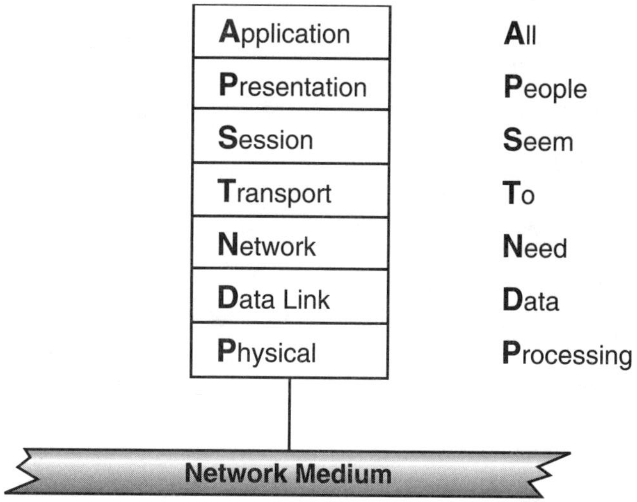

Figure 18.1
Layers of the OSI Model.

Figure 18.1 illustrates the origin of the term "protocol stack." The OSI model breaks the communication process into layers. At each layer, different protocols are selected to solve the needs of a particular communication environment. These protocols are "stacked" one on top of the other until the communication capability is complete. A protocol stack, then, is a set of compatible, layered protocols that have been implemented on a particular computer. Two common examples of protocol stacks are IPX/SPX, the standard NetWare protocols, and TCP/IP, the most widely implemented protocol stack in the computer industry.

A *protocol stack* is a hierarchical set of protocols that coordinate to perform a complete communication process. Each layer makes use of the services provided by the layer below it; and each layer provides services to the layer above it. Formally, layer N services layer $N+1$, and layer N is serviced by layer $N-1$.

Two computers must be running the same protocol stacks if they are to communicate; each layer in one computer's protocol stack must interact with a corresponding layer in the other computer's protocol stack (see fig. 18.2). The figure originates the path of a message starting in the transport layer. The message travels down the protocol stack, through the network medium, and up the protocol stack of the receiving computer. If the transport layer in the receiving computer understands the protocols used in the transport layer that originated the message, the message can be delivered.

Provided the protocol stacks on two computers are compatible, it is possible for different computer types to communicate. TCP/IP, for example, is available for almost any computer and operation system currently being made. If a Macintosh and a Unix workstation are both running TCP/IP, it is possible for the Mac to access files on the Unix workstation.

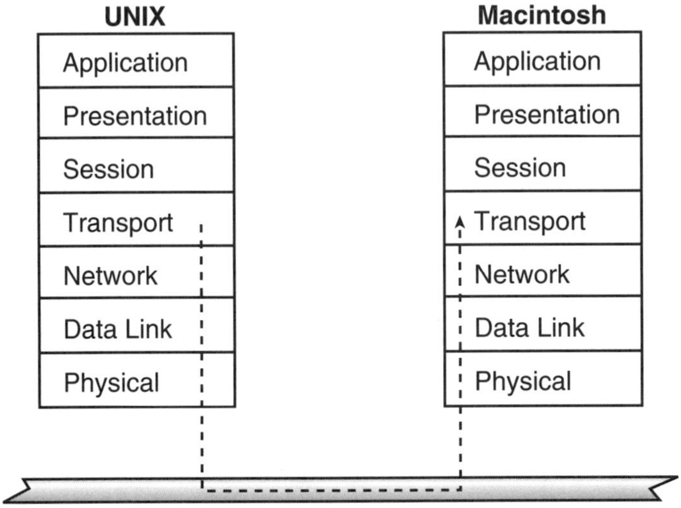

Figure 18.2
Peer communication between protocol stacks.

How Peer Layers Communicate

To communicate with its peer layer in another computer, each protocol layer adds its personal information to the message being sent. This information takes the form of a header added to the beginning of the message (see fig. 18.3).

Headers are added as the message is prepared for transmission, and headers are removed (*stripped*) by the receiver after the information in the header has been utilized.

Notice that the data for each layer consists of the header and data of the next higher layer. Because the data format is different at each layer, different

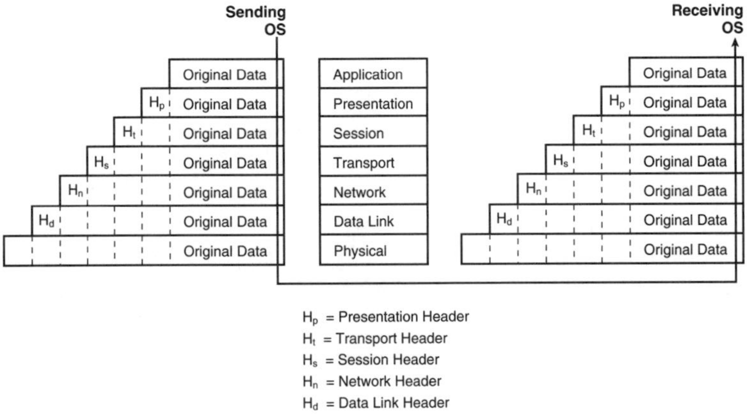

Figure 18.3
Adding headers to messages.

terms are commonly used to name the data package at each level. Table 18.1 summarizes these terms by layer.

Note The physical layer does not append a header because it is concerned with sending and receiving information on the individual bit level. The bits are assembled into longer message units in the data link layer.

Table 18.1
Data package names and the OSI reference model.

Layer	*Data Package Names*
Application	Message (and packet)
Presentation	Packet
Session	Packet
Transport	Datagram, segment (and packet)
Network	Datagram (and packet)
Data Link	Frame (and packet)
Physical	Bit (and packet)

As you can see in the table, *packet* is a generic term applicable to all layers. It is the term, therefore, to be used for non-layer-specific discussion in later chapters.

Questions

1. The layers of the OSI model (in order) are included in which of the following choices?

   ○ A. Physical, data link, network, transport, system, presentation, application

   ○ B. Physical, data link, network, transport, session, presentation, application

   ○ C. Physical, data link, network, transform, session, presentation, application

   ○ D. Presentation, data link, network, transport, session, physical, application

2. In the OSI model, what is the relationship of a layer (*N*) to the layer above it (layer *N*+1)?

   ○ A. Layer *N* provides services for layer *N*+1.

   ○ B. Layer *N*+1 adds a header to information received from layer *N*.

   ○ C. Layer *N* utilizes services provided by layer *N*+1.

   ○ D. Layer *N* has no effect on layer *N*+1.

3. Which *three* of the following statements regarding protocol stacks are true?

   ☐ A. A given protocol stack can run on only one computer type.

   ☐ B. Layers add headers to packets received from higher layers in the protocol stack.

   ☐ C. A protocol stack is a hierarchical set of protocols.

   ☐ D. Each layer provides services for the next highest layer.

4. Which *two* of the following terms are used to describe data units at the network layer?

   ☐ A. Datagram

   ☐ B. Message

   ☐ C. Frame

   ☐ D. Packet

5. Which *two* of the following terms are used to describe data units at the data link layer?

   ☐ A. Datagram

   ☐ B. Message

   ☐ C. Frame

   ☐ D. Packet

Answers

1. B
2. A
3. B, C, D
4. A, D
5. C, D

CHAPTER 19

Transmission Media

Network clients must have a channel through which they can communicate with network servers. The channel that carries messages between clients and servers is called the transmission media.

The media for local area networks usually consist of one of the following:

- *Cable (coaxial, twisted-pair, or fiber-optic)*
- *Wireless (radio, infrared, microwave)*

With wide area networks, you don't deal with media so much as you deal with services. You buy wide area network services from a commercial provider or connect to an existing network such as the Internet. In its course through a wide area network, a packet may pass through many types of media, but you as a network administrator need not be concerned with the media being employed. Two networks that provide wide area network support are examined in this chapter:

- The public telephone network
- The Internet

In this chapter, you will learn about the following:

- What transmission media are
- Common transmission media and their characteristics
- Public network services that provide wide-area networking support

Network Transmission Media

Transmission media make it possible for the electronic signals in one computer to be transmitted to another computer. These electronic signals express data values in the form of binary (on-off) impulses. The signals are transmitted through the network using a combination of electronic devices (network boards, hubs, and so on) and transmission media (cables, radio, and so on) until they reach the desired destination computer where they again are converted into data signals inside the receiving computer.

All signals transmitted between computers consist of some form of *electromagnetic* (EM) waveform, ranging from radio frequencies, up through microwave, and infrared light. Depending on the frequency of the EM waveform being used, different media are used to transmit the signals. Figure 19.1 illustrates the range of electromagnetic waveforms, known as the *electromagnetic spectrum*, along with their associated frequencies.

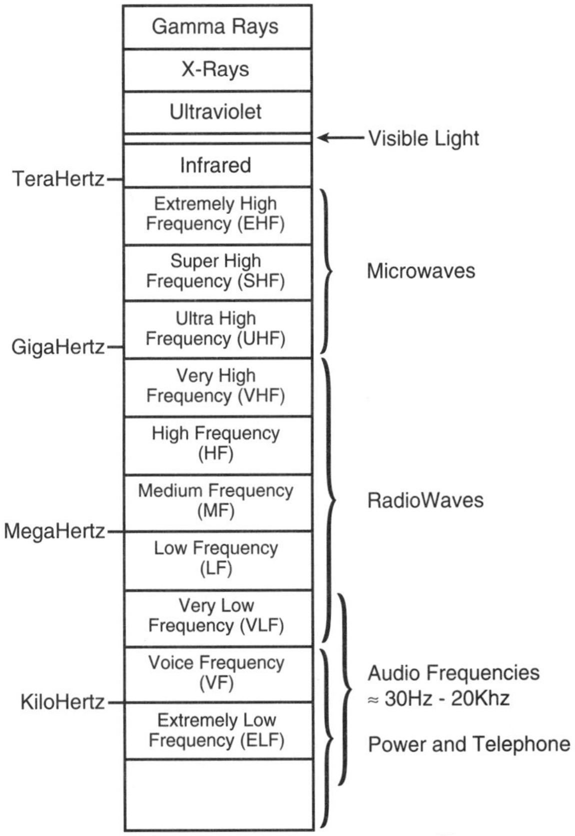

Figure 19.1
The electromagnetic spectrum.

Radio frequency waves are often used for LAN signaling. Radio frequencies can be transmitted using electrical cables (twisted-pair or coaxial) or using radio broadcast transmission.

Microwave transmissions can be used for tightly focused transmissions between two points. Microwaves are used to communicate between Earth stations and satellites. They also are used for line-of-sight transmissions on the Earth's surface. Microwaves also can be used in low-power forms to broadcast signals from a transmitter to many receivers. Cellular phone networks are examples of systems that use low-power microwave signals to broadcast signals.

Infrared light is ideal for many types of network communications. Infrared light can be transmitted relatively short distances and can either be beamed between two points or broadcast from one point to many receivers. Infrared and higher frequencies of light also can be transmitted through fiber-optic cables.

The next sections examine examples of network transmission media, and describe the advantages and disadvantages of each media type.

Characteristics of Transmission Media

Each media type has special characteristics that suit it to a specific type of service. You should be familiar with these characteristics:

- Cost
- Installation requirements
- Bandwidth
- Attenuation
- Immunity from electromagnetic interference

The last three characteristics require some explanation.

Bandwidth

Bandwidth is the measure of the capacity of a medium to transmit data. A medium that has a high capacity has a high bandwidth. A medium that has limited capacity has a low bandwidth. The term bandwidth comes about because it is a measure of the range of frequencies that the medium can carry.

Bandwidth can be understood through an analogy to water hoses. A half-inch garden hose that can carry waterflow from a trickle up to 2 gallons per minute might be said to have a bandwidth of 2 gallons per minute. A 4-inch firehose, however, might have a bandwidth of over 100 gallons per minute.

Transmission media have a lower frequency limit and an upper frequency limit. Frequencies are measured in *Hertz* (Hz), or cycles per second. The bandwidth of a voice telephone line is 400–4,000 Hz, meaning that the line can transmit signals with frequencies ranging from 400–4,000 cycles per second.

Data transmission rates frequently are stated in terms of the bits that can be transmitted per second. An Ethernet LAN theoretically can transmit 10 million bits per second and has a bandwidth of 10 megabits per second (Mbps).

The bandwidth that a cable can accommodate is determined in part by the cable's length. A short cable can generally accommodate greater bandwidth than a longer cable. This is one reason all cable designs specify maximum lengths for cable runs. Beyond those limits, the highest frequency signals can deteriorate and errors might be introduced into data signals.

Attenuation

Attenuation is a measure of how much a signal weakens as it travels through a medium. This course does not discuss attenuation in formal terms, but with regard to the impact of attenuation on performance.

Attenuation is a second reason cable designs must specify limits in the lengths of cable runs. When signal strength falls below certain limits, it might be difficult for the electronic equipment that receives the signal to isolate the original signal from the noise that is present in all electronic transmissions. The effect is exactly like trying to tune in distant radio signals. Even if you are able to lock into the signal on your radio, the sound produced generally contains more noise than the sound produced for a local radio station.

Electromagnetic Interference

Electromagnetic interference (EMI) consists of outside electromagnetic noise that distorts the signal in a medium. When you listen to an AM radio, you often hear noise caused by nearby motors or lightning. This is an example of EMI. Some network media are more susceptible to EMI than others.

Cable Media

Three types of cable media are discussed in this section:

- Coaxial
- Twisted-pair
- Fiber-optic

Coaxial Cable

Coaxial cables were the first cable types used in LANs. Shown in figure 19.2, coaxial cable gets its name because two conductors share a common axis; the cable is most frequently referred to as *coax*. The components of a coaxial cable are as follows:

- A center conductor, which is usually solid copper wire (although stranded wire can be used)
- An outer conductor that forms a tube surrounding the center conductor. This conductor can consist of braided wires, metallic foil, or both. Because this conductor also protects the inner conductor from EMI, it is most frequently called the *shield*.
- An insulation layer that also keeps the outer conductor spaced evenly from the inner conductor
- A plastic encasement (jacket) that protects the cable from damage

Types of Coaxial Cable

All coax cables have a characteristic measurement called *impedance*, which is given in ohms. It is important to use a cable with the proper impedance in any given situation. Here are some types of coaxial cable frequently used on LANs:

- RG-8 and RG-ll, 50-ohm cables used with thick Ethernet
- RG-58, a 50-ohm cable used with thin Ethernet
- RG-59, a 75-ohm cable used for cable TV
- RG-62, a 93-ohm cable used with ARCnet

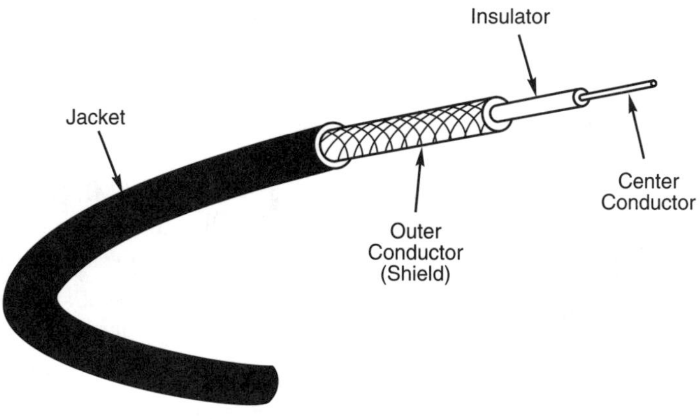

Figure 19.2
The structure of coaxial cable.

Characteristics

You will want to be familiar with the following characteristics of coaxial cable.

Installation

Coaxial cable typically is installed in two configurations: daisy-chained from device to device (Ethernet) and stars (ARCnet). You will learn the details of Ethernet cabling in Chapter 20, "Transmission Media Connections."

The Ethernet cabling shown in figure 19.3 is an example of thin Ethernet, which uses RG-58 type cable. Devices connect to the cable by means of T-connectors. Cables are used to provide connections between T-connectors. One characteristic of this type of cabling is that the ends of the cable run

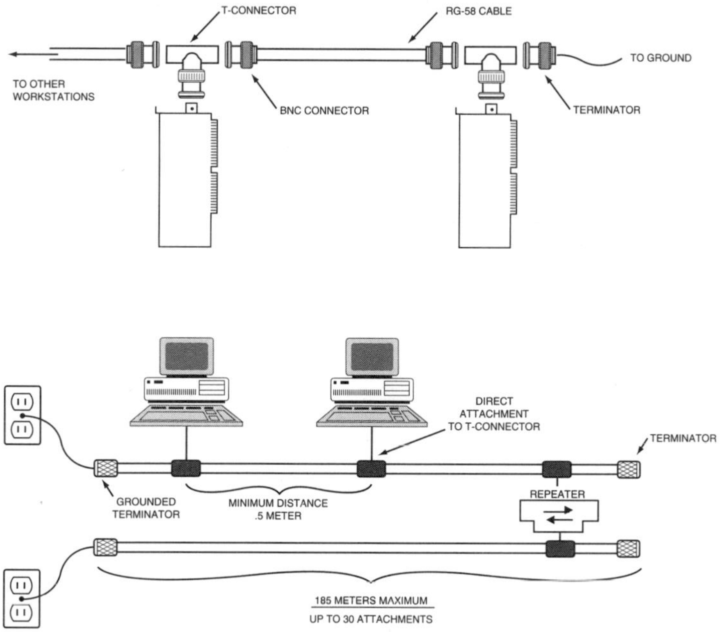

Figure 19.3
Coaxial cable wiring configurations.

must be terminated by a special connector called a terminator. The *terminator* contains a resistor that is matched to the characteristics of the cable. The resistor prevents signals that reach the end of the cable from bouncing back and causing interference.

Coaxial cable is reasonably easy to install. The cable is robust and difficult to damage, and connectors can be installed with inexpensive tools and a bit of practice. The device-to-device cabling approach can be difficult to reconfigure, however, when new devices cannot be installed near an existing cabling path.

Cost

The coaxial cable used for thin Ethernet falls at the low end of the cost spectrum, whereas thick Ethernet is among the more costly options. Detailed cost comparisons are made after the remaining cable types have been introduced.

Bandwidth

LANs that employ coaxial cable typically have a bandwidth ranging from 2.5 Mbps (ARCnet) to 10 Mbps (Ethernet). Thicker coaxial cables have higher bandwidth, and the potential bandwidth of coax is much higher than 10 Mbps. This potential, however, is not taken advantage of by current LAN technologies.

Attenuation

All media suffer from attenuation, but coax has better attenuation characteristics than other copper cables such as twisted-pair. LANs employing coaxial cable are limited to a few thousand meters in length.

EMI Characteristics

All copper media are sensitive to EMI, although the shield in coax makes the cable fairly resistant to EMI. Coaxial cables, however, do radiate a portion of their signal, and this radiated signal can be detected by electronic eavesdropping equipment.

Twisted-Pair Cables

Twisted-pair cable has become the dominant cable type for all new network designs that employ copper cable. Several reasons account for the popularity of twisted-pair cable, with the most significant being low cost. Twisted-pair cable is inexpensive to install and has the lowest cost-per-foot of any cable type.

Figure 19.4 shows a basic twisted-pair cable, which consists of two strands of copper wire twisted together. The twists are an important part of the characteristics of twisted-pair cable. Twisting reduces the sensitivity of the cable to EMI and also reduces the tendency of the cable to radiate radio frequency noise that interferes with nearby cables and electronic components. The radiated signals from the twisted wires tend to cancel each other out. (Antennas, which are purposely designed to radiate radio-frequency signals, consist of parallel, not twisted, wires.)

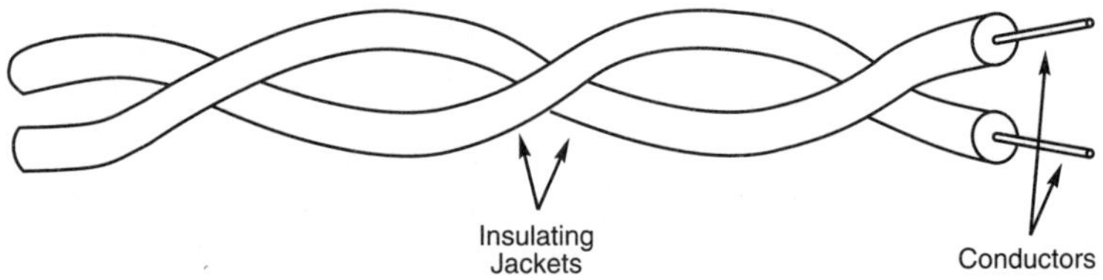

Figure 19.4
A twisted-pair cable.

Twisting also controls the tendency of the wires in the pair to cause EMI in each other. Whenever two wires are in close proximity, there is a tendency for the signals in each wire to produce noise in the other. Noise caused in this way is called *crosstalk.* Twisting the wires in the pair reduces crosstalk in much the same way that twisting reduces the tendency of the wires to radiate EMI.

Two types of twisted-pair cable are used in LANs: shielded and unshielded.

Shielded Twisted-Pair (STP) Cable

The first twisted-pair cables used in LANs were shielded twisted-pair, similar to the cable shown in figure 19.5, which shows IBM Type 1 cable, the first cable type used with IBM Token Ring. Early LAN designers employed shielded twisted-pair cable because the shield further reduces the tendency of the cable to radiate EMI and reduces the cable's sensitivity to outside interference.

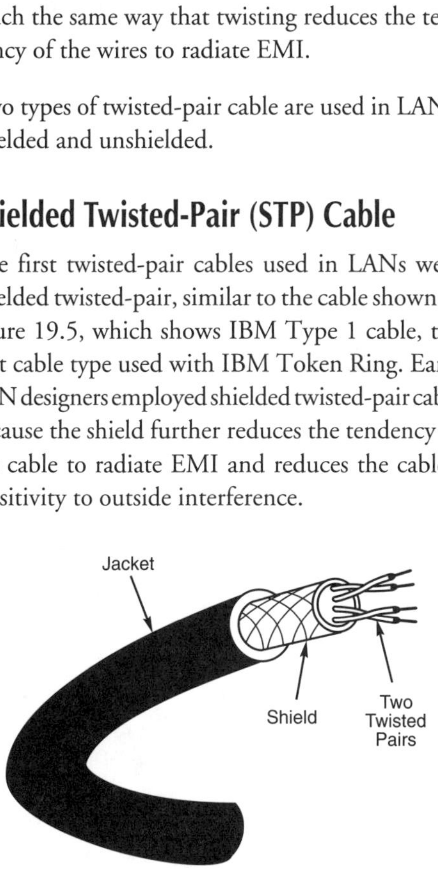

Figure 19.5
A shielded twisted-pair cable.

Coaxial and STP cables use shields for the same purpose. The *shield* is connected to the ground portion of the electronic device to which the cable is connected. A *ground* is a portion of the device, serves as an electrical reference point, and usually is literally connected to a metal stake that is driven into the ground. A properly grounded shield tends to prevent signals from getting into or out of the cable.

The IBM Type 1 cable shown in figure 19.5 includes two twisted-pairs of wire within a single shield. Various types of STP cable exist, with some shielding each pair individually and others shielding several pairs. The exact configuration used is chosen by the engineers who design the cabling system. IBM designates several twisted-pair cable types for use with their Token-Ring network design, and each cable type is appropriate for a given kind of installation. A completely different type of STP is the standard cable for Apple's AppleTalk network.

Because so many different types of STP cable exist, it is difficult to state precise characteristics. Here, however, are some general guidelines.

Cost

STP cable costs more than thin coaxial or unshielded twisted-pair cables. STP is less costly, however, than thick coax or fiber-optic cable.

Installation

Different network types have different installation requirements. One major difference is the connector used. Apple LocalTalk connectors generally must be soldered during installation, requiring some practice and skill on the part of the installer. IBM Token Ring uses a so-called *unisex* data connector (the connectors are both male and female), which can be installed with common tools such as a knife, wire stripper, and a large pliers.

In many cases, installation can be greatly simplified by using pre-wired cables. You need to learn to install the required connectors, however, whenever your installation requires use of bulk cable.

> **Note** Most connectors require two connector types to complete a connection. The traditional designation for connector types is male and female. The male connector is the connector with pins, and the female connector has receptacles into which the pins insert. In a standard AC wall outlet, the outlet itself is female and the plug on the line cord is male.
>
> These designations originated when electrical installation was a male province, and the terms male and female gradually are being replaced. A commonly used alternative is "pins and sockets."
>
> The IBM data connector is called a unisex connector because the connector has both pins and sockets. Any IBM data connector can connect to any other IBM data connector.

STP cable tends to be rather bulky. IBM Type 1 cable is approximately $1^{1}/_{2}$ inches in diameter. Therefore, it can take little time to fill up cable paths with STP cables.

Capacity

STP cable has a theoretical capacity of 500 Mbps, although few implementations exceed 155 Mbps with 100-meter cable runs. The most common data rate for STP cable is 16 Mbps, the top data rate for token-ring networks.

Attenuation

All varieties of twisted-pair cable have attenuation characteristics that limit the length of cable runs to a few hundred meters, although a 100-meter limit is most common.

EMI Characteristics

The shield in STP cable results in good EMI characteristics for copper cable, comparable to the EMI characteristics of coaxial cable. This is one reason STP might be preferred to unshielded twisted-pair cable in some situations. Like all copper cables, STP is sensitive to interference and is vulnerable to electronic eavesdropping.

Unshielded Twisted-Pair Cable

Unshielded twisted-pair (UTP) cable does not incorporate a braided shield. The characteristics of UTP are similar in many ways to STP, differing primarily in attenuation and EMI characteristics. As shown in figure 19.6, several twisted pairs can be bundled together in a single cable. These pairs are typically color coded to distinguish the pairs.

Figure 19.6
A multi-pair UTP cable.

UTP cable is a latecomer to high-performance LANs because engineers only recently solved the problems of managing radiated noise and susceptibility to EMI. Now, however, a clear trend toward UTP is in operation, and all new copper-based cabling schemes are based on use of UTP.

UTP cable is available in the following five grades or categories:

- Categories 1 and 2 are voice-grade cables, suitable only for voice and for low data rates (below 4 Mbps). At one time, Category 1 was the standard voice-grade cable for telephone systems. The growing need for data-ready cabling systems, however, has caused Category 1 and 2 cable to be supplanted by Category 3 for new installations.

- Category 3 is the lowest data grade cable and is generally suited for data rates up to 16 Mbps. Some innovative schemes, however, make it possible to support data rates up to 100 Mbps with Category 3 cable. Category 3 is now the standard cable used for most telephone installations.
- Category 4 is a data-grade cable suitable for data rates up to 20 Mbps.
- Category 5 is a data-grade cable suitable for data rates up to 100 Mbps. Most new cabling systems for 100 Mbps data rates are designed around Category 5 cable.

Note In a UTP cabling system, the cable is only one component. All connecting devices also are graded, and the overall cabling system only supports the data rates permitted by the lowest grade of component in the system. In other words, if you require a Category 5 cabling system, it is essential to ensure that all connectors and connecting devices are designed for Category 5 operation.

Category 5 cable also requires more stringent installation procedures than the lower cable categories. Installers of Category 5 cable require special training and skills to understand these more rigorous requirements.

UTP cable offers an excellent balance of cost and performance characteristics.

Cost

UTP cable has the lowest cost of any cable type, although properly installed Category 5 tends to be fairly high in cost. In some cases, existing cable in buildings can be used for LANs, although it is important to verify the category of the cable and also to know the length of the cable in the walls. Distance limits for voice cabling are much less stringent than for data-grade cabling.

Installation

UTP cable is easy to install. Some specialized equipment might be required, but the equipment is low in cost and can be mastered with a bit of practice. Properly designed UTP cabling systems easily can be reconfigured to meet changing requirements.

As noted earlier, however, Category 5 cable has stricter installation requirements than lower categories of UTP. Special training is recommended.

Capacity

The data rates possible with UTP have pushed upward from 1 Mbps, past 4 and 16 Mbps, and to the point where 100 Mbps data rates are now common. In fact, all new copper-based standards provide at least the option of using UTP cable.

Attenuation

UTP cable shares similar attenuation characteristics with other copper cables. UTP cable runs are limited to a few hundred meters, with 100 meters the most frequent limit.

EMI Characteristics

Lacking a shield, UTP cable is more sensitive to EMI than coaxial or STP cables. The latest technologies make it possible to use UTP in the vast majority of situations, provided reasonable care is taken to avoid electrically noisy devices such as motors and fluorescent lights. Nevertheless, UTP might not be suitable for noisy environments such as factories. Crosstalk between nearby unshielded pairs limits the maximum length of cable runs.

Fiber-Optic Cable

In almost every way, fiber-optic cable is the ideal cable for data transmission. Bandwidths are extremely high, there are no problems with EMI, cables are durable, and cable runs can be several kilometers long. The two disadvantages of fiber optic are cost and more difficult installation.

Figure 19.7 shows two types of fiber-optic cable. In each case, the center conductor is a fiber consisting of highly refined glass or plastic designed to transmit light signals with little loss. The fiber is coated with a cladding that reflects signals back into the fiber to reduce signal loss. A plastic sheath protects the fiber.

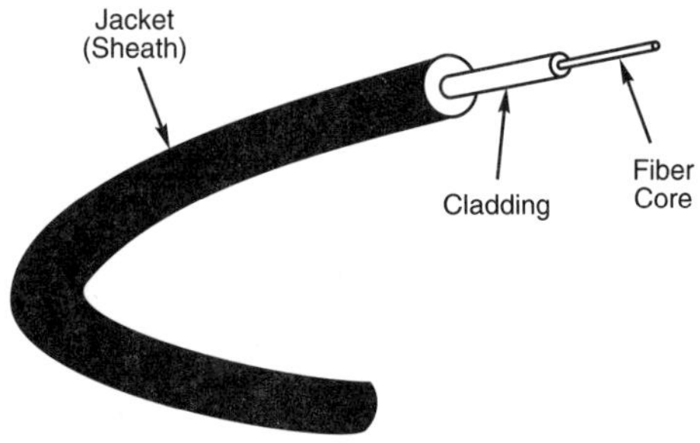

Figure 19.7
A fiber-optic cable.

Loose and tight cable configurations are available. Loose configurations incorporate a space between the fiber sheath and the outer plastic encasement; this space is filled with a gel or other material. Tight configurations include strength wires between the conductor and the outer plastic encasement. In both cases, it is the job of the plastic encasement to supply the strength of the cable. The gel layer or strength wires protect the delicate fiber from mechanical damage.

Although the figure shows cables with single fibers, it is common to bundle multiple fibers into cables. A small-diameter cable can incorporate an astonishing number of optical fibers, making fiber-optic cable ideal for cabling when cable paths are clogged.

Optical fiber cables do not transmit electrical signals. Instead, the data signals must be converted to light signals. Light sources include lasers and *light-emitting diodes* (LEDs). LEDs are inexpensive, but produce a fairly poor quality of light that is suitable for less-stringent applications.

A laser is a light source that produces an especially pure light that is monochromatic (one color) and coherent (all waves are parallel). The most commonly used source of laser light in LAN devices is called an *injection laser diode* (ILD). The purity of laser light makes lasers ideally suited to data transmissions because long distances and high bandwidths are possible. Lasers, however, are expensive light sources and are used only when their special characteristics are required.

The end of the cable that receives the light signal must convert the signal back to an electrical form. Several types of solid-state components can perform this service. The most common are types of photodiodes.

Optical fibers have several characteristics:

- **Mode.** Single-mode cables support a single light path and are commonly used with lasers. Multi-mode cables support multiple light paths and are best suited to lower-quality light sources such as LEDs. At a much higher cost, single-mode cables with laser light sources support the longest cable runs and the greatest bandwidth. Figure 19.8 illustrates the difference between single- and multi-mode cables.

- **Core diameter.** The cores of fiber-optic cables are small enough to be measured in microns (millionths of a meter). The symbol for micron is µ.
- **Cladding diameter.** This dimension also is given in microns.

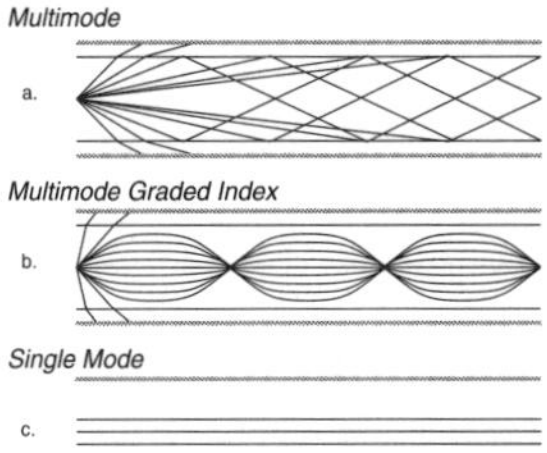

Figure 19.8
Modes of fiber-optic cables.

The following are common types of fiber-optic cables:

- 8.3 micron core/125 micron cladding/ single-mode
- 62.5 micron core/125 micron cladding/multimode
- 50 micron core/125 micron cladding/ multimode
- 100 micron core/140 micron cladding/ multimode

Note the small core diameters of these cables. One of the significant difficulties of installing fiber-optic cable arises when two cables must be joined. The small cores of the two cables must be lined up with extreme precision to prevent excessive signal loss.

Fiber-Optic Characteristics

Like all cable types, fiber-optic cables constitute a blend of advantages and disadvantages.

Cost

The cost of the cable and connectors has fallen significantly in recent years. The electronic devices required are significantly more expensive than comparable devices for copper cable. An Ethernet network board for UTP cable now can cost less than $100. Network boards for use with fiber-optic cables, however, frequently cost in excess of $1,000 each. Fiber-optic cable is also the most expensive cable type to install.

Installation

Greater skill is required to install fiber-optic cable than is needed for most copper cables. Improved tools and techniques, however, have reduced the training required. Still, greater care is required because fiber-optic cables must be treated fairly gently during installation. Every cable has a minimum bend radius, for example, and fibers are damaged if the cables are bent too sharply. It also is important not to stretch the cable during installation.

Capacity

Bandwidths for fiber-optic cables can range as high as 2 Gbps (billion bps). Fiber-optic cable can support high data rates even with long cable runs. UTP cable runs are limited to less than 100 meters with 100 Mbps data rates. Fiber-optic cables can transmit 100 Mbps signals for several kilometers.

Attenuation

Attenuation in fiber-optic cables is much lower than in copper cables. Fiber-optic cables are capable of carrying signals for several kilometers.

EMI Characteristics

Because fiber-optic cables do not use electrical signals to transmit data, they are totally immune to electromagnetic interference. They also are immune to a variety of electrical effects that must be taken into account when designing copper cabling systems.

Note: When electrical cables are connected between two buildings, a common problem to be dealt with is differences between the ground potentials (voltages) between the two buildings. When a difference exists (as it frequently does), current flows through the grounding conductor of the cable, even though the ground is supposed to be electrically neutral and no current should flow. When current flows through the ground conductor of a cable, the condition is called a *ground loop*. The results of ground loops are electrical instability and various types of anomalies.

Because fiber-optic cable is immune to electrical effects, the best way to connect networks in different buildings is by putting in a fiber-optic link segment.

Because they are not electrical in nature, the signals in fiber-optic cables cannot be detected by electronic eavesdropping equipment that detect electromagnetic radiation. Fiber-optic cable is, therefore, the perfect choice for high-security networks.

Summary of Cable Characteristics

Table 19.1 summarizes the characteristics of the four cable types discussed in this chapter.

Table 19.1
Comparison of Cable Media

Cable Type	*Cost*	*Installation*	*Capacity*	*Attenuation*	*EMI*
Coaxial	Medium < Cat 5 UTP > Cat 3 UTP Thin<STP Thick>STP <Fiber	Inexpensive/ Easy. May be difficult to reconfigure	10 Mbps typical	Less than STP or UTP. Limited to range of few kilometers	Less sensi- tive than UTP, but still subject to EMI and eavesdropping
Shielded Twisted-Pair	Medium >UTP =Thin coax <Thick coax <Fiber	Moderate cost/ Fairly easy. More difficult than UTP and coax	16 Mbps typical. Up to 500 Mbps	Limits range to several hundred meters	Less sensi- tive than UTP, but still subject to EMI and eavesdropping
Unshielded Twisted-Pair	Lowest	Inexpensive/ Easy	1-100 Mbps with 100- meter runs	Limits range to several hundred meters	Most sensi- tive to EMI and eaves- dropping
Fiber-Optic	Highest	Expensive/ Difficult	10 Mbps to 2 Gbps. 100 Mbps typical	Lowest. Range of 10s of kilometers	Insensitive to EMI and eavesdropping

When comparing cabling types, it's important to remember that the characteristics you observe are highly dependent on the implementations. At one time, it was argued that UTP cable would never reliably support data rates above 4 Mbps, but 100 Mbps data rates are now commonplace with UTP.

Some comparisons are fairly involved. Although fiber-optic cable is costly on a per-foot basis, it is possible to construct a fiber-optic cable that is many kilometers in length. To build a copper cable that length, you would need to install repeaters at several points along the cable to amplify the signal. These repeaters could easily exceed the cost of a fiber-optic cable run.

Wireless Media

Cable lends itself to fixed installations and moderate distances. When end points are widely separated or when they are moving, it might be desirable to investigate wireless media. Several wireless media are available, of which the following will be considered:

- Radio
- Microwave
- Infrared

Radio

The radio portion of the electromagnetic spectrum extends from 10 KHz to 1 GHz. Within this range are numerous bands, or ranges of frequencies that are designated for specific purposes. The following are frequency bands with which you are probably familiar:

- Shortwave
- VHF (Very High Frequency): television and FM radio
- UHF (Ultra High Frequency): television

Within the United States, the use of radio frequencies is controlled by the Federal Communications Commission (FCC). The majority of frequency allocations are licensed; an organization is granted an exclusive license to use a particular range of frequencies within a certain limited geographic area. Thus, there only can be one television Channel 5 within an area. Channel 5 allocations are spread out so that they do not interfere with each other. A licensed frequency allocation guarantees the license owner a clear, low-interference communication channel.

A few frequency ranges are unlicensed, meaning that they can be used freely for the purpose specified for those frequencies. The FCC has designated three unlicensed frequency bands: 902–928 MHz, 2.4 GHz, and 5.72–5.85 GHz. The 902 MHz range has been available the longest and has been used for everything from cordless telephones to model airplane remote control. Because the 902 MHz range is quite crowded, many vendors are pushing development of devices for the less crowded 2.4 GHz band. Equipment for the 5.72 GHz remains expensive and is used infrequently.

Use of an unlicensed frequency is done at the user's risk, and a clear communication channel is not guaranteed. Equipment used in these frequency bands, however, must operate at a regulated power level to limit range and reduce the potential for interference.

Radio transmissions can be omnidirectional or directional. A radio station typically transmits an omnidirectional (all-directional) signal that can be received by all radios within the broadcast area. In some circumstances, a directional transmission might be used to direct all of the transmission power toward a specific reception point.

Various types of antennas are used depending on the desired transmission and reception characteristics. Several antenna types are shown in figure 19.9.

- Broadcast towers generally are omnidirectional, although the specific radiation pattern can be adjusted to match the FCC restrictions for a particular licensee.
- Dipole antennas receive a fairly broad range of frequencies and are moderately directional.
- A random-length wire can be used for transmission or reception. Random-length means that the antenna length is not specifically chosen for the frequency being transmitted or received. The antenna on a typical AM/FM radio is a random-length wire.
- A beam antenna uses multiple elements to tune the antenna for a specific frequency range and directiveness. A common antenna design is called the Yagi. A beam antenna is used to produce a fairly focused beam that can be aimed at a specific reception point (although the effect is not completely directional, and some signal leaks in all directions).

Characteristics of Radio Transmission

The characteristics of radio transmissions change dramatically with frequency. Low-frequency radio supports limited data rates, but has a significant advantage in that it can frequently communicate past the horizon. Shortwave operators are familiar with this phenomenon, and it is common for them to be able to monitor transmissions from the other side of the Earth.

As frequency increases, transmissions become increasingly line-of-sight. AM radio broadcast frequencies range from the KHz to the low MHz range. You might have had the experience of picking up an AM radio station that is several states away, particularly late at night. This can occur because AM radio transmissions can bounce off some phenomena in the atmosphere. Some transmissions can bounce a considerable distance.

FM transmissions, however, seldom can be received past the horizon. You will seldom clearly receive an FM broadcast beyond a range of 100 miles. This is partly a function of power, but the primary cause of the range limitation is the inability of FM frequencies to go beyond the horizon.

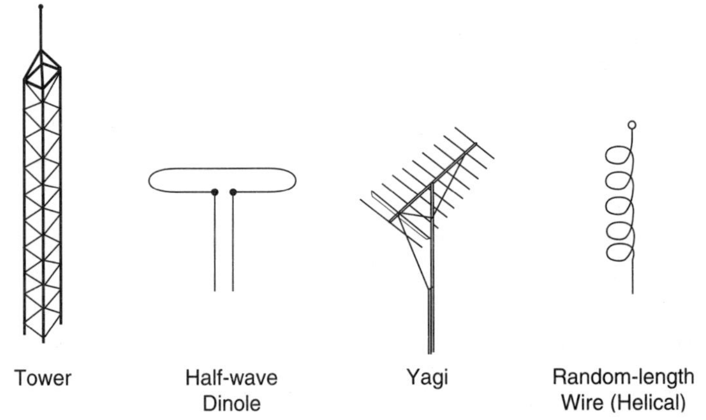

Figure 19.9
Representative antenna types.

On a line-of-sight basis, however, high-frequency transmissions attenuate less rapidly than low-frequency transmissions.

Lower-frequency radio waves can penetrate solid materials to a greater degree than higher frequencies. Very low radio frequencies can be used to communicate with submerged submarines, although the data rates are extremely slow. Penetration capability is also a function of power. Higher-power transmissions penetrate building walls more effectively than lower-power transmissions.

As you can see, designing a radio system to have the ideal characteristics for an application requires a lot of design tradeoffs.

Three classes of radio frequency transmission are discussed in this chapter:

- Low-power, single frequency
- High-power, single frequency
- Spread spectrum

Low-Power, Single-Frequency Radio

Low-power systems are chosen to limit the interference between nearby radio systems. Transmission ranges might be as short as 20 to 30 meters. This approach resembles cellular telephone technology, which divides geographic areas into isolated, low-power cells, enabling frequencies to be reused in nearby cells.

Although low-frequency radio can penetrate building walls, the low power used with this radio class typically requires transmitters and receivers to have a line-of-sight path. The data rates possible with low-frequency radio do not support the data rates required for LANs.

It is theoretically possible to implement mobile stations with this radio class, although walls and low power limit the mobility that is possible.

Frequency Range

Any radio frequency can be used, but higher frequencies, typically in the GHz, generally are chosen to support higher data rates.

Cost

Cost depends on design, but can be low compared to other wireless media. As with most media, higher data rates come at a higher cost.

Ease of Installation

This characteristic is also dependent on design. Some single-frequency systems use licensed frequencies, and a license application must be filed with the FCC. In at least one case, however, a prominent vendor has obtained licenses in many major markets and handles the FCC paperwork for the customer.

Some single-frequency systems use unlicensed frequencies. Some troubleshooting might be needed to prevent interference from other nearby devices that use the same frequencies.

Capacity

Although the theoretical bandwidth of radio LANs is high, currently available products range from 1 to 10 Mbps.

Attenuation

Attenuation is high due to the low power levels used, but proper design turns this into an advantage by creating large numbers of independent areas that do not interfere with each other.

EMI Characteristics

EMI resistance is low, particularly in the 902 MHz band that is shared with other unlicensed devices. All radio LANs are vulnerable to electronic eavesdropping, although the low powers used typically reduce the range at which eavesdropping can occur to the confines of the building in which the LAN is housed.

High-Power Single-Frequency Radio

High-power radio has data capacity similar to low-power radio, but it can cover much larger areas. Transmissions can be line-of-sight or can be extended by bouncing signals off the atmosphere. Because power can be higher, this approach can result in practical mobile networking and can service stations on motor or marine vehicles.

Frequency Range

As with low-power radio, any part of the radio spectrum can be used. Frequencies in the GHz range are generally chosen to achieve high data rates.

Cost

High-power transmission equipment is considerably more expensive. Signal repeaters might be needed to extend the coverage area. Costs for high-power radio can be moderate to high.

Ease of Installation

High-power radio equipment must be operated under an FCC license by licensed personnel. Equipment must be maintained in proper order to remain within the terms of the license. Improperly installed and maintained equipment might function poorly and interfere with nearby radio services.

Bandwidth

Capacity can be high but typically falls between 1 and 10 Mbps.

Attenuation

Attenuation rates for high-power radio are fairly low. Signal repeaters can be employed to extend transmission range.

EMI Characteristics

Immunity to EMI is low, and the potential for eavesdropping is high. Signals might be easily intercepted anywhere within the broadcast area.

Spread Spectrum Radio

Spread spectrum is a technique originally developed by the military to solve several communication problems. Spread spectrum improves reliability, reduces sensitivity to interference and jamming, and is less vulnerable to eavesdropping than single-frequency radio.

Spread spectrum transmission uses multiple frequencies to transmit messages. Two techniques employed are direct sequence modulation and frequency hopping.

Direct sequence modulation breaks original messages into parts called *chips* (see fig. 19.10), which are transmitted on separate frequencies. To confuse eavesdroppers, decoy data also can be transmitted on other frequencies. The intended receiver knows which frequencies are valid, and can isolate the chips and reassemble the message. Eavesdropping is difficult because the correct frequencies are not known, and the eavesdropper cannot isolate the frequencies carrying true data. This technique can operate in environments with other transmission activity since different sets of frequencies can be selected. Direct sequence modulation systems operating at 900 MHz support bandwidths of 2–6 Mbps.

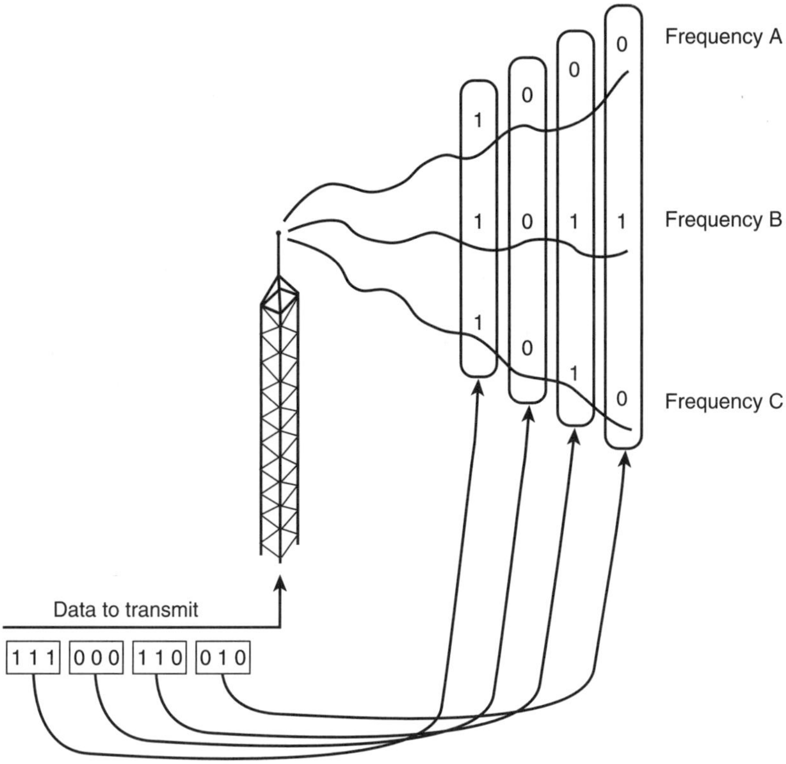

Figure 19.10
Direct sequence modulation.

Frequency hopping switches transmissions among several available frequencies (see fig. 19.11). Transmitter and receiver must remain synchronized for this technique to work. Some systems transmit on multiple frequencies simultaneously to increase bandwidth.

Frequency Range

Spread spectrum systems typically operate in unlicensed frequency ranges. 900 MHz devices are common, but 2.4 GHz devices are becoming available.

Costs

Costs are moderate compared to other wireless media.

Ease of Installation

This depends on the system design and the frequencies used. Installation complexity ranges from simple to somewhat complex.

Capacity

All 900 MHz systems support bandwidth capacities of 2–6 MHz. Newer systems operating in GHz frequencies can be expected to offer higher data rates.

Attenuation

This is determined by the frequency and power of the transmitted signals. Spread spectrum LANs typically operate at low power and exhibit high attenuation characteristics.

Figure 19.11
Frequency hopping.

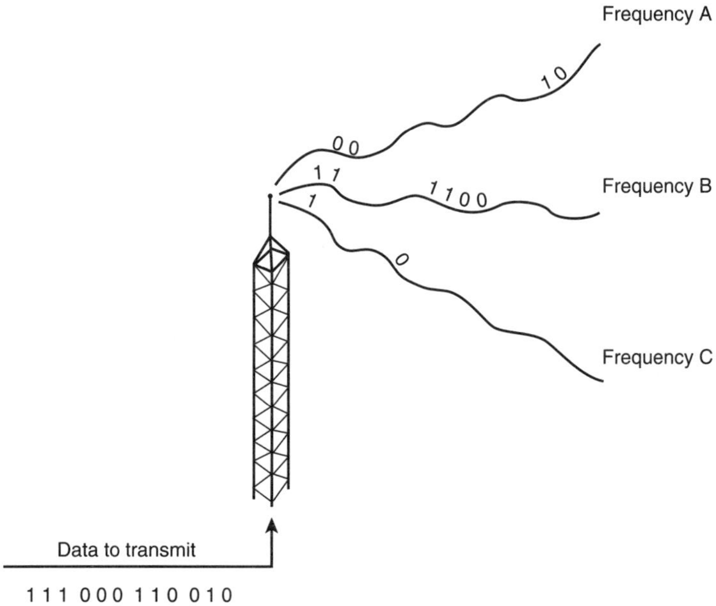

EMI Characteristics

Although individual frequencies are susceptible to EMI, the system can seek out clear frequencies on which to transmit. Overall resistance to EMI is, therefore, fairly high. Resistance to eavesdropping is high for the reasons cited earlier.

Microwave

As shown in figure 19.12, microwave communication can take two forms: terrestrial (ground links) and satellite links. The frequencies and technologies employed by these two forms are similar, but distinct differences exist between them.

Terrestrial Microwave

Terrestrial microwave communication employs Earth-based transmitters and receivers. The frequencies used are in the low-gigahertz range, limiting all communications to line-of-sight. You have probably seen terrestrial microwave equipment in the form of telephone relay towers, which are placed every few miles to relay telephone signals cross country.

Microwave transmissions are typically made using a parabolic antenna that produces a narrow, highly directional signal. A similar antenna at the receiving site is sensitive to signals only within a narrow focus. Since both the transmitter and receiver are highly focused, they must be carefully adjusted so that the transmitted signal is aligned with the receiver.

Microwave is frequently used as a means of transmitting signals where it would be impractical to run cables. If you need to connect two networks that are separated by a public road, you might find that you are not permitted to run cables above or below the road. In such a case, a microwave link is an ideal solution.

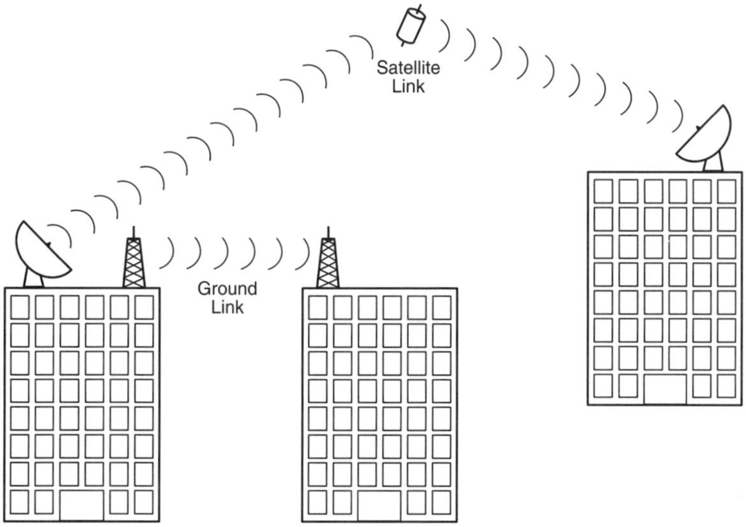

Figure 19.12
Terrestrial and satellite microwave links.

Some LANs operate at microwave frequencies, operate at low power, and use non-directional transmitters and receivers. Network hubs can be placed strategically throughout an organization, and workstations can be mobile or fixed. This approach is one way of enabling workstations to be mobile in an office setting.

In many cases, terrestrial microwave uses licensed frequencies. A license must be obtained from the FCC, and equipment must be installed and maintained by licensed technicians.

Frequency Range

Terrestrial microwave systems operate in the low-gigahertz range, typically at 4–6 GHz and 21–23 GHz.

Cost

Costs are highly variable depending on requirements.

Long-distance microwave systems can be quite expensive, but might be less costly than alternatives. A leased telephone circuit represents a costly monthly expense. When line-of-sight transmission is possible, a microwave link is a one-time expense that can offer greater bandwidth than a leased circuit.

Costs are decreasing for low-power microwave systems for the office. Although these systems do not compete directly in cost with cabled networks, when equipment must be frequently moved, microwave can be a cost-effective technology.

Installation

Licensing usually is required. Many equipment providers take care of licensing along with installation. Installation is a skilled operation generally requiring licensed technicians. Setup of transmitter and receiver sites can be difficult because antennas must be precisely aligned.

The requirement for a line-of-sight communication path might require purchase of access to suitable transmitter sites.

Bandwidth

Capacity can be extremely high, but most data communication systems operate at data rates between 1 and 10 Mbps.

Attenuation

Attenuation characteristics are determined by transmitter power, frequency, and antenna size. Properly designed systems are not affected by attenuation under normal operational conditions. Rain and fog, however, can cause attenuation of higher frequencies.

EMI Characteristics

Microwave systems are highly susceptible to atmospheric interference. They also might be vulnerable to electronic eavesdropping, and signals transmitted through microwave are frequently encrypted.

Satellite Microwave

Satellite microwave systems relay transmissions through communication satellites that operate in geosynchronous orbits 22,300 miles above the Earth. Satellites orbiting at this distance remain located above a fixed point on the Earth.

Earth stations use parabolic antennas (satellite dishes) to communicate with the satellites. Satellites can retransmit signals in broad or in narrow beams depending on which locations are to receive the signals. When the destination is on the opposite side of the Earth, the first satellite cannot transmit directly to the receiver and must relay the signal through another satellite.

Because no cables are required, satellite microwave communication is possible with most remote sites and with mobile devices, including ships at sea and motor vehicles.

The distances involved in satellite communication result in an interesting phenomenon: Because all signals must travel 22,300 miles to the satellite and 22,300 miles when returning to a receiver, the time required to transmit a signal is independent of distance. It takes as long to transmit a signal to a receiver in the same state as it does to a receiver a third of the way around the world. The time required for a signal to arrive at its destination is called *propagation delay.* The delays encountered with satellite transmissions range from 0.5 to 5 seconds.

Unfortunately, satellite communication is extremely expensive. Building and launching a satellite easily can cost in excess of a billion dollars. In most cases, organizations share these costs, or they purchase services from a commercial provider. AT&T, Hughes Network Services, and Scientific-Atlanta are among the firms that sell satellite-based communication services.

Frequency Range

Satellite links operate in the low-gigahertz range, typically at 11–14 MHz.

Cost

Costs are extremely high and are usually amortized across many users by selling communication services.

Ease of Installation

Earth stations can be installed by numerous commercial providers. Transmitters operate on licensed frequencies and require an FCC license.

Bandwidth

Bandwidth is related to cost, and firms can purchase almost any required bandwidth. Typical data rates are 1–10 Mbps.

Attenuation

Attenuation characteristics depend on frequency, power, and atmospheric conditions. Properly designed systems take attenuation into account. Rain and atmospheric conditions might attenuate higher frequencies.

EMI Characteristics

Microwave signals are sensitive to EMI and electronic eavesdropping. Signals transmitted through microwave frequently are encrypted.

Infrared Systems

You use an infrared communication system every time you control your television with a remote control. The remote control transmits pulses of infrared light that carry coded instructions to a receiver on the TV. This technology can be adapted to network communication.

Two methods of infrared networking are in use: point-to-point and broadcast.

Point-to-Point Infrared

Point-to-point networks operate by relaying infrared signals from one device to the next. An example of an infrared LAN is shown in figure 19.13. Transmissions are focused in a narrow beam, and the transmitter and receiver must be aligned carefully. Because the devices must be carefully placed and set up, point-to-point infrared is not suitable for use with devices that move frequently.

High-powered laser transmitters can be used to transmit data for several thousand yards when line-of-sight communication is possible. Lasers can be used in many of the same situations as microwave links, without the requirement of an FCC license. Consider infrared lasers for connections between buildings, particularly when they are separated by public rights of way.

Frequency Range

Infrared light falls in a range below visible light and has a frequency range of approximately 100 GHz to 1,000 THz.

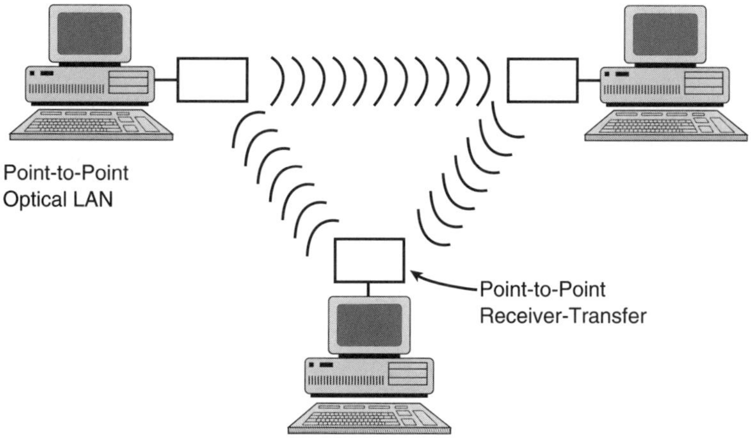

Figure 19.13
Point-to-point infrared networking.

Cost

The cost of point-to-point infrared equipment is higher than the cost for a comparable cabled network. Most systems use transmitters based on LED technology, and the hardware cost is moderate. Long-distance systems use high-powered laser transmitters, which can be quite costly.

Ease of Installation

Installation requires careful alignment of the transmitters and receivers. Lasers used in high-powered transmitters can be hazardous and can burn or damage eyes.

Bandwidth

Bandwidth ranges from about 100 Kbps to 16 Mbps.

Attenuation

Attenuation characteristics are determined by the quality of the transmission, by presence of obstructions, and by atmospheric conditions.

EMI Characteristics

Infrared devices are insensitive to radio-frequency interference but reception can be degraded by bright light. Because transmissions are tightly focused, they are fairly immune to electronic eavesdropping.

Broadcast Infrared

Instead of focusing transmissions in tight beams, broadcast infrared disperses transmissions so that they are visible to several receivers. At least two approaches are possible, as shown in figure 19.14. One approach is to locate an active transmitter at a high point so that it can transmit to all devices. Another is to place a reflective material on the ceiling; devices transmit toward the ceiling where the light signals are dispersed to other devices in the room.

Frequency Range

Infrared light falls in a range below visible light and has a frequency range of approximately 100 GHz to 1000 THz.

Cost

The cost of point-to-point infrared equipment is higher than the cost for a comparable cabled network. Because lasers produce a tightly focused beam, they are not very suitable to broadcast-type networks.

Ease of Installation

Installation is fairly simple because device alignment is not critical. It is essential that each device has clear transmission and reception pathways. Because these devices are sensitive to light interference, the control of ambient light is a significant installation concern.

Capacity

Typical bandwidths are less than 1 Mbps, although higher bandwidths are theoretically possible.

Attenuation

Attenuation characteristics are determined by the quality of the transmission, by presence of obstructions, and by atmospheric conditions. Typical ranges are limited to tens of meters.

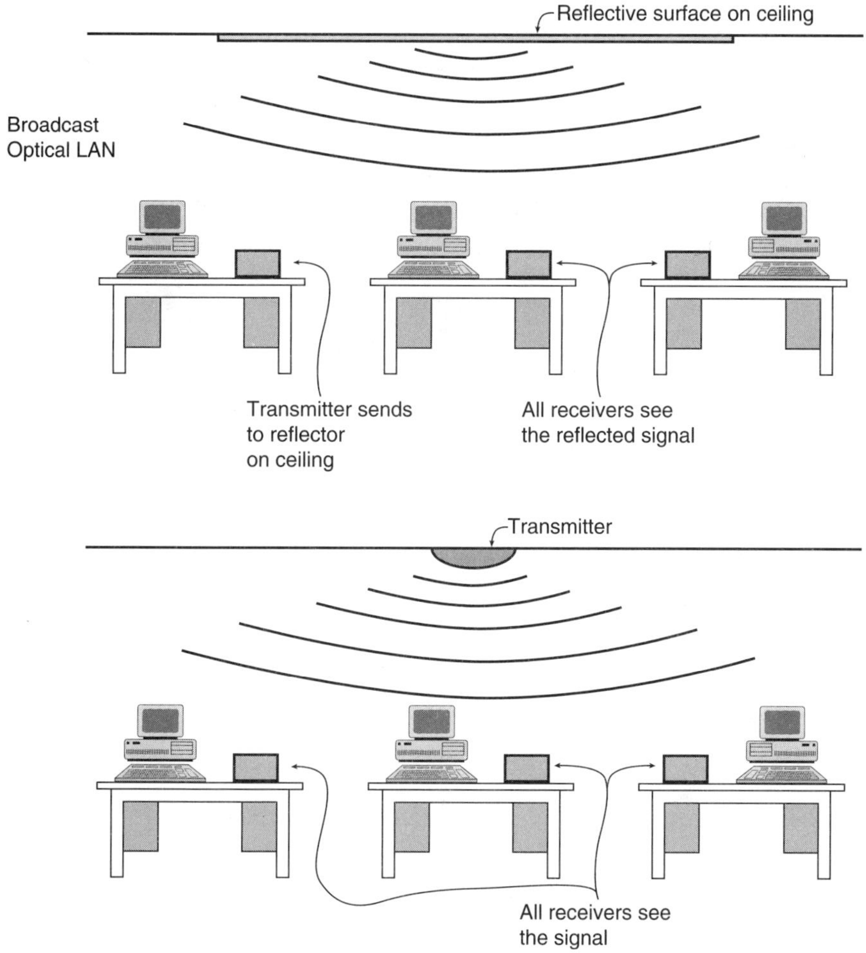

Figure 19.14
Two approaches to broadcast infrared networking.

EMI Characteristics

Infrared devices are insensitive to radio-frequency interference, but reception can be degraded by bright light. Because transmissions are tightly focused, they are fairly immune to electronic eavesdropping.

Summary of Wireless Media

Table 19.2 summarizes the characteristics of the wireless media discussed in this section.

Table 19.2
Comparison of Wireless Media

Media Type	*Frequency Range*	*Cost*
Low-power single frequency	All radio frequencies. Frequencies in the low GHz range are most common.	Moderate for wireless but higher than cabled devices
High-power single frequency	All radio frequencies. Frequencies in the low GHz range are most common.	More expensive than low-power
Spread spectrum	All radio frequencies. 902-928 MHz common in the US. 2.4 GHz most common worldwide.	Moderate
Terrestrial microwave	Usually low GHz, with 6 or 21–23 GHz most common.	Moderate to high but cost effective in many situations
Satellite microwave	Low GHz. 11–14 GHz most common.	High
Point-to-point infrared	100 GHz to 1000 THz	Low to moderate
Broadcast infrared	100 GHz to 1000 THz	Low for wireless, higher than cables systems

Public and Private Network Services

Communication must take place between distant points, but few organizations can justify the costs required to construct a private wide area network. Fortunately, a variety of commercial options are available that enable organizations to pay only for the level of service that they require. One option is the public telephone network. Another is to utilize a public network service, of which the Internet is an example.

The Public Telephone Network

Public telephone networks offer two general types of service:

- Switched services, which the customer pays for on a per-use basis
- Leased dedicated services, to which the customer is granted exclusive access

Switched services operate on the *Public Switched Telephone Network* (PSTN), which we know as the telephone system. Voice grade services have evolved

Installation	*Capacity*	*Attenuation*	*EMI Sensitivity*
Low difficulty	Below 1 Mbps to 10 Mbps	High	High EMI sensitivity. Vulnerable to eavesdropping.
High difficulty	Below 1 Mbps to 10 Mbps	Low	High EMI sensitivity. Vulnerable to eavesdropping.
Moderately difficult	2 to 6 Mbps	High	Some EMI sensitivity. Low eavesdropping vulnerability.
Difficult	Below 1 Mbps to 10 Mbps with higher rates possible	Depends on strength and atmospheric conditions	Low EMI sensitivity. Some eavesdropping vulnerability.
Very difficult	Below 1 Mbps to 10 Mbps with higher rates possible	Depends on frequency, signal strength, and atmospheric conditions	Low EMI sensitivity. Moderate eavesdropping vulnerability.
Moderately difficult	Below 1 Mbps to 16 Mbps	Depends on light purity and intensity as well as environmental conditions	Sensitive to intense light. Low eavesdropping vulnerability.
Low difficulty	Up to 1 Mbps	High	Sensitive to intense light. Low eavesdropping vulnerability.

to high levels of sophistication and can be adapted to providing many data services by using devices such as modems. Newer switched options are providing higher levels of service while retaining the advantages of switched access.

On a switched network, subscribers do not have exclusive access to a particular data path. The PSTN maintains large numbers of paths, but not nearly enough to service all customers simultaneously. When a customer requests service, a path is switched in to service the customer's needs. When the customer hangs up, the path is reused for other customers. In situations when the customer does not need full-time network access, switched service is extremely cost-effective.

In the United States, the following terms are used to describe components of the PSTN (see fig. 19.15):

- The *demarcation point*, or *demarc*, is the point at which outside wiring enters the customer's premises. The demarc is a specific point in the building at which customer wiring connects to the wiring of the local loop.

- *Subscriber wiring and equipment* consists of all wiring and equipment on the customer side of the demarc. These items are owned by the customer, and the customer is responsible for operation and maintenance.
- *Local loops* connect the demarc to a central office. The local loop can consist of unshielded twisted-pair wiring, fiber-optic cable, or a combination of the two.
- The *central office* (CO) switches connections between customer sites. It also supplies reliable, filtered power for the local loop.

  Central offices are interconnected by high capacity trunk lines.

  Central offices rely on long-distance carriers to communicate with COs that are outside of the local service area. Long-distance carriers use various combinations of fiber-optic, copper, and microwave media to provide high-capacity long-distance service.

When customers require full-time access to a communication path, one option is a dedicated, leased line. Several levels of service are available. Common options are T-1 (1.544 Mbps) and T-3 (44.736 Mbps). Leased lines enable a customer to lease a specified bandwidth between two specified points.

Many organizations need to communicate among several points. Leasing a line between each pair of

Figure 19.15
Elements of the Public Switched Telephone Service.

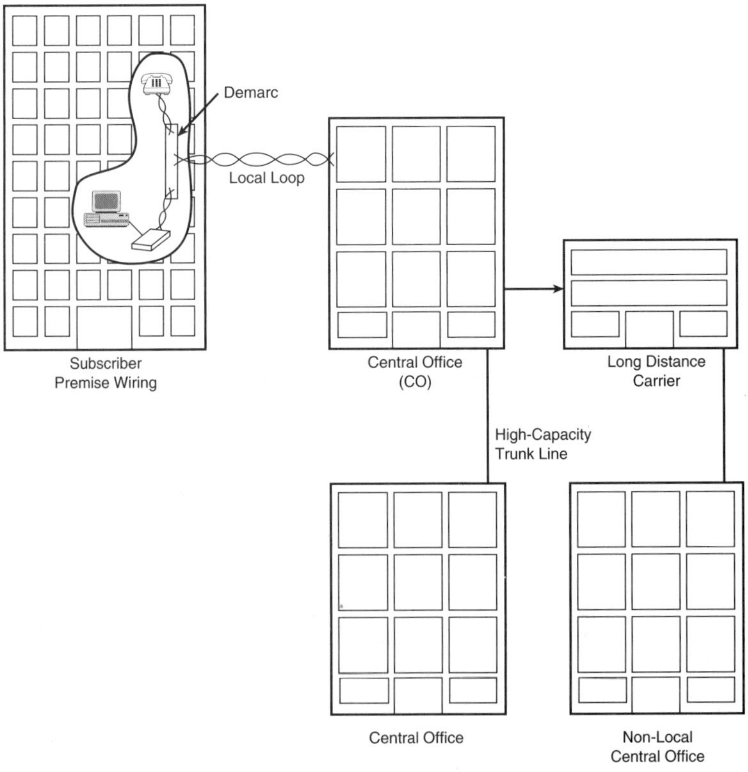

points can prove too costly. Many services now are available that route packets between different sites. Among the services available are X.25, Frame Relay, SONET (Synchronous Optical Network), and ATM. Each of these services has characteristics that suit it to particular uses, and all are available on a leased basis from service providers. An organization that needs to communicate among many sites simply pays to connect each site to the service, and the service takes on the responsibility of routing packets. The expense of operating the network is shared among all of the network subscribers. Because the exact switching process is concealed from the subscriber, these networks are frequently depicted as a communication cloud, as shown in figure 19.16.

Table 19.3 lists common network services and their associated bandwidths.

Table 19.3
Bandwidths of Network Services

Service	*Bandwidth*
Dedicated 56 KB (DDS)	56 Kbps
Switched 56	56 Kbps
X.25	56 Kbps
T1	1.544 Mbps
Switched T1	1.544 Mbps
Frame Relay	1.544 Mbps
SMDS	1.544 Mbps
ISDN	1.544 Mbps
E1 (Europe)	2.048 Mbps
T3	44.736 Mbps
ATM	44.736 Mbps

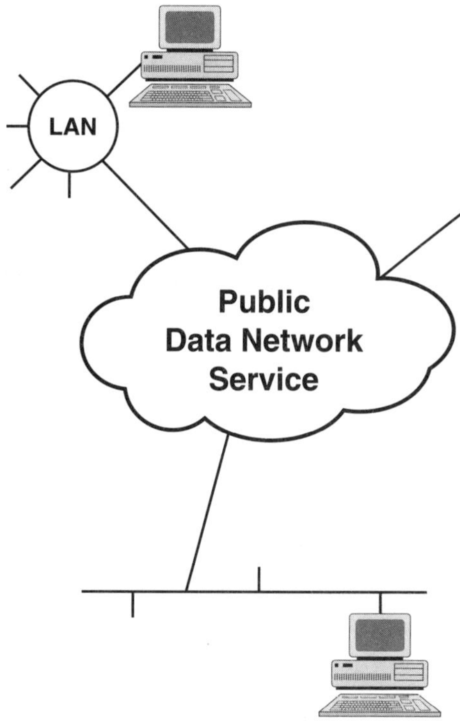

Figure 19.16
An example of a public network service.

These data rates can be compared to common LAN services such as Ethernet (10 Mbps) and token ring (4–16 Mbps).

The Internet

The Internet is a cooperative venture in which huge numbers of government agencies, educational institutions, and businesses have agreed to provide shared network services. Each organization on the Internet provides some amount of communication and computing capability that is freely shared with other network users. As a result of this cooperation, the Internet has grown to encompass computers in over 100 countries on all continents.

The United States has begun to encourage development of a national information infrastructure, popularly called the Information Superhighway. Research is underway to develop practical methods of establishing high-capacity media (>3 Gbps) with the capability of interconnecting large numbers of public and private networks.

Questions

1. Which of the following cable types supports the greatest cable lengths?
   - ○ A. Unshielded twisted-pair
   - ○ B. Shielded twisted-pair
   - ○ C. Large coaxial cable
   - ○ D. Small coaxial cable

2. Which *two* are advantages of UTP cable?
   - ☐ A. Low cost
   - ☐ B. Easy installation
   - ☐ C. High resistance to EMI due to twists in cable
   - ☐ D. Cables up to 500 meters

3. Which *three* are advantages of coaxial cable?
   - ☐ A. Low cost
   - ☐ B. Easy installation
   - ☐ C. Good resistance to EMI
   - ☐ D. Easy to reconfigure

4. Which *two* are disadvantages of fiber-optic cable?
   - ☐ A. Sensitive to EMI
   - ☐ B. Expensive hardware
   - ☐ C. High installation cost
   - ☐ D. Low bandwidth

5. Which of the following *three* cable types should be regarded as mature, well-proven technologies?
   - ☐ A. Level 3 UTP
   - ☐ B. STP
   - ☐ C. Fiber-optic
   - ☐ D. Level 5 UTP

6. Which of the following is a true statement?
   - ○ A. Telephone wiring can be reliably used for most UTP networks.
   - ○ B. Thin coaxial networks are easy to install and reconfigure.
   - ○ C. Fiber-optic cable supports cable runs of tens of kilometers.
   - ○ D. STP cable is insensitive to EMI.

7. Which cable type should be used to connect between two buildings?
   - ○ A. UTP
   - ○ B. STP
   - ○ C. Coax
   - ○ D. Fiber-optic

8. Which of the following cable types has the greatest data capacity?
   - ○ A. Category 5 UTP
   - ○ B. Thick coax
   - ○ C. Single-mode fiber-optic
   - ○ D. Multi-mode fiber-optic

9. Which statement is true of unlicensed radio frequencies?
   - ○ A. Anyone may use them.
   - ○ B. 902 MHz and 2.4 GHz are unlicensed frequency bands.
   - ○ C. The FCC prevents users from interfering.
   - ○ D. They are relatively uncrowded.

10. Which *three* of the following are antenna types?
    - ☐ A. Beam
    - ☐ B. Duplex
    - ☐ C. Dipole
    - ☐ D. Random-length wire

11. Which of the following radio transmissions is typically line-of-sight?
    - ○ A. AM
    - ○ B. FM
    - ○ C. Microwave
    - ○ D. None of the above

12. Which *three* of the following statements are true:
    - ☐ A. Attenuation of radio waves is less with high-power signals.
    - ☐ B. High-frequency radio LANs can penetrate office walls.
    - ☐ C. Radio-frequency LANs have high bandwidth.
    - ☐ D. Spread-spectrum technology reduces sensitivity to EMI.

13. Which *two* wireless technologies would be good choices for connecting two buildings on opposite sides of a highway?
    - ☐ A. Satellite microwave
    - ☐ B. High-power single-frequency
    - ☐ C. Terrestrial microwave
    - ☐ D. Broadcast infrared

14. Which *two* wireless technologies are sensitive to radio-frequency interference:
    - ☐ A. Microwave
    - ☐ B. Spread-spectrum
    - ☐ C. Infrared
    - ☐ D. High-power, single frequency

15. Which *two* statements are true of the public telephone network?
    - ☐ A. Switched services enable customers to pay on a per-use basis.
    - ☐ B. The demarc is the place at the Central Office where a user's connection attaches to the network.
    - ☐ C. Local loops connect subscriber wiring to the demarc.
    - ☐ D. Central offices switch calls between customer sites.

Answers

1. C
2. A, B
3. A, B, C
4. B, C
5. A, B, C
6. C
7. D
8. C
9. B
10. A, C, D
11. A
12. A, C, D
13. B, C
14. B, D
15. A, D

CHAPTER 20

Transmission Media Connections

This chapter covers a wide variety of devices that are used to connect networks. The devices discussed range from the lowly connector to exotic units, such as routers and CSU/DSUs. Novell divides these devices into two categories, describing them either as network or internetwork devices.

This course defines a network as "a single, independent network." What does this mean? By this definition, a network consists of a single, local cabling system. Any device on the network can directly communicate with any other device on the same network. A network by this definition does not have any connections to other, remote networks.

According to the course definition, an *internetwork* consists of multiple independent networks that are connected together and can share remote resources. It is said that internetworks consist of "logically separate but physically connected networks" that can be dissimilar in type. The device that connects the independent networks together must have a degree of "intelligence" because it must determine when packets will stay on the local network or when they will be forwarded to another remote network.

Connectivity devices perform the following functions:

- Attaching devices to media
- Connecting media segments together
- Utilizing media capacity effectively
- Connecting remote (logically separate) networks

Listed below are the devices to be examined:

- Network connectivity devices:

  Connectors

  Network interface boards

  Hubs

  Repeaters

  Bridges

  Multiplexors

  Modems

- Internetwork connectivity devices:

  Routers

  Brouters

  CSU/DSUs

When you complete this chapter, you will be able to do the following:

- Identify connecting hardware used in computer networking
- Identify connecting hardware used to connect internetworks
- Select connectivity devices to meet specific requirements

Connecting Hardware

Each connection type will specify connectors to be used. Several are discussed in this section.

Connectors for Multi-Wire Cable

A variety of physical layer standards require cables with large numbers of wires. The RS-232 serial interface commonly used for modems can utilize as many as 25 wires (although seldom are all wires actually implemented).

Several types of connectors are used for these types of connections, three of which are shown in figure 20.1. A wide variety of D-type connectors are available, of which the DB-25 and the DB-9 are shown. The number reflects the number of pins or sockets that the connector can accommodate. You will encounter DB-9 connectors in several places. Token-ring network cards are frequently equipped with DB-9 connectors.

The DIX connector is similar to a DB-15 connector, and is used to connect devices with thickwire Ethernet. The DIX connector differs from a standard DB-15 because the DIX is secured to the mating connector with a sliding clip instead of screws. The sliding clip is installed on the connector that has sockets, which is not shown in the figure. The connector shown in figure 20.1 is equipped with pins and with studs that mate with the sliding clip.

The fourth connector shown in figure 20.1 is a DIN connector. DIN connectors are available in various configurations, with different pin counts and pin arrangements. In networking, you are most likely to encounter DIN connectors when cabling Macintoshes into AppleTalk networks.

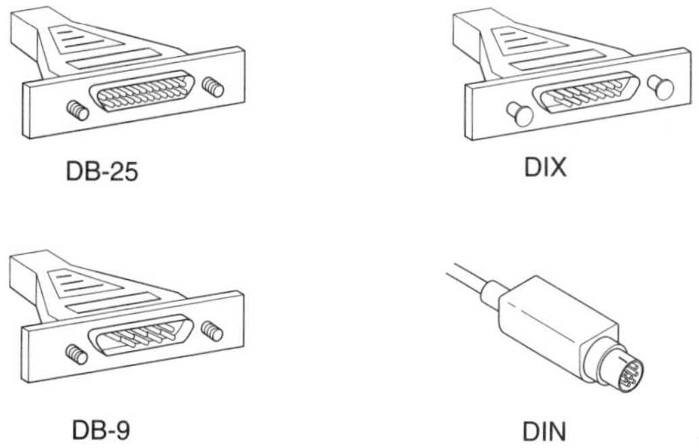

Figure 20.1
Connectors used with multi-wire cables.

Connectors for Twisted-Pair Cables

The most common connector used with UTP cables is the RJ-45 connector, shown in figure 20.2. These connectors are easy to install on cables and are extremely easy to connect and disconnect. The RJ-45 connector has eight pins. You also will occasionally encounter the RJ-11 connector, which resembles the RJ-45, but has only four pins.

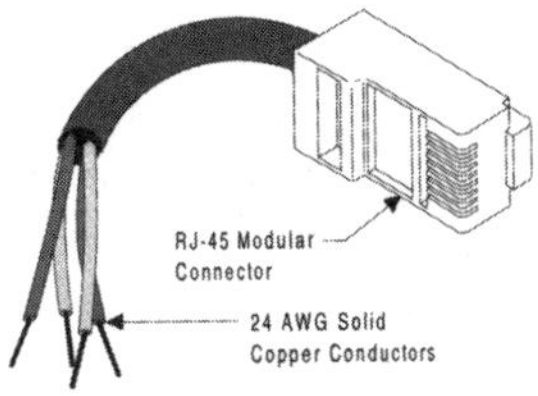

Figure 20.2
A RJ-45 connector.

Although AppleTalk and token-ring networks can both be cabled with UTP cable and RJ-45 connectors, both originated as STP cabling systems. For STP cable, AppleTalk employs a DIN-type connector, shown in figure 20.3. IBM uses the IBM Data Connector, also shown in the figure.

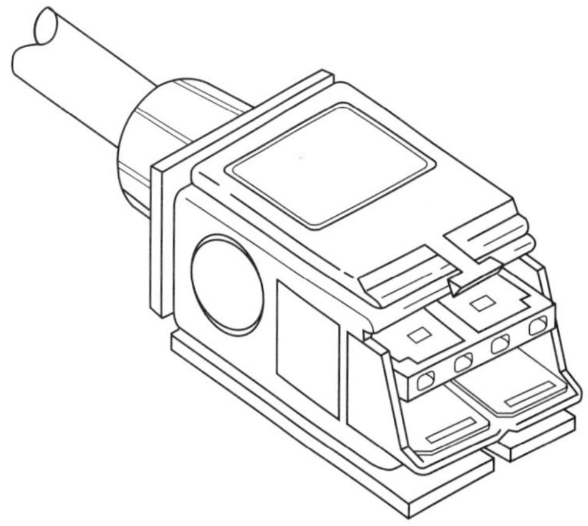

Figure 20.3
Connectors used with STP cable.

The IBM Data Connector is unusual because it does not come in two gender configurations. Any IBM Data Connector may be snapped to any other IBM Data Connector.

Most networking connections for STP token ring are made using IBM Data Connectors. The connection to the workstation, however, is made with a DB-15 connector. Figure 20.4 shows a PC that is set up to connect to a token-ring network.

Connectors for Coaxial Cable

Two types of connectors are commonly used with coaxial cable. The most common connector is the *Bayonette Connector* (BNC) connector, shown in figure 20.5. This figure shows several characteristics of thin Ethernet cabling, as follows:

- A T-connector is used to connect the network board in the PC to the network. The T- connector attaches directly to the network board, and a cable is never used at this point.
- BNC connectors attach cable segments to the T-connectors.
- Both ends of the cable must be terminated. A *terminator* is a special connector that includes a resistor that is carefully matched to the characteristics of the cable system.
- One of the terminators must be grounded. A wire from the connector is attached to a grounded point, such as the center screw of a grounded electrical outlet.

Thick Ethernet uses N-connectors, which screw on instead of using a twist-lock (bayonette) fitting (see fig. 20.6). As with thin Ethernet, both ends of the cable must be terminated and one end must be grounded.

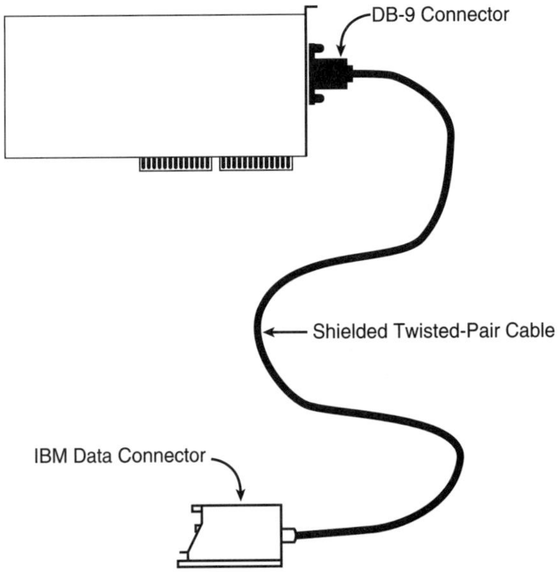

Figure 20.4
PC ready to connect to a token-ring network.

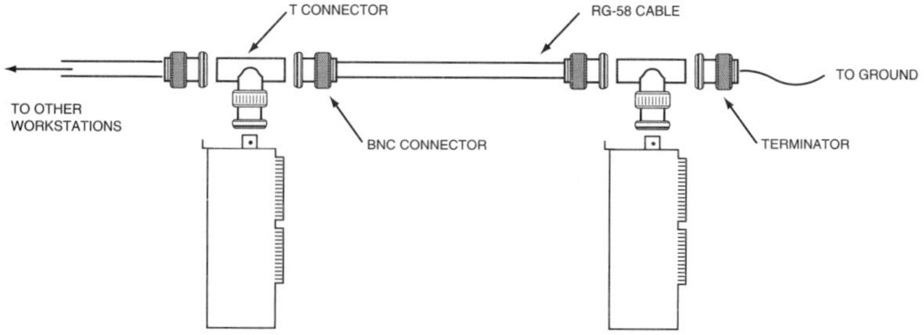

Figure 20.5
Connectors and cabling for thin Ethernet.

Workstations do not connect directly to the cable with thick Ethernet. The cable attachment is made with a *transceiver* (also called a *medium attachment unit* or MAU), which connects to the workstation with a cable called an *AUI cable.* Transceivers can connect to cables in the following two ways:

- They can connect by cutting the cable and using N-connectors and a T-connector on the transceiver. This, the original method, is now used infrequently.
- The more common approach is to use a clamp-on transceiver, which has pins that penetrate the cable without the need for cutting it. Because clamp-on transceivers force sharp teeth into the cable, they are frequently referred to as *vampire taps.*

Connectors for Fiber-Optic Cable

A variety of connectors are used with fiber-optic cable. The most common is the ST-connector, shown in figure 20.7. If two devices are to engage in two-way data exchange, two fibers are required, and you will frequently encounter fiber-optic cables with connectors in pairs.

When fiber-optic cable bundles must be interfaced to individual cables, a connection center will be used. Within the splice center, the individual fibers in the cable bundle can be connected to individual connectors that are used to connect to devices. Figure 20.8 illustrates a cabling system based on a splice center.

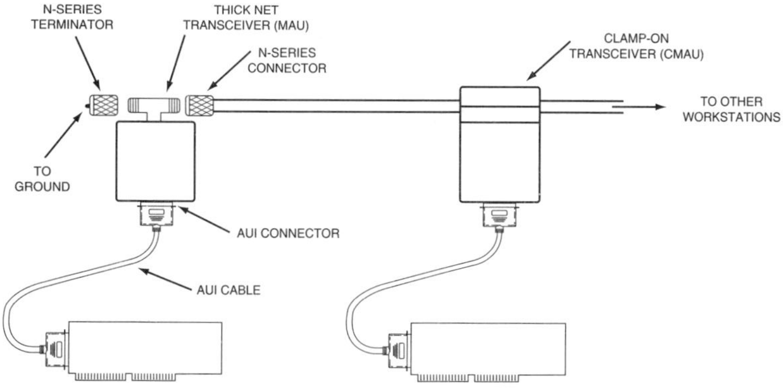

Figure 20.6
Connectors and cabling for thick Ethernet

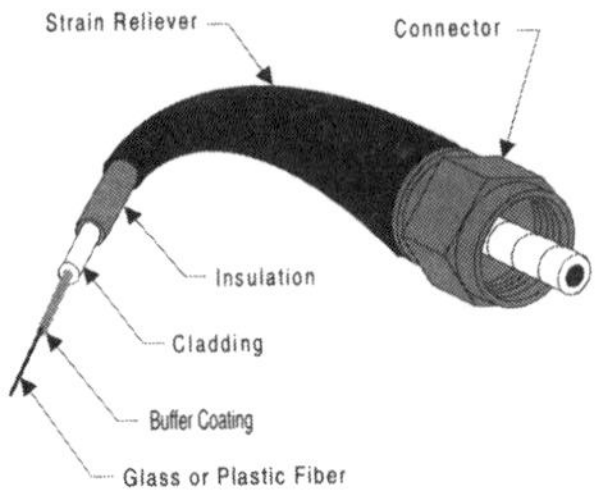

Figure 20.7
An ST connector used for fiber-optic cable.

Network Connectivity Devices

This section defines a variety of devices as "network connectivity devices." This definition focuses on the roles of these devices in local networks as opposed to internetworks.

Network Interface Boards

Each workstation must be equipped with hardware that enables the workstation to connect to the network. This course calls all such devices *network interface boards,* although they might not be boards at all:

- A *network interface card* (NIC) may be installed in one of the computer's expansion slots.
- The network interface circuitry may be built into the computer's main board. In this case, the connector is built into the computer's case.
- A transmission media adapter may be used.

Several types of transmission media adapters are in common use, including the following:

- Ethernet LANs use transceivers to connect DIX connectors on devices to network media. Transceivers are always used with thick coaxial cable and may be used with thin coax or

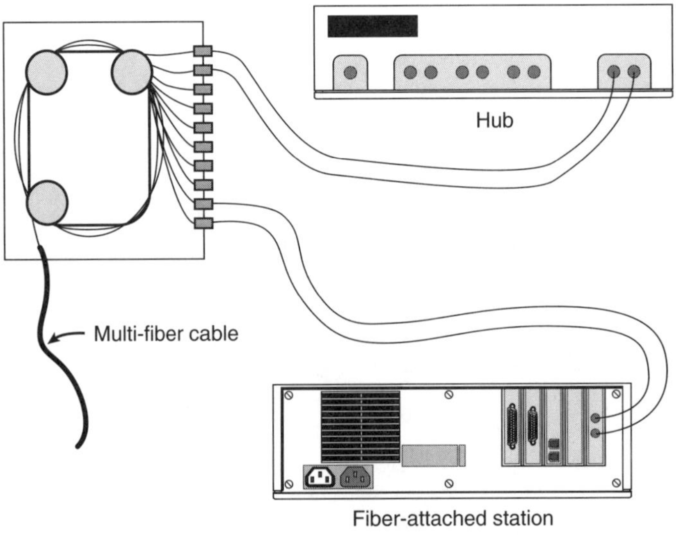

Figure 20.8
Fiber-optic cable.

UTP. NICs for thin and UTP Ethernet usually have the transceivers built in so that an external transceiver is not required.

- When UTP cable is used with token-ring networks, a media filter might be required when operating at 16 Mbps. The media filter prevents noise from getting out onto the LAN. Many token-ring NICs designed for 16 Mbps operation incorporate the media filter on the card.

Transceivers

Regardless of the form of the device, it will include a transceiver of some kind. A transceiver functions as both a *trans*mitter and a re*ceiver*.

The transmitter component translates the computer's internal signals to the signals required for the network. If the network uses UTP cable, the transceiver will supply the proper electrical signals to the proper type of connector. If the network uses fiber-optic cable, the transceiver will translate the computer's electrical signals into the light signals required for the network.

The receiver component performs the opposite service when signals are received from the network, translating them back to a form that matches the computer's internal requirements.

Network Interface Cards (NIC)

Also called an NIC, a *network interface card* is a network board that can be installed in a computer's expansion slot. NICs are the devices most commonly used to connect computers to networks.

NICs incorporate a transceiver, which can service several types of connectors. With the exception of thick Ethernet, NICs are available to connect directly to all types of networks.

Ethernet NICs are equipped with one, two, or possibly all three of the following:

- RJ-45 connector for UTP Ethernet
- BNC connector for thin Ethernet
- AUI connector for thick Ethernet

Token-ring NICs are equipped with one or both of the following:

- DB-15 connector for STP
- RJ-45 connector for UTP

Transmission Media Adapters

Novell uses the term *transmission media adapter* to describe a device that adapts one type of connector on the computer to a different type of connector that is required for the network. Several types of devices can be classified as transmission media adapters, including the following:

- **Transceivers (or MAUs).** Used to connect computers to thick coax Ethernets
- **Media filters.** Adapt a DB-15 token-ring connector to connect to a UTP network with an RJ-45 connector
- **Parallel port adapters.** Enable laptop computers to network by communicating through their parallel ports
- **SCSI port adapters.** Enable computers to connect to networks through a SCSI interface

Hubs

Coaxial cable Ethernet is the only LAN standard that does not use hubs to bring wiring together in a central location, as shown in figure 20.9. Hubs are also called *wiring concentrators*. You will encounter three types of hubs, as follows:

- Passive
- Active
- Intelligent

Passive Hubs

This type of hub is called passive because it does not contain any electronic components and does not process the data signal in any way. The only purpose of a passive hub is to combine the signals from several network cable segments. All devices attached to a passive hub see all the packets that pass through the hub.

Because the hub does not clean up or amplify the signals (in fact, the hub absorbs a small part of the signal), the distance between a computer and the hub can be no more than half of the maximum permissible distance between two computers on the network. If the network design limits the distance between two computers to 200 meters, the maximum distance between a computer and the hub is 100 meters.

ARCnet networks commonly use passive hubs.

Token-ring networks also can use passive hubs, although the industry trend is to utilize active hubs to obtain the advantages cited in the following.

Active Hubs

Active hubs incorporate electronic components that can amplify and clean up the electronic signals that flow between devices on the network. The process of cleaning up the signals is called *signal regeneration*. There are two benefits of signal regeneration: the network is more robust and less sensitive to errors, and distances between devices can be increased. These advantages generally outweigh the fact that active hubs cost considerably more than passive hubs.

Later in the chapter, you will learn about *repeaters*, which are also devices that amplify and regenerate network signals. Because active hubs function in part as repeaters, they are occasionally called *multiport repeaters*.

Intelligent Hubs

Intelligent hubs are active hubs that include something more. Several functions can add intelligence to a hub, as follows:

Figure 20.9
Network wiring with a hub.

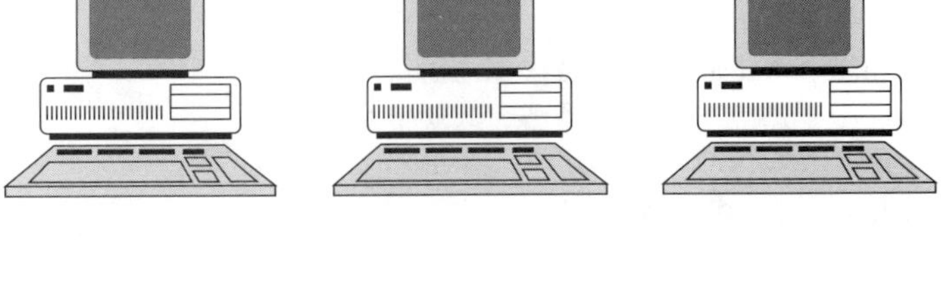

- **Hub management.** Many hubs now support network management protocols that enable the hub to send packets to a central network console. They also enable the console to control the hub, ordering, for example, a hub to shut down a connection that is generating network errors.
- **Switching hubs.** The latest development in hubs is the *switching hub*, which includes circuitry that very quickly routes signals between ports on the hub. Instead of repeating a packet to all ports on the hub, a switching hub repeats it only to the port that connects to the destination computer for the packet. Many switching hubs have the capability of switching packets to the fastest of several alternative paths. Switching hubs are replacing bridges and routers on many networks.

Repeaters

As you learned in Chapter 18, "The OSI Layered Protocol Model," all media attenuate the signals that they carry. Each media type, therefore, has a maximum range that it can reliably carry data. Figure 20.10 shows the use of a repeater to connect two Ethernet cable segments. The result of adding the repeater is that the potential length of the overall network is doubled.

Some repeaters simply amplify signals. Although this increases the strength of the data signal, it amplifies any noise on the network as well. Also, if the original signal has been distorted in any way, an amplifying repeater cannot clean up the distortion.

More advanced repeaters can extend the range of network media by both amplifying and regenerating the signals. Signal regenerating repeaters, for example, identify the data in the signal they receive and use the data to regenerate the original signal. This amplifies the strength of the desired signal while reducing noise, and clears up any distortion that might be present. The output of a regenerating repeater duplicates the original data signal.

It would be nice if repeaters could be used to extend networks indefinitely, but all network designs limit the size of the network. The most important reason for this limit is signal propagation. Networks need to work with reasonable expectations about the maximum time a signal might be in transit. This is known as *propagation delay*—the time it takes for a signal to reach the furthest point on the network. If this maximum propagation delay interval expires and no signals are encountered, a network error condition is assumed. Given the maximum allowed propagation delay, it is possible to calculate the maximum permissible cable length for the

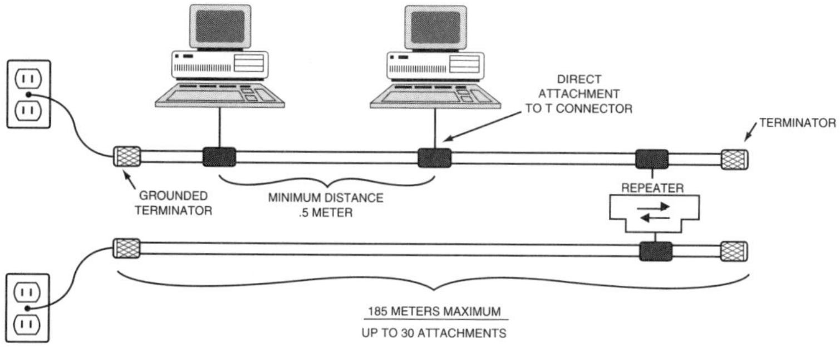

Figure 20.10

Using a repeater to extend an Ethernet LAN.

network. Even though repeaters enable signals to travel farther, the maximum propagation delay still sets a limit to the maximum size of the network.

Bridges

Bridges, on the other hand, are capable of extending the maximum size of a network. Although the bridged network in figure 20.11 looks much like the earlier example of a network with a repeater, the bridge is a much more flexible device.

A repeater passes on all signals that it receives. A bridge, on the other hand, is more selective and only passes on the signals that are targeted for a computer that is on the other side. A bridge can make this determination because a device on the network is identified by a unique address, and each packet that is transmitted bears the address of the device to which it should be delivered. The process works like this:

1. The bridge receives every packet on LAN A and LAN B.
2. The bridge learns from the packets which device addresses are located on LAN A and which are on LAN B. A table is built with this information.
3. Packets on LAN A that are addressed to devices on LAN A are discarded. So are packets on LAN B that are addressed to devices on LAN B. These packets can be delivered without the help of the bridge.
4. Packets on LAN A that are addressed to devices on LAN B are retransmitted to LAN B for delivery. Similarly, the appropriate packets on LAN B are retransmitted to LAN A.

Figure 20.11
Extending a network with a bridge.

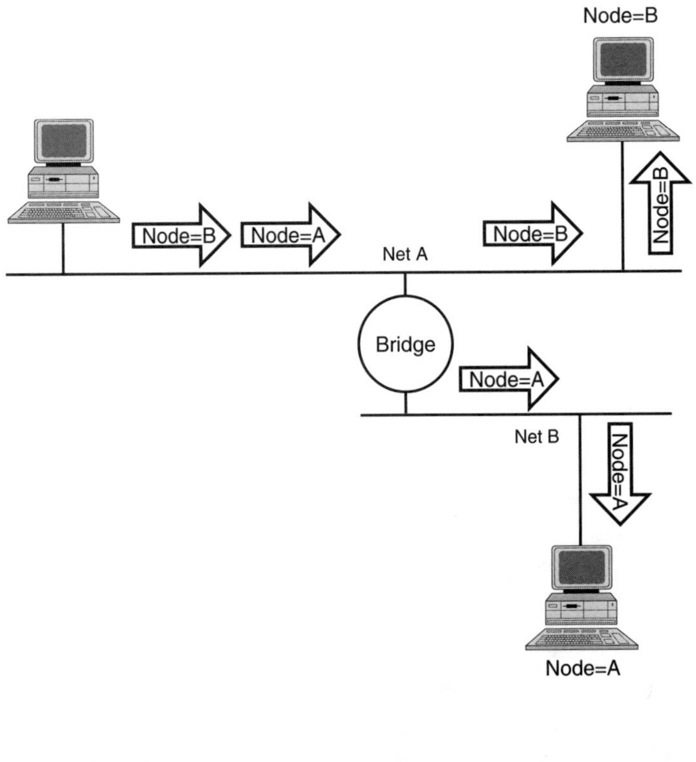

The address tables on older bridges needed to be manually configured by the network administrator. Newer bridges are called learning bridges—they function as described in step 2. *Learning bridges* automatically update their address tables as devices are added to or removed from the network.

Bridges accomplish several things. First, they divide busy networks into smaller segments. If the network is designed so that most packets can be delivered without crossing a bridge, traffic on the individual network segments can be reduced. If the Accounting and Sales departments are overloading the LAN, you might choose to divide the network so that Accounting is on one segment and Sales is on another. Only when Accounting and Sales need to exchange packets will a packet need to cross the bridge between the segments.

Bridges can also extend the physical size of a network. Although the individual segments are still restricted by the maximum size imposed by the network design limits, bridges enable network designers to stretch the distances between segments and extend the overall size of the network.

Bridges, however, cannot join dissimilar types of LANs. Bridges are dependent on the physical addresses of devices. Physical device addresses are functions of the data link layer, and different data link layer protocols are used for each type of network. A bridge, therefore, cannot be used to join an Ethernet segment to a token ring segment.

Note Device addresses are functions of the OSI data link layer, which is discussed in greater detail in Chapter 22, "OSI Data Link Layer Concepts." Therefore, bridges are said to function at the data link layer.

Multiplexors

Multiplexors solve a different type of connectivity problem. What if you have several signals to transmit, but only one path that the signals must share? A *multiplexor* is a device that combines several signals so that they can be transmitted together, and then enables the original signals to be extracted at the other end of the transmission. (The process of recovering the original signals is called *demultiplexing.*) Figure 20.12 shows how the process works.

Modems

Standard telephone lines can transmit only analog signals. Computers, however, store and transmit data digitally. *Modems* are capable of transmitting digital computer signals over telephone lines by converting them to analog form.

The process of converting one signal form to another (digital to analog in this case) is called *modulation.* The reverse process of recovering the original signal is called *demodulation.* The term modem is derived from this *mo*dulation/*dem*odulation process.

Modems can be used to connect computer devices or entire networks that are at distant locations. (Before digital telephone lines became available, modems were about the only way of linking distant devices.) Some modems operate constantly over dedicated phone lines. Others use standard *public switched-telephone network* (PSTN) dial-up lines and make a connection only when one is required.

Common uses for modems on LANs include the following:

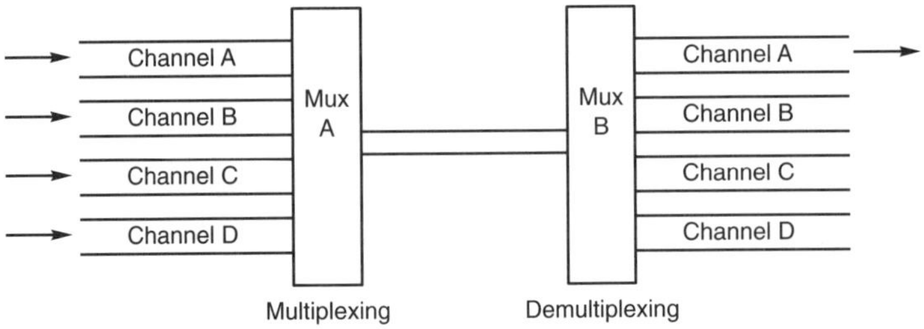

Figure 20.12
Multiplexing and demultiplexing a signal.

- Enabling users to call in and access the LAN
- Exchanging electronic mail between mail servers
- Transmitting and receiving faxes with a fax server
- Enabling LANs to exchange data on demand

Modems enable networks to exchange e-mail and to perform limited data transfers, but the connectivity made possible is extremely limited. By themselves, modems do not enable remote networks to connect to each other and directly exchange data. In other words, a modem is not an internetwork device. Nevertheless, modems may be used in conjunction with an internetwork device, such as a router, to connect remote networks through the PSTN, or an analog service, such as a 56 KB line.

The point is that a modem cannot enable remote networks to internetwork freely without the assistance of routers or brouters to manage the connection between the networks.

Note Modems do not necessarily need to connect through the PSTN. *Short-haul modems* are even frequently used to connect devices in the same building. A standard serial connection is limited to 50 feet, but short-haul modems can be used to extend the range of a serial connection to any required distance.

Many devices are designed to assume that modems will be used. When you want to connect such devices without using modems, you can use a *null modem cable*, which connects the transmitter of one device to the receiver of the other device.

Note A modem translates digital signals for transmission on analog phone lines. A codec (*co*der/*dec*oder) provides a similar service when analog signals are to be transmitted over digital phone lines, translating analog signals into digital form.

Internetwork Connectivity Devices

An *internetwork* consists of two or more independent networks that are physically connected, enabling them to communicate. The networks that make up an internetwork may be of quite different types. An internetwork might include Ethernet and token-ring networks, for example.

Earlier, you saw how bridges can be used to interconnect similar networks. When things get more complex, however, more advanced technologies might be required. This section discusses three such technologies: routers, brouters, and CSU/DSUs.

Routers

Recall that bridges subdivide networks by building tables that list which device addresses can be reached from a particular port on the router. This is a suitable strategy in relatively simple networks, but has shortcomings when networks become more complex.

Consider the network shown in figure 20.13. Let's examine why bridges are unsuitable for interconnecting the network segments in this manner.

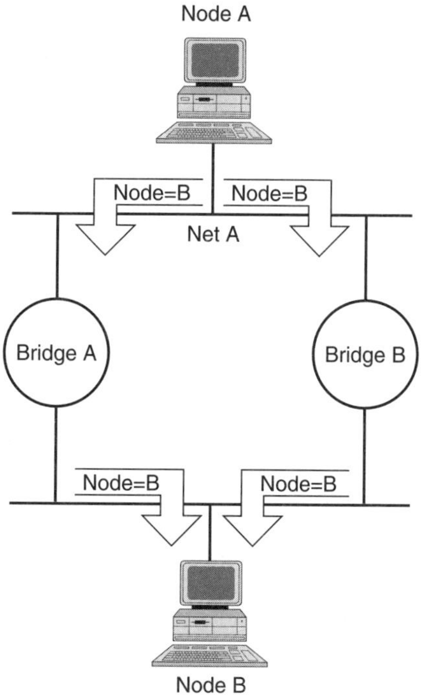

Figure 20.13
A complex network with bridges.

Both bridges are aware of the existence of Node B, and both will pick up the packet from Net A and forward it. At the very least, this means that the same packet will arrive twice at Node B.

A worse case, however, is that these relatively unintelligent bridges will start passing packets around in loops. This results in an ever-increasing number of packets that are circulating on the network and are never reaching their destinations. Ultimately, this activity will saturate the network.

So one restriction of bridges is that the network cannot include redundant paths. However, redundant paths are desirable because they enable the network to continue functioning when one path goes down.

Note

An algorithm called the *spanning tree algorithm* enables complex Ethernets to use bridges while redundant routes exist. The algorithm enables the bridges to communicate and to construct a logical network that does not contain redundant paths. The logical network is reconfigured if one of the paths fails.

Another problem is that the bridges cannot analyze the network and determine the fastest route over which to forward a packet. When multiple routes exist, this is a desirable capability, particularly in *wide area networks* (WANs) where some routes can be considerably slower than others.

Routers organize the large network in terms of logical network segments. Each network segment is assigned an address so that every packet has both a destination network address and a destination device address. Figure 20.14 shows a complex network based on routers.

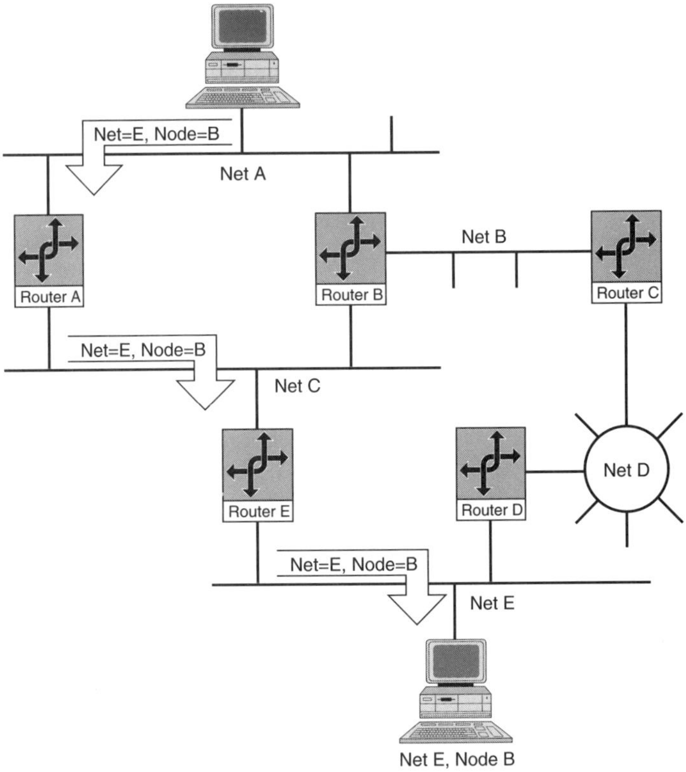

Figure 20.14
An internetwork with routers.

Note: Recall the section definition of an internetwork is that which consists of two or more logically separate, but physically connected, networks. By this definition, any network that is segment with routers is an internetwork.

Routers are more "intelligent" than bridges. Not only do they build tables of where networks are located, but they also use algorithms to determine the most efficient path for sending a packet to any given network. Even though a particular network segment might not be directly attached to the router, the router will know the best way to send a packet to a device on that network. Therefore, Router A knows that the most efficient step is to send the packet to Router C, not Router B.

Notice that Router B presents a redundant path to the path provided by Router A. Routers can cope with this situation Because they exchange routing information that ensures that packet loops will not occur. In figure 20.14, if Router A fails, Router B provides a backup message path, making this network more robust.

Routers can be used to divide large, busy LANs into smaller segments, much as bridges can be used. But that is not the only reason for selecting a router.

Routers are also capable of connecting different network types. Notice that the network in figure 20.14 includes a token-ring segment with the Ethernet segments. On such networks, a router is the device of choice.

Because they can determine route efficiencies, routers are usually employed to connect a LAN to a wide area network. WANs are frequently designed with multiple paths, and routers can ensure that the various paths are used most efficiently.

Note: Device addresses are functions of the OSI network layer, which will be discussed in greater detail in Chapter 23, "OSI Network Layer Concepts." Routers, therefore, are said to function at the network layer.

The network layer functions independently of the physical cabling system and the cabling system protocols—independently, that is, of the physical and data link layers. This is the reason that routers can easily translate packets between different cabling systems. Bridges cannot because they function at the data link layer, which is closely tied to a given set of physical layer specifications.

Brouters

A *brouter* is a router that can also bridge. A brouter attempts to deliver packets based on network protocol information. If a particular network layer protocol is not supported, the brouter bridges the packet using device addresses.

CSU/DSUs

When LANs are connected into wide area networks, the connection is frequently by means of the public telephone network. Connecting to some telephone media requires the use of a *channel service network/digital service unit* (CSU/DSU).

Network service providers design their media for a particular type of signal, and may require use of a CSU/DSU to translate the LAN signals to the signal format required. A CSU/DSU also isolates the local network from the public network to protect each network from noise and voltage fluctuations of the other.

Important Terms from This Chapter

A *network*, according to Novell study materials, is a "single independent network." On such a network, any device can communicate with any other device directly, without the need for a connection to a remote network. Under this definition, network connectivity devices are involved only in local network connectivity.

An *internetwork*, according to Novell study materials, consists of multiple independent networks that are connected together and can share remote resources. Internetwork connectivity devices facilitate connectivity between remote networks.

It is important to realize that "remote" does not necessarily mean "distant." An internetwork can be located entirely within a single building. The important distinction is whether the networks are logically separate, and actually has to do with protocol levels, which you will examine in greater detail in later sections. The crucial level is the network layer, which assigns an address to each network that makes up an internetwork. The following are ways to determine how a message was delivered:

- If a message can arrive at its destination using information that is available at the data link layer of the OSI model, then the message is being delivered by a network.

- If delivery requires use of the network address information that is available at the network layer, the message is being delivered through an internetwork.

Network connectivity devices, therefore, do not use network address information. Internetwork connectivity devices are capable of using network address information to assist in the efficient delivery of messages. The process of using network address information to deliver messages is called *routing.* The common feature that unites internetwork connectivity devices (routers and brouters) is that they can perform routing.

This distinction will become clearer to you as you progress through the rest of this section. Because each network in an internetwork is assigned an address, each network can be considered to be *logically separate*—that is, each network functions independently of other networks on the internetwork.

Note For the purposes of this section, CSU/DSUs are considered internetwork devices, but this is not strictly correct. The primary purpose of a CSU/DSU is to interface the network to a public data network. A given device may perform routing or it may depend on a separate router, depending on the vendor's hardware design.

Questions

1. Which *two* of the following are characteristic features of internetworks?
   - ☐ A. Multiple networks can be interconnected with bridges to form an internetwork.
   - ☐ B. Devices can communicate with devices on the local network.
   - ☐ C. Devices can communicate with devices on remote networks.
   - ☐ D. An internetwork can consist of segments that utilize different network protocols.
2. Which *two* of the following are characteristics of networks?
   - ☐ A. Devices can communicate with devices on the local network.
   - ☐ B. Devices can communicate with devices on remote networks.
   - ☐ C. Routers extend the range of a network.
   - ☐ D. A network can include network segments that utilize different protocols.
3. Which *two* of the following are functions of network connectivity devices?
   - ☐ A. Enabling devices to interface with media
   - ☐ B. Converting protocols between network segments
   - ☐ C. Connecting media segments together
   - ☐ D. Fully utilizing media capacity
4. Which *two* of the following are functions of internetwork connectivity devices?
   - ☐ A. Connecting remote networks
   - ☐ B. Enabling networks with different protocols to communicate
   - ☐ C. Attaching devices to media
   - ☐ D. Extending the range of network segments
5. The DB-15 connector is commonly used with ______.
   - ○ A. fiber-optic cable
   - ○ B. token-ring connections to NICs
   - ○ C. coaxial cable
   - ○ D. RS-232 serial interfaces
6. Which *two* connectors are frequently used with STP cable?
   - ☐ A. T-connectors
   - ☐ B. RJ-45 connectors
   - ☐ C. IBM unisex connectors
   - ☐ D. AppleTalk DIN connectors
7. Which *two* connectors are commonly used with coaxial cable?
   - ☐ A. DB-25 connectors
   - ☐ B. N-connectors
   - ☐ C. ST-connectors
   - ☐ D. BNC connectors

8. Which *three* are some advantages of active hubs?

   - ☐ A. They can regenerate network signals.
   - ☐ B. LANs ranges can be extended.
   - ☐ C. They are inexpensive.
   - ☐ D. They function as repeaters.

9. Which *two* networks can use passive hubs?

   - ☐ A. Ethernet
   - ☐ B. ARCnet
   - ☐ C. Token ring
   - ☐ D. All of the above

10. Which *two* statements are true of re-peaters?

    - ☐ A. Repeaters amplify signals.
    - ☐ B. Repeaters extend network distances.
    - ☐ C. Repeaters regenerate signals.
    - ☐ D. Repeaters can be used to extend the range of a network indefinitely.

11. Which *three* statements are true of bridges?

    - ☐ A. Bridges amplify and regenerate signals.
    - ☐ B. Bridges can connect logically separate networks.
    - ☐ C. Bridges use device address tables to route messages.
    - ☐ D. Bridges divide networks into smaller segments.

12. Modems can be used for which *three* of the following purposes?

    - ☐ A. To connect remote networks
    - ☐ B. To enable users to call in and access a LAN
    - ☐ C. To transmit and receive faxes
    - ☐ D. To extend the range of a serial interface

13. Which *three* features of routers are not features of bridges?

    - ☐ A. Regenerating signals
    - ☐ B. Connecting logically separate networks
    - ☐ C. Connecting networks using different protocols
    - ☐ D. Maintaining tables of network addresses

14. Which *two* of the following are functions of CSU/DSUs?

    - ☐ A. Connecting networks with different protocols
    - ☐ B. Connecting a network to some types of public telephone networks
    - ☐ C. Routing signals between logical networks
    - ☐ D. Isolating the local network from the public network

Answers

1. B, C
2. A, B
3. A ,C
4. A, B
5. B
6. C, D
7. B, D
8. A, B, D
9. B, C
10. A, B
11. A, C, D
12. B, C, D
13. B, C, D
14. B, D

CHAPTER 21

OSI Physical Layer Concepts

Although the OSI physical layer does not define the media used, the physical layer is concerned with all aspects of transmitting and receiving data on the network media. Specifically, the physical layer is concerned with transmitting and receiving bits. This layer defines several key characteristics of the physical network, including the following:

- *Physical structure of the network*
- *Mechanical and electrical specifications for using the medium (not the medium itself!)*
- *Bit transmission encoding and timing*

Although the physical layer does not define the medium, it defines clear requirements that the medium must meet, and physical layer specifications will differ depending on the physical medium to be used. Ethernet for UTP will have different physical layer specifications than Ethernet for coax, for example.

When you complete this chapter, you will understand the following:

- The purpose of the OSI physical layer
- Types of network connections
- Physical topologies
- Analog and digital signaling
- Bit synchronization
- Bandwidth use
- Multiplexing

Connection Types

All network connections consist of two types of building blocks:

- Multipoint connections
- Point-to-point connections

A *multipoint connection* enables one device to communicate with two or more devices. An example is shown in figure 21.1. All the devices attached using a multipoint connection share the same network transmission medium.

A *point-to-point connection* enables one device to communicate with one other device (see fig. 21.2). When two devices are connected through a point-to-point link, they have exclusive use of the data capacity of the link.

Larger networks can be constructed by adding point-to-point links. In this case, devices rely on other devices to relay their messages. Point-to-point links can even come full circle to form a ring, enabling messages to be passed from any device to any other device on the ring.

Physical Topologies

The physical topology of a network describes the layout of the network media. Different physical topologies have different characteristics in terms of performance, ease of installation, troubleshooting, and reconfiguration.

Physical Topologies Based on Multipoint Connections

In fact, only one topology is based on multipoint connections—the bus, shown in figure 21.3. Notice that all devices are connected to a common transmission media. In some cases, the common media is referred to as a *backbone network*.

Figure 21.1
Examples of multipoint connections.

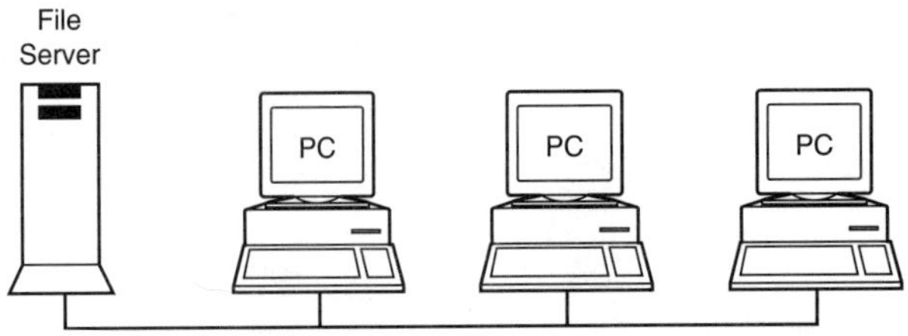

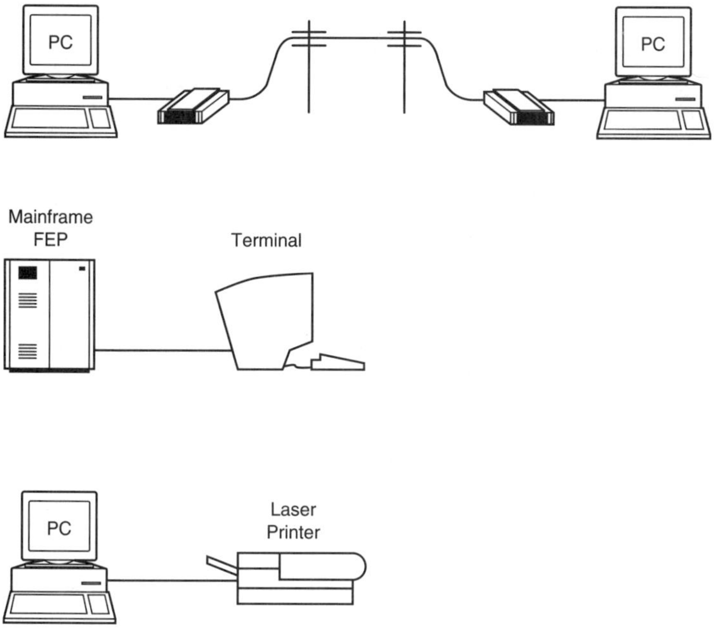

Figure 21.2
Point-to-point connections.

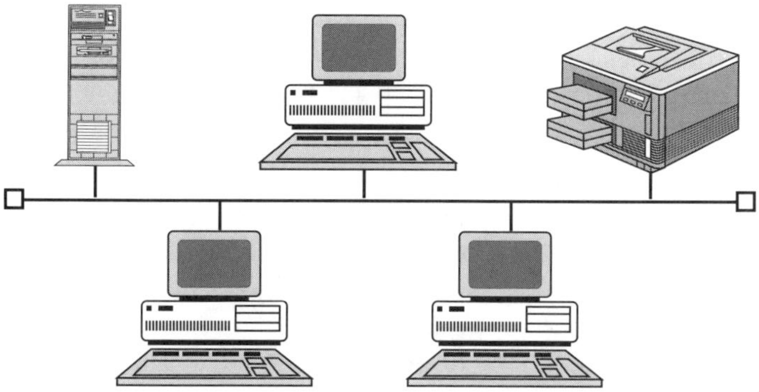

Figure 21.3
A bus physical topology.

Bus Characteristics

Chapters 19 and 20 discuss the cabling and connectors used for bus topologies. Recall that the ends of the cable must be terminated and that devices may be connected along the length of the cable. Connections are performed with T-connectors or with taps (transceivers) that attach directly to the cable and use a drop cable to connect to the workstation.

Typically, signals on a bus network are broadcast in both directions on the backbone cable, enabling all devices to directly receive the signal. With some unidirectional buses, however, signals travel in one direction only and can reach only downstream devices. In this case, the cable must be terminated in such a way that signals are reflected back on the cable and can reach other devices.

Installation

Bus installation is relatively simple and requires only basic tools and skill. Cable runs are generally fairly short because it is not necessary to run a separate cable to a central hub for each device on the network.

Bus networks such as Ethernet have carefully defined rules that must be adhered to for best network performance. Stations on a thick Ethernet cable, for example, should be attached at intervals that are multiples of 2 1/2 meters. All network media have attenuation characteristics that limit the lengths of cables and the number of devices that can be attached.

Reconfiguration

Bus networks can be difficult to reconfigure. If the main cable does not run close to the new device, it might need to be rerouted. Adding new devices often involves cutting the main cable to add a T-connector, which requires the network to be shut down. In the process, it is important to adhere to rules regarding maximum number of devices and distances at which taps are to be spaced.

Troubleshooting

Bus networks can be difficult to troubleshoot because a single fault can render the entire bus inoperative. A broken cable, for example, is the same as having two unterminated cables. Without termination, signals can reflect back into both cable segments interfering with transmissions and making the system inoperable. (In addition, of course, devices cannot communicate with devices that are on the opposite side of the break.) Because all devices are affected by a cable break, it can be difficult to isolate a break to the cable that falls between two devices.

Physical Topologies Based on Point-to-Point Connections

As shown in figure 21.4, several different topologies can be based on point-to-point connections, as follows:

- *Star topologies* utilize a point-to-point link (a "drop cable") to connect each device to a central hub.
- *Mesh networks* establish a point-to-point link between each pair of computers on the network. Because the number of required links rises rapidly as the number of computers increases, large mesh networks are not frequently used.
- *Hybrid mesh networks* are commonly used in wide-area networks. No attempt is made to provide a link between each possible pair of computers. Extra links, however, are installed to provide more direct paths, extra bandwidth, and some redundancy in case links fail.
- *Ring networks* utilize point-to-point links to connect devices together in a ring. Messages are forwarded around the ring and can reach any station in this way.
- *Cellular topologies* divide geographic areas into overlapping cells that are serviced by transmitter/receivers. Point-to-point radio links are established between a cellular data device and

the transmitter in a cell. These point-to-point links are constantly reconfigured as the data device moves through the cellular network. (Multipoint links may also be established under appropriate circumstances.)

Each of these topologies is examined in greater detail in the next sections.

The Ring Topology

The ring topology is circular, and signals typically travel around the ring in one direction only. Each device incorporates a receiver and a transmitter and serves as a repeater that passes the signal on to the next device in the ring. Because the signal is regenerated at each device, signal degeneration is low.

Installation

Installation is fairly simple, but the amount of cable required can go higher than with a bus. As with all networks, it is essential to stay within network design restrictions regarding cable lengths between devices, total ring length, and number of devices.

Reconfiguration

Rings can be difficult to reconfigure, particularly when devices are located at large distances.

Troubleshooting

The repeating function makes it fairly easy to isolate cabling faults. When a break is present in the cable, devices will still be able to transmit to downstream devices on the near side of the break. Fault isolation becomes a matter of determining which device is not receiving signals from its immediate upstream neighbor.

Some rings incorporate redundant paths that can be switched in when a cable break occurs. The redundant path takes the form of a second ring that transmits signals in opposite directions from the main ring. When a break occurs in the main ring, the counter-rotating ring can be used to route signals around the break.

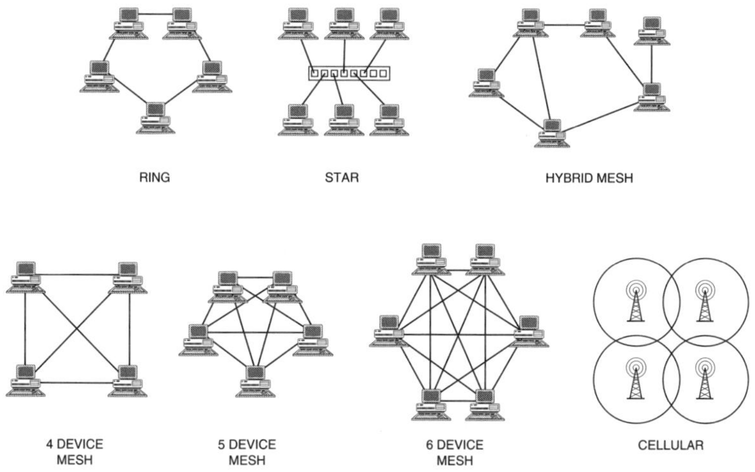

Figure 21.4
Physical topologies based on point-to-point connections.

The Star Topology

A star topology networks each device with a cable that connects it to a central hub. The hub receives signals from network devices and routes the signals to the proper destination. Star hubs can be interconnected to form tree or hierarchical network topologies.

Installation

The major installation difficulty is that a separate cable must be run to connect each device to a hub. Cabling requirements are generally considerably higher than for bus or ring physical topologies.

A significant concern with star topologies is that cable lengths between hubs and devices are limited, typically to 100 meters. Therefore, it is necessary to ensure that a hub is located within 100 meters of every potential device location

Reconfiguration

The payoff for cabling to a central hub is that networks are easy to reconfigure. Most adds and moves can be accomplished by simply moving a plug to a new hub port.

Troubleshooting

It is easier to troubleshoot stars than buses and, generally speaking, than rings. It is easy to build troubleshooting features into hubs, which can be monitored centrally.

When the cable to a device fails, it generally affects that device only. In cases where a device cable causes problems for the entire network, it is simple to disconnect the cable from the hub. Many managed hubs will automatically disconnect devices that are producing network errors.

Star topologies are subject to a single point of failure. If the hub fails, all devices are affected.

Mesh Topologies

Mesh networks consist of a point-to-point link between each pair of devices on the network. In most cases, the number of connections required limits the use of true mesh networks to a few stations. A five-device mesh network requires 24 ($4\times3\times2$) connections, but a six-device mesh requires 120 ($5\times4\times3\times2$)!

Two advantages can be stated for a mesh topology. The first is that every device has a guaranteed communication channel capacity with every other device. The other is a high level of fault tolerance. Even multiple media failures will probably leave the network capable of delivering messages to all devices.

More common is the hybrid network, which contains some redundant links, particularly to the most important devices or where the greatest capacity is needed. When it is essential that the network never go down, redundant links are a good form of insurance.

Installation

Mesh networks are difficult to install, with the difficulty increasing rapidly as the number of devices increases.

Hybrid mesh networks are most commonly in wide area networks, where the links consist primarily of leased communication services. Installation is primarily a matter of setting up routers, CSU/DSUs, and so on. WAN connections of this sort can get involved to install and manage.

Reconfiguration

Mesh networks can be extremely difficult to reconfigure.

Troubleshooting

Mesh networks are easy to troubleshoot because each device keeps track of every other device.

Hybrid mesh networks introduce concerns about how signals are routed through the network. This is a skilled task that calls for sophisticated diagnostic and management systems to ensure that the network operates smoothly.

Mesh networks are extremely robust because redundant links abound. They are, therefore, seldom subject to single points of failure. Performance can degrade, however, if failure of one link causes traffic on other links to rise to unacceptable levels.

Cellular Topology

Cellular networks divide the area being serviced into cells, each of which is serviced by a central station. Devices use radio signals to communicate with the central station, and the central station routes messages to other devices. Cellular data networks can be implemented on an office level or in large geographic areas.

Installation

Installation of office-based cellular LANs is quite different from installation of cable-based LANs. Much depends on the degree to which the office building supports the requirements of the cellular system that has been chosen. Transmitters are of limited power and cannot penetrate walls, so some building types are unsuitable. If hubs can be located so they can communicate clearly with devices, installation is relatively simple.

Reconfiguration

Within the area serviced by a hub, devices can be located and relocated easily. Hubs are often connected to other hubs using cable, however, and relocation of hubs can be more involved.

Troubleshooting

Troubleshooting depends on the network design. If hubs maintain a point-to-point link with devices, troubleshooting is simplified.

When a hub fails, all devices serviced by the hub lose service. Because devices are mobile, they can be relocated to a working area to restore service.

Digital and Analog Signaling

Signaling is the process of communicating information. The information being communicated can take one of two forms: analog or digital. Frequently, information in one form must be converted to the other. This frequently involves the use of some encoding scheme that enables the original information to be recovered from a signal after the signal has been received.

When an analog or digital signal is altered so that it contains information to be communicated, the process is called *modulation* or *encoding*. AM radio transmits information by modulating the radio signal, increasing or decreasing the amplitude (signal strength) depending on the information content. Many similar schemes are used to communicate information through different types of signals.

- *Analog information* is information that changes continuously and can take on many different values. The hands on an analog clock move constantly, displaying time on a continuous scale.

- *Digital information* is characterized by discrete states. A lightbulb is on or off, for example. A digital clock represents the time in one minute intervals and doesn't change its numbers again until the next minute. A digital clock can represent exact minutes, but nothing in between.

Figure 21.5 illustrates the difference between analog and digital signals. The analog signal is constantly changing and takes on values throughout the range of possible values. The digital signal takes on only two (or a few) specific states.

Digital Signaling Techniques

Computer data is inherently digital, and the majority of networks use digital signaling. This chapter examines two methods of modulating a digital signal to encode digital data, as follows:

- Current state
- State transition

Current State Encoding

This encoding technique assigns specific signal states to represent each possible data value. The signal is monitored periodically to determine its current state, from which a data value may be determined. A voltage of +5 might represent a binary 1 and a voltage of -5 might represent a binary 0, for example. Many different signal variations could be used. The important characteristic is that a given state represents one and only one data value. In figure 21.6, a high voltage represents a binary 0, while a low voltage represents a binary 1.

The following encoding schemes make use of current state encoding, although discussion of their specific characteristics is beyond the scope of this chapter:

- Unipolar
- Bipolar
- Return-to-Zero (NRZ)
- Biphase

State Transition Encoding

This encoding technique uses transitions in the digital signal to represent data. Following are a couple of ways this could be done:

- A transition from high to low voltage always represents a 1, and a transition from low to high voltage always represents a 0.

Figure 21.5
Analog and digital signals.

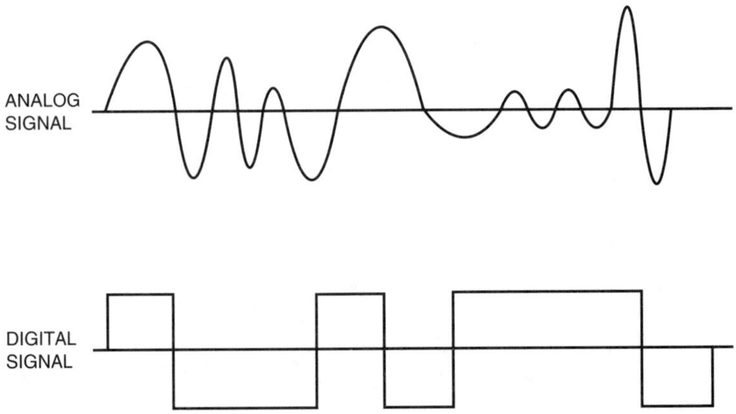

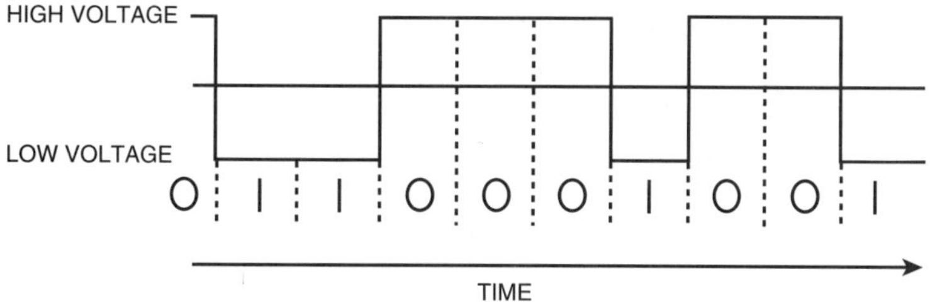

Figure 21.6
Current state encoding.

- Any transition always represents a 1, and the absence of an expected transition represents a 0. This scheme is depicted in figure 21.7.

The following encoding schemes make use of state transition encoding, although discussion of their specific characteristics is beyond the scope of this chapter:

- Bipolar-Alternate Mark Inversion (AMI)
- Non-Return-to-Zero (NRZ)
- Manchester
- Differential Manchester
- Biphase Space (FM-O)

Note The terms "current state" and "state transition" were invented by Novell for use in this course and are not standard terms in the industry.

The common industry term for current state is *level triggered* because recognition of a given state is triggered (initiated) by a specific signal level.

The common industry term for state transition is *edge triggered,* since either the leading or trailing edge of a signal transition (the edge of the signal transition) is used to signal that a state change has taken place.

Analog Signaling

Analog signals are constantly varying in one or more values. These changes in values can be used to represent data.

Analog wave forms frequently take the form of sine waves. The sine wave in figure 21.8 illustrates two characteristics that define an analog wave form, as follows:

- **Frequency.** Indicates the rate at which the waveform is changing. Frequency is associated with the wavelength of the waveform, which is a measure of the distance between two similar peaks on adjacent waves. Frequency is generally measured in Hertz (Hz), which indicates the frequency in cycles per second. Frequency is illustrated in figure 21.8.

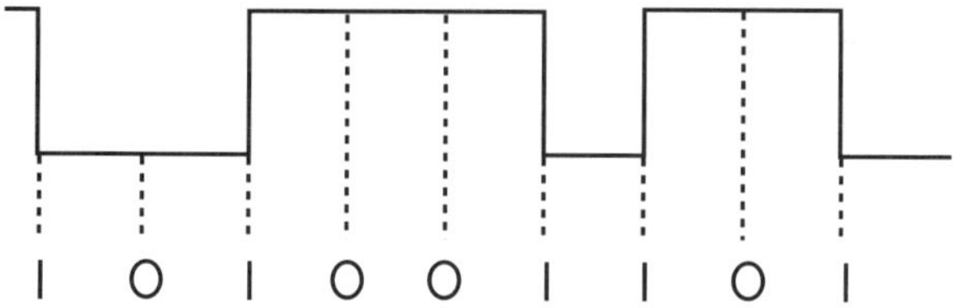

Figure 21.7
State transition encoding.

Figure 21.8
Two analog waveforms differing in frequency.

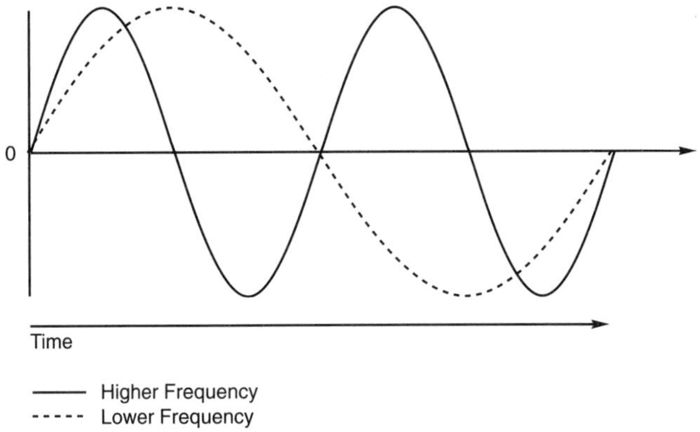

- **Amplitude.** The measure of the strength of the waveform. Amplitude is illustrated in figure 21.9.

A third characteristic, *phase*, can also be defined. Figure 21.10 illustrates waveforms that differ in phase. These waveforms have identical frequency and amplitude, but they do not begin their transitions at the same time.

- In figure 21.10, WAVE B begins to rise from the reference line at the same time that Wave A is peaking. Therefore, Wave B is 1/4 of a wave behind Wave A. If a complete wave is represented as having 360 degrees, Wave B lags behind Wave A by 90 degrees.
- In figure 21.11, notice that Wave B is a mirror image of Wave A. Because Wave B is 1/2 of a wave behind Wave A, Wave B lags behind Wave A by 180 degrees. Wave C is 1/3 of a wave behind A and lags behind Wave A by 120 degrees.

Each of these characteristics, frequency, amplitude, and phase can be used to encode data.

Figure 21.9
Two analog waveforms differing in amplitude.

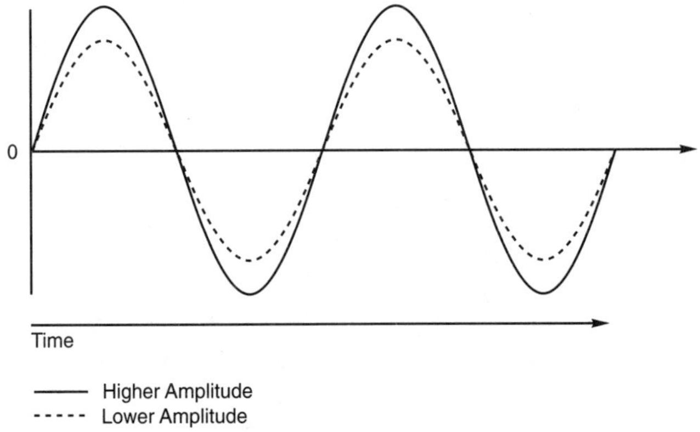

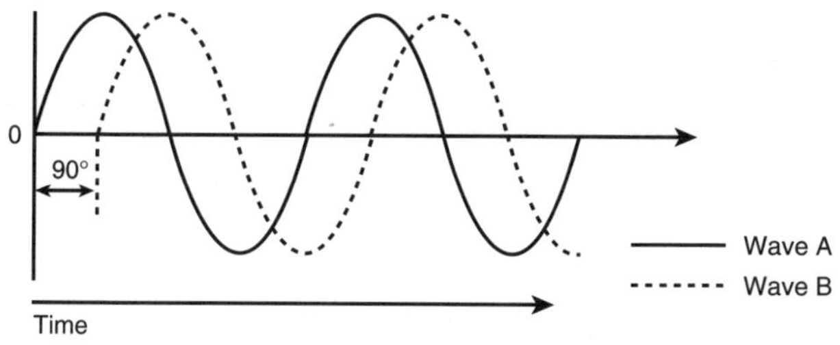

Figure 21.10
Two analog waveforms differing in phase.

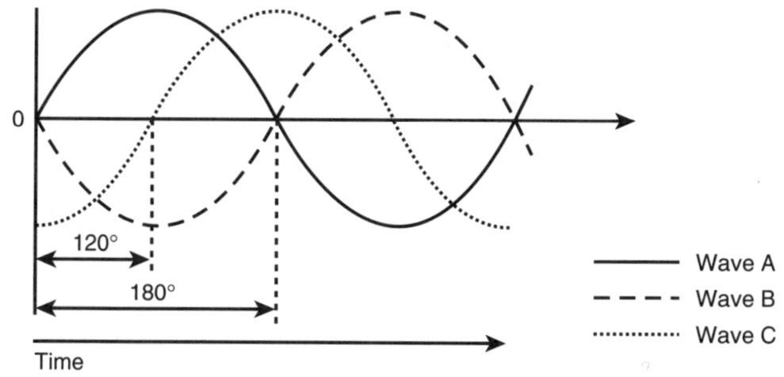

Figure 21.11
Three analog waveforms differing in phase by different amounts.

Amplitude Shift Keying

This is a current state method of modulation in that specific signal amplitudes are assigned specific data values. A high-amplitude signal, for example, might be assigned a value of 1, while a low-amplitude signal is assigned a value of 0. The first example in figure 21.12 illustrates amplitude shift keying.

Frequency Shift Keying

Frequency shift keying is also a current state modulation method. Specific frequency values are assigned specific data values. A high frequency, for example, might represent 0, while a lower frequency might represent 1. The second example in Figure 21.12 illustrates frequency shift keying.

Phase Shift Keying

Phase shift keying is a transition state modulation method. For example, a reference phase might represent 0, while a 180-degree phase shift would represent a 1 value. The process is illustrated in the third example of figure 21.12.

Bit Synchronization

With both current state and transition state modulation methods, the receiving device monitors the signal, looking for an expected characteristic. Timing is important because the receiver needs to know when it should check the incoming signal. If the check is made at the wrong time, erroneous data might be extracted.

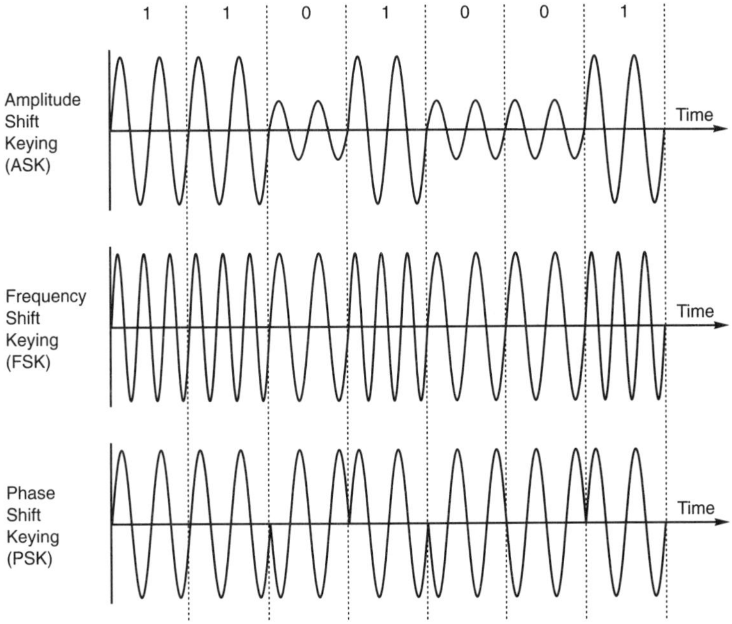

Figure 21.12
Keying methods for amplitude waveforms.

Two methods of coordinating signal timing follow:

- Asynchronous communication
- Synchronous communication

The methods differ primarily in the way they adjust the clocks of the sending and receiving devices.

Asynchronous Communication

Although the sender and receiver have internal clocks, these clocks are not directly synchronized. Each message begins with a start bit that enables the receiver to synchronize its internal clock with the timing of the message. Messages are kept short so the receiver's clock will not drift out of synchronization for the duration of the message. A *stop bit* signals that the message is complete. Asynchronous techniques are primarily used to transmit character data, and the message part of the transmission is limited to 7 or 8 bits.

To make the system work, the sender and receiver must reach a general agreement on the speed at which data is to be transmitted. You are probably familiar with the process of setting the data rate for modems. Even though the sending and receiving clocks are not directly synchronized, if they agree to transmit at, say 9,600 bits per second, their clocks can remain sufficiently synchronized to enable a single short transmission to be completed.

One characteristic to note is that the signals are intermittent and the transmission media is idle except when a transmission is actually taking place. No clock signals are transmitted to keep the receiver's clock synchronized with the sender's clock.

Synchronous Communication

Synchronous communication employs a clocking mechanism to ensure that the sending and receiving devices remain synchronized. Three techniques will be discussed, as follows:

- Guaranteed State Change
- Separate Clock Signals
- Oversampling

Guaranteed State Change

Some encoding techniques are designed to ensure that state changes occur at regular intervals. The receiving device adjusts its internal clock to match the frequencies of the state changes.

Signals of this type are called *self-clocking* because the clocking information is embedded in the signal itself and no other clocking mechanism is required.

Separate Clock Signals

The separate clock signal approach utilizes a separate communication channel to carry clocking information. The common RS-232 serial interface uses this approach. One of the wires in the cable carries clocking signals that enable the sending device to tell the receiver when it should monitor the incoming data.

This approach is useful over short distances, but becomes problematic with longer cables. Signals can travel through different wires in the cable at different rates, and at some point the clocking signal will no longer be synchronized with the signals on the data wires. RS-232 connections, for example, are typically limited to a maximum length of 50 feet for this reason.

Oversampling

With this technique, the receiver samples incoming data at a higher rate than the rate at which the data is being transmitted. If the receiver monitors at ten times the rate at which signal transitions are occurring, it is easy to determine when transitions have taken place. The extra samples also enable the receiver to determine when its clock is drifting and needs to be resynchronized.

Baseband and Broadband Transmissions

There are two ways to allocate the capacity of transmission media, as follows:

- **Baseband.** Devotes the entire capacity of the medium to one communication channel
- **Broadband.** Enables two or more communication channels to share the bandwidth of the communications medium

Baseband is the most common mode of operation. Most LANs function in baseband mode, for example. Baseband signaling can be accomplished with both analog and digital signals.

You have a great deal of experience with broadband transmissions, however, whether you know it or not. The TV cable coming into your house from an antenna or a cable provider is a broadband medium. Many television signals can share the bandwidth of the cable because each signal is modulated using a separately assigned frequency. You can choose the channel you want to watch by selecting its frequency with the television tuner. This technique of dividing bandwidth into frequency bands is called *frequency-division multiplexing* (FDM) and works only with analog signals. Another technique called *time-division multiplexing* (TDM) supports digital signals and will be described in the next section.

Figure 21.13 contrasts the difference between baseband and broadband modes of operation.

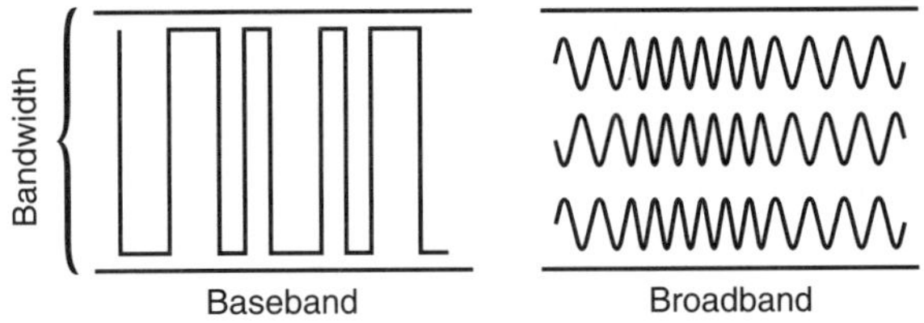

Figure 21.13
Baseband and broadband transmission modes.

Multiplexing

Multiplexing is the technique that enables broadband media to support multiple data channels. There are several times when multiplexing makes sense, as follows:

- **When media bandwidth is costly.** A high-speed leased line, such as a T-1 or T-3, is expensive to lease. Providing the leased line has sufficient bandwidth, multiplexing can enable the same line to carry mainframe, LAN, voice, video conferencing, and various other data types.
- **When bandwidth is idle.** Many organizations have installed fiber-optic cable that is being used only to partial capacity. With the proper equipment, a single fiber can support hundreds of megabits or even a gigabit or more of data capacity.
- **When large amounts of data need to be transmitted through low-capacity channels.** Multiplexing techniques can divide the original data stream into several lower-bandwidth channels, each of which can be transmitted through a lower capacity medium. The signals can be recombined at the receiving end.

Multiplexing is the process of combining multiple data channels for transmission on a common medium. *Demultiplexing* is the process of recovering the original separate channels from a multiplexed signal.

Multiplexing and demultiplexing are performed by a *multiplexor*, which usually has both capabilities. A multiplexor is sometimes called a *mux*.

The following two techniques are used to multiplex signals:

- Frequency-division multiplexing
- Time-division multiplexing

Frequency-Division Multiplexing

Figure 21.14 illustrates *frequency-division multiplexing*. The technique works by converting all data channels to analog form. Each of these analog signals can be modulated by a separate frequency (called a *carrier frequency*) that makes it possible to recover that signal during the demultiplexing process. At the receiving end, the demultiplexor can select the desired carrier signal and use it to extract the data signal for that channel.

FDM can be used in broadband LANs (a standard for Ethernet exists). One advantage of FDM is that it supports bi-directional signaling on the same cable.

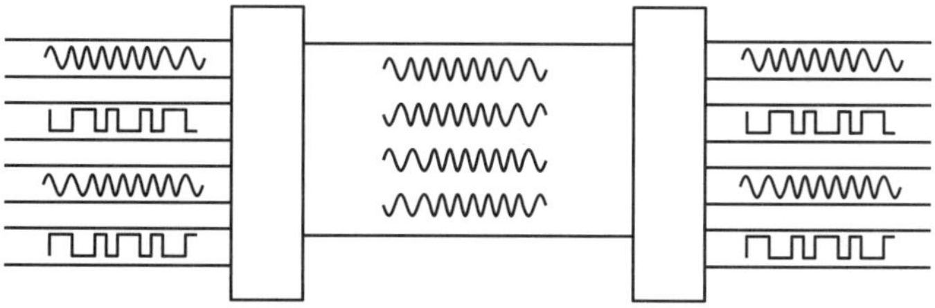

Figure 21.14
Frequency-division multiplexing.

Time-Division Multiplexing

Time-division multiplexing (TDM) divides a channel into time slots that are allocated to the data streams to be transmitted. Figure 21.15 illustrates the process. Provided that the sender and receiver agree on the time slot assignments, the receiver can easily recover and reconstruct the original data streams.

TDM transmits the multiplexed signal in baseband mode. Interestingly, this makes it possible to multiplex a TDM multiplexed signal as one of the data channels on an FDM system.

Conventional TDM equipment utilizes fixed time divisions and allocates time to a channel regardless of how busy that channel is. If a channel is not busy, its time slot is not being fully utilized. Because the time divisions are programmed into the configurations of the multiplexors, this technique often is referred to as *synchronous TDM.*

If it is important to use the capacity of the data medium more efficiently, a more sophisticated technique called *statistical time-division multiplexing* (StatTDM) may be used. A stat-mux uses the time-slot technique, but allocates time slots based on the traffic demand on the individual channels. Figure 21.16 illustrates the process. Notice that Channel B is allocated more time slots than Channel A, while Channel C is allocated the fewest time slots. Channel D is idle and no slots are allocated to it. To make this procedure work, the data transmitted for each time slot includes a control field that identifies to which channel the data in the time slot should be assigned.

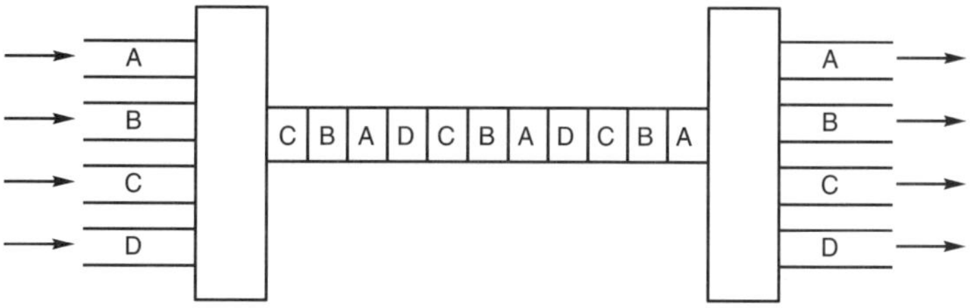

Figure 21.15
Time-division multiplexing.

Figure 21.16
Statistical time-division multiplexing.

Questions

1. Which *three* of the following are functions of the OSI physical layer?
   - ☐ A. Mechanical and electrical specifications for using the medium
   - ☐ B. Generating electrical signals on the medium
   - ☐ C. Network topology
   - ☐ D. Bit transmission encoding and timing

2. Which *three* of these network topologies consist of point-to-point links?
   - ☐ A. Bus
   - ☐ B. Ring
   - ☐ C. Star
   - ☐ D. Mesh

3. Which network topologies are subject to a single point of failure (that is, one failure can stop all network communication)?
   - ○ A. Mesh
   - ○ B. Bus
   - ○ C. Star
   - ○ D. Ring

4. Which *three* are advantages of star topologies?
   - ☐ A. Reconfiguration is simplified
   - ☐ B. Cable costs are minimized
   - ☐ C. Active hubs can regenerate signals
   - ☐ D. They are easy to troubleshoot

5. Which *two* are advantages of bus topologies?
   - ☐ A. Long cable runs are possible without signal regeneration.
   - ☐ B. They often require least amounts of cable.
   - ☐ C. They are well-proven technology.
   - ☐ D. They are easy to troubleshoot.

6. Which *two* are examples of analog data?
   - ☐ A. Light from a switched electric light
   - ☐ B. Sound from a radio
   - ☐ C. Morse code
   - ☐ D. A sine wave

7. Which *two* of the following are analog modulation techniques?
   - ☐ A. Phase shift keying
   - ☐ B. Binary modulation
   - ☐ C. State transition encoding
   - ☐ D. ASK

8. Which *two* of the following characteristics of an analog waveform are directly related?
   - ☐ A. Amplitude
   - ☐ B. Wavelength
   - ☐ C. Frequency
   - ☐ D. Phase

9. Which bit synchronization techniques can operate without a single-channel medium, such as a single pair of wires?

   - ☐ A. Guaranteed state change
   - ☐ B. Asynchronous
   - ☐ C. Oversampling
   - ☐ D. Separate clock signals

10. Which *two* techniques encode data in digital form for transmission on the media?

    - ☐ A. Time-division multiplexing
    - ☐ B. Frequency-division multiplexing
    - ☐ C. Phase shift keying
    - ☐ D. Current state encoding

Answers

1. A, C, D
2. B, C, D
3. C
4. A, C, D
5. B, C
6. B, D
7. A, D
8. B, C
9. A, B, C
10. A, D

CHAPTER 22

OSI Data Link Layer Concepts

Recall from the previous chapter that the OSI physical layer is concerned only with transmitting and receiving bits. Network communication, however, is considerably more involved than moving bits from one device to another. In fact, dozens of steps must be performed to complete the task of transporting a message from one device to another. This chapter examines the tasks performed by the data link layer.

Real messages consist not of single bits but of meaningful groups of bits. The data link layer receives messages called frames from upper layers (recall the description of OSI layer-to-layer communication in Chapter 18, "The OSI Layered Protocol Model"). A primary function of the data link layer is to disassemble these frames into bits for transmission and then to reconstruct frames from bits that are received.

The data link layer has other functions as well (although all functions may not be performed by a given network protocol stack). This layer performs the following tasks:

- Identifies devices on the network
- Controls (and possibly corrects) errors
- Controls access to the network medium
- Defines the logical topology of the network
- Controls data flow

Note The data link layer is conventionally divided into two sublayers:

- *Media access control* (MAC). This sublayer controls the means by which multiple devices share the same media channel.
- *Logical link control* (LLC). This sublayer establishes and maintains links between communicating devices.

This chapter covers the following data link layer topics:

- Logical topologies
- Media access control
- Addressing
- Transmission synchronization
- Connection services

Logical Topologies

Chapter 21, "OSI Physical Layer Concepts," introduces physical topologies, which describe how the media are physically arranged to build a network. Besides having a physical topology, a network has a logical topology that describes the path that a signal follows on a network. The logical and physical topologies of a network may be the same or different.

Token ring is the most dramatic example of a network having different physical and logical topologies. Figure 22.1 illustrates how computers are connected on a token ring. Each computer transmits signals to the receiver on the next computer. In this way, signals travel through each station on the cabling system, eventually completing a trip back to the station that originated them. Recall that a logical topology describes the manner in which signals travel on the network. It is easy to see why token ring networks have a *ring* logical topology.

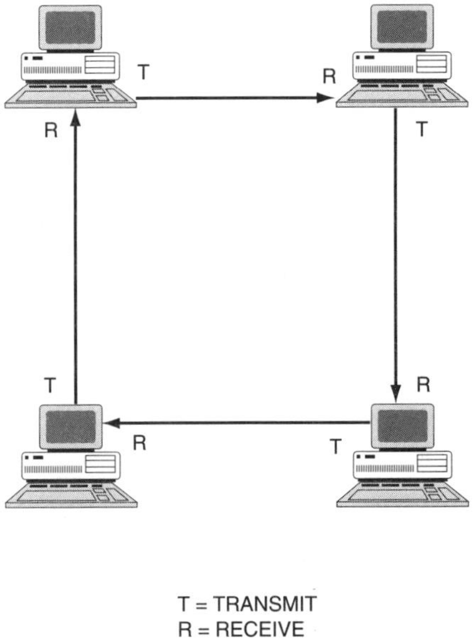

Figure 22.1
Logical topology of a token-ring network.

Token-ring networks, however, are never physically wired in rings. Hubs are used instead, and each computer is cabled to the hub by a drop cable. Figure 22.2 shows how the computers and cables are arranged. Notice the way the cables are connected within the hub so that the transmitter side of one computer connects to the receiver of the next computer. This is exactly the same logical relationship we saw in figure 22.1, and the logical topology is still a ring.

Due to the manner in which each computer is cabled individually to a hub, however, the physical topology of a token ring is a star.

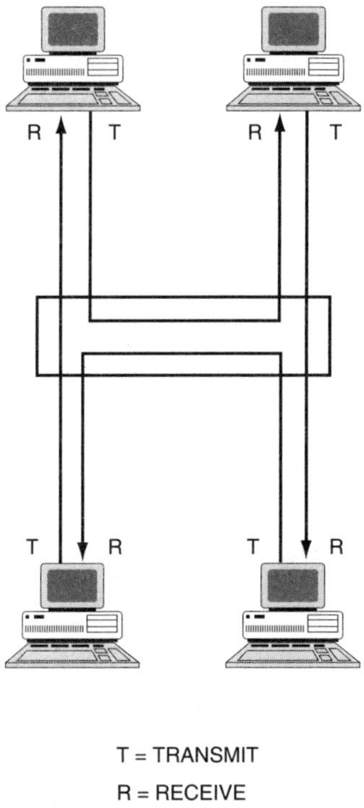

Figure 22.2
A logical ring is configured as a physical star.

Coax Ethernet is an example of a bus network where every station is connected to every other station in a multi-point physical topology. Also, every Ethernet station broadcasts signals to every other station, resulting in a bus logical topology as well. Ethernet, therefore, has a physical bus topology and a logical bus topology (see fig. 22.3).

A 10BASE-T Ethernet uses UTP cable and hub-based wiring, but it remains a logical bus because devices continue to communicate using multi-point communication. A 10BASE-T Ethernet, therefore, is a physical star but a logical bus.

Note The following are some rules of thumb for distinguishing between physical and logical:

- If you can see it or touch it, it is physical.
- If you can't see it or touch it, it is logical.

The following are rules of thumb for distinguishing between bus and ring networks:

- If signals from each computer are received by every other computer, the network is a bus.
- If each computer receives signals from only one other computer, the network is a ring.

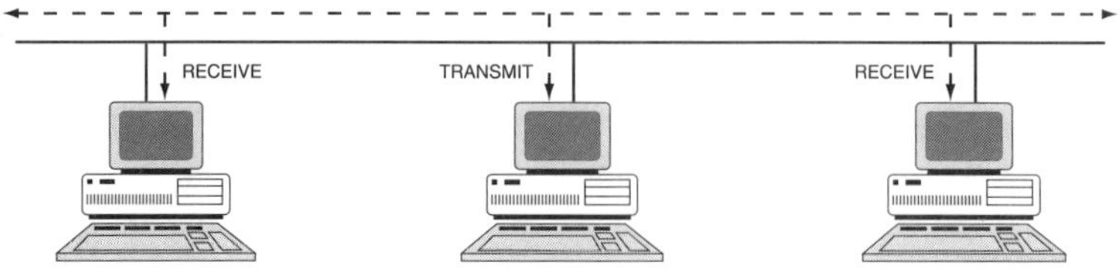

Figure 22.3
Ethernet is both a physical and a logical bus.

Media Access Control

Any given media channel can support only one signal at a time. If two computers transmit on the channel at the same time, their signals will interfere with each other, much as voices interfere when two people speak at the same time. Media access control is the process of controlling access to the media so that interference cannot take place.

This section discusses three forms of media access control:

- Contention
- Token passing
- Polling

Contention

With contention-based access control, any computer can transmit at any time. This system breaks down when two computers attempt to transmit at the same time, in which case a collision occurs (see fig. 22.4). Eventually, when a network gets busy enough, most attempts to transmit result in collisions and little effective communication can take place.

Mechanisms, therefore, are usually put into place to minimize the effects of collisions. One mechanism is *carrier sensing*, in which each computer listens to the network before attempting to transmit. If the network is busy, the computer refrains from transmitting until the network is quiet. This simple "listen before talking" strategy can significantly reduce collisions.

Another mechanism is *carrier detection.* With this strategy, computers continue to listen to the network as they are transmitting. If a computer detects another signal that interferes with the signal it is sending, it will stop transmitting. Both computers then wait a random amount of time and attempt to retransmit. Unless the network is extremely busy, carrier detection along with carrier sensing can manage a large volume of transmissions.

Both of these mechanisms used together form the protocol used in all types of Ethernet, which is called *Carrier Sense Multiple Access with Collision Detection* (CSMA/CD).

Apple's LocalTalk networks uses the protocol *Carrier Sense Multiple Access with Collision Avoidance* (CSMA/CA). *Collision Avoidance* uses additional techniques to further reduce the likelihood of collisions.

Note According to the course definitions, contention is an access-control *method.* CSMA/CD and CSMA/CA are *protocols* that incorporate contention-access methods.

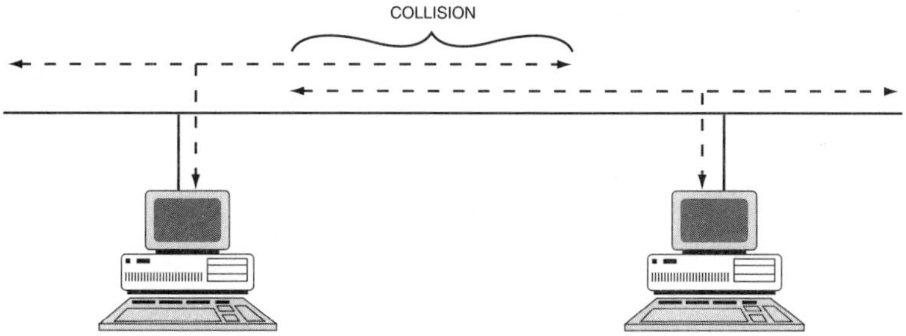

Figure 22.4
A collision on a contention-based network.

The following summarizes the characteristics of contention-access controls:

- Pure contention systems permit all stations to transmit whenever they want (although mechanisms are virtually always in place to limit transmission).
- Collisions always occur at some level on contention-based networks, with the number increasing geometrically as transmissions increase.
- CSMA/CD and CSMA/CA are two protocols that reduce the damage caused by collisions.

Although it sounds as if contention methods are unworkable due to the damage caused by collisions, contention (in particular CSMA/CD) is the most popular media access control method on LANs in the form of Ethernet. (In fact, no currently employed LAN standards utilize pure contention access control without adding some mechanism to reduce the incidence of collisions.)

Contention is a simple protocol that can be managed with simple software and hardware. Unless traffic levels exceed about 30 percent of bandwidth, contention works quite well. Contention-based networks offer excellent performance at low cost.

Because collisions occur at unpredictable intervals, however, no computer is guaranteed the capability to transmit at any given time. Contention-based networks are called "probabalistic" because a computer's chance of being permitted to transmit cannot be predicted.

Collisions increase in frequency as more computers use the network. When the number of computers on the network climbs to an unmanageable amount, collisions dominate network traffic and few frames are transmitted without error.

All computers on a contention-based network are equal. Consequently, it is not possible to assign certain computers higher priorities and therefore greater access to the network.

Note This course recommends contention access control for networks that experience bursty traffic—that is, large intermittent file transfers—and have relatively few computers.

Token Passing

Token passing utilizes a frame called a *token,* which circulates around the network. A computer that needs to transmit must wait until it receives the token frame, at which time it is permitted to transmit. When the computer is finished transmitting, it passes the token frame to the next station on the network. Figure 22.5 shows how token passing is implemented on a token-ring network.

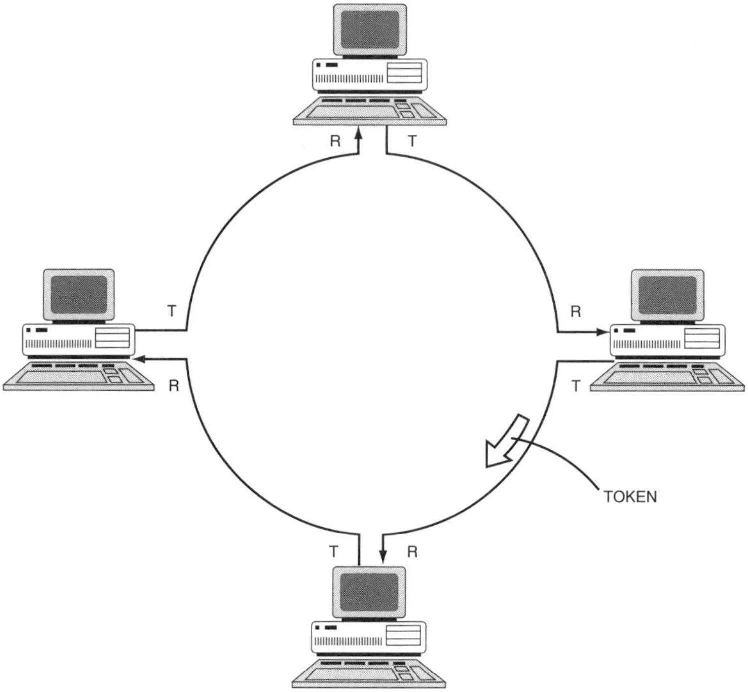

Figure 22.5
Token passing.

Several network standards employ token passing access control:

- The most common is token ring, defined by IEEE standard 802.5.
- IEEE standard 802.4 defines a bus network that also employs token passing. This standard is implemented only infrequently.
- FDDI is a 100 Mbps fiber-optic network standard that uses token passing and rings in much the same manner as 802.5 Token Ring.

Token passing methods can use station priorities and other methods to prevent any one station from monopolizing the network. Because each computer has a chance to transmit each time the token travels around the network, each station is guaranteed a chance to transmit at some minimum time interval.

Note: Token passing is more appropriate than contention under the following conditions:

- When the network is carrying time-critical data. Because token passing results in more predictable delivery, token passing is called deterministic.
- When the network experiences heavy utilization. Performance typically falls off more gracefully with a token passing network than with a contention-based network. Token passing networks cannot become gridlocked due to excessive numbers of collisions.
- When some stations should have higher priority than others. Some token passing schemes support priority assignments.

Comparing Contention and Token Passing

As an access control mechanism, token passing appears to be clearly superior to contention. You will find, however, that Ethernet, by far the dominant LAN standard, has achieved its prominence while firmly wedded to contention access control.

Token passing requires a variety of complex control mechanisms to make it work well. The hardware required is considerably more expensive than the hardware required to implement the much simpler contention mechanisms. The higher cost of token passing networks is difficult to justify unless the special features are required.

Because token passing networks are designed for high reliability, it is common to build network diagnostic and troubleshooting capabilities into the network hardware. This further increases the costs of token passing networks. Organizations must decide whether this additional reliability is worth the extra cost.

Conversely, though token passing networks perform better than contention-based networks when traffic levels are high, contention networks have superior performance under lighter loading conditions. The process of passing the token around (and other maintenance operations) eats into the available bandwidth. As a result, a 10 Mbps Ethernet and a 16 Mbps token ring perform comparably under light loading conditions, but the Ethernet costs considerably less. Figure 22.6 illustrates the performance characteristics you can expect from each access control method. (This figure reproduces the graph used for the course, and implies that token passing throughput will eventually reach a zero level, which cannot, in fact, happen, regardless of the loading conditions. Although a station's access to the network may be limited, access is guaranteed with each circuit of the token.)

Note The course materials emphasize that the comparisons being stated consider only pure contention-based networks, not networks that employ collision reduction schemes such as Ethernet. As noted, however, no current LAN standards employ contention as a media access control method without adding collision reduction techniques.

Polling

Polling is an access control method that employs a central device to regulate all access to the network. Polling is the most common access control method employed with mainframe computer networks.

The central device, called a *primary*, requests data from devices on the network, called *secondaries*. After it is *polled*, a secondary can transmit an amount of data that is determined by the protocols employed on the network. A secondary device cannot transmit unless it is polled by the primary.

Polling guarantees each device fair access to the network, and is suitable for use with time-critical data. In fact, polling has many of the advantages of token passing:

- Access times are predictable. Access is, therefore, deterministic.
- Priorities can be assigned.
- Collisions are eliminated.

A significant difference between polling and token passing is that polling centralizes control. This centralization can be an advantage from a management standpoint, but introduces a single point of failure. If the central control mechanism fails, the network stops functioning. Token passing uses more distributed control functions that are less subject to single points of failure.

Figure 22.6
Comparison of contention and token passing.

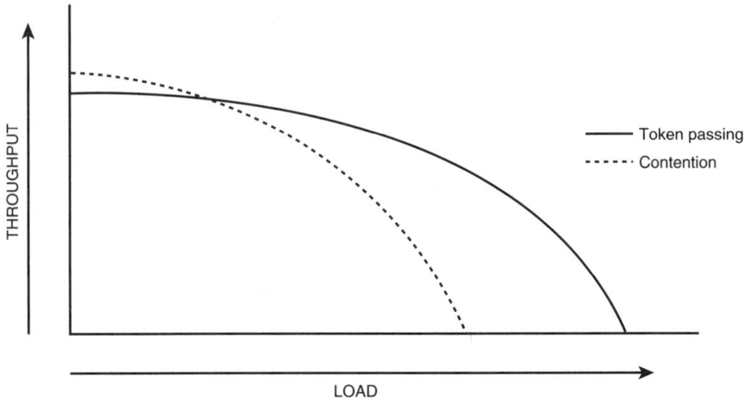

Because polling centralizes control, secondary devices cannot communicate directly with other secondary devices. Rather, they must use the primary as an intermediary.

Furthermore, because the primary must poll each secondary—whether or not the secondary has data to transmit—polling wastes large amounts of network bandwidth. This can result in excessive delays as some secondaries wait while others are polled.

Summary of Access Control Methods

Access Control Method	*Advantages*	*Considerations*
Contention	Simple software.	Access is probalistic (not guaranteed).
	Once access is gained, device has complete control of the medium.	No priority mechanism.
		Collisions increase geometrically with demand.
Token passing	Each device is guaranteed media access (deterministic).	More complex software and hardware.
	Priorities might be assigned.	Might require a central control device.
	Collisions are eliminated.	
	High throughput under heavy load.	

Access Control Method	*Advantages*	*Considerations*
Polling	Each device is guaranteed media access (deterministic).	Polling uses significant portion of network bandwidth.
	Priorities might be assigned.	Polling requires bandwidth overhead, even for devices that have nothing to transmit.
	Collisions are eliminated.	

Addressing

The data link layer maintains device addresses that enable messages to be sent to a particular device. The addresses used are called *physical device addresses,* which are unique addresses associated with the networking hardware in the computer. In most cases (for example, Ethernet and token ring) the physical device address is burned into the network interface card at the time the card is manufactured.

The standards that apply to a particular network determine the format of the address. Because the address format is associated with the media access control method being used, physical device addresses are frequently referred to as *MAC addresses.*

The device address is not actually used to route a message to a specific device. Frames on LANs are typically transmitted so that they are available to all devices on the network. Each device reads each frame far enough to determine the device address to which the frame is addressed. If the frame's destination address matches the device's own physical address, the rest of the frame will be received. If the addresses do not match, the remainder of the frame is ignored.

As Chapter 20, "Transmission Media Connections," explains, bridges can be used to divide large networks into several smaller ones. Bridges use physical device addresses to determine which frames should remain on the current network segment and which should be forwarded to devices on other network segments. Some bridges must be programmed with the device addresses for each attached network segment, but transparent or learning bridges can learn addresses by analyzing network traffic.

Because bridges utilize physical device addresses to manage frame routing, they function at the level of the data link layer and are data link layer connectivity devices.

Transmission Synchronization

Chapter 21 introduces the need to synchronize bit transmissions between sending and receiving devices. The data link layer, however, operates on data after the bits have been assembled to form characters, frames, or other data groups. At the data link layer, it is also necessary to synchronize frame transmissions. This section discusses three mechanisms:

- Asynchronous
- Synchronous
- Isochronous

Asynchronous Transmission

Asynchronous transmission does not use a clocking mechanism to keep the sending and receiving devices synchronized. Instead, bit synchronization is used to synchronize the devices for each frame that is transmitted.

Each frame begins with a start bit that enables the receiving device to adjust to the timing of the transmitted signal. Messages are kept short so that the sending and receiving devices do not drift out of synchronization for the duration of the message. Asynchronous transmission is most frequently used to transmit character data and is ideally suited to environments where characters are transmitted at irregular intervals, such as when users are typing in character data.

Figure 22.7 illustrates the structure of a typical frame used to transmit character data. This frame has four components:

- **A start bit.** Signals that a frame is starting and enables the receiving device to synchronize itself with the message.
- **Data bits.** Consist of 7 or 8 bits when character data is being transmitted.
- **A parity bit.** Optionally used as a crude method of detecting transmission errors.
- **A stop bit or bits.** Signal the end of the data frame.

Error detection in asynchronous transmission makes use of the parity bit. Several schemes are available for using the parity bit. The most common include the following:

- **Even parity.** The parity bit is set to ensure that an even number of 1 bits are sent. If the data field has three 1's, the parity bit will be set to 1 to produce a total of four 1 bits.
- **Odd parity.** The parity bit is set to ensure that an odd number of 1 bits are sent. If the data field has three 1's, the parity bit will be set to 0 to produce a total of three 0 bits.

Parity techniques can detect errors that affect one bit. They might, however, be unable to detect errors that affect two or more bits.

Asynchronous transmission is a simple, inexpensive technology ideally suited for transmitting small frames at irregular intervals.

Because start, stop, and parity bits must be added to each character to be transmitted, however, overhead for asynchronous transmission is high, in the neighborhood of 20 to 30 percent. This wastes bandwidth and makes asynchronous transmission undesirable for transmitting large amounts of data.

Asynchronous transmission is frequently used for PC-to-PC and terminal-to-host communication. Data in these environments is often of the bursty, character-oriented nature that is ideal for asynchronous communication. In both cases, it is also generally desirable to reduce costs of communication hardware, which is best achieved with asynchronous transmission.

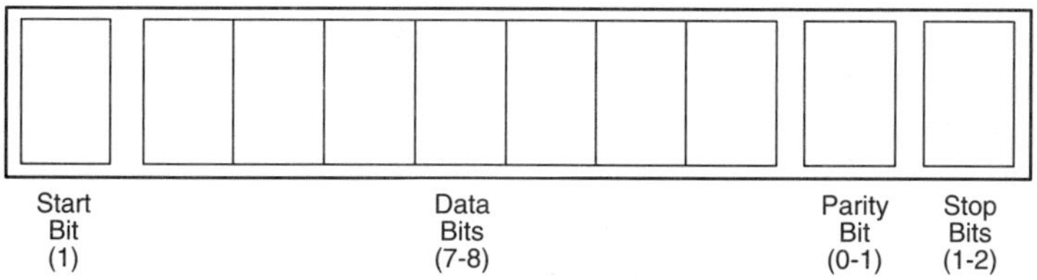

Figure 22.7
Structure of an asynchronous frame.

Synchronous Transmission

Communication can be made more efficient if the clocks on the transmitting and receiving devices are synchronized. This synchronization is accomplished in two ways:

- By transmitting synchronization signals with data. Some data encoding techniques, by guaranteeing a signal transition with each bit transmitted, are inherently self-clocking.
- By using a separate communication channel to carry clock signals, a technique that can function with any signal encoding technique.

Figure 22.8 illustrates two possible structures of messages associated with synchronous trans mission.

Both transmissions begin with a series of *synch signals*, which notify the receiver of the beginning of a frame. Synch signals generally utilize a bit pattern that cannot appear elsewhere in messages, ensuring that they will always be distinct and easy for the receiver to recognize.

A wide variety of data types can be transmitted. Figure 22.8 illustrates both character-oriented and bit-oriented data. Notice that multiple characters or long series of bits can be transmitted in a single data frame. Because the transmitter and receiver remain in synchronization for the duration of the transmission, frames may be of great length.

When frames are longer, parity is no longer a suitable method of detecting error. If errors are occurring, it is more likely that multiple bits will be affected and that parity techniques will not report an error properly. The technique used with synchronous transmission is the *cyclic redundancy check* (CRC). The transmitter uses an algorithm to calculate a CRC value that summarizes the entire value of the data bits. This CRC value is appended to the data frame. The receiver uses the same algorithm, recalculates the CRC, and compares the CRC in the frame to the value it has calculated. If the values match, it is virtually certain that the frame was transmitted without error.

An *end bit pattern* unambiguously indicates the end of a frame. As with the synch bits, the end bit pattern is frequently a pattern that cannot appear in the body of the data frame, eliminating confusion on the part of the receiver.

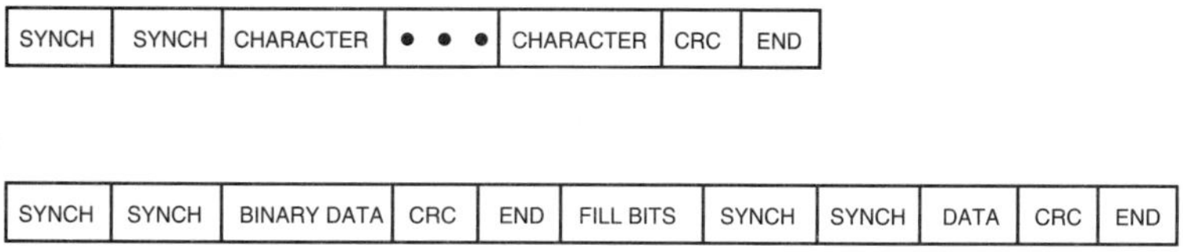

Figure 22.8
Structures of synchronous transmissions.

When synchronous transmission links are idle, it is common to transmit *fill bits* that keep the devices synchronized, eliminating the need to resynchronize devices when a new frame is transmitted.

Synchronous transmission has many advantages over asynchronous transmission. Overhead bits (synch, CRC, and end) are a smaller proportion of the overall data frame, making synchronous transmission far more efficient in its use of bandwidth. Synchronization enables the systems to utilize higher speeds and to improve error detection.

The disadvantage of synchronous transmission is primarily higher cost due to the more complex circuitry required. Consequently, synchronous transmission is employed primarily when high volumes of data must be transmitted.

Synchronous transmission is frequently used in mainframe-to-mainframe communication, and is also used to achieve high efficiency levels on LANs. Both Ethernet and token ring, for example, utilize self-clocking signals.

Isochronous Transmission

Isochronous transmission employs a common device that supplies a clocking signal shared by all devices on the network. The clocking device creates time slots. Devices with data to transmit monitor the network and insert data into open time slots as they become available. A given time slot can be filled to capacity with multiple frames.

Isochronous transmission guarantees transmission rates, is deterministic, and has low overhead. The technique, however, introduces a single point of failure; it is necessary to ensure that the clocking device is fault-tolerant.

Connection Services

Network connection services provide a variety of functions:

- Flow control determines the amount of data that can be transmitted in a given time period. Flow control prevents the transmitting device from overwhelming the receiver. Flow control can take place at several protocol levels, including the LLC sublayer.
- Error control detects errors in received frames and requests retransmission of frames. Error control is a function of the LLC sublayer.
- Sequence control enables receivers to reassemble data frames into their original order. Frame size is limited, and packet fragmentation and reassembly is necessary to transmit large messages. Sequence control is a function of the network layer.

Three types of connection services provide different combinations of the above services:

- **Unacknowledged connectionless services.** Provide no flow, error, or sequence control. When required, these services must be provided by higher protocol layers. Unacknowledge connectionless service provides high performance when network communication can be safely assumed to be reliable (as on most LANs).
- **Connection-oriented services.** Provide flow, error, and sequence control through use of acknowledgments. Connection-oriented services have higher overhead, reducing performance but improving reliability when network reliability is in question (as on most WANs).

- **Acknowledged connectionless services.** Use acknowledgments to provide flow and error control on point-to-point connections.

Flow Control at the LLC Sublayer

Flow control prevents receiving devices from being overwhelmed by faster transmitting devices. Two common techniques of flow control are guaranteed rate flow control and window flow control.

Guaranteed Rate Flow Control

With *guaranteed rate flow control*, the sending and receiving devices negotiate a mutually acceptable transmission rate. Typically, this transmission rate holds constant for the duration of a communication session.

To ensure that frames are received without error, some protocols require the receiver to acknowledge each frame as it is processed. If no error is detected, an acknowledgment frame is returned to the transmitter, instructing it to send the next frame. If errors are detected, the receiver does one of two things: it sends a retransmission request, or it simply waits until the transmitter times out and retransmits the frame.

Essentially, guaranteed rate flow control assumes that the receiver processes one message unit (bit or frame) for each unit transmitted. This rather inflexible approach often fails to make the most efficient use of transmitter, receiver, and media channel capacities.

Window Flow Control

Buffering is a technique that enables transmitters and receivers to operate with more flexibility. Buffers consist of memory that can receive data from the network and hold it until the receiver can process the data and acknowledge that it has been received.

Windowing is a technique that enables the transmitter to send several data frames prior to receiving acknowledgment from the receiver. Several frames may be buffered in the receiver as they are processed. The number of frames a transmitter can send without receiving an acknowledgment is known as a *window*.

Static window flow control limits the window size to a specific number of frames, usually defined by the number of frames that can fit in the receiver's input buffer. If the window size is 7, the transmitter can have as many as seven outstanding frames. An eighth frame cannot be transmitted, however, until one of the outstanding frames is acknowledged (see fig. 22.9).

Dynamic window flow control improves efficiency by enabling the communicating devices to adjust the window size. Other terms for this technique are *floating* or *sliding* windows. One dynamic window technique enables the receiver to send out a *choke frame* when its input buffer is nearing capacity. This choke frame signals the transmitter to slow down. After the transmitter adjusts its transmission rate downward, it will slowly increase its transmission rate until it receives another choke frame. In this way, bandwidth utilization is optimized.

Error Control

Two LLC error conditions can exist:

- When CRC errors are detected
- When expected acknowledgments are not received

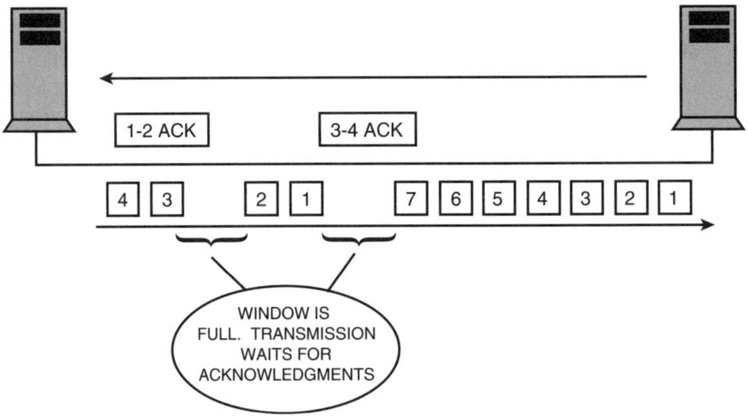

Figure 22.9
Window flow control.

Recall from earlier in this chapter that synchronous data frames incorporate a *cyclic redundancy check* (CRC) field that can be used to detect transmission errors. When a receiving device detects a CRC error, it can transmit a *negative acknowledgment* (NAK) that requests retransmission of the frame.

When acknowledged services are employed, the transmitter expects *acknowledgment* (ACK) frames from the receiver for each frame (or a group of frames in a windowed protocol). When a specified interval of time expires without an acknowledgment, the transmitter assumes that the frame was lost and retransmits it.

Questions

1. Which of the following statements is true?
   - A. Logical topologies are determined by the cabling system.
   - B. A physical bus network may be a logical ring.
   - C. A physical star network can be a logical ring.
   - D. Contention can be used as an access control medium on a physical ring.

2. Which protocol layer enables multiple devices to share the transmission medium?
   - A. Physical
   - B. MAC
   - C. LLC
   - D. Network

3. Which of the following is an error control mechanism?
   - A. Contention
   - B. Synchronous transmission
   - C. CRC
   - D. LLC

4. Which of the following layers establishes and maintains a link between communicating devices?
   - A. Physical
   - B. MAC
   - C. LLC
   - D. Network

5. Which of the following techniques uses network bandwidth most efficiently?
   - A. Static window flow control
   - B. Guaranteed rate flow control
   - C. Dynamic rate flow control
   - D. Dynamic window flow control

6. Which of the following access methods is centrally managed?
   - A. Contention
   - B. Token passing
   - C. Polling
   - D. Collision detection

7. Which *two* of the following services provides flow control?
   - A. Acknowledged connectionless
   - B. Unacknowledged connectionless
   - C. Unacknowledged connection-oriented
   - D. Connection-oriented

8. Which of the following access control methods is probabalistic?
   - A. Polling
   - B. Contention
   - C. Token passing
   - D. Sliding window

9. Which of the following methods relies on the internal clocks of transmitting and receiving devices?

   ○ A. Synchronous

   ○ B. Isochronous

   ○ C. Asynchronous

   ○ D. Nonsynchronous

10. Which of the following connectivity devices functions at the data link layer?

   ○ A. Repeater

   ○ B. Router

   ○ C. Hub

   ○ D. Bridge

Answers

1. C
2. B
3. C
4. C
5. D
6. C
7. A, D
8. B
9. C
10. D

CHAPTER 23

OSI Network Layer Concepts

The data link layer deals with communication between devices on the same network. Physical device addresses are used to identify data frames, and it is the responsibility of each device to monitor the network and receive frames that are addressed to that device.

The network layer involves communication with devices on logically separate networks that are connected to form internetworks. Because internetworks can be large and can be built of different types of networks, the network layer utilizes routing algorithms that can be used to guide packets from their source to their destination networks.

A key element of the network layer is that each network in the internetwork is assigned a network address that can be used to route packets. The nature of those addresses and how they are used to route packets defines the majority of topics in this chapter, which include the following:

- Addressing
- Switching
- Routing algorithms
- Connection services
- Gateway services

Addressing

You have already encountered the use of physical device addresses, which uniquely identify each device on a network. The network layer makes use of two additional address types, as follows:

- *Logical network addresses,* which are used to route packets to specific networks on the internetwork
- *Services addresses,* which route packets to specific processes running on the destination device

Logical Network Addresses

Logical network addresses are assigned when the networks are configured. If you have installed NetWare servers, you are familiar with the process of assigning a logical network address to each LAN that is attached to the server. One of the tasks a network installer must accomplish is to make sure that each network address is unique on a given internetwork. Network addresses enable routers to forward frames through the internetwork to the appropriate networks.

Service Addresses

The operating systems on most computers are capable of running several processes at once. When a packet arrives, it is necessary to determine which process on the computer should receive the data in the packet. This is achieved by assigning service addresses, which identify upper-layer processes and protocols. These service addresses are included with the physical and logical network addresses in the data frame. (Some protocols refer to service addresses as *sockets* or *ports.*)

Some service addresses, called *well-known addresses,* are universally defined for a given type of network. Other service addresses are defined by the vendors of network products.

Addressing Summary

A possible format of the address information for a packet is shown in figure 23.1. Three address components appear, as follows:

- *Physical (MAC) network addresses* identify a particular device as the source or destination of a frame.
- *Logical network addresses* identify a particular network on the internetwork as the source or destination of a packet.
- *Service addresses* identify a process or protocol on the computer that is the source or destination of a packet.

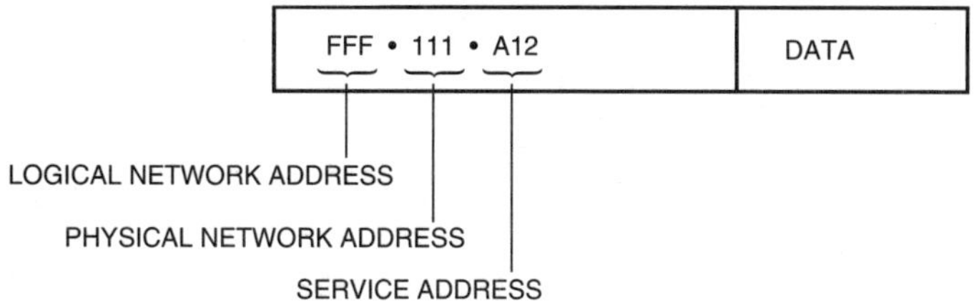

Figure 23.1
Address information showing physical and logical network addresses with a service address.

Switching

Many internetworks include redundant data paths that may be used to route messages. The following switching techniques may be used to route messages:

- Circuit switching
- Message switching
- Packet switching

Circuit Switching

As shown in figure 23.2, *circuit switching* establishes a path that remains fixed for the duration of a connection. Much as telephone switching equipment establishes a route between your telephone on the East Coast and a telephone you dial on the West Coast, circuit switching networks establish a path through the internetwork when the devices initiate a conversation.

Circuit switching provides devices with a dedicated path and a well-defined bandwidth.

Circuit switching is not without disadvantages, however. The process of establishing a connection between devices may be time-consuming. Because other traffic cannot share the dedicated media path, bandwidth may be inefficiently utilized. Because circuit switching networks must have a surplus of bandwidth, they tend to be expensive to construct.

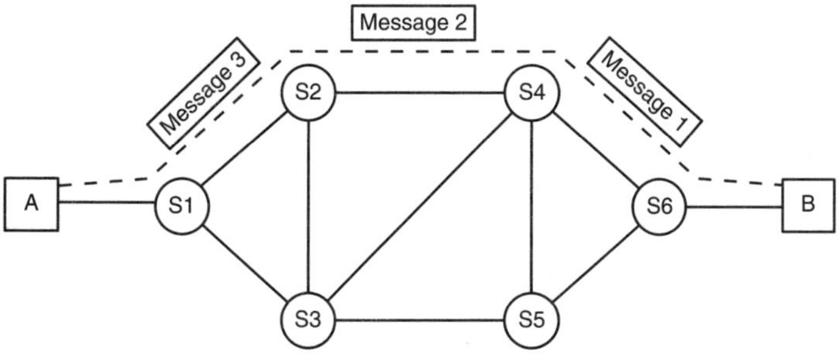

Figure 23.2
Circuit switching.

Message Switching

Message switching treats each message as an independent entity. Each message carries address information that describes the message's destination. This information is used at each switch to transfer the message to the next switch in its route. Message switches are programmed with information concerning other switches in the network that can be used to forward messages to their destinations. They may also be programmed with information about the most efficient routes. Depending on network conditions, different messages may be sent through the network by different routes, as shown in figure 23.3.

Message switching transfers the complete message from one switch to the next switch, where the message is stored before it is forwarded another time. Because each message is stored before it is sent on to the next switch, this type of network is frequently called a *store-and-forward* network. The message switches are often general-purpose computers. They must be equipped with sufficient storage (usually hard drives) to enable them to store messages until it is possible to forward them.

Electronic mail is a common application for message switching. Some delay is permissible when delivering mail, unlike the requirements when two computers are exchanging data in real time. Message switching uses relatively low-cost devices to forward messages and can function well with relatively slow communication channels. Other applications for message switching include group applications such as workflow, calendaring, and groupware.

Message switching has several advantages, as follows:

- Data channels are shared among communicating devices, improving the efficiency of using available bandwidth.
- Message switches can store messages until a channel becomes available, reducing sensitivity to network congestion.
- Message priorities may be used to manage network traffic.
- Broadcast addressing uses network bandwidth more efficiently by delivering messages to multiple destinations.

The chief disadvantage of message switching is that it is unsuitable to real-time applications, including data communication, video, and audio.

Figure 23.3
Message switching.

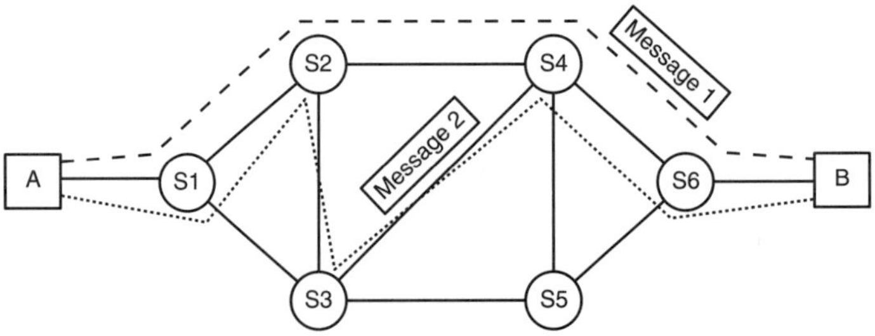

Packet Switching

In *package switching,* messages are divided into smaller packets. Each packet includes source and destination address information so that individual packets can be routed through the internetwork independently. As you can see in figure 23.4, the packets that make up a message may take very different routes through the internetwork.

So far, this looks a lot like message switching. The distinguishing characteristic is that packets are restricted to a size that enables the switching devices to manage the packet data entirely in memory, without the need to store the data temporarily on disk. Packet switching, therefore, routes packets through the network much more rapidly and efficiently than is possible with message switching.

Several methods of packet switching exist. The following two are discussed in this course:

- Datagram
- Virtual circuit

Datagram Packet Switching

Datagram services treat each packet as an independent message. Each packet is routed through the internetwork independently, and each switch node decides which network segment should be used for the next step in the packet's route. This capability enables switches to bypass busy segments and take other steps to speed packets through the internetwork. This is the specific approach that was shown in figure 23.4.

Datagrams are frequently used on LANs. Network layer protocols are responsible for delivering the frame to the appropriate network. Then, because each datagram includes destination address information, devices on the local network can recognize and receive datagrams that they are intended to receive.

Note Packet switching matches the need to transmit large messages with the fairly small frame size that can be accommodated by the physical layer. The network layer is responsible for fragmenting messages from upper layers into smaller datagrams that are appropriate for the physical layer. The network layer is also responsible for reconstructing messages from datagrams as they are received.

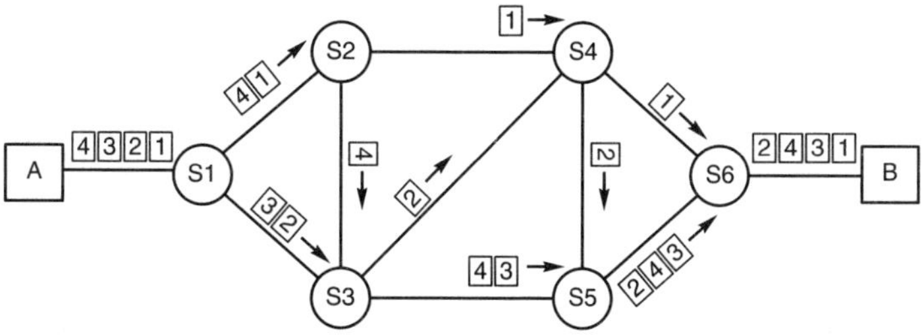

Figure 23.4
Packet switching.

Virtual Circuit Packet Switching

Virtual circuits operate by establishing a formal connection between two devices that are in communication. When devices begin a session, they negotiate communication parameters, such as maximum message size, communication windows, network paths, and so forth. This negotiation establishes a *virtual circuit*, a well-defined path through the internetwork through which the devices communicate. This virtual circuit generally remains in effect until the devices stop communicating.

Virtual circuits are distinguished by the establishment of a logical connection. *Virtual* means that the network behaves as though a dedicated physical circuit has been established between the devices that are communicating. Even though no such physical circuit exists, the network presents the appearance of a physical connection so far as the devices at the ends of the circuit are concerned.

Virtual circuits are frequently employed in conjunction with connection-oriented services, which are discussed later in this chapter.

Advantages of Packet Switching

Packet switching optimizes the use of bandwidth by enabling many devices to route packets through the same network channels. At any given time, a switch may be routing packets to several different destination devices, adjusting the routes as required to achieve the best efficiency possible at the present time.

Because entire messages are not stored at the switches prior to forwarding, transmission delays are significantly less than delays encountered with message switching.

Although the switching devices do not need to be equipped with large amounts of hard drive capacity, they might need a significant amount of real-time memory. Also, they must have sufficient processing power to run the more complex routing protocols that are required for packet switching. Among the new complexities is the need to recognize when packets have been lost so that retransmission can be requested.

Routing Algorithms

Routing is the process of forwarding messages through switching networks. In some cases, routing information is programmed into switching devices. However, preprogrammed switches cannot adjust to changing network conditions. Most routing devices, therefore, have the capability of discovering routes through the internetwork and storing the route information in route tables.

Route tables do not store only path information. They also store estimates of the time taken to send a message through a given route. This time estimate is known as the *cost* of a particular path. There are several methods of estimating routing costs, as follows:

- *Hop count* describes the number of routers that a message would cross before it reaches its destination. If all hops are assumed to take the same amount of time, the optimum path is the path with the smallest hop count.
- *Tic count* is an actual time estimate, where a *tic* is a time unit that is defined by the routing implementation.
- *Relative expense* is any defined measure of the cost (including the monetary cost) to use a given link.

After costs are established, routers can select routes either statically or dynamically, as follows:

- *Static route selection* uses routes that have been programmed in by the network administrator.
- *Dynamic route selection* uses routing cost information to select the most cost-effective route for a given packet. As network conditions change and are reflected in routing tables, the router can select different paths to maintain low costs.

Two methods of route discovery are discussed in this course: distance vector and link-state.

Distance Vector Routing

Distance vector routers advertise their presence to other routers on the network. Periodically, each router on the network will broadcast the information in its routing table. This information can be used by other routers to update their own router tables.

Figure 23.5 illustrates how the process works. In the figure, server S3 learns that server S2 can reach server S1 in three hops. Because Server S3 knows that Server S2 is one hop away, Server S3 knows that its cost to reach Server S1 through Server S2 is two hops.

Distance vector routing is an effective algorithm, but can be fairly inefficient. Because changes must ripple through the network from router to router, it might take a while for a change to become known to all routers on the network. In addition, the frequent broadcasts of routing information produce high levels of network traffic that can hurt performance on larger networks.

Note: Distance vector routing is the standard routing algorithm for NetWare and is used by the NetWare *Routing Information Protocol* (RIP). You can observe routing information including hop counts by typing **TRACK ON** at a NetWare 3.*x* or 4.*x* server console. Type **TRACK OFF** to cancel the display of routing information.

Figure 23.5
Distance vector routing.

Link-State Routing

Link-state routing reduces the network traffic required to update routing tables. Routers that are newly attached to the network can request routing information from a nearby router.

After routers have exchanged routing information about the network, routers broadcast messages only when something has changed. These messages contain information about the state of each link the router has with other routers on the network. Because routers keep each other updated, complete network routing updates are needed infrequently.

Note Link-state routing is employed by Novell's recently introduced *Network Link-State Protocol* (NLSP), which may be substituted for RIP on NetWare 3.*x* and 4.*x* servers.

Connection Services

In Chapter 22, you were introduced to three types of connection services, as follows:

- *Unacknowledged connectionless services*, which provide no flow control, error detection, or packet sequence control
- *Connection-oriented services*, which provide flow control and error detection with acknowledgments
- *Acknowledged connectionless services*, which use acknowledgments to provide flow and error control

The network layer also provides connection-oriented services, including flow control, error detection, and acknowledgments. Network acknowledgments are employed to provide flow control, error detection, and packet sequence control.

Network Layer Flow Control

The data link layer manages flow control based on the capacities of the devices that are in communication.

The network layer manages flow control to avoid congestion on the network. As you learned in the discussion about routing, the network layer determines the number of packets that will be sent through a given route. By routing packets around busy links, available network bandwidth is used more effectively and congestion is reduced. For this reason, network flow control is often referred to as *congestion control.*

Network layer flow control can permit devices to negotiate a guaranteed data rate. Static and dynamic windows may also be employed.

Receiving devices can control congestion by delaying before sending acknowledgments. Under these circumstances, the sender may assume that the packet was lost and retransmit it. To prevent unnecessary retransmission, some protocols define packets that signal congestion and enable receiving devices to explicitly request delays in transmission.

Network Layer Error Control

A variety of error conditions may be detected at the network layer.

Errors in data are typically detected using CRC algorithms. Because packet header information changes at each hop (addresses change), CRC values must be recalculated by each router.

Although the network layer can implement detection of lost and duplicate packets, these functions are typically handled by the transport layer.

Packet Sequence Control

Recall that packet switching networks may route packets by varying routes. As a result, the packets for a message might arrive at their final destination out of order. This can be the case for both datagram and connection-oriented services.

The network layer may be configured to handle packet sequence control, although that function is generally handled at the transport layer.

Gateway Services

Routers can handle interconnection of networks whose protocols function in similar ways. When the rules are sufficiently different on the two networks, however, a more powerful device is required.

A *gateway* is a device that can reconcile the different rules that are used on two different networks. Gateways are commonly required to connect LANs into mainframe networks, which have completely different protocol architectures than LANs. Mainframe networks, such as IBM's SNA, for example, do not use the same device address schemes as LANs employ (they differ in many other ways as well). It is necessary to "fool" the mainframe network into thinking that mainframe devices are on the LAN, and it is also necessary to make the mainframe look like a LAN, so far as devices on the LAN are concerned.

Note: Gateways may be implemented at the network layer or at higher layers in the OSI model, depending on where the protocol translation is required.

Questions

Because the material is so intertwined, study questions for this chapter can be found at the end of Chapter 27.

CHAPTER 24

OSI Transport Layer Concepts

The transport layer is the next layer of the OSI model. Lower layer protocols are concerned with delivering messages between devices. The transport layer, however, is concerned with delivering messages between processes running on those devices. Whenever a device is using a multitasking operating system, and multiple processes might be running on the device, it becomes essential that messages be delivered from one process on the transmitting device to the correct process on the receiving device.

The transport layer can implement procedures to ensure the reliable delivery of those segments to their destination devices. The term "reliable" does not mean that errors cannot occur, only that if errors occur, they will be detected. If errors such as lost data are detected, the transport layer either requests retransmission or notifies upper layer protocols so that they can take corrective action.

The transport layer enables upper layer protocols to interface with the network, but hides the complexities of network operation from them. Among it's functions, the transport layer breaks large messages into segments that are suitable for network delivery.

The following transport layer topics are covered in this chapter:

- Addressing
- Address/name resolution
- Segment development
- Connection services

Addressing

Transport layer addressing is concerned with delivering messages from a specific process on one computer to the correct process running on the destination computer. Messages can be identified in two ways: connection identifiers and transaction identifiers.

Connection Identifiers

A connection identifier (connection ID) might also be called a socket or a port depending on the specific protocol implementation. The *connection identifier* labels each conversation and enables a process to communicate with processes running on other devices. A numeric identifier is assigned to each conversation. A service, running at higher OSI levels, identifies communications with a connection ID number that enables the transport layer to direct lower layer addressing and deliver the messages as required.

Transaction Identifiers

Connection identifiers are used when two devices are engaged in multiple exchanges of data. Transaction identifiers are used when the exchange is a one-time event consisting of a request and a response. Only this simple exchange is tracked, no multiple-message conversations that might be occurring between the devices are tracked.

Address/Name Resolution

Network addresses are always binary numbers, which are often 32 bits in length. These numbers can be expressed in decimal or hexadecimal notation to make them easier for humans to identify. Long decimal and hex numbers, however, are not as recognizable as words. For that reason, some network protocols implement a scheme of logical alphanumeric names that humans use when specifying network devices. These names are translated into numeric network addresses by a service on the network. This translation can be performed by individual network devices or by a central name server.

Service-Requester-Initiated Address/Name Resolution

With this method, a device that requires address information broadcasts a packet requesting the information for a given name, address, or service. The device that corresponds to the name, address, or service responds with the required information.

Service-Provider-Initiated Address/Name Resolution

This method employs a central directory server (also called a name server) that collects information which is broadcast by devices on the network. Devices that require name or address information can request it from the directory server.

Segment Development

When messages from higher-level protocols exceed the size allowed by a protocol stack for a segment, the transport layer divides outbound messages into segments of a suitable size. The transport layer also recombines incoming segments into message formats required by upper layers.

The transport layer also can combine multiple small messages into a single segment to improve network efficiency. As shown in figure 24.1, each message component is identified by a connection identifier (CID). The CID enables the transport layer of the receiving device to deliver each message to the proper process.

Connection Services

Some services can be performed at more than one layer of the OSI model. In addition to the data link and network layers, the transport layer can have some responsibility for connection services.

Segment Sequencing

One connection-oriented service provided by the transport layer is segment sequencing. When large messages are divided into segments for transport, the transport layer must resequence the segments when they are received prior to reassembling the original message.

Error Control

When segments are lost in transmission, or when segments have duplicate segment IDs, the transport layer must initiate error recovery. The following strategies are available:

- Unique segment sequence numbers
- Virtual circuits, permitting only one virtual circuit per session
- Timeouts removed from the network segments that have been misrouted and have remained on the network past a specified time

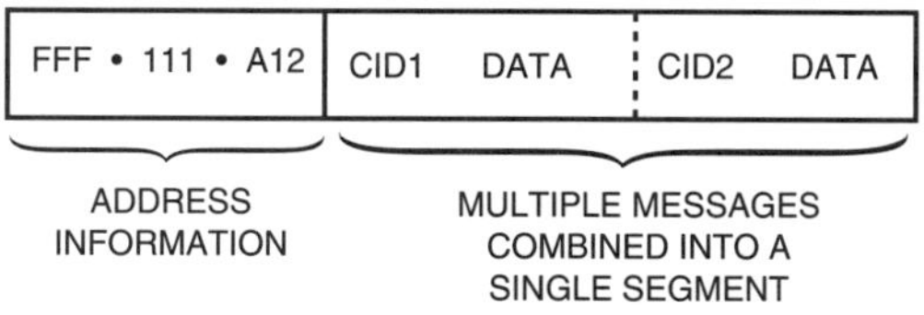

Figure 24.1
Identification of messages at transport layer.

The transport layer also detects corrupted segments by managing end-to-end error control using techniques such as checksums.

End-to-End Flow Control

The transport layer uses acknowledgments to manage end-to-end flow control between two connected devices.

Besides negative acknowledgments, some transport layer protocols can request the retransmission of the most recent segments. These acknowledgments are called *go back n* or *selective repeat* acknowledgments.

Go back *n* acknowledgments request retransmission of the last *n* packets. Selective repeat acknowledgments can request retransmission of specific packets.

This approach is useful when the receiving device's buffers overflowed before it was able to warn the transmitting device to cease transmission.

Questions

You will find study questions for this chapter at the end of Chapter 27, "OSI Application Layer Concepts."

CHAPTER 25

OSI Session Layer Concepts

The session layer manages dialogs between two computers by establishing, managing, and terminating communications.

The following two session layer topics are discussed in this chapter:

- *Dialog control*
- *Session administration*

Dialog Control

As illustrated in figure 25.1, dialogs can take three forms:

- **Simplex dialogs.** Involve one-way data transfers. An example is a fire alarm, which sends an alarm message to the fire station, but cannot (and does not need to) receive messages from the fire station.
- **Half-duplex dialogs.** Involve two-way data transfers in which the data flows in only one direction at a time. When one device has completed a transmission, it must "turn over" the medium to the other device so that it has a turn to transmit.

  CB radio operators, for example, converse on the same communication channel. When one operator is through transmitting he must release his transmit key so that the other operator may send a response.
- **Full-duplex dialogs.** Permit two-way simultaneous data transfers by providing each device with a separate communication channel. Voice telephones are full-duplex devices, and either party to a conversation may talk at any time. Most computer modems are capable of operating in full-duplex mode.

Costs rise for half- and full-duplex operation because the more complex the dialog technology is, the more expensive it is. Designers of communications systems, therefore, generally use the simplest dialog mode that satisfies the communication requirements.

Half-duplex communication can result in wasted bandwidth during the intervals when communication is being turned around. On the other hand, full-duplex communication generally requires a greater bandwidth than half-duplex communication.

Note

The Novell course materials associate simplex transmission with broadcast transmission, and therefore imply that simplex transmission is used with multiple receivers. This implication is incorrect, as the above-mentioned example of the fire alarm shows.

Simplex transmission may indeed be implemented as a broadcast technology. Commercial radio is an example of broadcast simplex transmission.

A CB radio is, however, an example of half-duplex communication that also operates in a broadcast mode. Many operators may listen in to CB radio communications. Many operators may also reply to transmissions by waiting for a break in the dialog and pressing the transmit key.

For the purposes of this course, simplex transmissions are defined as providing broad area coverage with the potential for reaching large target audiences.

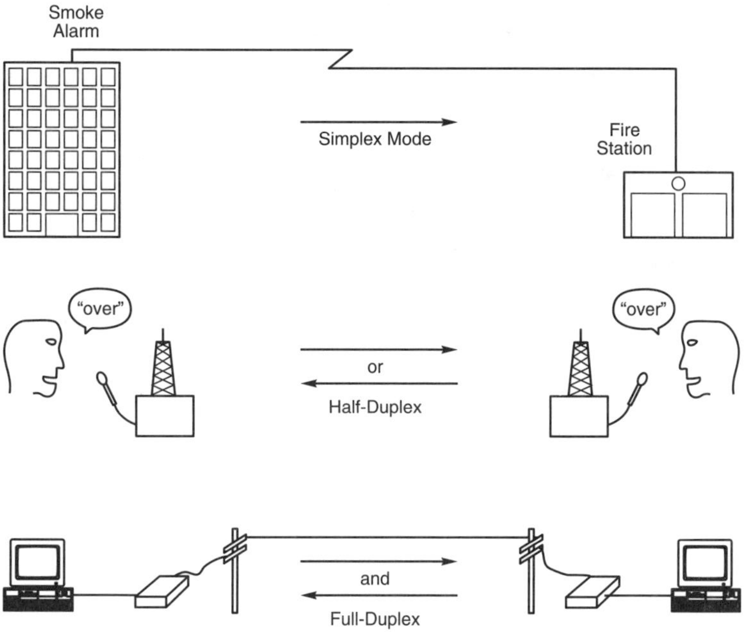

Figure 25.1
Simplex and duplex communication modes.

Session Administration

A *session* is a formal dialog between a service requester and a service provider. Sessions have at least three phases:

- **Connection establishment.** A service requester requests initiation of a service. During the setup process, communication is established and rules are agreed upon.
- **Data transfer.** Because of the rules agreed upon during setup, each party to the dialog knows what to expect. Communication is efficient and errors are easy to detect.
- **Connection release.** When the session is completed, the dialog is terminated in an orderly fashion.

Connection Establishment

Several tasks can be performed at the time a session is initiated:

- Specification of services that are required
- User login authentication and other security procedures
- Negotiation of protocols and protocol parameters
- Notification of connection IDs
- Establishment of dialog control, as well as acknowledgment of numbering, and retransmission procedures

Data Transfer

Once the connection has been established, the devices involved can initiate a dialog. Besides exchanging data, these devices exchange acknowledgments and other control data that manage the dialog.

The session layer can also incorporate protocols to resume dialogs that are interrupted. After a formal dialog has been established, devices recognize a lost connection whenever the connection has not been formally released. A device, therefore, realizes that a connection has been lost when it fails to receive an expected acknowledgment or data transmission.

Within a certain time period, two devices can reenter the session that was interrupted but not released.

Connection Release

This is an orderly process that shuts down communication and releases resources on the service provider.

Session Layer Topics and Methods

Dialog control	Simplex
	Half-duplex
	Full-duplex
Session administration	Connection establishment
	Data transfer
	Connection release

Questions

Study questions for this chapter can be found at the end of Chapter 27.

CHAPTER 26

OSI Presentation Layer Concepts

The presentation layer deals with the syntax, or grammatical rules, needed when communicating between two computers.

This chapter discusses two major services performed at the presentation layer:

- *Translation of data from one form to another*
- *Encryption/decryption of data*

Note: The name *presentation layer* has caused considerable confusion in the industry because some people mistakenly believe that this layer presents data to the user. However, the name has nothing to do with displaying data, which is performed instead by applications that are running above the application layer.

The presentation layer is so named because it presents a uniform data format to the application layer. As a matter of fact, this layer is not commonly implemented because most presentation layer functions are typically performed by applications.

Data Translation

An important goal to strive for when designing networks is to enable different types of computers to interchange data. Although this goal is seldom met completely, effective use of data translation techniques can make it possible for many types of computers to communicate.

The following discussion covers four forms of data translation: bit order, byte order, character code, and file syntax.

Bit Order

When binary numbers are transmitted through a network, they are sent one bit at a time. Consider the binary number 11110000. The transmitting computer could start at either end of the number:

- It could start at the *most-significant digit* (the MSD, which is the highest value digit) and send a 1 first.
- It could start at the *least-significant digit* (the LSD, which is the lowest value digit) and send a 0 first.

Unless the sending and receiving devices agree on bit-order conventions, they will change the values of the binary numbers that are being transmitted.

Byte Order Translation

A similar logic applies to byte orders. Complex values generally must be represented by more than one byte, but different computers use different conventions as to which byte should be transmitted first:

- Intel microprocessors start with the least-significant byte. Because they start at the small end, they are called *little endian.*
- Motorola microprocessors start with the most-significant byte and are called *big endian.*

Byte order translation might be needed to reconcile these differences.

Character Code Translation

Most computers use one of the following binary numbering schemes to represent character sets:

- ASCII, the *American Standard Code for Information Interchange,* used to represent English characters on all microcomputers and most minicomputers (see fig. 26.1)
- EBCDIC, the *Extended Binary Coded Decimal Interchange Code,* used to represent English characters on IBM mainframes (see fig. 26.2)
- Shift-JIS, used to represent Japanese characters

4	3	2	1	8 →	0	0	0	0	0	0	0	0	1	1	1	1	1	1	1	1
				7	0	0	0	0	1	1	1	1	0	0	0	0	1	1	1	1
				6	0	0	1	1	0	0	1	1	0	0	1	1	0	0	1	1
				5	0	1	0	1	0	1	0	1	0	1	0	1	0	1	0	1
0	0	0	0		NUL	DLE	SP	0	@	P	`	p	Ç	É	á	░	└	╨	∝	≡
0	0	0	1		SOH	DC1	!	1	A	Q	a	q	ü	æ	í	▒	┴	╤	ß	±
0	0	1	0		STX	DC2	"	2	B	R	b	r	é	Æ	ó	▓	┬	╥	Γ	≥
0	0	1	1		ETX	DC3	#	3	C	S	c	s	â	ô	ú	│	├	╙	π	≤
0	1	0	0		EOT	DC4	$	4	D	T	d	t	ä	ö	ñ	┤	─	╘	Σ	⌠
0	1	0	1		ENQ	NAK	%	5	E	U	e	u	à	ò	Ñ	╡	┼	╒	σ	⌡
0	1	1	0		ACK	SYN	&	6	F	V	f	v	å	û	ª	╢	╞	╓	µ	+
0	1	1	1		BEL	ETB	'	7	G	W	g	w	ç	ù	º	╖	╟	╫	τ	≈
1	0	0	0		BS	CAN	(	8	H	X	h	x	ê	ÿ	¿	╕	╚	╪	Φ	°
1	0	0	1		HT	EM	)	9	I	Y	i	y	ë	Ö	⌐	╣	╔	┘	Θ	·
1	0	1	0		LF	SUB	*	:	J	Z	j	z	è	Ü	¬	║	╩	┌	Ω	-
1	0	1	1		VT	ESC	+	;	K	[	k	{	ï	¢	½	╗	╦	█	δ	√
1	1	0	0		FF	FS	,	<	L	\	l	|	î	£	¼	a	╠	▄	∞	^{n}
1	1	0	1		CR	GS	_	=	M	]	m	}	ì	¥	¡	╜	═	▌	ø	^{2}
1	1	1	0		SO	RS	.	>	N	^	n	~	Ä	₧	«	╛	╬	▐	∈	■
1	1	1	1		SI	US	/	?	O	_	o	DEL	Å	ƒ	»	┐	╧	▀	∩	
					7-Bit ASCII Character Set								8-Bit IBM Extended ASCII							

Figure 26.1
The ASCII character code.

Note Novell and other vendors are beginning to incorporate Unicode in their products. *Unicode,* a 16-bit code that can represent 65,536 characters in English and other languages, is organized into code pages devoted to the characters required for a given language, improving portability of products between different language environments.

File Syntax Translation

When file formats differ between computers, they require translation. Some situations that might require file format translation include:

- Copying files between a Macintosh and a DOS PC. Macintosh files actually consist of two related files called a *data fork* and a *resource fork.* PC files, on the other hand, consist of single file.
- Copying files between DOS PCs and Unix workstations.

Properly done, these translations can be completely transparent. NetWare, for example, enables DOS, Macintosh, and Unix users to share the same files on a NetWare server by using a feature called *name space support.*

Encryption

It is often desirable to ensure that data on a LAN is absolutely secure. Even if an eavesdropper were successful in listening in, sensitive data can be encrypted so that it is unusable.

Encryption techniques employ a form of reversible data scrambling that renders data unreadable without a key. A *key* is a code word or number that allows the encryption/decryption software to scramble and unscramble the data.

Given time, every encryption can be broken. High-speed computers make it feasible to crack many codes by simply trying different key values until the right one is found. A great deal of effort, therefore, has gone into creating powerful encryption algorithms boasting a low probability of failure.

Figure 26.2
The EBCDIC character code.

				8	0	0	0	0	0	0	0	0	1	1	1	1	1	1	1	1
				7	0	0	0	0	1	1	1	1	0	0	0	0	1	1	1	1
				6	0	0	1	1	0	0	1	1	0	0	1	1	0	0	1	1
				5	0	1	0	1	0	1	0	1	0	1	0	1	0	1	0	1
4	3	2	1																	
0	0	0	0		NUL	DLE	DS		SP	&	—									0
0	0	0	1		SOH	DC1	SOS				/		a	j			A	J		1
0	0	1	0		STX	DC2	FS	SYN					b	k	s		B	K	S	2
0	0	1	1		ETX	DC3							c	l	t		C	L	T	3
0	1	0	0		PF	RES	BYP	PN					d	m	u		D	M	U	4
0	1	0	1		HT	NL	LF	RS					e	n	v		E	N	V	5
0	1	1	0		LC	BS	EOB	UC					f	o	w		F	O	W	6
0	1	1	1		DEL	IL	PRE	EOT					g	p	x		G	P	X	7
1	0	0	0			CAN							h	q	y		H	Q	Y	8
1	0	0	1			EM							i	r	z		I	R	Z	9
1	0	1	0		SMM	CC	SM				!		:							
1	0	1	1		VT					.	$	,	#							
1	1	0	0		FF	IFS		DC4		<	*	%	@							
1	1	0	1		CR	IGS	ENQ	NAK		(	)	-	'							
1	1	1	0		SO	IRS	ACK			+	;	>	=							
1	1	1	1		SI	IUS	BEL	SUB		|		?	"							

Two common techniques are the following:

- Private keys
- Public keys

Private Keys

Private keys use the same key to encrypt and decrypt the message. This has several disadvantages. The sender and receiver must be sure to inform each other of the key. If the key is intercepted, the message becomes vulnerable. Each time the key is changed, and private keys are changed often in case they are compromised, the new key must be communicated and is vulnerable to discovery.

Public Keys

A *public key* is used to encrypt messages, whereas a *private key* is used for decryption. The public key is created by a user by applying an algorithm to a private key, which is known only to the intended receiver of the message.

The sender of the message uses the public key to encrypt a message and does not know or need to know the private key. In fact, anyone who has a person's public key can encrypt a message for that person.

The receiver decrypts the message by combining the public key with the private key, known only to him- or herself.

The algorithms used for public key encryption are extremely complex and make it unlikely that even a super computer will stumble on the correct key within a reasonable period of time (your lifetime, for example). Nevertheless, the code makers are never far ahead of the code breakers, and more sophisticated encryption techniques are always under development.

Questions

Study questions for this chapter may be found at the end of Chapter 27, "OSI Application Layer Concepts."

CHAPTER 27

OSI Application Layer Concepts

The application layer is concerned with providing services on the network. These services include file services, print services, database services, and the other services discussed in Chapter 17, "Network Services."

A common misunderstanding is that the application layer is responsible for running user applications such as word processors. This is not the case. The application layer, however, does provide an interface whereby applications can communicate with the network.

The application layer performs two functions related to the utilization of services on the network. One function involves the advertisement of available services. Another function involves the use of the services.

Advertising Services

To inform clients of services that are available, the application layer advertises the services to the network. You encountered the use of service addresses when the network layer was discussed in Chapter 23, "OSI Network Layer Concepts." These service addresses provide the mechanism that enables clients to communicate with services.

The application layer can employ *active* and *passive* methods of advertising services.

Active Service Advertisement

When servers actively advertise their services, they broadcast messages announcing the services they offer. Most protocols consider these service advertisements to be valid for a limited time. Unless the information is refreshed within a specified time, clients remove the information from their service tables.

Clients also can transmit messages that request specific services. Servers respond with a list of services they support.

Note: NetWare employs an active service advertisement protocol called the *Service Advertisement Protocol* (SAP).

Passive Service Advertisement

Servers also can list their services and addresses with a central service registry. Clients query the directory to determine which services are available and how to access them—this is called *passive service advertisement.*

Service Use Methods

Clients can access services using three methods:

- OS call interruption
- Remote operation
- Collaboration

OS Call Interruption

Applications on client systems request services by placing service calls to their local operating systems. A *service call* is a formal procedure set up by the designers of an operating system that provides an interface with the programs the operating system supports. Normally, these service calls invoke services on the local client PC.

When a client is configured for network operation, OS call interruption intercepts service requests. Service calls that request local resources are forwarded to the client's OS. Service calls that request network resources are transferred to the network, where they are forwarded to the appropriate server. The process is shown in figure 27.1.

OS call interruption enables a client to utilize network services even when OS has no inherent networking capability.

Note: This is the service access method used by NetWare requesters for DOS and OS/2, as well as for other operating systems supported for NetWare such as Macintosh.

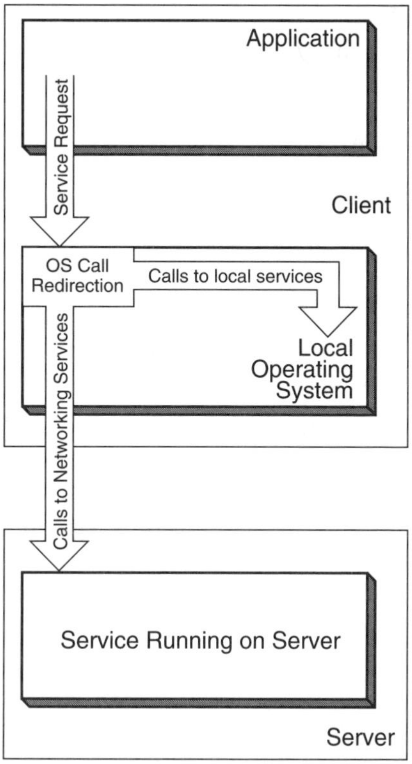

Figure 27.1
OS call interruption.

Remote Operation

When the client OS has network capability built-in, it can access the server by remote operation. The client OS interfaces directly with the network. Requests from the client OS appear to the server to be the same as requests from the server's own systems. In other words, the server is not directly aware of the separate existence of client systems.

Collaborative Computing

Some server and client operating systems are so advanced that the border between them blurs. The operating systems work together to coordinate the use of resources on the two respective computers. Recall from Chapter 16 the discussion of collaborative computing, which consists of far more than computers simply accessing each other's services. Indeed, computers participating in collaborative computing pool all of their resources. One computer can start a process on another, for example, to take advantage of some free processing cycles. This requires the participating operating systems to be capable of a high level of cooperation.

The following table summarizes the topics discussed in this chapter along with the associated methods.

Application Layer Topics and Methods

Topic	*Method*
Service advertisement	Active
	Passive
Service use	OS call interception
	Remote operation
	Collaborative processing

Questions

Here are some sample questions to help you evaluate your understanding of Chapters 23 through 27.

1. Which *two* address types are associated with individual devices?
   - ☐ A. Service
   - ☐ B. Network
   - ☐ C. Physical
   - ☐ D. Virtual

2. Which switching method employs virtual circuits?
   - ○ A. Message
   - ○ B. Circuit
   - ○ C. Packet
   - ○ D. All of the above

3. Which network layer is concerned with data encryption?
   - ○ A. Network
   - ○ B. Transport
   - ○ C. Session
   - ○ D. Presentation

4. Which network layer is concerned with delivering messages between processes on devices?
   - ○ A. Network
   - ○ B. Transport
   - ○ C. Session
   - ○ D. Presentation

5. Which network layer is concerned with address/name resolution?
   - ○ A. Network
   - ○ B. Transport
   - ○ C. Session
   - ○ D. Presentation

6. Which switching method makes the most efficient use of network bandwidth?
   - ○ A. Message
   - ○ B. Circuit
   - ○ C. Packet
   - ○ D. Methods are about equal

7. Which *two* connection services perform flow-control?
   - ☐ A. Unacknowledged connectionless services
   - ☐ B. Connection-oriented services
   - ☐ C. Acknowledged connectionless services
   - ☐ D. Unacknowledged connection-oriented services

8. What is another name for a message switching network?
   - ○ A. Connectionless
   - ○ B. Datagram
   - ○ C. Store-and-forward
   - ○ D. Virtual circuit

9. Which is the most common network switching method?
   - ○ A. Message
   - ○ B. Packet
   - ○ C. Circuit
   - ○ D. Virtual

10. Which *two* statements about virtual circuits are true?
    - ☐ A. They usually are associated with connection oriented services.
    - ☐ B. A virtual circuit represents a specific path through the network.
    - ☐ C. A virtual circuit appears to the connected devices as a dedicated network path.
    - ☐ D. Virtual circuits dedicate a communication channel to a single conversation.

11. Which of the following statements is true?
    - ○ A. Hop count is a measure of routing cost.
    - ○ B. Distance vector routing methods are technically simple and make efficient use of network bandwidth.
    - ○ C. Link-state routing protocols rely on tick counts to make routing determinations.
    - ○ D. Link-state routing protocols transmit routing information at regular intervals.

12. Which *three* of the following terms are related?
    - ☐ A. Port
    - ☐ B. Connection ID
    - ☐ C. Socket
    - ☐ D. Service address

13. Which switching method fragments messages into small units which are routed through independent paths?
    - ○ A. Message
    - ○ B. Packet
    - ○ C. Circuit
    - ○ D. Virtual

14. Which activity involves the use of connection IDs?
    - ○ A. Packet switching
    - ○ B. Routing
    - ○ C. Segment development
    - ○ D. End-to-end flow control

15. Which *two* of the following are transport layer error control strategies?
    - ☐ A. Using datagram packet switching
    - ☐ B. Utilizing unique segment sequencing numbers
    - ☐ C. Using time-outs to drop packets that have remained on the network too long
    - ☐ D. Using parity checking to detect errors

16. Which *two* of the following statements are true?

    ☐ A. The data link layer deals with device-to-device traffic.

    ☐ B. The network layer deals with traffic between upper layer processes.

    ☐ C. The transport layer deals with traffic between end-nodes.

    ☐ D. All of the above are true.

17. Which of the following methods of dialog control provides two-way communication?

    ☐ A. Simple duplex

    ☐ B. Simplex

    ☐ C. Half-duplex

    ☐ D. Full-duplex

18. Dialog control is a function of which layer of the OSI Reference Model?

    ○ A. Network

    ○ B. Transport

    ○ C. Session

    ○ D. Presentation

19. Which *threee* of the following are functions of session administration?

    ☐ A. Connection establishment

    ☐ B. Checksum error detection

    ☐ C. Data transfer

    ☐ D. Connection release

20. Which *two* of the following are functions of connection establishment?

    ☐ A. Resumption of interrupted communication

    ☐ B. Login name and password verification

    ☐ C. Determining required services

    ☐ D. Acknowledgment of data receipt

21. Which *two* of the following are possible functions of the presentation layer?

    ☐ A. Data encryption

    ☐ B. Presentation of data on display devices

    ☐ C. Data translation

    ☐ D. Display format conversion

22. Which *two* statements are true about public key data encryption?

    ☐ A. Encoded data is vulnerable should the public key become known.

    ☐ B. A public key is generated from a secret key.

    ☐ C. Public key encryption is less secure than private key encryption.

    ☐ D. The public key is used to encrypt messages, and a separate key is used to decrypt messages.

23. Which *three* of the following are possible functions of the application layer?

    ☐ A. Network printing service

    ☐ B. End-user applications

    ☐ C. Client access to network services

    ☐ D. Service advertisement

24. Which of the following methods is used by the NetWare requester to access network services?
    - A. Collaborative
    - B. OS call interception
    - C. Remote operation
    - D. Peer-to-peer communication

Answers

1. A, C
2. C
3. D
4. B
5. B
6. C
7. B, C
8. C
9. B
10. A, C
11. A
12. A, C, D
13. B
14. C
15. B, C
16. A, C
17. C, D
18. C
19. A, C, D
20. B, C
21. A, C
22. B, D
23. A, C, D
24. B

CHAPTER 28

Protocol Suites

In the preceding chapters, you have seen how the process of designing network protocols is usually done in pieces, with each piece solving a small part of the overall problem. By convention, these protocols are regarded as layers of an overall set of protocols called a protocol suite or a protocol stack.

You have seen one approach to defining the layers of a protocol stack. The OSI Reference Model is useful as a conceptual tool for understanding protocol layering. Although protocols have been designed in strict conformance with the OSI Reference Model, the OSI protocol suite has not become popular. The main influence of the Reference Model is as a conceptual framework in which to understand the process of network communication and in which to compare various types of protocols.

Protocols are real implementations, in program code and hardware, of the conceptual rules defined in the Reference Model. The tasks described in the Reference Model can be performed in various ways, depending on the goals of the network designers, and various protocol suites are in common use. Some protocols and protocol suites existed before the OSI Reference Model was published and can be matched only loosely to the seven-layer model.

In this chapter, you will get down to the task of examining a variety of actual protocols. In the process, you will apply what you have learned about the OSI Reference Model to several of the most popular protocol stacks.

This chapter examines the following protocol stacks:

- NetWare IPX/SPX
- Internet Protocols (TCP/IP)
- AppleTalk
- Digital Network Architecture (DNA)
- Systems Network Architecture (SNA)

Models and Protocols

Three stages take place before a protocol goes to work:

1. A model describes the general function of the protocol.
2. The protocol itself is defined in complete detail.
3. The protocol must be realized by software and hardware designers in real products.

Consider the process of designing a building. The architect first produces sketches that describe the general nature of the building. Then the architect, possibly working with a specialist in particular building trades, develops blueprints that describe every detail of the building. Finally, an actual building is constructed.

Protocols are the blueprints of networking. They are highly-detailed descriptions of all the functions at a given communication layer. Until the protocol is expressed in hardware and software, however, it cannot go to work.

The act of translating a protocol into hardware and software can be a difficult one, and different designers often have difficulty getting their equipment to interact without some tweaking, particularly in the early life stages of a protocol. Eventually, implementation of a protocol becomes fairly routine, but it always is advisable to inquire into the compatibility testing that has been performed on a new piece of equipment.

Because many problems are encountered when attempting to interconnect devices running different protocols, many organizations have pushed for *open systems* (sets of hardware and software standards that could be generally applied throughout the industry to ease communication difficulties).

The OSI Reference Model has been used as one strategy for developing open systems, and some vendors have redesigned existing protocol suites to make them more compliant with the OSI model. Others—a good example is the TCP/IP community—have argued that they already have a highly-functional set of protocols that are, in fact, open in the sense that they are freely available to everyone in the industry. As a result, the impact of the OSI model has been limited to the products of some manufacturers.

Figure 28.1 illustrates how the protocol suites discussed in this chapter relate to the layers of the OSI Reference Model.

NetWare IPX/SPX

The protocols utilized with NetWare are summarized in figure 28.2. The NetWare protocols have been designed with a high degree of modularity, making it easy to adapt to different hardware and to incorporate other protocols into the configuration. The discussion of NetWare protocols in this course is fairly brief considering the importance of these protocols to NetWare engineers. For a more detailed description, you might want to consult *NetWare: The Professional Reference, Fourth Edition* from New Riders Publishing.

Each of the protocols in figure 28.2 is discussed later in this chapter. Many of the features of the protocols are summarized in table 28.1.

Multiple Link Interface Driver (MLID)

MLIDs implement the *medium access control* (MAC) sublayer of the OSI data link layer. Practically speaking, MLID is Novell's name for the software that drives a network interface board. The specifications for writing MLIDs are defined by Novell's *Open DataLink Interface* (ODI) specification, which describes Novell's overall architecture for network protocols. An MLID must be written for each board design.

As such, the specific methods incorporated into a specific MLID depend on the underlying physical layer architecture. An MLID written for an Ethernet card uses contention access control, whereas an MLID written for a token-ring card uses token access.

The MLID is implemented in a software driver that usually takes its name from the model number of the network board being supported. An MLID for the Novell/Eagle NE2000 card, for example, is packaged in a file named NE2000.COM.

MLIDs are not dependent on any specific upper layer protocols. One feature of the ODI specification is that multiple protocols can access the same network interface board by linking to the same MLID.

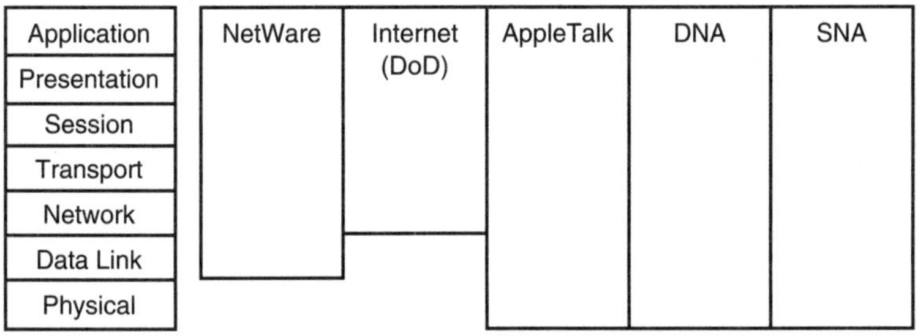

Figure 28.1
A comparison of various protocol suites to the OSI Reference Model.

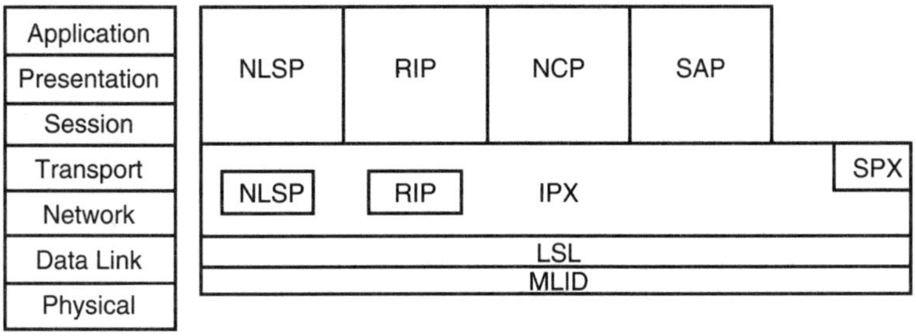

Figure 28.2
The NetWare protocol suite.

Multiple Link Interface Driver (MLID) Topics And Methods

OSI Layer	*Topics*	*Methods*
Data link (MAC sublayer)	Medium access	Contention Token passing Polling (Underlying physical layer defines MAC headers)

Link Support Layer (LSL)

The LSL implements the *logical link support* (LLC) sublayer of the OSI data link layer and functions as the interface between the MLID and the upper layer protocols.

When multiple upper layer protocol stacks are being used, the LSL software is responsible for passing packets to the appropriate protocol stack.

On NetWare DOS clients, the LSL sublayer is implemented in a file named LSL.COM.

Link Support Layer (LSL) Topics And Methods

OSI Layer	*Topics*	*Methods*
Data link (LLC sublayer)	Protocol specific	Interfaces MLID to upper layer protocols

Internetwork Packet Exchange Protocol (IPX)

IPX is a network layer protocol that provides connectionless (datagram) service. (IPX was developed from the XNS protocol originated by Xerox). As a network layer protocol, IPX is responsible for internetwork routing and for maintaining network logical addresses. Routing uses the RIP protocol (described below) to make route selections.

IPX relies on hardware physical addresses found at lower layers to provide network device addressing. It also makes use of *sockets*, upper-layer service addresses, to deliver packets to their ultimate destinations.

On the client, IPX support is provided as a component of the older DOS shell and the current DOS NetWare requester.

Internetwork Packet Exchange Protocol (IPX) Topics And Methods

OSI Layer	*Topics*	*Methods*
Network	Addressing	Logical network service
	Route selection	Dynamic
	Connection services	Connectionless

Router Information Protocol (RIP)

RIP uses the distance-vector route discover method to determine hop counts to other devices. Like IPX,

RIP was developed from a similar protocol in the XNS protocol suite. RIP is implemented as an upper-layer service and is assigned a socket (service address). RIP is based directly on IPX and performs network layer functions.

Router Information Protocol (RIP) Topics and Methods

OSI Layer	*Topics*	*Methods*
Network	Route discovery	Distance vector

Network Link Services Protocol (NLSP)

NLSP is a link-state routing protocol derived from an ISO protocol named IS-IS (intermediate system-to-intermediate system). NLSP supports fault-tolerant mesh and hybrid mesh networks with a high level of fault tolerance.

(This protocol is mistakenly named the NetWare Link Services Protocol in the course materials.)

Network Link State Protocol (NLSP) Topics And Methods

OSI Layer	*Topics*	*Methods*
Network	Route discovery	Link-state

Note Due to the frequency of messages required to advertise routing information, RIP has been a traditional bottleneck in NetWare performance, particularly with large internetworks that include slower wide-area links. NLSP is a newer protocol that can greatly improve performance of NetWare internetworks. It is shipped with 4.1 and is available as an upgrade for other NetWare implementations such as 3.*x* and earlier versions of 4.*x*.

Sequenced Packet Exchange (SPX)

SPX is a transport layer protocol that extends IPX to provide connection-oriented service with reliable delivery. Reliable delivery is ensured by retransmitting packets in the event of error. SPX is derived from a similar SPX protocol in the XNS network protocol suite.

SPX establishes virtual circuits called *connections*. The connection ID for each connection appears in the SPX header. A given upper-layer process can be associated with multiple connection IDs.

On the client, SPX support is provided as a component of the older DOS shell and of the current NetWare requester.

Sequenced Packet Exchange Protocol (SPX) Topics And Methods

OSI Layer	*Topics*	*Methods*
Transport	Addressing	Connection ID
	Segment development	Division and combination
	Connection services	Segment sequencing
		Error control
		End-to-end flow control

NetWare Core Protocols (NCP)

NCP provides numerous function calls that support network services such as file service, printing, name management, file locking, and synchronization. NetWare client software interfaces with NCP to access NetWare services.

It is interesting to note that most NetWare services do not rely on a transport layer protocol such as SPX. In almost all cases, NCP provides the upper layer protocol structure that provides services, connection management, and reliable delivery. In most cases, SPX is not required and can even be left out of the client configuration.

NetWare Core Protocols (NCP) Topics And Methods

OSI Layer	*Topics*	*Methods*
Transport	Connection services	Segment sequencing
		Error control
		End-to-end flow control
Session	Session administration	Data transfer
Presentation	Translation	Character code
		File syntax
Application	Service use	OS redirector or Collaborative (depend ing on client)

Service Advertising Protocol (SAP)

SAP is used by NetWare servers to advertise their services to the network. Each server identifies itself once a minute by transmitting a SAP packet. SAP users also can request service information by transmitting a service query packet. SAP implementations obtain service address information from IPX header information.

Service Advertising Protocol (SAP) Topics And Methods

OSI Layer	*Topics*	*Methods*
Session	Session administration	File transfer
Application	Service advertisement	Active

Internet Protocols

The Internet protocol suite (also commonly called the TCP/IP protocol suite) was originally developed by the United States Department of Defense (DoD) to provide robust service on large internetworks that incorporate a variety of computer types. In recent years, the Internet protocols have become increasingly popular and constitute the most popular network protocols now in use. If you want more detailed information about the Internet protocols than that provided in this course, you can consult *NetWare TCP/IP and NFS* from New Riders Publishing.

One reason for this popularity is that the Internet protocols are not owned by any one vendor, unlike the NetWare, DNA, SNA, AppleTalk, and various other protocols. The protocol suite evolves in response to input from a wide variety of industry sources. As such, the Internet protocol suite is the most open of the protocol suites and is supported by the widest variety of vendors. Virtually every brand of computing equipment now supports the Internet protocols.

Much of the popularity of the TCP/IP protocols comes from their early availability on Unix. The protocols were built into the Berkeley Standard Distribution (BSD) Unix implementation. Since then, TCP/IP has achieved universal acceptance in the Unix community and is a standard feature on all versions of Unix.

Figure 28.3 illustrates the relationship of the protocols in the Internet suite to the layers of the OSI Reference Model. Notice that the suite does not include protocols for the data link or physical layers. TCP/IP was designed to work over established standards such as Ethernet. Over time, TCP/IP has been interfaced to the majority of data link and physical layer technologies.

It should be noted that the Internet protocols do not map cleanly to the OSI Reference Model. The DoD model was, after all, developed long before the OSI model was defined. The model for the Internet protocol suite has four layers, which are also shown in figure 28.3. From this, you can see the approximate relationships of the layers of the two models. The functions of the layers of the DoD model are as follows:

- The *network access* layer corresponds to the bottom two layers of the OSI model. As previously mentioned, this was deliberately done to enable the DoD protocols to coexist with existing data link and physical layer standards.
- The *internet* layer corresponds roughly to the OSI network layer. Protocols at this layer are concerned with moving data between devices on networks.
- The *host-to-host* layer can be compared to the OSI transport layer. Host-to-host protocols enable peer communication between hosts on the internetwork. (At the time these protocols were designed, personal computers and workstations did not exist and all network computers were host computers. As a result, devices on TCP/IP networks are typically referred to as *hosts*. The concept of a client/server relationship did not exist, and all communicating hosts were assumed to be peers.)
- The *process/application* layer embraces functions of the OSI session, presentation, and application layers. Protocols at this layer provide network services.

A large number of protocols are associated with the Internet protocol suite.

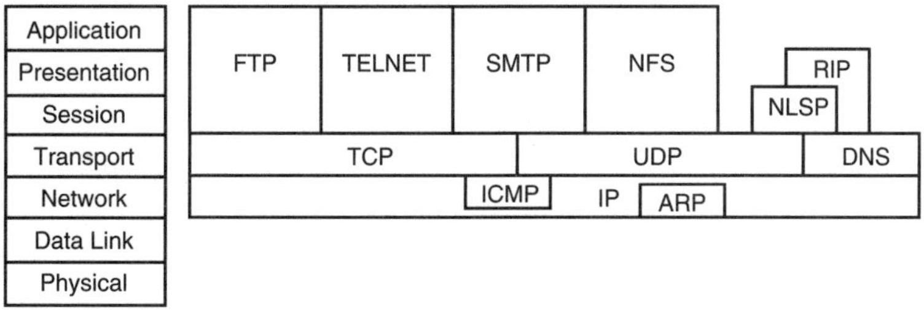

Figure 28.3
The Internet protocol suite.

Internet Protocol (IP)

IP is a connectionless protocol that provides datagram service, and IP packets are most commonly referred to as IP datagrams. IP is a packet-switching protocol that performs addressing and route selection. An IP header is appended to packets, which are transmitted as frames by lower level protocols. IP routes packets through internetworks by utilizing dynamic routing tables that are referenced at each hop. Routing determinations are made by consulting logical and physical network device information, as provided by the *Address Resolution Protocol* (ARP).

IP performs packet disassembly and reassembly as required by packet size limitations defined for the data link and physical layers being implemented. IP also performs error checking on the header data using a checksum, although data from upper layers is not error-checked. The following table shows IP topics and methods.

Internet Protocol (IP) Topics And Methods

OSI Layer	*Topics*	*Methods*
Network	Addressing	Logical network
	Switching	Packet
	Route selection	Dynamic
	Connection services	Error control

Internet Control Message Protocol (ICMP)

ICMP enhances the error control provided by IP. Connectionless protocols such as IP cannot detect internetwork errors such as congestion or path failures. ICMP can detect such errors and notify IP and upper layer protocols.

Internet Control Message Protocol (ICMP) Topics And Methods

OSI Layer	*Topics*	*Methods*
Network	Connection services	Error control
		Network-layer flow control

Routing Information Protocol (RIP)

RIP in the Internet protocol suite is not the same protocol as RIP in the NetWare suite, although the two serve similar functions. Internet RIP performs route discovery using a distance vector method, calculating the number of hops that must be crossed to route a packet by a particular path. A *hop* is defined as crossing a single router.

While it works well in localized networks, RIP has many weaknesses that limit its utility on wide-area internetworks. These weaknesses are similar to those of NetWare RIP and are causing RIP to be replaced gradually by the OSPF link-state protocol.

Routing Information Protocol (RIP) Topics And Methods

OSI Layer	*Topics*	*Methods*
Network	Route discovery	Distance vector

Open Shortest Path First (OSPF)

OSPF is a link-state route discovery protocol that is designed to overcome the limitations of RIP. On large internetworks, OSPF can identify the internetwork topology and improve performance by implementing load balancing and class-of-service routing.

Open Shortest Path First (OSPF) Topics And Methods

OSI Layer	*Topics*	*Methods*
Network	Route discovery	Link-state

Transmission Control Protocol (TCP)

TCP is an internetwork protocol that corresponds to the OSI transport layer. TCP provides full-duplex, connection-oriented transport. When the overhead of a connection-oriented transport is not required, the *User Datagram Protocol* (UDP) can be substituted for TCP at the transport (host-to-host) level.

TCP also provides message fragmentation and reassembly, and can accept messages of any length from upper layer protocols. TCP fragments message streams into segments that can be handled by IP. When used with IP, TCP adds connection-oriented service and performs segment synchronization, adding sequence numbers at the byte level.

In addition to message fragmentation, TCP can maintain multiple conversations with upper layer protocols and can improve use of network bandwidth by combining multiple messages into the same segment. Each virtual-circuit connection is assigned a connection identifier called a *port*, which identifies the datagrams associated with that connection.

Transmission Control Protocol (TCP) Topics And Methods

OSI Layer	*Topics*	*Methods*
Network	Addressing	Service
Transport	Addressing	Connection identifier
	Segment development	Division and recombination
	Connection services	Segment sequencing
		Error control
		End-to-end flow control

User Datagram Protocol (UDP)

UDP is a connectionless transport (host-to-host) layer protocol. UDP does not provide message acknowledgments, it simply transports datagrams.

Like TCP, UDP utilizes port addresses to deliver datagrams. These port addresses, however, are not associated with virtual circuits and merely identify local host processes. UDP is preferred over TCP when high performance or low network overhead is more critical than reliable delivery. Because UDP does not need to establish, maintain, and close connections, or control data flow, it generally outperforms TCP.

UDP is the transport layer protocol used with the *Simple Network Management Protocol* (SNMP), which is the standard network management protocol used with TCP/IP networks. UDP enables SNMP to provide network management with a minimum of network overhead.

User Datagram Protocol (UDP) Topics And Methods

OSI Layer	*Topics*	*Methods*
Transport	Addressing	Connection identifier
	Segment development	Combination
	Connection services	Connectionless (datagram)

Address Resolution Protocol (ARP)

The following three types of address information are used on TCP/IP internetworks:

- Physical addresses used by the data link and physical layers.
- IP addresses, which provide logical network and host IDs. IP addresses consist of four numbers typically expressed in "dotted-decimal" form. An example of an IP address is 134.135.100.13.
- Logical node names, which identify specific hosts with alphanumeric identifiers. These are easier for humans to recall than the numeric IP addresses. An example of a logical node name is MYHOST.COM.

Given a logical node name, ARP can determine the IP address associated with that name. ARP maintains tables of address resolution data and can broadcast packets to discover addresses on the internetwork. The IP addresses discovered by ARP can be provided to data link layer protocols.

Address Resolution Protocol (ARP) Topics And Methods

OSI Layer	*Topics*	*Methods*
Network	Address resolution	Matches logical (IP) and physical device addresses

Domain Name System (DNS)

DNS provides name/address resolution as a service to client applications. DNS servers enable humans to use logical node names to access network resources.

Domain Name System (DNS) Topics And Methods

OSI Layer	*Topics*	*Methods*
Transport	Address/name resolution	Service-provider initiated

File Transfer Protocol (FTP)

FTP is a protocol for sharing files between networked hosts. FTP enables users to log onto remote hosts. Logged-on users can inspect directories, manipulate files, execute commands, and perform other commands on the host. FTP also has the capability of transferring files between dissimilar hosts by supporting a file request structure that is independent of specific operating systems.

Note: NetWare users should note that FTP is more than simply a remote file access protocol. Users are not limited to reading and writing files unlike when they are logged into a NetWare server. FTP is a peer-to-peer protocol that enables users to initiate processes on the remote host.

File Transfer Protocol (FTP) Topics And Methods

OSI Layer	*Topics*	*Methods*
Session	Session administration	Connection establishment
		File transfer
		Connection release
Presentation	Translation	Machine-independent file syntax
Application	Network services	File services
	Service use	Collaborative

Simple Mail Transfer Protocol (SMTP)

SMTP is a protocol for routing mail through internetworks, and it makes use of the TCP and IP protocols. SNMP does not provide a mail interface for the user. Creation, management, and delivery of messages to end users must be performed by an e-mail application. (The most popular e-mail application on the Internet is named Eudora.)

SMTP is implemented by NetWare messaging gateways. SMTP also is provided with UnixWare.

Simple Mail Transfer Protocol (SMTP) Topics And Methods

OSI Layer	*Topics*	*Methods*
Application	Network services	Message services

Remote Terminal Emulation (TELNET)

TELNET enables PCs and workstations to function as dumb terminals in session with hosts on internetworks. TELNET implementations are available for most end-user platforms including Unix (of course), DOS, Windows, and Macintosh OS.

TELNET is provided as a part of NetWare XCONSOLE, NetWare NFS, FlexIP, and NetWareIP through UNICON. TELNET also is provided with UnixWare.

Remote Terminal Emulation (TELNET) Topics And Methods

OSI Layer	*Topics*	*Methods*
Session	Dialog control	Half-duplex
	Session administration	Connection establishment
		File transfer
		Connection release
Presentation	Translation	Byte order Character code
Application	Service use	Remote operation

Network File System (NFS)

NFS, developed by Sun Microsystems, is a family of file access protocols that are a considerable advancement over FTP and TELNET. Since Sun made the NFS specifications available for public use, NFS has achieved a high level of popularity. NFS consists of the following protocols:

- eXternal Data Representation (XDR) supports encoding of data in a machine-independent format. C programmers use XDR library routines to describe data structures that are portable between machine environments.
- Remote Procedure Calls (RPC) function as a service request redirector that determines whether function calls can be satisfied locally or must be redirected to a remote host. Calls to remote hosts are packaged for network delivery and transmitted to RPC servers, which generally have the capability of servicing many remote service requests. RPC servers process the service requests and generate response packets that are returned to the service requester.

Network File System (NFS) Topics And Methods

OSI Layer	*Topics*	*Methods*
Application	Network services	File services
	Service use	Remote operation

Remote Procedure Call (RPC) Topics And Methods

OSI Layer	*Topics*	*Methods*
Session	Session administration	Connection establishment
		File transfer Connection release

External Data Representation (XDR) Topics And Methods

OSI Layer	*Topics*	*Methods*
Presentation	Translation	Byte order
		Character code
		File syntax

AppleTalk

AppleTalk is the computing architecture developed by Apple Computer for the Macintosh family of personal computers. Although AppleTalk originally supported only Apple's proprietary LocalTalk cabling system, the suite has been expanded to incorporate both Ethernet and token ring physical layers.

AppleTalk originally supported networks of limited scope. The AppleTalk Phase 2 specification issued in 1989, however, extended the scope of AppleTalk to enterprise networks. The Phase 2 specification also enabled AppleTalk to coexist on networks with other protocol suites. Table 28.1 summarizes the differences between AppleTalk Phases 1 and 2.

Table 28.1
Comparison of AppleTalk Phases 1 and 2

Characteristic	*Phase 1*	*Phase 2*
Maximum zones on a network segment	1	255
Maximum nodes per network	254	About 16 million
Dynamic addressing based on	Node ID	Network+Node ID
supported link access protocols	LocalTalk Ethernet	LocalTalk IEEE 802.2 IEEE 802.5
Split-horizon routing	No	Yes

AppleTalk Phase 1 protocols do not support internetworks because addressing is limited to a unique node ID. This approach is called a *nonextended network* under Phase 2 terminology. Phase 2 also supports extended networks in which addressing is determined by a combination of a network and a node ID, and can make use of the hardware-based device IDs that are coded into Ethernet and token ring cards.

Figure 28.4 presents a layered perspective of the AppleTalk protocols. Each of these protocols is described in this chapter. Each AppleTalk protocol is briefly discussed below.

LocalTalk, EtherTalk, and TokenTalk Link Access Protocols (LLAP, ELAP, and TLAP)

These are link access protocols that integrate AppleTalk upper layer protocols with the LocalTalk, Ethernet, and token ring environments.

LLAP is a protocol developed by Apple for operation with the LocalTalk cabling system, a system based on shielded twisted-pair cabling. LocalTalk is suitable primarily for small, low performance networks. The maximum data rate is 230.4 Kbps (compared to 10 Mbps for Ethernet), and cable segments are limited to 300 meters in length and a maximum of 32 devices.

LLAP uses addresses called AppleTalk addresses that are developed dynamically on the network. LLAP is ideally suited to Apple's "plug and play" Macintosh philosophy because a Macintosh can discover a unique physical address when it connects to the network without the need for any configuration.

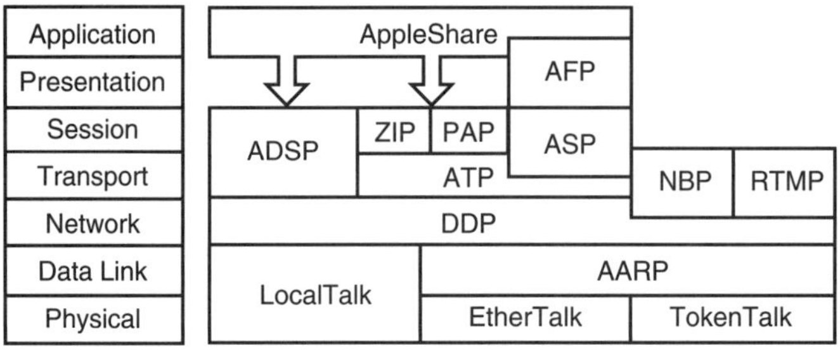

Figure 28.4
The AppleTalk protocol suite.

LocalTalk *Topics And Methods*

OSI Layer	*Topics*	*Methods*
Physical	Connection types	Multipoint
	Physical topology	Bus
	Digital signaling	State transition
	Bit synchronization	Synchronous
	Bandwidth use	Baseband
Data Link (MAC)	Logical topology	Bus
	Media access Addressing	Contention Physical device
Data Link (LLC)	Transmission synchronization	Synchronous
	Connection services	LLC flow control
		Error control

AppleTalk Address Resolution (AARP)

Both Ethernet and token ring make use of physical device addresses that are built into the interfaces when they are manufactured. AARP maps AppleTalk addresses to Ethernet and token ring physical addresses, enabling upper AppleTalk protocols to interface with the Ethernet and token ring physical layers.

AppleTalk Address Resolution Protocol (AARP) Topics And Methods

OSI Layer	*Topics*	*Methods*
Network/ Data Link	Address resolution	Matches logical names with physical device addresses

Datagram Delivery Protocol (DDP)

DDP is a network-layer protocol that provides connectionless service between two sockets. A *socket* is the AppleTalk term for a service address. A combination of a device address, network address, and socket uniquely identifies each process.

DDP performs network routing and consults routing tables maintained by RTMP to determine routing. Packet delivery is performed by the data link protocol operating on a given destination network.

Datagram Delivery Protocol (DDP) Topics And Methods

OSI Layer	*Topics*	*Methods*
Network	Addressing	Logical network service
	Route selection	Dynamic
	Interoperability	Network layer translation

Routing Table Maintenance Protocol (RTMP)

RTMP provides DDP with routing information based on a distance vector method similar to RIP.

Routing Table Maintenance Protocol (RTMP) Topics And Methods

OSI Layer	*Topics*	*Methods*
Network	Route discovery	Distance vector

Zone Information Protocol (ZIP)

ZIP organizes devices into zones, which organize service providers into logically named groups. Zones reduce the complexity of a network by limiting users network views to the devices they need.

ZIP functions with routers to organize service providers into zones and to resolve zone and network names.

Zone Information Protocol (ZIP) Topics And Methods

OSI Layer	*Topics*	*Methods*
Session	Protocol-specific	Organization of service providers into zones

Name Binding Protocol (NBP)

AppleTalk enables devices to have logical names in addition to their addresses. These names hide lower-layer addresses from users and from upper-layer processes.

NBP enables an application to match a logical name with it's associated address. Recall that AppleTalk addresses are dynamic and can change from session-to-session. NBP obtains up-to-date information that enables devices to use a logical name to determine address information even though the address varies.

Name Binding Protocol (NBP) Topics And Methods

OSI Layer	*Topics*	*Methods*
Transport	Address resolution	Service requestor initiated

AppleTalk Transaction Protocol (ATP)

ATP is a connectionless transport layer protocol. Reliable service is provided through a system of acknowledgments and retransmissions. Retransmissions automatically are initiated if an acknowledgment is not received within a specified time interval.

ATP reliability is based on transactions. A transaction consists of a request followed by a reply.

ATP is responsible for segment development and performs fragmentation and reassembly of packets that exceed the specifications for lower layer protocols. Packets include sequence numbers that enable message reassembly and retransmission of lost packets. Only damaged or lost packets are retransmitted.

AppleTalk Transaction Protocol (ATP) Topics And Methods

OSI Layer	*Topics*	*Methods*
Transport	Addressing	Transaction identifier
	Segment development	Division and combination
	Connection services	Error control

AppleTalk Session Protocol (ASP)

ASP is a session layer protocol that establishes, maintains, and releases sessions between service requesters and service providers. The focus of ASP is on providing file services. ASP works with ATP to provide a complete transport service. ATP messages are limited to eight packets, each with a maximum size of 578 bytes. ASP can generate multiple ATP transactions as required to control message overhead on large data transfers.

Multiple sessions can be maintained between service requesters and providers. Sessions can be requested by service requesters, but not by service providers.

AppleTalk Session Protocol (ASP) Topics And Methods

OSI Layer	*Topics*	*Methods*
Transport	Connection services	Segment sequencing
		End-to-end flow control
Session	Session administration	Connection establishment
		Data transfer
		Connection release

Printer Access Protocol (PAP)

PAP is a session layer protocol similar to ASP. As the name implies, the protocol provides printing services, but it also supports other types of connections between service requesters and providers.

PAP permits sessions to be initiated by both service requesters and service providers.

Printer Access Protocol (PAP) Topics And Methods

OSI Layer	*Topics*	*Methods*
Session	Session administration	Connection establishment
		Data transfer
		Connection release

AppleTalk Data Stream Protocol (ADSP)

Notice in figure 28.4 that ADSP provides a protocol stack that is an alternative to protocols that are layered onto ATP.

ADSP performs services associated with several network layers. It is considered a transport layer protocol in that it establishes, maintains, and releases sessions between sockets. At the session layer, ADSP substitutes for ASP and PAP.

ADSP replaces ATP at the transport layer and incorporates segment sequencing and sliding window flow-control. The service provided is full-duplex.

ADSP is not transaction-based like ATP. Instead ADSP uses a connection identifier and byte streams. ADSP provides better performance on lower-bandwidth channels than does ATP working with ASP or PAP.

AppleTalk Data Stream Protocol (ADSP) Topics And Methods

OSI Layer	*Topics*	*Methods*
Transport	Addressing	Connection identifier
	Segment development	Division and combination
	Connection establishment	Error control
		End-to-end flow control
		Segment sequencing

OSI Layer	*Topics*	*Methods*
Session	Session administration	Connection establishment
		Data transfer
		Connection release

AppleTalk Filing Protocol (AFP)

AFP provides file services and is responsible for translating local file service requests into formats required for network file services. AFP directly translates command syntax and enables applications to perform file format translations.

AFP is responsible for file system security, and verifies and encrypts login names and passwords during connection setup.

AppleTalk Filing Protocol (AARP) Topics And Methods

OSI Layer	*Topics*	*Methods*
Session	Session administration	Data transfer
Presentation	Translation	File syntax
	Encryption	Public key

AppleShare (ASP)

AppleShare provides the following three primary application services:

- The AppleShare File Server uses AFP to enable users to store and access files on the network.

It logs in users and associates them with network volumes and directories.

- The AppleShare Print Server uses NBP and PAP to support network printing. NBP provides name/address information that enables PAP to connect to printers. The AppleShare Print Server performs print spooling and manages printing on networked printers.
- The AppleShare PC enables PCs running MS-DOS to access AppleShare services by running an AppleShare PC program.

AppleShare Topics And Methods

OSI Layer	*Topics*	*Methods*
Application	Network services	File service
		Print service
	Service advertisement	Active
	Service use	Collaborative

Digital Network Architecture

Since it's introduction in 1974, the Digital Network Architecture (DNA) has evolved several times. It's current generation is called Phase V. DECnet is Digital's family of products that implement the DNA architecture.

As DNA has evolved, Digital has placed a strong emphasis on use of standards-based protocols and on achieving close conformance with the OSI Reference Model. A variety of ISO standards are incorporated into the DNA protocol suite.

Prior to DNA Phase V, DNA relied heavily on Digital proprietary protocols above the network layer. This stack—which includes Digital's NSP, Naming Service, Session Control, and other protocols—is still supported for the purpose of backward compatibility. Other pre-Phase V protocols also are supported at the lower network levels.

DNA Phase V introduced an alternative protocol stack based on ISO standards.

Figure 28.5 illustrates the layers of the DNA protocol suite. DNA is based on several physical and data link standards that are discussed in Chapter 29, "Other Protocols and Standards," including IEEE 802.X, FDDI, and X.25/LAPB.

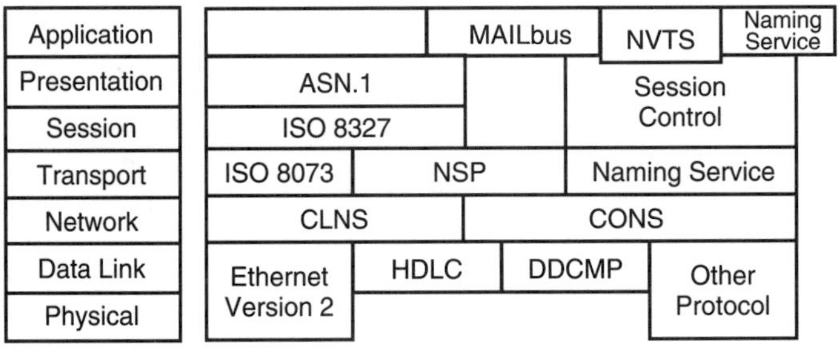

Figure 28.5
Protocols in the Digital Network Architecture.

Ethernet Version 2

Digital was joined by Intel and Xerox to develop the first version of Ethernet, physical and data link protocol. Since that time, the standard has been updated, and the current version is Ethernet Version 2.

Ethernet has the following characteristics:

- 10 Mbps signaling over coaxial cable.
- Media access control method is CARRIER-sense multiple access with collision detection (CSMA/CD).
- Signaling uses Manchester encoding.

The IEEE 802.3 standard was developed with slight modifications from Ethernet Version 2. Among those changes was a modification to the frame format, which makes 802.3 frames incompatible with Ethernet Version 2.

Note NetWare LANs can interface to DECnet networks using the NetWare for LAT product.

Ethernet Version 2 Topics And Methods

OSI Layer	*Topics*	*Methods*
Physical	Connection types	Multipoint
	Physical topology	Bus
	Digital signaling	State transition
	Bit synchronization	Synchronous
	Bandwidth use	Baseband
Data Link (MAC sublayer)	Logical topology	Bus
	Media access	Contention
	Addressing	Physical device

Digital Data Communications Message Protocol (DDCMP)

DDCMP is a data link protocol that dates from the earliest DNA implementations and remains as an optional Phase V protocol. DDCMP has the following capabilities:

- Asynchronous or synchronous service
- Half- or full-duplex modes
- Point-to-point or multipoint operation
- Connection-oriented error control using commands and acknowledgments along with CRC-based error detection
- LLC flow control and message sequencing (Digital uses the term *message* to describe data link level frames.)

Note At the time the DNA protocols were being defined, all users interacted with central computers by means of computer terminals. Terminal support was provided by the Local Area Transport protocol (LAT), which enables terminal server devices to support multiple terminals and multiplex their traffic over a single channel. LAT does not conform to the OSI network layer, in that packets do not incorporate routing information and cannot be routed on wide area networks.

NetWare networks can interface with the DNA environment using the product NetWare for LAT.

Digital Data Communications Message Protocol (DDCMP) Topics And Methods

OSI Layer	*Topics*	*Methods*
Physical	Connection types	Point-to-point
		Multipoint
Data Link (LLC Sublayer)	Transmission synchronization	Asynchronous
		Synchronous
	Connection services	LLC-Level flow control
		Error control
		Message sequencing

High-Level Data Link Control (HDLC)

HDLC is a data link protocol that supports transmissions over physical layer modem communication protocols. HDLC has the following features:

- Determines the data frame format and the frame transfer command syntax
- Supports asynchronous and synchronous communication
- Performs LLC flow control

High-Level Data Link Control (HDLC) Topics And Methods

OSI Layer	*Topics*	*Methods*
Physical	Connection types	Point-to-point
Data Link (LLC Sublayer)	Transmission synchronization	Asynchronous
		Synchronous
	Connection services	LLC-Level flow control

Connectionless-Mode Network Service (CLNS)

CLNS is a connectionless network layer service that incorporates the following three ISO protocols:

- ISO 8473 is a connectionless-mode network service that manages communication between end systems.
- ISO 9542 is a routing protocol that operates between *end systems* (devices) and *intermediate systems* (routers). This protocol, most frequently referred to as ES-IS, can be relatively simple because it does not need to perform internetwork routing.
- ISO 10589 is a routing protocol that operates between intermediate systems. IS-IS is a more complex protocol than ES-IS because it must be capable of determining routes through complex internetworks. Figure 28.6 illustrates the relationships of the two routing protocols.

These connectionless protocols are used to perform route discovery and selection, addressing, and switching.

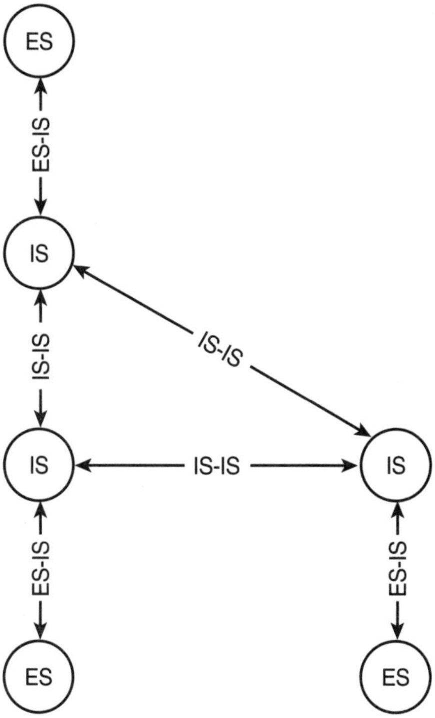

Figure 28.6
ES-IS and IS-IS routing protocols.

Connectionless-Mode Network Service (CLNS) Topics And Methods

OSI Layer	*Topics*	*Methods*
Network	Addressing	Logical network
	Route discovery	Link-state
	Route selection	Dynamic

Connection-Mode Network Service (CONS)

CONS is a connection-oriented network layer service based on the following protocols:

- ISO 8208 is an ISO version of the X.25 packet-switching protocol, which is discussed in Chapter 29.
- ISO 8878 is an additional protocol that enables X.25 networks to provide connection-oriented services.

CLNS is employed more commonly than CONS to provide network layer services.

Connection-Mode Network Service (CONS) Topics And Methods

OSI Layer	*Topics*	*Methods*
Network	Addressing	Logical network
	Route discovery	Link-state
	Route selection	Dynamic
	Connection services	Network layer flow control
		Error control
		Packet
		Sequence control

Connection-Oriented Transport Protocol Specification (ISO 8073)

ISO 8073 is a transport layer protocol that provides five service classes, tailored to different requirements. Network implementations can select a service level based on required levels of flow, error, and packet sequencing.

Connection-Oriented Transport Protocol Specification Topics And Methods

OSI Layer	*Topics*	*Methods*
Transport	Addressing	Connection identifier
	Connection services	Segment sequencing
		Error control
		End-to-end flow control

Network Services Protocol (NSP)

NSP was incorporated in the original DNA protocol suite. NSP is a connection-oriented transport protocol that manages normal or expedited full-duplex subchannels. End-to-end flow control is performed in response to congestion messages from network layer protocols. Either windowing or guaranteed flow rates can be used to control data flow.

Network Services Protocol (NSP) Topics And Methods

OSI Layer	*Topics*	*Methods*
Transport	Addressing	Connection identifier
	Connection services	Segment sequencing
		Error control
		End-to-end flow control

Session Control

Session Control is a DNA protocol that performs session and presentation layer functions. Functions performed by Session Control include:

- Address/name resolution.
- Transport connection management.
- Connection identifier management.
- Selection of protocol stacks. When devices initiate a session, Session Control negotiates a protocol stack that is supported on both systems.

Session Control Topics And Methods

OSI Layer	*Topics*	*Methods*
Transport	Address/name resolution	Service-requestor initiated
	Addressing	Connection identifier

OSI Layer	*Topics*	*Methods*
Session	Session administration	Connection establishment
		Data transfer
		Connection release

Session Protocol Specification (ISO 8327)

ISO 8327 is a session layer protocol that implements the specification ISO 8326, Session Service Definition. OSI 8327 provides the following services:

- Connection establishment, half-duplex data transfer, and connection release.
- Support for multiple transport layer connections for each session.
- Packet synchronization. The method uses tokens that can be used to request retransmission from any point.

ISO 8327 Session Protocol Specification Topics And Methods

OSI Layer	*Topics*	*Methods*
Session	Dialog control	half-duplex
	Session administration	Connection establishment
		Data transfer
		Connection release

Abstract Syntax Notation One with Basic Encoding Rules (ASN.1 with BER)

ASN.1 (ISO 8824) is a set of extensible syntax rules that establish data types and structures. The rules themselves are described in the Basic Encoding Rules. These protocols operate at the presentation DNA layer.

These standards are designed to facilitate data exchange between different systems by establishing a common set of data formats. These translations might include conversion between character sets, number representation systems, or other data types. The rules can be extended as required to embrace new data types.

Abstract Syntax Notation (ASN.1 with BER) Topics And Methods

OSI Layer	*Topics*	*Methods*
Presentation	Translation	Character code

File Transfer, Access, and Management (FTAM) and Data Access Protocol (DAP)

FTAM (ISO 8571) is an application layer file service protocol. The specification requires a certain set of document types and services, but permits vendors to create customized implementations of the protocol. Standard document types include binary, text, and hierarchical files. Standard services include file transfer and management.

Data Access Protocol (DAP)

DAP performs file services including file creation, deletion, storage, retrieval, and transfer.

File Transfer, Access, and Management (FTAM) and DAP Topics and Methods

OSI Layer	*Topics*	*Methods*
Application	Network service	File services

Network Virtual Terminal Service (NVTS)

This service enables multiple terminal types to access computer services. A virtual terminal is a conceptual representation of a computer display. Both the host and the terminal emulating device maintain a copy of this model, which serves as a common intermediate data representation that enables the host and device to exchange terminal data.

Network Virtual Terminal Services (NVTS) Topics And Methods

OSI Layer	*Topics*	*Methods*
Presentation	Translation	Character code (commands)
Application	Network service	Terminal service
	Service use	Remote operation

MAILbus and X.400 Message Handling System

These systems provide DNA electronic messaging services. The MAILbus family of products provides proprietary mail services and use the X.400 messaging specification to interface with other X.400-based systems.

MAILbus and X.400 Topics And Methods

OSI Layer	*Topics*	*Methods*
Application	Network service	Message service

Naming Service and X.500 Directory

Naming Service is an application-level naming service that provides address/name resolution. A *name service* enables humans to describe network services with logical, alphanumeric identifiers. These identifiers are translated to network addresses by the naming service.

X.500 is a standard for a naming service. Digital has stated that the DNA Naming Service will migrate toward conformance with X.500.

Naming Service and X.500 Topics And Methods

OSI Layer	*Topics*	*Methods*
Transport	Address/name resolution	Service-provider initiated
Application	Network service	Directory service

Systems Network Architecture (SNA)

Like DNA, IBM's Systems Network Architecture (SNA) evolved when terminals were the normal devices used to interact with centralized computers. SNA terminal networks are organized hierarchically, and when it was introduced in 1974, SNA supported only hierarchical networks. An example of an SNA network is shown in figure 28.7. The network hierarchy consists of a central control point (the host computer), controllers (communication controllers and cluster controllers), and terminals.

In 1984, SNA was updated to support distributed processing environments with a feature called *Advanced Peer-to-Peer Networking* (APPN). APPN can implement a distributed processing environment that can leverage the processing capabilities of mainframe hosts, minicomputers, and personal computers.

The next refinement of SNA, the Systems Application Architecture (SAA), was announced in 1987 and represents IBM's strategic direction.

SNA and the OSI Reference Model

SNA was not developed from a preconceived, carefully thought-out model from which protocols were developed. IBM literally was pioneering the development of computer networking, and new protocols were added to meet new needs and design criteria. One result of this is that multiple protocols

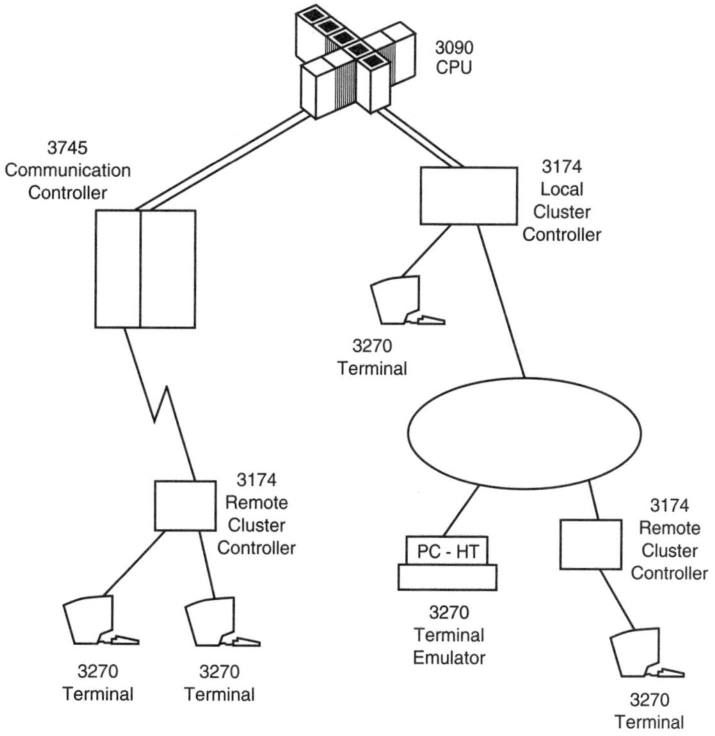

Figure 28.7
An example of an SNA network.

can be present at any given layer. Each protocol serves a somewhat different purpose in the overall scheme of SNA. As such, SNA does not consist of a protocol stack so much as it consists of multiple protocols that work together in different combinations to meet different needs.

SNA was a mature model by the time formulation of the OSI Reference Model was undertaken, and the SNA architecture had a significant influence on the definition of the OSI model. For that reason, this course includes a comparison of the two models.

In addition to showing the organization of the SNA protocols, figure 28.8 compares the layers of the OSI Reference Model to the layers of the SNA model.

The layers of the SNA model and their features are as follows:

- **Physical control** covers the same functions as the OSI physical layer. Both are concerned with the electrical, mechanical, interface, and control characteristics of the physical medium. IBM developed the Token Ring physical layer standard for this layer, but market forces have pushed IBM to extend SNA to embrace other popular physical layer standards such as Ethernet (IEEE 802.3).
- **Data link control** includes many functions of the OSI data link layer. The *Synchronous Data Link Control* (SDLC) protocol is the SNA data link protocol and is responsible for communication between master/primary nodes and slave/secondary nodes.
- **Path control** incorporates functions from two OSI layers. Path control is responsible for flow control, a data link layer function. Path control also is responsible for the routing and packet disassembly/assembly functions of the network layer.
- **Transmission control** is analogous to the OSI transport layer and provides end-to-end connection services. This layer also performs encryption/decryption, services OSI provides at the presentation layer.
- **Data flow control**, like the OSI session layer, controls dialogs.
- **Presentation services** perform data translation services similar to the OSI presentation layer, but also are responsible for sharing resources and synchronizing operations.
- **Transaction services** provide application services, supporting distributed processing and management services. *SNA Distributed Services* (SNADS) is an example of a distributed service.

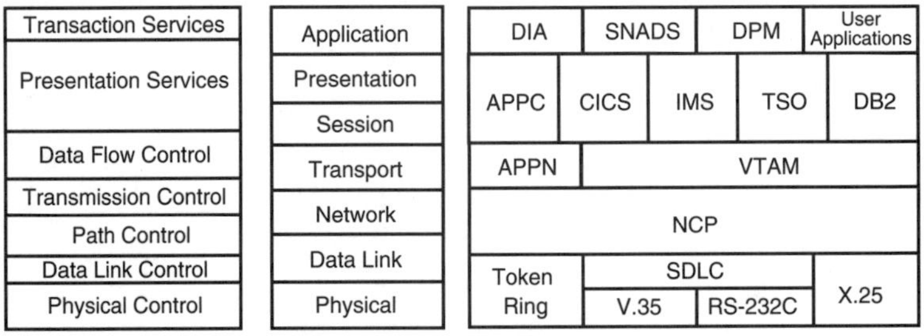

Figure 28.8
SNA protocols and the OSI Reference Model.

Network Addressable Units

SNA networks are organized hierarchically and consist of *network addressable units* (NAUs). An NAU is a hardware device or a program (or a combination of hardware and software) that can be addressed on the network. Two types of NAUs can be found: physical units and logical units.

A *physical unit* (PU) is a device consisting of the hardware, firmware, and software required to manage node communication. Communication controllers and cluster controllers are examples of physical units.

Note Under SNA terminology, a node is, by definition, a physical unit (PU). Terminals, printers, and other peripherals are not regarded as nodes.

Logical units (LUs) are the end points of network communication. (The course definition calls LUs "the 'entities' of the network.") Examples of LUs are peripherals such as terminals, printers, and programs that communicate by means of SNA.

SNA defines several types of PUs and LUs, some of which are illustrated in figure 28.9. The types of each are discussed next.

Until the 1980s, virtually all devices on SNA networks operated in a master/slave relationship under which a master device, the control point, controls all network communication. Terminals, printers, and other peripheral devices function as slaves controlled by the master device, which uses polling to manage communication.

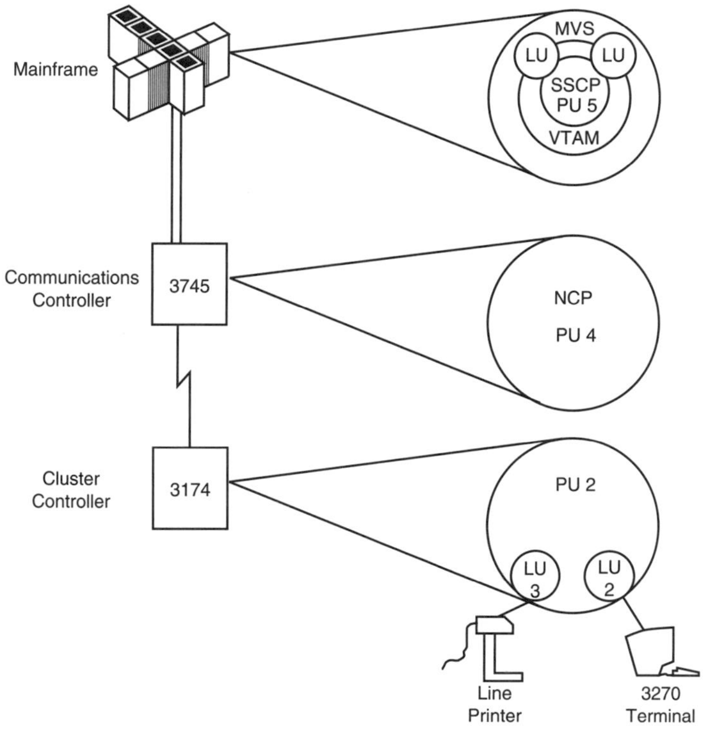

Figure 28.9
PUs and LUs in an SNA network.

During the 1980s, IBM introduced Advanced Program-to-Program Networking (APPN), which enabled LUs to communicate in a peer-to-peer fashion. LU Type 6.2 and PU Type 2.1 were introduced to support APPN.

Physical Units

SNA defines the following three types of physical units:

- **PU type 5** nodes are host nodes. A *host node* is the control point that manages networking in a domain. A *domain* consists of all the PUs, LUs, and other network resources that a given host can control. Domains can be divided into subareas. On SNA networks consisting of multiple hosts, terminals can be configured to access applications on more than one host.

  The host node runs a program called *Virtual Terminal Access Method* (VTAM), which provides the *System Services Control Point* (SSCP) service that controls all connection requests and network flow. All SNA network hierarchies are organized around an SSCP.

- **PU type 4** nodes are communication controllers. A *communication controller* is a device that runs a *Network Control Program* (NCP) and serves as a communication front-end for the host node. (For this reason, this device typically is called a front end processor.) A communication controller relieves the host node of the responsibility for directly supervising remote communication resources. The IBM 3745 is a type of communication controller.

- **PU Type 2** nodes are peripheral nodes. Typically, *peripheral nodes* are *cluster controllers*, devices that enable printers, terminals, and other devices to connect to the network. The IBM 3174 is a type of communication controller.

Note

The course materials state that terminals and printers are also examples of PU Type 2 devices. Terminals and printers, however, are more typically defined as logical units, which are discussed in the next section.

Logical units are the network end-points between which communication occurs. Quite often an LU consists of a software process that is running on a type 2 node (a cluster controller). This process in turn services data input and output for a particular terminal, printer, or other peripheral.

The most important thing about PUs and LUs is the *function*, not the hardware in which the function is performed. A terminal, for example, must be serviced by a PU Type 2 function as well as an LU Type 2 function. These two functions typically are performed by the hardware and software operating in a cluster controller.

Some SNA printers might be equipped with hardware that enables them to network as PU Type 2 devices, enabling them to network without a cluster controller. These printers, however, must still include the LU function as well as the PU function.

For purposes of this course, some types of terminals and printers might be considered to be Type 2 PUs.

The course also lists a PU Type 1—a type no longer in use—which is a type of terminal node.

All communication of PU Type 2 nodes is managed by the central control point, the SSCP. Two type 2 devices, therefore, cannot directly communicate.

PU Type 2.1 is a new subclass of PU Type 2 that enables the device to provide a control point. This control point enables type 2.1 PUs to engage in peer-to-peer communication.

Note: In summary, control points manage data communication on the network. Control points are found on type 5 PUs and type 2.1 PUs only.

Logical Units

Logical units are the endpoints of SNA communication and consist of physical devices (terminals, printers, etc.) and programs. The various LU types are summarized in table 28.2.

Key SNA Protocols

The following are brief descriptions of common SNA protocols.

Table 28.2
Logical Unit Types

LU	*Communication*	*Description Endpoints*
0	Program-to-program	An older LU type supporting program-to-program communication. Replaced by LU type 6.2.
1	Program-to-device	Master/slave. SNA character-stream data on printers, card readers, and hard copy terminals.
2	Program-to-device	Master/slave. Supports terminals using the 3270 protocol.
3	Program-to-device	Master/slave. Supports printers using the 3270 protocol.
4	Program-to-program	Master/slave, peer-to-peer, or program-to-device SNA character stream to printers.
6&6.1	Program-to-program	Peer-to-peer interprogram communication. (Such as CICS-CICS, IMS-IMS, CICS-IMS.)
6.2	Program-to-program	Peer-to-peer Advanced Program-to-Program Communication (APPC).
7	Program-to-device	Communication using 5250 data streams, such as terminals on AS/400, System 36, and System 38.

Token Ring

Token Ring is IBM's specification for a token-access LAN based on a ring logical topology. This specification was used as the basis for developing the IEEE 802.5 token ring standard. IBM Token Ring originally operated at 4 Mbps but has been extended to function at 16 Mbps data rates. The Token Ring specification describes various cable types, connectors, hubs, and wiring specifications.

Token Ring Topics And Methods

OSI Layer	*Topics*	*Methods*
Physical	Connection types	Point-to-point
	Physical topology	Star
	Digital signaling	State transition
	Bit synchronization	Synchronous
	Bandwidth use	Baseband
Data Link (MAC sublayer)	Logical topology	Ring
	Media access	Token passing
	Addressing	Physical device

Synchronous Data Link Control (SDLC)

SDLC is a high-performance data link protocol developed to support communication between computers and to function with dedicated or dial-up lines. SDLC supports point-to-point and multi-point communication in half- and full-duplex modes. SDLC frame types can be used to communicate data or to perform control functions.

Synchronous Data Link Control (SDLC) Topics And Methods

OSI Layer	*Topics*	*Methods*
Data Link (MAC sublayer)	Media access	Polling
	Addressing	Physical device
Data Link (LLC sublayer)	Transmission synchronization	Synchronous Synchronous
	Connection services	Flow control
		Error control

Network Control Program (NCP)

NCP is the protocol that manages network communication on front end processors. NCP functions at the data link and network layers and supports routing and gateway functions.

Network Control Program (NCP) Topics And Methods

OSI Layer	*Topics*	*Methods*
Data Link (MAC sublayer)	Media access	Polling
	Addressing	Physical device
Data Link (LLC sublayer)	Connection services	Flow control
Network	Addressing	Logical network
	Route selection	Static
	Gateway services	Network layer translation

Virtual Telecommunications Access Method (VTAM)

VTAM operates on the host control node and provides the *System Services Control Point* (SSCP) function for the network. The SSCP controls the network hierarchy and works in conjunction with NCPs running on front end processors. VTAM can manage single or multiple domains and supports interconnections between networks.

Virtual Telecommunications Access Method (VTAM) Topics And Methods

OSI Layer	*Topics*	*Methods*
Transport	Addressing	Connection identifier
	Segment development	Division and combination
	Connection services	End-to-end flow control
Session	Dialog control	Half-duplex
	Session administration	Connection establishment
		Data transfer
		Connection release

Advanced Peer-to-Peer Networking (APPN)

APPN is the SNA architecture for network peer-to-peer communication. Any PU Type 2.1 can communicate with other PU type 2.1 devices directly, without the need for an SSCP control node. Thus APPN supports networking without the requirement for a mainframe computer. APPN provides directory services, route discover, and window-based flow control.

Advanced Peer-to-Peer Networking (APPN) Topics And Methods

OSI Layer	*Topics*	*Methods*
Network	Addressing	Logical network
	Route discovery	
Transport	Connection services	Segment sequencing
		End-to-end flow control

Customer Information Control System (CICS)

CICS is a transaction processing environment used to build applications. Transaction processing is intended for critical applications, and CICS provides the security, transaction tracking, error recovery, transaction backout, and restart capabilities that are required in such demanding environments as banking and stocks trading.

Customer Information Control System (CICS) Topics And Methods

OSI Layer	*Topics*	*Methods*
Session	Dialog control	Half-duplex
	Session administration	Connection establishment
		Data transfer
		Connection release
Presentation	Translation	File syntax

Information Management System (IMS)

IMS is another application processing environment, and it supports both database and transaction management. The IMS Database Manager is a powerful hierarchical database that can operate under CICS or under the IMS Transaction Manager. IMS databases can be shared among various applications, with IMS scheduling activities and switching messages.

Information Management System (IMS) Topics And Methods

OSI Layer	*Topics*	*Methods*
Session	Dialog control	Half-duplex
	Session administration	Connection establishment
		Data transfer
		Connection release
Presentation	Translation	File syntax

Advanced Program-to-Program Communication (APPC)

APPC is the IBM specification that defines LU Type 6.2.

Advanced Program-to-Program Communication (APPC) Topics And Methods

OSI Layer	*Topics*	*Methods*
Transport	Addressing	Connection identifier
	Connection services	Segment sequencing
		End-to-end flow control
Session	Dialog control	Half-duplex
	Session	Connection establishment
		Data transfer
		Connection release

Distributed Data Management (DDM)

DDM uses an OS call redirection approach to provide remote file access to SNA applications. DDM receives service requests and executes them locally or directs them to a DDM server elsewhere on the network as appropriate.

Distributed Data Management (DDM) Topics And Methods

OSI Layer	*Topics*	*Methods*
Application	Network services	File
	Service use	OS call interception

SNA Distributed Services (SNADS)

SNADS provides asynchronous distribution by implementing a store-and-forward distribution service. This service complements the synchronous delivery supported by SNA session capabilities and is useful for distribution of messages and documents. Among its functions, SNADS provides an infrastructure for distribution of e-mail.

SNA Distribution Services (SNADS) Topics And Methods

OSI Layer	*Topics*	*Methods*
Application	Network services	File Message

Document Interchange Architecture (DIA)

DIA defines standards for data interchange between dissimilar computer systems, and coordinates storage, transfer, and retrieval of files.

Document Interchange Architecture (DIA) Topics And Methods

OSI Layer	*Topics*	*Methods*
Application	Network services	File

Questions

1. Which *two* protocols are designed to provide reliable delivery?

   - [ ] A. IPX
   - [ ] B. TCP
   - [ ] C. UDP
   - [ ] D. SPX

2. Which protocol enables clients to identify available NetWare servers?

   - ○ A. IPX
   - ○ B. NLSP
   - ○ C. SAP
   - ○ D. RIP

3. Which *three* protocols translate logical device names into device addresses?

   - [ ] A. DNS
   - [ ] B. NBP
   - [ ] C. SAP
   - [ ] D. X.500

4. If your network includes large numbers of NetWare servers, connected via a wide area network, which protocol should you evaluate as a means of reducing network traffic overhead?

   - ○ A. SPX
   - ○ B. SAP
   - ○ C. NLSP
   - ○ D. RIP

5. Which of the following protocols are most similar?

   - ○ A. NetWare IPX and Internet TCP
   - ○ B. NetWare NLSP and AppleTalk RTMP
   - ○ C. NetWare NLSP and DNA CLNS
   - ○ D. NetWare RIP and Internet OSPF

6. Which Novell protocol usually provides transport-layer functions?

   - ○ A. SPX
   - ○ B. IPX
   - ○ C. NLSP
   - ○ D. NCP

7. Which protocol suite provides the standards with the broadest industry support?

   - ○ A. AppleTalk
   - ○ B. Internet
   - ○ C. NetWare
   - ○ D. SNA

8. Which types of addresses are used on LocalTalk networks?

   - ○ A. Physical node numbers
   - ○ B. Static logical IDs
   - ○ C. Dynamic logical IDs
   - ○ D. Logical device names

9. Which protocol enables Ethernet and token ring networks to interface with AppleTalk protocols?

   - ○ A. RTMP
   - ○ B. AARP

- ○ C. LLAP
- ○ D. ZIP

10. Which protocol is responsible for matching user's logical device names with AppleTalk addresses?
    - ○ A. AARP
    - ○ B. ZIP
    - ○ C. NBP
    - ○ D. ATP

11. Which AppleTalk protocols provide session-level services?
    - ☐ A. ASP
    - ☐ B. PAP
    - ☐ C. ADSP
    - ☐ D. AFP

12. Which *two* components are required to enable a NetWare LAN to communicate with a Digital computer?
    - ☐ A. Ethernet v.2 support
    - ☐ B. IEEE 802.3 Ethernet support
    - ☐ C. TCP/IP
    - ☐ D. NetWare for LAT

13. Which *two* of these DNA protocols are regarded as presentation layer protocols?
    - ☐ A. ASN.1
    - ☐ B. NVTS
    - ☐ C. FTAM
    - ☐ D. MAILbus

14. Which *three* of the following statements are true regarding SNA network addressable units?
    - ☐ A. A PU type 2 is a communication controller
    - ☐ B. An LU 6.2 device is capable of program-to-program communication
    - ☐ C. A PU consists of the hardware and software required to manage the resources of nodes.
    - ☐ D. Control points are found on Type 5 and Type 2.1 PUs.

15. Which SNA protocols are required to implement peer-to-peer communication?
    - ○ A. DDM
    - ○ B. SNADS
    - ○ C. APPN and APPC
    - ○ D. NCP

Answers

1. B, D
2. C
3. A, B, D
4. C
5. C
6. D
7. B
8. C
9. B
10. C
11. A, B, C, D
12. A, D
13. A, B
14. B, C, D
15. C

CHAPTER 29

Other Protocols and Standards

This chapter discusses a variety of network protocols that you are likely to encounter. The following protocols are covered:

- *The IEEE 802 family*
- *Fiber Distributed Data Interface (FDDI)*
- *Serial Line Internet Protocol (SLIP) and Point-to-Point Protocol (PPP)*
- *CCITT/ITU X.25*
- *Frame Relay*
- *Integrated Service Digital Network (ISDN) and Broadband ISDN (B-ISDN)*
- *Asynchronous Transfer Mode (ATM)*
- *Synchronous Optical Network (SONET) and the Synchronous Digital Hierarchy (SDH)*
- *Switched Multimegabit* Digital Service (SMDS)

More information about many of these protocols can be found in NRP's NetWare: The Professional Reference, Fourth Edition.

The IEEE 802 Family

The *Institute of Electrical and Electronic Engineers* (IEEE) is the largest professional organization in the world and is extremely influential with regard to setting standards. The 802 committee of the IEEE has developed a series of standards for *local area networks* (LANs), *metropolitan area networks* (MANs), and *wide area networks* (WANs). These standards have been recognized and reissued by the *International Organization for Standardization* (ISO) as the ISO 8802 standards.

Twelve subcommittees oversee the 802 standards. (A thirteenth committee has been proposed for the developing 100-BASE-X standard.) Figure 29.1 illustrates the position each standard occupies in the OSI Reference Model. The following table summarizes the topics and methods associated with each standard.

802.2 Topics and Methods

Layer	*Topics*	*Methods*
Data link	Protocol specific	Identification of upper-layer protocols
LLC sublayer		

IEEE 802.2

The IEEE 802.2 standard defines an LLC sublayer that is utilized by other lower-layer protocols. Because a single LLC protocol layer is used by lower-layer protocols, network layer protocols can be designed independently of the network's physical layer and MAC sublayer implementations.

The LLC appends a header to packets that identifies which upper-layer protocols are associated with the frame. The header also declares which processes are the source and destination of each packet.

IEEE 802.3

The IEEE 802.3 standard defines a network derived from the Ethernet network originally developed by Digital, Intel, and Xerox. This standard defines characteristics related to the MAC sublayer of the data link layer and to the OSI physical layer. With one minor distinction—frame type—IEEE 802.3 Ethernet functions identically to DIX Ethernet v.2. The two standards can even coexist on the same cabling system, although devices using one standard cannot communicate directly with devices using the other. The following table about 802.3 summarizes the topics and methods associated with each layer.

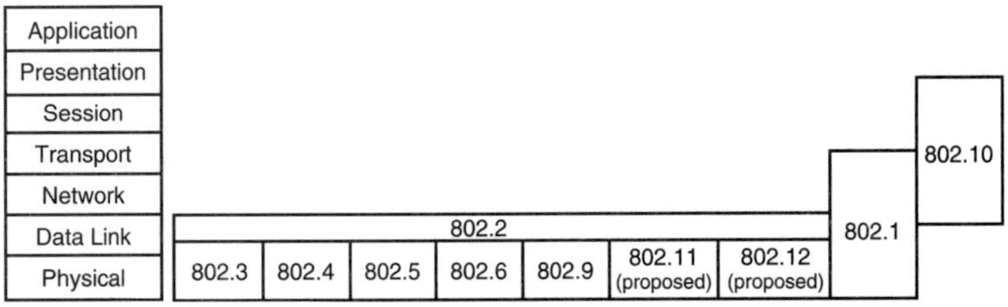

Figure 29.1
The relationship between the IEEE 802 standards and the OSI Reference Model.

802.3 Topics and Methods

Layer	*Topics*	*Methods*
Physical	Physical topology	1BASE5 star 10BASE5 bus 10BASE2 bus 10BROAD36 bus 10BASE-F star 10BASE-T star
	Connection types	Multipoint
	Digital signaling	State transition
	Bit synchronization	Synchronous
	Bandwidth use	Baseband (except 10BROAD36 broadband)
Data link (MAC sublayer)	Logical topology	Bus
	Media access	Contention
	Addressing	Physical device address

The MAC sublayer uses a variety of contention access called *Carrier Sense Multiple Access with Collision Detection* (CSMA/CD). This technique reduces the incidence of collision by having each device listen to the network to determine if it is quiet ("carrier sensing"); a device only attempts to transmit when the network is quiescent. This reduces but does not eliminate collisions because signals take some time to propagate through the network. As devices transmit, they continue to listen so they can detect a collision should it occur. When a collision occurs, all devices cease transmitting and send a "jamming" signal that notifies all stations of the collision. Then, each device waits a random amount of time before again attempting to transmit. This combination of safeguards significantly reduces collisions on all but the busiest networks.

The physical layer definition describes signaling methods (both baseband and broadband are available), data rates, media, and topologies. Several physical layer variants have been defined. Each is named following a convention that states the signaling rate (1 or 10) in Mbps, baseband (BASE) or broadband (BROAD) mode, and a designation of the media characteristics. The following are the 802.3 variants:

- **1BASE5** is a 1 Mbps network that utilizes UTP cable with a signal range up to 500 meters (250 meters per segment). A star physical topology is used.
- **10BASE5** uses a large diameter (10mm) "thick" coaxial cable with a 50-ohm impedance. A data rate of 10 Mbps is supported with a signaling range of 500 meters per cable segment on a physical bus topology. This variant is typically called *Thick Ethernet* or *Thicknet.*
- **10BASE2** is similar to Thicknet, but uses a thinner coaxial cable that can support cable runs of 185 meters. (In this case, the 2 only approximately indicates the cable range.) The transmission rate remains 10 Mbps and the physical topology is a bus. This variant is typically called *Thin Ethernet* or *Thinnet.*
- **10BASE-F** uses fiber-optic cables to support 10 Mbps signaling with a range of 4 kilometers. Three subcategories include 10BASE-FL (fiber link), 10BASE-FB (fiber backbone), and 10BASE-FP (fiber passive).

- **10BROAD36** is a broadband standard that supports channel signal rates of 10 Mbps. 75-ohm coaxial cable supports cable runs of 1,800 meters (up to 3,600 meters in a dual-cable configuration) using a physical bus topology.
- **10BASE-T** uses UTP cable in a star physical topology. The signaling rate remains at 10 Mbps. Devices might be up to 100 meters from a wiring hub.
- **100BASE-X** is a proposed standard that is similar to 10BASE-T but supports 100 Mbps data rates.

Note The industry is not in accord regarding the proper use of the name Ethernet. Xerox has placed the name Ethernet in the public domain, therefore no one can claim authority over it. Purists often claim that Ethernet refers only to the original Digital-Intel-Xerox standard. More frequently, however, the term is used to designate any network based on CSMA/CD access control methods.

It is usually necessary to be specific about the standard that applies to a given network configuration. The original standard is called Ethernet version 2 (the older version 1 is still in occasional use) or Ethernet-II. The IEEE standard is distinguished by its committee title as 802.3.

The distinction is important because Ethernet version 2 and 802.3 Ethernet use incompatible frame types. Devices using one frame type cannot communicate with devices using the other frame type. Fortunately, NetWare is conversant with both frame types on both servers and clients.

IEEE 802.4

The 802.4 standard describes a network with a bus physical topology that controls media access with a token mechanism. The standard was designed to meet the needs of industrial automation systems but has gained little popularity. Both baseband and broadband (using 75-ohm coaxial cable) configurations are available.

802.4 Topics and Methods

Layer	*Topics*	*Methods*
Physical	Physical topology	Bus
	Connection types	Multipoint
	Digital signaling	State transition
	Bit synchronization	Synchronous
	Bandwidth use	Baseband
Data link (MAC sublayer)	Logical topology	Ring
	Media access	Token passing
	Addressing	Physical device address

IEEE 802.5

The IEEE 802.5 standard was derived from IBM's Token-Ring network, which employs a ring logical topology and token-based media access control. Data rates of 1, 4, and 16 Mbps have been defined. The IEEE 802.5 standard does not describe a cabling system. Most implementations are based on the IBM cabling system, which uses twisted-pair cable wired in a physical star.

802.5 Topics and Methods

Layer	*Topics*	*Methods*
Physical	Physical topology	Star/Ring
	Connection types	Point-to-point
	Digital signaling	State transition
	Bit synchronization	Synchronous
	Bandwidth use	Baseband
Data link (MAC sublayer)	Logical topology	Ring
	Media access	Token passing
	Addressing	Physical device address

IEEE 802.6

The IEEE 802.6 standard describes a MAN standard called *Distributed Queue Dual Bus* (DQDB). Much more than a data network technology, DQDB is suited to data, voice, and video transmissions. The network is based on fiber-optic cable in a dual-bus topology. Traffic on each bus is unidirectional. When operated in pairs, the two buses provide a fault-tolerant configuration. Bandwidth is allocated using time slots, and both synchronous and asynchronous modes are supported.

802.6 Topics and Methods

Layer	*Topics*	*Methods*
Physical	Physical topology	Ring
	Connection types	Point-to-point
	Bandwidth use	Baseband
Data link (MAC sublayer)	Logical topology	Ring

IEEE 802.9

The IEEE 802.9 standard supports a 10 Mbps asynchronous channel along with 96 64-Kbps (6 Mbps total bandwidth) channels that can be dedicated to specific data streams. The total bandwidth is 16 Mbps. This standard is called *Isochronous Ethernet* (IsoEnet) and is designed for settings that have a mix of bursty and time-critical traffic.

IEEE 802.11

IEEE 802.11 is a standard for wireless LANs, currently under development. A CSMA/CD method has been approved, but the final standard is pending.

802.11 (Proposed) Topics and Methods

Layer	*Topics*	*Methods*
Data link (MAC sublayer)	Media access	Contention

IEEE 802.12

The IEEE 802.12 standard is based on a 100 Mbps proposal promoted by AT&T, IBM, and Hewlett-Packard. Called 100VG-AnyLAN, the network is based on a star wiring topology and a contention-based access method whereby devices signal the wiring hub of a need to transmit data. Devices can transmit only when granted permission by the hub. This standard is intended to provide a high-speed network that can operate in mixed Ethernet and Token Ring environments by supporting both frame types.

802.12 (Proposed) Topics and Methods

Layer	*Topics*	*Methods*
Physical	Physical topology	Star
	Connection types	Multipoint
	Bandwidth use	Baseband
Data link (MAC sublayer)	Logical topology	Bus
	Media access	Contention

Fiber Distributed Data Interface

Fiber Distributed Data Interface (FDDI) is a standard for fiber-based networks that was developed by the X3T9.5 committee of the *American National Standards Institute* (ANSI). The ISO has adopted FDDI as standard 9314. FDDI was developed for WANs but has been used in MANs and LANs as well.

As shown in figure 29.2, FDDI covers the physical layer and the MAC sublayer of the OSI Reference Model. Most frequently, the IEEE 802.2 standard is employed for the LLC sublayer.

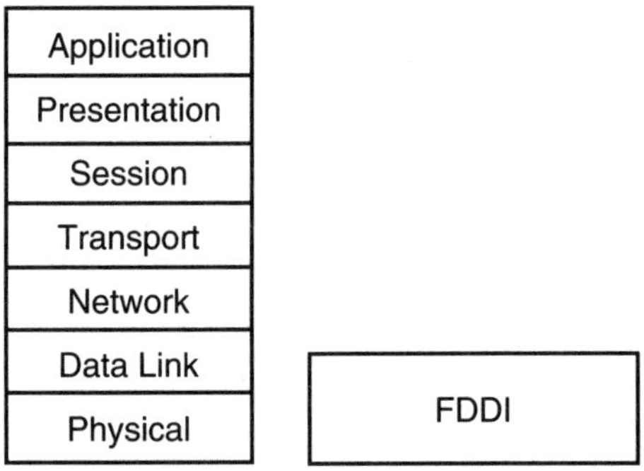

Figure 29.2
The relationship of FDDI to the OSI Reference Model.

FDDI is a 100 Mbps network that functions similarly to 802.5 Token Ring, and is based on token-passing access control and a ring topology. Originally developed for optical fiber cable, the standard has been extended so that it can be supported with copper UTP. Use of optical fiber cable enables FDDI to support physically large networks.

Although FDDI networks can be cabled as physical stars, stars might be impractical with larger networks, and FDDI networks are then typically cabled in physical rings. Stations can be attached in two ways as shown in figures 29.3A and 29.3B. Stations on a single ring configuration are called *single-attached stations.* On a single ring, failure of the medium at any point causes the network to fail.

To provide greater fault tolerance, FDDI is typically cabled with *dual-attached stations* (DASs) using two counter-rotating rings. As figure 29.3B shows, if the cable fails at any one point, the two rings are automatically reconfigured to maintain a complete ring transmission path. (Note that a failed link between single-attached stations cannot be corrected in this manner.) Under normal operation, both rings can be used for data and traffic can be balanced between rings. It is desirable, however, to design the network to half its dual-ring capacity and to half its size limit. If a ring failure occurs under these conditions, the total length of the two rings will be within specifications and the traffic will be manageable with only a single active ring.

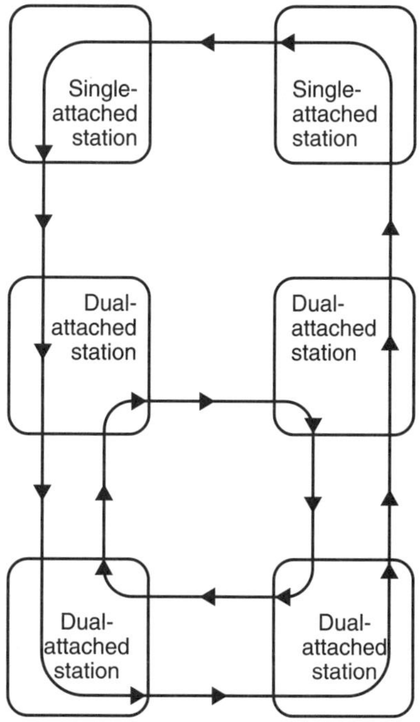

Figure 29.3A
Normal operation of an FDDI network with single- and dual-attached stations.

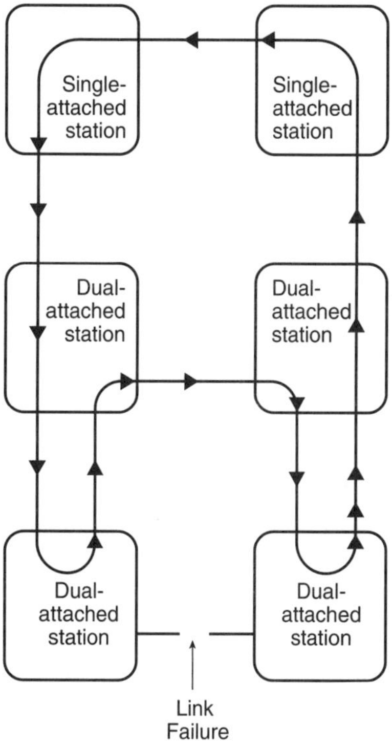

Figure 29.3B
Dual-attached FDDI stations correcting for a failed link.

FDDI Topics and Methods

Layer	*Topics*	*Methods*
Physical	Physical topology	Star or ring
	Connection types	Point-to-point
	Bandwidth use	Baseband
Data link (MAC sublayer)	Logical topology	Ring
	Media access	Token passing

Serial Line Internet Protocol and Point-to-Point Protocol

The *Serial Line Internet Protocol* (SLIP) and *Point-to-Point Protocol* (PPP) were designed to support dial-up access to networks based on the Internet protocols. SLIP is a simple protocol that functions at the physical layer, whereas PPP is a considerably enhanced protocol that provides physical layer and data link layer functionality. The relationship of both to the OSI model is shown in figure 29.4.

SLIP was developed to provide dial-up IP connections. It is an extremely rudimentary protocol that suffers from a lack of rigid standardization such that different implementations might not interoperate.

SLIP Topics and Methods

Layer	*Topics*	*Methods*
Physical	Connection type	Point-to-point

PPP was defined by the *Internet Engineering Task Force* (IETF) to improve on SLIP by providing the following features:

- Security using password login
- Simultaneous support for multiple protocols on the same link
- Dynamic IP addressing
- Error control

Different PPP implementations might offer different levels of service and can negotiate service levels when connections are made.

Figure 29.4
The relationship of SLIP and PPP to the OSI Reference Model.

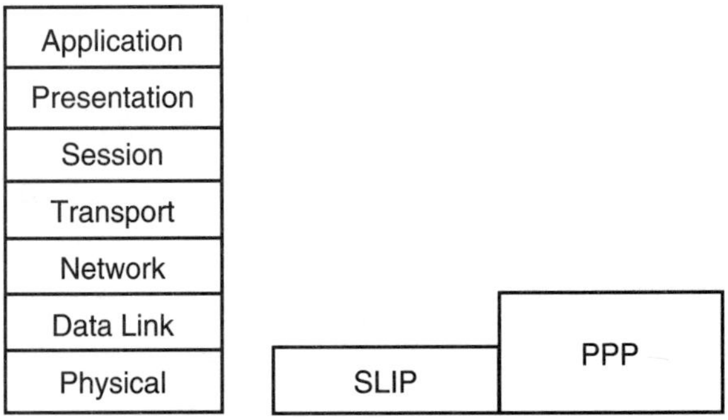

PPP Topics and Methods

Layer	*Topics*	*Methods*
Physical	Connection type	Point-to-point
Data link (MAC sublayer)	Addressing	Physical device
Data link (LLC sublayer)	Connection services	Error control

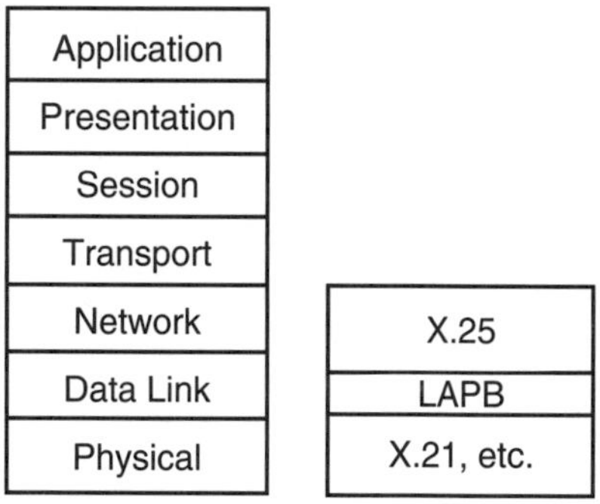

Figure 29.5
The relationship of X.25 to the OSI Reference Model.

CCITT/ITU X.25

X.25 is a packet-switching network standard developed by the *International Telegraph and Telephone Consultative Committee* (CCITT), which has been renamed the *International Telecommunications Union* (ITU). The standard, referred to as Recommendation X.25, was introduced in 1974, and is most commonly implemented in WANs.

As shown in figure 29.5, X.25 is one level of a three-level stack that spans the network, data link, and physical layers.

Physical layer connectivity is provided by a variety of standards including X.21, X.21bis, and V.32.

X.21 Topics and Methods

Layer	*Topics*	*Methods*
Physical	Connection type	Point-to-point
	Physical topology	Hybrid mesh
	Bit synchronization	Synchronous

Link Access Procedures-Balanced (LAPB) is a bit-oriented, full-duplex, synchronous data link layer LLC protocol.

LAPB Topics and Methods

Layer	*Topics*	*Methods*
Data link control (LLC sublayer)	Connection services	LLC flow
		Error control

X.25 packet-switching networks provide the options of permanent or switched virtual circuits. Although a datagram (unreliable) protocol was supported until 1984, X.25 is now required to provide reliable service and end-to-end flow control. Because each device on a network can operate more than one virtual circuit, X.25 must provide error and flow control for each virtual circuit.

X.25 networks are typically implemented with line speeds up to 64 Kbps. These speeds are suitable for the file transfer and terminal activity that comprised the bulk of network traffic when X.25 was defined. Such speeds, however, are inadequate to provide LAN-speed services, which generally require speeds of 1 Mbps or better. X.25 networks are, therefore, poor choices for providing LAN application services in a WAN environment.

Recommendation X.25 Topics and Methods

Layer	*Topics*	*Methods*
Network	Addressing	Channel (logical address maintained for each connection)
	Switching	Packet (virtual circuit)
	Connection services	Network layer flow control
		Error control

Frame Relay

Frame relay was designed to support the *Broadband Integrated Services Digital Network* (B-ISDN), which is discussed in the following section, "ISDN and B-ISDN." The specifications for frame relay address some of the limitations of X.25. Like X.25, frame relay is a packet-switching network service. Frame relay is standardized by ANSI and ITU (CCITT).

Unlike X.25, frame relay assumes a more reliable network. This enables frame relay to eliminate much of the X.25 overhead required to provide reliable service on less reliable networks. Frame relay relies on higher-level protocol layers to provide flow and error control.

Frame relay typically is implemented as a public data network and is, therefore, regarded as a WAN protocol. The relationship of frame relay to the OSI model is shown in figure 29.6. Notice that the scope of frame relay is limited to the physical and data link layers.

Frame relay provides switched and permanent virtual circuits. Frame relay services are typically implemented at line speeds of 56 Kbps up to 1.544 Mbps (T1).

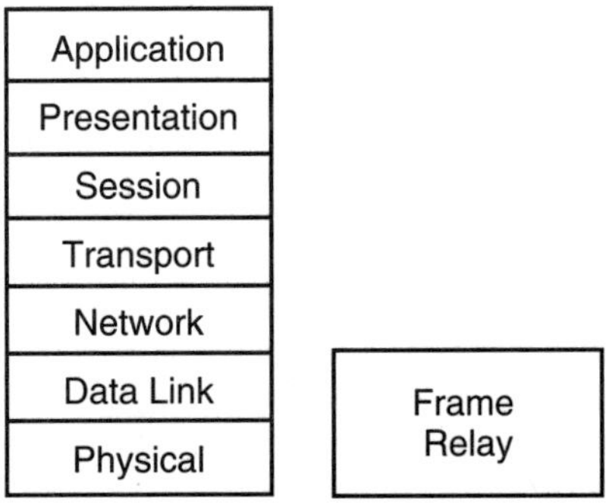

Figure 29.6
The relationship of Frame Relay to the OSI Reference Model.

Customers typically purchase access to a specific amount of bandwidth on a frame relay service. This bandwidth is called the *committed information rate* (CIR), a data rate for which the customer is guaranteed access. Customers may be permitted to access higher data rates on a pay-per-use, temporary basis. This arrangement enables customers to tailor their network access costs based on their bandwidth requirements.

Frame Relay Topics and Methods

Layer	*Topics*	*Methods*
Physical	Connection type	Point-to-point
	Physical topology	Hybrid mesh
	Switching	Packet (virtual circuit)
Data link	Connection services	LLC-level flow control (LLC sublayer)
		Error control (detection but not recovery)

ISDN and B-ISDN

Integrated Services Digital Network (ISDN) is a group of ITU (CCITT) standards designed to provide voice, video, and data transmission services on digital telephone networks. ISDN uses multiplexing to support multiple channels on high-bandwidth circuits. The relationship of the ISDN protocols to the OSI Reference Model is shown in figure 29.7.

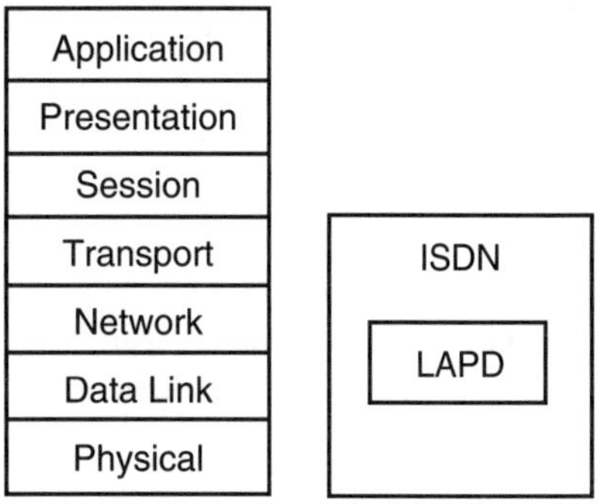

Figure 29.7
The relationship of ISDN protocols to the OSI Reference Model.

A variety of ISDN channel types are defined. These channel types, often called *bit pipes*, provide different types and levels of service. The various channels are described in the following list:

- A channel provides 4 kHz analog telephone service.
- D channels support 64 Kbps digital data.
- C channels support 8 or 16 Kbps digital data, generally for out-of-band signaling.
- D channels support 16 or 64 Kbps digital data, also for out-of-band signaling. D channels support the following subchannels:
    - p subchannels support low-bandwidth packet data.
    - s subchannels are used for signaling (such as call setup).
    - t subchannels support telemetry data (such as utility meters).
- E channels provide 64 Kbps service used for internal ISDN signaling.
- H channels provide 384, 1,536, or 1,920 digital service.

The following three standard channel combinations have been defined:

- *Basic rate* includes two B channels and one D channel.
- *Primary rate* includes one D channel, 23 B channels (in the U.S. and Japan), or 30 B channels (in Europe and Australia).
- *Hybrid* provides one A channel and one C channel.

ISDN functions as a data transmission service only. Acknowledged, connectionless, full-duplex service is provided at the data link layer by the LAPD protocol, which operates on the D channel.

ISDN Topics and Methods

Layer	*Topics*	*Methods*
Physical	Multiplexing	Time-division multiplexing
Network	Switching	Packet
		Circuit

LAPD Topics and Methods

Layer	*Topics*	*Methods*
Data link (MAC sublayer)	Addressing	Physical device
Data link (LLC sublayer)	Connection services	LLC flow control Frame sequencing

Broadband ISDN is a refinement of ISDN that is defined to support higher bandwidth applications such as video, imaging, and multimedia. Physical layer support for B-ISDN is provided by *Asynchronous Transfer Mode* (ATM) and the *Synchronous Optical Network* (SONET). SONET is discussed further in the following section. Typical B-ISDN data rates are 51 Mbps, 155 Mbps, and 622 Mbps over fiber-optic media.

Synchronous Optical Network and the Synchronous Digital Hierarchy

Bell Communications Research developed SONET, which has been accepted as an ANSI standard. SONET is regarded as a WAN standard.

A similar set of standards, published by the ITU (CCITT), is called the *Synchronous Digital Hierarchy* (SDH). Regional variations of SDH, including SDH-Europe, SDH-SONET (North America), and SDH-Japan, have been defined to accommodate local differences. Figure 29.8 illustrates the relationship of the SONET/SDH standards to the OSI Reference Model.

Data rates for SONET are organized in a hierarchy based on the *Optical Carrier* (OC) speed and the corresponding *Synchronous Transport Signals* (STS) employed. The basic OC and STS data rate is 51.84 Mbps. Higher data rates are provided in multiples of the basic rate. Thus OC-48 is 48×51.84 Mbps = 2488.32 Mbps.

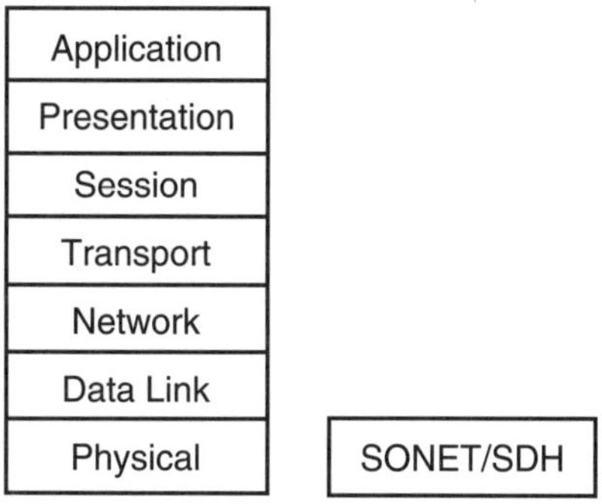

Figure 29.8
The relationship of SONET/SD to the OSI Reference Model.

SDH data rates begin at 155.52 Mbps and are calculated in multiples of that rate. Thus an SDH-16 has a data rate of 2488.32 Mbps, equivalent to the SONET STS-48 data rate.

SONET/SDH Topics and Methods

Layer	*Topics*	*Methods*
Physical	Connection type	Point-to-point
	Physical topology	Mesh
		Ring
	Multiplexing	Time-division

Asynchronous Transfer Mode (ATM)

ATM is a high-bandwidth switching technology developed by the ITU *Telecommunications Standards Sector* (ITU-TSS). An organization called the *ATM Forum* is responsible for defining ATM implementation characteristics. ATM can be layered on other physical layer technologies such as FDDI and SONET. The relationships of these protocols to the OSI model are shown in figure 29.9.

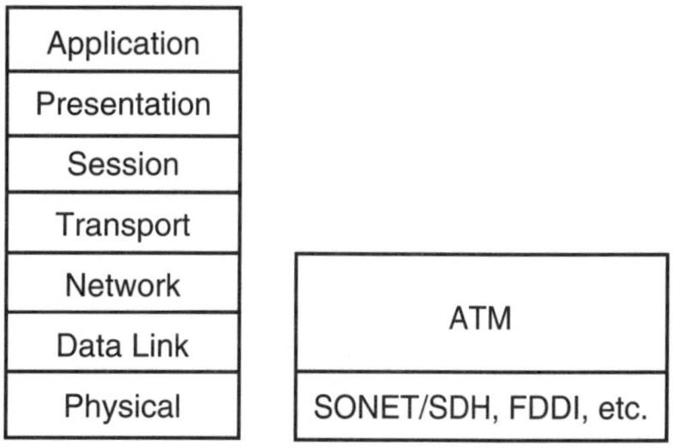

Figure 29.9
The relationship of ATM to the OSI Reference Model.

ATM has several characteristics that distinguish it from other switching technologies discussed in this course. ATM is based on fixed-length, 53-byte cells, whereas other technologies employ frames that vary in length to accommodate different amounts of data. Because ATM cells are uniform in length, switching mechanisms can operate with a high level of efficiency.

The unit of transmission for ATM is called a *cell.* All cells are 53 bytes in length and consist of a 5-byte header and 48 bytes of data. The 48-byte data size was arrived at by the standards committee as a compromise between the needs of audio and data transmission. Audio information must be delivered with little latency (delay) to maintain a smooth flow of sound. Audio engineers preferred a small cell so that cells would be more readily available when needed. For data, however, large cells reduce the overhead required to deliver a byte of information.

Asynchronous delivery is another distinguishing feature of ATM. *Asynchronous* refers to the characteristic of ATM whereby transmission time slots do not occur periodically, but are granted at irregular intervals. ATM uses a technique called *label multiplexing,* which allocates time slots on demand. Traffic that is time critical, such as voice or video, can be given priority over data traffic that can be delayed slightly with no ill effect. Channels are identified by cell labels, not by specific time slots. A high-priority transmission need not be held until its next time slot allocation. It might only be required to wait until the current 53-byte cell has been transmitted.

Other multichannel technologies utilize time-division techniques to allocate bandwidth to channels. A T1 (1.544 Mbps) line, for example, might be time-division multiplexed to provide 24 voice channels. With this technique, each channel is assigned a specific time slot in the transmission schedule. The disadvantage of this technique is that an idle channel does not yield its bandwidth for the creation of other channels.

Devices communicate on ATM networks by establishing a virtual path, which is identified by a *virtual path identifier* (VPI). Within this virtual path, virtual circuits can be established, which are in turn associated with *virtual circuit identifiers* (VCIs). The VPI and VCI together make up a three-byte field that is included in the cell header. Other networks, such as a routed Ethernet, require a six-byte physical address as well as a network address to uniquely identify each device on an internetwork. ATM can switch cells with three-byte identifiers because VPIs and VCIs apply only to a given device-to-device link. Each ATM switch can assign different VPIs and VCIs for each link. Up to 16 million circuits can be configured for any given device-to-device link.

The following three characteristics define the classes of ATM service:

- **Time relation between source and destination.** Some data types require a precise time relationship between transmission and reception of cells.
- **Bit rate.** Constant and variable bit rates are available. Many audio and video signaling techniques require constant bit rates. Newer techniques based on data compression might have the capability to function on variable-rate services.
- **Connection mode.** Connection-oriented and connectionless services are available.

Using these characteristics, the following service classes have been defined:

- **Class A.** Timing required, constant bit rate, connection-oriented.
- **Class B.** Timing required, variable bit rate, connection-oriented. Data for this class must be delivered with a constant delay.
- **Class C.** No timing, variable bit rate, connection-oriented.
- **Class D.** No timing, variable bit rate, connectionless.
- **Class X.** Unrestricted, variable bit rate, connection-oriented or connectionless.

Although ATM was developed primarily as a WAN technology, it has many characteristics of value for high-performance LANs. An interesting advantage is that ATM makes it possible to use the same technology for both LANs and WANs.

ATM Topics and Methods

Layer	*Topics*	*Methods*
Data link	Transmission synchronization	Isochronous
	Connection services	Error control
Network	Switching	Cell switching
	Route selection	Static

Switched Multimegabit Digital Service (SMDS)

Switched Multimegabit Digital Service (SMDS) is a technology developed by Bell Communications Research in 1991. SMDS is related to ATM in that it transports data in 53-byte cells. SMDS supports cell switching at data rates of 1.544–45 Mbps.

SMDS is a connectionless data link layer service. IEEE 802.6 (DQDB metropolitan area network) is the primary physical layer standard employed with SMDS, although other physical layer standards are supported as well. Figure 29.10 illustrates the relationships of these protocols in the context of the OSI model.

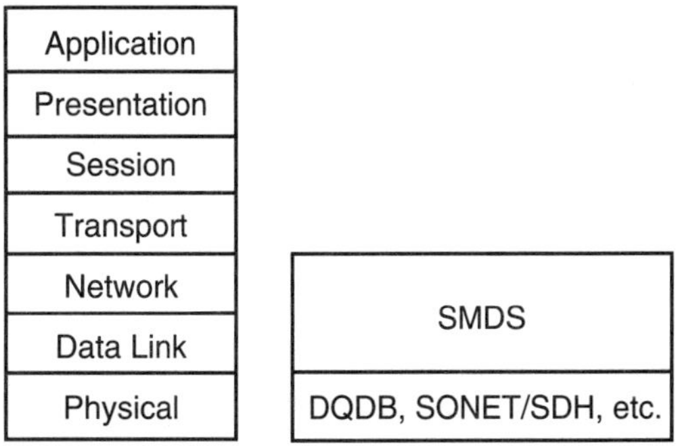

Figure 29.10
The relationship of SMDS to the OSI Reference Model.

SMDS Topics and Methods

Layer	*Topics*	*Methods*
Data link (LLC sublayer)	Transmission synchronization	Isochronous
Network	Switching	Cell switching

Questions

1. Which *two* of the following are regarded as WAN protocols?
   - ☐ A. Frame relay
   - ☐ B. SLIP
   - ☐ C. IEEE 802.6
   - ☐ D. X.25
2. Which protocols are commonly used with IEEE 802.2?
   - ○ A. IEEE 802.3
   - ○ B. IEEE 802.5
   - ○ C. IEEE 802.6
   - ○ D. All of the above
3. What is the primary characteristic that distinguishes a cell from a packet?
   - ○ A. Cells are generally smaller than packets.
   - ○ B. Cells do not incorporate physical addresses.
   - ○ C. All cells have the same fixed length.
   - ○ D. Packets cannot be switched.
4. What are the primary differences between Ethernet version 2 and IEEE 802.3 Ethernet?
   - ○ A. They require different network hardware.
   - ○ B. IEEE 802.3 Ethernet functions at a higher data rate.
   - ○ C. They use different frame formats.
   - ○ D. Ethernet version 2 does not use CSMA/CD media access control.
5. Which *two* of these protocols are intended primarily for use on fiber-optic cable?
   - ☐ A. Frame relay
   - ☐ B. FDDI
   - ☐ C. SONET
   - ☐ D. X.25
6. Which *two* of these standards use token passing for media access control?
   - ☐ A. IEEE 802.4
   - ☐ B. IEEE 802.6
   - ☐ C. Frame relay
   - ☐ D. FDDI
7. Which *two* of these standards are designed to support audio data?
   - ☐ A. IEEE 802.10
   - ☐ B. ISDN
   - ☐ C. ATM
   - ☐ D. Frame relay
8. Which *two* of these network standards are well suited to delivering time-critical data?
   - ☐ A. X.25
   - ☐ B. IEEE 802.5
   - ☐ C. Frame Relay
   - ☐ D. ATM

Answers

1. A, D
2. D
3. C
4. C
5. B, C
6. A, D
7. B, C
8. B, D

CHAPTER 30

Tasks of Network Administrators

The job of network managers involves a wide variety of responsibilities, the basic concepts for some of which this chapter discusses, including the following topics:

- *Configuration management*
- *Fault management*
- *Performance management*
- *Security management*
- *Accounting management*

This book assumes you have had some experience as a network administrator, so discussion is brief and to-the-point, and no review questions follow.

Configuration Management

Configuration management is a process of tracking the components of a network and the configurations of those components. A detailed history of changes to the network is a tremendous aid for troubleshooting. When a problem occurs, the first thing you want to know is, "What's changed?" A configuration management database can tell you.

Following are just a few of the things your configuration management procedures should track:

- All hardware that has vital data, such as firmware (ROM) revisions, when installed (for example, a design change without a new model number), and configuration details, such as interrupts, addresses, and so forth
- Workstation configuration files, such as CONFIG.SYS and AUTOEXEC.BAT, to which many problems trace owing to users making changes
- Network software, such as NetWare shell and Requester versions
- Software licenses, to ensure that your network operates within the bounds of the license terms
- Problems encountered and related solutions; history tends to repeat itself, so the solutions to many problems might already be known and recorded

You can manage proper configuration most easily if you use software designed for that purpose. Novell offers the *NetWare Management System* (NMS). Commercial NetWare configuration management products include Bindview and Cheyenne Monitrix.

Fault Management

Fault management involves using tools and procedures that anticipate network problems and help correct them when they occur.

When failures do occur, having the proper tools can improve the rapidity with which you can isolate and diagnose the fault. Many of these tools have evolved to the point that they report events that are not apparent as problems but that betray a degradation in the network. If a network card generates increasing numbers of damaged packets that must be retransmitted, the right tools report the condition before the NIC fails or generates so many errors that it degrades overall network performance.

Fault management includes some of the following practices:

- **Data archiving and backup.** Properly speaking, archiving and backup are not part of fault management procedure, other than that a good set of backup tapes, properly stored, ensures against catastrophic data loss. Novell's standard for data archiving and backup is the *Storage Management Services* (SMS).
- **Fault-tolerant design.** You can configure many network components in a fault-tolerant configuration such that one hardware failure cannot halt the network. NetWare provides the following three levels of server fault tolerance:
  - **SFT I (hot fix).** Enables servers to recover from minor failure in hard drive media
  - **SFT II (disk mirroring and duplexing).** Enables hard drives to operate in parallel so that a single hard drive failure does not cause data loss or service interruption

- **SFT III (server duplexing).** Enables pairs of servers to operate in parallel so that even complete failure of a single server does not cause data loss or service interruption

You can achieve network fault-tolerance by designing in redundant data paths, fault-tolerant hubs, uninterruptible power supplies, and other such features.

- **Network management systems.** Protocols for network management include the *Simple Network Management Protocol* (SNMP—a protocol in the TCP/IP suite that is *the* dominant network management protocol) and *Common Management Information Protocol* (CMIP). Devices that run these protocols (such as routers, hubs, switches, managed NICs, and so on) can generate network management messages that are directed to a network management console that analyzes incoming management information and generates network performance statistics and alerts. The console also can possess the capability to remotely manage network devices. On managed network hubs, for example, the console might automatically shut down a hub port that generates high numbers of errors. Novell's NetWare Management System is an SNMP management console for which you can use "snap-in" accessory products to extend its capabilities.

- **Protocol analyzers receive all packets on the network and decode them for analysis.** Many network problems betray themselves in the form of abnormal packets. Network managers can capture packets from the network data stream and examine them for abnormalities. The latest versions of protocol analyzers perform much of the analysis automatically and assist with the rest. Some even incorporate expert systems that can intelligently diagnose network problems. Novell offers a software-based protocol analyzer, called LANalyzer for Windows.

- **Cable testers are available at many levels of sophistication.** The best cable testers isolate faults to a specific area of a cable and even inform you when a cable is operating, but not performing up to specification.

Performance Management

Performance management is the proactive companion to fault management. Monitoring the performance of a network provides "baseline" data that is a snapshot of the network performing well under normal conditions, which proves valuable for identifying deteriorating network performance and as a standard of comparison when network failures occur.

You might monitor the following parameters:

- **Response time.**
- **Throughput.**
- **Network load.** A measure of network traffic as a percentage of total performance capacity.
- **Errors.** All networks display some errors, but rising error levels are a clear indication of an impending problem.

Performance management enables you to plan future network enhancements, in addition to helping you anticipate problems. As network demand rises, you can add capacity before users become aware of problems.

Security Management

Anyone who has managed NetWare has dealt with *security management.* One of your tasks is to anticipate security threats and install safeguards. You might consider selecting some of the following security provisions:

- Establishing user and group security
- Restricting internal and external access to data
- Conducting security risk assessments
- Establishing security policies
- Protecting the network from viruses
- Auditing the network to detect security breaches

NetWare 4 provides for auditing the network, by supporting the establishment of network auditors who can function independently of network administrators. NetWare 4 network auditors can monitor all network operations to detect security breaches, including those that supervisors perform.

Accounting Management

Accounting management involves assessing the costs of using network resources. Some organizations use this information to charge departments for network use. These charges can be used to provide incentives for using LAN resources intelligently. User demand for additional LAN storage capacity and performance tends to rise rapidly if not controlled.

Other organizations simply use accounting information to control costs and plan improvements. When network enhancements are anticipated, accounting data can aid in assessing the cost/performance ratio of various options.

PART PART PART PART PART PART PART PART

IV

Service and Support

CHAPTER 31

Troubleshooting the Network

It is wonderful when everything works as it should, but there is a finite life to everything. This means that no matter how well your network might be operating today, it is only a matter of time before there is a failure in cards, cabling, or any other component from which the network is built.

This chapter explores the following two components of network management:

- *Preventing problems*
- *Troubleshooting*

Regardless of how well you do the first, an occasion will come when you will have to do the second. This chapter places primary emphasis on details that can easily become test fodder. Your purpose for reading this chapter is that you want to be able to answer questions on the Novell tests. Aside from that, the material is presented in as practical a manner as possible, and lends itself well to use in the real world.

Problem Prevention

Preventing problems after a network is up and running is one of the primary jobs of an administrator. Because there are so many different types of problems that can occur, one cannot plan for all eventualities. The possibilities, however, can be divided into the following four categories:

- Physical
- Electrical
- Security
- Viruses

The following sections examine each of these.

Physical Problems

Temperature is one of the most critical environmental components affecting a computer's operation—whether a server or a workstation. Ambient temperature figures in, but more importantly is the temperature inside the computer. There can be as much as a 40 degree difference between the inside and outside of a computer due to the heat generated by the components. One reason for leaving computers turned on all the time is to prevent the internal temperature from fluctuating too greatly.

> Note
>
> When new equipment arrives, you should allow it to adjust to room temperature before using it. This assures that there will not be undue thermal strain on the components, should they have been bouncing around in a frozen FedEx truck for three days.

It is critical that a server have adequate ventilation to keep from overheating, otherwise "chip creep" can occur wherein integrated circuits lose their seating and contact with the socket. It is equally important that ambient air, which is sucked into the machine, be filtered and be of as high a quality as possible. A consistent temperature in the room should be maintained, and particles such as smoke and dust should be filtered out as much as possible with appropriate filtration devices.

Electrical Problems

Whereas physical problems can deteriorate a server or other computer slowly, electrical problems tend to do it immediately. They can destroy components, trash data, and make you wonder why you didn't keep the job at ChemLawn.

The four types of electrical problems are as follows:

- **Crosstalk.** Crosstalk is when two wires interfere with the magnetic fields of each other. The best solution is to use proper cable shielding and to avoid physical proximity between cables.
- **Static.** It is not the build up that wreaks damage, it is the sudden discharge. What makes it dangerous is that it can build to phenomenal levels before discharging all at once. Also known as *Electro-Static Discharge* (ESD), it must be beyond 3,000 volts for you to even feel it, but charges of 20 and 30 volts

can damage equipment. The best solution to avoiding ESD is to use static discharge equipment and ground cords.

You should always ground yourself and any equipment on which you will be working. Never directly touch any electrical leads and always use antistatic bags to store components. You also can control static by keeping ambient humidity low.

Note Styrofoam is a common carrier of static buildup. It is highly recommended that Styrofoam cups not be left near servers or workstations.

- **Transients.** Transients are sudden, high voltage bursts of current. Also known as spikes, transients usually occur randomly and last for less than one second. The randomness makes them hard to isolate, and they can often be associated with trouble farther down a power line, such as a blackout or lightning strike. Suppressor diodes are the best line of defense, as well as putting computers on their own circuit with isolated grounds.
- **Line noise.** Low in voltage and low in current, noise usually occurs in an observable pattern. Most of the time, the culprit is another electrical device such as a microwave oven, a motor, or even the ballast of a fluorescent lamp. The best solution is to properly ground equipment and avoid running cable near other sources of interference.

When discussing noise, there are two acronyms commonly used. *Radio Frequency Interference* (RFI) is caused by microwaves, ovens, and appliances. *Electromagnetic Interference* (EMI) is caused by lights, radar, and industrial tools.

Security

Network security, and the implementation thereof, is the responsibility of the system administrator. *Electronic Data Processing* (EDP) Environmental Security entails thoroughly thinking through all the risks in your installation and creating a plan for dealing with them.

The following are four types of threats:

1. Destruction
2. Corruption
3. Disclosure
4. Interruption

To deal with the possibility of these threats, the administrator should think about each network segment and evaluate what potential risks there are. Next, he should evaluate and implement steps to minimize those risks effectively.

Some examples of security that can be implemented include the following:

- Restricting login times to business hours
- Requiring regular password changes
- Requiring unique passwords
- Turning off modems after working hours
- Building RAID and redundancy into the server

Encryption also can be used to keep an intruder from understanding data that he intercepts. Beginning with NetWare 3.11, encryption is now standard, providing the SET command has ALLOW UNENCRYPTED PASSWORDS set to OFF.

Viruses

In simple terms, *viruses* are programs that interfere with the normal flow of processing. Viruses interfere by changing files and configurations, or by attaching themselves to everything they come in contact with and growing exponentially.

Viruses, by nature, require some action to activate them, and so they attach themselves to executable files. Those files are usually denoted by their extension, which can be BAT, EXE, or COM. Overlays, OVL files, provide other opportunities, however, as do FAT tables and boot sectors.

Very rarely have there been occurrences of viruses shipping with retail software. Most of the time, viruses enter the workplace through pirated software, downloaded shareware, or other suspect software. In a perfect world, the best solution is to prevent anyone other than the system administrator from installing software on the network. In this sense, "network" refers to all things physically attached—not only the server, but all workstations, too.

Given that there is no perfect world, and that you often cannot prevent installation of software on an individual's workstation, you must contend with the possibility of a virus attack. To do so, you should perform the following:

- Regularly back up the server and workstations
- Routinely scan for viruses with third-party software
- Flag EXE and COM files as Read-Only and Execute-Only
- In the PUBLIC and LOGIN directories, grant only Read and File Scan rights
- Check every disk for viruses before you install
- Discourage the downloading of BBS software
- Be prepared for action

Bear in mind that NetWare includes some safeguards against virus attacks. For one thing, the NetWare FAT table is different from that of workstations and cannot be attacked. Therefore, NetWare viruses are not as common as DOS viruses, and most virus attacks occur on workstations, as opposed to the server.

Troubleshooting

After a problem has occurred, prevention is a meaningless word and troubleshooting comes into play. The overall goal of troubleshooting is to restore service in a timely manner. The following are the four steps to the basic troubleshooting model:

1. Gather information.
2. Develop an attack plan.
3. Isolate the problem and execute the plan.
4. Document what was done.

By following these four steps, you can successfully restore a network to its fully operational state in the most efficient time possible. The importance of the fourth step cannot be overstated; it is easy to see where an experienced administrator has an advantage over an inexperienced one.

Note There are several questions you should ask when someone first reports a problem (and before you ever arrive on site). As rudimentary as these questions might seem, taking the time to ask them will save you an enormous amount of time in the long run.

- **Has it ever worked?** Quite often, when a user calls to complain about something that doesn't work, it might be because she just in-stalled it or has made some other major change that she does not want to mention without prodding.
- **When did it work last?** If the accounting clerk is calling to complain about a printer that is not printing checks, it can be worth knowing that the printer in question has been offline for the last year and a half.
- **What has changed since then?** You should consider, for example, whether you have moved from one building to another, or rearranged your offices? Did you pull your own cable through the ceiling?

The four step troubleshooting model discussed earlier suggests the following steps to solving workstation problems:

1. Rule out any possibility of user error.
2. Check the physical site to verify that all is as it should be. Make certain that an electrical cord or printer cable did not come unplugged.
3. Power everything down and then back up.
4. Back up data if there is a question of storage media (a hard drive or drives).
5. Eliminate as much overhead as you can. If the problem is with a workstation, reduce the CONFIG.SYS and AUTOEXEC.BAT files to the bare minimum and try the process again. Be certain that all *terminate-and-stay-resident* (TSR) programs that do not need to boot to get on the network are commented out of the AUTOEXEC.BAT file.

Whether solving problems on a workstation or server, you should always think in terms of dollars. During the hypothesis stage, consider what all the possibilities are and try those that cost the least first. Keep in mind that dollars are associated not only with any components that might need replacement, but also with downtime and the time of the administrator.

Documents and Records

As mentioned earlier, the importance of documentation cannot be overstated. The importance of *good* documentation can never be surpassed by any other tool. Even on the smallest of networks, time and money can be saved by documenting problems and keeping good records.

You should maintain three types of records—those relating to the LAN system, the history surrounding it, and the resources available.

For the LAN system, there should be a detailed map identifying the location of users, and all tangible components: printers, routers, bridges, and so forth. You also should keep an inventory of the components and documentation on cabling and the workstations.

The history of the LAN should include user profiles, what the purpose of the LAN is, a log of past problems, and usage information. Not only can this come in handy when an administrator is trying to diagnose a problem, but also when said administrator meets a bus somewhere other than the bus stop. Should a change in administrators take place, there is no better way to keep a business on its feet than to have its network thoroughly documented.

The documentation regarding available resources should include information about the protocols and routing in use, as well as the LAN architecture. The most important resource of all, however, is people. You should have a chart of people and phone numbers readily available for when problems become too difficult for the administrator. VAR numbers, manager numbers, and any other emergency personnel numbers should be kept in an easy to find location.

Diagnostic Software

Third-party, diagnostic software is used to provide information about hardware. That hardware can be virtually anything from the server to a workstation to a cable. A considerable number of packages are available at a variety of prices. The most important consideration should be that they offer information that is useful to you.

Check It PRO is one program that can give quick facts about your hardware and operating system. It can also benchmark the components and show information about the interrupts.

There are a variety of programs with similar features. The following shows an example of output generated at a workstation with System Information—one of the tools available in Norton Utilities:

```
        Computer Name: IBM AT
     Operating System: DOS 6.20
  Built-in BIOS dated: Friday, January 15, 1988
       Main Processor: Intel 80386              Serial Ports: 2
         Co-Processor: Intel 80387            Parallel Ports: 3
 Video Display Adapter: Video Graphics Array (VGA)
    Current Video Mode: Text, 80 x 25 Color
 Available Disk Drives: 13, A: - C:, F: - I:, P:, S:, V:, X: - Z:

DOS reports 639 K-bytes of memory:
   254 K-bytes used by DOS and resident programs
   385 K-bytes available for application programs
A search for active memory finds:
   640 K-bytes main memory     (at hex 0000-A000)
   128 K-bytes display memory  (at hex A000-C000)
   128 K-bytes extra memory    (at hex C000-E000)
 1,024 K-bytes expanded memory
ROM-BIOS Extensions are found at hex paragraphs: C000

  Computing Index (CI), relative to IBM/XT: Testing...                          73.0
       Disk Index (DI), relative to IBM/XT: Not computed. No drive specified.

Performance Index (PI), relative to IBM/XT: Not computed.
```

Much of the same workstation information can be achieved with newer versions of DOS and MSD utility. The following is an excerpt from a report run on the same machine with this utility:

```
   Microsoft Diagnostics version 2.01    1/24/95    7:44pm   Page  1
========================================================================

----------------------- Summary Information ------------------------

              Computer: Gateway/Phoenix, 486DX
                Memory: 640K, 15104K Ext, 1024K EMS, 1024K XMS
                 Video: VGA, ATI , Ultra
               Network: Novell, Shell 4.10.00
            OS Version: MS-DOS Version 6.20, Windows 3.10
                 Mouse: Serial Mouse 7.05
        Other Adapters: Game Adapter
           Disk Drives: A: B: C: F: G: H: I: P:
             LPT Ports: 3
             COM Ports: 2

---------------------------- Computer ----------------------------

         Computer Name: Gateway
     BIOS Manufacturer: Phoenix
          BIOS Version: 680486 ROM BIOS PLUS Version 0.10 G21-2
         BIOS Category: Phoenix PC/AT Compatible BIOS
         BIOS ID Bytes: FC 81 00
             BIOS Date: 01/15/88
             Processor: 486DX
     Math Coprocessor: Internal
              Keyboard: Enhanced
              Bus Type: ISA/AT/Classic Bus
        DMA Controller: Yes
        Cascaded IRQ2: Yes
     BIOS Data Segment: None

---------------------------- Network ---------------------------

                  Network Detected: Yes
                      Network Name: Novell
          MS-DOS Network Functions: Not Supported
                   NetBIOS Present: No
                     Shell Version: 4.10.00
                          Shell OS: MS-DOS
                  Shell OS Version: V6.20
                     Hardware Type: IBM_PC
                    Station Number: 3
           Physical Station Number: 0060:8C84:A8DD
                     IPX Installed: Yes
                     SPX Installed: Yes
                 ODI/LSL Installed: Yes
```

Regardless of which utility you use, you should run reports regularly and store them in a place where they are easily accessible. When problems arise, immediately run the utility again and look for any discrepancies that signal problems.

Questions

1. To reduce problems with static electricity, ______.
   - ○ A. place a humidifier in the computer room
   - ○ B. use proper antistatic protection such as grounded hardware
   - ○ C. keep Styrofoam cups away from computers
   - ○ D. all of the above

2. Which of the following is *not* a type of electrical problem?
   - ○ A. Electro-Static Discharge
   - ○ B. Crosstalk
   - ○ C. Ephemeral
   - ○ D. Transients

3. EMI includes all of the following except ______.
   - ○ A. appliances
   - ○ B. radar
   - ○ C. power tools
   - ○ D. ignition systems

4. Noise is ______.
   - ○ A. low voltage, low current
   - ○ B. low voltage, high current
   - ○ C. high voltage, low current
   - ○ D. high voltage, high current

5. Encrypted passwords ______.
   - ○ A. are the default with NetWare 3.1*x*
   - ○ B. can be turned on starting with NetWare 3.12
   - ○ C. can be implemented with Check It PRO
   - ○ D. couldn't keep my big brother out

Answers

1. D
2. C
3. A
4. A
5. A

CHAPTER 32

Using Research Tools in Troubleshooting

Anyone who has ever dealt with computers and computer networks knows that increasing the number of computers arithmetically increases the number of problems logarithmically. The number of computer components and peripherals on the market today makes it impossible for network administrators to go without updated research tools at their fingertips. These factors have in no small part influenced Novell's decision to include the knowledge of three basic research tools into their certification curriculum and testing procedures.

This section covers in-depth the tools that Novell has suggested NetWare network administrators use to manage a NetWare network. This chapter reviews Novell's *Network Support Encyclopedia* (NSEPro), Novell's online NetWare assistance database (NetWire), and the Micro House Technical Library, an invaluable hardware reference tool. Each of these products are *query specific* (the data that the program returns depends directly on user input), so the examples that show how the programs work use realistic scenarios.

Any network administrator who uses these three products can shorten the time required to get a system into an operational status. Testing of this portion of the Service and Support CNE examination is three hours, during which you have available a CD-ROM that has NSEPro and the Micro House Technical Library. You need to reference material on these disks much as you would in a real-world situation.

Note: All NSEPro available is Windows-based. At the same time, when taking the Service & Support test, the machines use a DOS-based version.

NSEPro

Novell's Network Support Encyclopedia is designed to be your front line against outdated software and driver revisions, as well as an answer source for frequently asked NetWare-related questions. Novell distributes it to subscribers monthly on compact disk (and you should install it as soon as you get it).

NSEPro was basically reserved for NetWare and network-related subjects, until February of 1995, when Novell decided to include WordPerfect and QuattroPro in it. Although the move makes sense from Novell's standpoint—and you should peruse these capabilities for future reference—you should not expect questions on WordPerfect or QuattroPro on the CNE exam.

Installing NSEPro

Installing NSEPro is similar to installing other CD distributed software. If your hard drive is large enough (presently over 170 MB), and you use NSEPro frequently, Novell suggests that you copy all of the data and *Folio* (the database application software) onto your nonremovable media. Should you want to install only NSEPro but not the downloadable files, you only need 100 MB. And if you have next to no available drive space for the NSEPro data, you can select to install only the Windows files necessary to launch NSEPro from your CD. Either of the first two instances not only obviously speeds program access over running applications directly from compact disks, but you then can store your CD in a safe place until a time when your NSEPro data might become corrupted.

If you know how to install software into Windows, you know how to install NSEPro. You can select File, New, Item, Browse, and so on, to install the different modules, or you can use the Windows File Manager application to install the package (the preferred method). To use File Manager to install NSEPro, first open File Manager and select the drive letter that corresponds to your CD-ROM device. Run SETUP.EXE, and you are prompted for which of the three installations you want to use. That's it. One warm or cold system reboot and you can access your NSEPro infobase.

To install NSEPro in a DOS-only environment, simply move over to your CD-ROM device and type **INSTALL <*drive_letter*> [DFILES/NODFILES]**. You want to modify your path environment to include your working NSEPro directory, or move to the NSEPro directory when you want to run the Network Support Encyclopedia.

Using NSEPro

Invoking NSEPro in DOS is as simple as typing **NSEPRO**. If you install NSEPro onto a network, you need a minimum of write rights for the encyclopedia directory. If not, you cannot create a swap file for your graphics and other data. When you initiate NSEPro, you initially are taken to the main menu from which you can select the manual you want.

As with most DOS- and Windows- compatible applications, the MS Windows version is much more user-friendly and less keyboard intensive. After you install NSEPro into your Windows environment, you have an NSEPro program group that consists of your different NSEPro modules. Simply point to the application you want to invoke, double-click the mouse, and navigate the infobase as you please (see fig. 32.1).

Running Queries

Because the NSEPro infobase includes such a vast amount of data, you really do need to familiarize yourself with NSEPro search methods. The most basic form is to search in binary, in which you want to use the "and" and "or" operands. Using generic terminology returns a large number of finds or "hits."

As shown in figure 32.2, if you were to perform a simple search on "ne2000" (a network interface card), the infobase would return 4,996 hits. Nobody really wants to wade through almost five thousand documents, so you might narrow the search by "anding" the ne2000 parameter with the vendor's eagle or smc (which would be 727 and 4,213 hits total in the infobase, respectively), which would drop the number to a slightly (but only marginally) more manageable 3,604. To further

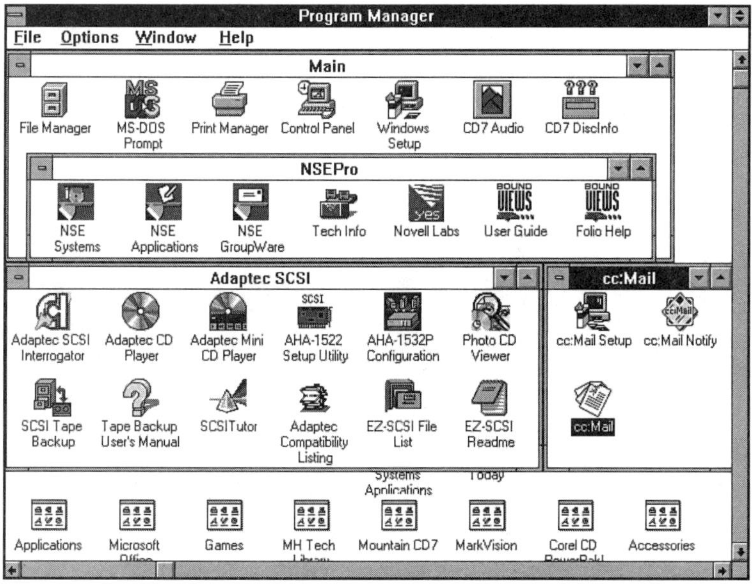

Figure 32.1
The NSEPro Windows program group allows direct access to the different applications.

reduce the number and limit the search, you might "and" the outcome from the previous search concatenation with the term "ethernet," which would bring the outcome to a much more manageable 273. If you were to find 273 acceptable, you would select OK and review the query table of contents.

By focusing the search, the NE2000 NIC example was reduced from almost 5,000 to a much more manageable number. Whether you are in What's New, Service and Support, File Updates, or any of the other NSEPro databases, you have the same basic search and management toolbelt. If you run NSEPro from within MS Windows, you have eight different buttons across your screen. The various buttons enable you to do the following tasks:

- **Query.** Enables you to search the database by selecting combinations of search parameters and keywords
- **Clear Query.** Enables you to clear your previous query criteria so you can easily initiate a new search
- **Next (hit).** When you run a query that returns multiple matches, you can move from one instance to the next by selecting the next button
- **Previous (hit).** Opposite of the next button; you can move back up to the previously matched search criteria instance
- **Backtrack.** Enables you to back through your searches and links so that you can modify your criteria
- **Trail.** Enables you to see the trail you've created with your links and queries and select any part of your trail to move directly to that point
- **Contents.** Enables you to switch from the actual document and the table of contents
- **Print.** Enables you to open your Windows print dialog box and print your search results

You also can run NSEPro from within a DOS environment. The selections in DOS follow the basic MS DOS format; that is, you can select from File, Edit, View, Search, Window, and Help. The display is less graphical than the Windows counterpart, but you basically have a similar representation of the manuals included in the Windows counterpart (see fig. 32.3).

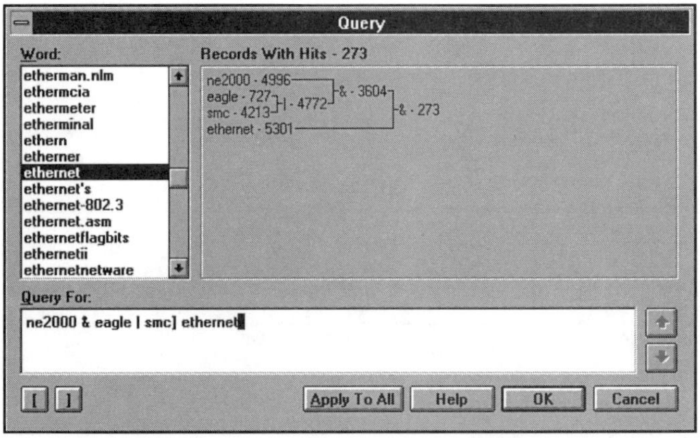

Figure 32.2
The Query dialog box used to search the NSEPro infobase.

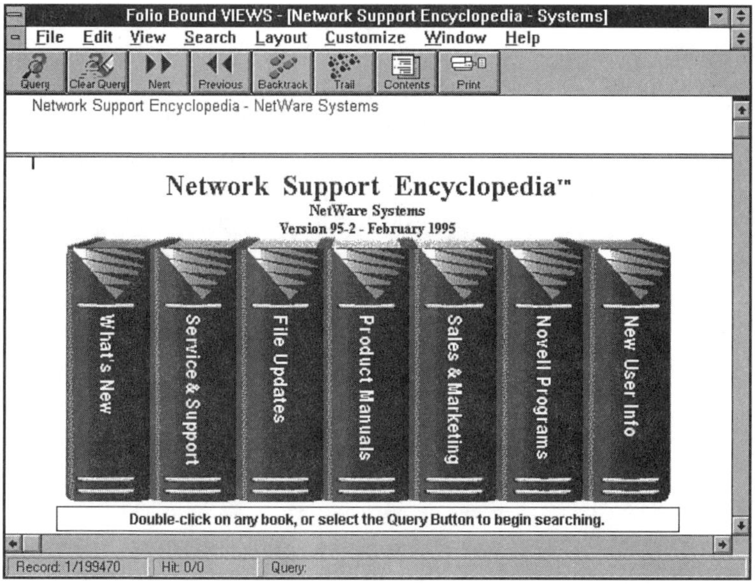

Figure 32.3
Double-click on the spine for the manual you want.

What's New

Anything new or added to NSEPro is covered in this section. Review this section for changes in format for data presentation, as well as any other noteworthy program or driver modifications.

NetWare Support Encyclopedia Modules

As NetWare grows and interfaces with new and different platforms, operating systems, and peripherals, this area will afford you information on various NetWare-related modules.

Service and Support

The Service and Support section is arguably the most used and important section of the CD. It contains the following subsections:

- **Technical Information Documents.** Technical documents and FYI documents written by Novell engineers and technicians
- **Files, Patches, and Fixes.** Names of files available to download from the NetWire BBS, including descriptions of the file names, upload dates, locations, and briefly what the files do
- **Third Party Files.** Items like network interface drivers or "requesters" for various operating systems
- **NetWare Application Notes.** Electronic version of the AppNotes published monthly by Novell, covering new NetWare technologies, implementations, and fine-tuning (for example, NFS and TCP/IP installation and tuning parameters)
- **Novell Professional Developer Bullets.** Another periodical, but more directed toward NetWare-specific application development than addressing the needs of NetWare network administration
- **Novell Lab Bulletins.** Reflect the status of NetWare-compatible third-party products that Novell is testing for compatibility. NetWare

compatibility as confirmed by Novell helps network administrators increase the probability of products purchased for certain applications functioning properly

- **Training-Related Information.** Included in the Service and Support section of NSEPro and includes many typical questions and answers regarding training, classes, and other training-related issues
- **Service Providers Guide.** Geographical representation of third-party support providers and the number of Novell certified personnel on their staffs
- **Top Issues.** Most frequently asked questions and answers, particularly useful for newly released products or product versions
- **Printing Decision Trees.** Enables you to methodically address many NetWare-related problems, beginning from the most logical starting point (as determined by Novell after extensive problem analysis), through a multitude of analytic decisions, drawing conclusions depending on your previous answers; useful for most NetWare problem solving

File Updates

The File Updates section of NSEPro is designed to ensure that critical NetWare and Novell network-related files are up-to-date for a network administrator. Because the number of support are as vast as they are varied, they have been clustered into logical groups for review and download. This issue of NSEPro has fifteen different categories.

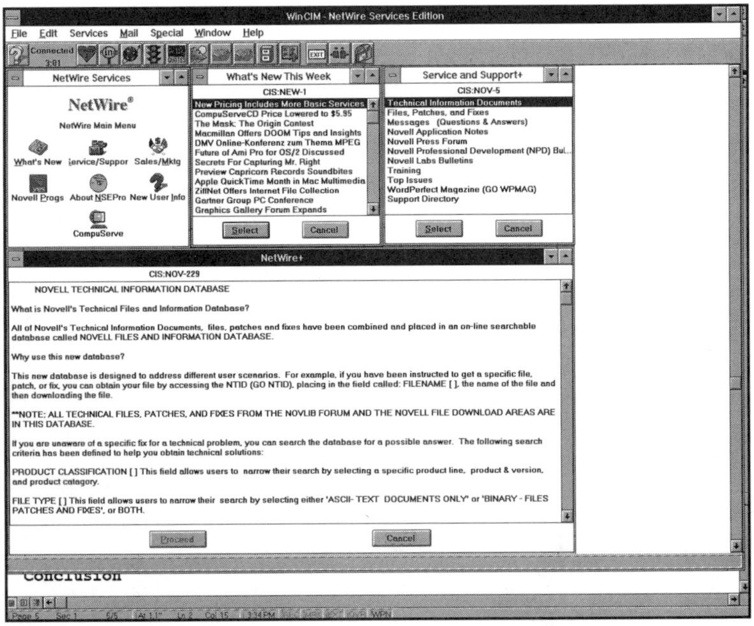

Figure 32.4
By focusing your search criteria, you can travel both up and down your threaded path.

Product Manuals

You can find literally dozens of NetWare and Novell product manuals in electronic form in this area. Granted, NetWare literature has shrunk significantly since version 2.*x*, but having manuals available on one thin media is a vast improvement over even the most concise of documentation.

Sales and Marketing

Network administrators frequently underuse the Sales and Marketing tool. Although the terms "sales" and "marketing" basically go 180 degrees against network administration and engineering, the *NetWare Buyer's Guide* is a tool that you simply cannot overuse. Network administrators have no major use for the sales tools themselves, but the buyer's guide provides an invaluable list that has brief descriptions of all Novell-developed products.

Novell Programs

This section contains information about Novell Education Certification Programs such as CNE, NPA, and NUI.

New User Information

New User Information is a great place to start when you first use NSEPro, because it has hints and tips on maximizing time in NSEPro.

NetWire

If you purchased this book, you are more than likely technically literate and familiar with modems and bulletin board systems (BBSes). NetWire is Novell's bulletin board system developed so people who had NetWare network technical questions had an expedient way to get answers to their questions around the clock. The foundation of the NetWire user interface is the CompuServe Information Manager for Windows and DOS (WINCIM), which provides user-friendly access to NetWire via CompuServe.

When you use WINCIM to access NetWire, a user-friendly graphical interface greets you. If you decide to connect to the NetWire system, WINCIM dials the specified CompuServe account and automatically logs you in to the NetWire forum. The main menu for NetWire closely resembles the modules in NSEPro.

Although many people believe BBSes are frivolous and nothing more than an extension of the corporate coffee pot (where people sit and chat), you can use NetWire to do things like ask questions in a variety of forums to perform database searches. Take a look at figure 32.4.

Micro House Technical Library (MHTL)

If you have ever worked with computer hardware, you know that even when you limit the manufacturers and products you use in your network, that versions, as well as form factors, change frequently. And each change basically forces you to relearn how to configure the product, set the jumpers, set the BIOS settings, and on and on. A demo version of MHTL is included with this book.

Even the likes of Stephen Hawking could not memorize all the settings and parameters for the products on the market. Micro House Technical Library to the rescue. The MHTL ships on a compact disk and contains information on almost every product that you might encounter while working with computer hardware. Included on the CD are such items as the following:

- BIOS settings for IDE drives
- Jumper settings for popular drives, network interface cards, and other peripheral boards
- A diagnostic program that determines the BIOS settings of your computer

The easiest way to learn how to use the Micro House Technical Library tool would be to follow a couple of examples step-by-step. You can go in one of three basic directions after you boot the MHTL program (see figs 32.5 and 32.6). The first route you might follow is the Hard Drive Encyclopedia.

Imagine that you have acquired a computer that has lost its CMOS battery and that you must reenter the BIOS information. You can tell by looking that the hard drive is a Seagate ST251-1. You need only click on the Hard Drive Encyclopedia button from the MHTL main menu, click on the Hard Drives button from the Hard Drive submenu, then enter what information you know about the drive into the appropriate fields (see fig. 32.7). After you enter the appropriate information, click on the Search button and the MHTL program searches its database for a search map. If you have entered the information correctly, the odds are that MHTL has the information and you soon see a list of the hard drive settings as suggested by the drive's manufacturer.

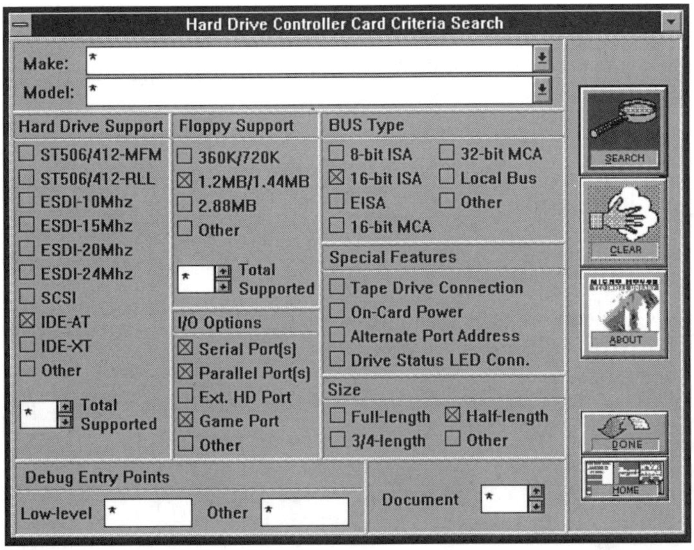

Figure 32.5
The Mircro House Technical Library hard drive search window.

Figure 32.6
The Micro House Technical Library is widely recognized as the resource guide for network hardware configuration.

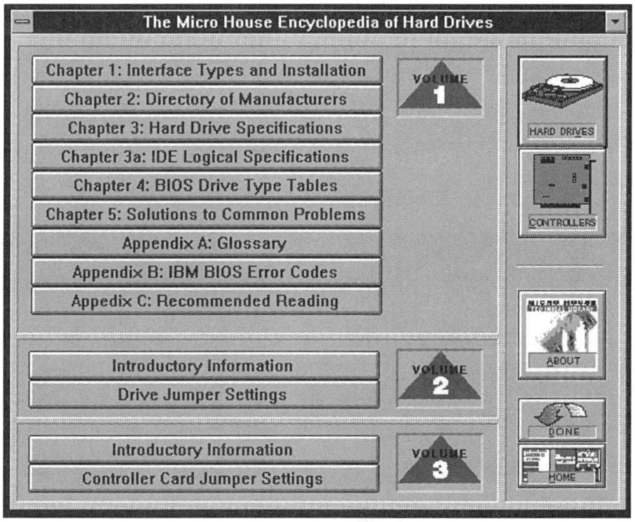

Figure 32.7
The Hard Drive Encyclopedia submenu enables you to access various aspects of hard drive specifications and related data.

Now, assume that your BIOS was actually wiped out due to a surge in your power source, and that your IDE controller was smoked, too. You need to find a controller to replace the one that has passed away and you want MHTL to help.

Buckets and buckets of hard drive controllers are available, so you want to narrow your focus as much as possible. First, open the Hard Drive Encyclopedia module by selecting the Like button from the main menu. Then, select the Controllers button (refer to fig. 32.7) rather than the Hard Drives button as in the last example. The Hard Drive Controller Card Criteria Search menu appears.

Here, you select the specific parameters you want the product to match; suppose you need a 16-bit ISA IDE-AT half-length card. Further, you want the card to have a 1.2 MB/1.44 MB controller, a serial port, a parallel port, and a game port. After you select the appropriate boxes, you would press the Search button.

Search results show that twenty-two products meet the search criteria (see fig. 32.8). Now you review each product to see whether you like or dislike any additional features before you buy. Suppose you're familiar with Acculogic products and have liked them in the past.

To see the configuration settings for the Acculogics IDE-4/PLUS board, you would simply double-click on the respective Acculogic line on your display. MHTL really shines here in most network administrators' eyes. You are then presented with a series of spreadsheets that display all the possible switch settings, jumper configurations, and additional specifications (see fig. 32.9). If you want to see what the board physically looks like, use your cursor to select the See Diagram #1 button.

Pressing the See Diagram #1 button brings up a physical representation of the board and any switch, jumper, accessory chip, and connectors locations (see fig. 32.10). The different locations are cross-referenced with the text mentioned in the last paragraph. With this information on CD, most frustration of many network administrators goes the way of the 8-track cassette tape. And if you do not have a photographic memory, you can print the different pages in a variety of sizes and alignments.

Now let's say that not only was the BIOS lost and the IDE controller toasted, but that your motherboard is dysfunctional, and what the heck, as long as the case is open, you want a new network interface card, too. You already have seen basic searching in the hard drive section of the MHTL application. Now, you would select the Main Boards Encyclopedia and Network Interface Technical Guide buttons respectively rather than the Hard Drive Encyclopedia button from the main menu.

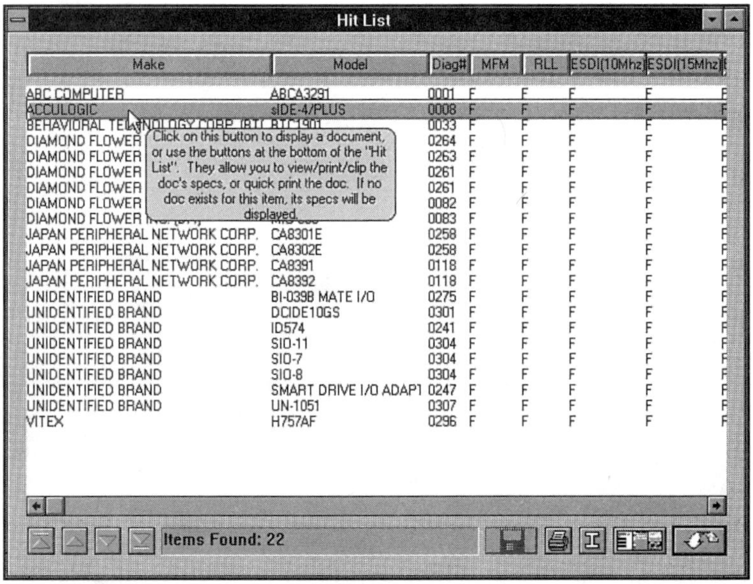

Figure 32.8
Our search for a 16-bit ISA IDE controller with additional criteria has resulted in a list of twenty-two products.

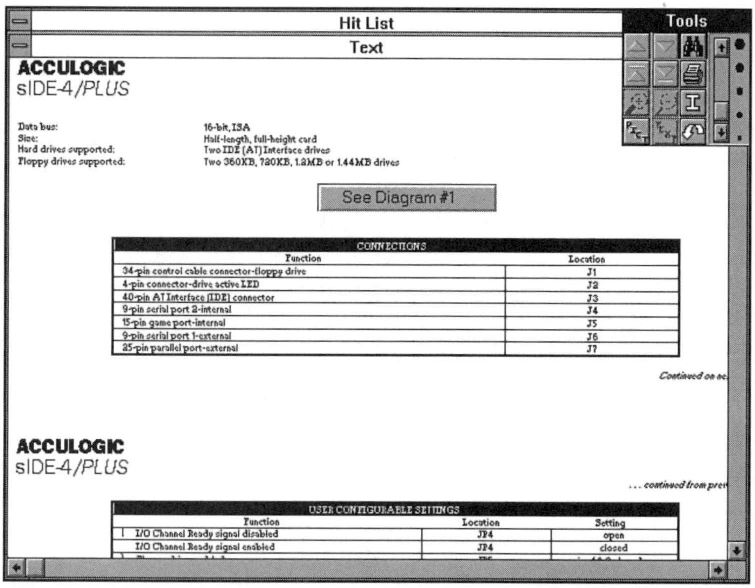

Figure 32.9
The text associated with the various products in the MHTL is as extensive as many expensive hardware encyclopedias.

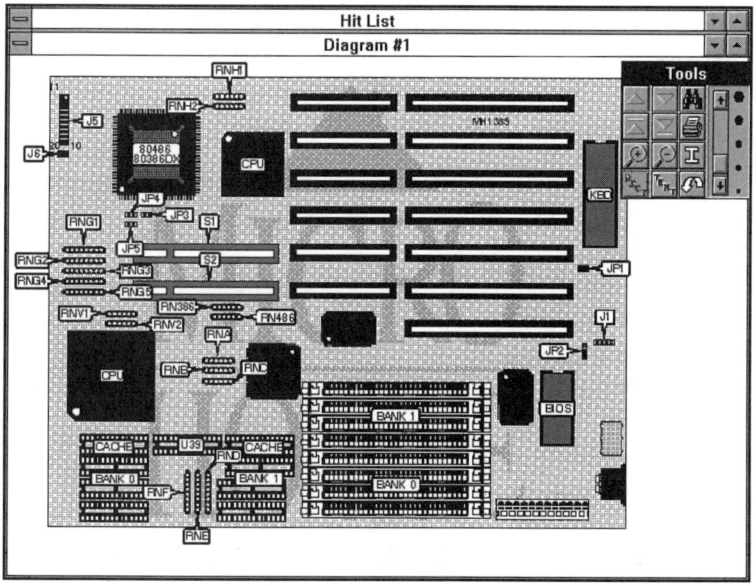

Figure 32.10
Being able to see a representation of the motherboard and match the references to a text chart is invaluable to any network administrator.

The motherboard section of the program enables you to select your criteria much as you did in the hard drive example, but you can select the type of processor, the bus clock speed, the number and type of slots, and other motherboard-related criteria.

You decide you want a 80386/80486/Pentium-compatible board that can handle up to sixty-six MHz. After you narrow your choices, you scrutinize the resulting list and decide you want a TMC Research Corporation PAT34PV board, which can support 32 MB of RAM, a 256 KB cache, and uses AMI BIOS. Good enough, but what is the form factor? As in the drive and controller example, you would double-click on the PAT34PV line, which would bring up the board specifications and chip/connector/jumper location text, and the Diagram button. Click on the Diagram button to bring up a visual layout drawing of the motherboard (refer to fig. 32.10).

In the spirit of avoiding too many redundant details, selecting a network interface card is very much the same. Suffice it to say that having drawings of the different boards, as well as the specifications, is more than just a luxury. Most network environments use few combinations of hardware to ease the support burden. When one comes out, make the new one look the same as the old one, and put the new one in. But what happens when a product you use moves from one vendor to another (which happens frequently)? You know what the board looks like and you usually know a few of the specifications. But do you now know the model number or the manufacturer?

If not, you can enter as much information as you know and then take a look at the board to confirm that you're ordering the right product. For this example, suppose you know that the board is an Ethernet board with 10BASE-T, 10BASE2, and an AUI port. It also has a status LED and is a 10-bit card. You would first enter the proper information into the Network Interface Card Criteria Search menu (see fig. 32.11) and review the listing that results from the MHTL search (see figure 32.12). Fortunately, the second NIC on the list matches the NIC you removed from the computer (except the labels have changed). Figure 32.13 displays the network interface card, which helps an administrator configure the NIC.

After you master searching the MHTL database for one type of product, you should pretty much know how to search for other products. And as for the ways you can use Micro House Technical Library to maximize your computer skill productivity, you can confidently purchase and support virtually any type of desktop computer on the market today.

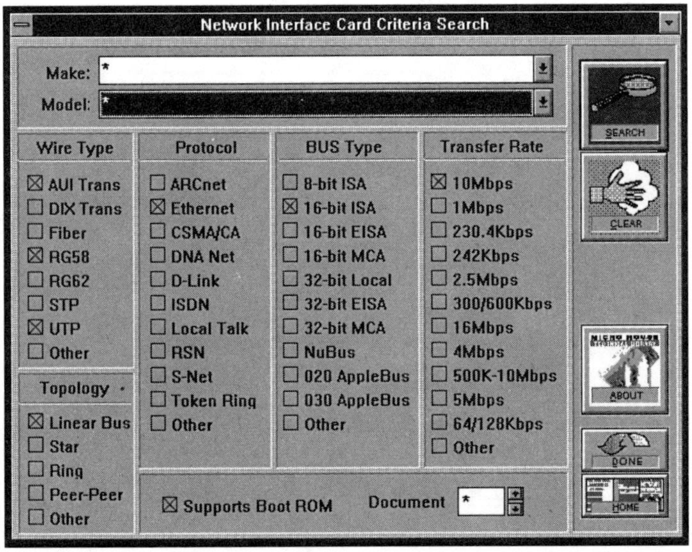

Figure 32.11
The Network Interface Card Criteria Search menu enables you to select many different hardware/topology/protocol combinations for your search.

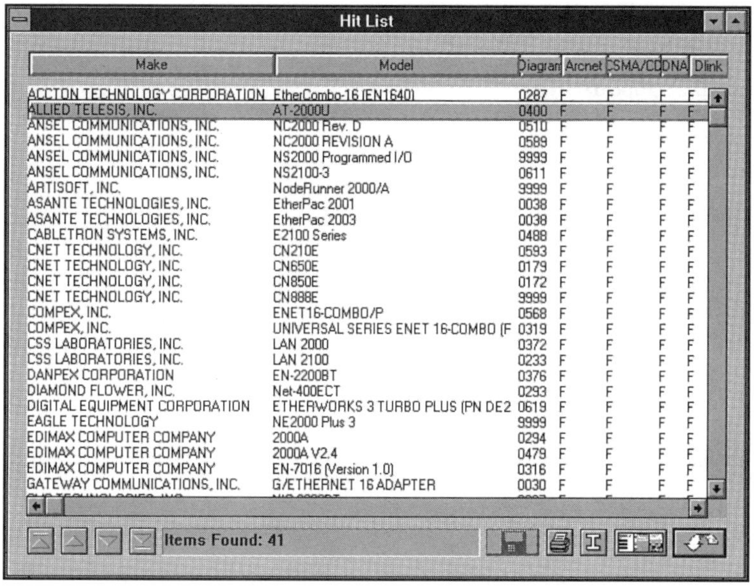

Figure 32.12

The network interface card Hit List affords you enough initial data to drastically narrow your search.

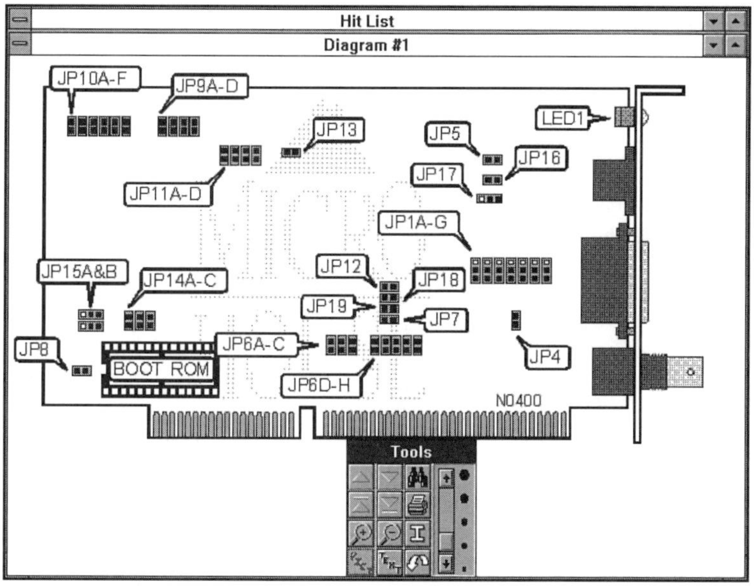

Figure 32.13

The network interface card display helps the network administrator determine how to configure his or her NIC.

Questions

1. Which is not a spine title that appears in NSEPro?

   ○ A. What's New

   ○ B. Sales & Marketing

   ○ C. Patches

   ○ D. Product Manuals

2. The best source of information on network hardware configuration is ______.

   ○ 1. Micro House Technical Library

   ○ 2. NetWire

   ○ 3. NSEPro

   ○ 4. NetWare documentation

3. What is the required hard drive space needed to copy all of NSEPro onto your hard drive?

   ○ 1. 150 MB

   ○ 2. 170 MB

   ○ 3. 190 MB

   ○ 4. 210 MB

Answers

1. C
2. A
3. B

CHAPTER 33

Working with Network Adapter Cards and Cabling

In this chapter, you learn about several of the network interface components used when configuring a NetWare LAN. Proper planning, research, and verification of certified NetWare-compatible components is an integral part of building an efficient network. The items discussed in this chapter include the following:

- *ARCnet board settings, cabling, and troubleshooting*
- *Ethernet board settings, cabling, frame types, and troubleshooting*
- *Token Ring board settings, cabling, and troubleshooting*
- *FDDI cabling, advantages, disadvantages, and troubleshooting*

During the planning phase of a network implementation project, many hardware choices are available. The verification of component compatibility and confirmation of Novell certification of all hardware and software to be integrated is obtained from several sources. Vendor documentation, FAXBACK phone numbers, technical support lines, and peers are good sources for verification. Novell provides a technical support desk that can be reached by dialing 1-800-NETWARE. Access to the technical bulletins in a NetWare Support Encyclopedia can provide some of the information needed.

Without verification that the hardware you want to use has been tested thoroughly using NetWare, you do not know what compatibility problems may occur. If you do not choose hardware that has been verified at the Novell Labs, you will have a much more difficult time troubleshooting problems. You also will not have Novell support to help fix problems. Spending some time at this phase saves you money in the long run. Novell also offers a service called FAXBACK where you can have certain documents sent to your fax. A master document containing all the titles of the documents on FAXBACK helps you choose which item will provide the information you need. In the U.S. or Canada, call 1-800-233-3382 or 1-801-429-5363.

Note Diagnose and correct incompatibilities between the network adapter card and the CPU data bus.

After you have obtained the equipment to build your network, you must configure the hardware to avoid conflicts. Conflicts among different pieces of hardware occur when their settings match or overlap. Unless the hardware has special features to avoid conflicts, you must be aware of the areas where conflicts are most likely to occur. The following list contains the most common conflicts that occur when configuring a PC adapter card:

- Interrupt conflicts
- Base I/O and memory address conflicts
- Page memory range conflicts
- DMA channel conflicts
- Node address conflicts

Keep in mind that conflicts are internal to the individual PC. A common misconception is that all network boards on the same network must share the same settings. This is not true and is impractical to enforce unless all your machines are identical in their components. Look at each client individually for configuration information.

Interrupts are dedicated to certain resources. It is possible to use a dedicated interrupt by disabling an unneeded resource. For example, if you do not need a second COM port, you can disable COM2 by using the PC's configuration program, setting switches or jumpers on the system board, or removing the board that supports COM2. This frees up INT 3 for use with a LAN card.

The following is a list of additional items to research as part of the planning process:

- Cabling specifications and requirements
- Hard drive specifications and requirements
- Software drivers to ensure that they are certified with the version of operating system to be used

Now that you have an idea of what needs to be verified, the next section details information about ARCnet, Ethernet, and Token Ring specifications.

Note: Differentiate among media types and physical media protocols.

Exploring ARCnet Specifications

ARCnet is an acronym for Attached Resource Computer NETwork, which was founded by the Datapoint Corporation. Novell uses the term RX-Net to denote its form of this architecture and TRX-Net for the Turbo version. ARCnet uses a token-bus packet passing scheme.

Note: A Turbo version is an updated RX-Net version that hands packets off to the communications buffers rather than attempting to place the *NetWare Core Protocol* (NCP) packets in a *File Server Process* (FSP) buffer.

ARCnet operates at 2.5 Mbps throughput and can be connected using RG-62/U coax cable or *unshielded twisted-pair* (UTP) wiring. Although ARCnet can support up to 255 node numbers on a single network, systems of this size are not practical.

Figure 33.1 shows the components of a typical ARCnet card. This card is configured for use with twisted-pair wiring. ARCnet cards for use with coax cable have a *Bayonet Navy Connector* (BNC) twist-on connector. You will find jumpers or DIP (Dual In-line Package) switches for setting the following characteristics:

- Node number
- Base I/O address
- Memory address
- Interrupt
- Network timeout

The node number and network timeout are unique to ARCnet and are described later in this chapter.

Each *network interface card* (NIC) on an ARCnet network is assigned a node number. This number must be unique on each network and in the range of 1 to 255.

ARCnet manages network access with a token mechanism. The token is passed from the lowest number node to higher number nodes in ascending order. Lower numbered addresses get the token before the higher numbered addresses.

Traffic is controlled by assigning sequential numbers to nodes using the same order in which they are cabled. Choosing random numbers can create a situation in which a node numbered 23 can be a whole building away from the next number, 46, but in the same room as numbers 112 and 142. The token has to travel in a haphazard manner that is less effective than if you numbered the three clients in the same office sequentially, 46, 47, and 48, and the client in the other building 112. With this configuration, the packet stays within the office before venturing on to other stations.

ARCnet was one of the topologies used early on in networking and is rarely used as the topology of choice in current LAN environments. ARCnet, however, still is a functional and cost-effective means of networking.

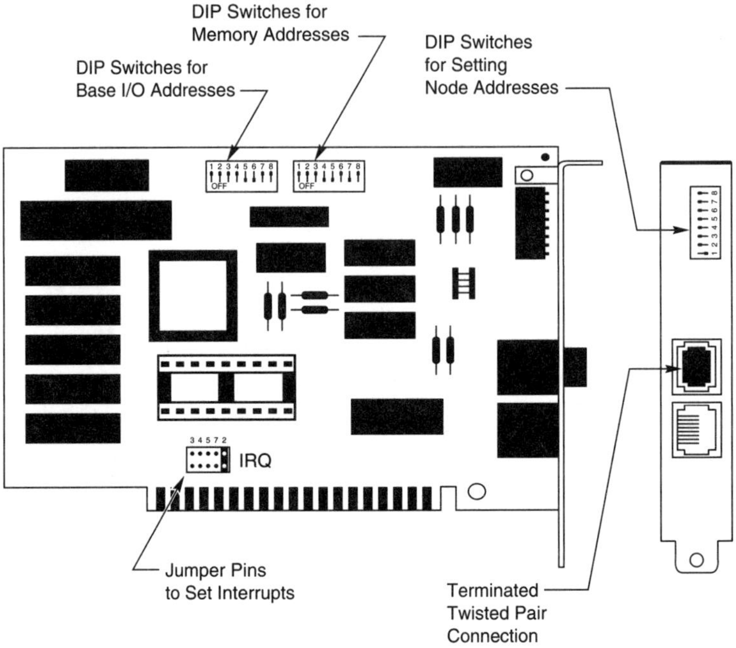

Figure 33.1
Example of an ARCnet NIC.

ARCnet Board Settings

Depending on the vendor design specifications of your ARCnet card, most base I/O addresses, node addresses, and memory addresses are set by DIP switches. These addresses are set using a binary mode calculation with an on or off setting in the required switch block. Interrupt settings are made by jumper combinations at marked locations on the network interface card. Many types and brands of ARCnet cards are on the market today. Refer to the MicroHouse Technical Library, the documentation for the NIC or, as a last resort, call the technical support group for the specific vendor of the component.

Most ARCnet cards require a shared memory address. Many manufacturers use the area of D000:0 to DFFF:0 as the default. Standard DOS memory is limited to the first 640 KB of a PC's memory. However, extended or expanded memory managers can be used to make memory above 640 KB available for use by DOS programs. If memory above the 640 KB line (above hex address A000:0) is used for network boards, however, the memory becomes unavailable for use by a memory manager. This makes it difficult to optimize a PC's upper memory area. If a network card requires a memory area such as D000:0-DFFF:0, the memory available for use by DOS memory managers is reduced by 64 KB.

ARCnet Cabling

The ARCnet topology uses coax, twisted-pair, or fiber-optic cabling to connect network devices. An ARCnet network is used primarily with either coax or twisted-pair cable. Coax is an RG-62/U type cable and is terminated with 93-ohm terminators.

Twisted pair uses stranded 24- or 26-gauge wire or solid core 22-, 24-, or 26-gauge type cable and is terminated with 100-ohm terminators. Many ARCnet networks use a mix of both coax and UTP cabling. UTP cable is simple to install and provides a reliable connection to the clients, whereas coax provides a means to span longer distances.

ARCnet can run off a linear bus topology using coax or twisted-pair as long as the cards support BUS. The most popular installations of ARCnet run off two types of hubs:

- *Active hubs* have active electronic signals that amplify signals and split them to multiple ports. The number of ports on an active hub varies with the manufacturer, but eight is typical. A port on an active hub can be connected to a port on another active device (such as another active hub or an NIC) or to a passive hub.

- *Passive hubs* cannot amplify signals. Each hub has four connectors. Because of the characteristics of passive hubs, unused ports must be equipped with a *terminator*, a connector containing a resistor that matches the ARCnet cabling characteristics. A port on a passive hub can connect only to an active device (an active hub or an NIC). Passive hubs can never be connected to passive hubs.

One of the greatest flexibilities of ARCnet is that you can integrate connections from active hubs to a linear bus connection as long as you terminate at the last connection point.

A maximum time limit of 31 microseconds is allotted for an ARCnet signal. This is also called a time-out setting. Signals on an ARCnet can travel up to 20,000 feet during the 31-microsecond default time-out period. You can sometimes extend the range of an ARCnet by increasing the time-out value. However, 20,000 feet is the distance at which ARCnet signals begin to seriously degrade. Extending the network beyond that distance can result in unreliable or failed communication. Therefore, the time-out parameter and cabling distance recommendations should be increased only with great caution.

The maximum cable distances between individual components in an ARCnet network are dependent on how the components are connected (see table 33.1).

In cabling ARCnet networks with coax cable, you must follow several rules:

- Never connect a passive hub to another passive hub directly.

- Passive hubs should never be used to connect two active hubs.

- Passive hubs are only used to connect an active hub and a node.

- Unused connectors on active hubs do not need to be terminated.

- Unused connectors on passive hubs must be terminated using a 93-ohm terminator.

Figure 33.2 shows an ARCnet configuration using active and passive hubs. Active hubs are required to extend the network for long distances and to configure networks that have more than four nodes. Passive hubs are used as an economical means of splitting a port on an active hub to support three devices.

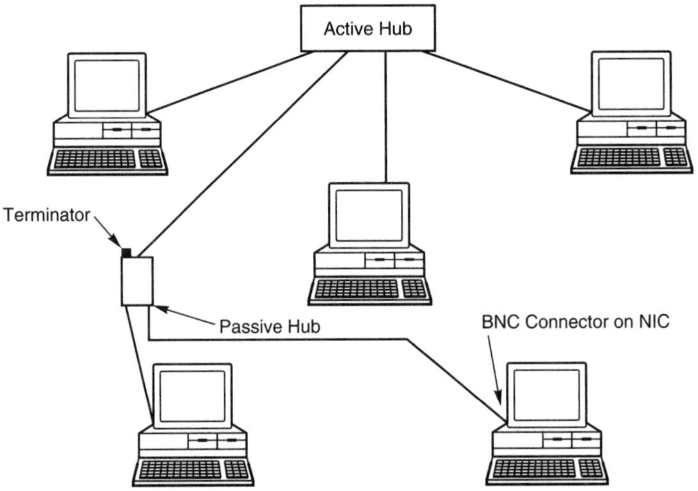

Figure 33.2
Example of an ARCnet topology using active and passive hubs and coax cable.

Table 33.1
Maximum ARCnet Cable Distances

Maximum Distance	*From*	*To*
2,000 feet	Network node	Active hub
2,000 feet	Active hub	Active hub
100 feet	Active hub	Passive hub
Not supported	Passive hub	Passive hub
100 feet	Network node	Passive hub
2,000 feet	Network node	Network node
20,000 feet	Farthest node	Farthest node

ARCnet Troubleshooting

Note Troubleshoot common problems with cards, cables, and related hardware for the three most common networking topologies.

Common sources of problems on ARCnet networks are as follows:

- No more than one node can have a given node address on the same network. If two or more nodes share an address, one of the two clients will either lose its network connection or will not be able to find a network.

- Missing terminators might not present visible problems on a small network. Missing terminators cause data retransmits on smaller systems, eventually appearing as transmit timeout errors or network errors.
- Using a terminator with an incorrect ohm rating. Coax uses 93 ohm; twisted-pair uses 100 ohm. A terminator's value in ohms depends on the impedance of the cable. The cable's impedance and the terminator's value should always match.
- The ARCnet bus using NICs that do not use the same impedance level. Signals will become attenuated and/or reflected, causing interference with other signals on the wire.
- Failed NICs.
- Failed active hubs (or a port on that hub).
- Cable lengths that exceed specifications (refer to table 33.1). Twisted-pair, cabled in a bus rather than a star, cannot have more than ten NICs per segment. This number varies with different manufacturers. ARCnet UTP installed in a bus configuration is generally used only in very small networks of six nodes or less. This configuration has the major drawback of halting the network if a single cable is disconnected. In an ARCnet bus configuration, the network must be brought down to make any changes or service to the ARCnet cards.
- Coax connectors not built or crimped correctly. Twist-on connectors are responsible for more intermittent errors on a network than most other failures because of their design.

Twist-on coax connectors became popular in the IBM 3XXX systems. These systems used RG-62 coax cable and operated at 1.5 Mbps throughput. The twist-on connectors are not recommended for use on any modern LAN cable system because of the higher data rates employed.

The primary characteristics of ARCnet are as follows:

- The maximum time it takes for the ARCnet signal to travel the length of the network is 31 microseconds.
- The maximum distance an ARCnet signal can travel between the two nodes farthest away from each other is 20,000 feet.
- The absolute maximum number of ARCnet nodes that can occupy a given network segment is 255. An ARCnet segment consists of all cabling and nodes that share a given network address.

Understanding Ethernet Specifications

Ethernet was originally developed by the Xerox Corporation, Digital Corporation, and the Intel Corporation in the early 1970s. Ethernet is also known as a *spanning tree topology* because the networks expand by branching in tree structures that do not allow redundant paths between nodes. Ethernet uses the *Carrier Sense Multiple Access/Collision Detection* (CSMA/CD) media contention access method and supports a maximum throughput of 10 Mbps. The Ethernet and 802.3 protocols are described in the Ethernet Frame Types section of this chapter.

> **Note** The origins of Ethernet are commemorated in the initials DIX, which is a 15-pin connector used to interface Ethernet components. The acronym DIX is derived from the combination of leading letters of the founding Ethernet vendors: Digital, Intel, and Xerox.

The term Ethernet commonly refers to original Ethernet (which has been updated to Ethernet II) as well as the IEEE 802.3 standards. However, Ethernet and the 802.3 standards differ in ways significant enough to make standards incompatible in terms of packet formats. At the physical layer, Ethernet and 802.3 are generally compatible in terms of cables, connectors, and electronic devices.

Today, NetWare 3.11 uses the IEEE 802.3 frame format as a default on its networks. However, a variety of other Ethernet frame formats are supported. NetWare 3.12 and 4.*x* use the IEEE 802.2 frame format as the Ethernet frame type default. To change this default, change the frame type in the NET.CFG file. Add this frame type if you need to communicate with networks using older Ethernet frame types.

Ethernet is generally used on light-to-medium traffic networks, and performs best when a network's data traffic is sent in short bursts. Ethernet is the most popular network standard. It has become especially popular in many university and government installations.

Ethernet Board Settings

Most older versions of Ethernet NICs are configured using jumpers to set addresses and interrupts. Current models of NICs can be configured using a diagnostic program that enables changing of interrupt and memory address settings stored in a special memory chip on the NIC.

An example of an Ethernet NIC is shown in figure 33.3. Some of the features of these cards are as follows:

- Shared memory selection; most Ethernet cards do not require the use of shared memory
- I/O address
- Interrupt
- Connectors
- Active connector selection jumpers
- Socket for a remote boot PROM

Ethernet cards can have one, two, or possibly all three of the following connectors:

- BNC connectors support coax cabling
- RJ-45 connectors support 10BASE-T (UTP) cabling
- DIX connectors are used to connect to external transceivers

With some cards, DIP switches or blocks of jumpers are used to select the active connector. In many cases, however, the active connector can be selected with configuration software.

A limitation of 1,024 nodes (physical addresses) per network address exists on an Ethernet network. Addresses are assigned by IEEE to the vendor for the first three bytes of a six-byte address. The vendor is responsible for assigning the rest of the address and ensuring unique IDs.

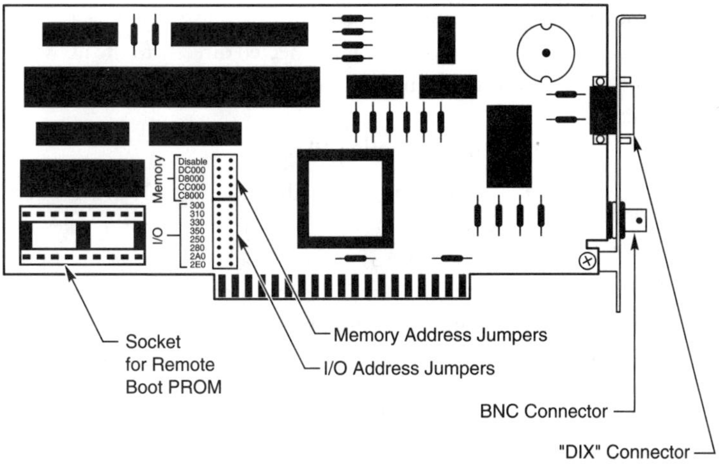

Figure 33.3
Features of an Ethernet NIC.

As with the Token Ring cards, the card's manufacturer "burns" a unique node address into ROM on each NIC. Unless you override the burned-in address, address conflicts cannot occur on an Ethernet. Vendors sometimes label their cards with the node address. If the address is not visible, use the diagnostic disk supplied by the vendor.

Ethernet Cabling

A variety of cables can be used to implement Ethernet networks. Traditionally, Ethernet networks have been cabled with coaxial cables of several different types. Fiber-optic cables are now frequently employed to extend the geographic range of Ethernet networks.

The contemporary interest in using twisted-pair wiring has resulted in a scheme for cabling using unshielded twisted-pair. The 10BASE-T cabling standard, which uses UTP in a star topology, is described later.

Ethernet remains closely associated with coaxial cable, however. Two types of coaxial cable still used in small and large environments are thin net (also known as cheapernet) and thick net. The Ethernet networks have different limitations based on thin net and thick net cable specifications. The best way to remember the requirements is to use the 5-4-3 rule of thumb for each cable type.

The 5-4-3 Rule

The 5-4-3 rule states that the following can appear between any two nodes in the Ethernet network:

- Up to five segments in a series
- Up to four concentrators or repeaters
- Three segments of (coax only) cable that contain nodes

10BASE2

The 10BASE2 cabling topology, also referred to as thin net, generally uses the on-board transceiver of the network interface card to translate the signals to and from the rest of the network. Thin net cabling can use RG-58A/U or RG-58C/U coaxial type cable, 50 ohm terminators, and T-connectors that directly attach to the BNC connector on the NIC.

A grounded terminator must be used on one end of the network segment.

Note: A *transceiver* is a device that takes the digital signal from the node and translates it to communicate on a baseband cabling system. NICs that support thin net or 10BASE-T cable generally have built-in transceivers. External transceivers are used for thick Ethernet although they may be used for thin net and UTP as well.

Use RG-58A/U cable for Ethernet topology, not RG-58U, which is for use with cable TV setups.

Advantages of 10BASE2

The main advantage of using 10BASE2 in your network is cost. When any given cable segment on the network does not have to be run further than 185 meters, 10BASE2 is often the cheapest network cabling option.

10BASE2 is also relatively simple to connect. Each network node is connected directly to the network cable using a T-connector attached to the NIC.

Troubleshooting 10BASE2

The first step in troubleshooting a 10BASE2 network is to ensure that you have met the rules for using 10BASE2. Several additional rules must be adhered to in 10BASE2 Ethernet environments, including the following:

- The minimum cable distance between clients must be 1.5 feet, or 0.5 meters.
- Pig tails, also known as drop cables, from T-connectors should not be used to connect to the BNC connector on the NIC. The T-connector must be connected directly to the NIC.
- You may not go beyond the maximum network segment limitation of 607 feet, or 185 meters.

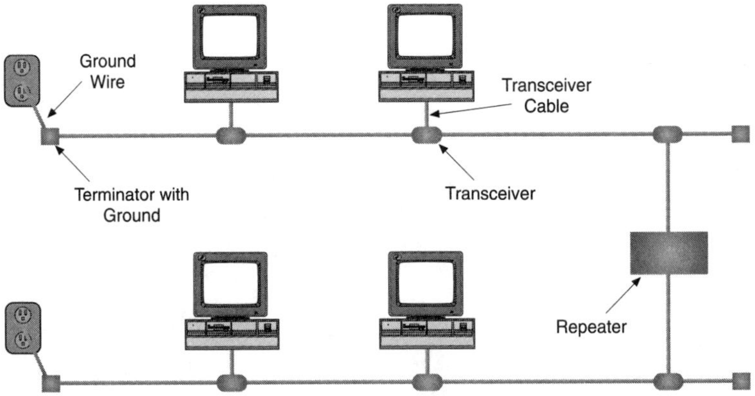

Figure 33.4
Two segments using 10BASE2 cabling.

- The entire network cabling scheme cannot exceed 3,035 feet, or 925 meters.
- The maximum number of nodes per network segment is 30 (this includes clients and repeaters).
- A 50-ohm terminator must be used on each end of the bus with only one of the terminators having either a grounding strap or a grounding wire that attaches it to the screw holding an electrical outlet cover in place.
- You may not have more than five segments on a network. These segments may be connected with a maximum of four repeaters, and only three of the five segments may have network nodes.

Additional troubleshooting tips are found in the Ethernet Troubleshooting section of this chapter.

As mentioned previously, the IEEE 802.3 standard for Thinnet is 10BASE2. This standard describes a 10 Mbps baseband network with a maximum segment length of approximately 200 meters (the actual limit, as stated previously, is 185 meters). Figure 33.4 shows two segments using 10BASE2 cabling.

10BASE5

The 10BASE5 cabling topology, also referred to as thick net, uses an external transceiver to attach to the network interface card (see Fig. 33.5). The NIC attaches to the external transceiver by an *Attachment Universal Interface* (AUI) cable to the DIX connector on the back of the card. The external transceiver clamps to the thick net cable. As with thin net, each network segment must be terminated at both ends, with one end using a grounded terminator. The components of a thick net network are shown in figure 33.6.

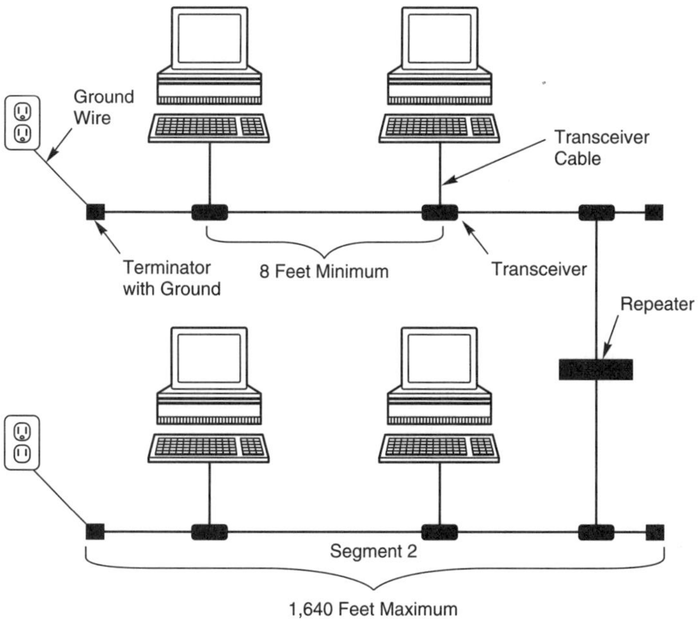

Figure 33.5
Two segments using 10BASE5 cabling.

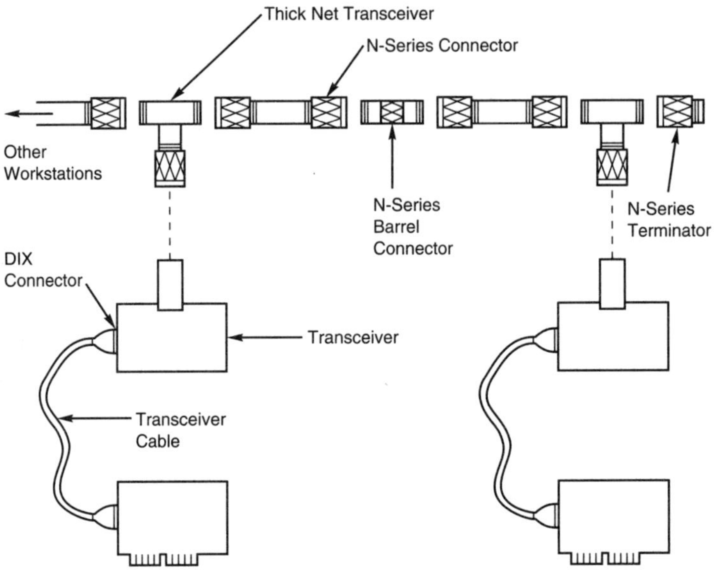

Figure 33.6
Components of a thick Ethernet.

Note: RG-11 is a 75-ohm cable. 10BASE5 requires 50 ohms.

Advantages of 10BASE5

The primary advantage of 10BASE5 is its ability to exceed the cable lengths to which 10BASE2 is restricted. However, it does have restrictions of its own that should be considered when installing or troubleshooting a 10BASE5 network.

Troubleshooting a 10BASE5 Network

As with 10BASE2 networks, the first consideration when troubleshooting a 10BASE5 network should be the cabling rules and guidelines that have been established. Several additional guidelines, along with the 5-4-3 rule, must be followed in thick Ethernet networks:

- The minimum cable distance between transceivers is 8 feet, or 2.5 meters.
- You may not go beyond the maximum network segment length of 1,640 feet, or 500 meters.
- The entire network cabling scheme cannot exceed 8,200 feet, or 2,500 meters.
- One end of the terminated network segment must be grounded.
- Drop cables can be as short as required, but cannot be longer than 50 meters from transceiver to NIC.
- Cable segments that are cut and connected using a "Vampire Tap" should come from the same cable spool to ensure that each connected piece carries the identical electrical cabling to the other.
- The maximum number of nodes per network segment is 100. (This includes all repeaters.)

Additional troubleshooting tips are found in the Ethernet Troubleshooting section of this chapter.

The IEEE 802.3 standard that describes thick net is 10BASE5. This standard describes a 10 Mbps baseband network that can have segments up to 500 meters long. Figure 33.7 shows two segments using thick net and the appropriate hardware.

Thin net and thick net cable can be combined to extend the distance of an Ethernet network topology. The following formula can be used to define the maximum amount of thin net cable that can be used in one network segment combination:

Maximum length of thin net that can be used = 1,640 feet (Length of new network segment to be added)

Note A linear bus topology is more economical than wire because it is not necessary to have a separate cable run for each client. However, some local problems on a linear bus have the capability of bringing the entire network down.

If a break is in the cable or a streaming NIC is in the channel, the entire network can go down. Streaming is more frequently referred to as a broadcast storm. This occurs when a network card fails, and the transmitter floods the cable with traffic, just like a faucet that is stuck open. At this point, the network becomes unusable.

10BASE-T

The trend in wiring Ethernet networks is to use *unshielded twisted-pair* (UTP) cable. UTP or 10BASE-T cable is one of the three most popular implementations for Ethernet. It is based on the IEEE 802.3 standard.

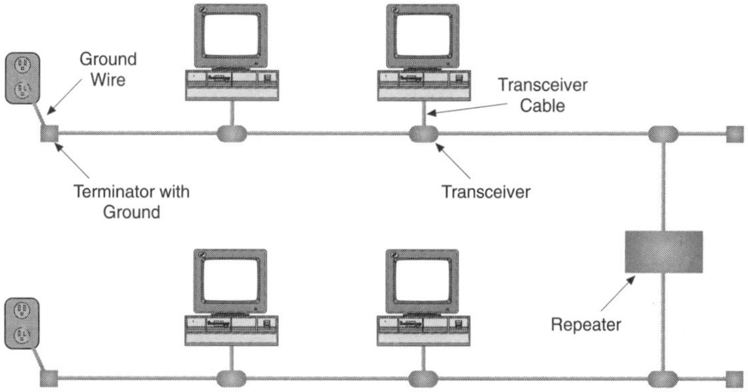

Figure 33.7
Example of thick net Ethernet cabling.

10BASE-T cabling is wired in a star topology. However, it functions logically like a linear bus. The cable uses RJ-45 connectors, and the network interface card can have RJ-45 jacks built into the back of the cards. External transceivers attached to a DIX connector found in combination with RJ-45 or BNC connectors on the NIC can be used to connect standard Ethernet cards into a twisted-pair topology. Figure 33.8 shows Ethernet cabling using twisted-pair cabling and a hub, also called a concentrator.

Advantages of 10BASE-T

The star wiring of 10BASE-T provides several advantages, particularly in larger networks. First, the network is more reliable and easier to manage because 10BASE-T networks use a concentrator (a centralized wiring hub). These hubs are "intelligent" in that they can route network traffic around a bad cable segment, and they can detect defective cable segments. This makes it easier for you to locate and repair bad cable segments.

10BASE-T enables you to design and build your LAN one segment at a time, growing as your network needs grow. This makes 10BASE-T more flexible than other LAN cabling options.

10BASE-T is also relatively inexpensive to use compared to other cabling options. In some cases where a data-grade phone system has already been used in an existing building, this cabling can be used for the LAN.

Note Networks with star wiring topologies can be significantly easier to troubleshoot and repair than bus wired networks. With a star network, a problem node can be isolated from the rest of the network by simply disconnecting the cable and directly connecting it to the cable hub. If the hub is considered "intelligent," management software developed for that hub type, as well as the hub itself, can disconnect the suspect port.

Figure 33.8
Example of twisted-pair Ethernet cabling.

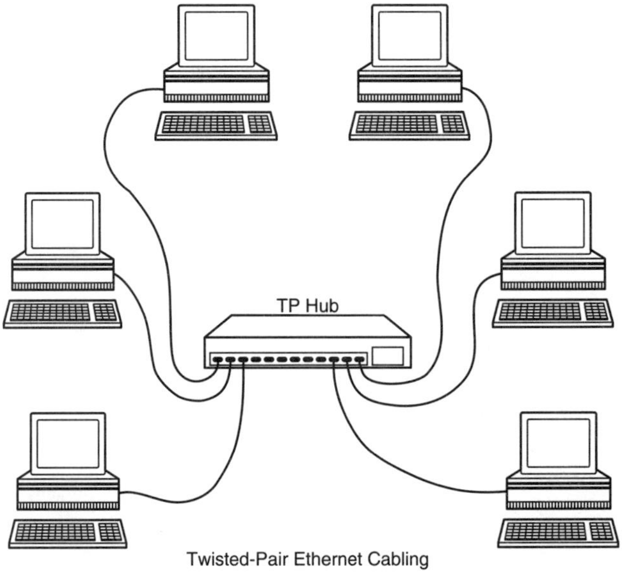

Troubleshooting 10BASE-T

The first step in troubleshooting a 10BASE-T network is to ensure that your network meets the rules for using 10BASE-T. The rules for a 10BASE-T network are as follows:

- The maximum number of network segments is 1,024.
- The cabling used should be 22, 24, or 26 *American Wire Gauge* (AWG), and be rated for an impedance of 85 to 115 ohms at 10 MHz.

Note Unshielded twisted-pair uses a terminator resistance level of 100-200 ohms; shielded twisted-pair uses 150 ohms.

- The maximum number of nodes is 512, and they may be connected on any three segments, with five being the maximum number of available line segments.
- The maximum unshielded cable segment length is 328 feet, or 100 meters.

Note You should be able to translate cable segment lengths from feet to meters, or from meters to feet. A meter is equivalent to 39.37 inches.

Additional troubleshooting tips are found in the Ethernet Troubleshooting section of this chapter.

Note 10BASE-T requires that the UTP cable system be compliant with the Level IV standard. Level IV is cable-certified to operate at 10 Mbps throughput.

Ethernet Frame Types

In order for information to be transmitted successfully across an Ethernet network, the sending and receiving network nodes must agree in advance on the structure of the information being transmitted. The sending node must organize the information in an orderly and predictable manner so that the receiving node can find and interpret the transmitted information. This orderly arrangement of information traveling across an Ethernet network is known as an *Ethernet frame.* Different Ethernet frame types describe different standards that specify the protocol structure (configuration of the media).

There are four possible Ethernet frame types. The same Ethernet frame type must be loaded at both the server and accessing clients in order for proper communication to take place. The four available frame types are ETHERNET 802.3 (also known as raw ETHERNET), ETHERNET 802.2, ETHERNET SNAP, and ETHERNET II.

Raw ETHERNET (802.3) was developed before the IEEE 802.3 standard was completed and released. Therefore, ETHERNET 802.3 is not in complete compliance with the IEEE standard. ETHERNET 802.3 is used only on IPX/SPX Novell networks. ETHERNET 802.3 does not contain a field to specify which protocols may be contained within the packet. The lack of this field is one feature of ETHERNET 802.3 that makes it almost exclusively unique to Novell's NetWare 2.2 and NetWare 3.*x* Operating Systems.

Common features of the ETHERNET 802.3 standard include the following:

- A frame size between 64 and 1,518 bytes

- A preamble in the first line of the header (it contains alternating ones and zeroes to synchronize the communicating stations)
- A one-byte *Start Frame Delimiter* (SFD) field that follows the preamble and designates the beginning of the frame
- A six-byte field that specifies the address of the station to which the packet is being sent
- An originating address indicating the client, server, or router from where the packet was last sent
- A two-byte field that specifies the length of the data portion of the packet, and which must not have a length greater than 1,500 bytes to be considered valid
- A data field which must be no shorter than 46 bytes and no longer than 1,500 bytes
- A four-byte *Cyclical Redundancy Check* (CRC) or Frame Check Sequence that helps to ensure that the transmitted data is valid

ETHERNET 802.2 is fully compliant with the IEEE 802.3 standard. ETHERNET 802.2 is the default frame type used in NetWare 3.12 and NetWare 4.*x* networks. Common features of the ETHERNET 802.2 standard include the following:

- All of the same fields as the 802.3 specification
- Three additional *Logical Link Control* (LLC) fields, one byte long, that act much like an 802.3 header
- A frame size between 64 and 1,518 bytes

ETHERNET SNAP (SubNetwork Address Protocol) is fully compliant with ETHERNET 802.2 and is actually considered an enhancement to the 802.2 specification. Common features of the ETHERNET SNAP standard include the following:

- Two of the LLC fields, which contain fixed data indicating that this is a SNAP packet
- A type field as the third of the LLC fields, which enables the packet to carry other high-level protocols within the frame structure, thus ensuring compatibility and making it possible for network operating systems to carry protocols over other types of media, such as Token Ring

ETHERNET II frame types support TCP/IP for NetWare 3.11. Common features of the ETHERNET II frame type include the following:

- A packet type field located immediately after the source address field, which is the location of the packet length field in other ETHERNET frame types
- A combined preamble and Start Frame Delimiter field that are referred to jointly as the preamble

Although four ETHERNET frame types are available, load only the frame type that you need to use on your network server. If it is necessary in order to support multiple upper-layer protocols, you can load more than one frame type on a server.

Each LAN NIC in the server must have at least one protocol bound to it. To bind a protocol to a NIC, first LOAD the NIC drivers, then bind the protocol to the NIC as in the following:

```
LOAD NE2000 port=320 int=5
frame=ETHERNET_802.3     NAME=ENE5
BIND IPX TO ENE5 NET=BAC1234
```

Ethernet Troubleshooting

Trend measurement and analysis can be applied to all network types. The use of a sophisticated protocol analyzer, such as LANalyzer for WINDOWS and simpler tools, along with your own experience and knowledge, are two other effective troubleshooting techniques for Ethernet networks. This section covers the latter option.

When troubleshooting an Ethernet network, begin with the more obvious physical problems. For example, check to make certain that all connectors are tight and properly connected. Make certain that ground wires and terminators are used when required. Also, be certain that manufacturer's specifications are met, and that cable lengths, maximum number of nodes, and so on, are correct.

Consider the following when troubleshooting Ethernet networks:

- With 10BASE-T, make sure that the cable used has the correct number of twists to meet the data grade specifications.
- Check for electrical interference. Electrical interference can be caused by tying the network cable together with monitor and power cords. Outside interference also can be caused by fluorescent lights, electric motors, and other electrical devices.
- Make sure that connectors are pinned properly and crimped tightly.
- Check the cable lengths to make sure that distance specifications are not exceeded.
- If excess shielding on coax cable is exposed, make sure it is not grounding out the connector.
- Make sure that coax cables are not coiled tightly together.
- Check the grade of the cable being used. For 10BASE2, RG-58/U is required. All 10BASE5 cable must meet Ethernet specifications.
- If using a linear bus setup, make sure that the topology rules are followed.
- Check for missing terminator or terminators with improper impedance ratings.
- Check for malfunctioning hardware, such as a bad NIC, transceiver, concentrator, T-connector, or terminator. Check to make certain that connectors have not been mixed up, such as ARCnet connectors being used on an Ethernet network.
- Test the continuity of the cable, using various physical testing devices, such as an Optical Time Domain Reflectometer, or software, such as Novell's COMCHECK utility.
- If the Fileserver not found error message appears, check for a mismatch in the Ethernet frame type between the server and the client.
- Verify that the LAN card is working properly. Clean the connector fingers (do not use an eraser because it leaves grit on the card); pull the card and replace it with one that you know is in working order; or run the NIC's diagnostics software.
- If NIC resource conflicts seem to be a potential cause of network problems, remove all cards except the file server NICs, then replace them one at a time until the conflicting card is found. Then correct the NIC settings and continue checking NICs one at a time. If you are installing new NICs, avoid using the common COM port interrupts of 3 and 4 to prevent potential Ethernet card conflicts.

- Make sure that all the component cables in a segment are connected together. A user who moves his client and removes the T-connector incorrectly can cause a broken segment.

Understanding Token Ring Specifications

Token Ring uses a token-passing architecture that adheres to the IEEE 802.5 standard. The topology is physically a star, but logically uses a ring to pass the token from station to station. Each node must be attached to a concentrator called a *multistation access unit* (MSAU or MAU).

Token Ring network interface cards can run at 4 Mbps or 16 Mbps. 4 Mbps cards can run only at that data rate. However, 16 Mbps cards can be configured to run at 4 or 16 Mbps. All cards on a given network ring must be running at the same rate.

As shown in figure 33.9, each node acts as a repeater that receives token and data frames from its *nearest active upstream neighbor* (NAUN). After a frame is processed by the node, the frame is passed downstream to the next attached node. Each token makes at least one trip around the entire ring. It then returns to the originating node. Workstations that indicate problems send a "beacon" to identify an address of the potential failure. You will learn more about this topic later in this chapter.

Practical TIP To find out if any beacon messages have been sent on your Token Ring network, review your System Error Log, found in SYSCON through Supervisor Options.

Token Ring Board Settings

As with the Ethernet cards, the node address on each NIC is burned in at the manufacturer and is unique to each card. The node address in some cases can be overridden by vendor-specified software instructions. (Check with the vendor of the component.) A maximum of two Token Ring cards can be installed in any node, with each card being defined as the primary or alternate Token Ring card in the machine. A typical Token Ring card is shown in figure 33.10.

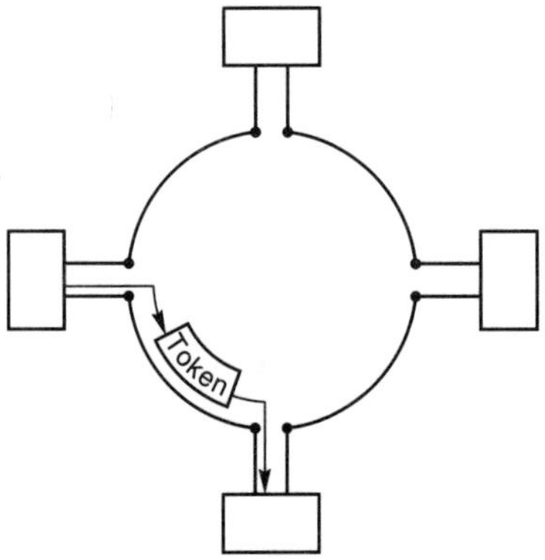

Figure 33.9
Operation of a Token Ring.

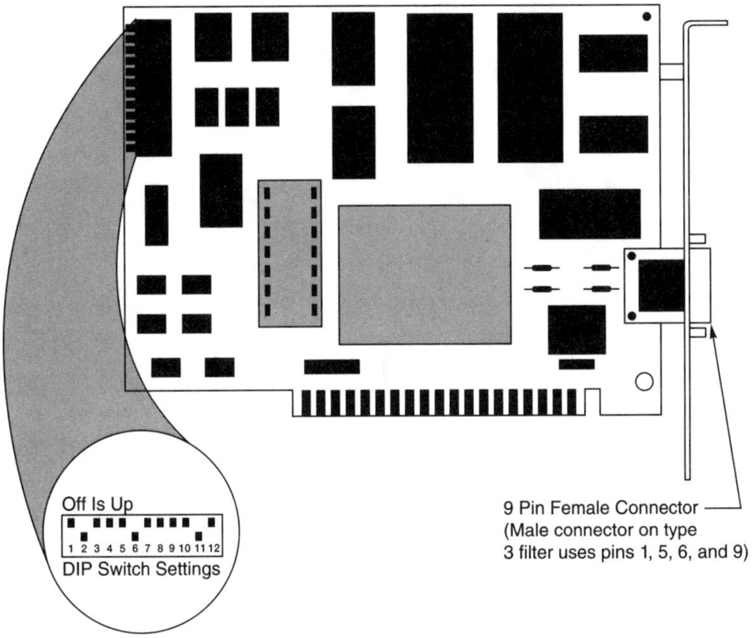

Figure 33.10
Features of a Token Ring NIC.

The following are features of a Token Ring NIC:

- DIP switches (see table 33.2)
- 9-pin female connector
- Remote boot PROM socket

Note: When loading two Token Ring NICs in a NetWare file server, make sure that you configure the primary card at port address of A20. The alternate card must be set at A24. For v3.1*x* or v4.*x*, in the AUTOEXEC.NCF file or at the file server console, use the following example commands:

```
LOAD TOKEN PORT=A20 INT=2 MEM=CC000
NAME=CARD1

LOAD TOKEN PORT=A24 INT=3 MEM=DC000
NAME=CARD2
```

The interrupt and base memory address on each Token Ring NIC must be set to avoid conflicts with all other components. Table 33.2 defines the proper DIP switch settings for an IBM 16/4 Token Ring card.

Each Token Ring card comes with a diagnostic disk that provides testing for the adapter. Refer to the appropriate documentation for your card for more detailed instructions.

Token Ring Cabling

Traditional Token-Ring networks used shielded twisted-pair cable. The following are standard IBM cable types for Token Ring:

- **Type 1.** A braided shield surrounds two twisted pairs of solid copper wire. Type 1 is used to connect terminals and distribution panels, or to connect between different wiring closets that are located in the same building. Type 1 uses two STPs of solid-core 22 AWG wire for long, high data grade transmissions within the building's walls.

Table 33.2
IBM 16/4 Token-Ring Switch Settings

Switch Blk (Off is Up, On is Down)	*1*	*2*	*3*	*4*	*5*	*6*	*7*	*8*	*9*	*10*	*11*	*12*
ADDRESS												
CC000	Off	On	On	Off	Off	On						
DC000	Off	On	Off	Off	Off	On						
INTERRUPT												
2							Off	Off				
3							On	Off				
6							Off	On				
7							Off	Off				
PRIMARY									Off			
ALTERNATE								On				
SHARED RAM												
8 KB										On	On	
16 KB										Off	On	
32 KB										On	Off	
64 KB										Off	Off	
DATA RATE												
16 Mbps												Off
4 Mbps											On	

- **Type 2.** Type 2 uses a total of six twisted pairs; two are STPs (for networking), four are UTPs (for telephone systems). Additionally, this cable type incorporates two unshielded twisted pairs that can be used for voice circuits. This cable is used for the same purposes as Type 1, but enables both voice and data cables to be included in a single cable run.
- **Type 3.** Type 3 has unshielded twisted-pair copper with a minimum of two twists per inch, used as an alternative to Type 1 and Type 2 cable because of its reduced cost. It has four UTPs of 24 AWG solid-core wire for networks or telephone systems. Type 3 cannot be used for 16 Mbps Token-Ring networks. It is used primarily for long, low data-grade transmissions within walls. Signals will not travel as fast as with Type 1 cable because Type 3 does not have the shielding used by Type 1.
- **Type 5.** With Type 5, fiber-optic cable is used only on the main ring. Type 5 can use two 100-um or 140-um optical fibers in one fiber jacket.
- **Type 6.** A braided shield surrounds two twisted pairs of stranded copper wire. It is made up of two 26 AWG stranded-core STPs. This cable supports shorter cable runs than Type 1, but is more flexible due to the stranded conductors.

Type 6 is the IBM standard for patch cables and extension cables, used also in wiring closets.

- **Type 8.** Type 8 uses a single 26 AWG stranded-core STP and is especially designed for use under carpet.
- **Type 9.** Type 9 is the same as Type 6 cable except that it is designed to be fire-resistant for use in plenum installations. It uses two STPs of solid-core 26 AWG wire and is used for long runs within the walls of a building.

Token ring cabling is used to connect clients to the MSAU, or to connect one MSAU to another. Cables that connect between MSAUs are called patch cables. Patch cables may also be made of IBM Type 6 cable.

Note: Novell defines Token-Ring cabling in terms of two types of systems:

- Small movable
- Large non-movable

The small movable system supports up to 96 clients and file servers and 12 MSAUs. It uses Type 6 cable to attach clients and servers to IBM Model 8228 MSAUs. Type 6 cable is a shielded twisted-pair cable with stranded conductors. This cable is flexible, but has limited distance capabilities. The characteristics of this cable make it suitable for small networks and for patch cords.

The large non-movable system supports up to 260 clients and file servers, with up to 33 MSAUs. This network configuration uses IBM Type 1 or Type 2 cable. These are shielded twisted-pair cables with solid-wire conductors suitable for carrying signals greater distances than are possible with Type 6. The large nonmovable system also involves other wiring needs such as punch panels or distribution panels, equipment racks for MSAUs, and wiring closets to contain the previously listed components.

The MSAU is the central cabling component for IBM Token-Ring networks. The 8228 MSAU was the original wiring hub developed by IBM for Token-Ring networks. Figure 33.11 shows 8228 MSAUs. Each 8228 has ten connectors, eight of which accept cables to clients or servers. The other connectors are labeled RI (ring in) and RO (ring out). The RI and RO connectors are used to connect multiple 8228s to form larger networks.

8228s are mechanical devices that consist of relays and connectors. Their purpose is to switch clients in and out of the network. Each port is controlled by a relay powered by a voltage sent to the MSAU from the client. When an 8228 is first set up, each of these relays must be initialized with a setup tool shipped with the unit. The setup tool is inserted into each port and held there until a light indicates that the port is properly initialized.

IBM Token Ring networks use two types of connectors. NICs are equipped with a nine-pin D-connector. MSAUs, repeaters, and most other equipment use a special IBM data connector. Two types of cables are employed:

- *Patch cables* have IBM data connectors at both ends. These cables interconnect MSAUs, repeaters, and most other Token-Ring components.
- *Token Ring adapter cables* have an IBM data connector at one end and a nine-pin connector at the other. Adapter cables connect client and server NICs to other network components that use IBM data connectors.

Figure 33.11 shows an example of a network cabling several clients and MSAUs. The distances noted in the figure are based on the rules for the small movable cabling system.

When you are connecting a Token-Ring network, make sure that you do the following:

1. Initialize each port in the 8228 MSAU by using the setup tool shipped with the MSAU (wait for the click) before connecting a cable.
2. If using more than one MSAU, connect the RO port of each MSAU with the RI port of the next MSAU in the loop. This must physically complete a circle or ring.

A variety of rules must be observed when configuring Token Rings. The following rules apply to small, movable Token-Ring networks:

- The minimum patch cable distance between two MSAUs is eight feet.
- The maximum patch cable distance between two MSAUs is 150 feet. Patch cables come in standard lengths of 8, 30, 75, and 150 feet for Type 6.
- The maximum patch cable distance connecting all MSAUs is 400 feet.
- The maximum adapter cable distance between an MSAU and a node is 150 feet.

A small movable IBM cable system consists of the following:

- Maximum 96 nodes
- Maximum 12 MSAUs
- Uses Type 6 cable

A large non-movable IBM cable system consists of the following:

- Maximum 260 nodes
- Maximum 33 MSAUs
- Uses Type 1 or Type 2 cable

Note

Token-Ring networks also can be cabled using UTP cabling, which IBM calls Type 3 cable. The IEEE 802.5 standard describes 4 Mbps Token Ring using UTP cable. However, level 5 UTP is currently used for 16 Mbps Token Ring.

When using UTP wiring, a media filter must be installed between the NIC and the UTP cable. Some newer Token Ring NICs have built-in media filters and RJ-45 jacks ready to interface with UTP wiring.

Token Ring Troubleshooting

When troubleshooting a Token-Ring network, as with troubleshooting other types of networks, begin with the more obvious physical problems, checking such things as connectors to see if they are tight and properly connected. You also should check to see that manufacturer's specifications are met, and that cable lengths, maximum number of nodes, and so on, are correct.

When troubleshooting Token-Ring networks, you also should look for the following:

- Any base I/O, DMA shared memory, or interrupt conflicts with other boards.
- The version of the client or server software driver, to make sure that its revision level is compatible with your NIC (drivers are different for file servers and clients).

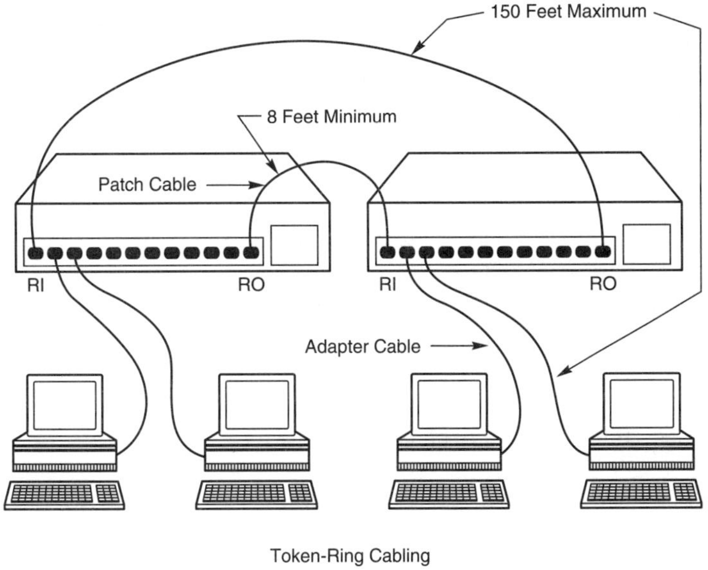

Figure 33.11
An example of Token-Ring cabling using MSAUs.

- Proper connections of MSAUs, with ring out ports connecting to ring in ports throughout the ring. In troubleshooting problems that you have first isolated to a particular area of the network, if you suspect the MSAU, isolate it by changing the ring in and ring out cables to bypass the MSAU. If the ring is now functional again, consider replacing the MSAU. You may also find that if your network has MSAUs from more than one manufacturer, they are not wholly compatible. Impedance and other electrical characteristics may show slight differences between manufacturers, causing intermittent network problems.
- Other MSAU problems. Some MSAUs other than the 8228 are active and require a power supply. These MSAUs fail if they have a blown fuse or a bad power source.
- Correct attachments of patch cables and the adapter cable. Remember, patch cables connect MSAUs together, and the adapter cable connects the NIC to the MSAU. Patch cables, adapter cables, and MSAUs are common sources of problems. Isolating the problem is easier to do if you have a current log of your network's physical design. Once you have narrowed down the problem, you can isolate potential problem areas on the network from the rest of the network, and then use a cable tester to find the actual problem.
- A failed NIC. Try substituting another one known to work properly. NICs that have failure rates that exceed a preset tolerance level may actually remove themselves from the network.
- A bad MSAU or MSAU port. Ports may need to be reinitialized with the setup tool. Removing drop cables and reinitializing each MSAU port is a "quick fix" that is useful on relatively small Token-Ring networks.
- Incorrect card speeds; for example, a 16 Mbps card is inserted into a 4 Mbps ring or vice versa. Neither situation is correct. The speed of the NIC is displayed when the Token-Ring driver is loaded at the client.

- The wrong type of cable for the speed of the network.
- Bent or broken pins on the adapter cable.
- Duplicate node addresses. If you are overriding the burned-in network addresses, it is possible that duplicate node addresses may be set.
- The Type 3 media filter, if connecting to a 4 Mbps twisted-pair network.

One of the advantages of a Token-Ring network is its built-in ability to monitor itself. This process provides electronic troubleshooting and, when possible, repair processes. When it is not possible for the Token-Ring network to make its own repairs, a process called *beaconing* is helpful. Beaconing narrows down the portion of the ring where the problem is most likely to exist. This potential problem area is referred to as the *fault domain.*

The Beaconing Process

The design of the Token Ring network itself contributes greatly to the ability of the beaconing process to troubleshoot its own network. The design includes two types of network stations known as Active Monitors and Standby Monitors. Only one Active Monitor can exist on a network at a time. All other stations are Standby Monitors.

Generally, the first station that is powered-up and becomes part of the network is automatically the Active Monitor station. The responsibility of the Active Monitor station is to announce itself to the next active downstream station as the Active Monitor station, and request that station to announce itself to its next active downstream station. The Active Monitor station sends out this beacon announcement every seven seconds.

Once each station has announced itself to its next active downstream neighbor, the announcing station becomes the nearest active upstream neighbor (NAUN) to the downstream station. Each station on a Token-Ring network has an upstream neighbor as well as a downstream neighbor.

Once each station is aware of its NAUN, the beaconing process continues every seven seconds. If for some reason a station does not receive one of its expected seven-second beaconed announcements from its upstream neighbor, it attempts to notify the network of its lack of contact from the upstream neighbor. It sends a message out onto the network ring, which includes the following:

- The sending station's network address
- The receiving NAUN's network address
- The beacon type

From this information, the ring can determine which station may be having a problem and attempt to fix the problem without disrupting the entire network. This problem fix is known as *autoreconfiguration.* If the autoreconfiguration is unsuccessful, manual correction is required. Figure 33.12 shows a Token-Ring network utilizing the beaconing process.

The preceding section detailed common characteristics of ARCnet, Ethernet, and Token Ring. Other components also must be examined for conflicts and proper configuration. The next section describes these items.

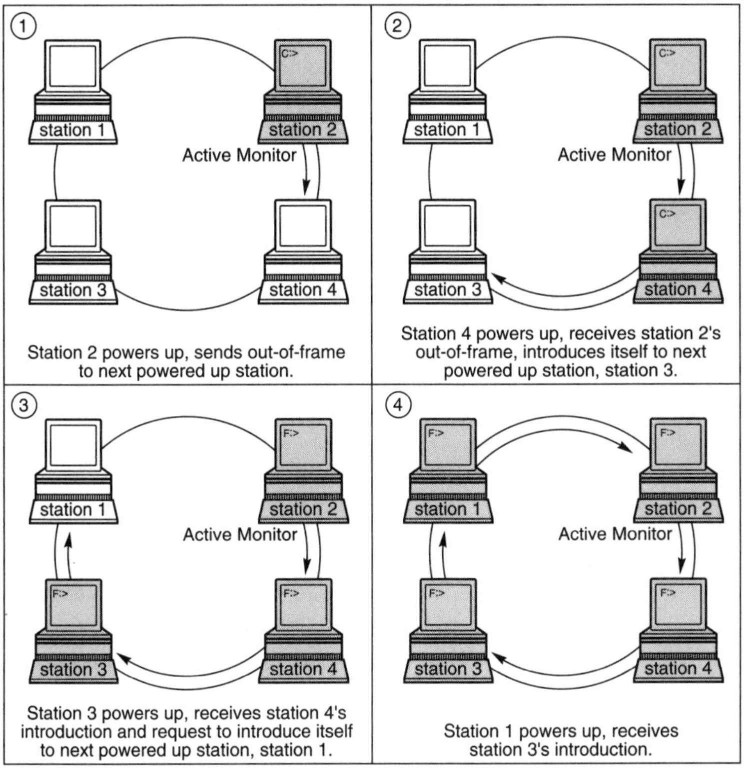

Figure 33.12
Token Ring beaconing.

Understanding FDDI

Fiber Distributed Data Interface is a LAN standard that, like Token Ring, follows the IEEE 802.5 standard for accessing the network. FDDI carries both LED and laser-generated LAN communications through fiber-optic cables.

Note Decide when it is appropriate to consider the installation of FDDI.

Fiber optic cable is primarily made of pure glass that is pulled into very thin wires or fibers. Many of these fibers are bundled together to form a core. This core is surrounded by another layer of glass called *cladding*. The LED sends the signals through the core of this cable, and the cladding contains these signals to the core. The signal on each fiber can go in only one direction at a time. The bundle of fibers enables the LED to send multiples of signals at a time.

Unlike Token Ring and its related network interface cards that transfer data across the network at speeds of 4 or 16 Mbps, FDDI transfers information at a rate of 100 Mbps. In addition, FDDI is structured to take advantage of two rings, rather than one. This Dual Counter Rotating Rings structure enables FDDI to transfer data across one ring while it performs backup and other services on the second ring.

In addition, FDDI uses multiple tokens and has the ability to bypass network stations designated as low priority, so it can provide faster service to high-priority network stations.

Like a Token-Ring LAN, FDDI uses a token to transfer data frames around the network. After the data frame is processed by the correct network station, the token is passed on to the next attached network node.

The second ring in the FDDI network rotates in the opposite direction of the first ring. This counter-rotation enables the network to compensate for a break in the fiber. If one ring in the network becomes broken due to a problem at one of the network stations, those stations located on either side of the break can isolate the break in the fiber by forming a single ring (wrapping) from their own ports, as shown in figure 33.13.

Each network station can be attached to either one ring or to both rings, depending on the class of the connected station. There are two types of station classes: Class A and Class B.

Class A stations, also called *Single Attached Stations* (SAS), can be attached to only one ring at a time. Only Class B stations, or Dual attached Stations (DAS), can be connected to both rings simultaneously. This designation of station classes helps to keep unstable network devices from breaking both network rings.

Another method of isolating faulty nodes in the network is through the use of wiring concentrators. Wiring concentrators function in theory much like the Token-Ring MSAU. They act as centralized cabling connection devices for network stations. Unlike MSAUs, however, wiring concentrators are capable of communicating with stations and verifying the integrity of the station-to-concentrator connection.

Advantages of Using FDDI

The ability to isolate a break in the cable and continue network communication makes FDDI an extremely reliable cabling option. FDDI has several other advantages.

FDDI overcomes some of the performance problems experienced by traditional Token-Ring networks. It accomplishes this by implementing a standard that provides fair and timely access to the network.

Increased reliability is another advantage of using FDDI. That reliability comes in several forms, including the following:

- **Information security.** Fiber-optic cable is difficult to wiretap.
- **Physical security.** Fiber-optic cable is more resistant to cable breakage than are other types of cabling.
- **Electrical security.** Fiber-optic cable is not susceptible to electrical interference and does not conduct electricity.

FDDI also can transmit network packets over its cable for distances that are significantly longer than other types of cabling. For example, on a fiber-optic cable with no cable bends or breaks that would otherwise reduce the integrity of the transmission, information theoretically can travel hundreds of miles.

FDDI also has built-in management of three aspects of the network, including the following:

- **Ring Management (RMT)** is responsible for finding and resolving faults in the network ring.

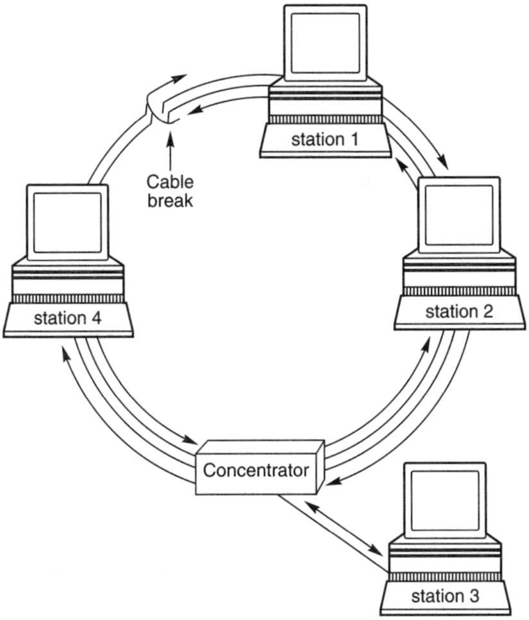

Figure 33.13
Isolated cable break in an FDDI network.

- **Connection Management (CMT)** is responsible for controlling stations that are inserting themselves into the network, or removing themselves from the network.
- **Station Management (SMT)** makes it possible for special high-level programs to monitor the ring.

As noted earlier, FDDI networks are substantially faster than Token-Ring networks, capable of communicating at a rate of 100 Mbps. They accomplish this speed not only as a result of the type of cable (fiber optic) that they use, but also as a result of their use of multiple tokens and their ability to service only the high-priority network stations, bypassing the low-priority stations whenever necessary.

A fiber-optic cable is also significantly lighter in weight than is, for example, twisted-pair cabling with an equivalent bandwidth.

Note: Don't look directly at fiber-optic cable without eye protection. To check to see whether a fiber-optic port is transmitting, darken the room and place a piece of paper in front of the port. If it is transmitting, a light will be reflected onto the paper.

Disadvantages of Using FDDI

There are two primary disadvantages of using FDDI in your network. First, because of the complexity and newness of FDDI technology, you need a great deal of expertise to install and subsequently maintain an FDDI network.

Second, although the cost of the cable itself is comparable to that of unshielded twisted-pair (UTP) cabling, the concentrators and LAN adapters are relatively expensive. For example, a typical FDDI concentrator runs between $1,000 and $1,500 per network node. Therefore, the overall cost of an FDDI network for a LAN of any size can quickly become quite costly.

FDDI Cabling

Various types and wavelengths of fiber-optic cables are available. A typical fiber-optic cable consists of a core made from silica, surrounded by a primary and secondary buffer, and then enclosed in a jacket. Kevlar may be added to provide strength.

The important thing to remember about choosing a fiber-optic cable is to select one based on its intended use, and to match the cable to its appropriate connectors. Figure 33.14 shows a typical duplex fiber-optic cable.

FDDI Troubleshooting

As with troubleshooting all types of networks, begin by looking for the obvious problems, such as loose connectors, damaged cables, and so on. After ruling out these types of problems, consider other possible causes. Look first at those problems considered typical of FDDI networks:

- Incorrect cable type for actual distance between nodes. On an FDDI network where network information must travel thousands of feet, Multimode Fiber should be used. When distances between nodes begin to reach tens of thousands of feet, or exceed distances of two kilometers, Single-Mode Fiber is necessary.
- Problems with communicating between network nodes. Even small breaks in a fiber-optic cable can result in network communication problems. There are several ways to detect cable problems, except for one that requires special equipment. If a break in a segment of the cable is a complete break, you can detect the break using a flashlight. Otherwise, you can use an optical power meter and a source of light energy to test the cable. If either of these methods is insufficient, you can use the most expensive method, an *Optical Time Domain Reflectometer* (OTDR).
- Dirt on connectors is another cause of communication problems between network nodes. Data is transmitted through fiber-optic cables using light. Therefore, it is important that you keep connectors free from dust and dirt. You can clean connectors using any type of lint-free cloth dampened with alcohol. Do not use water or any type of cleaning fluids other than alcohol.
- Communication problems also can be caused by bad connectors or by a segment of the cable that is open (incorrectly terminated). A loss of optical power that exceeds 13.0 decibels is an indication that cable problems of this nature may exist. To correct these problems, replace faulty connectors and properly close any open cable segment.
- A delay of up to four milliseconds in communication is not unusual for fiber-optic cable. If communication delays are a problem, consider using NetWare's Packet Burst Protocol to send multiple rather than single frames across the network, thus reducing transmission delay.
- When the network does not efficiently handle transmissions across cable that exceeds 50 meters, or which requires 10 Mbps or more throughput, this problem may be directly related to the type of fiber-optic cable. If you are using plastic fiber-optic cable in your network, consider replacing all or at least some of this cable with glass cable. Speed can be affected by the type of fiber-optic cable used.

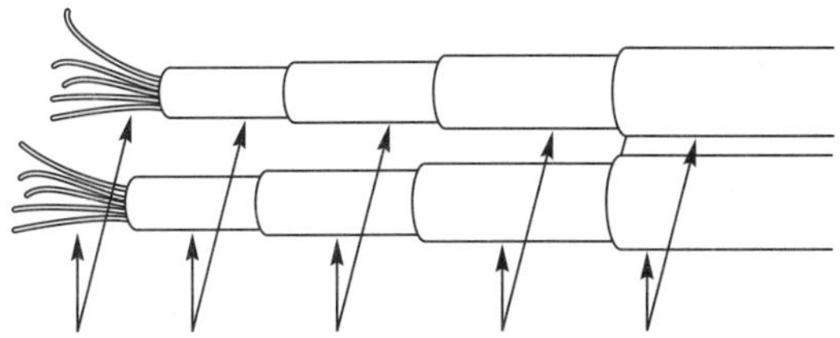

Figure 33.14
Fiber-optic duplex cable assembly.

- The path that network information must travel should be the most efficient. If you are using bridges instead of routers in your network, consider switching to network routers. NetWare network routers, or routers such as CI500 and Wellfleet that are certified by Novell, can choose the best path for any given packet. They are somewhat slower than bridges, however, because of the increased processing that they perform. The design of FDDI translation bridges makes routers the preferred choice for FDDI networks running NetWare.

Which Topology Should I Use?

As a network administrator or support engineer, you have to make some tough decisions on the best type of topology to incorporate into your network environment. It is similar to choosing what type of vehicle and size of engine you need to drive your loads on local streets, freeways, or highways. You need to consider using Token Ring (4 Mbps or 16 Mbps) or Ethernet (10 Mbps). You also need to consider which type of cabling system you need for your network.

The factors that are involved in your choice include the following:

- Type of applications and their percentage of overall use
- Flexibility of setup
- Cost
- Knowledge level of your support or vendor source
- Availabilty of replacement or add-on components

No one topology is better than another. Your choice is dependent on how the factors affect your network environment.

Choose the Ethernet topology for those types of networks with a light-to-medium workload. If you are using standard applications, such as word processing, spreadsheets, gateway host sessions, electronic mail, and calendaring packages, Ethernet will work efficiently.

Ethernet has a maximum throughput of 10 Mbps. (Standard loads usually are working around 8-9.1 Mbps.) The cost is nominal, and interchangeable components are readily available. Clients can attempt to transmit more quickly rather than waiting their turn, as is done with the Token Ring topology.

The disadvantage of Ethernet is that the size of the data frames in the packets may require more traffic to pass along the data files on the media. Also, the collision-oriented system can be degraded with the heavy use of database, imaging, multimedia, or CAD/CAM applications.

Token Ring topology is a choice for networks that tend toward heavy workloads. The size of the data frame in the packet is larger than in Ethernet. Token Ring can handle large file transfers, such as database, CAD/CAM, and multiple accesses to imaging files, more easily. Token Ring runs at 4 Mbps or 16 Mbps on many types of media. Some applications of 16 Mbps Token Ring speed are not always as efficient as using the 4 Mbps or the Ethernet 10 Mbps.

Token Ring is more reliable because no collisions occur with the token passing scheme. The disadvantages of Token Ring are cost, station transmission capabilities, and the overhead for management of the token scheme. Also, the more clients you add to a ring, the more that performance can be degraded. Consider splitting the ring into smaller rings with fewer clients attached.

Use your best judgment on your network setup. Where your applications reside, the location of your workloads, and the availability of your network components will determine whether you should use one topology or perhaps mix them.

Questions

1. Which is the least important when configuring a client?
   - ○ A. Avoiding conflicts
   - ○ B. How other clients are configured
   - ○ C. Checking that cables meet specifications for their intended topology
   - ○ D. Matching drivers to operating system revisions

2. Which statement about ARCnet is false?
   - ○ A. ARCnet can be cabled in star or bus.
   - ○ B. ARCnet uses RG-62/U for coax.
   - ○ C. ARCnet has the unique feature time-out setting of 31 microseconds.
   - ○ D. ARCnet can span a distance of 25,000 feet.

3. Which combination is not supported?
   - ○ A. Passive hub to passive hub
   - ○ B. Active hub to passive hub to active hub
   - ○ C. Active hub to passive hub
   - ○ D. Network node to passive hub

4. Which is not a feature of an Ethernet board?
   - ○ A. Ethernet boards usually have DIX connectors.
   - ○ B. Ethernet boards can have thick (DIX), thin (BNC), or twisted-pair (RJ-45) connectors.
   - ○ C. Ethernet boards have internal transceivers for thin net.
   - ○ D. Ethernet boards have a time-out setting.

5. Which level cable is correct for 10BASE-T?
   - ○ A. Level I
   - ○ B. Level II
   - ○ C. Level IV
   - ○ D. Level VI

6. Which statement about Token Ring cabling is true?
   - ○ A. Small, movable systems support up to 96 clients and 12 MSAUs. Token Ring networks cannot use UTP cabling.
   - ○ B. The maximum patch cable distance between two MSAUs is 75 feet.
   - ○ C. The minimum patch cable distance is 2.5 feet.
   - ○ D. Token-Ring uses Type 2, Type 4, and Type 6 cabling.

7. Which *two* of the following statements regarding FDDI are true?
   - ☐ A. It follows the IEEE 802.5 standard.
   - ☐ B. Like Token Ring, it uses only a single token.
   - ☐ C. FDDI can transfer data at speeds of 100 Mbps.
   - ☐ D. Stations must attach to the cable by a concentrator.

8. FDDI stands for ______.
   - ○ A. Fiber-based Data Distribution Interface
   - ○ B. Fiber Distributed Data Interface
   - ○ C. Fiber Optic Data Distributed Interface
   - ○ D. Fiber Data Distribution Interface

9. Plastic and glass fiber-optic cables can be used equally well in all situations except ______.
   - ○ A. when the cable distance is less than 50 meters
   - ○ B. when the cable has an open condition
   - ○ C. when stations are attached using a concentrator
   - ○ D. when throughput of 10 Mbps or greater is required

10. Which of the following is one advantage that FDDI has over Token Ring?
    - ○ A. Fiber optic cable is difficult to wiretap.
    - ○ B. FDDI is capable of isolating cable breaks.
    - ○ C. FDDI provides fair and timely access to the network.
    - ○ D. FDDI has built-in ring management.

11. What is the main advantage of using 10BASE2 when network segments do not have to exceed 185 meters?
    - ○ A. It is relatively simple to connect.
    - ○ B. Drop cables can be used, making it easier to troubleshoot.
    - ○ C. Each node connects directly to the cable.
    - ○ D. It is the least expensive of the cabling options.

12. Which *three* of the Ethernet cabling options requires that each end of the bus be terminated?
    - ☐ A. 10BASE2
    - ☐ B. 10BASE5
    - ☐ C. 10BASE-T
    - ☐ D. Thin net

13. Which of the cabling options is considered the trend for wiring Ethernet networks?
    - ○ A. 10BASE2
    - ○ B. 10BASE5
    - ○ C. 10BASE-T
    - ○ D. Thick net

14. Which of the following is not an advantage in using 10BASE-T for cabling a network?
    - ○ A. It is easier and more reliable to manage.
    - ○ B. Centralized hubs make it easier to detect bad cable segments.
    - ○ C. Beaconing helps to isolate cable breaks.
    - ○ D. It is relatively inexpensive to use.

15. Which of the following Ethernet frame types is designated as raw Ethernet?
    - ○ A. ETHERNET_802.2
    - ○ B. ETHERNET_802.3
    - ○ C. ETHERNET_SNAP
    - ○ D. ETHERNET_II

Answers

1. B
2. D
3. A
4. D
5. C
6. C
7. A, C
8. B
9. B
10. A
11. D
12. A, B, D
13. C
14. C
15. B

CHAPTER 34

Troubleshooting Network Storage Devices

In this chapter, you will learn about the advantages and disadvantages of different types of storage devices that can be used on the network. There are many storage devices that have evolved throughout the history of the computer industry. Understanding how these devices operate and what their limitations are is an important function of a network administrator's job. The following are the types of storage devices that will be discussed in this chapter:

- *Hard drives*
- *CD-ROM players*
- *Magneto-optical drives*

Hard Drives

The hard drive is perhaps the most important storage device on your network. Great care and attention must be given to the hard drive because it is the core of the file server. The operating system that gives a network its functionality must reside on that core drive. If that core drive fails, the entire network will go down. A network administrator is responsible for developing a design for fault tolerance in protecting the core of the network. You also must be able to diagnose potential failure points and be proactive in preventative maintenance. An experienced network administrator must be able to do capacity planning and know how to react in a contingency management mode.

The terminology in the computer industry uses the term *fixed disk* to mean *hard disk*. The fixed disk or the *platters* are contained in the hard drive casing, as opposed to inserting a removable disk in the floppy drive (see fig. 34.1). The technology of a hard drive enables it to provide speed, reliability, and a lot of storage in a small space in one location.

The device that enables the communication between the hard drive and the CPU is called the *disk controller card.* The disk controller card can be built into the motherboard, as part of the drive or as a separate component. The controller interprets the commands from the CPU and sends the interpreted signals to either seek, read, or write data to the hard drive.

Warning The drive casing is sealed by the manufacturer in a dust- and moisture-free environment. Do not open this drive casing for any reason—dust particles can scratch your platters. They can become inoperable and you could lose valuable data.

The hard drive is made up of many components that work in unison and can be described as an electronic wonder. The drive contains a spindle motor that rotates the platters inside the drive casing. The voice coil actuator moves the read/write heads to the needed position on the disk platter. The time it takes for the read/write heads to find the correct track is called *seek time.*

After the track has been located, the amount of time it takes for the needed piece of data to rotate under the read/write head is called *drive latency.* The combination of seek time and drive latency (the total amount of time it takes to get to the data on the platter) is called *access time.* To "settle" a drive is the time it takes for the head to stabilize above the track after the process or the motion for seeking data has stopped.

The *data transfer rate* is the speed at which data is moved from the disk to the electronic "brains" of the CPU. The amount of data moved is measured in megabytes per second. All these timing features in a hard drive are important to how quickly data can be accessed on the network.

Note A cluster is the minimum unit of space for the storage of a file allocated by DOS. A block is the minimum unit of space (usually 4 KB) for the storage of file information by NetWare.

Types of Hard Drive Interfaces

There are several types of hard drive interfaces and encoding schemes used with these interfaces in the networking environment. As a network administrator or support engineer, you should become familiar with each type because of the varied install base that still exists. An early example of a type of

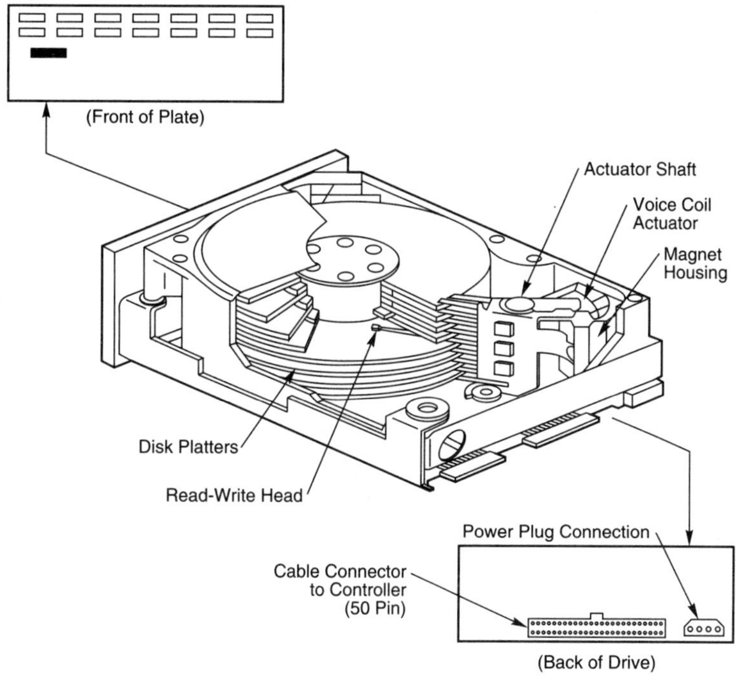

Figure 34.1
Internal components of a hard drive.

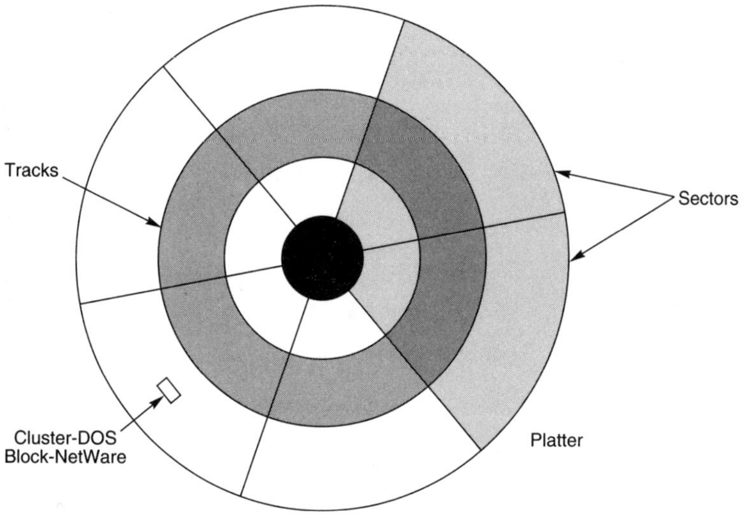

a hard drive is an ST-506 model manufactured by Seagate. The ST-506 originally was built for 5MB size drives. The *Run Length Limited* (RLL) or the *Modified Frequency Modulation* (MFM) encoding scheme is used for the larger ST-506 drives.

Note MFM is referred to as double-density recording and is used as a coding system to pack more information on hard disks. MFM is still used today on floppy disks and small hard drives.

RLL has increased data density capabilities over MFM by the way it manipulates electronic flux transitions. Fluxes are defined as the way the magnetic field handles the 0s and 1s of digital information. The RLL handles a higher data throughput over the MFM encoding scheme.

Integrated Drive Electronics (IDE) Drives

The Integrated Drive Electronics drive uses the mechanics of having the controller interface integrated with the electronic controls of the hard drive. The IDE terminology often is identified as an AT-type interface with the cable connector for the controller built into the CPU's motherboard. The IDE drive is a cost-effective solution that uses the RLL encoding scheme. Even though the IDE solution has widely replaced the ST-506 drives, there are some limitations on using IDE drives with NetWare:

- Unless a special nonstandard BIOS is used, there is a maximum drive capacity of 528MB.
- IDE does not support drive command overlapping, nor can it multitask I/O. If you are mixing IDE drives in a file server with other types of drives, the network operating system must wait for the IDE to complete any commands issued before the network operating system can issue any commands to any other drives.
- IDE does not support any optical or tape drives (the SCSI interface does).
- IDE does not support bus-mastering.

Note It is recommended that you never do a low-level format on an IDE drive. If you do this repair task, you could erase the manufacturer's bad block information that is written in a special format on the IDE drive.

Enhanced Small Device Interface (ESDI) Drives

The Enhanced Small Device Interface uses one cable for floppy control, one for hard drive control, and one for data. The ST-506 drive uses the same cabling system, but it is not interchangeable with the ESDI drive. The ESDI drive became more popular than the ST-506 because of its capability of having a higher performance level and using a larger storage capacity. The ESDI also can store information about bad tracks onto the disk, and the interface is designed to work with tape systems. The popularity of ESDI was fairly short-lived, however, and SCSI drive systems have replaced ESDI as the drives of choice on network servers.

Older ESDI drives are supported by the computer's BIOS. Newer drives that have 1,024 or more cylinders do not work well in older ESDI machines. Drives that have more than 1,023 cylinders and 33 sectors per track are not likely to be supported by DOS versions before v3.3. The controllers of XTs, ATs, and Western Digital WD1002 controllers cannot recognize the cylinder count above 1,023 in larger drives.

Note If you are using PS/2 CPUs as file servers (older ones came with ESDI drives) and early versions of NetWare, be careful in updating disk information with the reference disk after NetWare has been loaded. The older operating systems wrote the Cold Boot Loader to part of the track 0 on the ESDI drive.

When the reference disk updates drive information, it writes to track 0 and it will write on top of the cold boot loader. You will have to use your backup copy of the NET$OS.EXE file and boot from a floppy drive to get the server back up. If you want to boot from the hard drive again, you have to rebuild the file server from scratch.

Small Computer Systems Interface (SCSI) Drives

The Small Computer Systems Interface provides an expansion bus architecture that allows up to seven SCSI-type devices (hard drives, CD-ROM, tape units). These can all be the same tape device, be used in combination, or be only one device on one bus slot (see fig. 34.2). These devices are attached to the cable chain that is attached to the SCSI controller card installed in a server or a client.

The devices that are installed internally in the CPU use ribbon cables designed for SCSI. External devices attach by cables that are built with the appropriate connectors for each of the devices attached to the SCSI chain.

The SCSI arbitration scheme allows a faster data transfer rate among the devices attached to each bus slot chain. The advantage in using SCSI is that the CPU does not have to intervene with the processing on the chain in order for the SCSI devices to complete their operations. The SCSI controller has its own BIOS that will run in the upper memory area of the CPU. It also uses hardware port addresses, memory addresses, and DMA channels to ensure compatibility with other components in the CPU.

Each SCSI address can support a controller that provides access to one or two hard drives. An *advanced SCSI programming interface* (ASPI) device driver is provided by the manufacturer and is needed to coordinate communications between

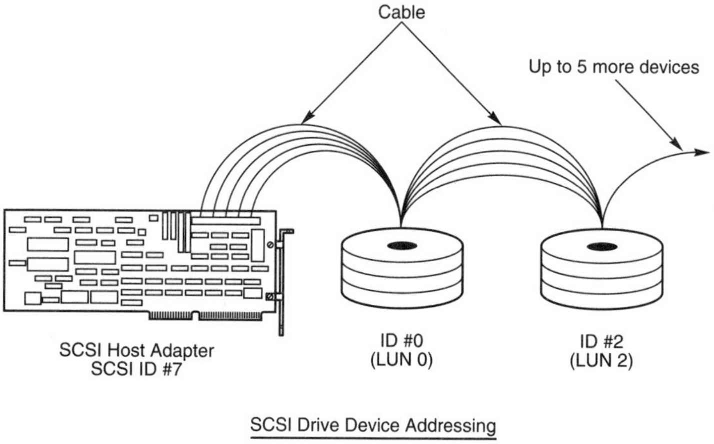

Figure 34.2
SCSI drive device addressing.

different types of devices. There are SCSI controllers that are available with connector ports for use with floppy disk drives. If you want to use the floppy controller already built into your CPU, you can disable the floppy controller on the SCSI board.

The SCSI bus must be terminated at both ends (see fig. 34.3). A SCSI device driver cannot interpret the difference between the original signals or returned signals as an Ethernet bus does. To prevent confusion caused by reflected signals, terminators are used to absorb or prevent signals from becoming unstable. Each SCSI device connected to this terminated bus must have a unique address. This unique address is called a *Logical Unit Number* (LUN).

The American National Standards Institute (ANSI) X3T9.2 committee sets the standards for the SCSI interface. The newest SCSI standard, SCSI-2, defines the protocols, hardware, and command set to run devices other than hard disks. The older SCSI standard could not reliably control the devices beyond the hard drive setup. It is not recommended that you mix SCSI-1 and SCSI-2 standards in the same host, unless the SCSI adapter provides a method of handling both standards. The ISA bus has a transfer data rate maximum of 2 MB per second, whereas the SCSI-2 can transfer data at 4 MB, and, during the FAST operation, can transfer data up to 10 MB per second. You should use the EISA, MCA, or PCI bus with the appropriate SCSI interface cards for the FAST SCSI-2 operation to work efficiently.

There is an implementation of SCSI called WIDE SCSI-2 that is not used as much as the FAST SCSI-2 standard, as WIDE SCSI-2 is fairly new. WIDE SCSI-2 uses a second data path that offers the capability of 20 MB per second data transfer rate. The WIDE SCSI-2 controller integrates the 68-pin SCSI cable and the differential signaling process. Standard SCSI devices use a 50-pin cable and the single-ended signaling process. There are SCSI host adapters that have a combination of connection slots for a SCSI internal bus with both 68-pin and 50-pin cables. These combination type adapters use either the differential or single-ended signaling process, but not both.

You cannot mix the differential and single-ended devices on the same SCSI bus—they are electronically incompatible. If you have both types of SCSI devices, use one adapter for WIDE SCSI using differential signaling, and another adapter that uses the single-ended devices. Future implementations for the WIDE SCSI devices will develop enhancements for using single-ended signaling.

Tips for Working with SCSI Devices

The use of SCSI devices is rapidly becoming an industry standard. These devices are flexible, affordable, and are relatively easy to install. As a network administrator or support engineer, you should use the following tips in setting up a SCSI environment:

- When selecting your hardware and software, make sure the revision levels are current and that each can work within the same bus with the other devices.
- Use all SCSI-2 devices when designing a network. Older SCSI-1 hard disks will mix with SCSI-2 equipment if you have to use available resources.
- Use SCSI host adapters that use a software setup for jumper and termination settings. Then you do not have to remove the card from the CPU each time you need to change the settings.

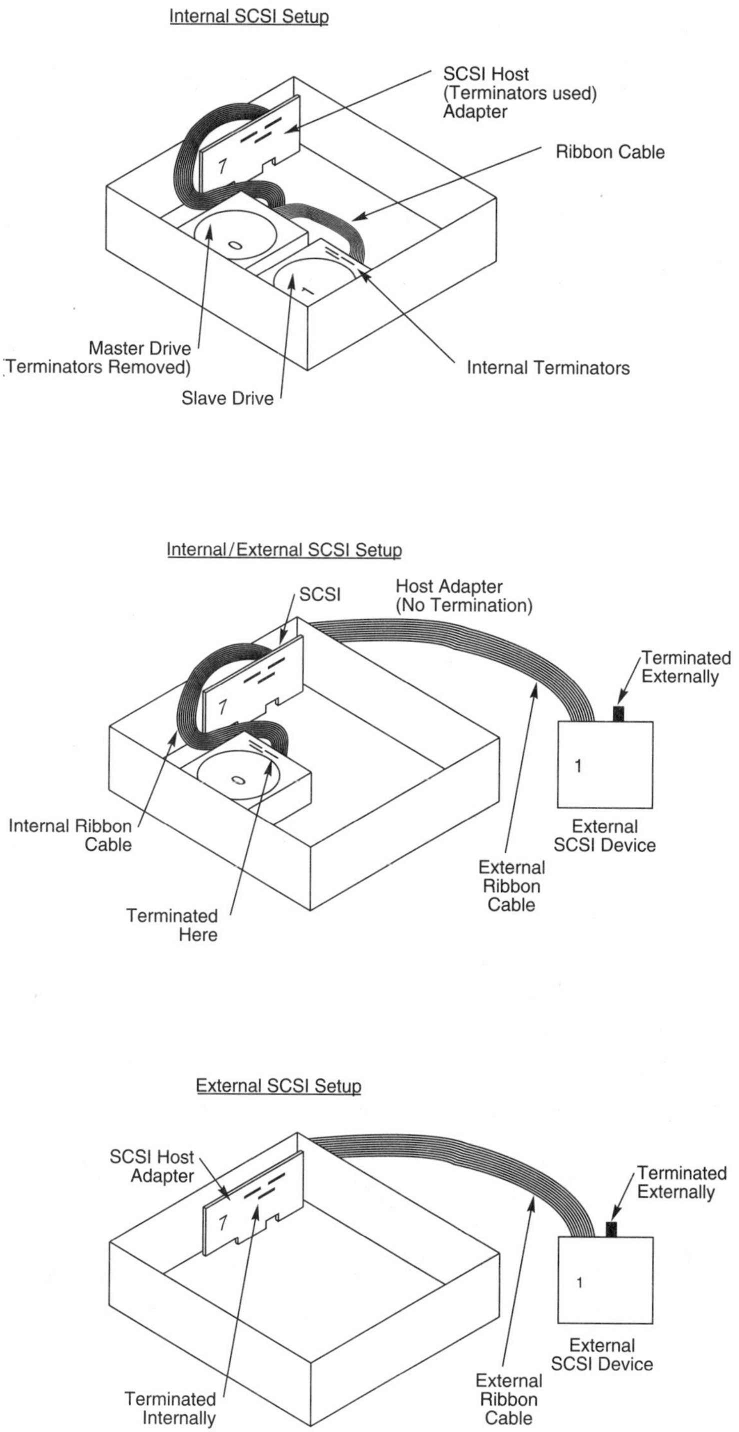

Figure 34.3
Termination of SCSI internal/external setups.

- Make sure that you use the proper pin number and connector size for the SCSI host adapter and the devices attached to complete the bus. Watch for cables with FAST SCSI-2 adapter connections attaching to the standard Centronics connector on the external SCSI devices. Unfortunately, the proper SCSI connector cables are not always shipped to meet the needs in your environment.
- Always confirm that each SCSI bus is properly terminated and that the cables are fitting snugly into the connector slots. The maximum length for a SCSI bus is 19 feet, 10 inches. Make sure that the external disk subsystems are using cables that match the proper impedance level.
- The SCSI bus requires a stable current for the signals to operate properly. Verify that your host adapter and other SCSI devices are supplying the necessary terminating power.
- Make sure your SCSI host adapter's BIOS, port address, IRQ, and DMA channel addresses do not conflict with other components in the CPU.
- Make sure that each SCSI device has a unique identifier number (LUN). Each SCSI adapter has a default address of 7 set by the manufacturer. The first bootable hard disk must have a SCSI LUN of 0. Other standard SCSI devices on the bus should be numbered 1-6 in the sequential order that the devices are located in the SCSI chain. Some Hewlett-Packard and IBM PS/2 CPUs use a SCSI adapter with an ID of 7 and the devices on the bus start at LUN 6; then each device is numbered sequentially downward to 0.
- It is best not to mix models of SCSI adapters if they are being used in the same computer. The ASPI software manager that is used by the adapter is written uniquely for that card. Mixing ASPI managers—even by the same manufacturer but different models—can cause operating conflicts.
- SCSI host adapters can coexist with other types of hard disks and their controllers. Still, it is best to keep device models consistent in the computer.

Note There are many third-party software utilities that can be used to determine what drive interface is used in a client or file server. Tools such as CHECKIT PRO, as shown in figure 34.4, can assist a network administrator in determining the needed details.

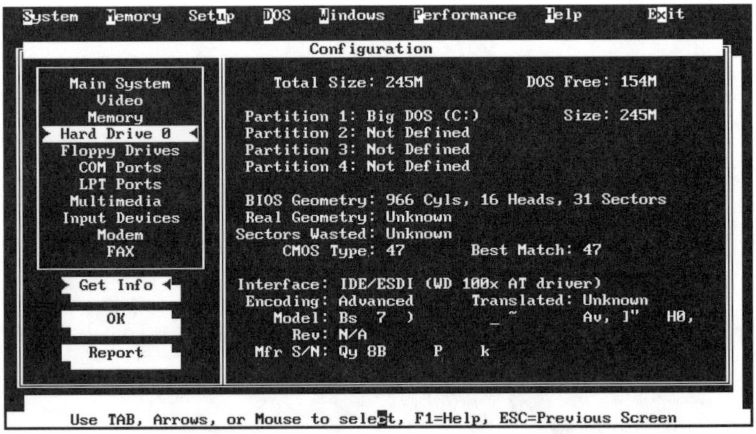

Figure 34.4 *CHECKIT PRO Hard Drive information screen example.*

Disk Coprocessor Boards (DCBs)

Disk Coprocessor Boards are controller cards that offload the I/O from the CPU onto the DCB's own coprocessor chip. This frees up the CPU's processor to assist in improving network performance. DCBs also are referred to as *Host Bus Adapters* (HBAs) in Novell literature.

A file server can handle up to four DCB channels. A *disk channel* is a DCB and its disk subsystems. Each DCB can handle a maximum of eight SCSI controllers, with each controller supporting up to two disk drives. SCSI external disk subsystems can be daisy-chained off the DCB port on the end of the card (see fig. 34.5). DCBs are developed for the ISA (AT bus), EISA, and Micro-channel architecture. Development of DCBs today is done by third-party vendors.

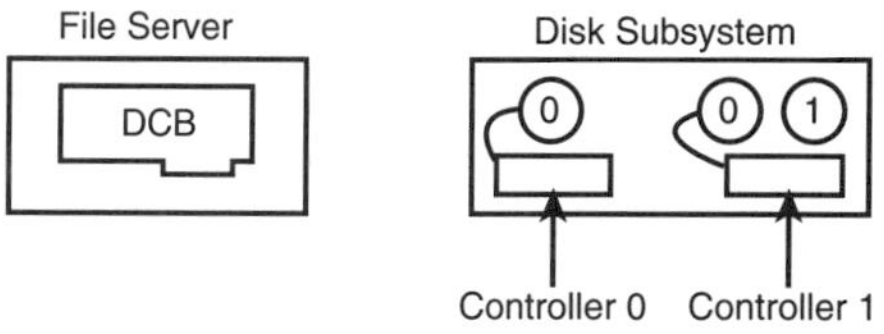

Figure 34.5
Disk Coprocessor Board configuration.

The original DCBs were developed by Novell and had an 80188 on-board processor. The DCB also served as a UPS monitor that could gracefully down a server in the event of a UPS "battery low" condition. DCBs also were used as a keycard for serialization of early versions of NetWare 2.*x*. The DISKSET utility is required for using Novell's DCBs to send disk and drive configuration information to the EEPROM on the DCB. Any physical adds or deletions to the controller or disk drive setup required the use of DISKSET. Current DCBs by third parties use the utilities provided by the vendor. Most extended channel disk subsystems or internal multiple drives today use internal SCSI cards in the file server instead of DCBs.

Although the DCB was at one time the preferred method for constructing high-performance disk storage systems, many current SCSI controllers offer much higher performance.

- A file server can handle up to 4 DCB channels.
- A disk channel consists of a DCB and the disk subsystems that attach to it.
- Each DCB can handle a maximum of eight SCSI controllers.

Proper integration of hardware components in a network is integral for efficient LAN performance. Verification from vendors and Novell Technical Support can help in your network planning. You must pay attention to potential conflicts for interrupts, memory addresses, and node addresses. Cabling limitations, hard drive requirements, addressing and termination, and certified software drivers also must be considered. If you do the proper homework and planning, you will reduce the chances of cost overruns and unplanned down time.

Setting Up Hard Drives

The hard disk is the most important device in a file server for storing both data and the applications that provide the glue for the network to function. The speed, the capacity, and the reliability of the hard disk can make or break your everyday operations (and maybe your sanity!). Understanding the hard disk, using the proper setup features, and performing proactive maintenance is an important function of a network administrator.

Working with Jumpers on the Hard Drive

When the hard drive arrives from the manufacturer and is unpacked from the box, all the jumpers on the drive are set at default options. These settings may or may not work in your computer. As a network administrator or support engineer, you must confirm that the settings on the drive will work for the interface type and encoding scheme required for that computer. Depending on your drive type, the following jumpers might need to be set directly on the drive:

- **ACT.** Set primarily on IDE and SCSI drives, and lights an external LED to indicate that the drive is active.
- **Drive Select.** Used primarily by ESDI, MFM, and RLL drives, depending on the number of drives and if you are using a flat or twisted cable.
- **C/D or DS.** Used by IDE to determine if the drive is to be a C or a D drive.
- **SCSI Address.** A unique address set by three jumpers that define a binary number. The manufacturer sets this address at 0. Check your drive documentation for all SCSI drives—this setting can vary with different vendors.
- **DSP.** Used by IDE to designate when a cable is being shared or which one of the drives is the master drive.

The controller card (if used by the drive) might need to have the following jumpers set:

- **Controller Interrupt.** You also might need to establish this setting in the STARTUP.NCF file on your file server when the DSK file is loading. Usually, this setting is made by the manufacturer and should be left at this default setting.
- **Base I/O.** This should not conflict with any other device in the computer. This is set as a default from the manufacturer and rarely is changed unless there is a conflict.
- **DMA Channel.** NetWare does not recommend sharing a DMA channel between two devices. There are some ESDI and SCSI controllers that may need to have this setting verified.
- **Base BIOS Address.** Some controller cards use ROM BIOS and may need to have this set. Addresses over E000h may not be supported by some motherboards. Conflicts may arise with this setting and network interface cards or VGA cards.

Types of Cables Used with Hard Drives

The cable setup is important; it should be installed so that the pins in the connectors on the cable can receive and transmit the proper signals for data transfer. As a network administrator or support engineer, you must be aware of different cable types and proper installation of these cables. Improper installation can cause the loss of data and the potential destruction of drive components. Use the following recommendations when working with drive cables:

- Make sure that the colored stripe (usually red) is attached to Pin 1 on the controller card and to the hard drive (see figure 34.6).
- In an AT standard computer, the floppy and hard drive cables have different twists and cannot be interchanged.

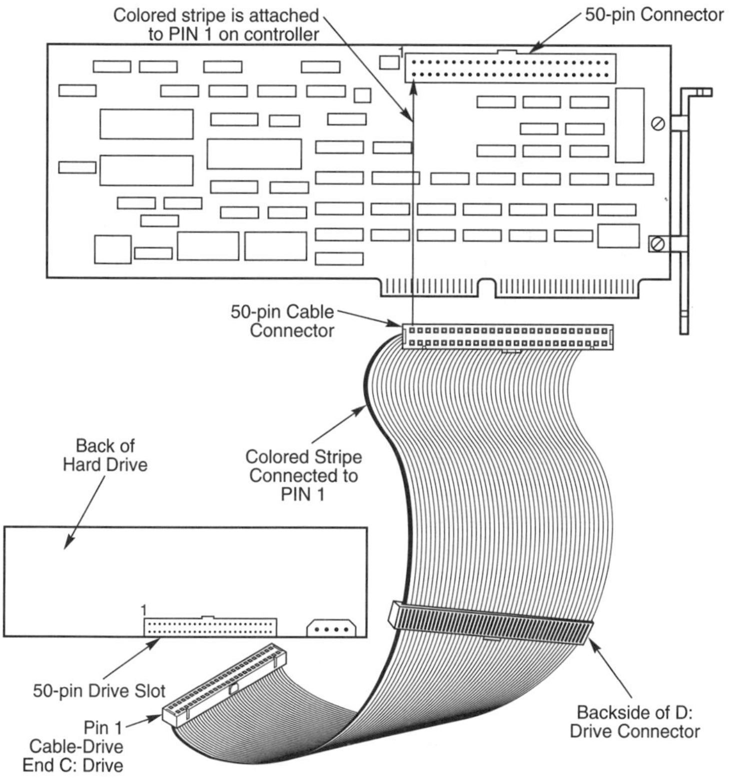

Figure 34.6
Proper connection of Pin 1 between a hard drive and a disk controller card.

Practical TIP MFM and RLL hard drive cables have five twisted lines, and a floppy cable has seven twisted lines.

Floppy cables have the twists in the lower pin numbers.

- Small-numbered wires: twisted, smaller drive (that is, floppy disk drive).
- High-numbered wires: twisted, larger drive (that is, hard drive).

- A SCSI cable may have 25 or 50 pins on the connector, and the bus it is attached to must have exactly two terminated ends. Terminators may be found near the connector slot on the SCSI device in packs of three resistors.
- An IDE cable must not be longer than 18 inches, and it uses a 40-pin cable.
- You need three cables to connect two RLL or MFM drives to one controller: two data cables and one control cable. The control cable regulates the way the disk functions. If you are using two drives, remove the terminator that is on the drive in the middle of the chain (see fig. 34.7).

Figure 34.7
Types of drive cables.

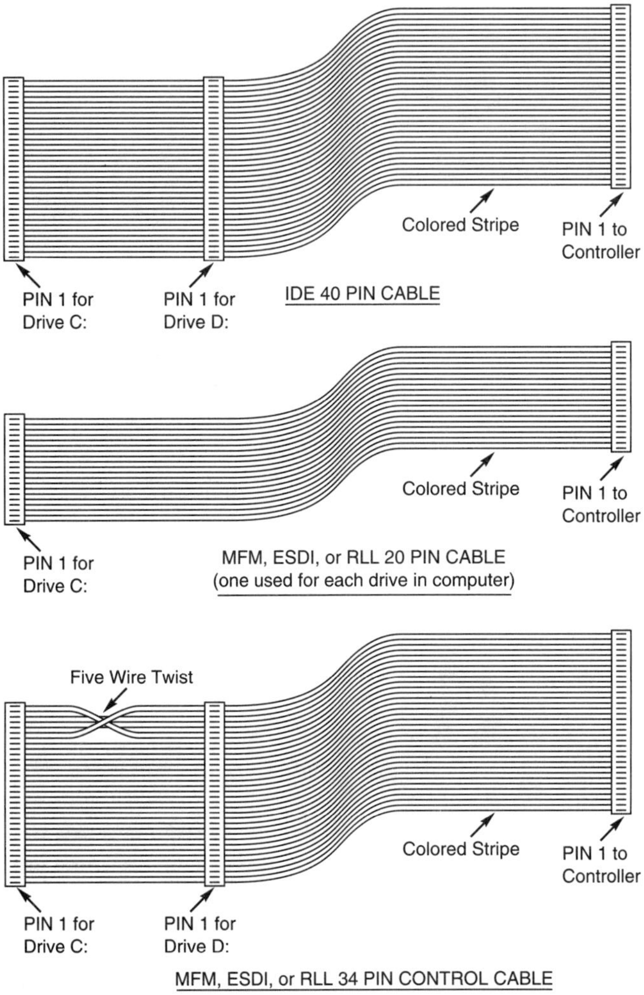

Formatting the Hard Drive

Physical installation of a hard drive into a computer, setting the jumpers, and connecting the cables are the initial necessary tasks in preparing the drive for network use. When you receive a new hard drive or are reusing an existing drive, you must prepare these drives in the required format so that data can be stored on them.

There are four important steps in preparing a hard drive to operate as it is designed:

1. Low-level formatting
2. Entering CMOS setup information
3. Establishing partitions
4. Performing a high-level DOS format

Low-Level Formatting

Low-level formatting usually is done by the manufacturer of the drive at the factory. It is a destructive process and should only be done as the last resort in attempting to repair a drive. A low-level format is the process of defining sectors and the bad spots on the hard drive. Sectors provide the marking points (or indexes such as in a phone book) where information can be read, retrieved, or written.

There are third-party programs such as CKLLFMT in the CheckIt PRO software package. Some versions of DOS or the advanced drive diagnostics disk for the drive include low-level format utilities. You should check with the manufacturer of your drive for the proper procedure and program to do a low-level format.

A low-level format not only establishes sector IDs, it marks off bad sectors, tests the disks by performing a surface analysis, temporarily fills each sector, and sets the interleave ratio entered. Besides using a low-level format to give a new hard drive the directions on getting started, a low-level format can be done to remark the sectors of a drive that have been previously used, make an attempt at repairing a drive that is exhibiting a large number of errors, or change the interleave ratio.

Practical TIP If for some reason you have to low-level format a drive, make sure you format the drive in the same temperature and in the same position it will be used—flat or sideways. The temperature and gravity environment are very important to disk drives.

Setting the Interleave Ratio

Establishing the interleave ratio helps the drive to manage the flow of information between the computer and the disk better. Setting the interleave factor is not as necessary a concern for newer drives. Older drives used to be faster than what the CPU's microprocessor could handle; therefore, the interleave factor was developed to slow the drive down but still make it functional. The interleave ratio can help prevent bottlenecks if it is set properly.

Note Technology has enabled newer drives to set sector sparring, which is similar to NetWare's hot fix. This new feature will reserve one sector on every track for the remapping of bad sectors. This reduces the capacity of your new drive and should only be used if there are a lot of problems with the drive.

The physical sector arrangement and the logical arrangement of how the sectors are numbered in a track determines the interleave ratio (see fig. 34.8). An interleave factor is chosen by setting a ratio for the computer to use in determining how it is to read disk information. A ratio is defined as the length of a sector and the distance between two logical sectors. One sector is used as the starting point for measuring the length of an interleave. Setting an interleave factor too low or high can impede performance.

Practical TIP IDE drives use cache and really have no need for an interleave setting. Some SCSI drives and all MFM encoded drives can manage interleave ratios. The following interleave ratios are recommended:

continues

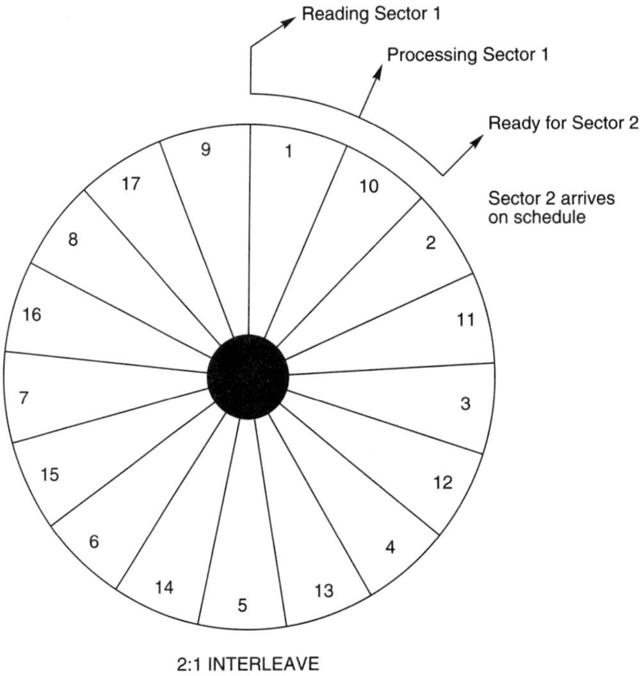

Figure 34.8
Sector reading by a hard drive set at a 2:1 interleave ratio.

- 1:1 for machines running NetWare that are 10 Mhz or faster, using 286 or 386 system boards. DOS machines at 20 Mhz or faster using 286 or 386 motherboards use this interleave. All 486 machines use 1:1.
- 2:1 for machines running DOS that are 10–16 Mhz and are using 286 or 386 motherboards.
- 3:1 for 6–8 Mhz AT class computers and for XT type machines running DOS applications.
- 4:1 for all 4.77 Mhz XT class machines.

Establishing Partitions

The hard drive must be partitioned after a low-level format has been completed. Modern drives that are new out of the box are already low-level formatted and ready to be partitioned. The operating system must be compatible with the format of the logical structure of the hard disk. The logical structure is set up with a DOS program called FDISK (see fig. 34.9). FDISK sets the partitions needed on a hard drive.

Note For NetWare 3.*x* and above file servers, a DOS partition of only 10 MB is recommended. DOS must be installed in a Primary DOS partition, which must be configured as the drive's Active partition. This can be done with an FDISK program.

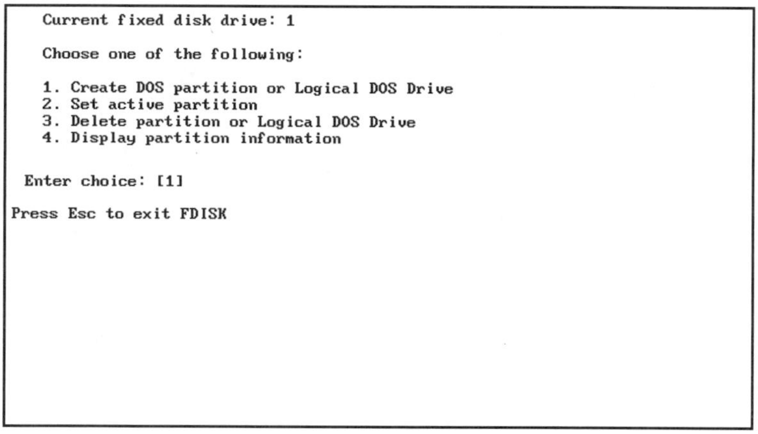

```
   Current fixed disk drive: 1

   Choose one of the following:

   1. Create DOS partition or Logical DOS Drive
   2. Set active partition
   3. Delete partition or Logical DOS Drive
   4. Display partition information

 Enter choice: [1]

Press Esc to exit FDISK
```

Figure 34.9
Opening screen using an FDISK program to partition hard drives.

The DOS operating system recognizes the rest of the NetWare-ready hard drive as a non-DOS partition. After the NetWare operating system is loaded, NetWare identifies the DOS partition as *Physical partition #0* and the NetWare partition as *Physical partition #1.*

Practical TIP The low-level format utility that is shipped with a SCSI drive is the best program to use if you need to perform the low-level format process. Generic-type low-level format utilities usually will not work with the SCSI drives.

Entering CMOS Setup Information

The *Complementary Metal-Oxide Semiconductor* (CMOS) is a battery-operated chip that is found on the motherboard of the computer. The CMOS chip is an important microprocessor found primarily in the newer generation of personal computers. This chip is important to the operation of the computer because it is responsible for telling the electronics of the PC what is contained in the CPU and the location of these components in the scheme of being able to operate together. The CMOS chip provides the electronic current management for the positive and negative electrons that provide the flow of electrical signals to the components.

Practical TIP If your computer shows unexplained erratic behavior or is losing the date or time, replace the battery with a new one that meets the same voltage requirements. This voltage number is printed or stamped on the battery.

The CMOS must be told what type of components the computer has and where they are located. The information about the hard drive is an important setup requirement in CMOS. You can get to CMOS with most computers during the power-up process by pressing Ctrl+Alt+Esc. You also can view CMOS information through third-party utilities such as CheckIt PRO, as shown in figure 34.10. The CMOS setup characteristics require the TYPE number of the drive, which is found marked on the drive or in the manufacturer's documentation. The type information includes the number of cylinders, heads, sectors, and the size of the hard drive. If the drive requires write precompensation information, the CMOS asks for this detail also.

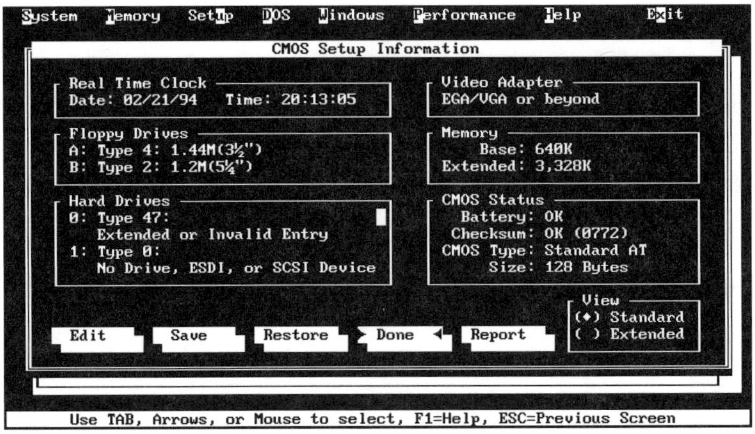

Figure 34.10
CMOS Setup Information found by CHECKIT PRO.

The drive you install does not have to match one of the CMOS drive types perfectly. IBM's CMOS Type 1 is used for most ESDI drives. The Type 1 represents a 10 MB drive, and at power-up the BIOS from the ESDI controller card overwrites this information to what is needed for ESDI operations. SCSI drives use the Type 0 or Not Installed parameter. The MicroHouse Technical Library has an extensive listing of drive types from which to find a type that closely represents your drive. Choose a type that has the cylinder count that is equal to or less than the number of cylinders available on your drive. Do not use a type that exceeds the megabyte size or the number of heads on your physical drive.

Note Write precompensation is used primarily by older drives. This process manages the timing of retrieval of information from the platters as the sectors get closer together toward the center of the drive. The magnetic field that is passed to the read/write heads on a hard drive is made stronger to handle the changes in the geometric division of the drive as the read/write heads move to the center of the disk. As a default, write precompensation is determined by taking the maximum number of cylinders on that individual drive and dividing that number by two.

High-Level DOS Format

The fourth part in setting up a hard drive is performing a high-level format. The DOS program FORMAT accomplishes this task on a new or used drive. The high-level format can be used to erase all the files in an entire DOS partition.

For a file server to have a bootable partition, you must format the primary DOS partition with the following command:

```
FORMAT /S
```

The /S parameter places the hidden DOS system information files and the COMMAND.COM in the DOS partition. The format process also accomplishes the following tasks:

- Creates a blank root directory (except when using the /S parameter)
- Creates a DOS boot sector and a DOS *file allocation table* (FAT)
- Scans the disk and notes the bad sectors

It is a benefit to have a DOS bootable partition on a NetWare 3.*x* and above file server. The server boots up faster from the hard disk. You can set the necessary statements to remotely reboot a server. You also can load a communication package on the DOS partition, down the server, then have an on-site person set the server as a host. Then you could dial in to copy updated files, such as DSK or NLM drivers, or maybe run CheckIt PRO to investigate server details.

Before you format a used drive that already contains data, make sure you back up all the files you need to protect. Low-level formats never allow the data to be recovered by an unformatted utility. There are some third-party utilities that can recover high-level formats, provided the hard drive has not been written to since the format was performed. Professional data recovery services such as On-Track can assist in recovering data from a destroyed drive. As a network administrator or support engineer, you should be aware that most disks have bad sectors—don't panic if you see a few. A manufacturer considers a hard drive to be acceptable to be shipped if the bad sectors are less than 1 percent of the total size of the drive.

NetWare Drive Information

NetWare calculates a unique device code for each device on the bus or for each hard drive. System error messages use this code to display failure messages. As an example, the device code 20010 refers to the first drive (0) on the second controller (1) on the first host bus adapter (0) on the first instance the ISADISK.DSK driver (20) is found. NetWare uses the ISADISK device driver for ST-506 drives using RLL or MFM encoding schemes. These types of drives have the disk controller and the host bus adapter on the same physical drive. The controller digit found in the device code always is zero. The IDE type drives can use the ISADISK.DSK file or preferably the IDE.DSK device drivers. The SCSI drivers are provided by the manufacturer of the host adapter card. The device code for SCSI is always set to 0.

Practical TIP

The device drivers that come in the core package of a new 3.11 operating system box are slightly outdated. Although they are operational, enhanced ISADISK and IDE drivers are available on NetWire or on NSEPRO.

When a 3.*x* server is setting up the operating system, it establishes the hot fix redirection area first. NetWare considers the location from the beginning of the NetWare data area to the end of the NetWare data area as a *logical partition.* A NetWare logical partition holds the NetWare operating system files and the data that is loaded to be accessed by the network users. Each logical partition has its own identifying number. A NetWare logical partition can be made up of more than one physical partition, contiguous with a physical partition, or be made as part of a physical partition. NetWare uses physical partition numbers for housekeeping tasks performed by the operating system. Logical partition numbers are used for mirrored drive designation.

After you set up NetWare partitions through the INSTALL.NLM, you also must establish volume information. NetWare 3.*x* (20) enables volumes to be spanned across multiple hard drives. Volume segments are made up of the same volume information on different hard disks. There can be up to 8 segments on a hard drive and 32 segments per volume. Performance can be improved by spanning volumes. The disadvantage to spanning is that the loss of one drive and its partial volume segment can cause the loss of access to the entire volume. RAID, mirroring, or duplexing can help prevent the loss of an entire volume from happening.

Working with RAID Drives

The network environment of today has evolved from having only a file server, a printer, and a few client stations, to having large enterprise designs requiring unlimited availability. The critical nature of data accessibility requires that network administrators or support engineers provide the best storage and recovery solutions as cost effectively as possible. The reliability of the network is not required for just the file server, but for the client also. The early history of the computer environment lacked the flexibility of the PC world, and the critical data needed was kept on a mainframe machine. Data manipulation on a mainframe requires many lines of code and cooperation from several differently skilled computer technicians. With the flexibility of the PC environment, extra precautions must be made in protecting against human or mechanical error.

The *Redundant Array of Inexpensive Drives* (RAID) can work with NetWare's *System Fault Tolerance* (SFT) features to protect data in a network environment. The use of RAID enables you to set up the best disk array design to protect your system. RAID is defined in detail as the architecture of combining two or more disks to create a large virtual disk structure to develop a source for redundancy of data. In a disk array, the drives are coordinated into different levels of RAID to which the controller card distributes the data as it is designed to do.

RAID uses a format of splitting data among drives at the bit, byte, or block level. The term *data striping* refers to the capability of arranging data in different sequences across drives. An example demonstration of this data splitting is shown in figure 34.11.

Your input in designing the most reliable drive setup for your network is an important responsibility. You must choose the best RAID implementation level that will meet your users' requirements in data integrity and cost. There are seven levels of RAID available on the market today. The numbers that represent RAID levels are 0, 1, 2, 3, 4, 5, and 10. A higher number does not necessarily mean that it is a better choice than the lower number. You must select the best for your environment. The following paragraphs present a brief discussion of each of the seven available levels.

RAID 0

Level 0 uses data striping and block interleaving. This level distributes the data block-by-block across the disk array in the same location across each drive. Data can be read or written to these same sectors from either drive, improving performance. The failure of a single drive can bring down the system. Redundancy of data is not provided.

RAID 1

Drives are paired or mirrored with each byte of information being written to each identical drive. You can duplex these devices by adding a separate host adapter for each drive. Mirroring provides a better performance benefit than that of RAID 0. If one drive in the pair fails, the other drive can continue to operate. This level can get expensive with the cost of drives to meet your needs for capacity. You will need to make sure your power source has enough wattage to handle the additional devices.

RAID 2

This level uses data striping with bit interleave. This means that data is written across each drive in succession, one bit at a time. Faulty bits are isolated

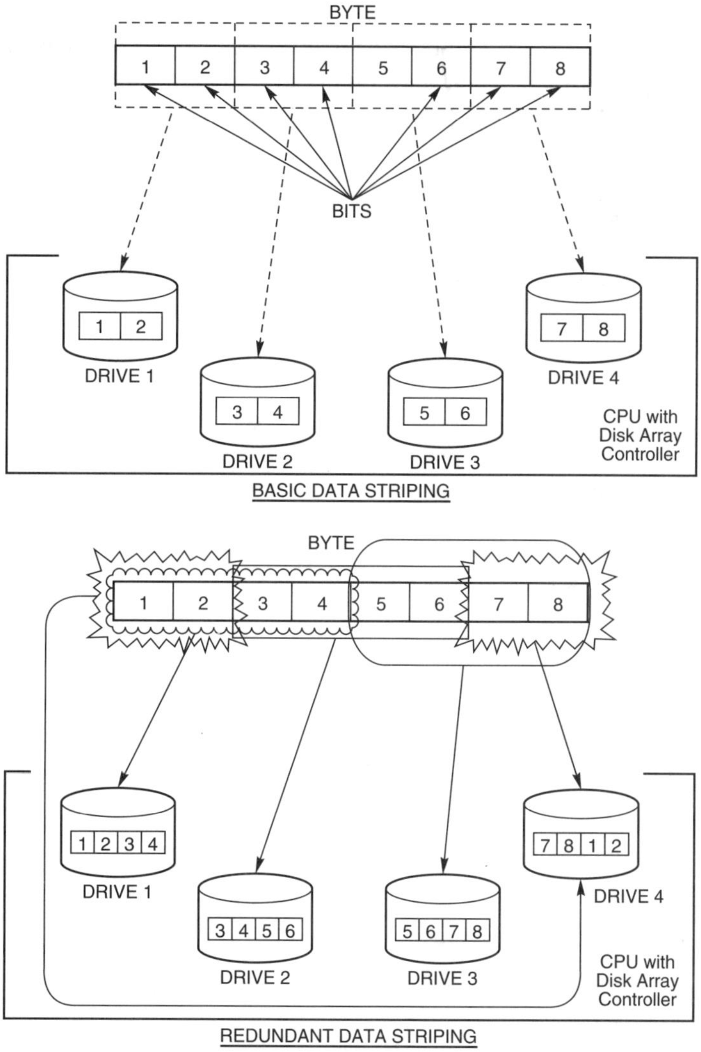

Figure 34.11
Examples of data striping.

by using checksum-capable drives. This level does not require total data redundancy. RAID 2 drives are transmitting in a parallel mode, enabling a faster data transfer rate. The write mode can be slower because each drive is working on every write attempt. The data used for checksum information is redundant. This level is not effective or cost-efficient for use in personal computers.

RAID 3

This level uses bit interleave data striping with parity checking capabilities. Data striping is done across the drives, one byte at a time. There usually are four or five drives at this level, with one drive dedicated for parity information to ensure the integrity of the data. RAID 3 has a very high data transfer rate and can handle long data transfers. This level is more reliable than RAID 2. Parity maintenance can be an overhead problem and cause the write performance to slow because the parity drive must be accessed for every write. There also could be major system problems if any two drives fail. The failure of a single drive will not affect the availability of data; the array controller will use the parity drive to reconstruct the contents of the failed disk. RAID 3 is not ideal for NetWare 3.*x*. As a default, NetWare accesses data in 4 KB blocks, which is not considered a long transfer rate.

RAID 4

This level uses block interleave data striping with parity checking. This means that this level uses a single parity drive, as does RAID 3, and uses block data striping, as does RAID 0. The drives in this RAID level function individually, with an individual drive reading a block of data. The combination of multiple drives has the ability to do multiple simultaneous reads. The block-level striping process is more efficient than RAID 3 byte-level striping. The downfalls of this level are the same as RAID 3, with the addition of the parity drive not being used to store data. If the array controller fails, the entire array cannot function.

RAID 5

This level uses block interleaved data striping with distributed check-data on all drives in the array. RAID 5 is efficient in handling small blocks and has quicker transfer rates because reads and writes can happen in parallel mode. The capability of virtual redundancy at an inexpensive cost is a benefit of RAID 5. This level is not as fast as RAID 0 or RAID 1 because it distributes parity information across all drives. Large file transfers are done in blocks and can be slower than RAID 3, which uses parallel bytes. RAID 5 efficiency goes up as the number of disks in the array increases. You can use hot spares mounted in the array cabinet. These extra drives can be picked up by the array automatically, replacing the failed drive. The data will be rebuilt to the added drive to function in sequence with the rest of the array as if nothing happened. This failed drive can then be replaced on the fly.

RAID 10

This level is defined as data that is duplicated across two identical RAID 0 arrays or hard disk drives. All data that is contained on a physical drive in one array is mirrored on a drive in the second array. RAID 10 uses the similar concept that NetWare's SFT III mirrored file servers use.

When you are choosing RAID for the customer, consider the following factors to make the best selection:

- The importance of the applications and data to the cost of downtime and lost business
- The number of users and the amount of drive capacity needed
- The size of the data blocks and whether they require direct or sequential access on the drives
- The proportion of reads to writes to the I/O activity, and the maximum transfer rate needed

There are many vendors that offer RAID solutions. Some examples of these vendors include AST, Compaq, Dell, IBM, and Storage Dimensions. Dell Computer offers a reliable high-end file server that uses RAID 10, PCI bus architecture, a Pentium processor, and FAST SCSI-2 host adapters. This combination can be used for the mission-critical environment using NetWare.

Understanding Disk Mirroring and Disk Duplexing

Disk mirroring and disk duplexing are two important system fault tolerance features added in SFT II to protect information in the event of hardware failure.

Disk Mirroring

Disk mirroring is defined as two hard drives—one primary and one secondary—using the same disk channel (controller cards and cable). The process is illustrated in figure 34.12. Disk mirroring is most commonly configured using disk drives contained in the server. You soon see that duplexing enables you to configure a more robust hardware environment.

All changes to the primary disk are duplicated on the secondary so that the secondary is a mirror image of the primary. In the event that the primary drive fails, users can access data on the secondary drive as if nothing happened. Disk mirroring can be done internally in a file server if enough drive and card slots are available. A DCB can be used to provide access to an external disk subsystem. Disk drives must be the same logical size, terminated properly, and addressed correctly.

Disk Duplexing

In the event of a disk channel failure (controller card or cable), access to all data on the channel is stopped. A message is displayed on the file server console screen (if your users do not let you know about it first). Even though drives can be mirrored, if they are connected to the same disk controller, all disk activity on the mirrored pair ceases.

Disk duplexing performs the function of simultaneously writing data to disks located on different channels. As figure 34.13 illustrates, each hard disk in a duplexed pair is connected to a separate hard disk controller. This figure shows a configuration in which the drives are housed in separate disk subsystems. Each subsystem has a separate power supply. This is a more reliable setup than is possible with mirroring, because a failure of one disk drive power supply does not disable the server, which continues to work with the system that remains under power.

A duplex configuration has two disk channels. In this example, each channel has two disks. NetWare identifies the drives by their channel and drive numbers, as shown in figure 34.13.

Duplexing enables NetWare to perform split seeks, in which NetWare seeks with both drives of a duplexed pair and retrieves data from the first drive on which the data is found. Split seeks are a distinct advantage of duplexing when compared to mirroring and can significantly improve a server's file access time.

Working on the same channel is analogous to going to a baseball game when only one gate is open to the stadium. You can enter or exit through only one gate (channel) at the stadium (file server), and the crowd (data) can get backed up on both sides. If more than one gate (another channel) is open, the crowd (data) does not get backed up on both sides of the fence (file server or workstation).

Note Duplexing protects information at the hardware level with duplicate channels (controller cards and cables) and duplicate hard drives (refer to fig. 34.12).

continues

Mirroring uses one controller card and two hard drives (refer to fig. 34.13). The point of failure for this setup is primarily the controller card or the cable connecting the drives to the controller card. Disk duplexing uses two controller cards and a minimum of one drive per controller card. The point of contention for failure is reduced with duplicate hardware.

Figure 34.12
How disk duplexing works.

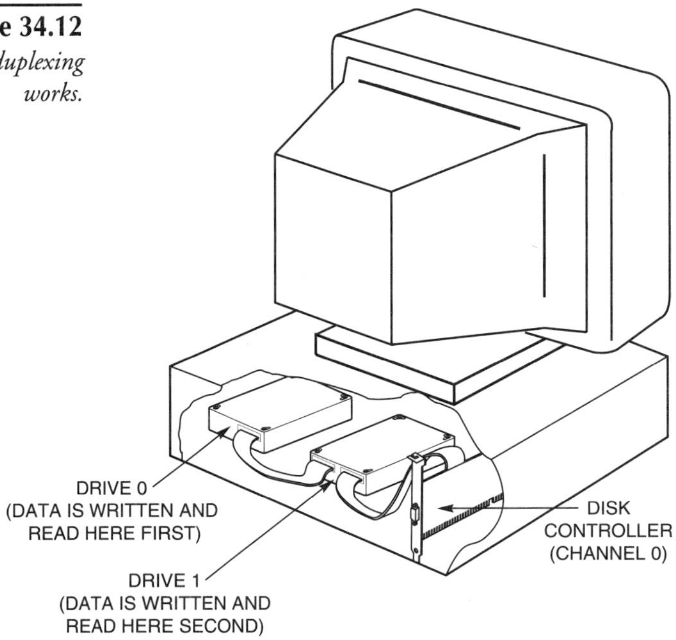

Disk Mirroring or Duplexing in Version 3.*x*

Use the INSTALL.NLM to mirror or duplex in 3.*x*. The following example is done on a network drive after the original operating system installation was completed. The following steps must be completed to install a disk pair as mirrored or duplexed:

1. Install the hardware components with the correct termination and hardware addresses. Document the model of the controller card and drives.
2. Bring the server up and at the file server console (or through RCONSOLE) load the

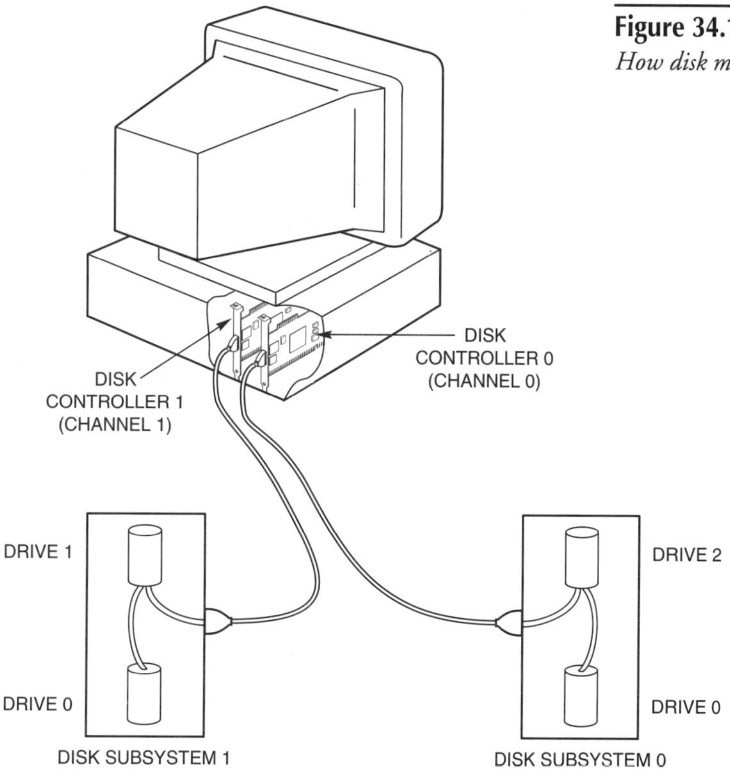

Figure 34.13
How disk mirroring works.

INSTALL.NLM. From the Installation Options menu, select Disk Options. The screen shown in figure 34.14 displays the Available Disk Options menu.

3. Select Mirroring and press Enter. The Partition Mirroring Status screen appears as shown in figure 34.15. This screen contains the status of all the drives in the 3.*x* file server to be edited. Select the drive designated as Logical Partition #1 to be the primary drive and press Enter.

4. The screen displays the Mirrored NetWare Partitions menu as shown in figure 34.16. Press Insert to add another partition to the Mirrored NetWare Partitions screen. The menu screen shown in figure 34.17 then displays the Available Partitions from which to choose.

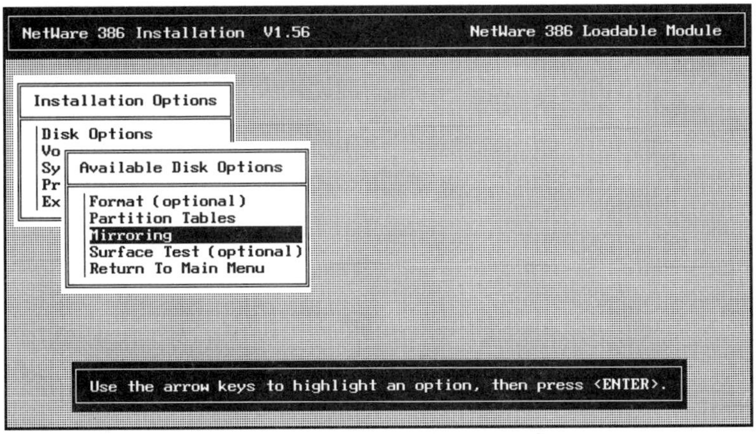

Figure 34.14
The Available Disk Options menu in INSTALL.

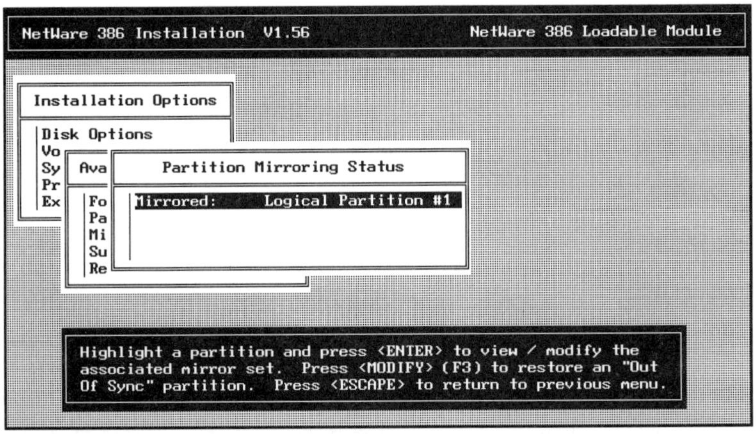

Figure 34.15
The Partition Mirroring Status display in INSTALL.

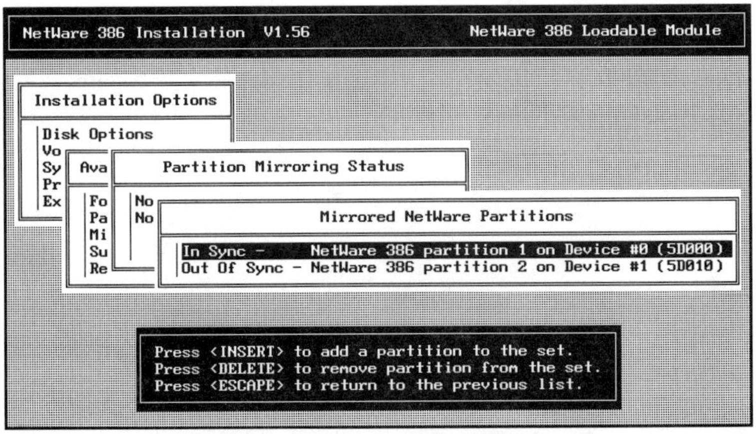

Figure 34.16
The Mirrored NetWare Partitions display in INSTALL.

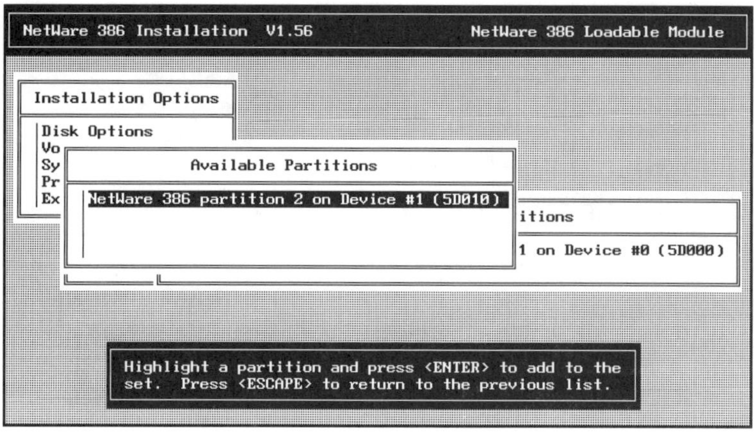

Figure 34.17
Display of partitions available for assignment as mirrors.

Highlight an available partition and press Enter. The Device numbers come from the addressing and termination of the SCSI drive installation.

5. The Mirrored NetWare Partitions screen menu (see fig. 34.18) displays the In Sync status of the primary mirrored partition. In Sync means that the designated partition is unmirrored and has no data problems. The Partition 2 shows an Out Of Sync status. Within ten seconds, the Partition 2 drive begins synchronizing with Partition 1.

   To check the status of the remirroring process, press Alt+Esc to get to the colon prompt. The message Remirroring partition # appears, indicating that the process has begun.

   The synchronization process takes several minutes, depending on the size of the drive being mirrored.

6. The Partition Mirroring Status menu screen (see fig. 34.19) then shows confirmation of the logical partition as being mirrored when the synchronization process from step 5 is completed. The partitions are now mirrored and in operation.

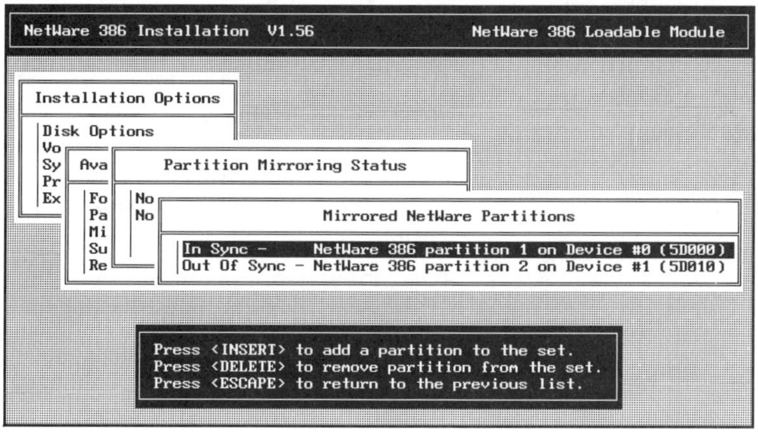

Figure 34.18
The Mirrored NetWare Partitions box displaying information about an out-of-sync mirrored pair.

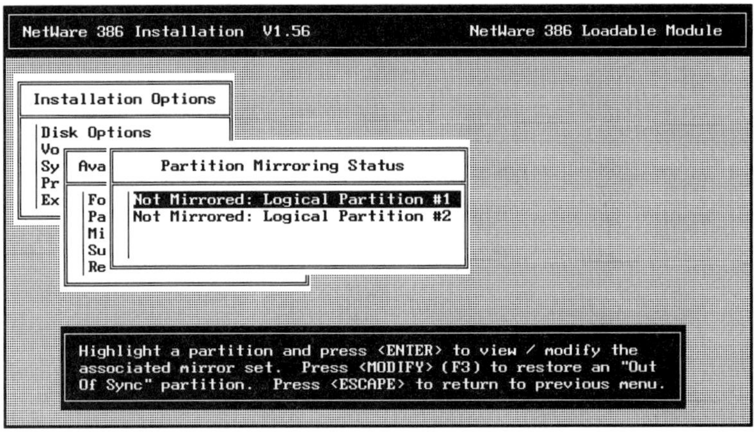

Figure 34.19
Mirrored drives in process of synchronization.

Press Esc until you exit from the INSTALL.NLM. You now can continue to do normal processing.

Note The mirroring process should be performed during nonproduction hours, and all user logins should be disabled.

Tips for Working with Mirrored/ Duplexed Drives

As a network administrator or support engineer, you must plan appropriately the use of mirrored/ duplexed drives in your file server. Improper setup or lack of monitoring these types of hard drive setups can cause loss of data and destruction of hardware. As part of your maintenance process, use the following recommendations in your planning design:

- Mirroring and duplexing should not take the place of backups—keep doing them on a regular basis.
- Always load the disk drivers in the same order—the internal controllers should be loaded first, in the order they are to be addressed.
- NetWare does not differentiate between mirroring or duplexing in its system messages.
- Periodically check the status of your mirrored or duplexed drives to see if they are still "in synch." Check the physical and the logical window using the INSTALL.NLM on the file server.
- As part of your network documentation, keep a record of the device codes of your hard drives. This could help you troubleshoot the load order of your disk drivers using system messages.
- IDE drives should not be used as duplexed drives because of how the built-in controllers piggyback each other in a master/slave relationship. If the primary drive goes down, the second drive will also. Exceptions to this rule are the use of a motherboard that has dual IDE ports or the use of paddle boards.

Working with CD-ROM Drives

CD-ROM players can enhance your network environment by adding flexibility to your resources for multitudes of information. You can have a CD-ROM player attached as a device on your SCSI bus that is connected to your file server. A CD-ROM drive can be found that has multiple drive bays, with each bay recognized as a volume on the server. For 3.1*x*, software packages such as SCSI-Express and Corel SCSI can do this volume setup. NetWare 3.12 has a CDROM.NLM that enables the CD-ROM to be seen as a built-in volume. The client can use a locally attached CD-ROM player with the proper MSCDEX driver extensions and parameters loaded in the CONFIG.SYS and AUTOEXEC.BAT files. The CD-ROM unit in the NetWare environment must be ISO-9660-compliant.

The following are the advantages of a CD-ROM player in a networked environment:

- The file formats are standardized and can be accessed easily.
- There is access to more volumes of information. Keyword searches on some applications increase data resources in one setting.
- Media is lightweight, can be stored easily, and costs for duplication are low.

The following are the disadvantages of a CD-ROM player:

- CD-ROM players can get expensive, but continually are coming down in price.
- CD-ROM players are slower than hard disks. Modern hard drives are 20 times faster than the 200–300-millisecond seek rate of the CD-ROM. Newer CD-ROM players coming to the market that are available for networks will have 3X and 4X speed capabilities.

Tips for Working with CD-ROM Players

CD-ROM players can be an enhancement to any network. A network administrator or support engineer must be knowledgeable in this hardware arena. As with any other device included in your network environment, improper planning can cause expensive data recovery and troubleshooting delays. Use the following tips when using CD-ROM players in your network:

- Check for incompatibilities by having the CD-ROM player and the hard drive on the same SCSI controller. Review the manufacturer's documentation and check the software vendor's requirements.
- Some CD-ROM players require a "caddie" box for the CD-ROM platter to be placed in before it can be inserted into the player. Make sure your users know about this—failure to properly use a caddie box can result in severe damage to your CD. (*Please* read your documentation before using the player!)
- Do not install a CD-ROM player in a drive bay in the CPU that is located directly above a hard drive in the CPU casing. The magnetic fields created by the CD-ROM unit can erase data from the hard drive.
- The error message Invalid drive specification means that the MSCDEX file is loaded too low in your AUTOEXEC.BAT file. The error message Disc not High Sierra Format means

you need to upgrade the version of your currently installed MSCDEX extension drivers to work with the newer ISO-9660 CD-ROM format.

Working with Magneto-Optical Drives

Magneto-optical Drives (M-O) are used to capture text, audio, video, and other types of integrated media in a combined format on the optical platter. M-O drives are used as a compromise between *digital access tape* (DAT) drives which are an inexpensive, slower medium, and hard drives which are expensive, yet faster in speed. M-O drives are faster than tape and more expensive than hard drives.

The use of optical drives can replace the standard tape and hard drives for backup, archiving (which is the best use for M-O), and storage of data-intensive applications such as CAD/CAM type programs. The setup of M-O drives is similar to tape backup units; they can be jukeboxes, external, or internal devices. M-O should not be confused with *Write Once Read Many* (WORM) systems because WORM drives cannot have the data changed on the optical-type disk after it has been written.

A magneto-optical drive operates with the use of laser beams and magnetism. An M-O disk is coated with layers on which spiral grooves have been molded. To write data, a polarized laser beam is reflected onto the surface of the M-O platter. The reflection is measured for its rotation on the plane of the disk that has been polarized magnetically. The data is then interpreted from how the rotation is magnetically oriented. Reverting the magnetic orientation to the way it was directed prior to the M-O disk being written to will erase data.

The following are the advantages of magneto-optical disks:

- **Removable Media.** Disks can be removed and are capable of being changed with another M-O disk.
- **Capacity.** M-O can handle capacities from 650 MB to 1,000 GB and can be loaded into jukeboxes for increased capacity of data accessibility.
- **Random Access.** M-O supports many read/write operations, unlike streaming tape cartridges.
- **Durability.** Head crashes are impossible because of the use of laser beams.
- **Backup.** It can be used for large unattended backups and archiving of data.

The following are the disadvantages of magneto-optical disks:

- **Cost.** Very expensive currently. Drive prices range from $3,500 to $5,000, and the optical disk platter ranges in price from $180 to $300.
- **Speed.** Magneto-optical drives are not as fast as SCSI drives. M-O drives need a double pass to the platter to write any data.
- **Size.** These drives are too big to fit inside laptops. This may interfere with the requirements for the mobile network of today.

Questions

1. The most important storage device on the network is ______.

   ○ A. fixed disk

   ○ B. CD-ROM

   ○ C. magneto-optical disk

   ○ D. floppy disk

2. Communication between the hard drive and the CPU is handled by which device?

   ○ A. NIC

   ○ B. Fixed disk cable

   ○ C. Disk controller card

   ○ D. Floppy drive cable

3. The time it takes for the read/write heads to find the correct track on a fixed disk is known as ______.

   ○ A. access time

   ○ B. transfer rate

   ○ C. megabytes per second

   ○ D. seek time

4. Which of the following is *not* one of the components of a hard drive?

   ○ A. Spindle motor

   ○ B. Voice coil actuator

   ○ C. Platter

   ○ D. Cluster block

5. Which of the following is *not* a limitation of an Integrated Drive Electronics (IDE) drive?

   ○ A. It cannot multitask I/O.

   ○ B. It has a maximum drive capacity of 528M even when a special non-standard BIOS is used.

   ○ C. It does not support any optical or tape drives, as does the SCSI interface.

   ○ D. It does not support bus-mastering.

6. The main reason that you should never do a low-level format on an IDE drive is that ______.

   ○ A. you might erase the manufacturer's bad block information

   ○ B. you might be unable to access the IDE drive again to reestablish it

   ○ C. it removes the drive's ability to support overlapping and multitasking of I/O

   ○ D. electronic flux transitions of the drive might be reversed

7. Which *two* of the following are cited as reasons why ESDI drives have become more popular than ST-506 drives that use the same cabling system?

   □ A. ESDI drives are interchangeable with ST-506 drives.

   □ B. ESDI drives are capable of performing at higher levels.

   □ C. ESDI drives allow the Cold Boot Loader to be written to track 0, freeing disk space for data storage.

   □ D. ESDI drives have a larger storage capacity.

8. Which drive type provides an expansion bus that allows up to seven types of devices to be connected?

   ○ A. IDE

   ○ B. ESDI

   ○ C. SCSI

   ○ D. ASPI

9. Which of the following is NOT true of the WIDE SCSI-2 implementation of SCSI?

   ○ A. It uses a 50-pin cable and the single-ended signaling process.

   ○ B. It uses a second data path offering up to 20 MB per second data transfer rate.

   ○ C. It implements a 68-pin SCSI cable with the differential signaling process.

   ○ D. It is not used as much as the FAST SCSI-2 standard.

10. Which drive device is rapidly becoming the industry standard?

    ○ A. ASPI

    ○ B. ESDI

    ○ C. SCSI

    ○ D. IDE

11. If you do not want to remove the SCSI host adapter each time you need to change its settings, you should do which of the following?

    ○ A. Make sure that the same cabling is used for all SCSI devices on the network.

    ○ B. Make sure that you use a SCSI host adapter that uses software for setup of jumpers and termination settings.

    ○ C. Make sure that each SCSI device has a unique identifier number.

    ○ D. Make sure that all SCSI devices are the same, using either all SCSI-1 or all SCSI-2 devices.

12. The SCSI LUN required for the first bootable hard disk on all except for some HP and PS/2 machines is ______.

    ○ A. 0

    ○ B. 1

    ○ C. 6

    ○ D. 7

13. One primary use of the third-party tool called CHECKIT PRO is ______.

    ○ A. to set up hard drives for storage

    ○ B. to modify jumpers on the drive

    ○ C. to enable you to mix SCSI devices

    ○ D. to determine a workstation's drive interface

14. Which of the following is not a jumper that might have to be set on the hard disk?

    ○ A. ACT

    ○ B. IDE

    ○ C. DS

    ○ D. DSP

15. Although usually set for the controller card by the manufacturer, you might need to put which setting into the STARTUP.NCF file of a network server?
    - ○ A. Controller interrupt
    - ○ B. Base I/O
    - ○ C. DMA channel
    - ○ D. Base BIOS address

Answers

1. A
2. C
3. D
4. D
5. B
6. A
7. B, D
8. C
9. A
10. C
11. B
12. A
13. D
14. B
15. A

CHAPTER 35

Troubleshooting the DOS Workstation

Several versions of DOS are installed in the workplace today. Many businesses, either for economic reasons or because they have never seen a need to upgrade, are still running version 3.3. If upgrade decisions are made on a departmental basis, then it is possible that one LAN administrator could be supporting PCs running versions 3.3, 4.x, 5.0, and 6.x.

Not only do all of these Microsoft versions exist, but there are also DOS versions from IBM and Novell. Novell's DOS was acquired in a purchase of Digital Research. DR DOS 5.0 gave way to DR DOS 6.0, which in turn gave way to Novell DOS 7. All of these combine together to make a fine stew for the administrator to stay on top of.

The majority of problems arise when one resource is accessed by more than one entity, for example, memory. This chapter examines these problems as well as the following topics:

- Working with IPX/NETX
- Working with ODI
- Working with the DOS Requester
- Working with Remote Boot
- Troubleshooting with TRACK
- Diagnosing conflicts
- Conflict resolution
- PC memory
- DR DOS

Working with IPX/NETX

Figure 35.1 depicts the *Internetwork Packet Exchange* (IPX) architecture and shows how the components work together. NCP is the NetWare Core Protocol going to the server, while the NetWare shell is going to the workstation. The LAN driver could be Ethernet, ARCnet, Token Ring, or any other.

With NetWare, as with any client/server system, one station interacts with another as the client makes requests of the server. The IPX.COM and the NetWare shell carry out this interaction between the two components.

> **Note:** The command IPX I shows information about the version of IPX running on your workstation.

The purpose of IPX is to function as a go-between for the NIC card and communication link. This is described in the Administration sections of this book, and it is strongly encouraged that you review the specific coverage there. Here, suffice it to say that IPX is responsible for communication functions and management of the sockets used in the workstation. It also is responsible for ascertaining the address of the network segment to which the workstation is connected, the network number, and the node address.

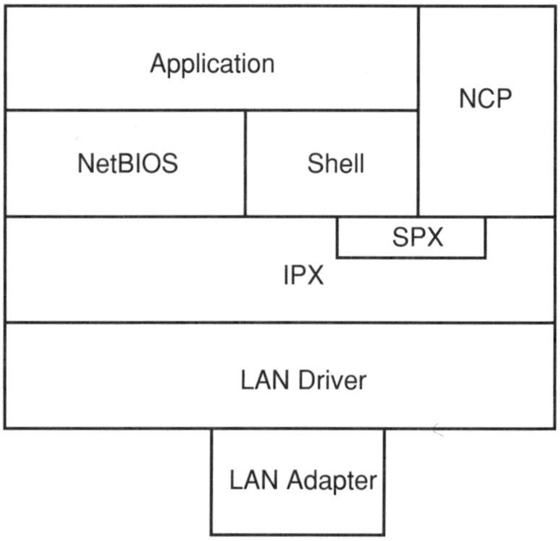

Figure 35.1
The IPX architecture for a DOS workstation.

The NetWare Core Protocol regulates how connection control information is passed. Every server packet must have the connection number and a sequence number assigned to it. The only purpose for the sequence number is to ascertain when a packet is lost.

What To Do If You Cannot Connect to the Server

The following steps should be followed if a workstation cannot connect to the server:

1. Verify proper seating of the NIC and connection of the cables.
2. Verify that the NIC is set to the same configuration as the IPX.COM.
3. Look for conflicts in interrupts, memory, and hardware addresses.
4. Verify that the server LAN driver is bound to IPX.

The Watchdog

When users leave a workstation, they should log out from the server to clear their connection and free resources. The Watchdog process, running at the server, routinely sends a poll to workstations to verify if they are active or not. If they are not active for a specified period of time, they automatically are cleared.

Working with ODI

ODI is nothing more than a specification of how the data link layer works in the OSI model. Developed by Novell and Apple in 1989, it provides support for multiple protocols on the same network with one driver. Up to four network cards can be active in the same machine, and drivers can be unloaded as easily as they were loaded. This means that IPX and TCP/IP can live in network harmony, and ODI drivers have replaced IPX.COM in the workplace.

The components of ODI, as discussed in the Administration sections, include:

- LSL.COM
- The LAN driver
- IPXODI.COM (which includes SPX)

The *Multiple Link Interface Driver* (MLID) is a part of the LAN driver specification, which controls communication between the board and the LSL. Figure 35.2 illustrates the interaction between the components.

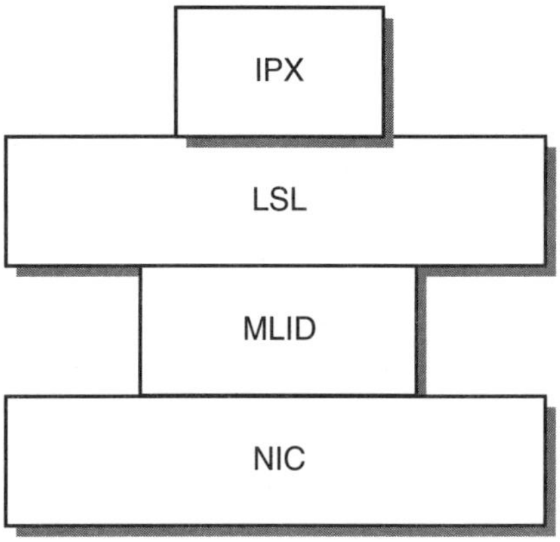

Figure 35.2
The ODI architecture.

Protocol stacks figure into the equation as they receive packets from the LSL. They operate independently of the board type and remove the header information that is pertinent only to them. Protocol stacks include TCP/IP, AppleTalk, OSI, and IPX/SPX.

Troubleshooting ODI

The first step when trying to diagnose ODI workstations is to check the board and cabling to make certain there are no obvious physical problems. Next, check that you have an ODI LAN driver for the board. Following that, boot with a bare-bones AUTOEXEC.BAT and CONFIG.SYS—loading no drivers of any kind. When booted, load LSL, the LAN driver, IPXODI, and the NETX.

Note: Any of the four networking components can be unloaded in the opposite order they were loaded by following their command with a *U*:

NETX U

IPXODI U

{LAN driver} U

LSL U

If problems persist, turn your attention to the NET.CFG file. Within that file, main headings must be left-justified, with other entries indented by a tab or space. Headings must precede each section and end with a carriage return, but case sensitivity does not apply. The following is an example of a NET.CFG file:

```
Link Driver NE2000
        INT 5
        PORT 340
        MEM D0000
        FRAME ETHERNET 802.2
NETWARE DOS REQUESTER
        FIRST NETWORK DRIVE=F
```

INT must match the IRQ set on the board, while PORT gives the I/O address. MEM shows the memory range used by the board, and FRAME is used with boards that support multiple types. Other entries that can be present, or needed, include the following:

- **DMA.** Allows the DMA channels to be configured
- **NODE ADDRESS.** Used to override hard coded board addresses
- **SLOT.** Makes the driver see a specific board first
- **PROTOCOL.** Signifies that existing LAN drivers can handle new protocols

Working with DOS Requester

The DOS Requester replaces NETX and all the variants that Novell traditionally shipped with successive versions of NetWare. Providing complete backward compatibility, it uses a modular approach to anticipate future enhancements.

Within DOS, the COMMAND.COM file serves as the shell. It accepts commands and determines whether the request can be handled internally, or if a search of the PATH statement directories is necessary to find an executable file to carry out the command. When NetWare is installed, the DOS Requester encompasses the DOS shell and intercepts commands before they get there. It then decides whether the command typed in is a NetWare command—in which case it directs it appropriately—or a DOS command—in which case it passes it through to the DOS shell for regular processing. Figure 35.3 symbolizes the relationship between these two shells.

The Requester actually is more than one entity; it is composed of a number of VLM files. Each VLM (Virtual Loadable Module) is a TSR program that can be loaded and unloaded by VLM.EXE as needed. These are stored, by default, in the NWCLIENT subdirectory on the workstation, and are loaded and unloaded by the manager (VLM.EXE). If the VLMs are in another directory, there must be a VLM= line in NET.CFG to point to the appropriate path.

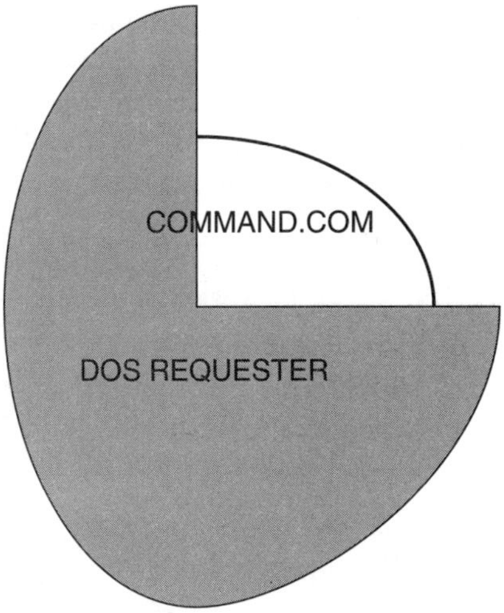

Figure 35.3
The relationship between the DOS Requester and the DOS shell.

Installing the DOS Requester

The steps to installing on a client machine are as follows:

1. Run INSTALL.EXE. This creates the NWCLIENT directories and copies in the VLMs.
2. Give the Windows path when prompted, if you are using Windows.
3. Give the configuration information when prompted—this is used to build the NET.CFG file.

The files you should see are shown in the following table.

VLM File	*Function*
AUTO.VLM	Automatic reconnect
BIND.VLM	Protocol bindery service
CONN.VLM	Connection table manager
FIO.VLM	File input\output
GENERAL.VLM	Miscellaneous NETX functions
IPXNCP.VLM	Transport protocol using IPX
NETX.VLM	Shell compatibility
NWP.VLM	Protocol multiplexer
PRINT.VLM	Print redirector
REDIR.VLM	DOS redirector
RSA.VLM	Encryption
TRAN.VLM	Transport protocol multiplexer

Working with Remote Boot

With diskless workstations, there is a read-only memory chip on the NIC. The code within that chip is executed on boot-up and is responsible for contacting the server and getting the necessary information to establish a communication link. Typically, the ROM size is 8 KB.

DOSGEN is the utility used to create the remote image the workstation communicates with on the server. Reasons for using diskless workstations include the following:

- Cost
- Convenience

- Security
- Speed

The created image appears to the workstation as a virtual drive, and the workstation functions as if there were a drive installed within it. To the workstation, the image is seen as a floppy from which it is booting, thus it needs files such as the following:

- CONFIG.SYS
- AUTOEXEC.BAT
- IPX
- NETX

It also needs the necessary command to get to the LOGIN routine (this can be within the AUTOEXEC.BAT file).

The file NET$DOS.SYS is created and placed in the working directory; it must be flagged as sharable to properly function.

Note: Remote booting DOS 5 requires RPLFIX run against the existing NET$DOS.SYS. The sole purpose of this utility is to change parameters since COMMAND.COM is larger in 5.0 than other DOS versions.

Troubleshooting with TRACK

TRACK is a console command used to diagnose router and server problems. It shows the network, server, and connection request information on a Router Tracking Screen. Information is depicted as it comes in and goes out. TRACK ON turns the monitor screen on, while TRACK OFF removes it.

The two requests to keep in mind are *Router Information Protocols* (RIP) and *Service Advertising Protocols* (SAP). RIPs are transmitted from routers to servers to advertise their presence, and SAPs are sent by print servers, gateways, and all servers to denote their presence.

A file server is seen by a workstation when it is "SAPing." Thus, the workstation knows it is there and attempts to connect to it—preferably the one within the nearest proximity. If a file server is not SAPing, there can be a problem with IPX not being bound to the card, or volumes not being mounted.

When a workstation shell loads, TRACK should report the following three things on the console if all is working as it should:

1. Get Nearest Server
2. Give Nearest Server *server_name*
3. Route Request

SLIST can be detrimental in isolating problems if a message of Unknown file server appears when the user tries to log in at the workstation.

Diagnosing Conflicts

Interrupt Request Channels (IRQ) conflicts can take a long time to diagnose. This is because the connection might work properly for a considerable amount of time, then die off at unexpected moments. IRQ conflicts do not happen until two devices attempt to access the same IRQ at the same time.

IRQs are directly tied to hardware components such as modems and printers. When a call is made to their device, the CPU puts other jobs on a wait status and processes the request made of that interrupt—in essence, they are interrupting other processing. A number of utilities can be used to diagnose IRQ problems, and Check It PRO is one worth noting. On DOS machines running version 6.*x*, MSD can offer similar information. The following listing depicts an example of an MSD report.

Normally, COM1 and COM3 use IRQ4, while COM2 and COM4 use IRQ3. It also is worth noting that early machines (XTs) have only eight interrupts, and newer ones have sixteen (numbered 0-15).

The I/O address gives the memory range reserved by the CPU. These are areas set aside specifically for each interrupt. If more than one device is using the same address, conflicts occur. The range of CA000 to DFFFF is safe for network adapter configurations.

Conflict Resolution

System configuration, once the domain of dip switches, now resides in CMOS memory. Usually, you can access CMOS during bootup by pressing a key sequence, which can be anything from the Esc key to Ctrl+Alt+Ins. The necessary key sequence is determined by the hardware manufacturer, and there is no standard throughout the industry.

The EISA Configuration Utility is a menu-driven approach to configuring EISA boards and solving conflicts. It reads the CFG file that comes with the board, and Verification Mode can be used to automatically check to see if conflicts can occur with other devices.

```
Microsoft Diagnostics version 2.01    1/24/95    7:44pm    Page  6
    ========================================================================

    --------------------------- IRQ Status ------------------------------

    IRQ  Address    Description       Detected            Handled By
    --  --------  ---------------  -----------------  ---------------
      0  2AB6:0000  Timer Click       Yes                 win386.exe
      1  0A79:1923  Keyboard          Yes                 Block Device
      2  08B4:0057  Second 8259A      Yes                 Default Handlers
      3  08B4:006F  COM2: COM4:       COM2:               Default Handlers
      4  0364:02C2  COM1: COM3:       COM1: Serial Mouse  MS$MOUSE
      5  08B4:009F  LPT2:             Yes                 Default Handlers
      6  08B4:00B7  Floppy Disk       Yes                 Default Handlers
      7  0070:06F4  LPT1:             Yes                 System Area
      8  08B4:0052  Real-Time Clock   Yes                 Default Handlers
      9  F000:9C54  Redirected IRQ2   Yes                 BIOS
     10  166A:01D4  (Reserved)                            3C509
     11  08B4:00E7  (Reserved)                            Default Handlers
     12  08B4:00FF  (Reserved)                            Default Handlers
     13  F000:9C45  Math Coprocessor  Yes                 BIOS
     14  08B4:0117  Fixed Disk        Yes                 Default Handlers
     15  F000:FF53  (Reserved)                            BIOS
```

Working with PC Memory

The following list shows the memory detail displayed with DOS 6's MSD utility.

When the 8088 CPU was first designed, it divided the 1 MB address space into several areas, including 640 KB for application usage. To maintain compatibility, subsequent CPUs have kept the same scheme. Memory optimizers, such as MEMMAKER (MS DOS) and OPTIMIZE (QEMM), enable you to avoid manual memory tuning and automatically configure your system for optimal memory performance.

Real Mode is the term used to indicate the backward compatibility between subsequent models of CPU boards and the 8088. All x86 machines, when running in real mode, act as if they were running an 8086 chip.

Protected mode is the native mode for all CPUs from 80286 on up. Protected mode refers to the fact that memory is not used without first requesting it from the operating system.

```
------------------------------ Memory -------------------------------

     Legend:  Available "  "  RAM "##"  ROM "RR"  Possibly Available ".."
       EMS Page Frame "PP"  Used UMBs "UU"  Free UMBs "FF"
     1024K FC00 RRRRRRRRRRRRRRRR FFFF  Conventional Memory
           F800 RRRRRRRRRRRRRRRR FBFF                 Total: 640K
           F400 RRRRRRRRRRRRRRRR F7FF             Available: 442K
      960K F000 RRRRRRRRRRRRRRRR F3FF                        452976 bytes
           EC00                  EFFF
           E800                  EBFF  Extended Memory
           E400                  E7FF                 Total: 15104K
      896K E000                  E3FF
           DC00 PPPPPPPPPPPPPPPP DFFF  MS-DOS Upper Memory Blocks
           D800 PPPPPPPPPPPPPPPP DBFF            Total UMBs: 28K
           D400 PPPPPPPPPPPPPPPP D7FF       Total Free UMBs: 0K
      832K D000 PPPPPPPPPPPPPPPP D3FF    Largest Free Block: 0K
           CC00 UUUUUUUUUUUUUUUU CFFF
           C800 ...UUUUUUUUUUUUU CBFF  Expanded Memory (EMS)
           C400 RRRRRRRRRRRRRRRR C7FF           LIM Version: 4.00
      768K C000 RRRRRRRRRRRRRRRR C3FF    Page Frame Address: D000H
           BC00 ................ BFFF                 Total: 1024K
           B800 ................ BBFF             Available: 1024K
           B400 ................ B7FF
      704K B000 ................ B3FF  XMS Information
           AC00 ................ AFFF           XMS Version: 2.00
           A800 ................ ABFF        Driver Version: 2.05
           A400 ................ A7FF     A20 Address Line: Enabled
      640K A000 ................ A3FF     High Memory Area: In use
                                                 Available: 1024K
                                        Largest Free Block: 1024K
```

Memory Types

Conventional memory, also known as base memory, is everything within the first 640 KB that is available to DOS applications. The following 384 KB is known as upper memory and is used by adapter cards, video, and serial ports. This completes the first 1 MB, or 1,024 KB of memory. Expanded memory is nothing more than pages of memory that can be swapped in and out of the upper memory space.

Extended memory comes next, and it is everything above the 1 MB space. High memory is a subset of extended memory and comprises the first 64 KB of extended memory. Within the range of 1,024 KB to 1,088 KB, it is available to DOS applications with an XMS memory manager.

Figure 35.4 illustrates this concept.

Loading LAN drivers into high memory can free up more of the lower 640 KB for applications. This is accomplished by placing lines in CONFIG.SYS similar to the following:

```
DEVICE=C:\DOS\HIMEM.SYS
DEVICE=C:\DOS\EMM386.SYS NOEMS
DOS=HIGH,UMB
```

This is followed up in the AUTOEXEC.BAT file with this:

```
LH LSL
LH 3C509 (or your card type)
LH IPXODI
LH NETX
```

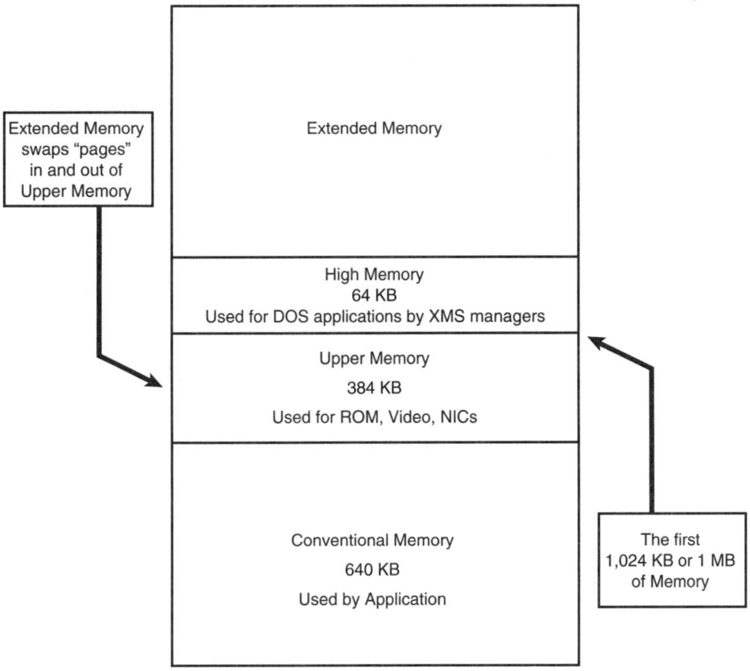

Figure 35.4
The Memory Model.

DR DOS

DR (Digital Research) DOS, from Novell, is a workstation operating system fully compatible with Microsoft's DOS. It features data compression, disk defragmentation utilities, a read/write cache, task switching, and enhanced memory management.

Enhancements have been made to the following external DOS commands:

- CHKDSK
- DISKCOPY
- HELP
- MEM
- REPLACE
- TREE
- UNDELETE
- XCOPY

Typing any command and following it with /H or /? displays all the options available. The following are additional features DR DOS offers over other products:

- DISKMAX is the set of compression utilities.
- DOSBOOK offers online documentation of the available commands.
- HIDOS.SYS is a driver for configuring memory on 80286 and earlier machines.
- HIDOS=ON, HIBUFFERS=xx are used in conjunction to move the operating system out of base memory.
- LOCK is used to lock the keyboard and keep anyone from using it without entering the password. This provides additional security at the workstation level.
- SETUP is a full screen menu used to configure any of the DOS features, including TASKMAX, MEMMAX, and DISKMAX.
- TASKMAX is the task switcher, enabling you to move between DOS programs in much the same manner as Windows does.

Questions

1. Which of the following is a connectionless protocol?
   - ○ A. SPX
   - ○ B. IPX
   - ○ C. NCP
   - ○ D. NetBios
2. The utility used to generate workstation files on the local drive is ______.
   - ○ A. WSUPDATE
   - ○ B. DOSGEN
   - ○ C. IPXODI
   - ○ D. WSGEN
3. Which *three* of the following are network communication protocols:
   - ☐ A. TCP
   - ☐ B. SPX
   - ☐ C. NFS
   - ☐ D. IPX
4. Unloading drivers is accomplished by ______ and ______.
   - ☐ A. using the U option
   - ☐ B. running the command a second time
   - ☐ C. specifying the drivers in reverse order of their load
   - ☐ D. using a memory management utility to remove the TSRs
5. Features of the DOS Requester do not include ______.
   - ○ A. backward compatibility
   - ○ B. modular design
   - ○ C. architecture independent protocol support
   - ○ D. the use of current technology
6. The Protocol Mulitplexer is loaded with which VLM?
   - ○ A. NWP.VLM
   - ○ B. MULTI.VLM
   - ○ C. NDS.VLM
   - ○ D. RSA.VLM
7. How many interrupts do XT machines have?
   - ○ A. 2
   - ○ B. 4
   - ○ C. 8
   - ○ D. 16
8. How many interrupts do current machines have?
   - ○ A. 2
   - ○ B. 4
   - ○ C. 8
   - ○ D. 16

Answers

1. B
2. D
3. A, B, D
4. A, C
5. C
6. A
7. C
8. D

CHAPTER 36

Troubleshooting Network Printing

Network printing is one of the most difficult processes to install and maintain. Because the process is so mechanical in nature, a series of problems can occur. When they do occur, the cause is not always visible. This chapter explores the issue from two sides:

- *Preventing problems*
- *Troubleshooting*

Before you consider taking the certification test, you should review the administrative topics pertinent to printing that are covered in the book's two administration course sections. The following topics are of particular interest:

- PCONSOLE
- PRINTCON
- PRINTDEF
- PSERVER
- RPRINTER

You should know how to create a print server and print queue; assign print servers to file servers; configure ports and printers; and manage queue and spool assignments.

Preventing Problems

Most of the steps used to prevent printer problems can be thought of as common sense precautions. They include cleaning paper and ribbon paths on a regular basis and vacuuming paper particles from inside the unit.

Temperature ranges and humidity should be kept as constant as possible, and there should be adequate space for ambient air to circulate around the printers. Laser printers should never be pointed directly at anyone, for the thermal radiation they give off can be harmful.

Troubleshooting

Printer problems can be broken into the following subcategories:

- Physical problems
- Print queues
- Print servers
- Remote printers
- Printer configuration
- Printer utilities
- PostScript printers

When diagnosing a problem, check the obvious components first. Make certain the electrical cord and printer cord are firmly attached and connected to the appropriate place. If there are any lights on the printer that indicate the power is on, check that they are lit. Also check to be sure that any switch boxes, electrical or A/B type, are working properly.

After you are convinced that the connections are functioning as they should be, turn the printer off and on again, and try sending your print job once more. If this attempt is unsuccessful, run a self-test on the printer and verify that it is working properly as a stand-alone. If it is, try printing to it again with a different application, such as a print screen, to see if the application is the culprit.

Physical Problems

Physical problems are the easiest problems to verify, and the first for which you should check. You should begin by checking the cables, as mentioned already. Next, make sure that the paper is not jammed, and that there is a ribbon or toner cartridge in working condition in the unit. If the ribbon is damaged or the toner cartridge is empty, replace the faulty component and try again.

Note

Parallel printing is four to six times faster than serial printing, and the faster the machine's CPU, the more obvious this becomes. Novell recommends that parallel printers be used as often as possible. The maximum standard cable length for parallel printers is 10 feet (150 by some manufacturers) compared to the standard of 50 for serial printers (500 by some manufacturers).

Parallel printers are, moreover, universally compatible, although serial printers are not. Only limited error checking is available on parallel printers; serial printers have parity checking, which slows printing speed by 10 percent.

Print Queues

The print queue's physical representation is the directory on the file server where the print jobs wait until they are printed by the print server. Problems can occur if you run out of hard drive space, or if the queue has become corrupted. You can monitor job entries with PCONSOLE to show their status.

Note If problems occur when using NPRINT, check for older versions of IPX and update them.

One of the first things you should do when a user complains that a job won't print is use PCONSOLE to verify that the job is still in the queue. If it is not in the queue, the application might not be network-aware. Check to see that CAPTURE is active on the workstation before going further.

Print Servers

If the job is still in the queue, and all the physical checks appear correct, re-enable the server's capability to service queues. Verify that the latest version of PSERVER.NLM is running; then, using PCONSOLE, take the print server down and bring it back up again.

Note PSERVER needs 512 KB of memory. An additional 10 KB is needed for every extra printer added to the server.

When using PSERVER.EXE (as opposed to PSERVER.NLM), make sure that your SPX CONNECTIONS are set to at least 60.

Note NETERR.ZIP is a file of utilities useful for problem solving with print servers and a variety of other hardware devices. It is highly recommended that this file be downloaded from NOVLIB on NetWire or taken from NSEPro and extracted for use.

Remote Printers

Remote serial printers demand constant attention. If the error message Not Connected appears, RPRINTER has not yet been run to activate the defined printer.

If RPRINTER has been run, and there are still problems, the problems might be attributed to a lack of memory, older versions of the software, or an incompatible PC clone.

Many times, conflicts can occur between RPRINTER and the NIC card installed in the machine. If such is the case, change the interrupt setting on the card to solve the problem.

Routers between RPRINTER workstations and print servers can cause problems and cause the remote printer to periodically hang. If such is the case, increase the NET.CFG parameters for the following two fields:

- SPX ABORT TIMEOUT
- IPX RETRY COUNT

Printer Configuration

PRINTDEF and PRINTCON are utilities used to create printer and job definitions. It is imperative that the printer definitions be correct in order for the print jobs to function as efficiently and error-free as possible. Often, a slight problem in the configuration means that short jobs will print without any errors, but large graphics jobs will fail.

Printer Utilities

You can solve many printing problems by upgrading older printer utilities, such as PSERVER.EXE and others, to the newest ones available. The latest utilities can be found on NSEPro or on the NOVLIB forum of NetWire.

Incorrect buffer sizes can cause characters to get lost on a printout. If such is the case, use PCONSOLE to increase the buffer size.

You can use PRINTCON when files are printing with improper page breaks. Redefine the configuration and change the Timeout Count.

PostScript Printers

PostScript is a printer language created by Adobe that provides a method of interfacing with a printer to create high-end, high-quality graphics. A great many PostScript problems can be solved by updating application drivers to the latest available.

It is important to verify that any cartridges used on the printer to generate PostScript are properly inserted and seated. It is also highly recommended that when printing in PostScript, you use the following settings:

- **/NB.** No banner
- **/NT.** No tabs
- **/NFF.** No form feed

Questions

1. The standard maximum length of a serial cable is ______.
   - ○ A. 10 feet
   - ○ B. 30 feet
   - ○ C. 50 feet
   - ○ D. 500 feet

2. The Print Server does which of the following *three* tasks?
   - ☐ A. Stores print jobs in the queue
   - ☐ B. Sends data to a remote printer
   - ☐ C. Accepts data from the queue
   - ☐ D. Polls the queue for print jobs

3. Parity checking is used with print jobs sent ______.
   - ○ A. to a remote printer
   - ○ B. to a serial printer
   - ○ C. to a parallel printer
   - ○ D. to any printer

4. When unloading PSERVER.NLM because of a problem, you should ______.
   - ○ A. reboot the print server
   - ○ B. unload the NLMs in an orderly manner
   - ○ C. use PRINTCON to stop incoming jobs
   - ○ D. laugh like a pirate

5. RPRINTER is ______.
   - ○ A. used to define remote print jobs
   - ○ B. the main utility for establishing network printing
   - ○ C. a loadable server module for remote printing
   - ○ D. a utility used at a workstation to activate remote printing

Answers

1. C
2. B, C, D
3. B
4. B
5. D

CHAPTER 37

Network Optimization and Disaster Recovery

Let's think about the two most basic needs of network administrators—how to best utilize the software and hardware resources on hand, and how to best ensure that your precious data will be there when you need it. This section of the Service and Support test is arguably by far the most important aspect of administering any network.

The SET Parameter

NetWare is generally quite good at optimizing the SET parameters. You can degrade system performance drastically by altering memory SET parameters incorrectly. If the alterations are performed correctly, however, your system and peripherals will function optimally.

On the other hand, as with any popular network operating system, you must know how to change these parameters. With NetWare you can alter communications, memory, file caching, directory caching, file system, locks, transaction tracking, disk, and miscellaneous parameters by adding the necessary SET commands into the appropriate STARTUP.NCF or SYS:SYSTEM\AUTOEXEC.NCF files.

Unless you have a full understanding of the ramifications involved in changing the various SET commands, do not change them. Although the system should remain intact after you make the changes, the potential exists for devastating results.

Communications Parameters

The following paragraphs give explanations for the parameters and their defaults and options.

Console Display Watchdog Logouts: OFF [ON, OFF]

If this parameter is set to ON, a message is displayed at the console when a connection is cleared.

New Packet Receive Buffer Wait Time: 0.1 Seconds [0.1 to 20]

This parameter determines how long the system will wait after receiving a request for another packet. If you have an EISA NIC in your server, you should not have to worry about your system granting too many receive buffers during high usage periods.

Maximum Physical Receive Packet Size: 1130 [618 to 4202]

As indicated by the name, this parameter establishes the maximum size of the packets that a system can receive. The parameter is configured in the STARTUP.NCF. The default is 1 KB (with packet header). If you have a NIC that can transmit packets larger than 512 bytes, you should increase this number to equal the largest packet size supported by your NIC.

Maximum Packet Receive Buffers: 100 [50 to 2000]

Use MONITOR to establish the number of service processes and packet receive buffers that your system is currently using. Increase the number in increments of 10 until you have 5 buffers per EISA or microchannel board, or until each workstation has 10.

Number of Watchdog Packets: 10 [5 to 100]

This value represents the number of watchdog packets that your server will send without receiving a reply before it disconnects the workstation.

Delay between Watchdog Packets: 59.3 Seconds [1 to 626.2]

Simply put, this is the amount of time that exists between sending the watchdog packets if the system receives no reply.

Delay before First Watchdog Packet: 240 Seconds [15.7 to 172.3]

This is the amount of time that a system will wait without receiving a request from a workstation before the system sends a watchdog packet to that workstation.

Memory Parameters

The following paragraphs give explanations for the parameters and their defaults and options.

Cache Buffer Size: 4096 Bytes [4096, 8192, or 16384]

If your block allocation size is smaller than 4096, increasing this value will diminish your system performance. If, however, your block allocation sizes are larger than 4096, system performance will increase if you increase this value.

Maximum Alloc Short-Term Memory: 2097152 [50000 to 16777216]

This critical memory pool stores drive mappings, loadable module tables, queued broadcast messages, open and locked files, service request buffers, and user connection information. The default 2 MB should be sufficient for 250 users with 26 drive mappings apiece.

Auto Register Memory above 16 Megabytes: ON [ON, OFF]

Care should be taken when altering this variable. If you install a NIC or disk controller that uses 24-bit address lines, only 16 MB of memory can be accessed properly. If your server can address more than 16 MB and you have installed one of the aforementioned EISA boards, only low memory will be addressed (in lieu of high), and the low memory that is being used by the NOS may become corrupted.

File Caching Parameters

The following paragraphs give explanations for the parameters and their defaults and options.

Maximum Concurrent Disk Cache Writes: 50 [10 to 100]

Increasing this variable increases the efficiency of write requests. Decreasing, on the other hand, increases read efficiency. If your dirty cache buffers rises above 70 percent of the total cache buffers, you should increase this number.

Dirty Disk Cache Delay Time: 3.3 Seconds [0.1 to 10]

This parameter sets the duration that your NOS will hold a write request before writing the data to the disk. This parameter is best left at the default.

Minimum File Cache Report Threshold: 20 [0 to 1000]

Your server will warn you when it has allocated some number greater than the minimum. Although changeable, this variable should be left at default in the vast majority of installations.

Minimum File Cache Buffers: 20 [20 to 1000]

As named, this variable sets the minimum number of file cache buffers that can be allocated at any given point in time. Increasing this number too high decreases resources available for other server processes.

Directory Caching Parameters

The following paragraphs give explanations for the parameters and their defaults and options.

Dirty Directory Cache Delay Time: 0.5 Seconds [0 to 10]

This parameter determines the amount of time that the system will wait until a directory table write request is written to disk. Increasing this parameter increases both system performance and the possibility of directory table corruption.

Maximum Concurrent Directory Cache Writes: 10 [5 to 50]

In a manner similar to the previous Maximum Concurrent Disk Cache Writes, when you increase this variable, you increase write efficiency at the cost of cache reads. The converse is also correct.

Directory Cache Allocation Wait Time: 2.2 Seconds [0.5 to 120]

How long will the operating system wait between allocating allocation buffers? Here is where this value is determined. If you notice that when you run DIR or NDIR the response time is lagging, try reducing this parameter.

Directory Cache Buffer Nonreferenced Delay: 5.5 Seconds [1 to 120]

Logically, some time must pass before your NOS can overwrite a nonreferenced directory entry with another. Increasing this value will increase allocated directory cache buffers and increase performance.

Maximum Directory Cache Buffers: 500 [20 to 4000]

This value is permanent until a server is rebooted and determines how large the directory cache is. Increase this number if directory searches are sluggish.

Minimum Directory Cache Buffers: 20 [10 to 2000]

This parameter is inverse parameter to the previous Maximum Directory Cache Buffers. For obvious reasons, don't set the Minimum Directory Cache Buffers greater than the Maximum Directory Cache Buffers.

File System Parameters

The following paragraphs give explanations for the parameters and their defaults and options.

Maximum Extended Attributes per File or Path: 32 [4 to 512]

This variable establishes the number of extended attributes that a file or path can have. This applies to all volumes on the server.

Immediate Purge of Deleted Files: OFF [ON, OFF]

If this self-explained variable is set to ON, no SALVAGE features will be able to recover deleted files. If set to OFF, deleted files are salvageable.

Maximum Subdirectory Tree Depth: 25 [10 to 100]

This variable determines how deep your deepest directory tree can be. Increasing this variable requires more system memory.

Volume Low Warn All Users: ON [ON, OFF]

If you value the data on your system and are not one to check your system variables regularly, you will want to leave this option ON so you are alerted if your drives approach full. If you change this option to OFF, you should run VOLINFO or CHKVOL daily.

Volume Low Warning Reset Threshold: 256 [0 to 100,000]

After you receive an initial warning that your volume is getting low (as set in Volume Low Warning Threshold), space is freed up by deleting files. Volume Low Warning Reset Threshold determines the amount of threshold space that must be exceeded for a second volume low warning.

Volume Low Warning Threshold: 256 [0 to 1,000,000]

Because this value is in blocks rather than bytes, you will first need to establish your system's block size (determined when you set up your volume during installation). If you want your system to warn you when your volume has only 5 MB left, you need to divide your desired volume-free size by your block size to establish the number of blocks that will trigger the warning. If your volume block size is 4 KB, then you would select 1280 blocks to be warned at 5 MB.

Turbo FAT Re-Use Wait Time: 329.6 Seconds [0.3 to 1 Hour 5 Minutes 54.6 Seconds]

If a program randomly accesses a file containing greater than 64 FAT entries, a turbo FAT index is automatically built. These builds take time, so a rebuild wait time is implemented so your NOS doesn't immediately rebuild the index every time a file is closed.

Minimum File Delete Wait Time: 65.9 Seconds [0 to 7 days]

This is an extremely valuable variable in environments where people delete files by accident. Since this situation could happen in just about every network in existence, increase this value if you have the resources. Realize, however, that this value is absolute, and that deleted files will not be purged until this time limit has been met (even if the volume is full and users are not able to create new files).

File Delete Wait Time: 329.6 Seconds [0 to 7 days]

Similar to the Minimum File Delete Wait Time, this value lets the system know when a deleted file may be marked as purgeable. Because NetWare tries to keep a minimum of $^1/_{32}$ of the total volume for new files, if your free space drops below $^1/_{32}$ and files are marked as purgeable, they will automatically be purged. At this point the file is history and can not be salvaged.

NCP File Commit: ON [ON, OFF]

Files can typically flush all pending file writes to disk.

Don't mess with this parameter unless you know what you are doing or a Novell representative instructs you to do so.

Maximum Percent of Volume Used by Directory: 13 [5 to 50]

How much of a volume may be used as directory space? This parameter provides the answer.

Maximum Percent of Volume Space Allowed for Extended Attributes: 10 [5 to 50]

This value is typically fine at the default setting, and is addressed only when the volume is being mounted.

Lock Parameters

The following paragraphs give explanations for the parameters and their defaults and options.

Maximum Record Locks per Connection: 500 [10 to 10,000]

A setting of 500 is usually more than sufficient in non-SQL environments (and even when you are in one). This parameter enables you to determine how many records each connection can establish. You might need to increase the value if you have a system-to-system *pipeline* in which multiple users will use one connection.

Maximum File Locks per Connection: 250 [10 to 1000]

If you have one connection that needs more than 250 files locked at one time, you have a unique environment! Suffice it to say that the default value should be fine.

Maximum Record Locks: 20,000 [100 to 200,000]

See the aforementioned Maximum Record Locks Per Connection, and take it to the server level. Changing this parameter is pretty straightforward.

Maximum File Locks: 10,000 [100 to 100,000]

This parameter enables you to set the number of files you can lock per connection.

Transaction Tracking Parameters

The following paragraphs give explanations for the parameters and their defaults and options.

Auto TTS Backout Flag: OFF [ON, OFF]

Although the default is OFF, if it is more important for your system to automatically boot after crashing, you might want to consider changing this value to ON. This enables your system to automatically back out of any incomplete transactions without asking you if it may do so.

TTS Abort Dump Flag: OFF [ON, OFF]

If you change the Auto TTS Backout Flag to ON, you will probably want to change this value to ON as well. If you do so, the system will create a log file that reflects what data has been backed out of the TTS.

Maximum Transactions: 10,000 [100 to 10,000]

Simply put, this parameter controls the number of transactions that can be performed at any given time on the system.

TTS Unwritten Cache Wait Time: 65.9 Seconds [11 to 659.1]

Certain transactional blocks are more courteous than others and for other blocks to be written to disk before they go. This value is the maximum time that any TTS block may wait in memory before being written to disk.

TTS Backout File Truncation Wait Time: 59 Minutes 19.2 Seconds [65.9 Seconds to 1 Day 2 Hours 21 Minutes 51.3 Seconds]

This parameter controls how long allocated blocks are available to the TTS backout file.

Miscellaneous Parameters

The following paragraphs give explanations for the parameters and their defaults and options.

Enable Disk Read After Write Verify: ON [ON, OFF]

If your media is "raided" or mirrored, then you may want to consider turning off this variable to increase performance. If not, or if you want to have a backup failsafe procedure in place, let your system verify that what it has just written to disk is the same as what was just in memory (default setting).

Maximum Outstanding NCP Searches: 51 [10 to 1000]

Normally your network will have only one NetWare Core Protocol directory search going on at any time. Ten searches are probably more than you will ever need, but if your network environment involves software that makes multiple NCP calls concurrently, you might need to increase this value. If your software needs this, it will let you know up front. Make any changes accordingly.

Allow Unencrypted Passwords: OFF [ON, OFF]

If you are running NetWare 3.0 or later, leave this OFF. Setting the variable to ON allows your passwords to be sent across your wire unencrypted.

New Service Process Wait Time: 2.2 Seconds [0.3 to 20]

This variable assigns how long the NOS waits after receiving a request for a new service before it actually allocates the new process.

Pseudo Preemption Time: 2000 [1000 to 10,000]

Certain types of software (NLMs) are CPU time-sensitive. Change this parameter only if your software suggests.

Display Spurious Interrupt Alerts: ON [ON, OFF]

This value should not be altered, because it reflects whether you have a hardware interrupt conflict in your file server. If this alarm is displayed at the system console, remove all unnecessary add-on boards and begin troubleshooting.

Display Lost Interrupt Alerts: ON [ON, OFF]

Again, this value should not be altered from the default value. An alarm will appear on the system console if a hardware interrupt call is made, but lost before the CPU can respond.

Display Disk Device Alerts: OFF [ON, OFF]

This is not a bad variable to change in any environment. Novell suggests turning this ON if you are experiencing hard drive problems.

Display Relinquish Control Alerts: OFF [ON, OFF]

This is a CPU watchdog control. If an NLM holds the CPU for more than 0.4 seconds, an alarm is displayed on the system console if this variable is turned ON.

Display Old API Names: OFF [ON, OFF]

This variable can be changed periodically to verify that new APIs are being used. Old APIs should still function, but they do so more slowly and should be updated.

Maximum Service Processes: 20 [5 to 40]

Increase this number only if you have sufficient resources (memory), and MONITOR reflects that you are using the number that is currently allocated.

Performance Modifications and Considerations

If your system requires that data be stored on the NetWare server in various file system formats, it is best that you do not mix file systems and name spaces on one volume. If you do require multiple name services on one volume, increase the Minimum Directory Cache Buffers setting, and the volume will mount more rapidly.

If you are going to implement more than one name space on a volume, install all name spaces on the volume when it is initially installed. If you are not able to do so and are adding a name space after your server has been running for some period of time, consider backing your system, re-installing the drive, adding all of the required name spaces, and then restoring the data. This will make efficient use of the Disk Directory Entry Table Blocks.

Monitoring with MONITOR

Whoever was on the development team of MONITOR.NLM is a friend to every network administrator. With MONITOR you have the ability to monitor various aspects of your network in real time, including various system utilizations, cache memory, network connections, drives, volumes, network drivers, modules, open file status, and memory usage.

When you invoke MONITOR.NLM, your initial screen will display information about the basic health of your system. Some information, such as file server up time, is nifty, but it is usually nothing more than a basis of bragging rights between network administrators. The remainder of the information is very pertinent indeed. The Utilization number reflects what percentage of your overall resources are being used. If this number is consistently over seventy, add memory and tune how these resources are being used. The Cache buffers numbers are also critical. If your Dirty Cache Buffers are close to or match your Total Cache Buffers, you have a bottleneck somewhere, and unless you find the source (that is, faulty cabling), your system will hang and need to be rebooted. Lastly, Current Disk Requests are transactions that are waiting for the disk to become available. Again, if your transactions get too stacked, your system will hang and need to be rebooted.

Connection Information

This section provides various information you need concerning connections.

List Active Connections

Displays connection time, network address, requests, kilobytes read, kilobytes written, semaphores, logical record locks, and open files for the user that is highlighted.

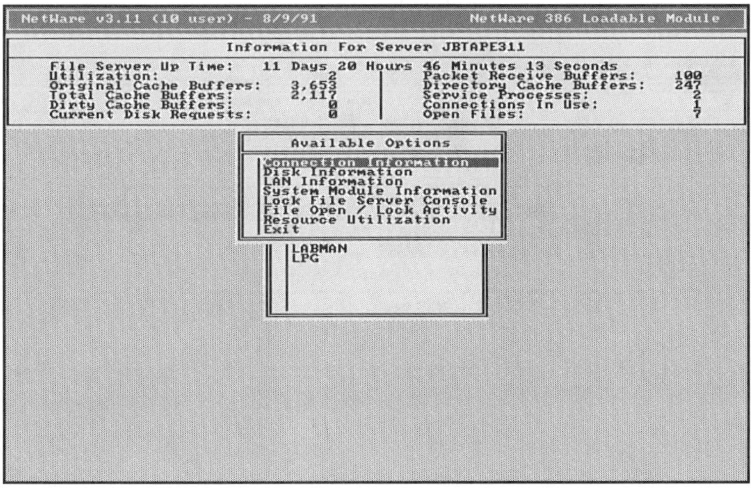

Figure 37.1
The MONITOR.NLM is an invaluable tool for anyone needing to tune a NetWare network.

List Physical Record Locks for a User

Show the beginning and ending offsets for locked files, how the record is locked, and the status of the file.

Clear a Connection

You can clear a connection using this section of the MONITOR program. Simply select the connection you want cleared, press Delete, and answer Yes when prompted to clear the connection. If you want to clear multiple connections, press F5 to select multiple connections before pressing the Delete key.

List Open Files

Lists the open files for the user that is highlighted. See figure 37.2.

Disk Information

This section discusses things you'll need to know about disks and other memory devices.

List System Hard Disks

This option enables you to view information about all system volumes. Select the desired drive from the drive list, and you will see a variety of information about the drive. Included is the driver for the disk, the disk size, partitions, mirror status, hot fix status, partition blocks, data blocks, redirection blocks, redirected blocks, and reserved blocks.

List Volume Segments per Hard Disk

This option displays basic information about a hard drive's volume segments.

Change the "Read After Write Verify" Status of the Hard Disk

Can change the read after write status between software level verify, hardware level verify, and disable verify events.

Flash the Hard Disk Light

Flashes the drive light.

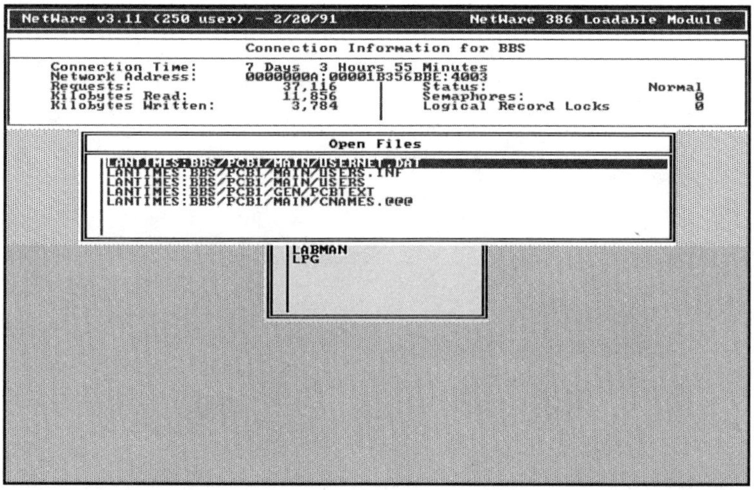

Figure 37.2
The Connection Information screen.

Activate/Deactivate a Hard Disk

Can switch a system drive between active and inactive.

Mount/Dismount a Removable Media Device

Makes it possible to mount and dismount devices such as magnetic optical or compact disk devices before they are removed. You can also view the status of the various removable devices from this utility (see fig. 37.3).

Lock/Unlock a Removable Media Device

It is good practice to lock a removable device prior to mounting it as a NetWare volume. This renders most eject buttons on removable media devices useless. Figure 37.3 shows the Drive Status screen.

LAN Information

This section covers information concerning details about local area networks.

LAN Drivers and Statistics

Displays information about the various network interface devices and connect points (see fig. 37.4). Included in the information is the driver name, version, node address, protocols, network address, total packets sent, total packets received, no ECB available count, send packet too big count, send packet too small count, receive packet overflow count, receive packet too big count, receive packet too small count, send packet miscellaneous errors, receive packet miscellaneous errors, send packet retry count, checksum errors, and hardware receive mismatch count.

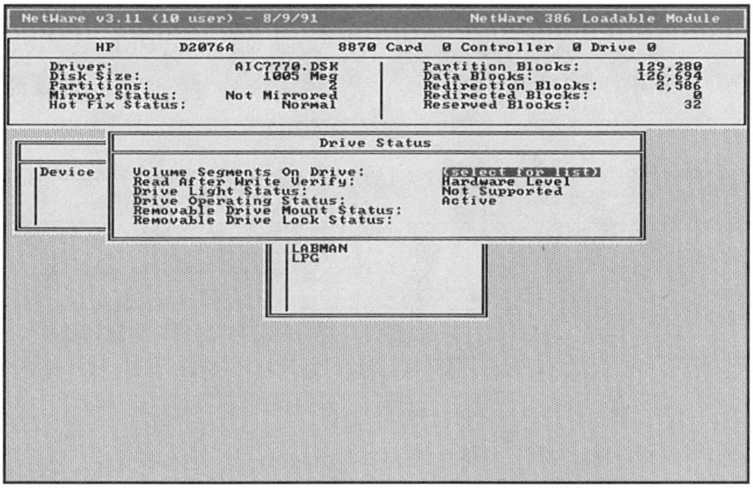

Figure 37.3
The Drive Status screen shows you pertinent information about your various hard drive media.

System Module Information

- List system modules (see fig. 37.5)
- List resources used by system modules

Lock File Server Console

- Lock the file server console
- Unlock the file server console

File Open/Lock Activity

- Check the status of a file
- View mounted volumes

Figure 37.6 shows the File Open/Lock Activity screen.

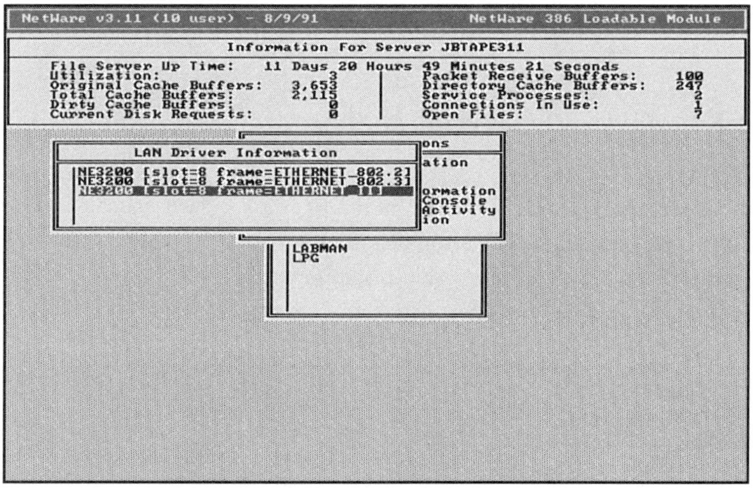

Figure 37.4
The LAN Information screen is your first reference point when using the MONITOR.NLM program.

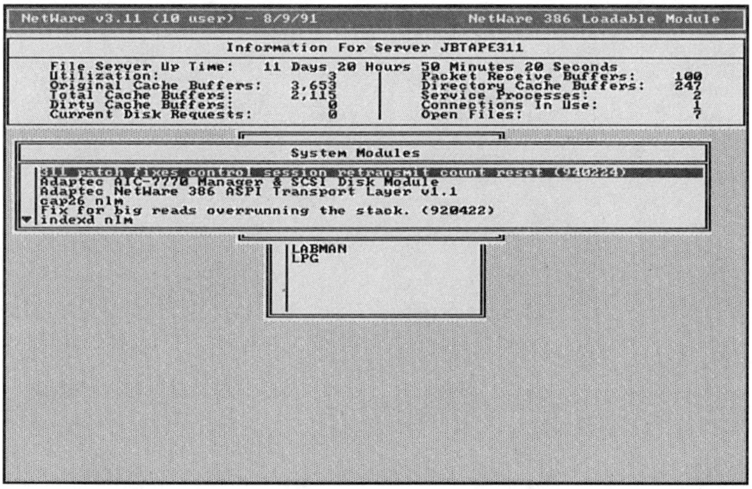

Figure 37.5
The System Modules screen affords you detailed information about your server status.

Resource Utilization

- View memory statistics
- View tracked resources

Figure 37.7 shows the Resource Utilization screen.

PATCHMAN

PATCHMAN is a utility available on NetWire and NSEPro that enables administrators to ensure that network modules are current and up to date. This is performed by means of the PATCHMAN.NLM that tracks and manages all official patches for

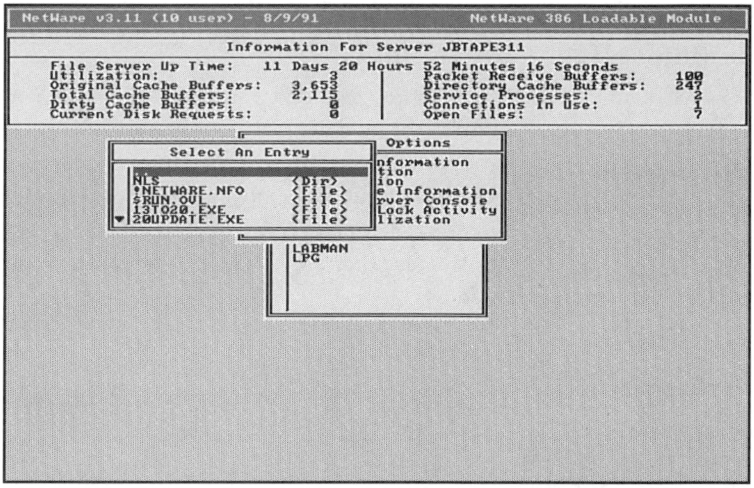

Figure 37.6
The File Open/Lock Activity screen lets you see at a glance what files a person presently has held open.

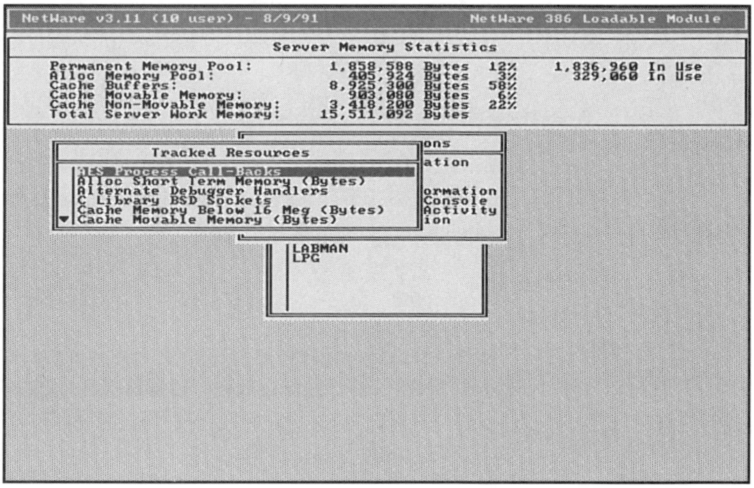

Figure 37.7
The Resource Utilization screen can give you detailed information about how your network resources are presently being used.

NetWare 3.11. The following list presents three basic types of patches for NetWare:

- **Dynamic.** Patches that can be loaded and unloaded at will. They are called *dynamic* because the server need not be powered down to have the changes take effect.
- **Semi-Static.** These semi-static patches can be loaded while the server is running (similar to dynamic patches), but cannot be unloaded unless you power down the server.
- **Static.** A *static* patch literally alters the SERVER.EXE file. It is good practice to back up your original SERVER.EXE prior to implementing any static patches.

Following is the PATCHMAN, dynamic, and semi-static patch installation procedure:

1. PATCHMAN is installed by first running the self-extracting file UPD311.EXE. This uncrunches the PATCHMAN.NLM that needs to be placed into the SYS:\SYSTEM directory.
2. Rename any patches that are currently on the system so that any new patches that have the same name as the current will not overwrite the old (in case you want to return the system to the pre-patch state).
3. Copy the new patches into the SYS:\SYSTEM directory.
4. Put LOAD PATCHMAN into the same script that holds your other system boot loadable modules.

To modify your SERVER.EXE file using a static patch, do the following steps:

1. Back your existing SERVER.EXE somewhere safe.
2. Copy the static patches into the directory that holds your existing SERVER.EXE file.
3. Patch your SERVER.EXE by typing the patch name followed by SERVER.EXE.

In the same way that you type MODULES to display the modules that are currently running on your server, you can type PATCHES to display what patches are currently in place in your server's memory. The patches will be grouped with regard to whether they are dynamic, semi-dynamic, or static.

Bridges, Routers, and Hubs

If your channel utilization exceeds 60 to 70 percent, split the channel with the bridge or router. The answer to the question of how much data should flow locally versus over bridges and routers, 80 percent should be local with a maximum of 20 percent over the bridge or router.

Bridges and routers do not always play well together. Routers cannot properly route packages when bridges are involved, and there is a possibility of data getting "trapped" in a segment of the topology.

Remember that no more than four repeaters can be included in any local topology. This includes many hubs that amplify the incoming signal prior to shipping it back out.

Speed should always be an issue. Realize that since routers need to make decisions as to how to route the packet, they typically take substantially longer to receive the packet and then send it along its merry way.

Protocol Analyzers

There is nothing quite like having a good protocol analyzer on your side when troubleshooting a network wire problem. If you have ever spent hours trying to find out where the intermittent break or short in a 10BASE2 cable is, even on a relatively small network, you can appreciate why so many administrators have sent buckets of money in the direction of the Hair Club for Men.

Spend just one evening, weekend, or holiday searching for cable gremlins, and you know that you can put almost no dollar value on a device that not only tells you how far and in what direction a problem exists, but what the problem actually is!

Realize that many protocol analyzers perform such intricate tasks such as capturing the packets and disseminating the information for you to review, but for the CNE exam you only need to know how to start an analyzer, stop the capture, and what data will help you analyze your problem.

Novell usesLANalyzer for Windows as its example for the CNE exam. This product is commercially available and is simple to use. It is not the most extensive network-monitoring package on the market today, but with it you can monitor real-time activity, identify trends, create reports, and troubleshoot your system.

When you use LANalyzer for Windows, you can monitor real-time activity either graphically or in text form. The main graphical dashboard display shows you in real time the packets per second, utilization percentage, errors per second, and the size of your capture buffer for your network, server, or router. These easy-to-read dials move accordingly with the respective network/server/router activity.

Identifying trends is an important aspect of troubleshooting any network. If you have a network card that is going bad and is "chattering" on your network, you will notice a network speed degradation that could possibly bring that segment to a halt. LANalyzer for Windows has a variety of charts that enable you to track trends. For the chattering NIC, the station monitor display would probably be most useful. If you were monitoring the station monitor screen while a NIC was merrily sending garbage away, you would probably notice an inordinate amount of data being generated from one station. Couple this discovery with minimal to no activity on the other stations and an increase in the error count, and your first action might be to swap out the NIC in the suspect machine to see if this rectifies your problem. Realize that just because one workstation is much more active than the others does not necessarily mean that the NIC is faulty. You might just have one workstation that is more communication-intensive than the others.

If you decide to frequent your LANalyzer for Windows program, you will undoubtedly want to set some thresholds for alarms within the program. "Settable" parameters include packets per second, utilization percentage, broadcasts per second, fragments per second, CRC errors per second, and server overload per minute. These parameters are self-explanatory, but unless you intend to scrutinize every aspect of your LANalyzer program every time you turn it on, take a moment to set your defaults so that you are alerted to any potential network problems.

Third-Party Disaster Recovery Products

Nowadays, when everybody seems to be coming out with backup and restoral products, it is important to take a look at a product's certified compliance. In the NetWare realm of backup products, the most popular certified compliance is *Storage Management System* (SMS) compliance. This standard began years ago with Novell's SBACKUP, but Novell has since released the standard to a standards committee in hopes that SMS will become the industry standard.

Without a standard, the backup and restore industry was becoming segmented. Segmentation is not necessarily a bad thing in the free-enterprise system; in this case, however, the end-user was frequently the loser. Frequently network administrators purchased "whiz-bang" backup utilities only to realize the utilities' shortcomings after a year or two. Upon attempting to contact the vendor to inquire about an upgrade path, network administrators frequently discovered that, in the cut-throat tape backup industry, their vendors had either gone away or merged with other companies. Often the vendors changed their formats (which were frequently not readable by other backup products anyway), which meant that if an administrator decided to purchase and use a new version (or merged product), past backups were history.

It cannot be stressed enough how important system backups are. Here are a few guidelines to follow when handling your backup procedures:

1. If a backup product does not allow for you to verify-after-write, don't buy it. You should always have this feature turned on.
2. Test the data that you back up. Ideally, you should have a mirror server identical to your online server. You can test that your backed-up data is valid by restoring it to your mirrored server. Realistically, you will only have a small area into which you can restore a small portion of your backup to ensure that the backup was valid.
3. Take an electronic look at your backup to verify that the data that you want to be backed up actually is. With many products, there is a log file that displays the names of all of the files that are backed to tape.
4. Obvious but necessary—do not ever overwrite your most recent tape.

Novell suggests that you verify that your data is indeed corrupted prior to restoring your server from tape. There are a couple of tools that can assist you in performing these tasks. The first is INSTALL.NLM. If you are having problems with drives or data, INSTALL displays useful information about the status of your drive and volume.

VREPAIR.NLM can be an invaluable tool when dealing with a suspect drive or volume. As invaluable as it is, however, if your hardware is damaged, there is nothing that you can do about it with software.

Burst Mode Advantages and Drawbacks

Normally, when a workstation makes a request to a server, the server responds with an acknowledgement that it has received a request. On smaller networks this is of little concern, but as your network grows, every little bit of optimization helps to keep the users from complaining about how slow their system is running. By enabling packet burst mode, you can increase performance on a larger LAN or WAN by expanding the size of the packet to over 512 bytes, as well as by allowing more than one packet to be included to the server before an acknowledgement is sent.

Although it might sound like enabling packet burst mode is a feature that should be implemented from the get go, by doing so you increase the possibility of damaging packets because of the congestion that will result in having to resend. This is where the argument for virtual loadable modules rather than NETX comes into play. NETX (or NET4, NET5, NET6, and so forth) is quite literal and will take packet sizes and order as law. VLMs, on the other hand, are more intelligent than NETX, and can dynamically adjust the packet window on the fly for both performance and speed. Although NETX's packet burst increases performance by an average of 38 percent, the VLM version displays an efficiency increase of 82 percent. Learn your VLMs and you will be happy that you did.

Questions

1. SET parameters can be changed ______.
   - A. in AUTOEXEC.NCF
   - B. in STARTUP.NCF
   - C. All of the Above
   - D. None of the Above

2. SET can be used to alter parameters for all except ______.
   - A. file caching
   - B. communications
   - C. palette colors
   - D. memory

3. Dirty Directory Cache Delay Time is used to determine the amount of time ______.
   - A. the system will wait until a directory table write request is written to disk
   - B. directory contents are stored in read-ahead buffers
   - C. the system will hold corrupted (dirty) data before discarding it
   - D. a user must wait before a response is given to their DIR request

4. By default, NetWare 3.0 and later use encrypted passwords.
   - A. True
   - B. False

Answers

1. C
2. C
3. A
4. A

PART V

Printing with NetWare

CHAPTER 38

Understanding Printing and NetWare Printing Services

One of the earliest—and continuous—benefits of networking your computer environment is the capability to share printers and related print services. A detailed understanding of printers and printing helps you take full advantage of this capability. To that end, this chapter discusses printers and printing in NetWare networks, and provides information about the following related topics:

- *Understanding printers and printing*
- *Identifying printing environments and components*
- *Understanding NetWare 2.x core printing*

Understanding Printers and Printing

As early printing design is based on printing through DOS applications, so too is much of today's network printing. Three methods of printing are commonly used in DOS-based applications. An understanding of these three methods may help you better understand network printing.

The following three printing methods are used by DOS-based applications:

- Interrupt 21 DOS function calls
- Interrupt 17 BIOS function calls
- Hardware direct I/O

The Interrupt 21 DOS function calls method is the simplest. Applications that use this method of printing simply send the print request directly to the printer, waiting until it is ready to accept its print job if it is presently busy with another. The drawback of this method is that it carries with it a great deal of printing overhead. The advantage is that it is readily compatible with most printing software and utilities.

The second method, the Interrupt 17 BIOS (Basic Input Output System) function call, is somewhat more complex than the first method. In this second method, the application accesses the printer by using the services of the ROM BIOS parallel printer port controller. Although somewhat more complex to use, this method provides additional features, including access to printer and controller status information.

The third method, hardware direct I/O (Input/Output), is the most direct of the three methods. This method ignores DOS and BIOS and instead interfaces directly with the printer. The main drawback to this approach is that the application itself must be correctly written to provide all interface with the printer. This method is useful for devices other than printers, if those devices need speed and minimal delay.

The first two options—Interrupt 21 DOS and Interrupt 17 BIOS—are compatible with NetWare printing redirection, using the CAPTURE command. The third method—hardware direct I/O—is not. It is better suited to video, serial devices, and similar devices.

Note

Applications that need to print to a serial device but which use this third printing method can still use the DOS MODE command to redirect the printing request from a parallel port to a serial port. To use the MODE command, type **MODE *parallel_port = serial_port*** and press Enter. Other options are available for use with the DOS MODE command, depending on which version of DOS you are running. Details about these other options can be found in your DOS manual.

Table 38.1 lists other printing-related terms and provides a brief explanation of and comments related to each term.

Table 38.1
Printer-Related Terms to Know

Term	*Description*	*Comments*
Redirection	Sending a print job to one location when it was originally intended for another location	The DOS MODE and NetWare CAPTURE commands can be used to redirect print jobs
Print Buffer	Temporary storage area for data being sent to a printer	There are three types of print buffers: external (between printer port and printer interface), internal (inside the printer), and memory-resident (in PC's memory)
Print Queue	A directory for temporarily storing print requests	Found on a NetWare file server
Spooling	Sending a print job to a queue on a NetWare server	CAPTURE, PCONSOLE, NPRINT, and NetWare-aware applications can use spooling
NetWare-aware	Capable of sending print jobs directly to NetWare print queues	Other networking software have network-aware printers
Print server	Responsible for polling print queues for job requests and routing the job to the correct network printer	Can be part of a NetWare server or a separate computer
Polling	Checking for jobs to be printed	Used with core printing services

Following are the three phases in the network printing process:

- Spooling
- De-spooling
- Printing

Spooling is the process of sending the actual print job across the network to a print queue. NetWare-aware applications and DOS applications with print services redirected to the network perform this process.

De-spooling is the process of transferring the print job from the print queue to the designated printer. Specialized NetWare Loadable Modules (NLMs) and Value Added Processes (VAPs) perform this function.

Note On NetWare 3 and 4 network file servers and on NetWare 3 multiprotocol routers, the NLM is PSERVER.NLM. On NetWare 3 and NetWare 2 external routers, the VAP is PSERVER.VAP. On dedicated DOS workstations in NetWare 2 or 3, the executable program is PSERVER.EXE.

Printing is the process of translating the print job into a printed document.

Identifying Printing Environments and Components

The different components associated with printing in a network environment (workstations, the NetWare Operating System, print servers, print queues, NetWare file servers, and printers) all play a role in the effective and efficient use of network printing. So too does the fact that NetWare printing services can support multiple workstation platforms (DOS, MS Windows, IBM OS/2, Apple Macintosh, and Unix BSD and AT&T hosts). In addition, the NetWare OS itself affects printing (core printing services provided in NetWare 2, or NetWare print services provided in NetWare 3 and 4). Each of these components and workstation platforms ultimately affect the quality of printing services on your network. Just how they can affect the quality of printing services on your network is important to developing an understanding of network printing.

The goal of printing services is to make their access and use as simple and as invisible as possible to network users. Supporting a variety of workstations on a NetWare network helps to accomplish that task. The workstations themselves contribute to this process whenever a network workstation is used to provide network printing services.

Workstations can provide printing services in two ways: through local printers and remote printers. A local printer, one attached to a workstation and accessible only to the workstation's user, does little to contribute to network printing services except for the service it provides to the local workstation. Having a printer attached to a workstation does not prevent the user from accessing files, printers, and print queues on the network, even though the local printer is not accessible by other network users.

On the other hand, remote printers are attached to workstations but can be accessed by other network users. Remote printers are accessible when the appropriate software is loaded at the workstation. In NetWare 2 and NetWare 3 environments, that software is the RPRINTER.EXE file. In NetWare 4 networks, that software is NPRINTER.EXE.

Besides direct attachment to a workstation, printers can be part of a network in the following ways:

- **Network direct.** Printers with a built-in network interface ("smart" printers) may be connected to the network cable at convenient locations.
- **External network direct.** Printers with external network interfaces can also be connected directly to the network cable.
- **Wide area remote.** Printers in LANs can be shared when LANs are connected using various communication methods to form WANs.
- **Print server.** A maximum of seven printers can be directly connected to a NetWare print server.

Note The main benefit of print servers is that print jobs can be directed to any printing device located anywhere on the network. In addition, there is no limit to the number of print servers that can be used on a network at one time. There can be only one print server per NetWare server, however.

The use of multiple print servers increases printing performance, and provides flexibility and convenience when placing printers on the network. Strategically placing printers, however, benefits not only the users and network administrators, but the efficiency of network printing as well.

Placing printers close to print servers, for example, generally increases printing performance. So too does placing the print server software on a dedicated PC instead of on a NetWare file server.

- **NetWare server.** A maximum of five printers can be directly connected to a NetWare server, provided that the print server software also is loaded on the NetWare server.

Note Not only can printers be directly connected to NetWare servers, but servers can also provide subdirectories (print queues) in which print jobs can be temporarily housed. Print jobs stored in these print queue subdirectories are recognizable by their Q file extension.

Various benefits are associated with using print queues on NetWare servers. First, certain network users can be assigned the responsibility of managing these queues. Those responsibilities may include deleting, ordering, holding, viewing, modifying, and flagging print jobs.

In addition, one or more servers can accept print requests from a single print queue (multiple printers assigned to a single queue), and a single server can service more than one print queue. The first option provides low-delay print services, and better distribution of print jobs. The second option provides distributed queue management, printing by form type, priority access to printers, cost-effective resource sharing, and job grouping by Print Description Language (PDL).

Finally, print management can be simplified by assigning queues to specific printers, and the priority of print jobs can be determined by the print queue into which the job is placed.

Understanding NetWare 2.x Core Printing

Core printing services are available only on NetWare file servers running versions earlier than NetWare 2.2. Using NetWare core printing services, you can attach a maximum of five printers directly to serial or parallel ports (COM1, COM2, LPT1, LPT2, and LPT3) on the NetWare file server, to be used as network printers. While in a very small network, connecting all printers to the file server may be sufficient, NetWare core printing services have two major drawbacks.

First, connecting all network printers to the file server adds the printing process to the server itself, thus possibly slowing other services normally provided by the NetWare file server. Second, print servers cannot be used, nor can workstation-attached or network-attached printers.

Installing NetWare 2.*x* core printing by using the Basic installation establishes some defaults. The defaults include: the creation of a print queue named PRINTQ_O on the server; generation of the NET$OS.EXE file with core printing included; the ability of all users (because they are members of group EVERYONE) to access and use these printers; and the establishment of polling at 15-second intervals, a time option that, depending on the network's demand for print services, may be too frequent or not frequent enough.

Note The following commands can be used with core printing services:

- **QUEUE.** To create a new print job (QUEUE *queue_name* CREATE), view a list of print queues (QUEUE), change a job's priority in the print queue (*queue_name* CHANGE JOB *n* TO PRIORITY *x*), remove a print queue (*queue_name DESTROY*), remove a job from the print queue (*queue_name* DELETE JOB n/*), and see a list of print jobs in the queue (*queue_name* JOBS).
- **PRINTER.** To alter or view a printer's configuration (PRINTER *n* CONFIG), assign a queue to a printer (PRINTER *n* ADD *queue_name*), or view available options for this command (PRINTER Help or PRINTER ?).
- **PSTAT.** To view the status of a printer from a workstation (PSTAT S=*server_name printer_name or printer_number*).

You can automate the process of loading the NetWare core printing services by placing the appropriate commands in the file server's AUTOEXEC.SYS file. To edit this file, start the SYSCON utility, choose Supervisor Options from the Available Topics menu, then choose Edit System AUTOEXEC File from the Supervisor Options menu (see fig. 38.1).

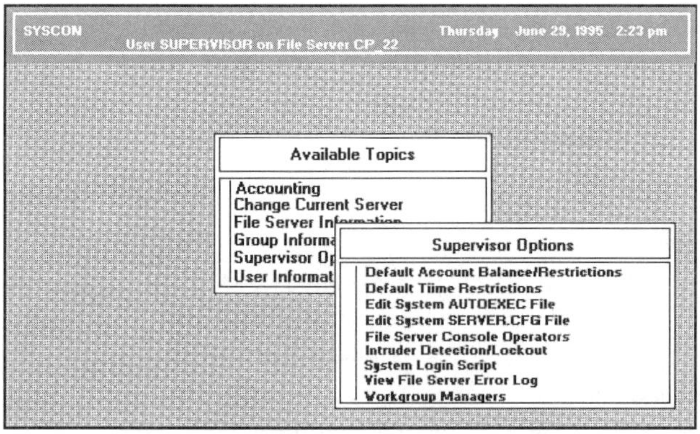

Figure 38.1
The SYSCON utility.

Questions

1. The printing method that enables the application to access the printer by using the ROM BIOS parallel printer port controller services is called ______.
   - ○ A. Interrupt 21 DOS function calls
   - ○ B. Interrupt 21 BIOS function calls
   - ○ C. Interrupt 17 BIOS function calls
   - ○ D. Hardware direct Input/Output
2. Which *three* printing methods are used by DOS-based applications?
   - ☐ A. Interrupt 21 DOS function calls
   - ☐ B. Interrupt 21 BIOS function calls
   - ☐ C. Interrupt 17 BIOS function calls
   - ☐ D. Hardware direct Input/Output
3. The ______ method of printing is *not* compatible with NetWare network printing redirection.
   - ○ A. Interrupt 21 DOS function calls
   - ○ B. Interrupt 21 BIOS function calls
   - ○ C. Interrupt 17 BIOS function calls
   - ○ D. Hardware direct Input/Output
4. A ______ is a temporary storage area used for data being sent to a printer.
   - ○ A. redirector
   - ○ B. print buffer
   - ○ C. spooler
   - ○ D. print server
5. The software responsible for polling print queues for job requests and then routing the job to the correct network printer is called the______.
   - ○ A. redirector
   - ○ B. print buffer
   - ○ C. spooler
   - ○ D. print server
6. The phase of printing that transfers the print job from the print queue to the designated printer is called______.
   - ○ A. redirecting
   - ○ B. spooling
   - ○ C. de-spooling
   - ○ D. printing
7. Of the following, which *three* perform de-spooling?
   - ☐ A. NPRINTER.EXE
   - ☐ B. PSERVER.NLM
   - ☐ C. PSERVER.VAP
   - ☐ D. PSERVER.EXE
8. In NetWare 2 and NetWare 3 environments, the software which must be loaded on a workstation to make that workstation's attached printer a remote printer is______.
   - ○ A. RPRINTER.EXE
   - ○ B. NPRINTER.EXE
   - ○ C. PSERVER.EXE
   - ○ D. RSERVER.EXE

9. A maximum of ______ printers can be directly connected to a NetWare file server.

   - A. 3
   - B. 5
   - C. 7
   - D. 9

10. Choosing the Basic installation option when installing core printing on a NetWare 2 network causes the ______ file to be generated by default.

    - A. RPRINTER.EXE
    - B. NET$OS.EXE
    - C. SERVER.EXE
    - D. NET$SYS.EXE

Answers

1. C
2. A, C, D
3. D
4. B
5. D
6. C
7. B, C, D
8. A
9. B
10. B

CHAPTER 39

Planning and Installing Basic Printing Services

You've heard the old cliché: Keep it simple. Sometimes simple is the best. Sometimes it is not. For example, using the NetWare 4 Basic Installation option to set up printing for your network certainly is simple, but that does not necessarily make it the best option because the simple setup may not truly meet your network's needs. To ensure that the network's needs are met, a well-planned and appropriately implemented network printing environment is necessary. This chapter deals with network planning and basic installation, and provides information about the following related topics:

- *Planning the printing environment*
- *Setting up and managing print queues*
- *Setting up and managing print servers and printers*

Planning the Printing Environment

There are two primary phases to planning a printing environment. The first is to understand what factors should be considered when you identify network printing requirements. The second is to understand the hardware, software, and other resources necessary for a well-designed network printing environment. This section discusses these two important phases of planning a printing environment.

Network Printing Requirements

The first step to determining network printing requirements is to conduct a needs analysis. A *needs analysis* is a study of current and future needs. Obtaining answers to the following types of questions should provide the basic information required to determine the printing needs of most network environments:

- How many current users need to print documents, and how many new users requiring access to print services are anticipated, in both the short and long term?
- How much printing does the average user do, based on the number of pages printed by each user in a single day?
- Do all users print to the same types of forms, or do forms vary (different size and shape of paper, preprinted documents, and so on)?
- How long can most users afford to wait for their printed documents, and will delays be detrimental to productivity?
- Is the layout of the building suitable to placing shared printers for ready access, or must additional printers be located so as to handle users who need easier access?
- Does the location of printers present any security issues, such as whether confidential data will have to be printed on a readily accessible printer?
- Have environmental factors such as excess noise, heating and cooling, fumes and odors, and so on been considered?

With the answers to these questions in hand, you can begin to decide such important issues as how many printers you will need, where the printers should be located, whether you will need only one or several print servers, and so on.

Network Printing Resources

Having analyzed your network's printing needs, you can then consider your available resources, as well as any additional resources you may need to provide. The following three types of resources should be considered:

- Physical (hardware)
- Applications and operating systems (software)
- Print services administrators (print server and print queue operators) and other human resources

Following are the physical resources to consider:

- The number and type (CPU) of workstations, and whether they can handle printers
- The number and type (not only CPU, but also version of NetWare OS) of file servers on the network, and their availability for printer attachment

- The number of print queues and print servers needed
- The number and types of printers available, including the amount of RAM available, types of interfaces they use, and fonts they provide
- Supplies needed to service the printers

Software resources to consider are the operating systems running at workstations (DOS, MS Windows, Unix, and so on), the NetWare OS versions running on network file servers, whether core printing services are to be used, and which applications are available to network users.

Print services administrators can include print queue operators as well as print server operators, in addition to the network Supervisor (or administrator, in NetWare 4) or users with Supervisor-equivalent rights.

Also to be considered are the rights end users will have to network printing services; the cost of providing printing services and service and support, both initially and as an ongoing benefit; and the training necessary not only for network users, but also for administrators, supervisors, and operators.

Setting Up and Managing Print Queues

Print queues (subdirectories located either in the SYS:SYSTEM directory on NetWare 2 and 3 servers, or on any volume in NetWare 4 servers) are an important part of network printing in all versions of NetWare—2, 3, and 4. In NetWare 2 and 3, print queues are bindery objects. In NetWare 4, print queues are NetWare Directory Services (NDS) objects. Print queues are used to maintain information about print jobs and print servers. Queue operator flags enable Supervisors, administrators, and print queue operators to control print queue access and use.

The PCONSOLE utility can be used to create and manage print queues in all versions of NetWare.

> **Note** The NetWare Administrator tool provided in NetWare 4 also can be used to create and manage print queues.

Using PCONSOLE, you can create print queues, rename or delete a print queue, view the Print Queue object ID, add or delete print queue operators and users, and modify operator flags. To use this utility, type **PCONSOLE** and press Enter. Next, choose Print Queue Information from the Available Options menu (see fig. 39.1). Now you can perform any of the listed tasks, some of which require that you have Supervisor rights.

To create a print queue, press the Insert key with the Print Queues screen open. At the New Print Queue Name prompt, type a name for the print queue, and then press Enter.

To rename a print queue, select a print queue from the list of print queues, press F3, delete the existing name, then type a new name and press Enter.

To delete a print queue, select a print queue from the list of print queues, press Delete, and answer Yes when prompted.

To view a print queue's object ID number, choose a print queue. From the Print Queue Information menu, choose Print Queue ID.

Figure 39.1
The PCONSOLE Available Options menu.

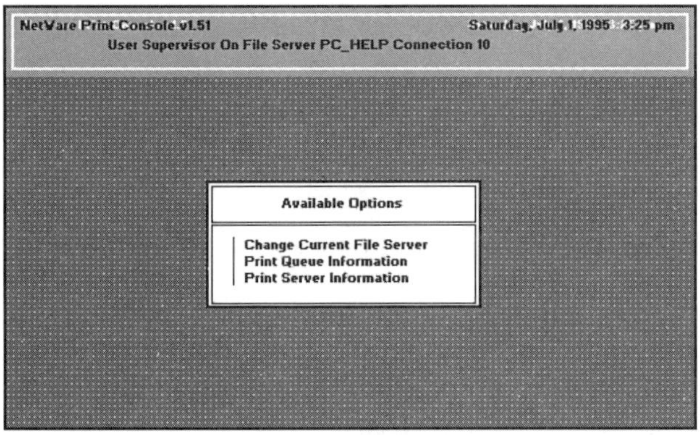

To add or delete a print queue operator, select a print queue from the list of print queues, then choose Queue Operators. Press Insert to see a list of queue operator candidates from which to choose. Select one and press Enter, or mark several by pressing F5, and then press Enter. To delete queue operators, select one or mark several with the F5 key, then press Delete. Answer Yes at the Delete Queue Operator prompt.

To add or delete a print queue user, select a print queue from the list of print queues, then choose Queue Users. Press Insert to see a list of queue users from which to choose. Select one and press Enter, or mark several by using the F5 key, and then press Enter. To delete queue users, select one or mark several with the F5 key, then press Delete. Answer Yes at the Delete User prompt.

Access to print queues by users and print servers can be managed and controlled by using NetWare's print queue operator flags. The following three operator flags can be modified:

- **Users can place entries in queue.** When set to No, users cannot add print jobs to the print queue.
- **Servers can service entries in queue.** When set to No, print servers cannot access the queue to service print jobs.
- **New servers can attach to queue.** When set to No, new print servers cannot attach to the print queue for the purpose of servicing print jobs.

To modify any of these operator flags, select the flag and press Y to toggle the flag on, or press N to toggle the flag off.

You also use print queues to view information about print jobs. Figure 39.2 shows a typical print queue entry.

Table 39.1 describes the function of each field in the Print Queue Entry Information screen, and provides additional information about some of the fields.

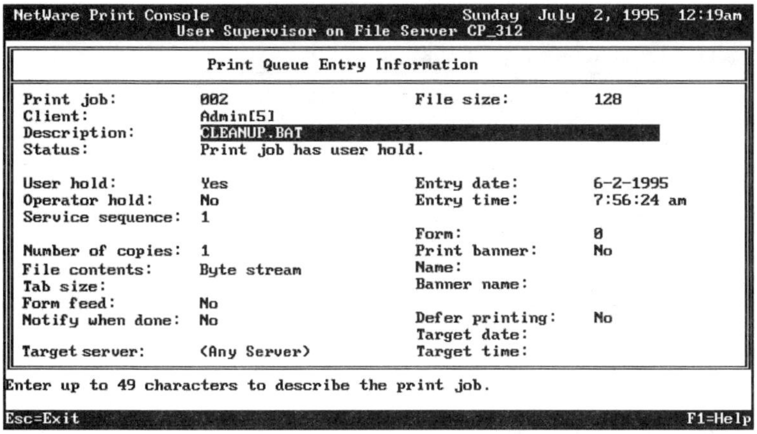

Figure 39.2
The Print Queue Entry Information screen.

Table 39.1
Print Queue Entry Information Fields

Field Name	*Description*	*Additional Information*
Print job	Number assigned to this print job request	Cannot be changed
Client	User's name and connection number	Cannot be changed
Description	Name of file being printed	
Status	Condition of print job	Shows whether job is on hold or ready to print
User hold	User can prevent job from printing by setting to Yes	
Operator hold	Queue operator can put any print job on hold	
Service sequence	Order in which job is to be printed	Queue operator can change job order to be printed

continues

Table 39.1, Continued
Print Queue Entry Information Fields

Field Name	*Description*	*Additional Information*
Number of copies	Quantity of copies to be printed, as requested by user	From 1 to 250, inclusive
File contents	If set to text, tabs replaced by spaces; if set to byte stream, data sent directly to printer	Choose Text or Byte stream
Tab size	Sets number of spaces to use when replacing a tab	Use 1 to 18, inclusive
Form feed	Prevents form feed from being sent to printer	
Notify when done	Notifies sender when print job is done	Set to Yes to notify, No to not notify
Target server	Print server to service this print job	"Any Server" indicates no server was specified
File size	Size of this file (in bytes)	Cannot be changed
Entry Date	Date job sent to queue	Cannot be changed
Entry Time	Time job sent to queue	Cannot be changed
Form	Name of form to be used for this job	Specified by form number
Print banner	Specifies whether to print a banner page	Set to Yes or No
Name	Text for upper part of banner page	Maximum of 12 alphanumeric characters

Field Name	*Description*	*Additional Information*
Banner name	Text for lower part of banner page	Maximum of 12 alphanumeric characters
Defer printing	Set to Yes to print at a later date and time	
Target date	Date when job is to be printed if Defer printing field is set to Yes	Use any standard format
Target time	Time when job is to be printed	Examples: 3 pm, 03:00:00, or 3:00 pm

Setting Up and Managing Print Servers and Printers

Print servers poll print queues looking for jobs to be printed. They then take ready-to-print jobs from print queues and send them to the appropriate print server.

The following three types of print servers differ in location and the type of file used to run them:

- **NetWare Loadable Module.** The NLM print server is created by loading the PSERVER.NLM file on a NetWare 3 or NetWare 4 file server. This type of print server can control a maximum of 16 printers on a NetWare 3 network, and a maximum of 255 printers on a NetWare 4 network.
- **Value Added Process.** The VAP print server is created by loading the PSERVER.VAP file on an external router (bridge) or a NetWare 2 (2.15c or higher) file server. This type of print server can control a maximum of 16 printers.
- **Executable.** The DOS executable print server is created by running the PSERVER.EXE file on a dedicated DOS-based NetWare workstation.

To create, configure, delete, or change a print server, use the PCONSOLE utility. To create a print server, start PCONSOLE and complete the following steps:

1. Choose Print Server Information from the Available Options menu.
2. Press Insert.
3. Provide a name for the print server (47 characters maximum) and press Enter.

Note Upon creation of a print server, a subdirectory is created in the SYS:SYSTEM directory, and a bindery object is created. When the print server is brought up the first time, a file called FILESERV is created. When additional print servers are brought up, information about those servers is added to this file, increasing its size by 48 bytes for each NetWare server added to the service list.

The following other configuration actions occur as print servers are configured:

- Each time a printer is defined for a print server, a file called PRINT.*nnn* (with *nnn* representing the printer's number) is created. This file contains such information as the name of the printer, its IRQ number, buffer size, baud rate, and so on.
- Each time a print queue is assigned to a printer, a file called QUEUE.*nnn* (with *nnn* representing the printer's number) is created. This file contains such information as the queue's name and its printing priority.
- Each time a notification list is added for a printer, a file called NOTIFY.*nnn* (with *nnn* representing the printer's number) is created. This file contains such information as the name and type of the object to be notified, and how much time should elapse before notification is first sent (as well as between notifications).

After you choose a print server from the list of print servers, you can delete the print server (see fig. 39.3) or modify various aspects of information related to the print server.

To modify print server information (that can be modified), you first choose the appropriate option from the Print Server Information menu, then complete the steps related to that option.

The following options are available for NetWare 2 and 3 print servers:

- **Change Password.** Provide a new password and press Enter, retyping the password at the prompt.

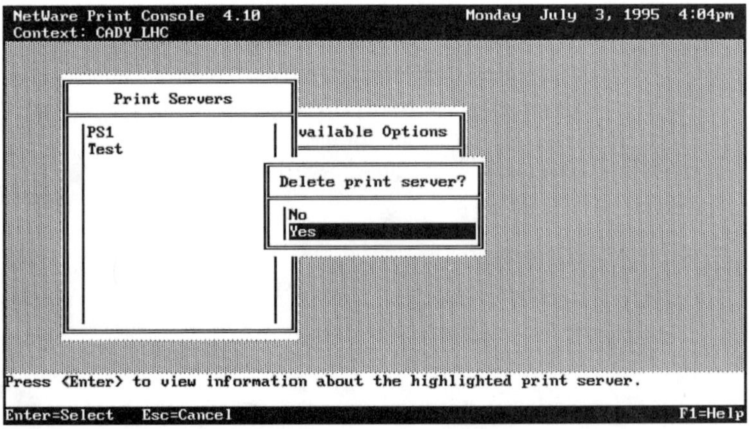

Figure 39.3
NetWare 4's prompt to delete a print server.

- **Full Name.** Type a descriptive name of no more than 62 alphanumeric characters, and press Enter.
- **Print Server Configuration.** Choose File servers to be Serviced, then choose one or more (mark with F5) NetWare servers, to authorize each server to service a print queue. (To discontinue service, press Delete after you choose the file servers.) To add a print server, press Insert, then provide a name and additional information (see the following Note).

Note

With this option, you can also configure printers to be serviced by this print server. You can use this option also to assign a permanent service mode (choose Queue service mode), create or edit a list of users to be notified when the printer needs attention (Notify List for Printer), or permanently assign a print queue to a printer (Queues Serviced by printer).

To configure printers being serviced by this print server, after choosing Printer Configuration from the Print Server Information menu, choose an existing printer number, provide the following information, then press Escape and, when finished, answer Yes at the Save changes prompt:

  - **Type of printer.** If the printer is directly connected to the print server's I/O port, choose a serial port such as COM1, or a parallel port such as LPT1. If the printer is connected to a DOS workstation running NPRINTER or RPRINTER, choose one of the Remote (parallel or serial) options.
  - **Method of port handling.** Choose either interrupt-driven or polling. At the Use Interrupts prompt, answer Yes (for quickest printing), then provide the correct interrupt number. If other devices use the same interrupt number as the port, choose No.
  - **Buffer size.** Enter the number of kilobytes for the print buffer. A maximum of 20 and a minimum of 3 are allowed.
  - **Starting form.** Provide the number of the form to be used when the print server is loaded.
  - **Queue service mode.** Enables you to choose to change forms as necessary, minimize form changes across queues, minimize form changes within queues, and service only currently mounted forms.
  - **Communication parameters.** Define information such as baud rate, data bits, stop bits, parity, and whether to use X-On/X-Off for serial printers.

- **Print Server ID.** View object ID shown for this print server, as well as the name of the NetWare server on which this print server was defined.
- **Print Server Operators.** Add or remove print server operators by using the Insert or Delete keys.
- **Print Server Users.** Add or remove users by using the Insert or Delete keys.
- **Print Server Status/Control.** Attach or detach a print server to/from a NetWare printer by choosing the File Servers Being Serviced menu option and adding (press Insert and choose from the list) or removing (select one or more servers and press Delete) attached servers.

The following options are available for NetWare 4 print servers (see fig. 39.4):

- **Printers.** View, add (press Insert), or delete (press Delete) printers assigned to this print queue.
- **Information and Status.** View type, version, print server's advertising name, and status of this print server, as well as the number of printers being serviced (if the print server is up), or the print server's status (Down) if it is not presently up and running.
- **Users.** View, add (press Insert), or delete (press Delete) users who can use this print server.
- **Operators.** View, add (press Insert), or delete (press Delete) operators responsible for this print server.
- **Description.** Add, view, or change (press F3) the description associated with this print server.
- **Password.** Add or change this print server's password.
- **Audit.** Enable and configure auditing of this print server, and view or delete the print server audit log.

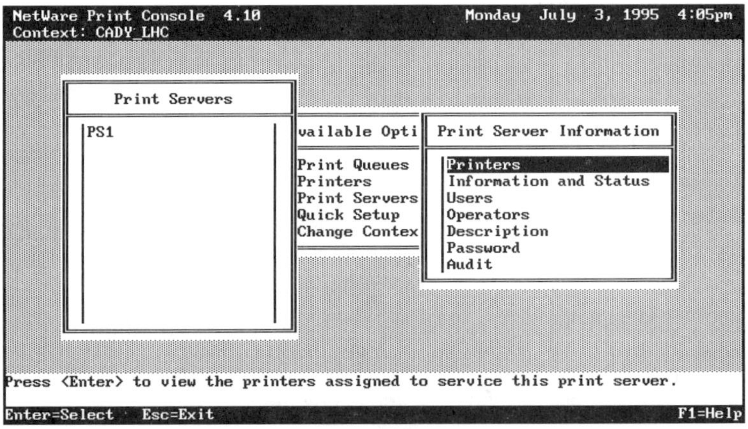

Figure 39.4
The Print Server Information menu.

Questions

1. The version of NetWare running on the file server is a ______ printing resource to be considered.
   - ○ A. hardware
   - ○ B. software
   - ○ C. administration
   - ○ D. human
2. The *two* phases of planning a printing environment are ______ and ______.
   - ☐ A. understanding network printing requirements
   - ☐ B. creating print queues and servers
   - ☐ C. understanding resources necessary for a well-designed network
   - ☐ D. conducting a needs analysis
3. The ______ is *not* a physical resource issue to be considered when designing network printing.
   - ○ A. workstation's CPU
   - ○ B. number of print servers
   - ○ C. OS running at the workstation
   - ○ D. supplies required for printers
4. In addition to PCONSOLE, the ______ utility can be used to create and manage print queues.
   - ○ A. NetWare User Tool
   - ○ B. PRINTCON
   - ○ C. PSERVER
   - ○ D. NetWare Administrator
5. Which of the following is *not* a print queue operator flag?
   - ○ A. Users can place entries in queue
   - ○ B. Operators can hold print jobs
   - ○ C. Servers can service entries in queue
   - ○ D. New servers can attach to queue
6. To view information about print jobs, use the ______ option in PCONSOLE.
   - ○ A. Print Job Description
   - ○ B. Current Queue Status
   - ○ C. Print Servers
   - ○ D. Print Queues
7. Of the following, which *three* are items of information provided on the Print Queue Entry Information screen?
   - ☐ A. Buffer Size
   - ☐ B. Print Job
   - ☐ C. Service Sequence
   - ☐ D. Operator Hold
8. Which of the following is *not* a type of print server?
   - ○ A. PSERVER.NLM
   - ○ B. PSERVER.VAP
   - ○ C. PSERVER.EXE
   - ○ D. PSERVER.VLM

9. When a print server is brought up the first time, a file called ______ is created.
   - A. FILESERV
   - B. PRINTSER
   - C. PRINTQ
   - D. PSERVER

10. If you want to assign a permanent service mode to a print server, you must ______.
    - A. choose Type of Printer and specify a port in PCONSOLE
    - B. choose Queue service mode from the Print Server Configuration option in PCONSOLE
    - C. load PSERVER.EXE on the file server and choose the appropriate print server
    - D. load PSERVER.VAP on a NetWare 3 file server

Answers

1. B
2. A, C
3. C
4. D
5. B
6. D
7. B, C, D
8. D
9. A
10. B

CHAPTER 40

Customizing Printing for DOS and Windows

Many applications are capable of interfacing directly with the network to provide printing services. Some applications are not. In addition, most MS Windows applications can access network printing, but there are some differences between local printing and network printing under MS Windows 3.1. Various NetWare programs can be used to accommodate not only those applications incapable of directly accessing network printing services, but also the variations expected while printing from within applications compatible with MS Windows 3.1.

This chapter, which provides information about printing on the NetWare network, is divided into the following two sections:

- Printing from DOS Applications
- Printing from MS Windows 3.1 Applications

Printing from DOS Applications

The following NetWare utilities provide printer control to DOS applications:

- PRINTDEF
- PRINTCON
- CAPTURE
- SMODE
- NPRINT
- RPRINTER
- NPRINTER
- NetUser (NetWare 3.12 and 4)
- NetWare Administrator (NetWare 4)

This section discusses these utilities and how to use them to customize printing and enable access to printer capabilities that may not otherwise be supported by the DOS application.

PRINTDEF

The PRINTDEF utility enables you to create custom definitions for network printers and forms. It stores these custom definitions in a server-wide database file called SYS:PUBLIC\NET$PRN.DAT. Network users can access this file, but it must be created by the network administrator. After printer definitions have been created, copies of definitions can be made (exported). Other existing printer definitions can also be copied (imported) by using the PRINTDEF utility.

To use this utility, type **PRINTDEF** and press Enter. The PrintDef Options menu opens (see fig. 40.1).

Choose the Print Devices option to create, change (edit), or delete network *printer definitions* (files containing strings of printer commands that control and specify the printer's actions). The names of these files end in the PDF extension. Choose the Forms option to create, change, or delete network

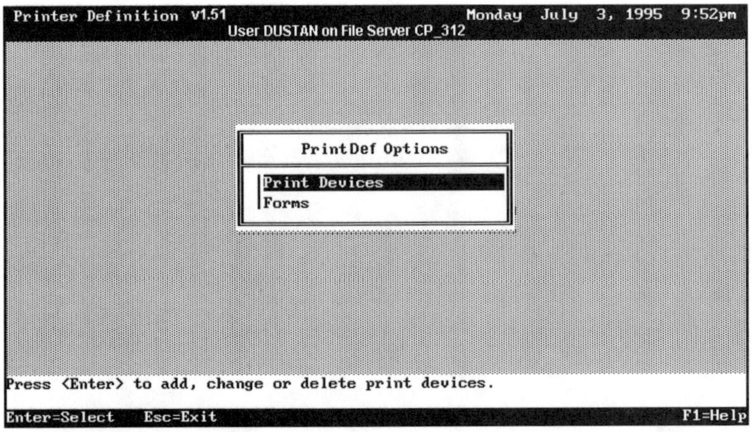

Figure 40.1
The PrintDef Options menu.

form types (definitions of paper or preprinted forms to be used in the printer). After the PRINTDEF database is created, it is used by PRINTCON, CAPTURE, and other printing-related utilities to accomplish various printing tasks.

Note The PRINTDEF utility in NetWare 4 is slightly different from its counterpart in NetWare 2 and 3. If you compare figure 40.2 to figure 40.1, you can see that the wording for menu names (Available Options versus PrintDef Options) and options (Printer Forms instead of Forms) is slightly different. Note also that the NetWare 4 version has a third option (Change Current Context), with which you can change your context in the NDS tree before creating, deleting, or modifying a print device or form.

To create, delete, or edit a printer definition, choose Print Devices from the Available Options (or PrintDef Options) menu. The Print Device Options menu (see fig. 40.3) is the same for all three versions of NetWare. Then complete the following steps:

1. Choose Edit Print Devices.
2. Choose a printer from the list of defined printers.

3a. Add a print device by pressing Insert, typing a name, and pressing Enter.

3b. Or, delete a print device by selecting the device, pressing Delete, and choosing Yes at the prompt.

3c. Or, edit a print device by choosing the device to be edited, then making changes to print modes and print functions.

Note To edit print device functions or modes, first choose either Device Functions or Device Modes from the Edit Print Devices menu. Next, choose either an existing function or an existing mode. (Alternatively, instead of choosing an existing function or mode, at this point you can add a new function or mode by pressing Insert and then providing a name for the function or mode.) Finally, edit the contents of the function or mode, then exit the PRINTDEF utility and save the changes.

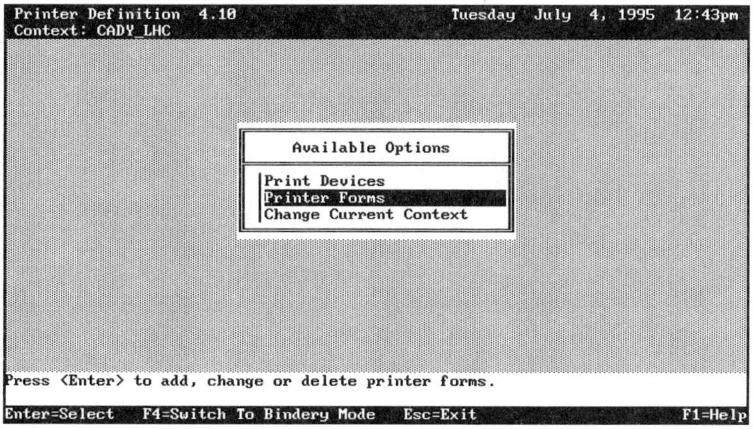

Figure 40.2
The Available Options menu in NetWare 4 version of PRINTDEF utility.

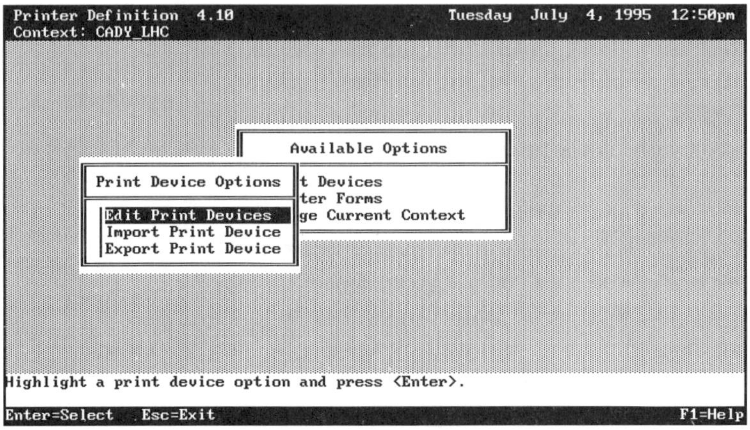

Figure 40.3
The Print Device Options menu.

To copy an existing printer definition into your PRINTDEF database (import), or from your PRINTDEF database to another one on another file server (export), choose Print Devices from the PrintDef Options menu, then complete the following steps:

1a. Choose Import Print Device.

1b. Or, choose Export Print Device.

2a. Type **SYS:PUBLIC** in the Source Directory field, and press Enter if you are importing a print device.

2b. Or, choose a print device (.PDF) file to export.

3a. Choose a file to import from the Available .PDFs list.

3b. Or, type the path to the location to which the print device file is to be copied (Destination Directory), as well as a name (without the PDF extension) for the print device file, and press Enter.

To create, delete, or edit a form type, choose Forms from the PrintDef Options menu, then complete the following steps:

1. Choose a form from the Forms list.
2. Add a form by pressing Insert, typing a name (12 characters maximum), pressing Enter, and giving the form a number (0 to 255, inclusive).

Note You can delete an existing form at this point by selecting (highlighting) it in the list of forms, then pressing Delete and choosing Yes when prompted. Or, you can edit a form by choosing it from the list of forms, then making necessary changes to the form's definition (length and width).

3. Provide the length of the form, based on the number of lines that can be printed on the page. You can enter any number from 1 to 255, inclusive.

   For example, if your printer can print 6 lines of text per inch of paper length, and your paper is 11 inches long, enter 66 (6 times 11).

4. Provide the width of the form, based on the number of characters that can be printed across the page in a single line. You can enter any number from 1 to 999.

For example, if your font size is 10 characters per inch and your page is 8 1/2 inches wide, enter 85 (10 times 8.5).

5. Save the form and exit the PRINTDEF utility.

PRINTCON

The PRINTCON utility enables both users and network administrators to set up print job configurations that help to customize the working environment. The CAPTURE, NPRINT, and PCONSOLE utilities can then use the custom print job configurations.

To use this utility, type **PRINTCON** and press Enter. From the Available Options menu (see fig. 40.4), you can then choose to accomplish any of the following tasks:

- **Edit Print Job Configurations.** Enables you to choose an existing print job configuration and modify various parameters set for this template, delete an existing print job configuration (select the configuration, press Delete, and answer Yes to the prompt to confirm), or rename a print job configuration (press F3, type a new name, and press Enter).
- **Select Default Print Job Configuration.** Enables you to choose which print job configuration to use as the default when you send a print request.
- **Copy Print Job Configurations.** Provides the capability to copy any individual user's PRINTCON.DAT database file to another user. Groups cannot have configurations set; therefore, a print job configuration must be created or copied for each user.

Note

In NetWare 4, significant changes have been made to the format of the PRINTCON database. In addition, a public database—instead of several private printing configuration databases—can be created (stored in SYS:PUBLIC). If your network does not include applications or utilities that use the PRINTCON.DAT databases created for individual users in the NetWare 2 or 3 environments, then delete these older DAT files from each user's SYS:MAIL*UserID* directory.

In addition, administrators can use the NetWare 4 NetWare Administrator utility to manage print job configurations.

Note also that in NetWare 4, the Copy Print Job Configurations option has been replaced by the Change Current Object option (see fig. 40.5). This option enables you to change your current user to that of another user, or to change your current container object.

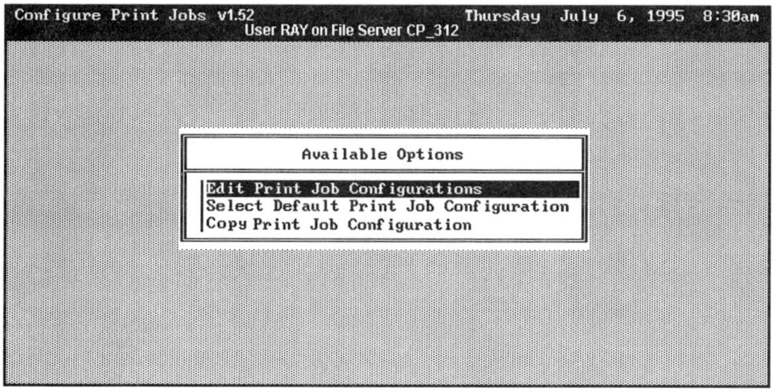

Figure 40.4
NetWare 2/3 PRINTCON Available Options menu.

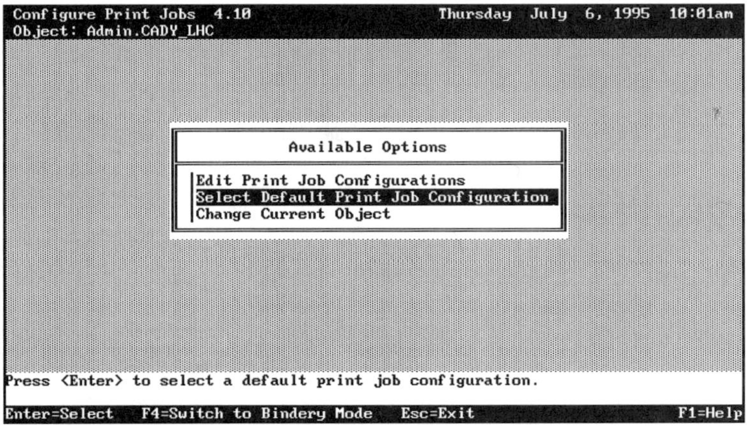

Figure 40.5
NetWare 4 PRINTCON Available Options menu.

When you create or edit a print job configuration, the parameters you work with are the same as those used with the CAPTURE and NPRINT utilities.

CAPTURE

The CAPTURE utility enables network users to customize their printing environment and accomplish a variety of printing-related tasks. For example, using the J (JOB) CAPTURE command option, the user can choose to apply a print job created by using the PRINTCON utility. You can use the J and other options when you issue the CAPTURE command, as well as when you create print job configurations. Several of the most commonly used CAPTURE options are shown in table 40.1.

Figure 40.6 shows the screen used to set options for print job configuration, using the NetWare 4 version of the PRINTCON utility. Note similarities between the field names in this figure and several of the CAPTURE options in table 40.1. The Notify and No Notify CAPTURE options, for example, are set by using a toggle (Yes/No) in the Notify when done field of this screen.

Table 40.1
Commonly Used CAPTURE Commands

Command	*Use*	*NetWare Version*	*Purpose*
All	ALL	4	Used with EC (ALL EC), ends capture of all LPT ports. Used with /?, provides online help
Autoendcap	AU	2, 3, 4	Automatically sends print job when application is closed

Command	*Use*	*NetWare Version*	*Purpose*
Banner	B	4	Specifies text to be placed in lower half of banner page. No more than 12 characters can be used
Local	L	2, 3	Specifies local port number
Notify	NOTI	2, 3, 4	Informs user when print job is finished
No Notify	NNOTI	3, 4	Does not inform user when print job is done
Printer	P	4	Specifies which printer is to receive print job
Server	S	4	Specifies NetWare server to which the print job should be directed if server is not the default server
Show	SH	2, 3, 4	Shows current status of CAPTURE command
Timeout	TI		Specifies how many seconds to wait after printing text has been received before the print job is deemed complete

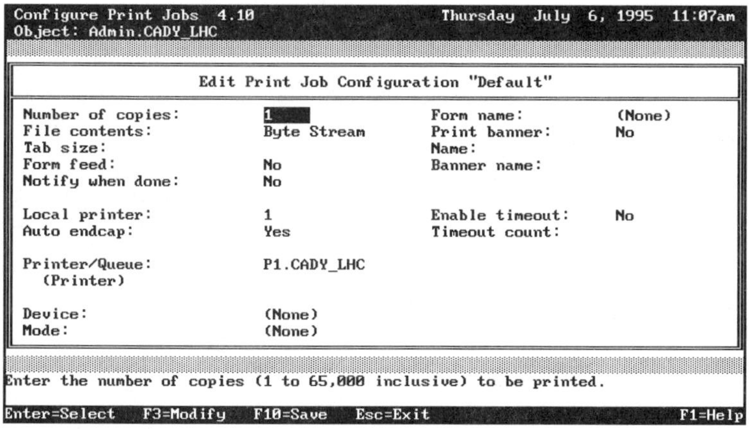

Figure 40.6

The Edit Print Job Configuration screen.

SMODE

The NetWare 2 and 3 SMODE command-line utility is used to modify how PCONSOLE, CAPTURE, and NPRINT function, so as to enable all currently logged-in users to use one PRINTCON database on a single file server. (In NetWare 4, the equivalent to using SMODE is to create and use a Public PRINTCON database stored in the SYS:PUBLIC directory on a NetWare 4 file server.)

Search mode (SMODE) is set to 0 by default. This setting causes all NetWare executable files to search the individual user's mail directory for a PRINTCON.DAT file. By changing the search mode setting to 5, NetWare executable files can use search drive mappings to find the PRINTCON.DAT file stored in SYS:PUBLIC, effectively using a global print job configuration instead of a private one.

To change the SMODE default of 0 to 5 for the PCONSOLE, CAPTURE, and NPRINT utilities to use, type the following nine lines of commands, pressing Enter after each command:

FLAG SYS:PUBLIC\PCONSOLE.EXE N

FLAG SYS:PUBLIC\CAPTURE.EXE N

FLAG SYS:PUBLIC\NPRINT.EXE N

SMODE SYS:PUBLIC\PCONSOLE.EXE /
➥Mode=5

SMODE SYS:PUBLIC\CAPTURE.EXE /
➥Mode=5

SMODE SYS:PUBLIC\NPRINT.EXE /
➥Mode=5

FLAG SYS:PUBLIC\PCONSOLE.EXE
SRO

FLAG SYS:PUBLIC\CAPTURE.EXE SRO

FLAG SYS:PUBLIC\NPRINT.EXE SRO

The first three commands set the flags on the PCONSOLE, CAPTURE, and NPRINT utilities to normal, so that their SMODE level can be changed. The next three commands change the SMODE level from the default of 0 to 5, for each of these three utilities. The last three commands change the flags on the three related utilities back to their original settings (-Shareable, Read-Only).

Note: Remember to remove the individual user's PRINTCON.DAT file from each users SYS:MAIL*UserID* directory.

NPRINT

As a workstation utility, NPRINT enables you to print DOS text files, or files preformatted by a DOS application program, to a network printer. You can use a variety of options with this command, most of which are the same as those used with the CAPTURE utility. The SHow, Autoendcap, NoAutoendcap, TImeout, Local, CReate, and Keep CAPTURE options do not apply to the NPRINT command.

RPRINTER

The RPRINTER utility enables you to connect or disconnect a *remote* printer (connected to a workstation) on a NetWare 3 network. NetWare 4 networks also can use remote printers, but they use NPRINTER instead of RPRINTER.

NPRINTER

As with RPRINTER on a NetWare 3 network, NPRINTER enables you to connect printers to workstations, which can then be accessed by other network users. NPRINTER.NLM is loaded on the NetWare 4 file server to provide remote printing services.

NetUser

This utility, available in NetWare 3.12 and NetWare 4 networks, is designed to enable users to add, modify, or delete their own print jobs. Figure 40.7 shows the NetUser utility Available Options menu running on a NetWare 4 file server.

NetWare Administrator

The NetWare Administrator utility can be used to create and administer printing services in the NetWare 4 environment. It is a GUI (*Graphical User Interface*) utility, which is run from inside MS Windows. Logged in to the network as the Administrator, you can accomplish the following tasks by using the NetWare Administrator utility:

- Create, control, monitor, and manage print queues
- Create, control, monitor, and manage print servers
- Delete, change, monitor, and reorder print jobs
- Assign print queue objects to printers, and printer objects to print servers

Printing from MS Windows 3.1 Applications

As with DOS-based network printing, a printer must be directly attached to the workstation, or the workstation must be connected to a network in order to print through MS Windows. In addition, a driver file for the printer must be available and properly configured to support the printer being accessed. MS Windows printer drivers can be used to access printing while still supporting the MS Windows environment and applications.

Note A print driver file is a DLL (dynamic link library) file with the DRV extension instead of a DLL extension. Print driver files are capable of communicating with a specific printer in order to translate application print requests into information the printer can use. MS Windows driver files enable users to access particular attributes of different printers. For example, a print driver makes it possible to specify such things as the margins to be used when printing a document, which typeface to use, which paper tray to choose from, and so on.

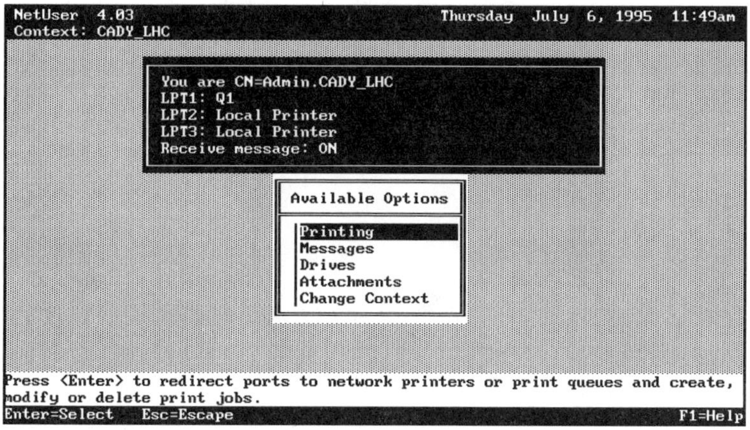

Figure 40.7
NetUser Available Options menu.

MS Windows applications access printing by using the GDI (Graphics Device Interface). GDI formats the output sent to the printer, as well as that sent to the monitor. Applications running under MS Windows use the GDI to call the active MS Windows Print Manager. From there, print jobs are formatted and printed one page at a time. When there is more to be printed than can be immediately sent to the printer, the additional print pages are stored in either the MS Windows TEMP directory, or the root directory of the default drive's hard disk. From either of these locations, jobs then can be sent directly to a NetWare print queue, to a local queue, or to a local printer port.

When the MS Windows Print Manager is not active or is not installed, GDI sends the data directly to a DOS device rather than to a print queue on the hard disk.

When the MS Windows Print Manager is installed and local printing is enabled, the formatted pages are sent by GDI to a queue file on the local hard disk, which the Print Manager controls.

When the Print Manager is enabled and network printing is available, the formatted pages are sent by GDI to a network queue file, bypassing the Print Manager's local queue file.

Note

The NetWare CAPTURE command can be used with MS Windows to redirect printing to a NetWare queue. By using the CAPTURE command, the user can specify which queue to use for print jobs. The command also enables users to monitor and manipulate jobs in the print queue before they are printed, and to otherwise exercise a greater degree of control over print jobs (after they have been sent to a print queue) than might be possible with local printing only.

You can use MS Windows 3.1 to set up printing for each application that needs print support, as well as for each type of printer being used. The setup for a specific printer is called the printer's *device context.* Most applications check the printer's device context before attempting to print. When a print request is made, MS Windows checks to see whether the application itself has established any specific print settings. If it has, MS Windows follows those settings. If it has not, MS Windows checks memory for the most recent print settings and uses those. If no print settings are stored in memory, MS Windows checks for print settings established in the WIN.INI file and uses those. If the WIN.INI file does not contain the necessary printer and port settings, MS Windows uses the defaults in its own setup to complete the print request (see fig. 40.8).

To take full advantage of MS Windows printing, you may need to set up printing by using the Printers dialog box in the MS Windows Control Panel (see fig. 40.9).

To install, configure, set up, or remove a printer, complete the following steps:

1. Open the MS Windows Control Panel.
2. Choose Printers.
3. Choose a printer, then choose one of the following:

    - **Setup.** To adjust settings such as DPI resolution (the number of dots per inch), paper tray to use, and so on
    - **Remove.** To remove or delete a printer from the list
    - **Set as default printer.** To choose the selected (highlighted) printer as the default print driver

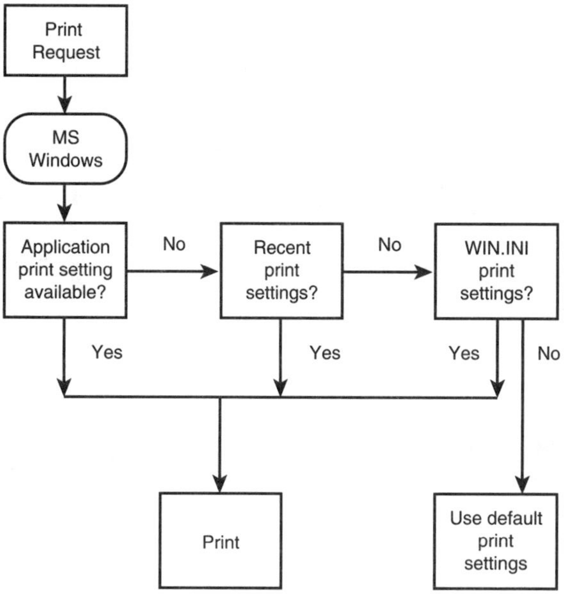

Figure 40.8
The steps taken by MS Windows when WIN.INI contains no printer settings.

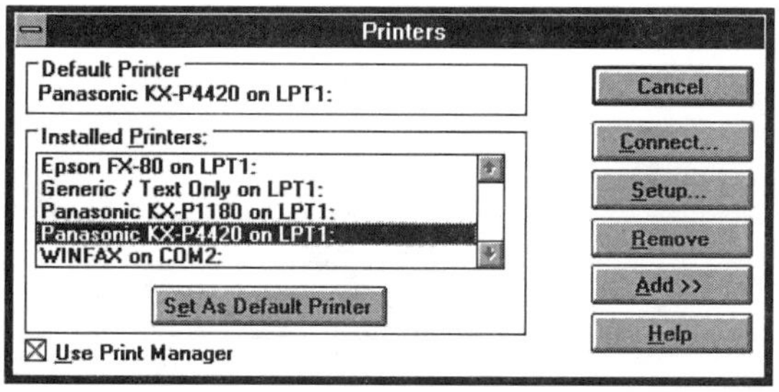

Figure 40.9
The MS Windows Printers window.

- **Connect.** To connect the printer to a local port (LPT or COM) or to a network drive

When you choose Connect and then choose Network to connect the printer to a NetWare network drive, the NetWare User Tools utility opens (see fig. 40.10). From this utility you choose to connect or disconnect a printer. In addition, you can make any printer connection a permanent one by marking the Permanent box.

Note Making a printer connection Permanent overrides CAPTURE redirection for the specified printer port.

You use the MS Windows Print Manager to set the following printing options:

- Priority (Low, Medium, or High)
- Alert Always
- Flash (or Ignore) if Inactive

- Network Settings
- Network Connections
- Printer Setup

Using the Print Manager, you can also view a NetWare print queue, temporarily pause any print job, resume a paused print job, or delete print jobs (see fig. 40.11).

The MS Windows WIN.INI file contains commands that help establish default printing settings.

The following main commands are included in the WIN.INI file:

- **Device=** Defines the default printer that MS Windows uses
- **DeviceNotSelectedTimeout=** Specifies how long MS Windows waits for a printer to be turned on before it sends a print request to a printer that currently is turned off (default is 15 seconds)

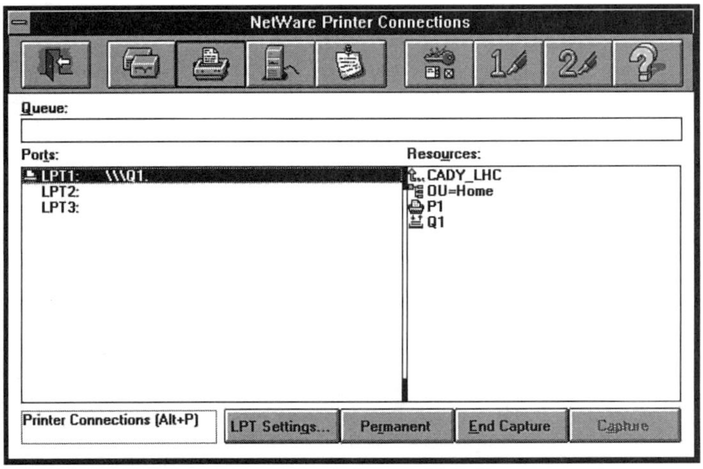

Figure 40.10
The NetWare User Tools Printer Connections window.

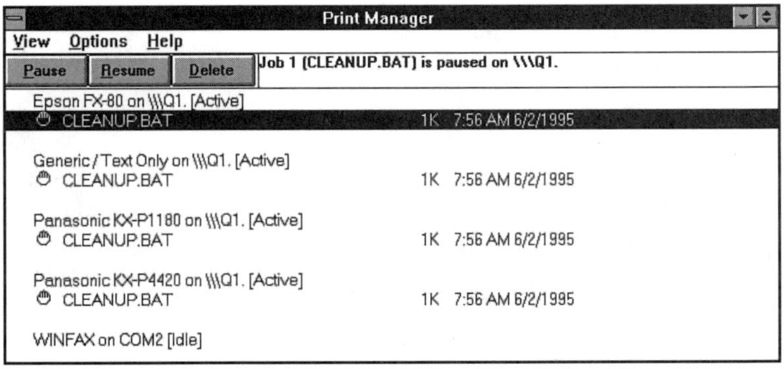

Figure 40.11
The Print Manager window.

- **DosPrint=** Uses Interrupt 21 for printing if set to Yes, or Interrupt 17 if set to No
- **Spooler=** Enables Print Manager, if set to Yes (the default); if set to No, disables Print Manager and does not display it in the Main window
- **TransmissionRetryTimeout=** Sets the number of seconds (default is 90) the printer will wait before sending out an error message when the printer is not accepting characters
- **LPT1:=** Specifies where the I/O port is redirected, if it has been redirected (such as the redirection that occurs when you use the NetWare User Tools to set a connection and specify it as Permanent)
- **LPT1-Options=** Lists all options associated with printing to this printer port, such as No Form Feed, number of copies to be printed, and so on (uses several of the same options used by the CAPTURE utility)

Questions

1. The PRINTDEF utility is used to ______.
   - ○ A. create custom printer and form definitions
   - ○ B. set up print job configurations
   - ○ C. customize user's printing environment
   - ○ D. connect or disconnect a remote printer

2. The file in which printer definitions are stored for server-wide use is called ______.
   - ○ A. NET$PRN.DBS
   - ○ B. NET$PRN.DAT
   - ○ C. NET$DAT.PRN
   - ○ D. NET$DBS.DAT

3. The ______ utility/command is used to set up job configurations to customize the user's environment.
   - ○ A. PRINTDEF
   - ○ B. PRINTCON
   - ○ C. SMODE
   - ○ D. CAPTURE

4. When creating or editing a print job configuration, many of the parameters that can be used are the same as those used in the ______ and ______ utilities.
   - ○ A. PRINTCON, PRINTDEF
   - ○ B. PRINTDEF, NPRINT
   - ○ C. NPRINT, CAPTURE
   - ○ D. CAPTURE, SMODE

5. The default setting for search mode (SMODE) is ______.
   - ○ A. 0
   - ○ B. 3
   - ○ C. 5
   - ○ D. 9

6. Which utility is used to connect or disconnect a remote printer?
   - ○ A. PRINTDEF
   - ○ B. PRINTCON
   - ○ C. SMODE
   - ○ D. RPRINTER

7. Of the following, which *three* are NetWare 2, 3, and 4 CAPTURE command options?
   - □ A. AUtoendcap
   - □ B. NoNOTIfy
   - □ C. NOTIfy
   - □ D. SHow

8. The ______ utility is designed to let users add, modify, or delete their own print jobs.
   - ○ A. NPRINTER
   - ○ B. RPRINTER

- ○ C. NetUser
- ○ D. NetWare Administrator

9. When the MS Windows Print Manager is not active, ______.
   - ○ A. GDI sends the formatted pages to a print queue on the local hard disk
   - ○ B. GDI sends the data directly to a DOS device
   - ○ C. GDI sends the formatted pages directly to a NetWare print queue
   - ○ D. GDI holds the print job until the Print Manager is activated

10. If you want to direct print jobs to a network printer by using the Printers option in the MS Windows Control Panel, you must choose ______.
    - ○ A. Capture
    - ○ B. Setup
    - ○ C. Set as default
    - ○ D. Connect

Answers

1. A
2. B
3. B
4. C
5. A
6. D
7. A, C, D
8. C
9. B
10. D

CHAPTER 41

Understanding Printing in NetWare 4

There are some basic differences between printing in the NetWare 4 (NDS) environment and printing in the NetWare 2 and 3 (bindery) environment. Other chapters in this section discuss NetWare 4 printing in contrast to NetWare 2 and 3. In this chapter, the following topics provide more detailed information about printing in the NetWare 4 environment:

- *NetWare 4 printing basics*
- *NetWare 4 printing configuration and administration*

NetWare 4 Printing Basics

Because NetWare 4 is based on NetWare Directory Services (NDS), print services must function in that environment as well. To some extent, print service configuration and administration in NetWare 4 is easier than in NetWare 2 or NetWare 3. Standard printing elements—print servers, print queues, and printers—are NDS objects in NetWare 4. As such, their administration is similar to that of other NetWare 4 objects.

Printing utilities such as PCONSOLE, PRINTCON, and PRINTDEF have been enhanced for NetWare 4 printing, functioning through bindery-emulation. In addition, the NetWare User Tools and NetWare Administrator utilities are available in NetWare 4, enabling you to administer and use NetWare print services.

NetWare 4 Printing Configuration and Administration

To administer NetWare 4 printing, you can use the NetWare Administrator utility as well as PCONSOLE. With the NetWare Administrator utility, you can accomplish the following tasks:

- Create, modify, and delete print queues and print servers
- Monitor, modify, reorder, and delete print jobs
- Control and monitor printers and print servers

Figure 41.1 shows the first screen of the NetWare Administrator utility.

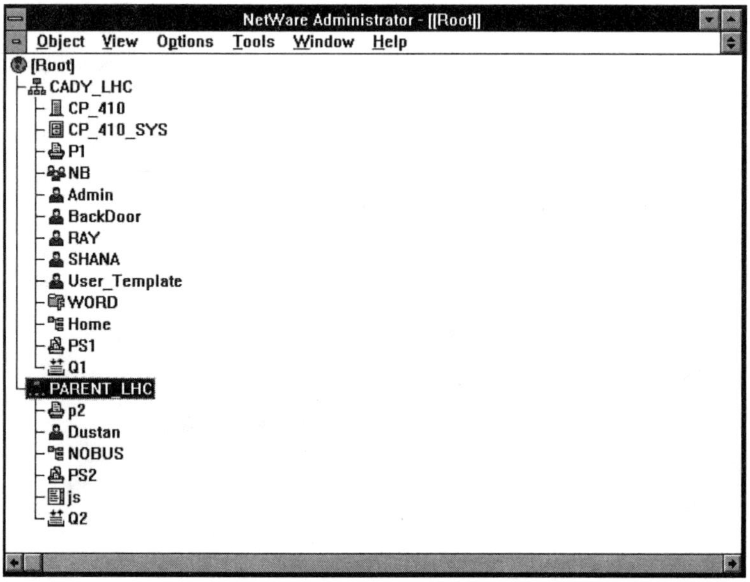

Figure 41.1
The main screen for the NetWare Administrator utility.

With the NDS tree expanded in the NetWare Administrator utility, you can create Print Server, Print Queue, and Printer objects by selecting (highlighting) the container in the NDS tree where you want to place the object, then choosing **C**reate from the **O**bject pull-down menu (see fig. 41.2).

Next, choose the type of object you want to create (Print Server, Print Queue, or Printer) from the New Object window (see fig. 41.3).

When the related Create *object_name* dialog box opens, provide the necessary information. For example, if you choose to create a Print Queue object, the Create Print Queue dialog box opens. You must provide a Print Queue **N**ame and a Print Queue **V**olume. You can also choose to either **D**efine Additional Properties for the Print Queue object, or to Create **A**nother Print Queue. In addition, you can choose to make this a NetWare Directory **S**ervice Print Queue, or to **R**eference a Bindery Queue (see fig. 41.4).

You can also move, rename, or delete Print Server, Print Queue, and Printer objects by selecting the object and choosing the related action from the **O**bject pull-down menu.

To rename a Print Queue object, for example, choose Re**n**ame from the **O**bject pull-down menu, and enter the new name in the Rename dialog box. If you want to, you can save the old name as well by marking the **S**ave Old Name box (see fig. 41.5).

You can also use NetWare Administrator to monitor, modify, reorder, and delete print jobs. To accomplish these tasks, you must choose either a Print Queue object or a Printer object. If you choose a Print Queue object and then open the Jobs List page for this Print Queue object (see fig. 41.6), you can perform various tasks (view details about the job, hold the job, delete the job, and so on) by choosing the corresponding button.

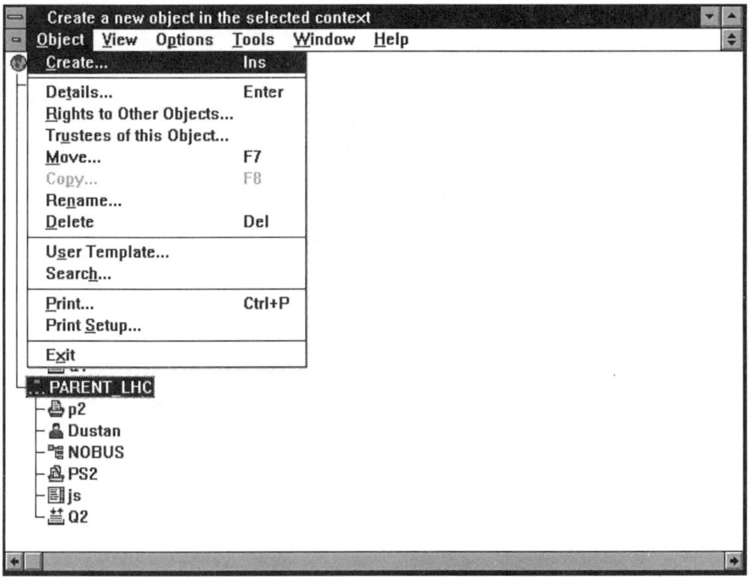

Figure 41.2
The Object pull-down menu.

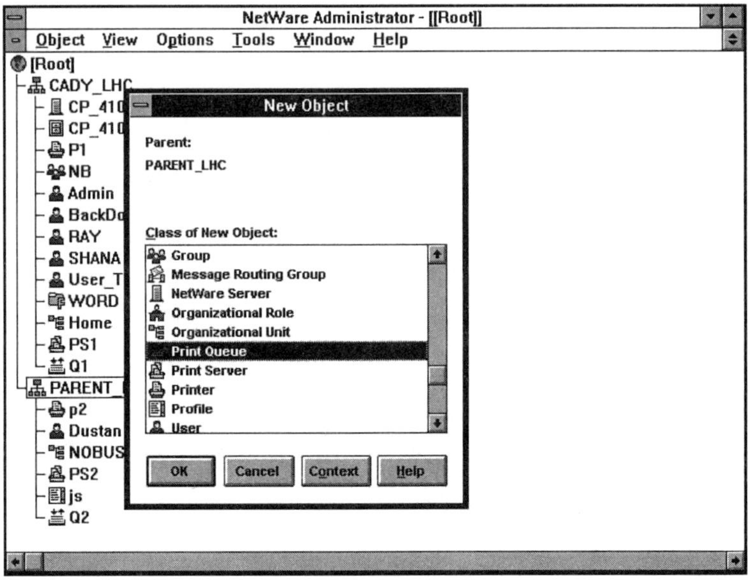

Figure 41.3
The New Object window.

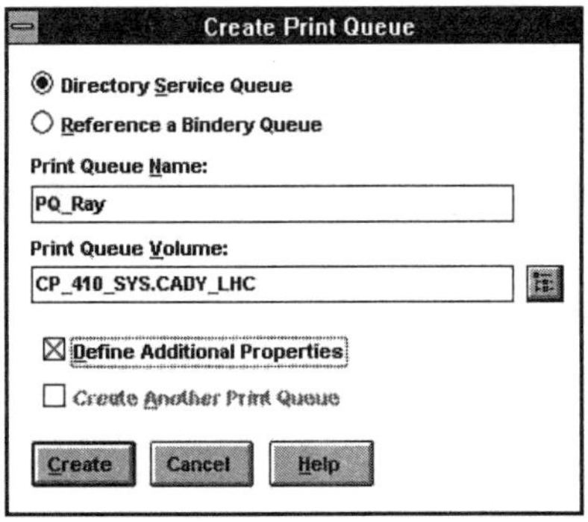

Figure 41.4
The Create Print Queue dialog box.

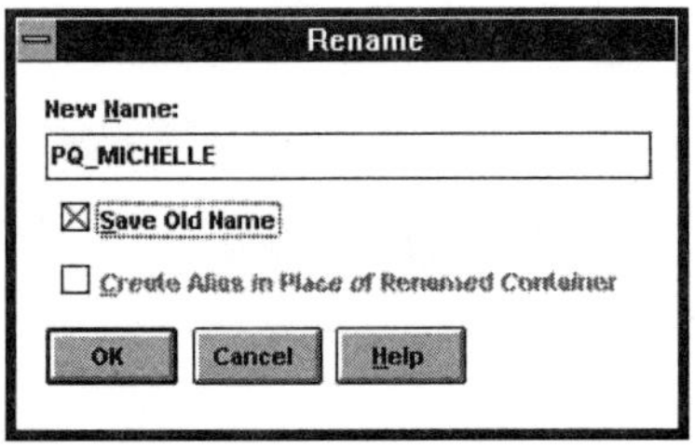

Figure 41.5
The Rename dialog box.

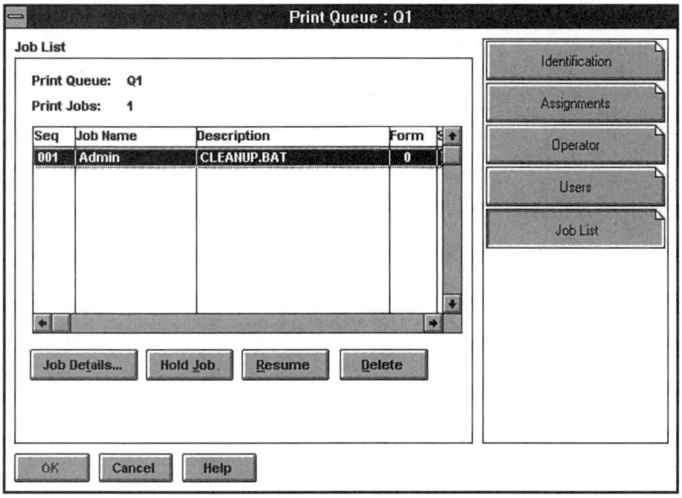

Figure 41.6
The Print Queue Jobs List page for Print Queue Q1.

You can also use the NetWare Administrator utility to control and monitor Printer objects and Print Server objects. To monitor a Printer object, for example, select the Printer object, choose De<u>t</u>ails from the <u>O</u>bject pull-down menu, then choose Configuration to open the Configuration page for this Printer object. Figure 41.7 shows a Configuration page.

From this page you can monitor information about the Printer object's configuration, such as the type of printer (Parallel or Serial), the type of banner, the service interval, buffer size, and so on. In addition, you can open the Printer Status page for this Printer object and monitor information such as the printer's status, which form is mounted, and so on.

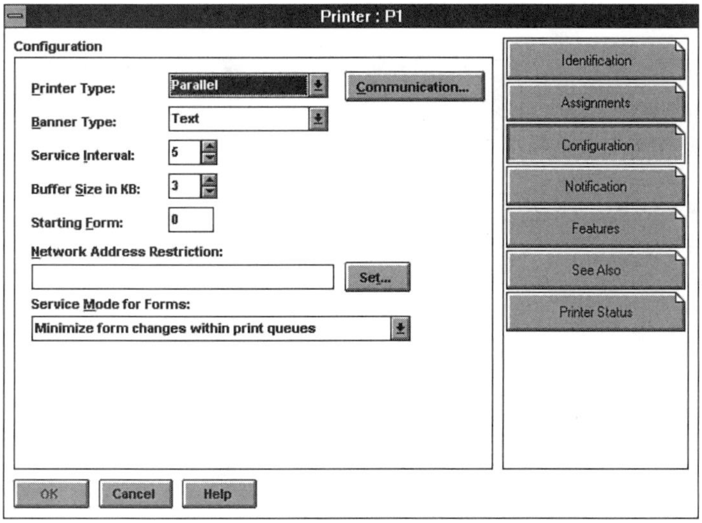

Figure 41.7
The Configuration page.

In addition to the NetWare Administration utility, the NetWare Tools and NetUser utilities are included in NetWare 4 to provide greater access to printing services. The NetWare Tools utility enables you to use the MS Windows drag-and-drop feature to capture printer ports to network print drives. Figure 41.8 shows the NetWare Tools utility with the NetWare Printer Connections window open.

The NetUser utility is used from DOS workstations to control printing. Its menu interface makes it possible for users to enable or disable printing redirection, set redirection parameters, and make printer redirection settings permanent. Figure 41.9 shows the Available Options menu for the NetUser utility.

Another significant change between NetWare 4 and earlier versions of NetWare is the addition of the Quick Setup option in the NetWare 4 version of the PCONSOLE utility (see fig. 41.10). With this option, the task of setting up the printing environment for a single Print Server, Printer, and Print Queue object is very quick and very easy.

NetWare 4 also provides a workstation and an NLM version of a utility called NPRINTER. NPRINTER enables users on the network to share printers attached to workstations and servers. (For DOS and OS/2 workstations, DOS and OS/2 versions of NPRINTER exist.) With the NPRINTER.NLM loaded at a NetWare 4 file server, up to seven printers can be attached to the server and shared by network users.

Printing in a NetWare 4 NDS environment and printing in a NetWare bindery environment differ in a few other ways.

First, in bindery-based versions of NetWare, print queues were always located on the SYS:SYSTEM volume. In NetWare 4, print queues can be located on any volume in the QUEUES directory.

Second, in NetWare 4, the ENDCAP command is not available as a separate command as it is in NetWare 3.1*x*.

Third, although NetWare 3.1*x* has three types of print servers—PSERVER.NLM, PSERVER.EXE, and PSERVER.VAP—NetWare 4 supports only one print server type: PSERVER.NLM.

Figure 41.8
The NetWare Tools NetWare Printer Connections window.

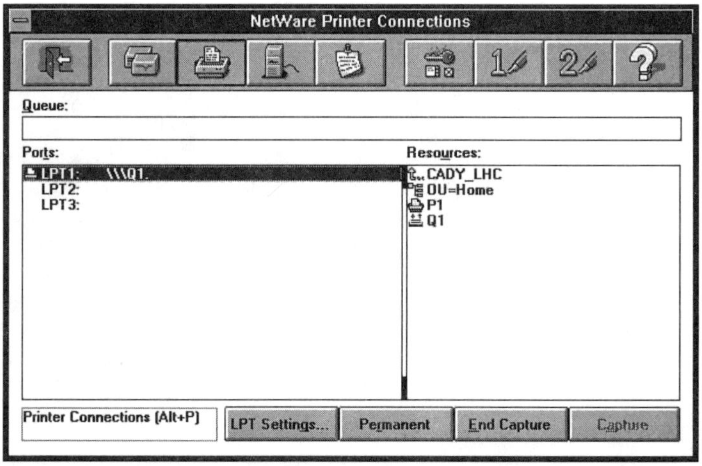

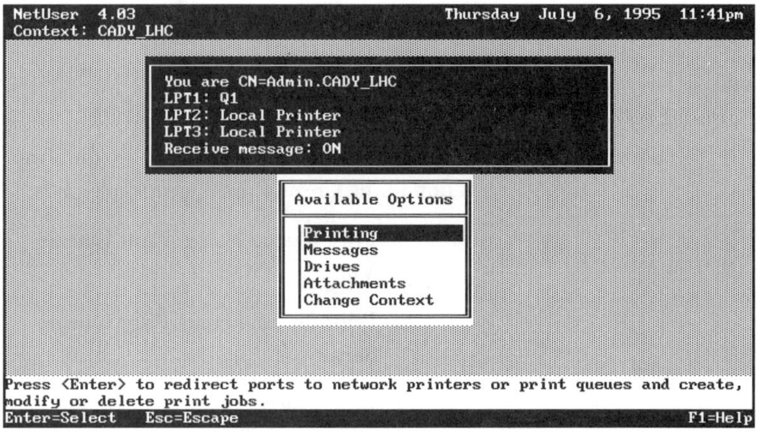

Figure 41.9
The NetUser Available Options menu.

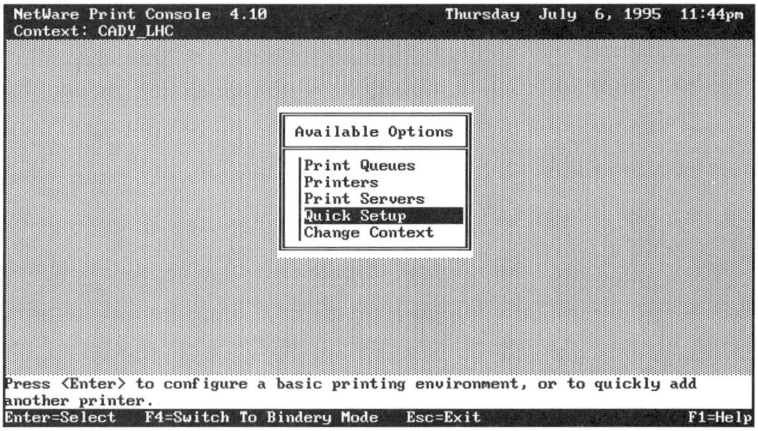

Figure 41.10
The PCONSOLE Available Options menu.

Fourth, print servers in the NetWare 3.1*x* environment can control a maximum of only 16 printers. In the NetWare 4 environment, however, Print Server objects can control up to 255 printers.

Finally, shared printers on a NetWare 4 network can only be connected to servers, DOS or OS/2 workstations, or directly to the network cable. In NetWare 3.1*x*, printers can be connected to NetWare servers, dedicated DOS print servers, external routers, DOS workstations, or directly to the network cable.

Questions

1. Which of the following utilities has *not* been enhanced for NetWare 4 printing services?
   - ○ A. NPRINT
   - ○ B. PRINTDEF
   - ○ C. PCONSOLE
   - ○ D. PRINTCON

2. Which *two* of the following are true?
   - ☐ A. NetWare Administrator provides many of the same capabilities as PCONSOLE.
   - ☐ B. PCONSOLE, PRINTCON, and PRINTDEF have all been enhanced for NetWare 4.
   - ☐ C. CAPTURE cannot be used with NetWare 4.
   - ☐ D. You must use the PCONSOLE utility to perform a quick printing setup.

3. The ______ utility *cannot* be used to set up or manage both NetWare 3 and NetWare 4 printing environments.
   - ○ A. PCONSOLE
   - ○ B. PRINTCON
   - ○ C. NetWare Administrator
   - ○ D. PRINTDEF

4. The ______ utility also can be used to administer printing in NetWare 4.
   - ○ A. PCONSOLE
   - ○ B. CAPTURE
   - ○ C. SMODE
   - ○ D. RPRINTER

5. To create a Print Queue object, you must provide at least ______ and ______ information in the Create Print Queue dialog box.
   - ○ A. Print Queue Name, Print Queue Volume
   - ○ B. Print Queue Name, Print Queue Server
   - ○ C. Print Queue Volume, Printer Name
   - ○ D. Print Queue Server, Printer Name

6. You can create, rename, or move a Print Queue object by first selecting the object, then choosing the related option from the ______ pull-down menu.
   - ○ A. View
   - ○ B. Window
   - ○ C. Options
   - ○ D. Object

7. Of the following, which *two* are provided with NetWare 4 and not with NetWare 3.1*x*?
   - ☐ A. Quick Setup option in PCONSOLE
   - ☐ B. PRINTCON and PRINTDEF
   - ☐ C. NetWare Administrator utility
   - ☐ D. NetWare User Administration utility

8. Open the ______ page to monitor information about a Printer object's configuration.

   ○ A. Assignments

   ○ B. Notification

   ○ C. Configuration

   ○ D. Features

9. The ______ utility makes it possible for users to enable or disable printing redirection, set redirection parameters, and make printing redirection permanent.

   ○ A. NETUSER

   ○ B. NETADMIN

   ○ C. NWUSER

   ○ D. NWADMIN

10. Which of the following is *not* a difference between printing in NetWare 3.1*x* and NetWare 4?

    ○ A. PSERVER.NLM is the only type of print server in NetWare 4.

    ○ B. NetWare 3.1*x* print servers can service up to 16 print servers only, whereas NetWare 4 print servers can service up to 255 printers.

    ○ C. Printers cannot be connected to external routers in a NetWare 4 environment.

    ○ D. None of the above

Answers

1. A
2. A, B
3. C
4. A
5. A
6. D
7. A, C
8. C
9. A
10. D

CHAPTER 42

Improving Network Printing Performance

Network printing performance depends on several factors, the most important of which are included in this chapter's discussions of the following topics:

- *Avoiding and correcting printing bottlenecks*
- *Troubleshooting network printing problems*

Avoiding and Correcting Printing Bottlenecks

Chapter 38, "Understanding Printing and NetWare Printing Services," discussed the following three phases of printing:

- **Spooling.** Sending the print job across the network to a print queue
- **De-spooling.** Transferring the print job from the print queue to the designated printer
- **Printing.** Translating the print job into a printed document

At any point in these three phases of printing, a *bottleneck* (a significant reduction in processing speed) can occur. Several factors can affect printing performance. An understanding of these factors can help you to find and correct performance problems with your network.

The following primary factors affect printing performance:

- How quickly the print job can travel between the printer port on the host computer and the printer (network interface speed)
- How effectively the application program and print drivers communicate (printer interface speed)
- How long and complex the document is that is being printed (spooling)
- How well the printing-related hardware handles the printing process (de-spooling)

When you consider the network interface speed, consider the design of the network itself, how traffic moves around the network (pattern), and the types of print information traveling across the LAN. For example, Token Ring networks can transfer data across the network at speeds ranging from 230.4 Kbps to 16 Mbps.

When you consider the printer interface speed, consider how the type of cable and connection affect how data is transferred to the printer. A parallel interface, for example, commonly transfers data at the rate of 1 Kbps to 40 Kbps.

Note

A printer with its own network interface, such as those that use the HP Jetdirect card, can be directly connected to the network through the printer's parallel port. The speed of printing for devices connected in this manner is determined primarily by the parallel interface the printer uses. These devices function, however, by taking the print job directly from the NetWare print queue and then printing it. These devices do not wait for a print server to poll the print queues and send the jobs to them.

When you consider spooling bottlenecks, consider such performance-affecting factors as the print drivers provided by the application requesting the print service, whether NetWare CAPTURE or *NetWare Core Protocol* (NCP) printing is being used, the speed and capability of the workstation's CPU and network board, and the topology of the network, as well as the NetWare server's configuration (network board, number of NLMs currently loaded, and so on).

When you consider de-spooling bottlenecks, consider such factors as the length of time between queries of the queue by the print server, where the print server is physically located on the network in relation to the printer, and the maximum performance of which the print server is capable.

You should also consider the printer's capabilities. Factors such as the printer's interface, the formatter, the print engine, language/context switching, multiple port and protocol selection all affect printing performance.

Printer Interface

Printer interfaces include elements such as the speed at which the printer can accept input, the capability of the printer's parallel port, and the size of the printer's print buffer. Printers that cannot accept print jobs from the network as quickly as the network sends them can create a bottleneck. This applies also to the capability of the parallel port. Many parallel ports can transfer and receive data at speeds from 1 to 14 Kbps. The use of a newer bidirectional, high-speed (up to 40 Kbps) printer port can reduce bottlenecks of this type. Larger print buffers also can reduce bottlenecks by allowing complete jobs to be sent to the printer and held until the formatter is ready for them.

Formatter

The printer's formatter converts print data signals into signals the printer engine can recognize. Those printer formatters that operate at speeds below the speed at which the parallel port can transfer and receive data become a bottleneck. When you use the bidirectional high-speed printer ports on a printer with a formatter that functions at a slower speed, you limit the speed of the printer to that of the printer's formatter.

Print Engine

The print engine takes the print data converted by the formatter and transfers the information to paper. The speed of the print engine is measured by using the number of lines per minute, pages per minute, or characters per second that the print engine is capable of managing.

Language/Context Switching

Some printers can accommodate different languages. Some automatically switch to the required language by examining the print data (context switching). Others accommodate a single language, which cannot be changed. Still others can accommodate different languages, but some method to enable the changes must be provided. Although the language change itself may initially be a little time-consuming, bottlenecking seldom occurs after the printer is changed. On the other hand, when automatic context switching is part of a printer's features, some bottlenecking may occur when the language used in different print jobs varies.

Multiple Port and Protocol Selection

Often, resources such as ports, protocols, fonts, macros, and so on must be downloaded to the printer before a print job can be completed. Sometimes, changing languages can necessitate that all this information be downloaded again. Printers that can retain this information, even when the language used changes, are less of a bottleneck than are those that necessitate downloading the information once again.

Troubleshooting Network Printing Problems

To effectively troubleshoot and solve network printing problems, you first need to understand the basics of printing on a NetWare network.

In NetWare versions 3.0 and higher, printing is a process separate from the NetWare Operating System. Printing is provided by separate software, called PSERVER, that can be added as a *NetWare Loadable Module* (NLM), *value-added process* (VAP), or as an *executable* (EXE) file on a workstation. The PSERVER software performs most of the NetWare printing process.

The Effect of Setting Up Printing Services

Using the NetWare Administrator (NetWare 4 only) or PCONSOLE utilities, you create print servers (or Print Server objects) and print queues (or Print Queue objects). When you create a print server, a directory for each print server is also created under the SYS:SYSTEM directory. The same is true for print queues, but the print queue directories are created on the same file server as the print queue. Alphanumeric characters are used to name both print server and print queue directories. Their names correspond to the Object ID number for print servers (found in the Print Server ID options of PCONSOLE's Print Server Information menu), and for print queues (found in PCONSOLE's Print Queue ID field for a chosen print queue).

> **Note** To see a list of print queues, type **LISTDIR** in the SYS:SYSTEM directory. NetWare 3.1*x* print queue directories are displayed with a QDR extension.

The print queue directory holds print jobs, SRV files, and a SYS file. Print jobs are placed in the print queue in the order they are sent. Each print job is assigned a number. After a print job is sent to a printer, the job is deleted from the print queue, and the job number becomes available for another print job to use. The print queue directory also contains a hidden SRV file for each print server to which the print queue sends print jobs. Print servers that are not currently available have zero bytes in their related hidden SRV file. The SYS file contains information required by the server to maintain the print queue. Information in this file includes such things as the number of the station that sent the print job, the ID number of the user who sent the print job, print job file names, and so on.

The print server directory contains four types of files, which contain information about the following:

- The file server this print server services (FILESERV)
- The printers being used (PRINT)
- The print queues being serviced by these printers (QUEUE)
- The users on the notify list for each printer (NOTIFY)

Because NetWare 3 can support as many as 16 printers per print server, as many as 16 sets of these files can be found in the print server directory. (Related files have the same extension; for example, all files in a set might have the extension .000 or .001.) When you run the PCONSOLE utility and make changes to print configurations, these files are updated. The updates become effective, however, only when the print server is brought down and then reloaded by typing PSERVER.

The Dynamics of Printing with NetWare

To use NetWare printing services, load and run the print server software—PSERVER.VAP (NetWare 2), PSERVER.NLM (NetWare 3 and 4), or PSERVER.EXE (dedicated workstation). Figure 42.1 shows what happens when you issue the PSERVER command. First, PSERVER checks its ID directory for information about the file servers it is to service. It then connects to each file server listed in the FILESERV file, and creates a table based on the information it finds in the PRINT, QUEUE, and NOTIFY files. Finally, it attaches print queues to their assigned printers.

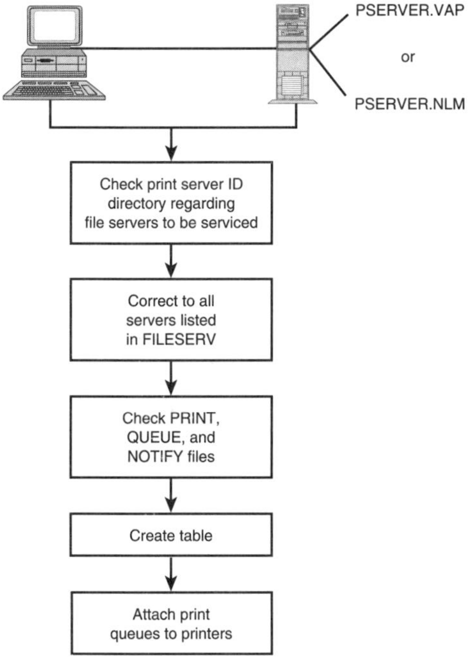

Figure 42.1
The dynamics of printing with NetWare.

After PSERVER is loaded and set up, it polls the assigned print queues and sends the print jobs it finds to the appropriate printer.

You can also provide network printing through a printer attached to a regular network workstation, if that workstation has a RPRINTER.EXE file loaded. When RPRINTER is loaded, the associated print server sends its configuration information to the workstation running RPRINTER. RPRINTER waits for a print job to be sent to it, then prints jobs as they are received. Because limited print buffer space is available, RPRINTER must notify PSERVER when it is ready for additional print job data (if the buffer cannot hold the entire print job when it first receives the job).

Printing Problems and Suggested Solutions

Printing problems are not uncommon, and most of them can be solved. With printing problems, as with medical problems, the first step toward solving the problem is correct diagnosis. Following are some common printing problems, their symptoms, and solutions:

- **Problem:** *Corrupted print queue or print server definitions.*

  Symptoms: Request for a print server password when none has been set; slow printing; RPRINTER errors that occur when network print data is sent or received.

  Solution: Delete and re-create print queues or print servers, and if necessary, any related subdirectories in the SYS:SYSTEM directory, if no corresponding PCONSOLE Print Server ID exists.

- **Problem:** *Faulty cabling, concentrators, terminators, network boards, or other printing-related hardware.*

  Symptoms: When you reboot the workstation to reestablish a lost connection, message indicates that RPRINTER is still in use

  Solution: Add settings to the SHELL.CFG or NET.CFG file to prevent the SPX connection from timing out before it receives a response. Add the following lines: IPX RETRY COUNT=35 and SPX ABORT TIMEOUT=700.

- **Problem:** *Conflicts between RPRINTER and the network interface board settings, or with other TSRs.*

  Symptoms: RPRINTER hangs when it loads.

  Solution: Change the settings on the network board, and rerun WSGEN to match the IPX to the new settings. If ODI drivers are used at the workstation, change the NET.CFG file to load the network board with the new settings. Also, before running RPRINTER, try unloading any other TSRs that may be loaded at the workstation.

- **Problem:** *Conflicts between PSERVER.EXE and the network interface board.*

  Symptoms: PSERVER.EXE hangs the workstation.

  Solution: Unload, then reload the print server to reset the print server. If this does not correct the problem, check various items of hardware such as the network board and the cabling for problems. Also, if you are using an older version of an IPX driver, update the driver to a newer version.

- **Problem:** *Third-party VAPS are in conflict with the PSERVER.VAP; the first LAN uses ARCNET topology and no workstations are powered on; the print server uses shadow RAM and is experiencing sporadic problems.*

  Symptoms: The PSERVER.VAP used on NetWare 2 networks hangs or *stops advertising its presence* (SAPs) on the network.

  Solution: Check the order in which third-party VAPs are loading, and eliminate those that are causing conflicts. You can also power up a workstation in the ARCNET LAN if none are currently running. Also, remove shadow RAM and run PSERVER without it to see whether that corrects the problem.

- **Problem:** *PostScript printers delete any print job that does not appear to be properly formatted for a PostScript printer. Banner pages and jobs sent in Text mode are seen as improperly formatted print jobs.*

  Symptoms: Print jobs containing graphics files are not printed when sent to PostScript printers.

  Solution: Use the /NT (No Tabs), /NB (No Banner), and /NFF (No Form Feed) parameters when you use CAPTURE or NPRINT on graphics jobs sent to PostScript printers. In addition, you can update the driver files for the PostScript printer, and add the following line to the SHELL.CFG or NET.CFG file: PRINT HEADER=*n* (replacing *n* with a number between 64 and 255).

- **Problem:** *Applications that print to plotters use the COM port, while NetWare uses LPT ports for printing.*

  Symptoms: Plotter printing jobs sent through a related application program do not print.

  Solution: Use the application to save the print job to a file, then use NPRINT or PCONSOLE to print the job.

- **Problem:** *The implementation method used for handshaking a serial printer to the network is not compatible with one or more printers.*

  Symptoms: Communication between serial printers and the network is nonfunctional or sporadic.

Solution: Use Novell's recommended pin-out for serial printer cabling, as shown in table 42.1.

Table 42.1
Serial Cable Pin-Out Recommended by Novell

Pin No. at PC	*Cable Type*	*Function*	*Pin No. at Printer*
(none)	9-pin	Frame Ground	1
1	25-pin	Frame Ground	1
3	9-pin	Transmit Data	2
2	25-pin	Transmit Data	3
2	9-pin	Receive Data	3
3	25-pin	Receive Data	2
7	9-pin	Request to Send	4
4	25-pin	Request to Send	4
8	9-pin	Clear to Send	20
5	25-pin	Clear to Send	20
6	9-pin	*Data Set Ready	6
6	25-pin	*Data Set Ready	6
5	9-pin	Signal Ground	7
7	25-pin	Signal Ground	7
1	9-pin	Data Carrier Detect	8
8	25-pin	Data Carrier Detect	8
7	9-pin	Data Terminal Ready	4
4	25-pin	Data Terminal Ready	4

* NetWare does not use Data Set Ready, but DOS does. Novell recommends tying pins 5 and 6 together to provide DOS printing support.

Questions

1. One of the primary factors that affects printing is ______.
   - ○ A. network interface speed
   - ○ B. application speed
   - ○ C. other network devices on the cable
   - ○ D. version of DOS being run

2. The ______ and ______ factors, which affect printing, are also steps in the printing process.
   - ☐ A. printing
   - ☐ B. spooling
   - ☐ C. queuing
   - ☐ D. de-spooling

3. Printers with their own network interface can be directly connected to ______.
   - ○ A. a print server
   - ○ B. a workstation
   - ○ C. the printer's parallel port
   - ○ D. the printer's print server

4. An element of a printer interface is ______.
   - ○ A. de-spooling
   - ○ B. the speed at which the printer can accept input
   - ○ C. print drivers provided by applications
   - ○ D. none of the above

5. The printer's ______ converts print data signals into signals the printer engine can recognize.
   - ○ A. language switch
   - ○ B. port selection
   - ○ C. context switch
   - ○ D. formatter

6. Printers that can switch automatically to the necessary language are said to have ______ ability.
   - ○ A. language switching
   - ○ B. port switching
   - ○ C. context switching
   - ○ D. formatter switching

7. Of the following, which *three* are elements of the printer's interface, which can be a cause of printing bottlenecks?
   - ☐ A. Speed of accepting input
   - ☐ B. Capability of the parallel port
   - ☐ C. Type of connection to the network
   - ☐ D. Size of the print job buffer

8. Which of the following is *not* a method of providing print services in NetWare 3.0 and later versions?
   - ○ A. PSERVER.VAP
   - ○ B. PSERVER.COM
   - ○ C. PSERVER.NLM
   - ○ D. PSERVER.EXE

9. The ______ file in the print queue contains information the server needs to maintain the print queue.
   - ○ A. SRV
   - ○ B. DRV
   - ○ C. 000
   - ○ D. SYS

10. If you are prompted for a print server password but no password was set, you must ______ to solve the problem.
    - ○ A. delete and re-create the print server and print queue
    - ○ B. change settings on the network board and rerun WSGEN
    - ○ C. unload and then reload the print server to reset it
    - ○ D. use the /NT, /NB, and /NFF parameters with the CAPTURE or NPRINT commands

Answers

1. A
2. B, D
3. C
4. B
5. D
6. C
7. A, B, D
8. B
9. D
10. A

CHAPTER 43

Using Alternative Printing Configurations

Printers are commonly attached to devices attached to the network, such as servers and workstations. Printers also can be attached directly to the network cable if those printers have interfaces that enable them to be placed anywhere on the network, including direct cable attachment, and if network software is provided to manage those printers. In NetWare, the QServer and RPRINTER software make possible the direct network connection of printers.

In order for printers to be successful when connected directly to the network cable, they must be capable of dealing with the variety of choices implemented on the network. For example, they must be capable of supporting the following:

- A variety of technologies, such as Ethernet, Token Ring, and Local Talk
- A variety of communication frame types, such as 802.2, 802.3, Ethernet II, and Ethernet SNAP
- A variety of protocols, such as TCP/IP, IPX/SPX, and AppleTalk

This chapter provides more detailed information on direct connection of printers and the associated network software, emphasizing the following topics:

- Alternate network printer interfaces and administration
- Remote printer administration and configuration

Alternate Network Printer Interfaces and Administration

Direct-connect printers use either an internal interface card to connect to the network (such as that used by the HP IIISi and HP 4Si), or an external connection device (such as that used by the HP JetDirect). The method of connection is a less important consideration in network printing, however, than the features or capabilities provided by the printers themselves.

Printer capabilities must be considered and may include any of those shown in table 43.1.

Table 43.1
Printer Capabilities

Capability	*Description*	*Function*
Duplexing	Prints one side, then turns the paper over and prints on the other side	Printing on both sides of paper
Multiple Input Ports	Simultaneously accepts multiple print jobs	Servicing print requests simultaneously
Resource Saving	Stores printer-related resource information in the printer's memory	Retaining downloaded fonts, forms, and so on to save time
Media Selection	Enables choice of what to print on—labels, paper, envelopes, and so on	Selecting the print media
Media Management	Enables choice of print trays when issuing a print job	Providing multiple types of print media

Capability	*Description*	*Function*
Language Switching	Provides choice of PCL or PostScript job printing language	Providing automatic or controlled switching
Plotters	Enables CAD packages to send print jobs across the network to plotters that can be connected directly to the network	Providing access to plotters for Computer Aided Design
Color Printers	Provides access to color printers	Enabling color print jobs to be used on the network

In addition to the printer's capabilities, consider the software method to be used for implementing direct-connect printers. The options are QServer mode and RPRINTER mode.

With the QServer mode, the printer's interface also functions as a print server. In addition to the network connection duties it performs, it is also responsible for polling print jobs directly from the network queue and then sending them to the printer. Benefits of this method include the fact that no external print server is needed, redundant printer traffic is prevented, and setup is relatively easy compared to setting up a printer that uses the RPRINTER mode.

The main disadvantage of the QServer mode is that it requires a user connection. On a network with limited available user connections, users may be prevented from connecting to the network if too many printers functioning under the QServer mode are connected to the network.

With the RPRINTER mode, the printer's interface emulates the RPRINTER communication method used by workstations connected to the network with a printer attached. The main benefit of using the RPRINTER mode is that a separate user connection is not required. In addition, this method provides reasonably good performance and does not require the use of unencrypted passwords, because the data itself is password protected from the NetWare server to the print server.

The main drawbacks associated with this method are the need for a Novell NetWare print server and the fact that setup requires more steps than setting up a printer running under the QServer mode.

Remote Printer Administration and Configuration

Because the HP JetDirect, HPIII, and HP4 printers are commonly used on NetWare networks when a direct-connect printer is required, an understanding of remote printer setup and administration of these printers is also commonly required. Two utilities are used to set up and administer these HP printers—JetAdmin and JetPrint.

JetAdmin

The JetAdmin program provides remote installation, configuration, management, troubleshooting, and monitoring of any printer using the HP JetDirect interface. For example, once you open the HP JetAdmin main menu and choose a printer, you can view the status of that printer (see fig. 43.1).

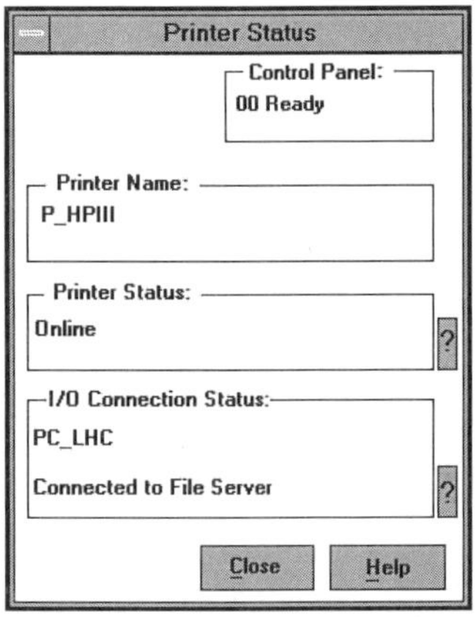

Figure 43.1
The HP JetAdmin Printer Status window.

The Printer Name area displays the name given to the printer when it was installed. The Printer Status area shows the current condition of the printer—Offline, Online, Out of paper, or Printing. Additional status information, such as Door open, Toner low, and so on, may also be displayed. The I/O Connection Status area displays any number of up to 38 different messages, each of which have context-sensitive help (F1) available to describe them.

You can also configure and manage the printer by using the JetAdmin software. Start JetAdmin from the DOS prompt (type **JetAdmin** and press Enter) or from MS Windows (choose the associated icon). Next, choose the printer to configure and choose Configuration. To configure Queue Server Mode, choose Queue Server Mode under Operating Mode; then assign a printer name, choose Add Queue, and add a New Queue.

To configure the Remote Printer Mode, choose Remote Printer from the Operating Mode option, provide a name for the printer, then choose a printer number and exit JetAdmin.

You can configure various aspects of the remote printer, such as printer drivers, advanced settings, notification, test pages, and user sheets. To use an MS Windows print driver for your JetDirect printer, make the copy available in the SYS:LOGIN\HP_PRINT directory on the NetWare server, if the one you need is not already stored there or needs to be updated. You can also modify printer settings or network interface settings.

The following are printer settings that you can modify:

- **JetDirect Broadcasts.** Sets the frequency at which broadcasts are made to locate the printer's interface on the network.
- **Queue Server job Poll Rate.** Sets the frequency at which print queues are polled for print jobs.
- **NetWare Protocol Restart.** Reinitializes the NetWare protocol.
- **PJL Settings.** Establishes how the HP JetDirect interface uses the Print Job Language.
- **Toner-Low Messages.** Determines which toner-low message is to be displayed (available only when operating in QServer mode).

- **Protocol Stacks.** Turns on or off other protocol stacks.
- **Frame Type Settings.** Chooses the frame type to be used.

JetAdmin printer network interface settings enable you to use the HP JetDirect interface in QServer mode, eliminating the need to assign the printer to a NetWare print server. You can also set the poll rate, adjusting it low to speed up the printing service or high to reduce the amount of network traffic.

You can also choose to Restart Server Connections, which restarts JetDirect interfaces and rereads the configuration files. You also can choose to Force Complete Re-Initialization Immediately, which restarts the NetWare protocol stack. This option stops jobs currently being printed, immediately implementing any changes in frame types, polling rates, and so on.

You can use Notification to specify which users or groups should be notified of printer problems. You can send a self-test page to the printer to verify its functionality by using the Test Page option, and you can send information about the printer to the printer by using the User Sheet option.

JetPrint

JetPrint is an HP utility designed to enable management of a remote printer from an MS Windows network client. You can install drivers, print by using the MS Windows drag-and-drop feature, view network printer and interface status, set up default print queues for use by MS Windows applications, and assign different sounds to different printer functions. The JetPrint main menu provides a list of printers and print queues from which to choose. It also provides information on the default printer, status of the selected printer, and print jobs submitted by users that are currently being serviced.

The JetPrint utility is a graphical utility, available through MS Windows. The main menu provides buttons from which to choose in order to perform various tasks:

- Exit closes the HP JetPrint Network Printing Utility main menu.
- Printer Setup enables you to specify information about the printer.
- Job Options enables you to set print job configuration information, such as whether a banner page should be printed and, if so, the banner name and user name to be used. It also enables you to set whether to enable the NetWare Form Feed option and whether to notify the user when the requested print job is complete.
- File Servers enables you to detach from NetWare servers (if no network drives are mapped or the server is not the NetWare server containing the default queue) or attach to NetWare servers (up to a maximum of eight).
- Search enables you to search for printer types associated with queues, or words or phrases that are part of the description of a queue.
- Preferences enables you to customize the user environment for JetPrint.
- Help enables you to search for and view information about the HP JetPrint utility and its associated fields of information.

When you choose the Preferences button and open the Preferences window (see fig. 43.2), you can set or choose to configure the following:

- Options
- ToolBar Buttons
- Prompt When
- Advanced Options

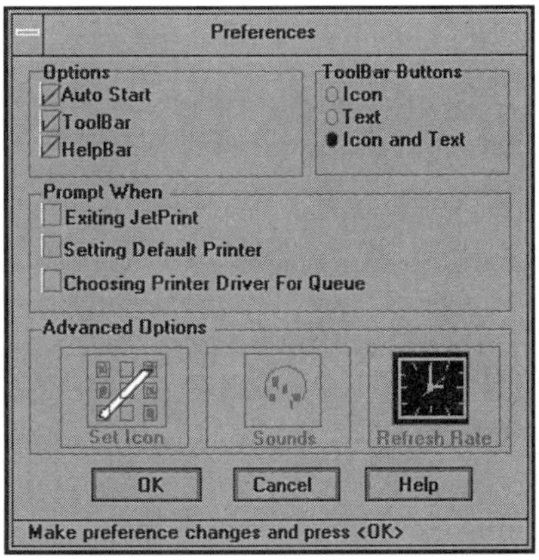

Figure 43.2
The HP JetPrint Preferences window.

The Options field can be toggled to include or not include Auto Start, ToolBar, and HelpBar. Those options toggled to On, as displayed by a check mark next to each option, are active when the JetPrint utility is running.

The ToolBar Buttons field enables you to choose whether to display the icon only, the text only, or both the icon and associated text on buttons within the HP JetPrint utility's button bar.

The Prompt When field enables you to specify when the utility is to prompt you. The options are when Exiting JetPrint, when Setting Default Printer, and when Choosing Printer Driver For Queue.

The Advance Options field enables you to choose from three advanced JetPrint options, which you then can configure. Those three advanced options are Set Icon, Sounds, and Refresh Rate.

If you choose the Set Icon button, you can choose any available MS Windows icon file to associate with a printer. The purpose of this configuration option is to make it easier for users to view graphically and choose the appropriate printer based on its capabilities, language selection, print options, or other features you choose to highlight by selecting a different icon.

If you choose the Sounds button, you can associate a given sound file (such as those you can choose from to play when you perform tasks such as closing MS Windows) with different printer events. The purpose of this configuration option is to inform the user of different printer-related events or conditions (such as when the printer is out of paper or has been taken offline) by using sound rather than just a message displayed on the user's workstation monitor.

If you choose the Refresh Rate button, you can set the frequency at which the JetPrint utility polls the NetWare server or printer to obtain printer and print job status information. This field cannot be set to a frequency of less than 15 seconds.

Questions

1. The ______ printer capability makes it possible to print on both sides of the paper.
   - ○ A. duplexing
   - ○ B. resource saving
   - ○ C. media selection
   - ○ D. media management

2. Direct-connect printers use either a/an ______ or a/an ______ interface.
   - ☐ A. internal
   - ☐ B. central
   - ☐ C. distributed
   - ☐ D. external

3. The ______ is *not* a printer capability.
   - ○ A. resource-saving capability
   - ○ B. QServer mode
   - ○ C. duplexing capability
   - ○ D. media-management feature

4. A ______ is a printing device that enables CAD packages to print on network printers.
   - ○ A. duplexor
   - ○ B. multiple input port
   - ○ C. color printer
   - ○ D. plotter

5. The main disadvantage of the QServer mode is ______.
   - ○ A. that it emulates the RPRINTER communication method
   - ○ B. that its interface also functions as a print server
   - ○ C. that it requires a connection
   - ○ D. that it does not require the use of unencrypted passwords

6. To view the name of the printer using the JetAdmin utility, look at the ______ area on the main menu.
   - ○ A. Printer Name
   - ○ B. Printer Status
   - ○ C. I/O Connection Status
   - ○ D. Control Panel

7. Of the following, which *three* are direct-connect printers?
   - ☐ A. HP JetDirect
   - ☐ B. HPIII
   - ☐ C. HP AppleWriter
   - ☐ D. HP4

8. A ______ is *not* a printer setting you can modify by using JetAdmin.
   - ○ A. JetDirect Broadcasts
   - ○ B. JCL Setting
   - ○ C. Queue Server job Poll Rate
   - ○ D. Protocol Stacks

9. The ______ button on the JetPrint utility main window enables you locate a print queue by a word in its description.
   - A. Printer Setup
   - B. Job Options
   - C. Search
   - D. Preferences

10. If you want to customize the user's environment for JetPrint, you must ______.
   - A. use the JetPrint Printer Setup option and set configuration information, such as whether to print a banner page
   - B. choose the Job Options button on the JetAdmin main menu
   - C. detach from the default file server
   - D. use the Preferences option of the JetPrint utility

Answers

1. A
2. A, D
3. B
4. D
5. C
6. A
7. A, B, D
8. B
9. C
10. D

CHAPTER 44

Printing Using Unix and Macintosh Devices

Both Unix and Macintosh workstations can access printers in a NetWare (DOS-based) network environment. Both the NetWare server and the Unix client must be configured in order for a Unix client to access NetWare printing services. Additional products (NetWare NFS or NetWare Flex/IP) are required in order for Unix clients to print to NetWare print queues. This is not true, however, for Macintosh clients. NetWare print services have been available for Macintosh clients since the early versions of NetWare 2 were released (NetWare 2.15).

In addition, NetWare clients may send print jobs to printers attached to Unix workstations by using the lpr (*line printer remote*) protocol and the NetWare-to-Unix gateway, providing the Unix host is correctly configured to service those print requests.

This chapter provides printing-related information on the following topics:

- Unix-to-NetWare Printing
- NetWare-to-Unix Printing
- Macintosh-to-NetWare Printing

Unix-to-NetWare Printing

Unix-to-NetWare printing requires that both the NetWare file server and the Unix client be set up for use before Unix systems can access NetWare network printers. Setting up the NetWare server includes such tasks as creating print queues and print servers, and assigning printers. This section explains the NetWare file server setup and the Unix client setup required before Unix users can print to NetWare printers.

NetWare File Server Setup

Setting up the NetWare file server for Unix-to-NetWare printing requires that NetWare print queues are first exported for use by lpd (line printer daemon), one of the two protocols used by Unix systems to send print jobs to other Unix systems. Several NLMs must be loaded in order to implement Unix-to-NetWare printing. Two of those NLMs are particularly important for setup (PLPD.NLM and PLPDCFG.NLM). The following are the NLMs used for Unix-to-NetWare printing:

- PLPD.NLM
- PLPDCFG.NLM
- PLPDMSG.HLP
- FILTER.NLM
- FLTRLIB.NLM
- POSTSCPT.PRO
- ENSCRIPT.PRO

By loading the PLPDCFG.NLM at the NetWare file server (see fig. 44.1), network administrators can then export NetWare print queues, identify those Unix systems that are considered to be *trusted hosts*—clients allowed to access the Unix-to-NetWare print gateway—and map Unix users to NetWare user accounts.

Figure 44.1
The PLPDCFG.NLM Main Menu.

To export NetWare print queues for use by Unix system clients, choose Select Print Queues for use by LPD from the Main Menu. Then choose which NetWare print queues will be accessible to Unix system users from the list of Available Print Queues. Choose a print queue from the list of Print Queues Selected. When the Print filter and Device configuration menu opens, provide information on the Print Filter to use (choose None, Line Printer, or Postscript), the Form Type (anyone previously defined using the NetWare PRINTDEF utility), the Print Device (type of printer such as HP4), and the Printer Mode (the command for the start of the job).

To choose which Unix hosts will be trusted hosts, choose Select Trusted Hosts from the Main Menu, then press the Ins key to see a list of Available Hosts. Choose a host to add to the Trusted Hosts List.

Note Unix hosts are listed in the HOSTS database in the SYS:ETC directory on the NetWare file server with the PLPDCFG.NLM and associated NLMs loaded. If the Unix host for which you are looking does not appear when the Available Hosts list opens, the database file does not contain an entry for that Unix host.

To map Unix users to NetWare user accounts, choose Select Username Mapping Mode from the Main Menu. Next, choose All Clients use same NetWare Account from the Current Mode menu (see fig. 44.2). This normally sets user GUEST as the default user for all Unix users to use when accessing NetWare print services. If only specific Unix users will be able to access NetWare print services, a table of Unix users and their associated NetWare User Name(s) can be created by using the Setup Table for Username Mapping option in the Current Mode menu. In addition, the Unix client user name can be used as the NetWare user name (choose the Use Client Username as NetWare Username option). Remember, Unix user names are case-sensitive and thus must be entered with case in mind. NetWare user names are not case-sensitive.

Figure 44.2
The Current Mode window.

Once the Unix-to-NetWare printing configuration is set up, the related print server can be loaded. To load the Unix-to-NetWare print server, type **LOAD PLPD** at the NetWare file server console and press Enter.

Unix Client Setup

One of the aspects of Unix that makes it an interesting operating system is that there are so many versions of it currently in use. NetWare supports several of those versions, two of which are considered to be the most commonly encountered—the BSD (Berkeley Source Distribution) and System V (a version from UniVel) versions.

The UnixWare (a version of the System V Unix OS) system administrator sets up access to NetWare servers running the NFS or Flex/IP products from the UnixWare desktop, using Printer_Setup found in System_Setup. To set up the UnixWare-to NetWare printer, the system administrator uses the following steps:

1. Choose the Printer button.
2. Select New and Remote Unix System.
3. Provide requested information, including the name of the printer, the type of printer, the name of the NetWare NFS or Flex/IP NetWare server (in the Remote System Name field), and the name of the NetWare queue (in the Remote Printer Name field).
4. Choose BSD at the `Remote Operating System is` prompt.
5. Add the new printer definition and a new icon in the Printer Setup window.
6. Select the printer's icon, then choose the Actions and the Set Remote Access buttons.

7. Enable BSD by choosing the NetWare NFS or Flex/IP server.
8. Save the changes to finish the setup.

The following are System V-based utilities for administering remote and local printing:

- lpstat to view printer status information
- lpsched/lpshut to control printer operation
- lp to send print jobs to a remote printer
- lpstat to view jobs in the queue
- cancel to delete jobs from a print queue

The Berkeley (BSD) uses a printing database file called Printcap to establish printing capabilities. To set up Unix-to-NetWare printing on a BSD system, use a text editor to add the following lines to this file. Then create the spool directory for the printer on the Unix host (use the Unix mkdir command and create the directory in the default directory (/var/spool). Once these steps are complete, start the printer by using the Unix lpc utility.

Include the following lines in the Printcap database file:

```
Printer Name:\
lp=:\
rm=<NetWare Server Name>:\
rp=<NetWare Queue Name>:\
sd=<Unix Spool Directory>:\
```

The following are BSD-based utilities for administering remote and local printing:

- lpstat to view printer status information
- lpc to control printer operation
- lpr to send print jobs to a remote printer
- lpq to view jobs in the queue
- lprm to delete jobs from a print queue

NetWare-to-Unix Printing

NetWare users can also print to printers attached to Unix systems if the NetWare-to-Unix print gateway is installed on a NetWare 3 or NetWare 4 server and configured, and if the Unix host is configured for NetWare clients to access the printers.

To install and configure the NetWare-to-Unix print gateway, complete the following steps:

1. Type **LOAD NFSADMIN -NWPRINT** (at the console of a NetWare NFS server) or **LOAD FLEXCON -NWPRINT** (at the NetWare Flex/IP server) and press Enter.
2. Add a printer to the list of Configured Unix Printers by pressing Ins, typing a descriptive name for the new printer in the Printer Name field of the UNIX Printer Setup Options window (47 alphanumeric characters maximum), and pressing Enter (see fig. 44.3)

Practical TIP You can also delete a printer by selecting the printer to delete, pressing Del, then answering Yes when prompted.

3. Choose the UNIX Host Name field and select a UNIX host from the Available UNIX Hosts list.
4. Choose the UNIX Printer Name field, and type the name of the UNIX printer.
5. Choose the NetWare Queues field and press Ins to display a list of Available NetWare Queues from which to choose, or press Ins again and type a name for a new queue in the Create Queue field and press Enter.

You can now exit the NFSADMIN or FLEXCON NLM utility and start the lpr print gateway by typing the following two commands at the NetWare file server console (press Enter after each command):

```
LOAD LPR_PSRV
LOAD LPR_GWY
```

Once the lpr print gateway is started, the Unix host must be configured. To configure the Unix host, complete the following steps:

1. If not already done, install the TCP/IP package on the Unix host by using the pkgadd program, and re-create the Unix OS kernel.
2. Log in to the Unix host as the root user.
3. Type **pmadm -l -p tcp -s** and press Enter. Then verify that values 0 and lpd exist for SVCTAG.
4. Type the following command (replacing *NetWare_FileServer_name* with the name of the file server) and press Enter:

   lpsystem -t bsd -R 5 -T 10
   ➥*NetWare_FileServer_name*

5. Define the printer on the UnixWare host (if it does not already exist) by typing the following command (replacing italicized items with the actual names associated with them, such as the type of printer in place of *Printer_Type*) and pressing Enter:

   lpadmin -p *Printer_Name* -v *Device* -T
   ➥*Printer_Type*

For a BSD-based Unix system, edit the Printcap database file to include the following lines, replacing the italicized items with the name associated with it (such as the name of the actual printer in place of *Printer Name*):

```
Printer Name ¦ Description:\
lp=Local Printer Port:\
rm=:\
rp=:\
sd=Spool Directory
```

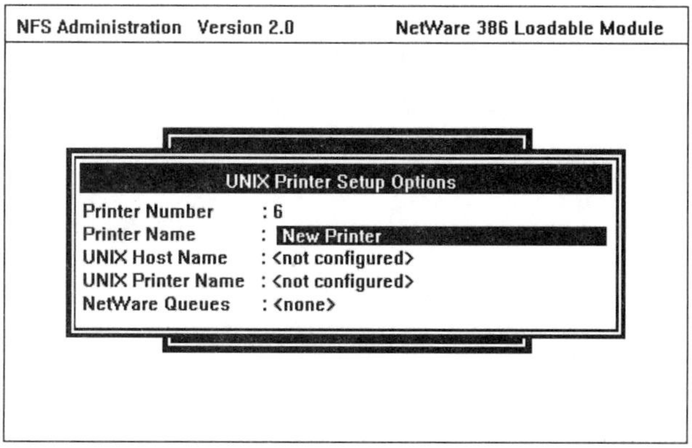

Figure 44.3
The UNIX Printer Setup Options window.

Macintosh-to-NetWare Printing

The NBP and PAP AppleTalk protocols enable communication between Macintosh clients and network printers. The ATPS.NLM is responsible for the front-end receipt of print data, as well as for the back-end distribution of print data to ATPS printers. To function properly, the ATPS.NLM must be configured. The ATPS.CFG file contains the configuration information for the ATPS.NLM. Once properly set up and configured, DOS, MS Windows, and other NetWare workstations can submit properly formatted print jobs to NetWare for Macintosh print queues. In addition, with NetWare for Macintosh v3.10-or-higher installed, Macintosh workstations with compatible print drivers loaded can print to non-AppleTalk printers attached to NetWare file servers.

Regarding printing in the Macintosh environment, keep the following in mind when preparing NetWare-compatible printing by using Macintosh:

- The Macintosh Chooser provides the capability of choosing a printer to which all print jobs then will be sent.
- AppleTalk printers can be attached to Macintosh computers or directly connected to the network.
- AppleTalk print services use the AppleTalk protocol architecture for sending print jobs from Apple workstations to printers or print queues.
- AppleTalk is compatible with LocalTalk, the Apple Computer, Inc., proprietary hardware interface, EtherTalk, TokenTalk, and networks using standard Token Ring or Ethernet media.
- AppleTalk printers use bi-directional communications, establishing a communications dialog before printing occurs; therefore, they require special drivers that support both AppleTalk protocol and bi-directional communications.

Note Because of the amount of network traffic created by bi-directional communication, the AppleTalk protocol is not recommended for wide area networks because of limited bandwidth.

- The Apple ImageWriter and Apple LaserWriter are the most commonly used AppleTalk network printers, and both include a printer interface that provides workstation or print server communication with the printer.
- The AppleTalk environment most commonly uses the PostScript page description language, supporting its own list of fonts—another feature that relies on bi-directional communication.

Several AppleTalk printing protocols are used for the various print devices used in the AppleTalk network:

- **Address Resolution Protocol.** The method whereby network nodes are arbitrarily assigned a node id (name) each time the node is activated on the network.
- **Datagram Delivery Protocol (DDP).** The connectionless delivery method for communication between the ATPS client and the printer. At this layer, two phases can be distinguished—phase I and phase II. Phase I networks are *nonextended* (a unique number must be assigned to each node). Phase II networks are *extended* (able to communicate across routers).

Note AppleTalk print services can use printer names to track printers (Name Binding protocol) and zone names to provide logical groupings of network nodes (Zone Information protocol).

- **AppleTalk Transaction Protocol (ATP).** The method of delivery service between ATPS clients and printers, considered to be very reliable because delivery is acknowledged by ATM and retransmission is reinitiated after a specified period of time if the first transmission is not acknowledged.
- **Printer Access Protocol (PAP).** The method of establishing communication between the workstation and printer. Used for communications related to connection setup and teardown, maintenance, and printer status.

NetWare print services can also be provided to most Macintosh users or other ATPS workstations by using NetWare for Macintosh AppleTalk print services. Unlike NetWare print queues, which receive data and store it in temporary print files, ATPS print queues establish and maintain bidirectional communication during the print request. This service is provided by the NetWare for the Macintosh print spooler. This is considered to be a front-end print service. In this front-end configuration, ATPS advertises NetWare print queues to appear to ATPS clients as if they were standard ATPS printer names. The NetWare PSERVER can service the NetWare print queue in this particular configuration.

Back-end print services are usually provided by the print server, such as NetWare's PSERVER.NLM and PSERVER.EXE files, or the NetWare for Macintosh ATPS print server. When binary data must be transferred to the printer, the ATPS back end requires an ATPS-compatible printer. Back-end print services include taking print jobs from the NetWare print queue, and sending the jobs across an AppleTalk network to an ATPS-compatible printer when the NetWare server is connected to an AppleTalk printer through an AppleTalk network.

Note Version 3.01 and later of NetWare for Macintosh enable the ATPS back-end process to be used without the front-end process when no ATPS clients are in use and the AppleTalk printer-to-NetWare network connection occurs across an AppleTalk network. This provides any workstation with access to a print queue with the capability of submitting print jobs to ATPS printers using CAPTURE or NPRINT commands.

Printing from a Macintosh application functions slightly differently (see fig. 44.4).

When a Macintosh application sends a print job, that print job is sent in a generic format called QuickDraw. A connection is made and a dialog is initiated between the Print Manager and the printer. The Print Manager then makes sure the printer is available or finds it on the network by using Name Binding Protocol (NBP). Next, the print driver converts the QuickDraw-formatted print job into printer commands, establishes a connection to the printer, then initiates print driver and printer interaction. The LaserPrep file, which specifies operating system and drive-related information from the computer to the printer, is then downloaded as needed, and any fonts needed for the print job are downloaded. Next, the print job is sent to the printer, the job is printed, the connection is terminated, and the job is complete.

Figure 44.4
The printing process for Macintosh applications.

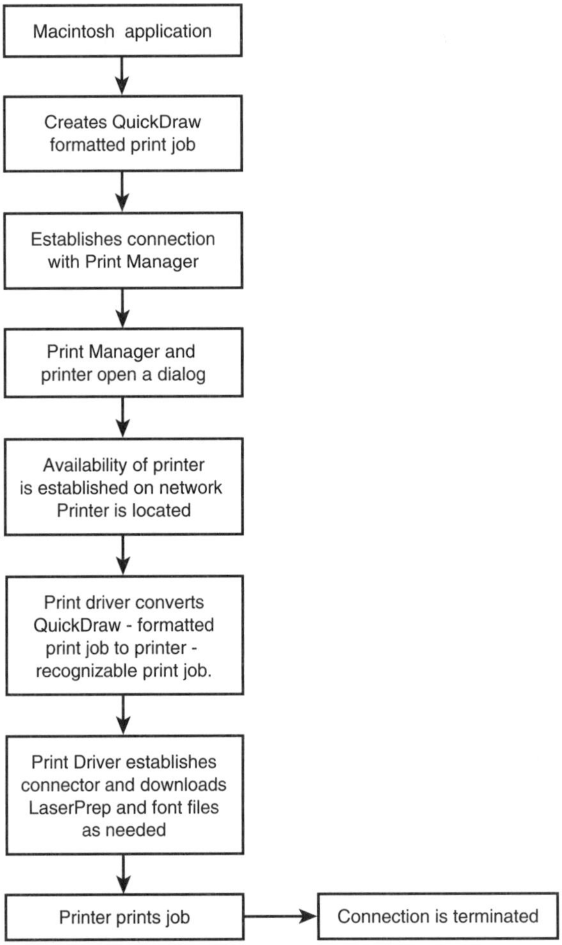

To configure AppleTalk print services, you can include the configuration options at the command line when you load AppleTalk print services, or you can provide the configuration information in a text file that can be referenced when AppleTalk print services are loaded. The configuration file used is called ATPS.CFG.

Practical TIP Use the NetWare Install console utility to create and edit the ATPS.CFG file.

Table 44.1 lists the configuration options that can be used at the command line or included in the ATPS.CFG file when loading AppleTalk print services.

Although some differences exist between printing with DOS or MS Windows applications and Macintosh applications, NetWare makes it relatively easy to print from the network from applications running under any of these operating systems.

Table 44.1
AppleTalk Print Services Configuration Options

Option	*Option Name*	*Description*
-o	Object Name	Name of the queue that accepts ATPS print jobs (31 characters maximum)
-p	Printer Name	Name of the AppleTalk printer, from which a default queue name consisting of the prefix of NW and the printer name can be created if the -o option is not included (31 characters maximum)
-wb	Without Back End	Assumes PSERVER or another print server other than an AppleTalk print server is to be used
-wf	Without Front End	Assumes no AppleTalk print spooler, and that PC users but not Macintosh or other ATPS users can use the queue
-z	Zone Name	If provided, gives the name of the zone in which the AppleTalk printer resides; otherwise, the internal network's zone is used as the default

Questions

1. The first step in setting up the NetWare file server for Unix-to-NetWare printing requires ______.

   ○ A. the administrator to load PLPD.NLM on the Unix host

   ○ B. that a trusted host be selected

   ○ C. Unix users to be mapped to NetWare user accounts

   ○ D. NetWare print queues to be exported for use by lpd

2. To choose Unix hosts as trusted hosts, choose the ______ and ______ options from the main menu of the NLM.

   ☐ A. Selected Trusted Hosts

   ☐ B. Username Mapping Mode

   ☐ C. PLPD

   ☐ D. PLPDCFG

3. The Unix lpd acronym refers to ______.

   ○ A. line printer display

   ○ B. live printer deployment

   ○ C. line printer daemon

   ○ D. live printer display

4. A list of trusted Unix hosts is contained in the ______ database file.

   ○ A. SYS:SYSTEM\DATABASE

   ○ B. SYS:PUBLIC\HOSTS

   ○ C. SYS:ETC\HOSTS

   ○ D. SYS:MAIL\HOSTDB

5. Load the Unix-to-NetWare print server by using the ______ NLM.

   ○ A. PLPDCFG

   ○ B. PLPDMSG

   ○ C. FILTER

   ○ D. PLPD

6. The NetWare-toUnix print gateway is configured by using the ______ or ______ NetWare loadable modules.

   ☐ A. NFSADMIN

   ☐ B. FLEXCON

   ☐ C. LPR_PSRV

   ☐ D. LPR_GWY

7. Of the following, which *three* are utilities used to control printer operation on System-V or BSD Unix systems?

   ☐ A. lpstat

   ☐ B. lpsched

   ☐ C. lpshut

   ☐ D. lpc

8. Edit the ______ database file to configure a BSD-based Unix host.

   ○ A. PrintDB

   ○ B. Printcap

   ○ C. PMADM

   ○ D. ATPS.CFG

9. Which protocol is used to provide connectionless delivery for communications between the ATPS client and the printer?

   ○ A. DDP

   ○ B. ARP

   ○ C. ATP

   ○ D. PAP

10. If the -o option to specify an object name is not included when loading AppleTalk print services, information provided by the ______ option is used to specify a default print queue.

    ○ A. -wf

    ○ B. -z

    ○ C. -p

    ○ D. -wb

Answers

1. D
2. A, D
3. C
4. C
5. D
6. A, B
7. B, C, D
8. B
9. A
10. C

PART PART PART PART PART PART PART PART

VI

NetWare 4.1 Installation

CHAPTER 45

Performing a Simple Installation

With each NetWare version, installation has become a little easier. NetWare 4 installation is substantially easier than some of the earlier versions of NetWare, particularly when you consider the complexity of the NetWare 4 design and the Simple Installation of NetWare 4.1 option provided with the NetWare 4 operating system. This chapter explains how to install NetWare 4 by using the Simple Installation option.

Installing NetWare 4 with the Simple Installation Option

To install NetWare 4, insert the CD-ROM into the CD-ROM drive on the computer that is to become the NetWare 4 file server.

Note: If one does not already exist, you must first create a small DOS partition (bootable DOS partition) and a large NetWare partition (secondary DOS partition) on the computer's hard disk. Do this by using the DOS FDISK command.

Change to the drive containing the NetWare 4.1 installation CD-ROM. (The examples used in the text of this chapter assume the drive letter assigned to the CD-ROM drive is drive letter D.) Then complete the following steps:

1. Type **INSTALL** and press Enter. The first NetWare Install screen opens. A menu is provided from which you choose what to install. Your choices include installing the NetWare server, installing a DOS/Windows client, or creating diskettes (see fig. 45.1).

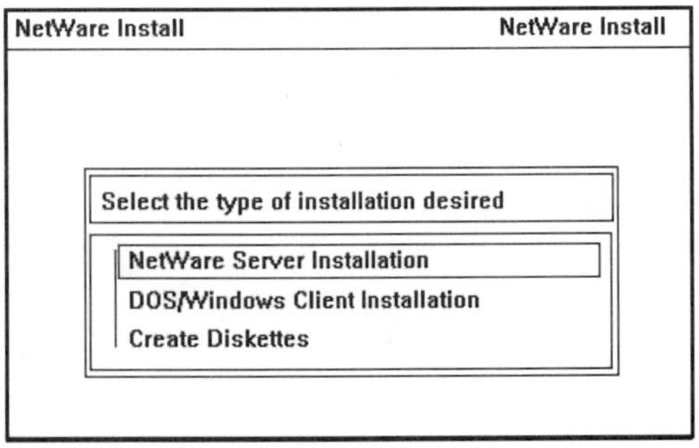

Figure 45.1
The first NetWare Install screen.

2. Choose NetWare Server Installation.

Note: NetWare 4.1 installation requires that memory management software such as that provided by MS Windows, QEMM, and so on *not* be loaded to activate protected mode memory when installing NetWare 4.1. If a memory manager is loaded and provided protected mode memory, a system message appears stating something similar to the following:

```
The processor is already in protected mode.

You need to remove or reconfigure your DOS
memory manager before installing NetWare.

Press <Enter> to continue.
```

To correct the problem, modify your workstation configuration file to *not* load the memory manager, then reboot your computer. Once NetWare 4.1 is installed, you can modify the configuration file to load the memory manager software again.

3. Choose NetWare 4.1 from the NetWare Installation Utility menu (see fig. 45.2).
4. Choose Simple Installation of NetWare 4.1 from the next NetWare Installation Utility screen that opens (see fig. 45.3).
5. Type a name for the NetWare 4.1 file server you are installing, then press Enter (see fig. 45.4).
6. When the Copy server boot files to DOS partition screen opens (see fig. 45.5), modify the Source path or Destination path as needed. The server files are copied to the DOS partition, and the copy process is generally quick. Progress is displayed as a percent complete as well as in graphic form on this screen and subsequent screens that flash by as the copy process proceeds.

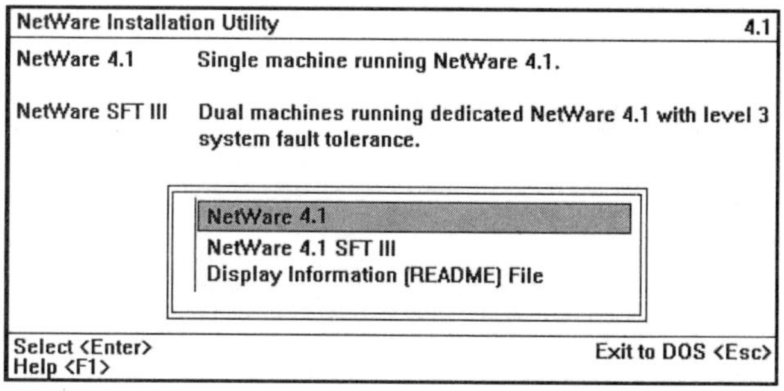

Figure 45.2
The NetWare Installation Utility screen.

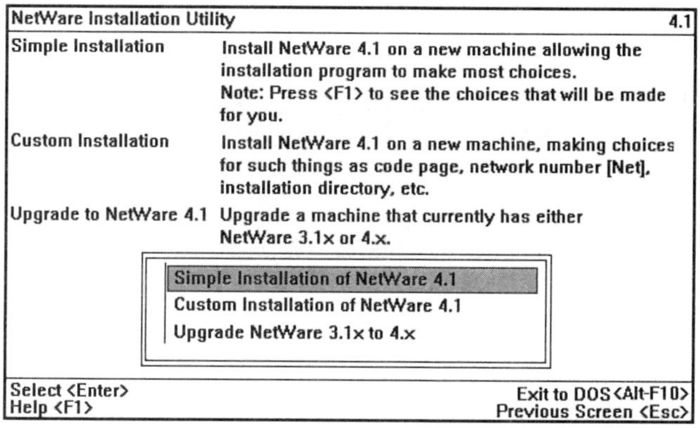

Figure 45.3
The NetWare Installation Utility screen specifying the server name.

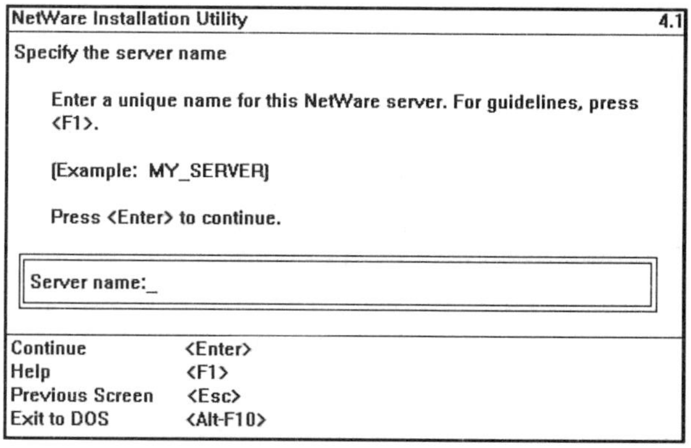

Figure 45.4
The prompt for server name screen.

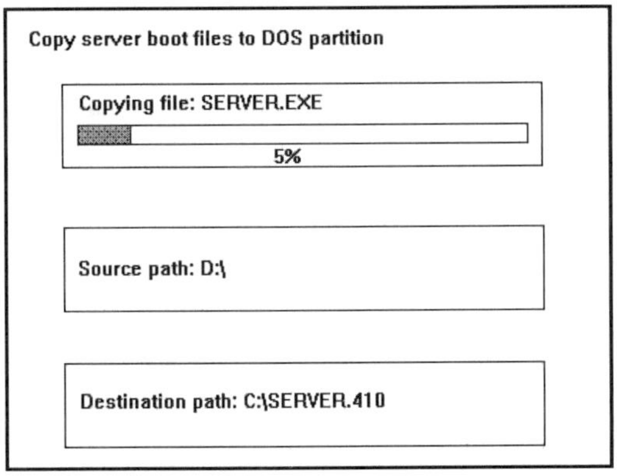

Figure 45.5
The Copy server boot files to DOS partition screen.

7. From the NetWare Server Installation 4.1 NetWare Loadable Module screen, choose the server disk driver from the list of known drivers. For example, if the disk drive used in this computer is an IDE or compatible disk drive, choose the IDE.DSK file from the list by highlighting (selecting) it and pressing Enter (see fig. 45.6).

Practical TIP You can use the arrow, PgUp, and PgDn keys to scroll through the list of available disk drivers. If the disk driver required for this particular computer is not displayed, you can install other disk drivers by pressing Ins and following the prompts. Other disk drivers are generally provided on a diskette by the drive manufacturer when the computer or disk drive is purchased.

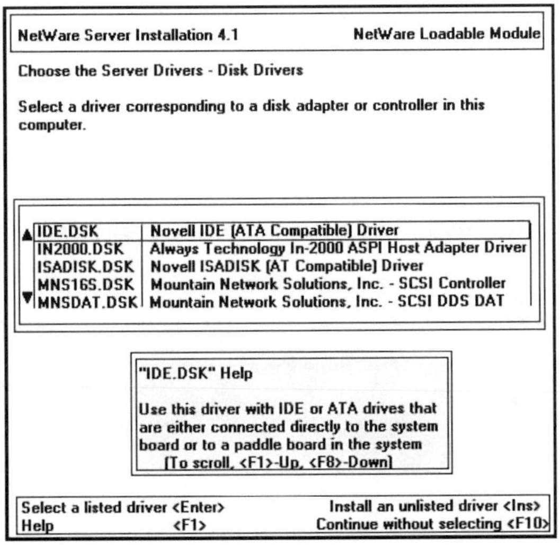

Figure 45.6
The disk driver installation screen.

8. When prompted to `Verify/Enter the driver parameters to be sure they match the hardware in this computer` (see fig. 45.7), verify or change the related parameters as needed. For example, be certain the Interrupt Number and Port Value are correct for the driver installed in this machine.

9. If necessary, install additional disk drivers by choosing Yes when prompted with `Do you want to select an additional disk driver?` (see fig. 45.8).

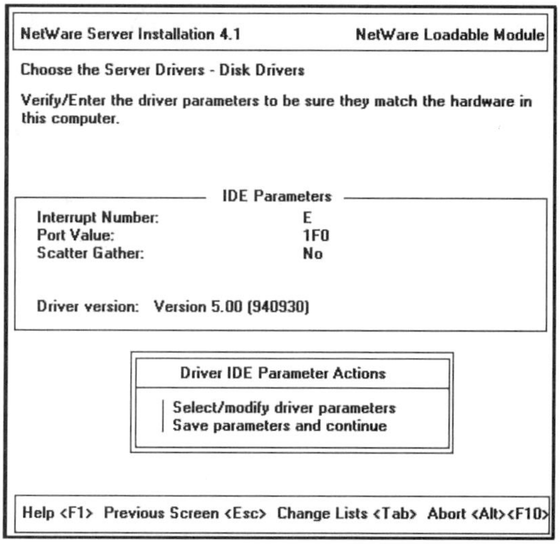

Figure 45.7
The disk driver verification screen.

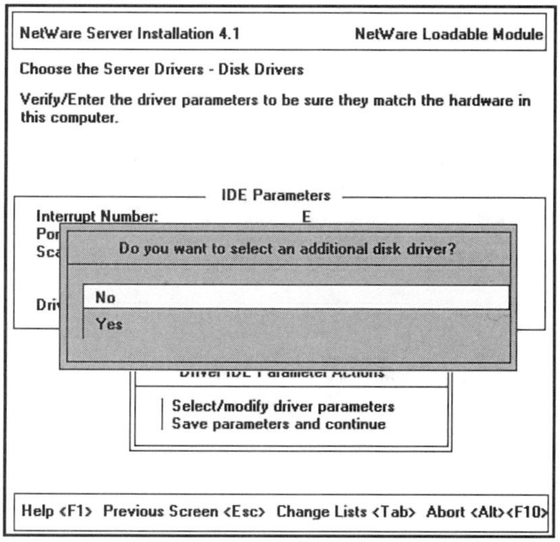

Figure 45.8
The install additional disk driver prompt.

10. After all disk drivers are installed and you answer No to the prompt to install additional disk drivers, the system scans for available network drivers and presents a list from which you must choose the driver for the network board installed in this machine (see fig. 45.9).

11. When prompted to `Verify/Enter the driver parameters to be sure they match the hardware in this computer` (see fig. 45.10), verify or change the related parameters as needed. For example, be certain the Interrupt Number and Port Value are correct for the driver installed in this machine. If necessary, change the number of retries from the default of 5 to a more suitable number. Then, choose to Save parameters and continue.

12. When prompted with `Do you want to select an additional network driver?`, choose Yes if necessary; otherwise, choose No.

13. A summary screen indicating what Disk and CD-ROM Drivers as well as what Network (LAN) Drivers are currently available opens. If the driver names listed are incorrect, correct them now by choosing Select additional or modify selected Disk/LAN drivers from the Driver Actions menu. Otherwise, choose Continue installation from the Driver Actions menu.

14. Wait while the installation software performs a variety of tasks, including checking for conflicts, then read the Warning that appears:

    `Warning:`

    `There is a slight chance that you may be using a NetWare driver that conflicts with the DOS CD-ROM driver. INSTALL cannot determine this for you. See <F1> for more information.`

    `If there is a driver conflict and INSTALL accesses the CD-ROM via DOS, the keyboard will LOCKUP. You then need to reboot your computer, restart the installation, and try to mount the CD-ROM as a NetWare volume the second time.`

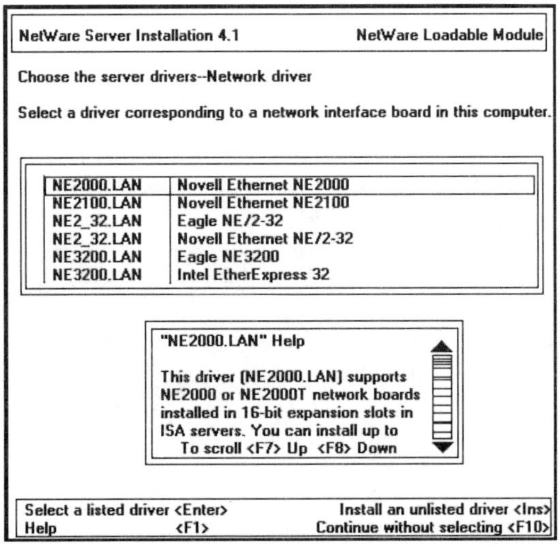

Figure 45.9
The network driver installation screen.

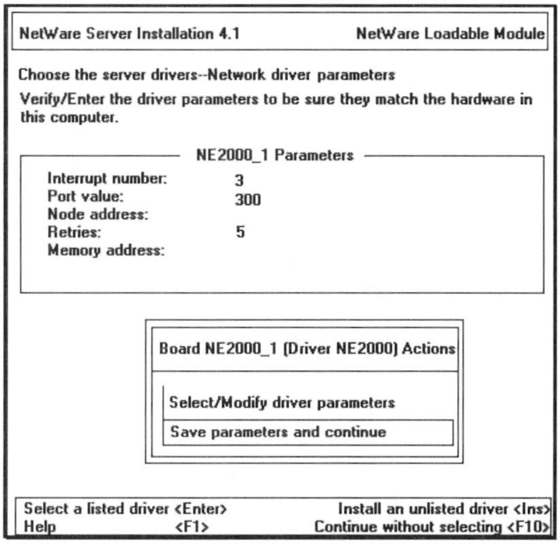

Figure 45.10
The network driver verification screen.

15. Choose Continue accessing the CD-ROM via DOS.

16. Because you partitioned the disk to provide both a DOS and non-DOS (NetWare) partition, read the screen that warns that some disk partitions already exist; then press Enter to continue with the installation.

17. When prompted to delete existing non-bootable disk partitions, choose Yes.

18. When prompted to specify the path from which license files will be installed (drive A is the default, press F3 to specify a different location), press Enter to continue.

19. After the source license document and related files are copied as needed, and you are prompted to Install NetWare Directory Services (NDS), choose one of the following options:

    `Yes, this is the first NetWare 4 server`

    `No, connect to existing NetWare 4 networks`

    If this is the first server being installed in your NetWare 4 network, choose the Yes option and continue.

20. Choose a time zone when the list of time zones appears (see fig. 45.11).

21. When prompted for an organization name, type the name you have chosen to represent your organization and press Enter. The screen notes the following:

    ```
    The organization name:
    - Is typically your company name but may also be a division or department name.
    - Uniquely identifies your NetWare 4 network (tree).
    - Should not be lengthy (abbreviate if necessary).
    - Cannot contain spaces.
    ```

22. Provide the administrator's password at the Admin Password: prompt (type and press Enter). This is the password that will be required each time the Admin user logs in to the network.

23. When prompted, retype the password and press Enter.

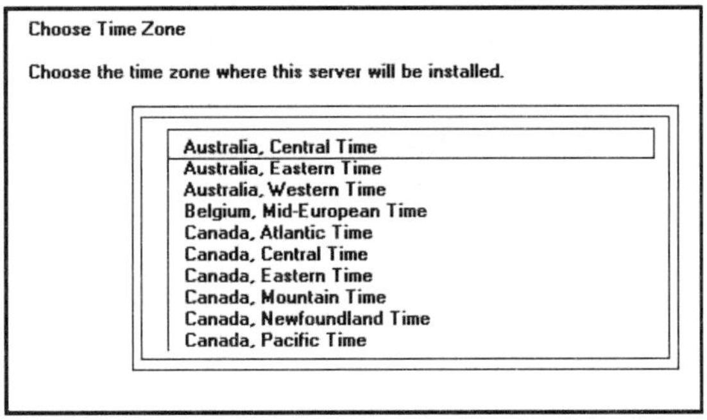

Figure 45.11
The time zone list.

NetWare Directory Services and other related NetWare 4 files are now copied to their assigned location. The For your information window opens displaying basic information about your NetWare 4 installation. After reading this screen and noting the information it provides, press Enter to continue. Figure 45.12 shows this information for a sample network.

24. When the rest of the files that need to be copied are copied, the Other Installation Options screen opens. From this screen, you can choose any one of four Other Installation Items/Products:

- Create a Registration Diskette
- Create DOS/MS Windows/OS2 Client Installation Diskettes
- Create NetWare UPGRADE/ MIGRATE Diskettes
- Install Online Documentation and Viewers

To choose one of these options, choose the Choose an item or product listed above option from the Other Installation Actions menu, and follow the prompts. Otherwise, choose Continue Installation from the Other Installation Actions menu.

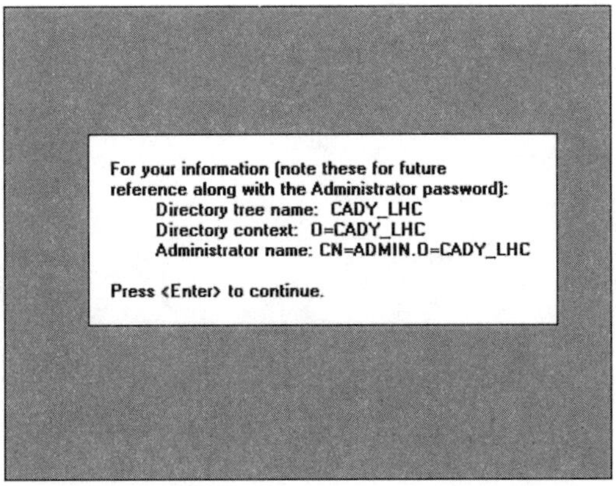

Figure 45.12
The For your information screen.

25. Once you choose Continue Installation, the installation process is complete. Press Enter to exit to the system console screen.

Although 25 steps might seem excessive, it looks much more cumbersome than it actually is. All choices that can be made for you (such as which type of LAN board is installed in this PC) are made. Compared to earlier versions of NetWare, using the Simple Installation option of NetWare 4.1 is a breeze.

Questions

1. Of the following, which one reflects the proper order of installation for a NetWare 4 server?
   - A. Provide a server name, copy server boot files, install driver files, choose a time zone, provide an organization name and a password for Admin.
   - B. Provide a server name, copy server boot files, install driver files, choose a password and name for the administrator, choose the time zone.
   - C. Provide a server name, install driver files, choose password, provide server name, provide organization name, choose a time zone.
   - D. Provide a server name, install driver files, copy server boot files, choose a time zone, provide an organization name and password.

2. The default destination path for installing the NetWare 4 server files is ______.
   - A. C:\NetWare4
   - B. C:\NetWare.410
   - C. C:\Server_4
   - D. C:\Server.410

3. Of the following, which one is *not* found on the Select the type of installation desired menu?
   - A. NetWare Server Installation
   - B. NetWare 4 Diskette Install
   - C. DOS/Windows Client Installation
   - D. Create Diskettes

4. When choosing disk drivers, to select one that is *not* on the list provided by Novell, press ______ to display additional drivers.
   - A. F1
   - B. Ins
   - C. Alt+F10
   - D. Esc

5. The following describes the ______ installation: Install NetWare 4.1 on a new machine allowing the program to make most choices.
   - A. Simple Installation of NetWare 4.1
   - B. Basic Installation of NetWare 4.1
   - C. Custom Installation of NetWare 4.1
   - D. Upgrade NetWare 3.1x to 4.x

6. The time zone to choose when installing a NetWare 4 server into an existing NetWare 4 tree should be ______.
   - A. the same as the time zone for the tree's [Root]
   - B. the same as the time zone for all other file servers in this tree
   - C. chosen based on the physical location of the file server being installed
   - D. chosen to reflect the country of the first server installed in the tree

7. Of the following, which *two* are true?
   - A. You can install only one disk driver per file server.
   - B. You can view a list of all installed disk and network drivers after driver installation is complete.

- ☐ C. You must type the name of the disk driver in the window when prompted.
- ☐ D. You can install more than one disk driver if you answer Yes to the prompt to install additional disk drivers.

8. Which of the following statements is *not* true?
   - ○ A. There is a slight chance you may be using a network driver that conflicts with the DOS CD-ROM driver.
   - ○ B. No DOS CD-ROM and network driver conflict can exist as long as INSTALL accesses the CD-ROM via DOS.
   - ○ C. If a CD-ROM and network driver conflict does exist, the problem can lock up the keyboard.
   - ○ D. If a conflict occurs between the CD-ROM and network driver, you can restart INSTALL and try to mount the CD-ROM as a NetWare volume.

9. When prompted to delete the existing nonbootable disk partition,______.
   - ○ A. answer No or you lose your NetWare volume
   - ○ B. answer Yes so that all of NetWare can be installed on the DOS volume
   - ○ C. answer No so that you do not lose any information on your existing NetWare volume
   - ○ D. answer Yes because this is a first-time install and, although the non-DOS volume exists, no information is yet stored on it

10. Which of the following statements about providing an organization name is *not* true?
    - ○ A. It is typically the same as the company name.
    - ○ B. It should use as many characters as necessary to be distinct and descriptive.
    - ○ C. It should uniquely identify your NetWare 4 network tree.
    - ○ D. It cannot contain spaces.

Answers

1. A
2. D
3. B
4. B
5. B
6. C
7. B, D
8. B
9. D
10. B

CHAPTER 46

Performing a Custom Installation

Although the simple installation is the easiest way to install NetWare 4.1, it is not always the method you need to follow. Sometimes you may prefer to perform a custom installation, specifying all parameters and options without having the installation program assume defaults. You can do that by using the Custom Installation of NetWare 4.1 option in the NetWare 4.1 INSTALL utility. This chapter discusses the use of the NetWare 4.1 Custom Installation option.

Using the NetWare 4.1 Custom Installation Option

The first phase of using the Custom Installation option involves the same steps as using the simple installation option. Follow these steps:

1. With the NetWare 4.1 operating system CD in the CD-ROM drive, change to that drive, then type **INSTALL** and press Enter.
2. Choose NetWare Server Installation from the Select the type of installation desired menu.
3. Choose NetWare 4.1 from the NetWare Installation Utility screen.
4. Choose Custom Installation of NetWare 4.1 from the next NetWare Installation Utility screen that opens.
5. Provide a name for the file server when prompted and press Enter.
6. When the randomly generated internal IPX number is displayed, press Enter to accept that number, or provide another number and press Enter.
7. When prompted, start the copying of the server boot files by pressing Enter.
8. Once the server boot files are copied, accept the defaults for Country Code, Code Page, and Keyboard Mapping by pressing Enter, or make changes as needed and press Enter.
9. When prompted, choose DOS file name format (recommended).
10. Choose No when prompted with `Do you want to specify any special startup set commands?` (see fig. 46.1).

Practical TIP If you need to set Auto Register Memory Above 16 Megabytes=OFF or Set Reserved Buffers Below 16 Meg=200, choose Yes and follow the prompts.

11. Choose No when prompted with `Add commands to AUTOEXEC.BAT to load SERVER.EXE?` (see fig. 46.2).

    SERVER.EXE is now loaded by the installation program. Once the NetWare 4.1 server is loaded, you are prompted to `Choose the Server Drivers - Disk Drivers`. Continue with the following steps.

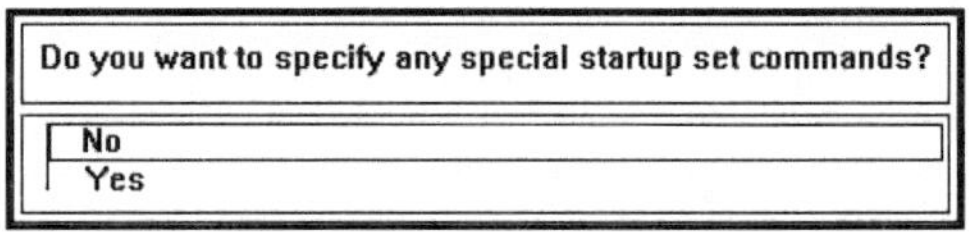

Figure 46.1
The specify set commands screen.

Figure 46.2
The prompt screen to update the AUTOEXEC.BAT file.

12. Choose the appropriate server disk driver from the list of known drivers to load it.
13. Choose Save parameters and continue when prompted with the Driver driver_name Parameter Actions menu.
14. Answer No when prompted with `Do You Want to load an Additional Disk Driver?`

15. When prompted with `Choose the Server Drivers - Network Drivers`, choose the LAN driver for this computer.

16. When prompted, modify the parameters to represent the settings on this computer's network board, then press F10 to save the parameter settings, choose Save parameters, and continue.

17. Choose No when prompted with `Do You Want to load an Additional LAN Driver?`

18. Choose Continue Installation.

19. Accept the default number for binding the protocol to the network board for each protocol you are using.

20. Read the Warning that appears:

```
Warning:

There is a slight chance that you may be
using a NetWare driver that conflicts with
the DOS CD-ROM driver. INSTALL cannot
determine this for you. See <F1> for more
information.
```

    If there is a driver conflict and INSTALL accesses the CD-ROM via DOS, the keyboard will LOCKUP. You will then need to reboot your computer, restart the installation, and try to mount the CD-ROM as a NetWare volume the second time.

21. Choose Continue accessing the CD-ROM via DOS.

22. Choose Automatically from the Create NetWare disk partition prompt, or choose Manually if you prefer, then set the partition size, hot fix, and mirroring configurations.

23. Choose Continue with Installation from the Disk Partition Options menu (see fig. 46.3).

24. Make any needed changes to NetWare volumes, such as adding additional volumes, if needed; then press F10 to continue.

25. When prompted, press Enter to install the NetWare files.

26. When the Select Optional NetWare Files window opens (see fig. 46.4), unmark boxes of file groups you do not want to have installed. For example, if you do not have any UNIX systems in your network, you can unmark the NetWare UNIX Utilities (1 MB) box.

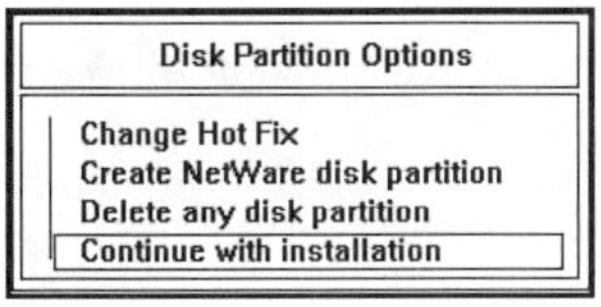

Figure 46.3
The Disk Partition Options window.

27. When you are prompted to Install NetWare Directory Services (NDS), choose one of the following options:

    `Yes, this is the first NetWare 4 server`

    `No, connect to existing NetWare 4 networks`

    If this is the first server being installed in your NetWare 4 network, choose the Yes option and continue.

28. Choose a time zone when the list of time zones appears.

29. When prompted for an Organization Name, type the name you have chosen to represent your organization and press Enter. As the screen notes:

The organization name:

- Is typically your company name but may also be a division or department name.
- Uniquely identifies your NetWare 4 network tree.
- Should not be lengthy (abbreviate if necessary).
- Cannot contain spaces.

30. Provide (type and press Enter) the administrator's password at the `Admin Password:` prompt. This is the password that will be required each time the Admin user logs in to the network.

31. When prompted, retype the password and press Enter.

    NetWare Directory Services and other related NetWare 4 files are now copied to their assigned location. A For your information window opens displaying basic information about your NetWare 4 installation. After reading this screen and noting the information it provides, press Enter to continue.

32. When all the rest of the files that need to be copied are copied, the Other Installation Options screen opens. From this screen you can choose any one of four Other Installation Items/Products:

    - Create a Registration Diskette
    - Upgrade 3.1x Print Services
    - Create DOS/MS Windows/OS2 Client Installation Diskettes
    - Create NetWare UPGRADE/MIGRATE Diskettes
    - Install Online Documentation and Viewers
    - Create NetWare BOOTDISK Diskettes
    - Install NetWare for Macintosh

    To choose one of these options, choose the option that reads Choose an item or product listed above from the Other Installation Actions menu (see fig. 46.5), and follow the prompts. Otherwise, choose Continue Installation from the Other Installation Actions menu.

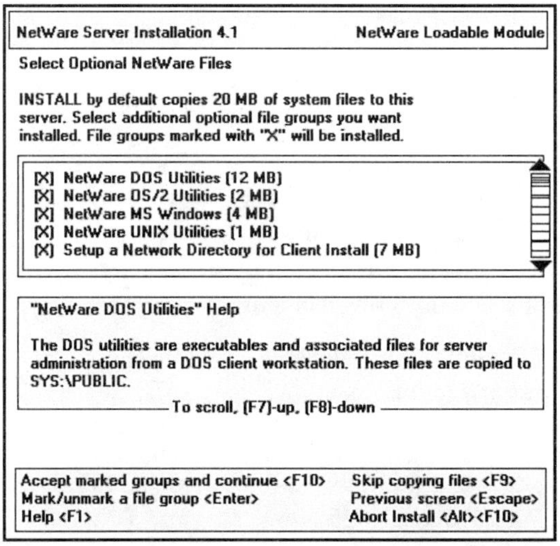

Figure 46.4
The Select Optional NetWare Files window.

33. Once you choose to Continue Installation, the installation process is complete. Press Enter to exit to the system console screen.

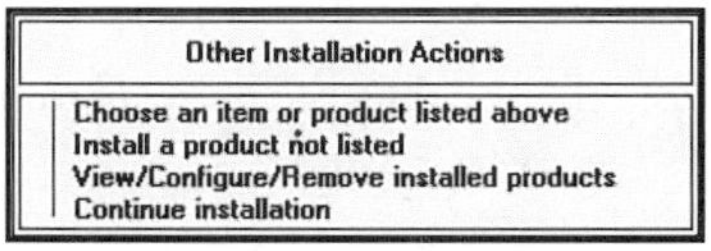

Figure 46.5
The Other Installation Actions menu.

The Custom Installation option of NetWare 4 lets you exercise greater control over the installation process than does the Simple Installation option. Although keeping the installation as simple as possible is often the best approach, there may be times, such as when you have an obscure LAN board installed in the PC, when you prefer to more closely control the installation of NetWare 4.1. The Custom Installation option gives you that control.

Questions

1. The ______ is a randomly generated number that can be changed.
   - ○ A. Network number
   - ○ B. Internal IPX number
   - ○ C. File server number
   - ○ D. IPX number
2. The ______ format is recommended.
   - ○ A. DOS file name
   - ○ B. DOS extended name
   - ○ C. DOS basic name
   - ○ D. DOS basic file name
3. After choosing the ______, you can choose to specify special startup set commands.
   - ○ A. DOS file name format
   - ○ B. Internal IPX number
   - ○ C. Custom installation option
   - ○ D. Basic installation option
4. Before providing or accepting the randomly generated IPX number, you must first provide ______.
   - ○ A. the Auto Register Memory above 16 MB set command
   - ○ B. a name for this NetWare 4.1 file server
   - ○ C. disk driver parameters
   - ○ D. the name and settings for the LAN driver
5. During installation, SERVER.EXE is loaded ______.
   - ○ A. after providing parameters for the network board
   - ○ B. after binding the protocol to the network board
   - ○ C. before choosing the appropriate server disk driver from a list of known drivers
   - ○ D. before choosing whether to add the command to load SERVER.EXE to the AUTOEXEC.BAT file
6. In which order do you load drivers during the installation of NetWare 4.1?
   - ○ A. LAN, then disk
   - ○ B. Disk, then LAN
   - ○ C. LAN, then bind, then disk
   - ○ D. Bind, then LAN, then disk
7. Of the following, which *three* are listed on the Disk Partition Options menu?
   - ☐ A. Change Hot Fix
   - ☐ B. Delete Hot Fix
   - ☐ C. Create NetWare Disk Partitions
   - ☐ D. Delete any Disk Partitions
8. The ______ option is found on the Select Optional NetWare Files screen.
   - ○ A. Create NetWare Disk Partitions
   - ○ B. Change Hot Fix
   - ○ C. Delete Hot Fix
   - ○ D. Setup a network directory for client install

9. If you choose to copy the NetWare DOS utilities, they are copied to ______.

   ○ A. SYS:PUBLIC

   ○ B. SYS:ETC

   ○ C. SYS:SYSTEM

   ○ D. SYS:MAIL

10. Of the following, which does *not* apply to providing an organization name?

    ○ A. It must be unique to identify the NetWare 4 tree.

    ○ B. It may contain spaces.

    ○ C. It should be short when possible.

    ○ D. It is typically the same as the company name.

Answers

1. B
2. A
3. A
4. B
5. C
6. B
7. A, C, D
8. D
9. A
10. B

CHAPTER 47

Migrating a NetWare 3 Server to NetWare 4.x

If your network currently contains NetWare 3 file servers, you can upgrade them to be NetWare 4 file servers. Although NetWare 3 servers can be useful in a NetWare 4 network if bindery emulation and NETSYNC are implemented, the sooner you upgrade your NetWare 3 servers to NetWare 4, the easier your network administration becomes.

There are two approaches you can take to upgrading your NetWare 3 file servers: the across-the-wire upgrade and the in-place upgrade. The most important difference between the two is what happens to the NetWare 3 file server when the upgrade occurs.

When an across-the-wire migration is performed, the source server is left intact. Copies of the upgraded NetWare 3 server information are sent to the NetWare 4 server. The NetWare 3 server still exists and is unchanged. The across-the-wire migration thus preserves the information about current users, their associated trustee assignments, and any related account restrictions. It also preserves the current accounting methods, print queues, and print servers.

The in-place migration, however, converts the current NetWare 3 file server to a NetWare 4 file server, after which the NetWare 3 file server no longer exists.

This chapter discusses migrating a NetWare 3 server to NetWare 4 by using these two approaches:

- The across-the-wire migration
- The in-place migration

Performing an Across-the-Wire Upgrade

An across-the-wire upgrade enables you to migrate bindery information and data from your NetWare 3 file server (*source*) to a NetWare 4 file server (*destination*) by using the MIGRATE.EXE utility located on a NetWare 4 file server. The NetWare MIGRATE.EXE utility enables you to choose which information in the NetWare 3 bindery and which data files will be upgraded, thus creating a customized NetWare 4 server.

The bindery information being migrated is transferred first to a working directory on the workstation where it is then converted into a format the NetWare 4 NDS database can understand. The converted information is then transferred to the NetWare 4 server by using *bindery services*, an emulation of the flat bindery structure found in pre-NetWare 4 file servers, so that the objects within the NDS database can become part of the NDS tree (see fig. 47.1). Any NetWare 3 user names that are the same as user names in the NetWare 4 NDS database are merged.

Note: NetWare 3 system files, including the system login script, are not migrated. User login scripts are migrated, however. If you choose, you can run the UIMPORT utility and convert the NetWare 3-based login scripts to the NetWare 4.

Data files that have the same name on the NetWare 4 server as they do on the NetWare 3 server are not copied to the NetWare 4 destination server. Files that are not copied are noted in the migration report, however.

Sometimes directories on the destination server have the same name as those on the source server. If this is the case, the files that are contained within those directories on the source server are merged into the same-name directories on the destination server. If you do not want this to occur, rename one or more of the directories before performing the migration.

Before performing an across-the-wire migration, you may also want to see whether any user names on the NetWare 4 server are the same as any of those on the NetWare 3 server. User names are merged when the migration is performed. Invalid user account information may thus be transferred to the NetWare 4 server if the users are not actually the same. It may be best to rename the user login name for duplicate users before performing the migration to reduce the amount of cleanup you must do after the migration.

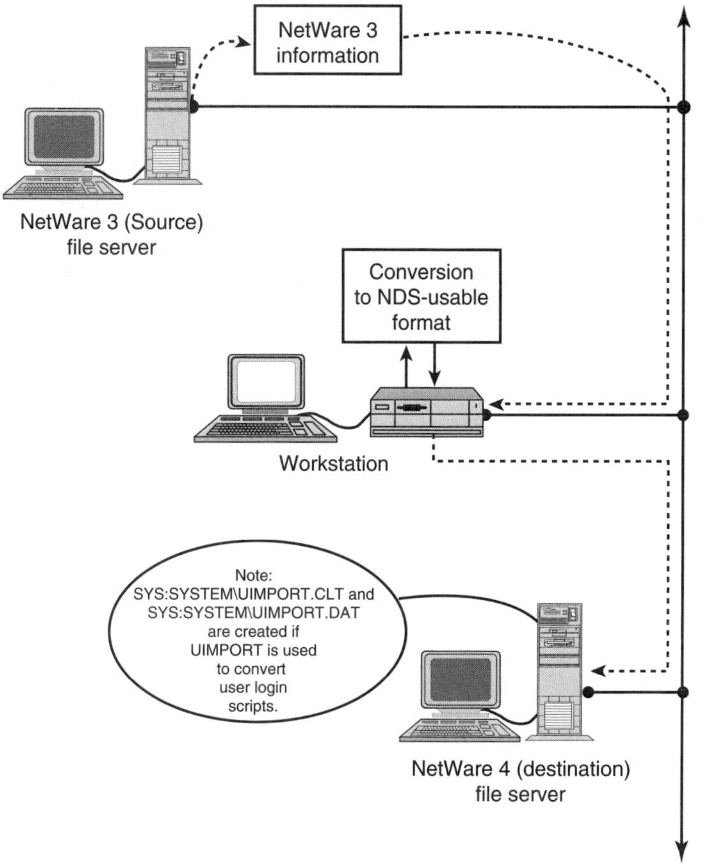

Figure 47.1
The across-the-wire migration process.

To complete an across-the-wire migration, follow these steps:

1. Ensure that all users are logged out and files closed, then clean up the NetWare 3 file server. To clean up the file server, consider performing any or all of the following tasks:
   - Delete any files you do not want to migrate (OLD, TMP, and so on).
   - Delete VAP files, because they are not compatible with NetWare 4.
   - Rename any files or directories that are named using other than the DOS 8.3 naming convention (except for Macintosh or OS/2 files) or they will not be migrated.
   - If necessary, modify the source server's directory structure so that no more than 25 levels exist, because that is the maximum number of levels the utility can migrate.

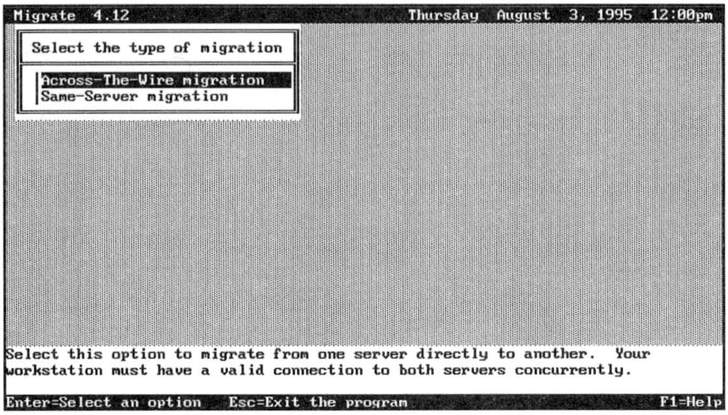

Figure 47.2
The Select the type of migration menu.

- Run BINDFIX to clean up the NetWare 3 bindery.

In addition, before running the migration, delete the following files from the SYS:SYSTEM directory:

- LARCHIVE.EXE
- LRESTORE.EXE
- MACBACK.EXE
- NARCHIVE.EXE
- NRESTORE.EXE

2. Log in to the NetWare 4 server by using bindery emulation (/B). For example, if your NetWare 4 file server is called FS_4, type the following at the workstation and press Enter:

```
LOGIN FS_4/Supervisor /B
```

3. Change to the directory (or CD-ROM drive) where the MIGRATE.EXE file is located, then type **MIGRATE** and press Enter.
4. Choose Across-The-Wire migration from the Select the type of migration menu (see fig. 47.2).
5. Choose NetWare 3.*x* from the Select the source LAN type menu (see fig. 47.3).
6. Choose NetWare 4.*x* from the Select the destination LAN type menu (see fig. 47.4).
7. Fill out the migration utility configuration form (see fig. 47.5).

Note One of the items you must pay particular attention to when migrating is the type of information to be migrated. You can choose what is to be migrated from the Select information to migrate menu (see fig. 47.6).

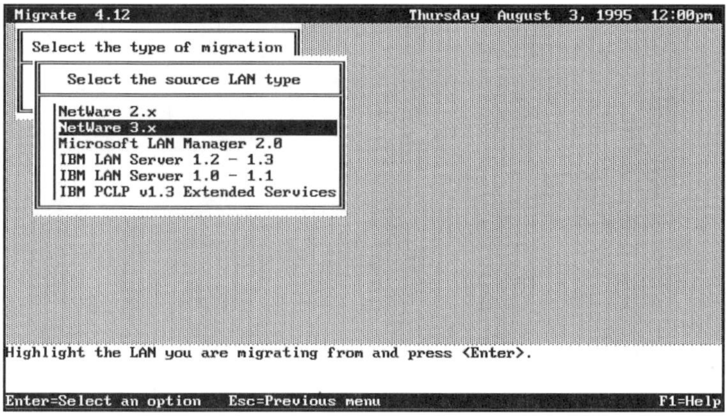

Figure 47.3
The Select the source LAN type menu.

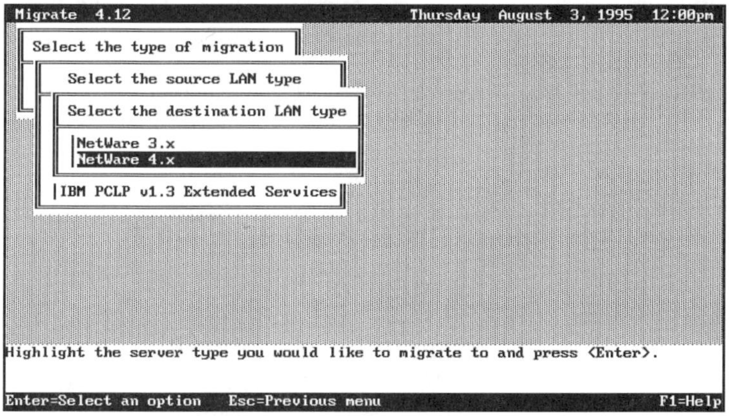

Figure 47.4
The Select the destination LAN type menu.

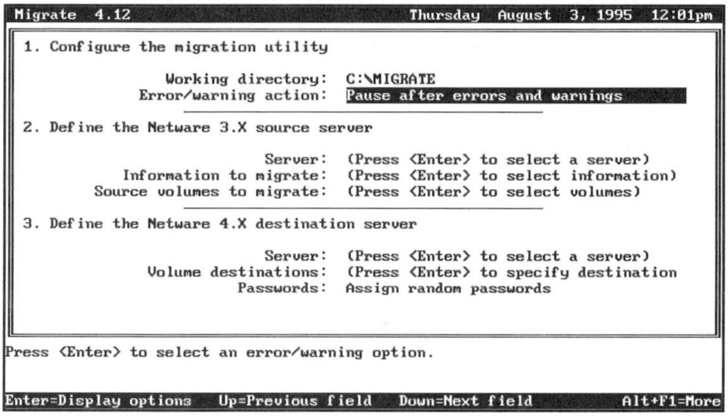

Figure 47.5
The migration utility configuration menu.

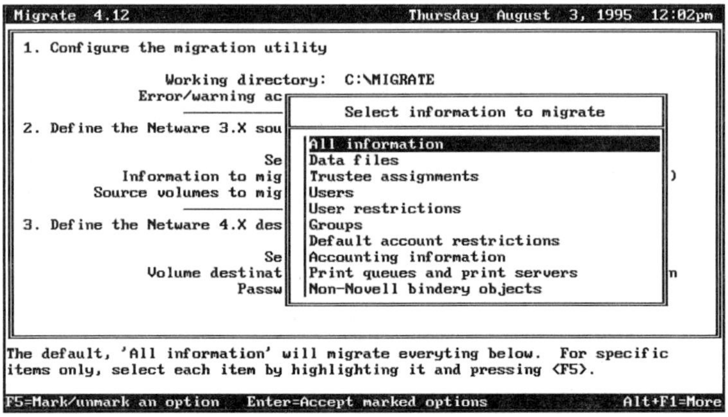

Figure 47.6
The Select information to migrate menu.

8. When the Migration Utility Configuration form is completed, press F10.
9. From the Select a migration action menu, choose Start the migration.
10. When the migration is complete, choose View migration reports from the Select a migration action menu to view information related to the migration process.
11. Choose Exit to DOS.

Next, you must run the MIGPRINT utility to migrate printing services.

1. Type **MIGPRINT /s=*source* /d=*destination* /VOL=*Q_volume* /O=*file*.**

   Replace *source* with the name of the source server, *destination* with the name of the NetWare 4 destination server, *Q_volume* with the name of the print queue volume if not using SYS:, and *file* with the name of a file to migrate to if you do not want to use the default file.

2. Complete the process by following the instructions provided on the MIGPRINT screen.
3. Exit MIGPRINT and perform any necessary cleanup.

Running an In-Place Upgrade

An in-place upgrade enables you to migrate your NetWare 3 file server to a NetWare 4 file server on the NetWare 3 server. When you finish the in-place upgrade, your NetWare 3 file server is a NetWare 4 file server with its bindery information merged into the NetWare 4 NDS database.

The in-place upgrade has almost all the same guidelines and processes applied to it as does the across-the-wire upgrade. For example, you still need a bindery connection to a NetWare 4 file server so that you can run the in-place upgrade. Also, all users must be logged out of the NetWare 3 file server. In addition, data and bindery files are treated the same in the in-place upgrade as they are in the across-the-wire upgrade.

Recall that the most important difference between the across-the-wire and the in-place upgrade is that once the upgrade is done, you no longer have the original NetWare 3 file server. It is important, therefore, that you perform a backup of your NetWare 3 server before beginning the in-place upgrade. If you experience any problems during the upgrade, you can then restore the backup and start over. In addition, you need to back up all data separately so that you can restore it to the NetWare 4 server after the in-place migration is run.

Use the following steps to execute an in-place upgrade:

1. Ensure that all users are logged out and files closed; then clean up the NetWare 3 file server. To clean up the file server, consider performing any or all of the tasks you perform for cleaning up the NetWare 3 file server.
2. Change to the directory (or CD-ROM drive) where the MIGRATE.EXE file is located; then type **MIGRATE** and press Enter.
3. Choose Same-Server migration from the Select the type of migration menu.
4. Choose NetWare 3.x from the Select the source LAN type menu.
5. Choose NetWare 4.x from the Select the destination LAN type menu.
6. Fill out the migration utility configuration form, including specifying the destination server, which can be chosen from a list (see fig. 47.7).

Note: In addition to the type of information to be migrated, you must also indicate what is to be done about passwords when migrating (see fig. 47.8).

7. Complete the same-server migration, then choose Exit (return to DOS) to exit the utility (see fig. 47.9).

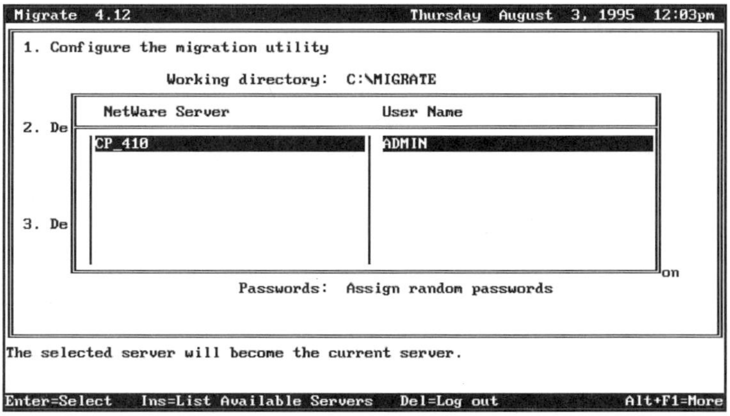

Figure 47.7
The Select NetWare Server list.

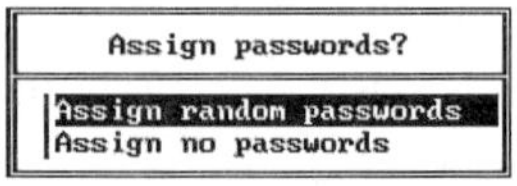

Figure 47.8
The Assign passwords? menu.

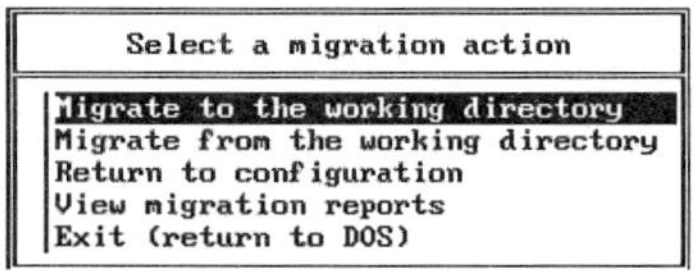

Figure 47.9
The Select a migration action menu.

Both the across-the-wire and in-place upgrades provide the same end result: a NetWare 4 file server. Using the across-the-wire method leaves the original NetWare 3 server intact, whereas the in-place upgrade converts the NetWare 3 server to a NetWare 4 server. The upgrade option you choose may, therefore, depend on the result you desire.

Questions

1. The most important difference between in-place and across-the-wire upgrades is ______.
   - ○ A. that one uses the MIGRATE.EXE utility and the other uses the MIGPRINT.EXE utility
   - ○ B. the fact that user objects are combined
   - ○ C. how much of the data is transferred
   - ○ D. what happens to the NetWare 3 file server when the upgrade occurs

2. When performing an across-the-wire migration, the bindery information is transferred first to ______.
   - ○ A. the workstation
   - ○ B. the new 4.*x* server
   - ○ C. the NDS database
   - ○ D. the hard disk of the older 3.*x* server

3. The ______ is/are *not* migrated.
   - ○ A. user login scripts
   - ○ B. system login script
   - ○ C. data files
   - ○ D. bindery information

4. If the 4.*x* server has directories with the same name as the 3.*x* server, what occurs?
   - ○ A. The directory is copied and renamed.
   - ○ B. The files in the 3.*x* server are not transferred.
   - ○ C. The files in the directories are combined but no new directory of the same name is created.
   - ○ D. The problem is recorded in the error report and the upgrade is aborted.

5. The ______ files should be deleted before updating because they are not compatible with NetWare 4.
   - ○ A. VAP
   - ○ B. EXE
   - ○ C. BAT
   - ○ D. MAC

6. Which of the following is *not* an option on the Select the source LAN type menu?
   - ○ A. NetWare 2.*x*
   - ○ B. IBM LAN Server 1.2 - 1.3
   - ○ C. Microsoft LAN Manager 1.0
   - ○ D. NetWare 3.x

7. Of the following, which *two* are terms associated with migration?
   - ☐ A. Source
   - ☐ B. Original
   - ☐ C. Restored
   - ☐ D. Destination

8. Run the ______ utility after running MIGRATE.EXE to upgrade printing services.
   - ○ A. UPPRINT
   - ○ B. MIGPRINT
   - ○ C. PRINTUPD
   - ○ D. PRINTUPG

9. Which of the following is *not* a true statement regarding in-place upgrades?

   ○ A. The original 3.*x* file server can still be used.

   ○ B. The original 3.*x* file server is no longer available.

   ○ C. The original 3.*x* file server can be restored from a backup if necessary (and one was created).

   ○ D. Once begun, the upgrade cannot be stopped.

10. Of the following, which one is *not* an option found on the Select information to migrate menu?

    ○ A. All information

    ○ B. Data files

    ○ C. Default account restrictions

    ○ D. Novell-only bindery objects

Answers

1. D
2. B
3. B
4. C
5. A
6. C
7. A, D
8. B
9. A
10. D

CHAPTER 48

Accessing the NDS Tree from a Workstation

With the NetWare 4 server installed and configured, each user's workstation must be prepared so it can provide that user with access to network resources. Preparing a workstation means the appropriate software must be loaded and configured. In addition, some workstation configuration files must be modified and some must be added. The user can then log in to the network.

This chapter discusses the following topics:

- *Installing and configuring the NetWare DOS Requester*
- *Modifying workstation configuration files*
- *Logging in to the NetWare 4 server*

After the workstation has been prepared—the NetWare DOS Requester is installed and the configuration files are modified—the user can begin the login process. This chapter explains how to accomplish all three of these tasks.

Installing and Configuring the NetWare DOS Requester

The NetWare DOS Requester consists of several files whose function is to provide support for workstations running DOS and MS Windows. Its primary file is VLM.EXE, which acts as a manager for the other files (*.VLM files). The VLM files provide services such as connection, file, print, and so on.

To log in to a NetWare 4 network, each workstation must have a LAN board installed and configured, be cabled to the network, and load the NetWare DOS Requester. Before users can load the NetWare DOS Requester on the workstation, it must be installed and configured. Installation and configuration of the NetWare DOS Requester and associated files is usually the responsibility of the network administrator.

Practical TIP Before installing the NetWare DOS Requester, install the network board in the workstation and load the LAN driver. If you complete this step before running the NetWare DOS Requester, the installation program determines the LAN board type and its current configuration without having to prompt you to provide that information.

The NetWare DOS Requester may be installed across the network or from disk.

If you choose to install the NetWare DOS Requester across the network, first log in to the network, then map a drive to SYS:PUBLIC on the NetWare 4 file server. Change to that drive, then use the DOS CD command and change to the CLIENT\DOSWIN subdirectory on that drive.

If you choose to install the NetWare DOS Requester from disk, first create the appropriate disks if you have not yet done so. To create the disks for installing the NetWare DOS Requester, you use the NetWare 4 installation program. To create disks, insert the NetWare 4 installation CD-ROM into the drive, type **INSTALL** and press Enter. From the Select the type of installation desired menu, which opens in the NetWare Install window, choose the Create Diskettes option; then follow the screen prompts, inserting and labeling disks as needed. You need five disks labeled WSDOS_1 through WSDOS_5.

Once you create the disks, insert the NetWare Client for DOS and MS Windows Disk 1 (WSDOS_1) disk into the drive, swapping out disks WSDOS_1 through WSDOS_5 when prompted. Change to the disk drive containing the WSDOS_1 disk.

Whether you are installing the NetWare DOS Requester across the network or from disk, complete the following steps:

1. Type **INSTALL** and press Enter.
2. When the NetWare Client Install screen opens (see fig. 48.1), accept the default of C:\NWCLIENT for the destination directory, or change the default to a directory where you want the client installation software to install the necessary files.

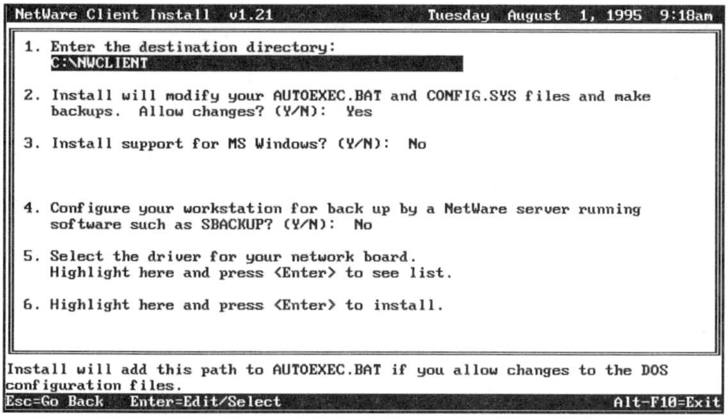

Figure 48.1
The NetWare Client Install v1.21 screen.

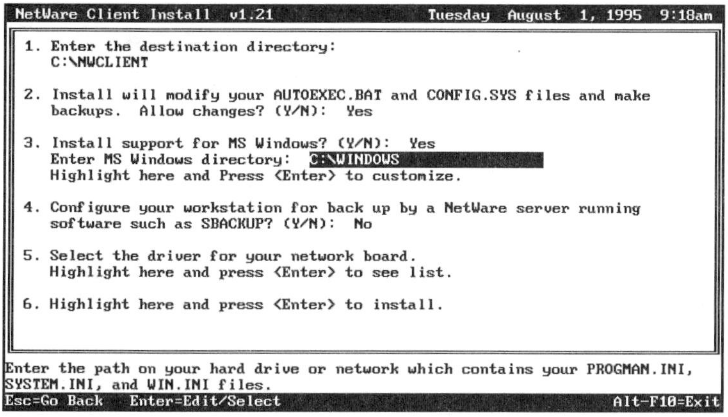

Figure 48.2
Step 3 of the NetWare Client Install v1.21 screen.

3. Choose step 2 on the NetWare Client Install screen and either accept the default of Yes to enable the installation program to make changes to the AUTOEXEC.BAT and CONFIG.SYS files, or choose No.

   If you choose No, the existing files are not changed. Instead, new files are created and saved with a NEW extension (AUTO-EXEC.NEW and CONFIG.NEW).

4. Choose step 3 on the NetWare Client Install screen and either choose to not install support for MS Windows (the default option), or type **Y** to change this option to Yes.

   If you choose Yes, this portion of the NetWare Client Installation screen changes (see fig. 48.2). The default directory of C:\WINDOWS is placed on the Enter MS Windows directory: field, and another field (Highlight here and Press <Enter> to customize.) is made available.

Modify the default MS Windows directory if your MS Windows files are not stored in the default directory. Choose the Highlight here and Press <Enter> to customize field. The screen shown in figure 48.3 opens.

If your workstation needs to be able to use country codes other than its current default codes, change the "Do you plan to use more country codes than the one currently running on your machine? (Y/N):" field to read Yes.

If you want this workstation to be able to access a shared directory, set the "For network administrators only: Do you want to set the shared MS Windows path? (Y/N):" field to Yes, then enter the path for this directory in the "Enter the path to the shared directory:" field (see fig. 48.4).

When you finish modifying the Customize Support for MS Windows screen, press F10 to save your changes.

5. Set the "Configure your workstation for back up by a NetWare server running software such as SBACKUP? (Y/N):" field to Yes if you want to be able to back up the hard disk(s) on this workstation by using the file server's backup

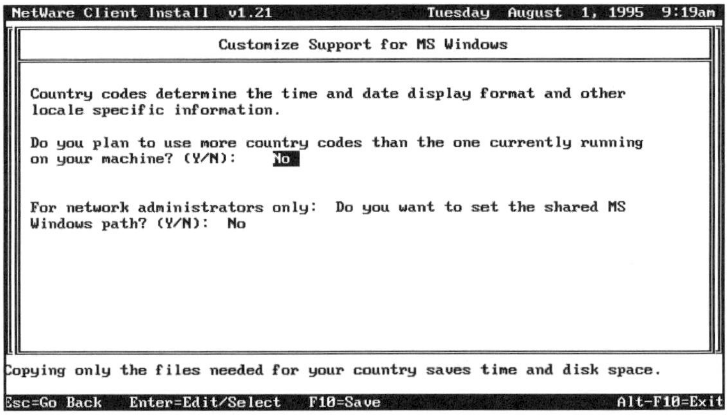

Figure 48.3
The Customize Support for MS Windows screen.

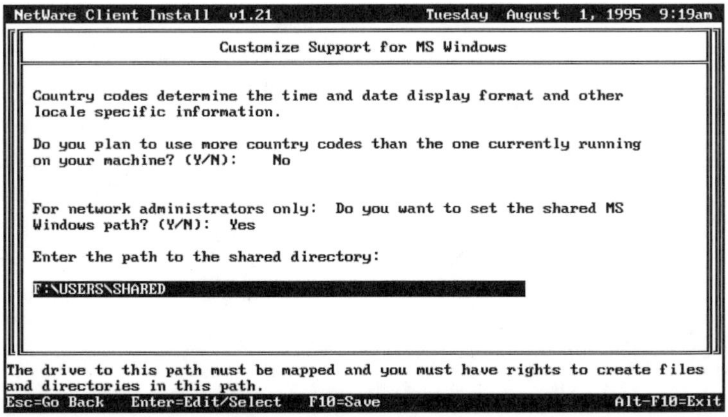

Figure 48.4
The shared directory installation field.

software. Otherwise, leave this field at its default setting of No.

If you choose to have this workstation backed up from the file server, after changing the step 4 field to Yes, the Configure TSA for Storage Management Services (SMS) window opens.

In this window, provide the necessary information in the following fields:

- Enter the SMS server name. Type the name of the file server to be used for backing up this workstation's hard disks.
- Enter a name for your workstation. Type a name that can be used by the backup software and administrator to distinguish this workstation in the list of workstations that can be backed up.
- Enter an optional password. Type a 10-character maximum password to be used when the backup administrator attempts to access the hard disk(s) on this workstation to back up the contents (see fig. 48.5).
- From Backup Drives, select hard drives to be backed up. Press Enter to see the list; then choose which hard drives are to be backed up (see fig. 48.6).

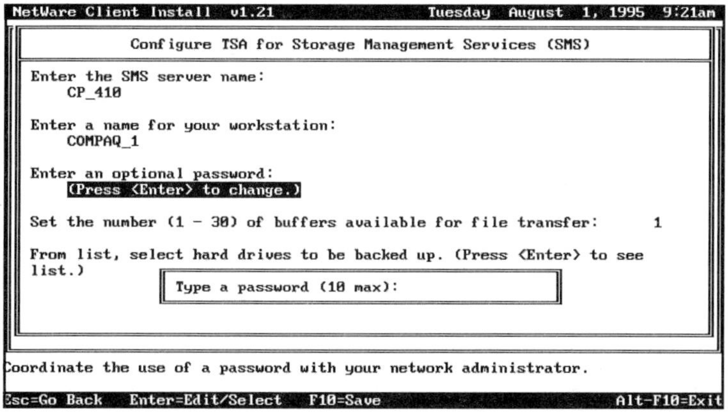

Figure 48.5
The Configure TSA for Storage Management Services (SMS) window.

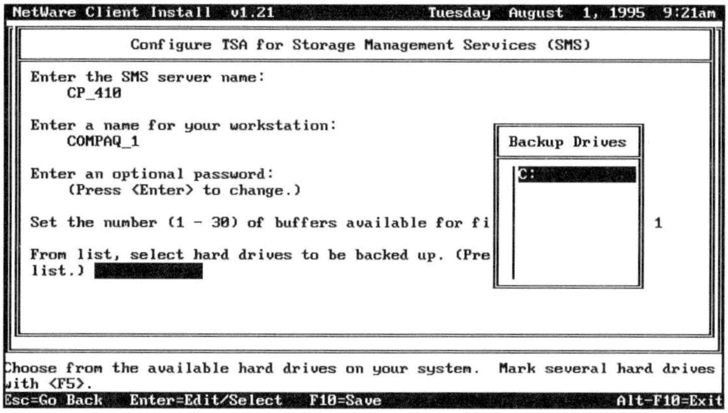

Figure 48.6
The Configure TSA for Storage Management Services (SMS) window with Backup Drives menu.

When you finish configuring the information contained on this screen, press F10 to save the changes.

6. Select (highlight) step 5 on the NetWare Client Install screen (Select the driver for your network board.) and press Enter.

   If you installed the LAN board and associated driver before running the NetWare Client Install on this workstation, the Install program can obtain the information it needs regarding the LAN board type and its configuration without prompting you for additional information (see fig. 48.7). Press Enter to continue.

   If you did not pre-install the LAN board and load the associated driver before starting the client install, you must provide the NetWare Client Install with the information about the type of board installed in this workstation and its associated configuration information (hardware interrupt number, optional node address, and slot). You also have to provide the frame type for Ethernet drivers. Frame type 802.2 is the default for NetWare 4.

7. Select the "Highlight here and press <Enter> to install" field and press Enter (see fig. 48.8). The file copy and configuration process begins.

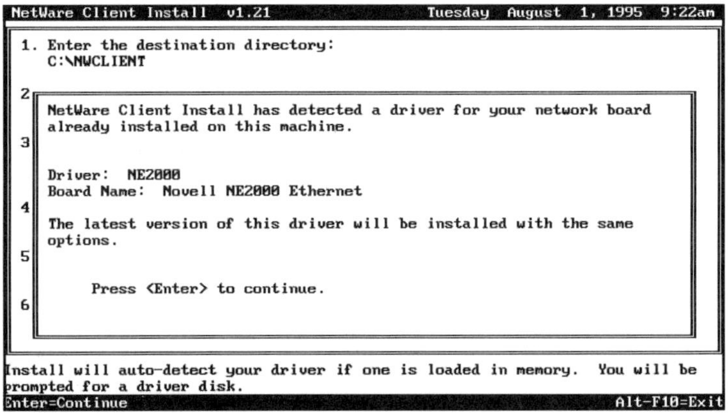

Figure 48.7
The NetWare Client installation driver screen.

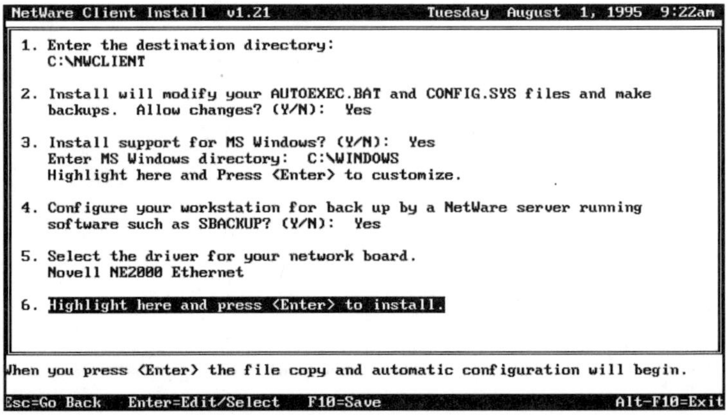

Figure 48.8
Step 6 highlighted to continue installation.

The installation of the NetWare Client proceeds, displaying the name of each file as it is copied and the percent complete for the entire process (see fig. 48.9).

Note: If the workstation contains any NetWare Client files that are a newer version than the one being copied to the workstation, you are notified and asked whether to replace the newer file with the older file. Answer No to the `Use version on installation diskette?` prompt, unless you have a specific reason for using an older file (see fig. 48.10).

8. When The Install Utility is finished screen is displayed, the installation is complete (see fig. 48.11). Press Enter to exit to DOS, or press Ctrl+Alt+Del to reboot the workstation and load the configuration files.

Note: If you choose to update the existing AUTOEXEC.BAT and CONFIG.SYS files, the new files are used when the computer is rebooted. You can then log in to the network from this workstation. (The older versions of these files are saved as BNW files, which can be renamed if you need to restore the old files.)

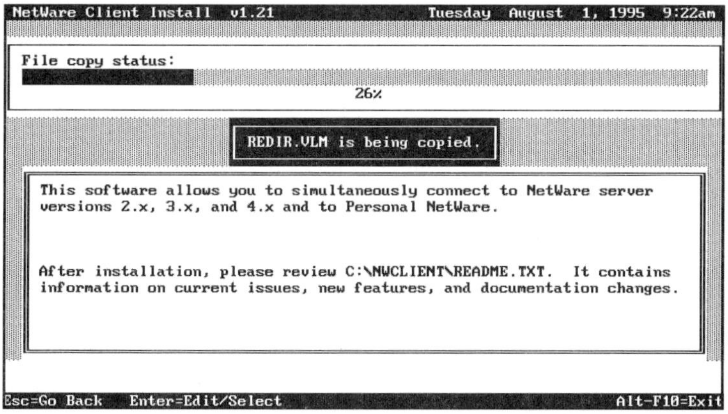

Figure 48.9
A sample NetWare Client file copy screen.

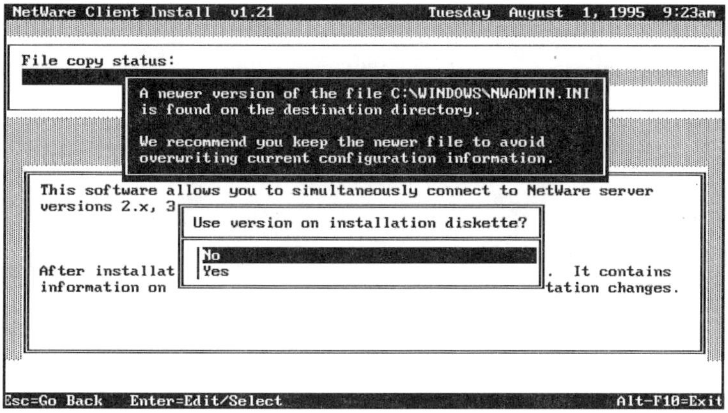

Figure 48.10
The prompt to replace a newer version of the file with the older version.

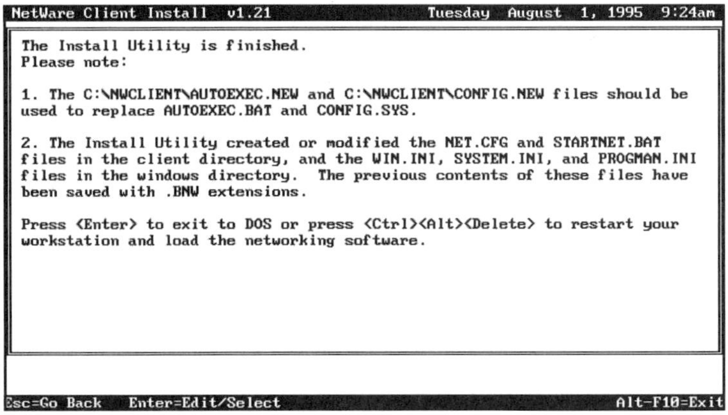

Figure 48.11
The Install Utility is finished screen.

Note If you choose not to update these files, the new versions of these files are created and saved with a NEW extension. You can view and edit these versions with a text editor. You also can rename them if you choose to use them later.

The NetWare Dos Requester installation process places current versions of the files needed for the workstation to connect to the file server onto the PC. You can customize the installation process to accomodate a PC running MS Windows in addition to DOS, or save space on the hard disk by not installing the MS Windows file if the workstation uses only DOS. The installation process also allows you to decide whether to let the modification of configuration file be handled by the installation program. The other option is to manually modify those same configuration files. Either way, the files must contain the required configuration information.

Modifying Workstation Configuration Files

Whether you chose to save the configuration files or to update them, you can view the related files and see what changes have been or would have been made. The following changes are made to the current configuration files or saved to the NEW copies of these files:

- AUTOEXEC.BAT

  This file now calls the STARTNET.BAT file, which loads the NetWare DOS Requester and related files—LSL.COM, LAN driver (such as NE2000.COM), IPXODI.COM, and VLM.EXE (see fig. 48.12).

- CONFIG.SYS

  This file includes the LASTDRIVE=command (see fig. 48.13).

- NET.CFG

  This file contains the LAN driver information under the Link Driver *driver_name* heading (see fig. 48.14). It also includes the PREFERRED TREE= and FIRST NETWORK DRIVE= statements under the NetWare DOS Requester heading. In addition, it includes the NetWare DOS TSA heading with associated entries if you respond Yes to the `Configure your workstation for back up by a NetWare server running software such as SBACKUP? (Y/N)` prompt when you install the DOS and MS Windows client software.

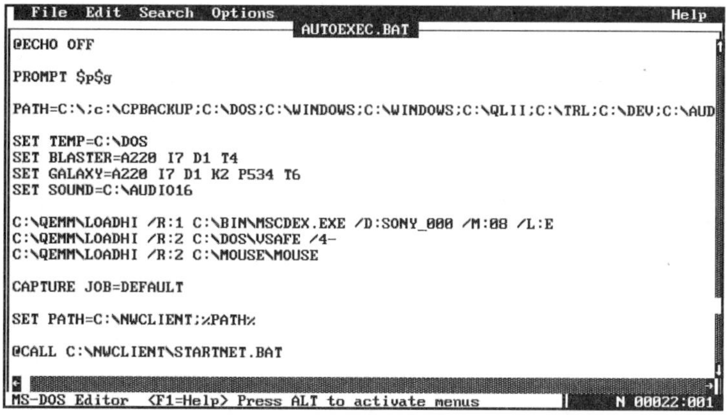

Figure 48.12
A sample revised AUTOEXEC.BAT file.

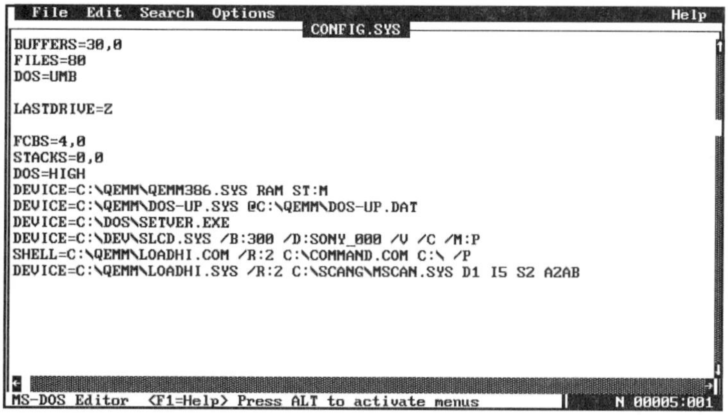

Figure 48.13
A sample revised CONFIG.SYS file.

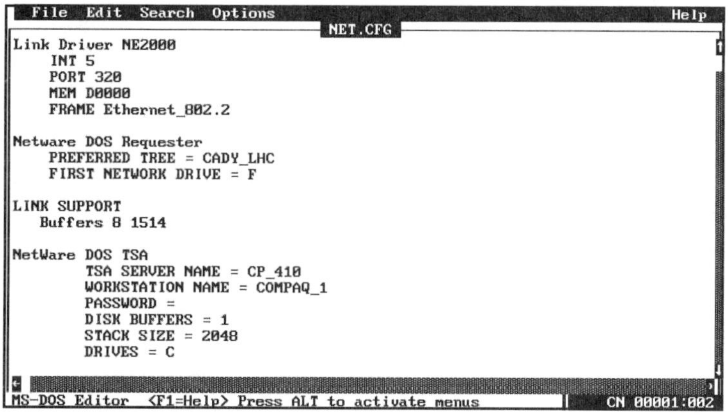

Figure 48.14
A sample revised NET.CFG file.

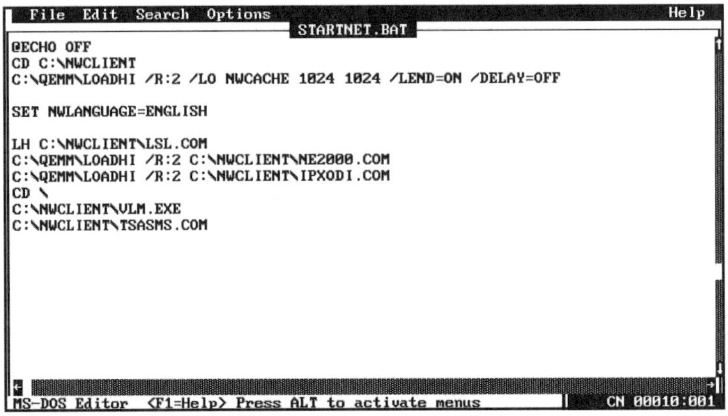

Figure 48.15
A sample revised STARTNET.BAT file.

- STARTNET.BAT

  This file is created to provide an alternative to loading the required files for network connection from the AUTOEXEC.BAT file (see fig. 48.15).

With the needed configuration files modified as necessary, the login process can be performed. It can even be made a little smoother by the addition of one other item to the NET.CFG file, as explained in the following section.

Logging In to the NetWare 4 Server

To ensure a smooth login, the PREFERRED TREE statement should be added to the workstation's NET.CFG file if it does not already exist. Once the workstation has been booted and all the required client files accessed and loaded, the user can log in to the network.

NetWare 4 login requires the user to follow NetWare 4 name context rules when logging in.

> **Note** The only exception occurs when bindery emulation is running on the NetWare 4 file server at the user's context. If bindery emulation is running, users can log in by using their old login procedure (LOGIN *server/user_name*). Their access to services may be limited, however.

Under NetWare 4, type the correct login statement to resemble the following example:

LOGIN *server*.CN=*user_name*.O=*organization*

Replace *server* with the name of the file server the user is to use for logging in. Replace *user_name* with the user's Login ID. Replace *organization* with the organization name. Include any organizational units if the user's login is lower in the NDS Tree structure.

For example, the default Login ID for the network administrator is Admin. If the organization is CADY_LHC, and the file server name is CP_410, the Admin user types the following command to log in:

```
LOGIN CP_410\.CN=ADMIN.O=CADY_LHC
```

If the user's name is located at a lower level in the NDS tree, the complete context needs to be included in the user's NET.CFG file (NAME CONTEXT=) or must be typed at the prompt when logging in. If the NAME CONTEXT is set for the user, users can log in with only the LOGIN command and their user names.

Questions

1. The NetWare Client Installation software can be found in the ______ directory on a NetWare 4 file server.

   ○ A. SYS:PUBLIC\DOSWIN\CLIENT

   ○ B. SYS:PUBLIC\CLIENT\DOSWIN

   ○ C. SYS:SYSTEM\CLIENT

   ○ D. SYS:SYSTEM\DOSWIN\CLIENT

2. An AUTOEXEC file with a NEW extension indicates that ______.

   ○ A. the installation was done without updating the existing AUTOEXEC.BAT file

   ○ B. the INSTALL program is not yet finished

   ○ C. the installation was done and the existing AUTOEXEC.BAT file was renamed to AUTOEXEC.NEW

   ○ D. the installation program requires the AUTOEXEC.NEW file be renamed to AUTOEXEC.BAT before the user can log in

3. If you choose to provide support for MS Windows during the client installation process, you ______.

   ○ A. can change the MS Windows default directory

   ○ B. cannot change the MS Windows default directory

   ○ C. can install MS Windows at the same time you install the client software

   ○ D. cannot also modify the AUTOEXEC.BAT and NET.CFG files

4. The installation field that enables you to choose to configure the workstation for backup is numbered as step ______.

   ○ A. 2

   ○ B. 3

   ○ C. 4

   ○ D. 5

5. To start the installation process, press Enter on the field numbered as step ______.

   ○ A. 3

   ○ B. 4

   ○ C. 5

   ○ D. 6

6. Which of the following statements is *not* true?

   ○ A. If your LAN driver is loaded, the INSTALL utility can read the configuration.

   ○ B. You configure the LAN driver after specifying whether to configure your workstation for backup.

   ○ C. The information in the destination directory field is added to the AUTOEXEC.BAT file even when you do not allow changes to this file.

   ○ D. Choosing to back up the workstation requires you to provide the name of the file server.

7. Of the following, which *three* are files that may be modified during the client installation?

   ☐ A. AUTOEXEC.BAT

   ☐ B. CONFIG.SYS

   ☐ C. STARTNET.BAT

   ☐ D. NET.CFG

8. When the INSTALL utility is finished, you can press ______ to exit to DOS.

   ○ A. Esc

   ○ B. Enter

   ○ C. Ctrl+Alt+Del

   ○ D. Tab

9. Which file calls the STARTNET.BAT file if changes are allowed to the workstation's configuration file?

   ○ A. AUTOEXEC.BAT

   ○ B. CONFIG.SYS

   ○ C. NET.CFG

   ○ D. INSTALL.BAT

10. If you want to update the existing AUTOEXEC.BAT and CONFIG.SYS files, the older versions are ______.

    ○ A. renamed with a BNW extension

    ○ B. copied over

    ○ C. modified and stored under their original names

    ○ D. not changed, because updating the existing files is only an option if you do not use MS Windows on your workstation

Answers

1. B
2. A
3. A
4. C
5. D
6. C
7. A, B, D
8. B
9. A
10. A

CHAPTER 49

Managing NDS Objects

All resources in the NetWare 4 environment are referred to as NDS objects. Objects have properties associated with them. A property is some aspect of an object that helps to define that object. All properties have values associated with them. The value of a property is its actual identifying factor.

For example, all User objects have a Name property. The value of the Name property is whatever has been assigned to that property. In the case of the network administrator User object, the value of the Name property is Admin.

The network administrator and other authorized users create NDS objects. NDS objects can be created at different levels in the NDS tree. Levels in the NDS tree structure are defined by the type of object.

For example, an Organization object defines a level in the NDS tree structure because it can have the [Root] level of the tree above it, the Country level of the tree above it, and Organizational Unit objects—which define a level of the NDS tree themselves—below it. The location of an object (its level) within the NDS tree structure is known as its *context.*

This chapter discusses context as it relates to workstations, conventions used when naming NDS objects, how to create various NDS objects including but not limited to Organization and Organizational Unit objects, and how to use the Search option of the Object menu in the NetWare Administrator utility. The following topics are covered:

- Understanding context
- Naming NDS objects
- Creating NDS objects
- Searching the NDS tree

Understanding Context

When you access the NDS tree, you are accessing a specific container within that tree. The container you are currently accessing is referred to as your *current context.* When you change from one container to another, you are changing your current context. Your current context affects how you access objects in the NDS tree. If you want to access an object that is in the same container as your current context, you can access that object by referring to the object's name.

For example, if your current context is set to the Payroll Organizational Unit container in the CSC organization (see fig. 49.1), and you want to access a printer called HP1 in the Payroll Organizational Unit container, you refer to the Payroll printer object by its Common Name (CN) of HP1 (CN=HP1).

If, on the other hand, your current context is set to the Accounting Organizational Unit container in the CSC Organization (.OU=Accounting. O=CSC), and you want to access the HP1 Printer

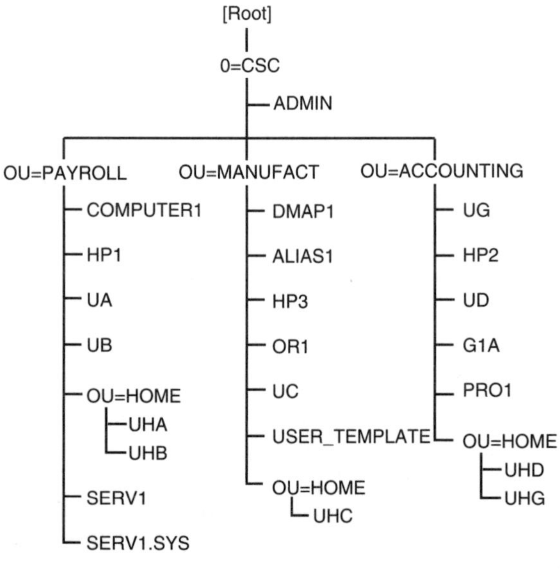

Figure 49.1
A sample NDS tree structure for the CSC organization.

object in the Payroll Organizational Unit container of the CSC organization (.OU=Payroll.O=CSC), you refer to the Printer object by its complete name in order to access it. In this example, this Printer object's complete name is the following:

```
.CN=HP1.OU=Payroll.O=CSC
```

The same philosophy of context holds true whether you are accessing a Printer or other NDS object, or logging in to the NDS tree (accessing your User object).

For example, if your User object name is UA (refer to fig. 49.1), the context in which your User object is located is .OU=Payroll.O=CSC. To access your User object and log in to the NDS tree, therefore, you must either set your current context to be .OU=Payroll.O=CSC, or specify your complete User object name when you log in. In this example, your complete User object name is the following:

```
CN=UA.OU=Payroll.O=CSC
```

To set current context for a user, place the Name Context= statement in the NET.CFG file on the user's workstation. Using figure 49.1 as an example again, to set User object UA's name context, place the following line to the NetWare DOS Requester section in the NET.CFG file of this user's workstation:

```
NAME CONTEXT="OU=PAYROLL.O=CSC"
```

If users need to log in to the network from a workstation other than their own, or if their current context is set to other than that of the context for the User object, users then have to specify their User object's complete context when they type the LOGIN command.

Again using figure 49.1 as an example, user UA has to type the following line at the DOS prompt in order to log in to the NDS tree—if user UA's name context is not set in the NET.CFG file or the current context is different from the context in which the user object resides:

```
LOGIN .CN=UA.OU=PAYROLL.O=CSC
```

How can you tell what your current context setting is? NetWare provides a utility called the CX utility that enables you to view your current context and the NDS tree structure before you log in to the NDS tree. By using CX, you can determine where your current context is set. You can also view the structure of the NDS tree, and change your current context by using the CX utility.

To see your current context, type **CX** and press Enter.

To view the NDS tree, including all its Organization, Organizational Unit, and leaf objects, type **CX /r /a /t** and press Enter. Depending on your current context, a display similar to the one shown in figure 49.2 is provided.

Practical TIP

The /R option changes your context to [Root]. The /A option specifies that All objects within the specified context are to be displayed. The /T option tells CX to display all containers. You can also use one or more trailing periods (CX .) with the CX command to move up the NDS tree structure one or more containers at a time, depending on the number of trailing periods used. In addition, you can change your current context to [Root] by specifying [Root], as in CX [Root].

To change your current context by using the CX utility, type **CX *new_context***, replacing *new_context* with the exact context to which you want to change. For example, to change from the Payroll Organizational Unit (shown in figure 49.1) to the Accounting Organizational Unit, type the following line and press Enter:

```
CX .OU=ACCOUNTING.O=CSC
```

Figure 49.2
A sample display of the NDS tree structure using CX.

```
*** Directory Services Mapping ***

[Root]
 ├CADY_LHC
 │  ├CP_410
 │  ├Admin
 │  ├CP_410_SYS
 │  ├Q1
 │  ├PS1
 │  ├P1
 │  ├RAY
 │  ├SHANA
 │  ├NB
 │  ├Home
 │  │  └RMC
 │  ├User_Template
 │  ├WORD
 │  ├BackDoor
 │  ├TGroup
 │  ├AppleT1
 │  ├Parent_PS2
 │  ├Contura
 │  ├OR_Admin
 │  └SMS_Backup
>>> Enter = More    C = Continuous    Esc = Cancel
```

Naming NDS Objects

All NDS objects have a name. The name associated with leaf objects is referred to as its Common Name (CN). The name associated with an Organization (O) object or an Organizational Unit (OU) object is identified by the abbreviation for its container type—O or OU, respectively. The same is also true for a Country (C) object. It is identified by the abbreviation for its container type—C.

When you create an object in the NDS tree, you must give it a name. Object names should be descriptive but as short as possible, particularly if they are Organization or Organizational Unit object names. Limiting the length of an object's name also reduces the number of characters that must be typed to specify that object, change context, set a name context in the NET.CFG file, and so on.

You should pay particular attention to the object's name in relationship to the number of levels in your NDS tree. For example, an NDS tree with only five levels can afford to have longer object names. Because only 256 characters are recognizable when a context is set or a change context command is entered at the DOS prompt, NDS trees with a larger quantity of levels necessitate object names that are short.

Other object-naming conventions include the following:

- The Country object name must be exactly two characters in length and use the internationally recognized two-digit abbreviation for the country.
- If network clients will be running software installed before NetWare 4 was installed, do not use special characters, such as the period (.), in the object's name.
- The object's name may not be longer than 64 characters.

Creating NDS Objects

There are three types of NDS objects—[Root], container, and leaf. Container objects are Country (C), Organization (O), and Organizational Unit (OU). There are 17 leaf objects, several of which are commonly created and managed by network administrators.

The DOS-based NETADMIN utility and the MS Windows-based NetWare Administrator utility are used to create NDS objects.

To create NDS objects by using the NETADMIN utility, log in to the network as a user with the appropriate rights for creating NDS objects. Next, start the utility by typing **NETADMIN** at the DOS prompt and pressing Enter. Then, complete the following steps:

1. Choose Manage objects from the NetAdmin options menu (see fig. 49.3).
2. Select (highlight) the container into which you want the object to be placed when it is created.
3. Press Ins.
4. Choose an object type from the Select an object class list (see fig. 49.4).
5. Provide additional information as prompted, and press F10 to save the information.

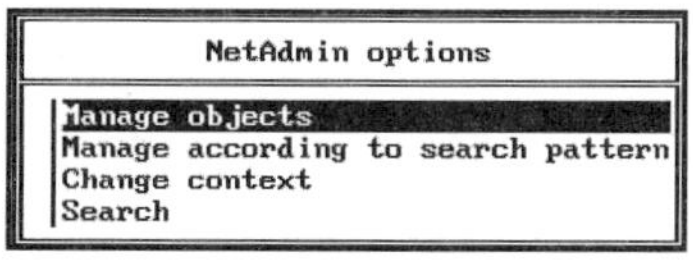

Figure 49.3
The NetAdmin options menu.

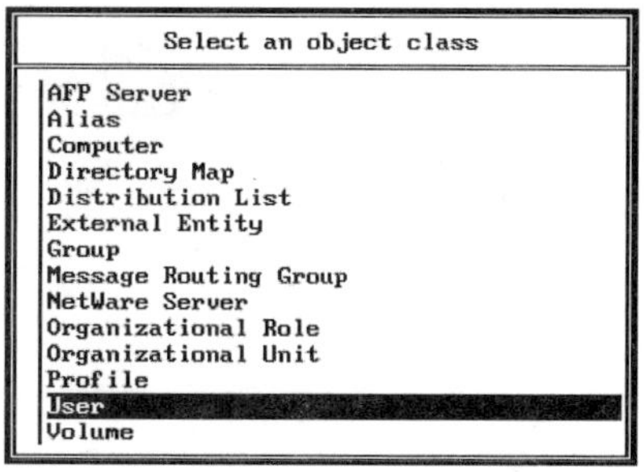

Figure 49.4
The Select an object class list.

To create NDS objects by using the NetWare Administrator utility, log in to the network as a user with the appropriate rights to create NDS objects, start Windows, and choose the NetWare Administrator icon. Then, complete the following steps:

1. Open the Browser and expand the directory tree so that you can see the container into which you want to place the object when it is created.
2. Select (highlight) the container to hold the new object.
3. Choose Create from the Objects pull-down menu (see fig. 49.5).
4. Choose the type of object to be created from the New Object list (see fig. 49.6).
5. Provide at least the minimum information required to create the object (determined by the type of object), and press Create to create the new object.

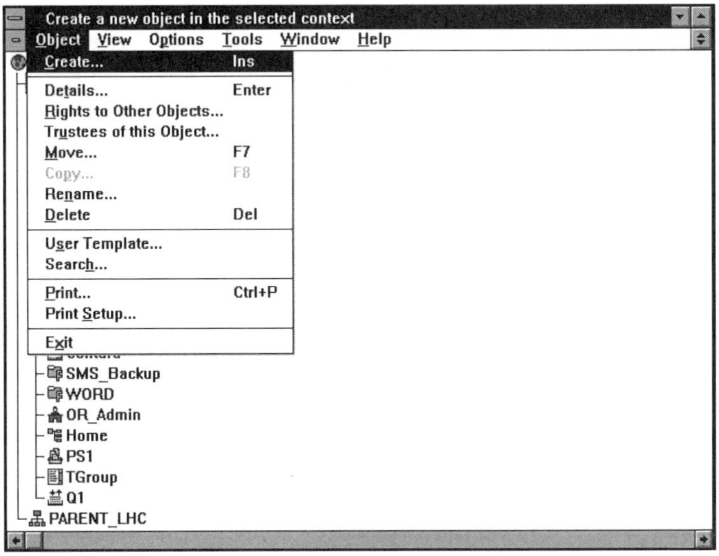

Figure 49.5
The NetWare Administrator browser window with Object menu.

Creating User Objects

To create a User object, follow the steps previously outlined for creating objects with the NetWare Administrator utility. Provide a Login Name and Last Name for this user. You can also mark the Use User Template, Define Additional Properties, and Create Home Directory boxes so that you can perform other tasks closely associated with creating a new User object (see fig. 49.7). Then, choose Create.

Figure 49.6
The New Object list.

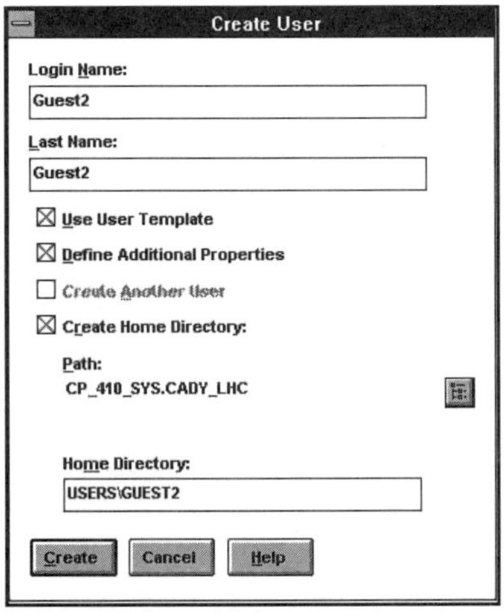

Figure 49.7
The Create User dialog box for a User object.

When the Identification page for this User object opens, you can provide additional information, such as the user's Given Name, Telephone Number, and so on (see fig. 49.8).

In addition, there are other pages that you can choose to perform additional tasks. For example, if you choose the Group Membership page and then choose the Add button, you can add this user as a member of one or more groups (see fig. 49.9).

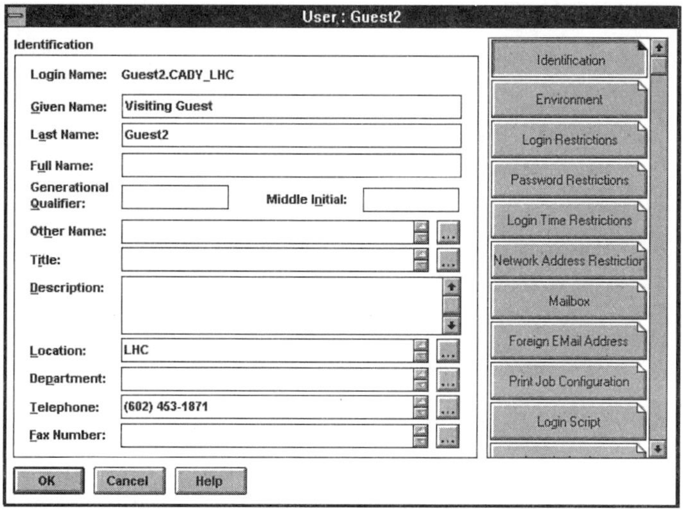

Figure 49.8
The User object Guest2's Identification page.

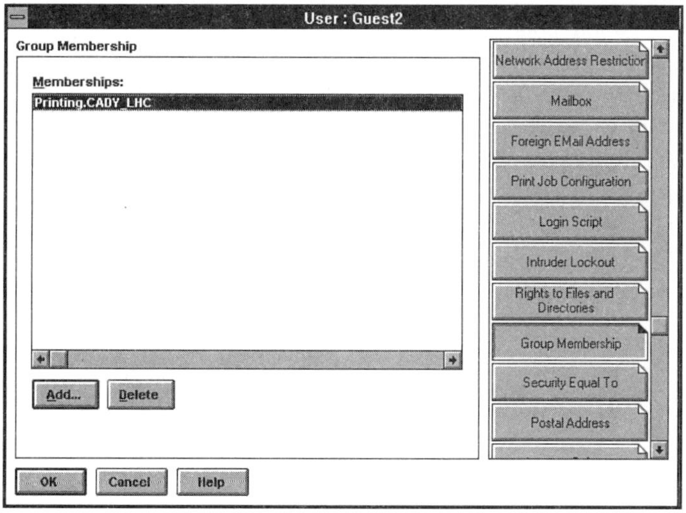

Figure 49.9
The Group Membership page.

Creating Group Objects

You can create Group objects and then add users to the list of members. To create a group object, follow the general steps previously outlined for creating objects by using the NetWare Administrator; then choose Group from the New Object list.

Next, provide a name for the group (Group Name), mark the Provide Additional Properties box, and choose Create (see fig. 49.10).

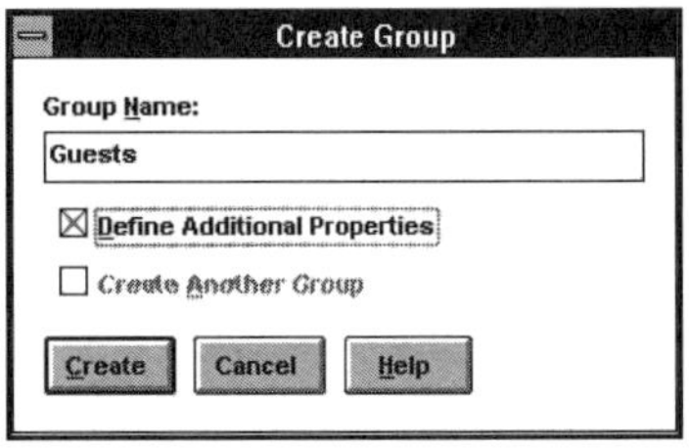

Figure 49.10
The Create Group dialog box.

You can now provide additional information about the group—such as Other Name, Description, Department, and so on—on the Identification page. In addition, you can choose the Members page and add members to this group, assign rights to files and directories for this group (choose the Rights to Files and Directories button), and so on.

Creating User Templates

When you create a User object, you have the option of using a template that you previously defined. A template, like all other resources in NDS, is an object. It is created the same way as any other object by following the previously noted basic instructions for creating an object with the NetWare Administrator. You choose User from the Create Objects list and provide information as requested. Specifically, the login name for this User object must be User_Template. You can then mark appropriate boxes to specify additional information just as you can when you create a regular network user object. You can even specify where a home directory should be created for this User object.

Once a User_Template is created in a container, if you choose to apply the template when you create other users in the same container, the information setup for the User_Template User object is applied to new User objects when they are created.

You can then define Login Restrictions, Group Memberships, and any other items you wish to associate with each new User object by choosing the associated page for the User_Template User object and filling in the necessary information.

To limit concurrent connections to two (2) for each new User object created, for example, set the Login Restrictions page for the User_Template to reflect a limit of 2 connections (see fig. 49.11).

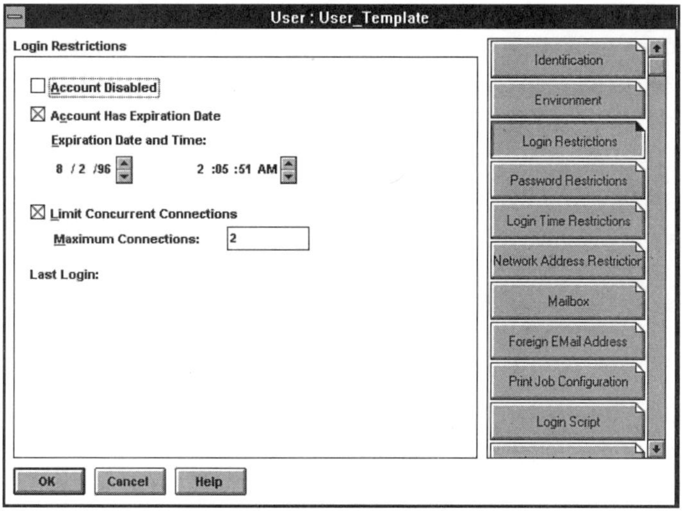

Figure 49.11
The User_Template Login Restrictions page.

Creating Alias, Organizational Unit, Profile, Computer, and Other Objects

To create other types of objects—such as Alias, Organizational Unit, Profile, Computer, and so on—follow the same basic instructions previously provided for running the NetWare Administrator. All objects are created following these basic steps. The primary difference is the type of information you provide.

When creating an Alias object, for example, you provide a name for the object and specify the object to which the Alias is being created (see fig. 49.12).

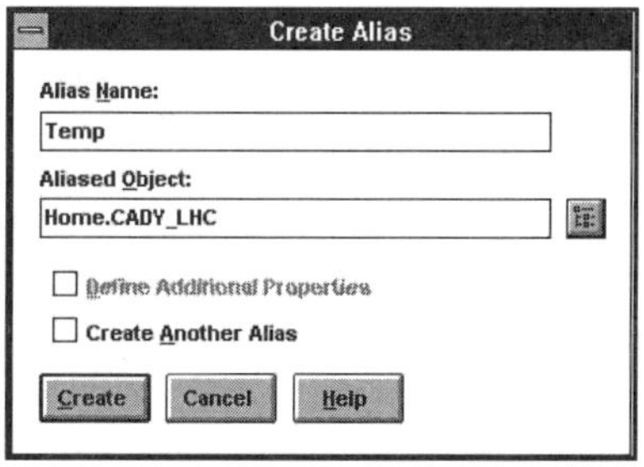

Figure 49.12
The Create Alias object window.

Organizational Units require only that you provide a name for the Organizational Unit. You can, however, provide additional information by marking the Define Additional Properties box. You can also mark the Define User Defaults box and have the User_Template applied automatically to any User objects created in this container (see fig. 49.13).

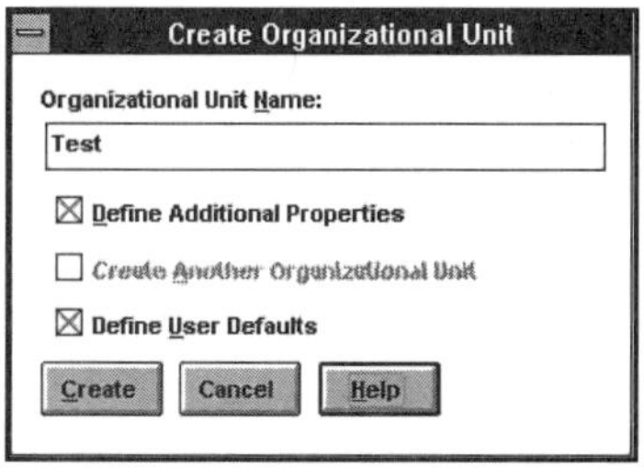

Figure 49.13
The Create Organizational Unit window.

The Profile object is an NDS object that contains a login script that can be applied to any set of users who need to share common login script commands, but whose User object does not reside in the same container.

The Computer object is an NDS object used to store inventory-type information about computers on the network other than file servers, such as routers and workstations.

The Printer object represents a physical printer attached to the network.

The Print Queue object represents a directory on the network to which print jobs can be sent and stored until they can be serviced.

The Print Server object represents a NetWare file server with the print server software installed.

All these objects, and others, are created the same way that the User, Group, Organization, Organizational Unit, and other objects are created. Regardless of what object you are creating, you first select the container into which that object is to be placed. Sometimes, once the object is created, it needs to be moved from one container to another.

Moving Objects

To move an object from one container to another by using the NetWare Administrator, complete the following steps:

1. If necessary, expand the NDS tree so that the container from which the object is being moved (as well as the container *into* which the object is being moved) can be seen.
2. Select (highlight) the object.
3. Choose Move from the Object pull-down menu.
4. Browse the tree to locate the container where the object is to be moved. That container's context will then display in the Destination field (see fig. 49.14).
5. Choose OK.

You can view the object in its new location by collapsing the NDS tree structure and then expanding it.

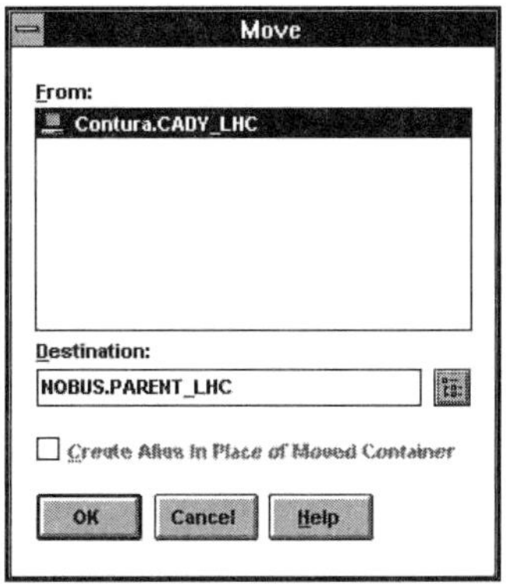

Figure 49.14
The object Move dialog box.

Searching the NDS Tree

If you cannot locate an object in the NDS tree, you can use the Search feature to help you find the object. To use the Search feature, choose Search from the Object pull-down menu. Specify what Object class to search for, where the search should begin, and what it should include (see fig. 49.15). Then choose OK to start the search.

Once the search is complete, a list of objects found is displayed (see fig. 49.16).

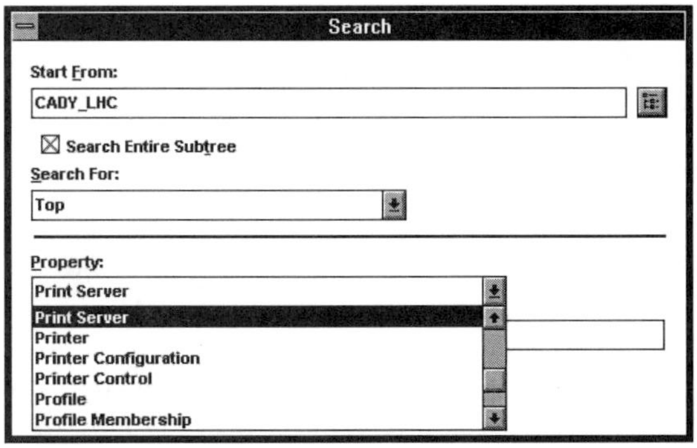

Figure 49.15
The Search dialog box.

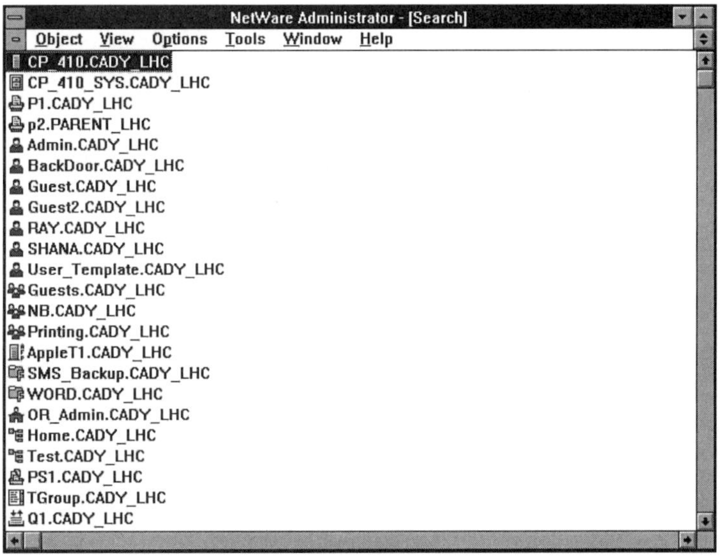

Figure 49.16
The results of Search.

Questions

1. Current context can be defined as ______.
   - ○ A. the container you are currently accessing
   - ○ B. the OU in which your User object resides
   - ○ C. the O in which your User object resides
   - ○ D. the container in which your closest printer resides

2. Use the ______ option with CX to start the NDS tree display at the [Root].
   - ○ A. /A
   - ○ B. ...
   - ○ C. /T
   - ○ D. /R

3. If you need to see every container in the entire tree, use the ______.options with the CX command.
   - ○ A. /R /T
   - ○ B. /A /R
   - ○ C. /T /A /R
   - ○ D. /T /R

4. To create objects by using the NETADMIN utility, choose ______ from the NetAdmin options menu.
   - ○ A. Manage objects
   - ○ B. Manage according to search pattern
   - ○ C. Change context
   - ○ D. Search

5. The maximum number of characters allowed for an object name is ______.
   - ○ A. 21
   - ○ B. 32
   - ○ C. 64
   - ○ D. 256

6. To place users in a group, choose the ______ page from the User's Details.
   - ○ A. Identification
   - ○ B. Login Restrictions
   - ○ C. Group memberships
   - ○ D. Manage objects

7. Of the following, which *three* are items of information you can provide for a User object?
   - ☐ A. Given Name
   - ☐ B. Telephone Number
   - ☐ C. Country of Birth
   - ☐ D. Generation Qualifier

8. To find an object in the NDS tree, use the ______ option in the Object pull-down menu.
   - ○ A. Find
   - ○ B. Create
   - ○ C. Search
   - ○ D. Locate

9. To establish a reference to another object, create a ______ object.
   - ○ A. Profile
   - ○ B. User

- C. Group
- D. Alias

10. Which of the following statements is *not* true?
    - A. You can specify that the User_Template be applied to all new users created in a container at the time you create the container.
    - B. Both the NETADMIN and NetWare Administrator utilities enable you to search for NDS objects.
    - C. You cannot move an object once it has been created.
    - D. You can create Group objects and then add users to the list of members, or add the User to a Group list from within the User's Details dialog.

Answers

1. A
2. D
3. C
4. A
5. C
6. C
7. A, B, D
8. C
9. D
10. C

CHAPTER 50

Implementing NDS Security Controls

Security in NetWare 4 environments can be categorized into two groups—file system and NDS security. File system security in NetWare 4 has changed only slightly from that of NetWare 3. NDS security, however, is new to NetWare 4 and is the subject of this chapter. The following topics explain how to implement various NDS security controls in a NetWare 4 network:

- *Understanding NDS security*
- *Creating workgroup managers*
- *Granting the Supervisor right to the File Server object*

Understanding NDS Security

Several key terms apply to NDS rights. Understanding these key terms and the effect they have on NDS security is key to understanding NDS security:

- Trustees
- Access Control List
- Object and Property Rights
- Inheritance and the Inherited Rights Filter (IRF)
- Effective Rights

Trustees

Every object in the NDS database, and every directory and file in a NetWare 4 file server's file system can have one or more trustees associated with it. A *trustee* is an NDS object (usually a User or Group object, but may also be a container or other NDS object) that has been given access and certain rights to another object.

You make an NDS object a trustee of another NDS object by adding the object to the Access Control List (ACL) property of another object.

Access Control List

The ACL of an object is a property of that object. The ACL keeps information about who or what is allowed to access that object. It contains not only a list of trustees, but also information on what rights (object and property) the object has to it, as well as its Inherited Rights Filter (IRF).

Object and Property Rights

In addition to the file system rights of earlier versions of NetWare, NetWare 4 has two types of NDS rights—object and property.

Object rights control who or what has access to an object, and the type of access. There are five types of object rights:

- *Supervisor* gives unrestricted access to the object and to all its properties. An object with the Supervisor object right to another object can view, delete, or rename that object, or create other objects below it in the NDS tree if that object is a container object.
- *Browse* makes it possible for the user to see the object in the NDS tree structure.
- *Create* enables the user to create other objects within the container object to which this object right applies. Because objects cannot be created below a leaf object in the NDS tree structure, this object right is valid only for container objects.
- *Delete* gives the user the right to delete this object from the NDS tree.
- *Rename* makes it possible for the user to change the name of the object for which this right has been granted.

Property rights control what another object can do to the properties of the object to which it has rights. Property rights can be assigned to all properties of an object or to individual properties of the object. There are five types of property rights:

- *Supervisor* gives unrestricted access to all properties of the object. An object with the Supervisor property right can modify the value assigned to any of the object's properties.

- *Compare* enables the value of a property of an object to be compared with any other value, returning either a True or False response.
- *Read* enables the user to read the values of the object's properties. Giving the Read property right to a user also gives that user the Compare property right because the Compare property right is a subset of the Read property right.
- *Write* makes it possible for the object granted this right to add, change, or delete values given to the properties for which this right is assigned.
- *Add* or *Delete Self* enables the trustee to add itself to or remove itself from a property that contains a list of names, such as a group membership or mailing list.

Practical TIP Both the Supervisor object right and the Supervisor property right can be prevented from flowing down the NDS tree structure by screening it out by using the Inherited Rights Filter.

Inheritance and the Inherited Rights Filter (IRF)

As with file system rights, NDS rights flow down through the hierarchy. Rights granted to an object at one container flow down to objects within that container, as well as to other containers within that container, and so on down through the NDS tree until those rights are changed.

NDS rights can be changed by assigning different rights or by stopping the flow of rights down the NDS tree structure. To stop the flow of rights, NDS provides an *Inherited Rights Filter* (called the Inherited Rights Mask in NetWare 3) or *IRF* for each object in the NDS tree.

The IRF, by default, allows all rights to flow down the NDS tree structure to the object. To prevent rights from flowing to the object, block (remove) the right from the IRF.

To modify the IRF, use the NetWare Administrator utility. With the Browse window open, select the object whose IRF you want to modify, then complete the following steps:

1. Choose the Trustees of this object from the Object pull-down menu.
2. Choose the Inherited Rights Filter button on the Trustees of object_name dialog box (see fig. 50.1).
3. Modify property rights or object rights by marking or unmarking the boxes associated with each right (see fig. 50.1).

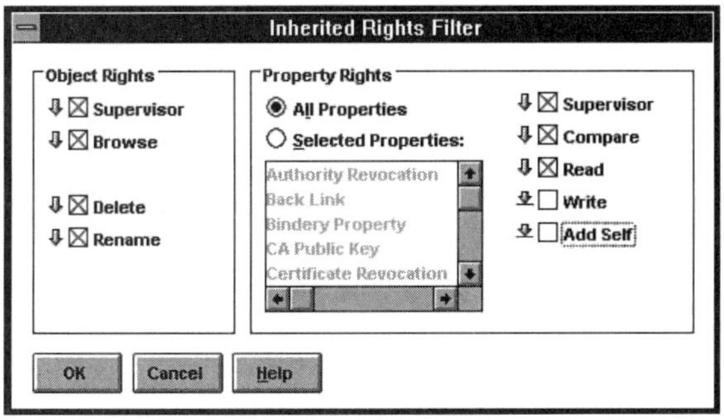

Figure 50.1
The Inherited Rights Filter dialog box.

Effective Rights

An object's effective rights are those rights that the object actually has to another object. Effective rights are determined by using one or the other of the following formulas:

+ All rights granted at or above this object (include rights granted as the result of being a member of a group, an object in a container that is a trustee of the object or which is in a container above the container of the object, and any other way an object can receive rights)

- Any rights removed by using the IRF

Effective rights

Note: Rights granted at this level may equal effective rights.Rights may be granted either directly to the object at this level, or to another object at this level for which this object has been made a trustee. If rights have been granted both ways, the two or more sets of rights are added together to get the effective rights.

When determining effective rights, consider the rights that are granted to two additional NDS objects—[Root] and [Public].

When a NetWare 4 file server is added to the NDS tree, the [Root] object receives the Read property right to the File Server object, thus giving the Read property right to all objects in the NDS tree. This gives all users the capability of seeing directories and files in the file server's file system.

The [Public] object is given the Browse object right at the root of the NDS tree when it is created, thus giving the Browse object right to all other objects in the NDS tree. This gives all users the capability of seeing the NDS tree structure even before logging in to the network.

Creating Workgroup Managers

A workgroup manager is effectively an administrator of a section of the NDS tree. To create a workgroup manager, first make the object (usually a User object) a trustee of the container at the top section of the NDS tree for which you want this object to be a workgroup manager. Once the User object is a trustee of the container, give the User object the appropriate rights.

Making a User Object a Trustee of Another Object

To make a User object a trustee, complete the following steps:

1. Open the NetWare Administrator utility in MS Windows.
2. Open the Browse window if not already open (choose Browse from the Tools pull-down menu).
3. Expand the tree so that you can view the appropriate container object (double-click on the highest container displayed).

4. Select (highlight) the container object to which you want to assign the User object as a trustee.
5. Choose Trustees of this object from the Object pull-down menu.
6. Choose the Add Trustee button on the Trustees of object_name dialog box (see fig. 50.2).
7. Change (double-click on) the context in the Directory Context: field until the object you want to give a trustee assignment to is listed in the Objects area of the Select Object dialog box (see fig. 50.3).

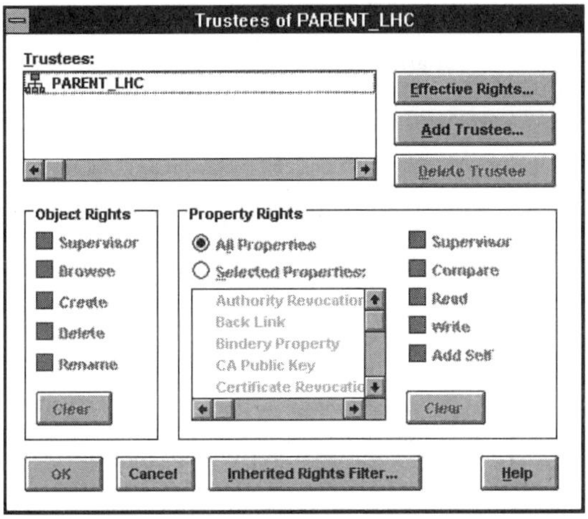

Figure 50.2
The Trustees of object_name dialog box.

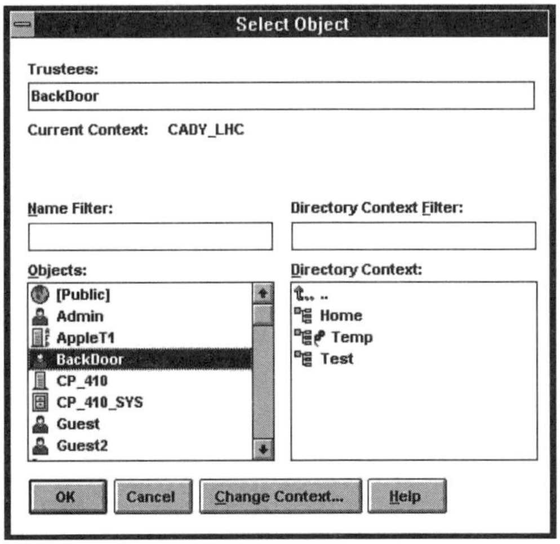

Figure 50.3
The Select Object dialog box.

8. Choose OK. The trustee now appears in the Trustees list for this object.

The next step in the process of creating workgroup managers is to give the trustee the rights required to effectively manage other User objects.

Granting Rights to a Trustee

To give the trustee the rights to this container required to administer objects within and below this container effectively, complete the following steps:

1. With the name of the trustee highlighted in the Trustees of object_name dialog box for this container (completing the previous steps 1 through 8 puts you at this dialog box), mark all five rights displayed under the Object Rights area.
2. Choose All Properties in the Property Rights area of the Trustees of object_name dialog box for this container.
3. Mark all five rights displayed under the Property Rights area of the Trustees of object_name dialog box for this container (see fig. 50.4).
4. Choose OK.

You have now effectively created an administrator or workgroup manager for that section of the NDS tree. You can view the workgroup manager's effective rights to any object in this container, including any containers below this one.

Viewing Effective Rights

To view a workgroup manager's effective rights, complete the following steps:

1. Change your context to the container in the tree where you want to view the workgroup manager's effective rights.
2. With the container selected in the Browse window, open the Trustees of object_name dialog box for the container. (Choose Trustees of object from the Object pull-down menu.)

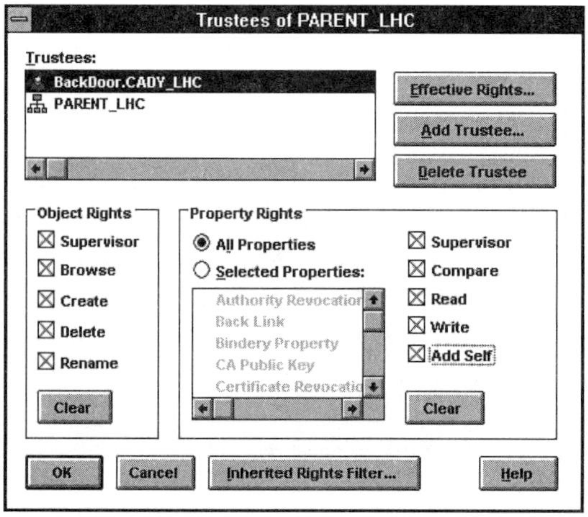

Figure 50.4
The Trustees of PARENT_LHC dialog box.

3. Choose the Effective Rights button from the Trustees of object_name dialog box.
4. When the Effective Rights dialog box opens, choose the Browse button (located at the end of the Object Name field).
5. Change the context to that of the workgroup manager trustee so that the workgroup manager's User object is displayed in the Objects area of the Select Object dialog box.
6. Choose the workgroup manager's User object, then choose the OK button.
7. View the effective rights to this object for this workgroup manager. (Effective rights are darkened and rights that the object does not have appear gray.)

Figure 50.5 displays the effective rights for the workgroup manager User object Backdoor in the K_Resources.PARENT_LHC container.

Granting the Supervisor Right to the File Server Object

For every NetWare 4 file server in the NDS tree, a File Server object exists. The File Server object is created when the NetWare 4 file server is installed into the NDS tree. By default, the user who installs the file server (usually the Admin user) is given the Supervisor property and object rights to the File Server object. The Supervisor right then flows down into the file server directory structure giving the user Supervisor rights to all directories and files on the file server.

You can give other users the Supervisor right to the server object as well. If you do, those users also have the Supervisor right in the file server's file system.

Note Use caution when granting this right to the ACL of an object, as it may result in giving full access to the file system.

To prevent the Supervisor right from flowing into the file system, you can block the Supervisor right by removing it from the File Server object's IRF.

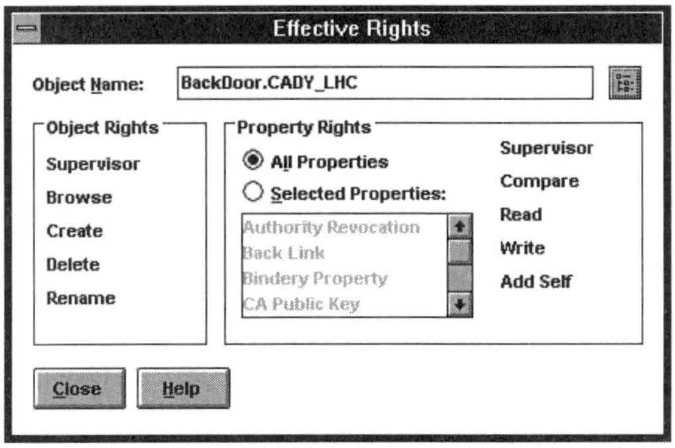

Figure 50.5
The Effective Rights dialog box.

Questions

1. A ______ is an NDS object that has been given access and certain rights to another object.
   - ○ A. ACL
   - ○ B. Trustee
   - ○ C. User
   - ○ D. Container

2. The security term that describes what holds information about who or what is allowed to access an object is that object's ______.
   - ○ A. ACL
   - ○ B. Trustee
   - ○ C. User
   - ○ D. Container

3. The ______ right is *not* an NDS object right.
   - ○ A. Supervisor
   - ○ B. Browse
   - ○ C. Compare
   - ○ D. Rename

4. The NDS object right that makes it possible for users to see objects in the NDS tree structure is ______.
   - ○ A. Supervisor
   - ○ B. Browse
   - ○ C. Compare
   - ○ D. Rename

5. The ______ property right is a subset of the Read property right.
   - ○ A. Supervisor
   - ○ B. Browse
   - ○ C. Compare
   - ○ D. Rename

6. To screen the Supervisor right from flowing down into the file system, use the ______.
   - ○ A. Delete object right
   - ○ B. Inherited Rights Mask
   - ○ C. Inherited Rights Filter
   - ○ D. SYSCON utility

7. Of the following, which *three* are Object rights?
   - □ A. Supervisor
   - □ B. Browse
   - □ C. Create
   - □ D. Remove

8. To assign a user as a workgroup manager, you must first ______.
   - ○ A. make the user a trustee of the container
   - ○ B. give the user security equivalence to [Public]
   - ○ C. create a Workgroup Manager object
   - ○ D. set the container's IRF to block out the Supervisor right

9. When determining a User object's effective rights, which *two* other NDS objects must be considered?

   ☐ A. [Root]

   ☐ B. [User]

   ☐ C. [Public]

   ☐ D. [Container]

10. If you want to see a user's actual rights at any given container in the NDS tree, you must set the context to that container, open the trustees dialog box for the container, then choose the ______.

    ○ A. Effective Rights button

    ○ B. Rights to Files and Directories button

    ○ C. Rights to other objects dialog box

    ○ D. Object rights area of the dialog box

Answers

1. B
2. A
3. C
4. B
5. C
6. C
7. A, B, C
8. A
9. A, C
10. A

CHAPTER 51

Working with NetWare 4.x Servers

One main advantage of using NetWare 4 networking technology is the capability of sharing resources such as printers, backup devices, and so on. Another important feature of NetWare 4 is that it can be successfully managed by using a variety of NetWare Loadable Modules (NLMs) provided by NetWare 4.

This chapter discusses managing two of several possible shared resources—printing and backup. It also discusses several management NLMs—SERVMAN, DSREPAIR, INSTALL (for enabling and managing compression on a volume), and DOMAIN. These shared resources and NLMs are discussed under the following three topics:

- Managing NDS printing services
- Managing NDS backup and restore services
- Using SERVMAN, DSREPAIR, INSTALL, and DOMAIN NLMs

Managing NDS Printing Services

Managing NDS printing services requires that you be able to accomplish the following tasks:

- Create and manage printing objects
- Provide advanced printing functionality
- Use Quick Setup in PCONSOLE
- Prepare print servers and provide remote printing

Creating and Managing Printing Objects

There are three types of printing objects you create in order to set up NDS print services. Those objects are Print servers, Print queues, and Printers. All three objects can be created by using the NetWare Administrator utility.

To create any of these three objects, first open the NetWare Administrator utility, then open the Browse window. Expand the NDS tree until you see the container where you want to create these objects, then select (highlight) that container. Next, choose Create from the Object pull-down menu (see fig. 51.1). Complete one or more of the following sets of steps described in the following three sections, depending on the type of object you want to create.

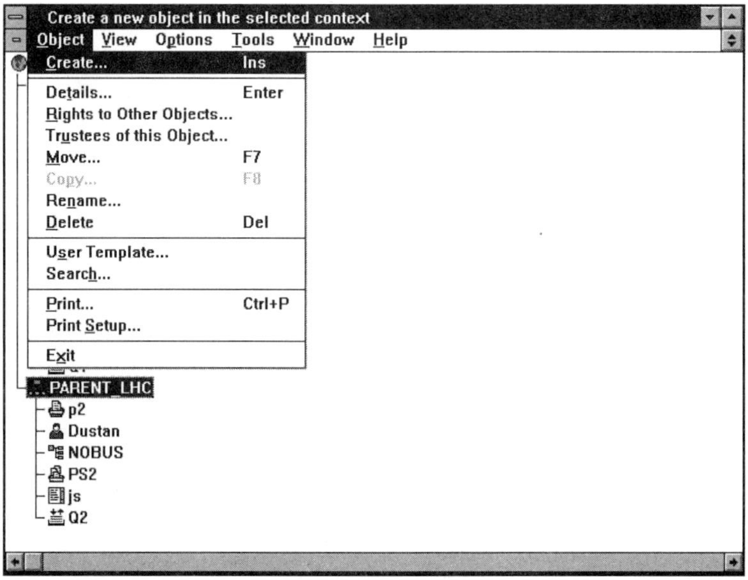

Figure 51.1
The Object pull-down menu.

Create a Print Server Object

To create a Print Server object, complete the following steps:

1. Choose Print Server from the New Object window.
2. In the Create Print Server dialog box, provide the required information—a Print Server Name (see fig. 51.2).

   You can also choose either to Define Additional Properties for the Print Server object or to Create Another Print Server.

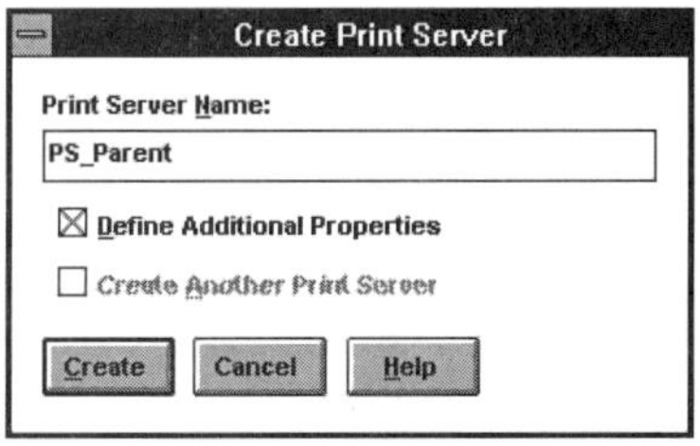

Figure 51.2
The Create Print Server object dialog box.

Create a Print Queue Object

To create a Print Queue object, complete the following steps:

1. Choose Print Queue from the New Object window.
2. In the Create Print Queue dialog box, provide the required information—a Print Queue Name and a Print Queue Volume (see fig. 51.3).

   You also can choose either to Define Additional Properties for the Print Queue object or to Create Another Print Queue. In addition, you can choose to make this a NetWare Directory Services Print Queue or to Reference a Bindery Queue.
3. Choose Create.

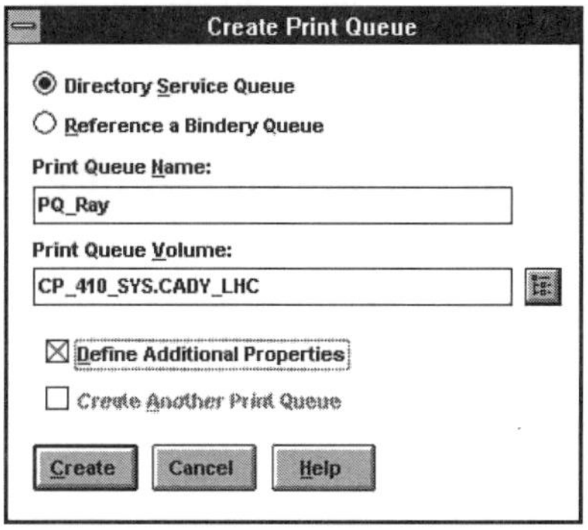

Figure 51.3
The Create Print Queue object dialog box.

Create a Printer Object

To create a Printer object, complete the following steps:

1. Choose Printer from the New Object window.
2. In the Create Printer dialog box, provide the required information—a Printer Name (see fig. 51.4).
3. Choose Create.

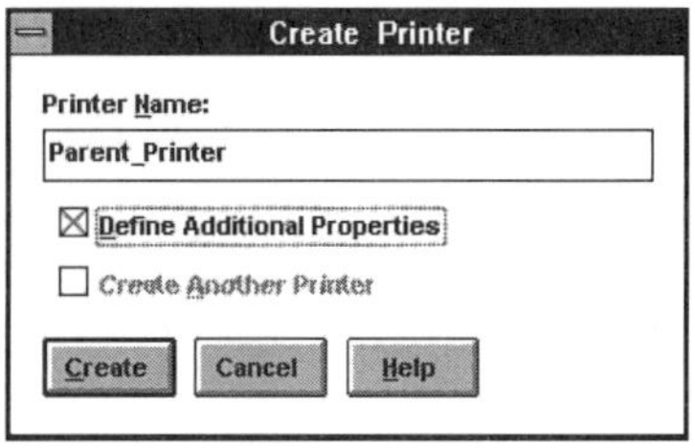

Figure 51.4
The Create Printer object dialog box.

Printer objects, Print Queue objects, and Print Server objects can also be managed by using the NetWare Administrator utility. By using NetWare Administrator, you can delete and rename printing objects, as well as define additional property information.

Providing Advanced Printing Functionality

Advanced print functionality includes such things as creating print devices and print forms and adding print job configurations. Each of these advanced printing functions is described in this section.

Create a Print Device

To create a print device for users to access when placing print job requests, complete the following steps:

1. Start the PRINTDEF utility.
2. Choose Print Devices from the Available Options menu.
3. Choose Edit Print Devices (see fig. 51.5).
4. When the Defined Print Devices list opens, press Insert.
5. Type in a name for the New Print Device and press Enter.
6. Choose the print device you just defined from the Defined Print Devices list.
7. Choose Device Functions and later, if necessary, Device Modes and provide the necessary information.

Create a Print Form

To create a print form, complete the following steps:

1. Start the PRINTDEF utility.
2. Choose Printer Forms from the Available Options menu.
3. Press Insert to add a form.
4. Provide a form name, form number, and the length and width of the paper being used for the form.
5. Save the new printer form by pressing F10.

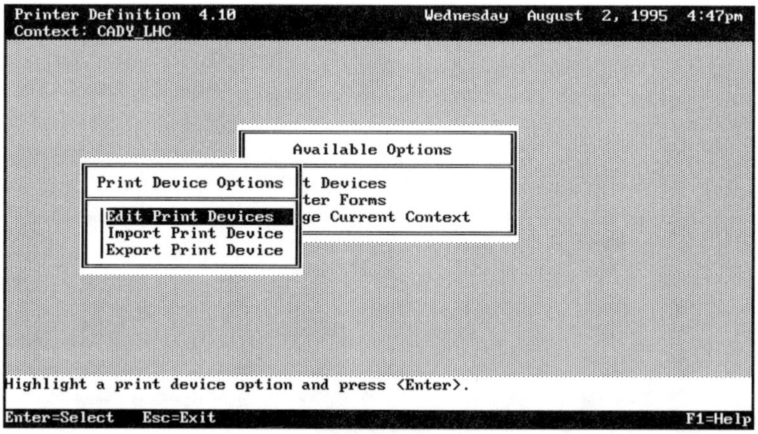

Figure 51.5 *The Print Device Options menu.*

Create a Print Job Configuration

To add print job configurations to a container for users to access, complete the following steps:

1. Start the NetWare Administrator utility and expand the tree so you can view and then select the level (container) at which you want the print job configuration to be added.
2. Choose Details from the Object pull-down menu.
3. Choose Print Job Configuration.
4. Choose the New button, then fill in at least the required fields on the Print Job Configuration window (see fig. 51.6). Required fields are Print Job Name and a printer or print queue object for the print job configuration to use (Printer/Queue).

Note By creating a print job configuration in a container, all user objects in that container have access to the print job configuration by default. To create a print job configuration for use by only a specific user, create the print job configuration at the User object level.

Using Quick Setup in PCONSOLE

The PCONSOLE utility simplifies basic printing setup for a parallel printer. To use Quick Setup, start the PCONSOLE utility, then complete the following steps:

1. Choose Quick Setup from the Available Options menu (see fig. 51.7).
2. When the Print Services Quick Setup window opens, verify that the information it contains is correct, then make any needed modifications (see fig. 51.8).
3. Press F10 to save the setup.

Preparing Print Servers and Providing Remote Printing

Print servers are NetWare file servers with print server software loaded. To prepare a print server for use, type at the file server console and press Enter. Replace *printserver_name* with the name of the print server object you created.

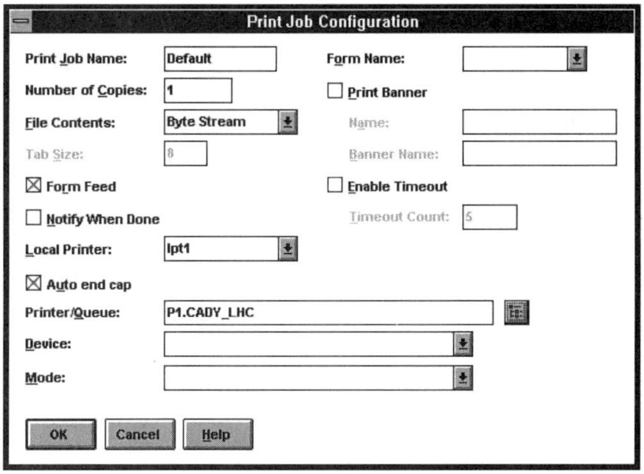

Figure 51.6
The Print Job Configuration window.

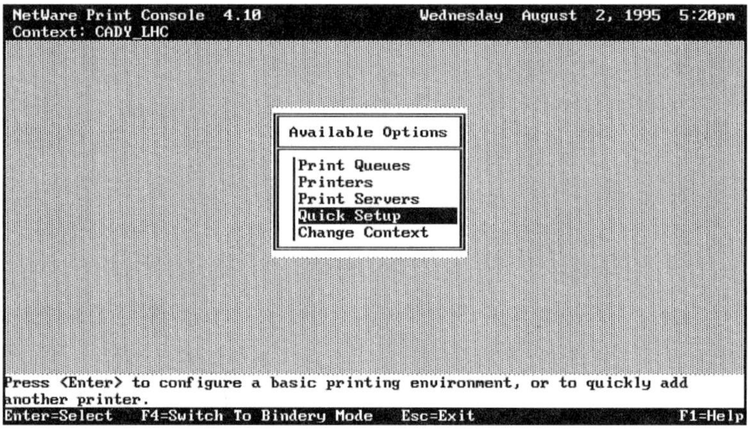

Figure 51.7
The Available Options menu.

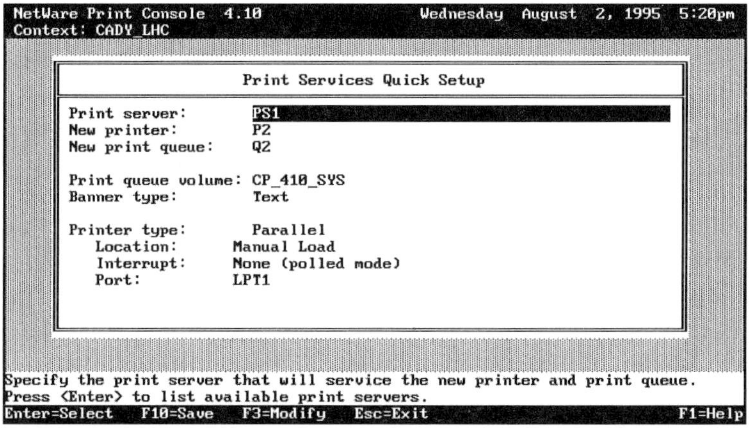

Figure 51.8
The Print Services Quick Setup window.

To provide remote printing from a printer connected to a workstation, load the NPRINTER.EXE software at the workstation. Next, press F4 to open the prompt to provide the printer name. Type the name of the printer object or press Ins to browse the NDS tree and choose the printer object.

Managing NDS Backup and Restore Services

The SBACKUP utility is NetWare's implementation of SMS (Storage Management Services), the architecture that provides backup and restore capabilities for various network target devices, including DOS workstations, OS/2 workstations, NetWare file servers, and NDS and BTRIEVE databases.

You run SBACKUP by loading it at the console of a NetWare file server that has a backup device installed (called the Host server). You can then choose the appropriate option from the SBACKUP menu to back up or restore network data.

Note For more detailed information on the SBACKUP utility and the SMS architecture, refer to Chapter 6, *Using NetWare Console Commands*, and Chapter 11, *Securing and Backing Up a NetWare 4.x Network.*

Using SERVMAN, DSREPAIR, INSTALL, and DOMAIN NLMs

The SERVMAN, DSREPAIR, INSTALL, and DOMAIN NetWare Loadable Modules all help the network administrator monitor and manage the network.

SERVMAN

The SERVMAN NLM enables you to perform a variety of configuration tasks that were previously done mostly from the console prompt by using the SET command, or from inside the file server's configuration files. When you type at the file server's console and press Enter, the SERVMAN Server General Information screen and Available Options menu open (see fig. 51.9).

By using SERVMAN, you can set communication parameters such as Reply to Get Nearest Server. To modify these and other communication parameters, choose Server Parameters from the Available Options menu. Next, choose Communications from the Select a parameter category. Find the communication parameters you want to modify and change the contents of the associated fields (see fig. 51.10).

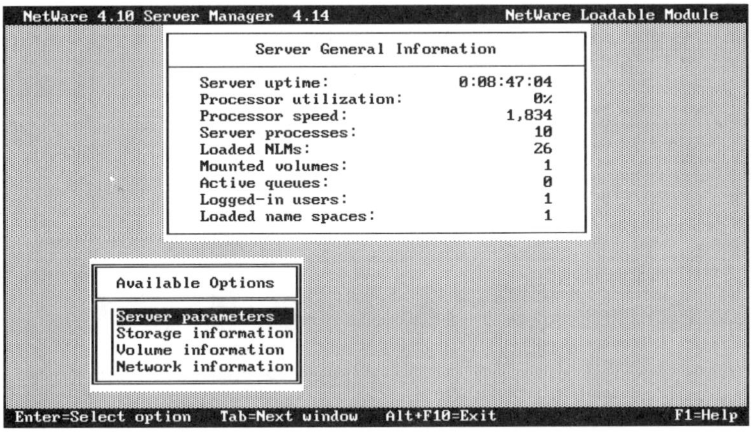

Figure 51.9
The main screen for the SERVMAN.NLM.

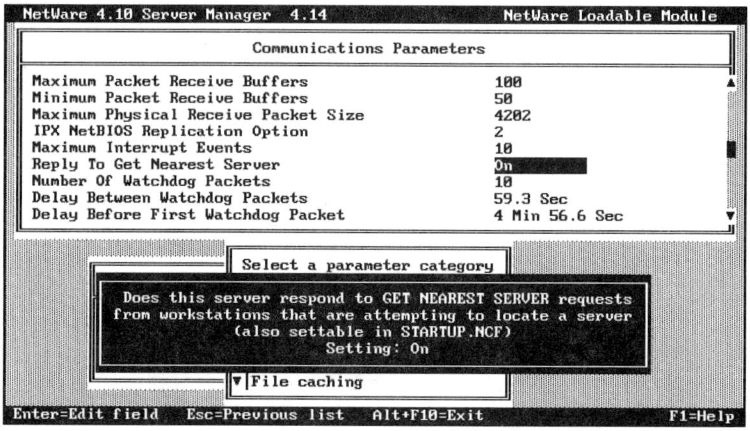

Figure 51.10
The Communications Parameters screen.

You also can change File system parameters such as Days untouched Before Compression. To modify these and other File system parameters, choose Server Parameters from the Available Options menu. Next, choose File system from the Select a parameter category. Find the file system parameters you want to modify and change the contents of the associated fields (see fig. 51.11).

You also can change Time parameters such as Start of Daylight Savings Time and End of Daylight Savings Time. To modify these and other Time parameters, choose Server Parameters from the Available Options menu. Next, choose Time from the Select a parameter category. Find the time parameters you want to modify and change the contents of the associated fields (see fig. 51.12).

You also can change NCP parameters such as Display NCP Bad Component Warnings and Display NCP Bad Length Warnings. To modify these and any variety of other parameters, choose the category for the parameters you want to modify, then choose the field and modify its contents.

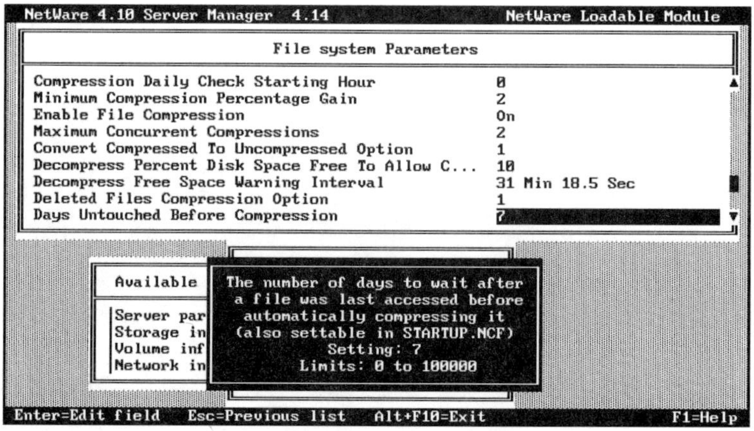

Figure 51.11
The File system Parameters screen.

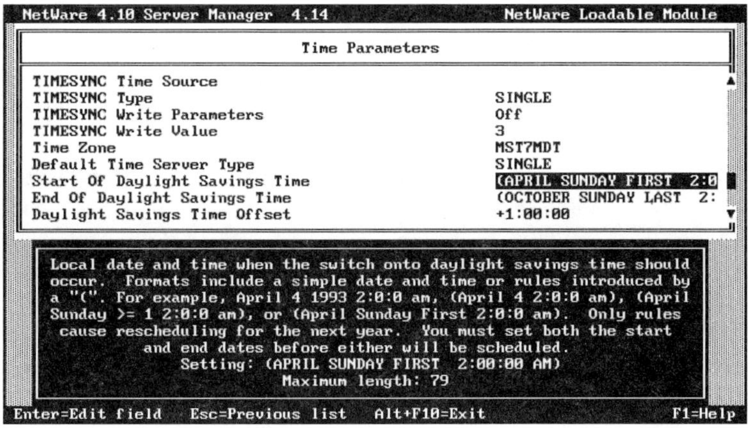

Figure 51.12
The Time Parameters screen.

When you finish modifying all the appropriate fields, you can exit and unload the SERVMAN.NLM.

Note For additional information on SERVMAN, refer to Chapter 15, *Optimizing a NetWare 4.x Network.*

DSREPAIR

The DSREPAIR NLM is primarily used to make repairs to the NDS database. Before running DSREPAIR, type **DISABLE LOGIN** at the console and press Enter. Then run DSREPAIR by typing **LOAD DSREPAIR** at the system console and pressing Enter.

Run the database repair by selecting Unattended full repair from the Available options menu (see fig. 51.13) and pressing Enter.

When you have completed the repair of the NDS database, type **ENABLE LOGIN** at the console and press Enter.

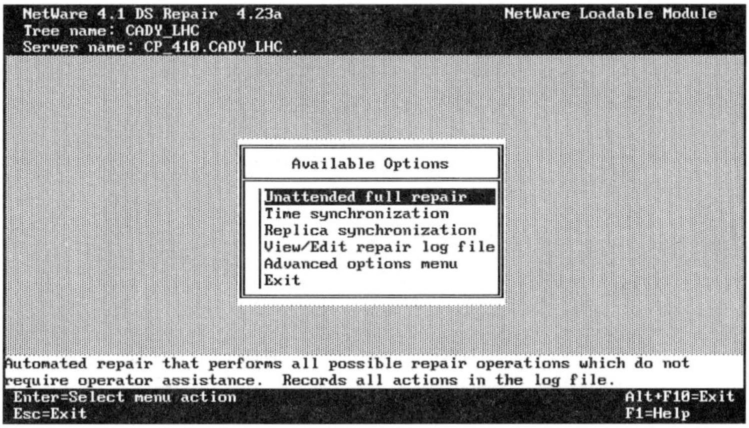

Figure 51.13
The DSREPAIR Available Options Menu.

INSTALL

The INSTALL NLM is used to perform a variety of tasks, one of which is editing the file server's startup files. When you need to load NLMs each time the file server is booted, you can put the command to load each NLM into the file server's STARTUP.NCF file.

To use the INSTALL NLM to edit the STARTUP.NCF file, type LOAD INSTALL at the file server console and press Enter. When the INSTALL NLM loads and the Installation options menu opens, choose NCF files options.

Next, choose Edit STARTUP.NCF from the Available NCF Files Options menu (see fig. 51.14). Modify the file to include the necessary commands. For example, add the command to load the DOMAIN.NLM.

You also use the INSTALL NLM to view the status of file compression. To accomplish this, choose Volume options from the Installation options menu. Choose a volume, then view the resulting volume information, which includes information about the status of file compression for this volume.

DOMAIN

The DOMAIN.NLM enables you to load other NLMs and modules into a protected area of memory, if you choose to do so. If you use the DOMAIN.NLM, you must load it before loading other NLMs, disk drivers, or name spaces. Once loaded, you can use the DOMAIN command to change between the OS (*Operating System*) domain and the OSP (*OS_Protected*) domain.

For example, to load the DOMAIN NLM, change to the OSP domain, then load an NLM called TEST.NLM, use the following four commands. The last one resets the domain to the OS domain so that NetWare modules can be loaded into the OS domain:

LOAD DOMAIN

DOMAIN OSP

LOAD TEST

DOMAIN OS

Figure 51.14
The Available NCF Files Options menu.

Questions

1. Which of the following is *not* a task associated with managing NDS printing services?
   - ○ A. Creating and managing print objects
   - ○ B. Providing advanced printing functionality
   - ○ C. Sending print jobs to a printer
   - ○ D. Preparing print servers
2. The *three* types of NDS print objects are ______, ______, and ______.
   - ☐ A. Printers
   - ☐ B. RPrinters
   - ☐ C. Print Servers
   - ☐ D. Print Queues
3. When you create a Print Queue object, the dialog box into which you enter a Print Queue object name is called ______.
   - ○ A. Print Queue
   - ○ B. Printer
   - ○ C. Create Print Queue
   - ○ D. Additional Properties
4. The two required fields for creating a Print Queue object are ______ and ______.
   - ☐ A. Print Queue Name
   - ☐ B. Print Volume Assigned
   - ☐ C. Print Queue Assigned
   - ☐ D. Print Queue Volume
5. The ______ utility enables you to provide advanced printing functionality.
   - ○ A. Network Administrator
   - ○ B. PRINTDEF
   - ○ C. NETADMIN
   - ○ D. PRINTCON
6. The Print Device Options Menu is part of the ______ utility.
   - ○ A. PCONSOLE
   - ○ B. PRINTDEF
   - ○ C. PRINTCON
   - ○ D. NETADMIN
7. Of the following, which *two* are required fields when creating a Print Job Configuration?
   - ☐ A. Print Job Name
   - ☐ B. Printer object
   - ☐ C. Print Server name
   - ☐ D. File Server Volume
8. Of the following, which one is *not* supported by the SBACKUP utility?
   - ○ A. DOS workstations
   - ○ B. MAC workstations
   - ○ C. OS/2 workstations
   - ○ D. BTRIEVE databases
9. The ______ NLM enables you to choose which ring into which to load NLMs?
   - ○ A. SERVMAN
   - ○ B. DSREPAIR
   - ○ C. INSTALL
   - ○ D. DOMAIN

10. If you want to change the Reply to get nearest server configuration parameter to OFF, you can use the ______ utility.

    ○ A. SERVMAN

    ○ B. DSREPAIR

    ○ C. INSTALL

    ○ D. DOMAIN

Answers

1. C
2. A, C, D
3. C
4. A, D
5. B
6. B
7. A, B
8. B
9. D
10. A

CHAPTER 52

Putting It All Together

The concept of NDS is that everything in the networking environment is treated as an object. Information about all objects is stored in one database. To simplify network log in, reduce the database to manageable chunks (partitions), and provide security of the NDS database, various partitions of the NDS database are copied (replicated) to different NetWare 4 network file servers.

By now, you understand the basic concepts of NDS, how to create and manage objects, and how to design an NDS tree to meet your company's goals. The final aspects of the NetWare 4 network that you need to understand are discussed in this chapter under the following two topics:

- *Partitioning the NDS database*
- *Replicating the NDS database*

Partitioning the NDS Database

Partitioning the NDS database means logically dividing it into smaller, more manageable sections. There are two main rules associated with partitioning. First, each partition must include at least one container object. Whether one or more container objects is included in a partition, the name of the top container is also the name of the partition. Second, the [Root] of the NDS tree must be at least part of a partition if it is not a partition by itself.

In figure 52.1, a sample NDS tree structure is displayed. This tree structure has had its partition boundaries defined as illustrated by the dotted-line boxes. As you can see from this figure, the [Root] and Organization have become a separate partition, and each of the two Organizational Units has also become a separate partition.

In the example shown in figure 52.1, the first container to be created was one that included [Root], the RMCCHIR container, and the RECORDS container. This partition was created by default when the first NetWare 4 file server (FS_RMC) was installed and the NDS Tree was created. This partition is called the [Root] partition.

The second partition was created when the second file server (FS2_RMC) was installed. This second partition is called the Financial partition. It too was created by default because a NetWare 4 file server was installed into each of these containers.

Figure 52.1
Partitioning the NDS tree.

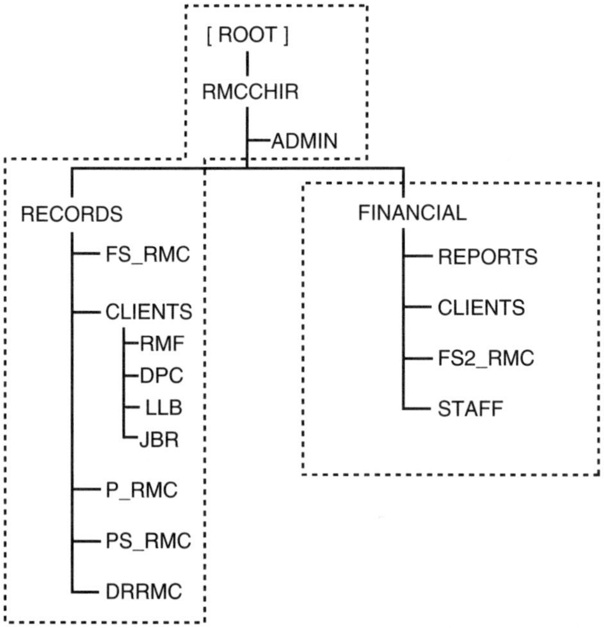

If, as the network administrator, you choose to create additional partitions, you can do so. In figure 52.1, the only possibility for an additional partition at this time is the container called CLIENTS under the RECORDS container. You can make that container a partition of its own if you have the Supervisor right to the parent container. Because the top container of this new partition is called CLIENTS, this partition is called the CLIENTS partition.

To create partitions, first choose Partition Manager from the Tools pull-down menu in the NetWare Administrator utility (see fig. 52.2).

Change the display of containers until the container you want to create as a separate partition is displayed. Select (highlight) that container.

Next, choose Create as new partition, and when prompted with the Confirmation dialog box, choose Yes (see fig. 52.3).

When prompted with the Partition Manager prompt indicating the process involved in the partitioning process (see fig. 52.4), choose OK.

When the partitioning process is complete, the container displays as a partition (shows the partition icon and displays the parent container's name in red) in the Partition Manager dialog box.

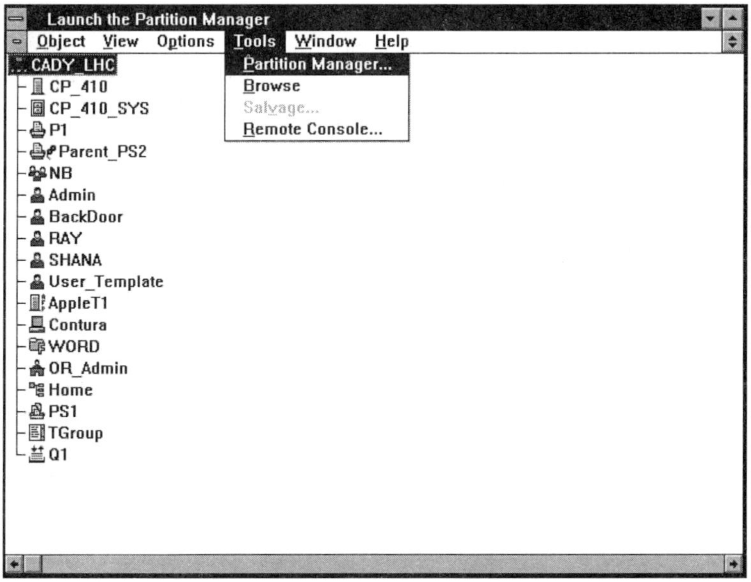

Figure 52.2
The Tools pull-down menu.

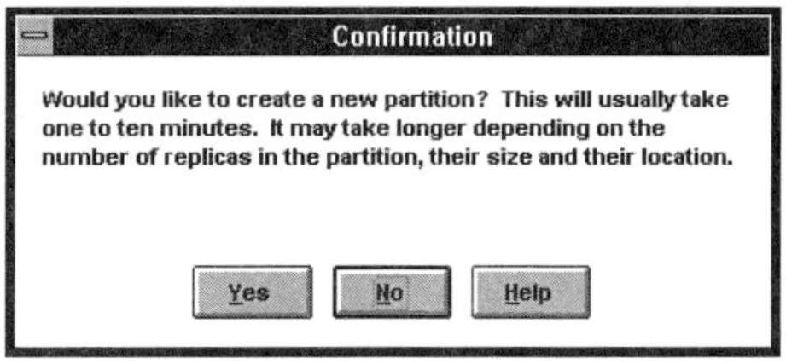

Figure 52.3
Confirmation to create a new partition.

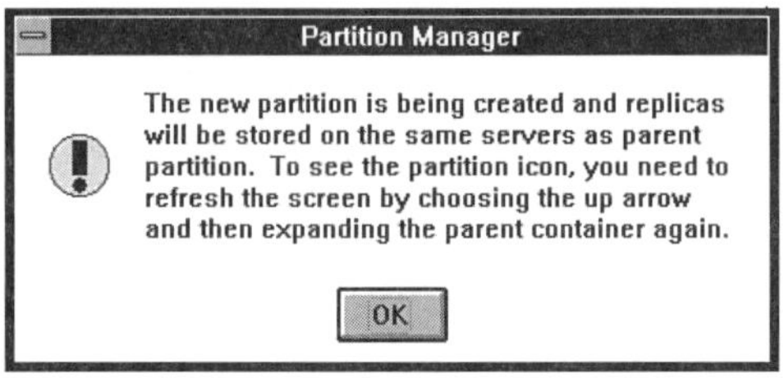

Figure 52.4
The Partition Manager prompt.

Replicating the NDS Database

When you partition the NDS tree, the master record for the partition is saved on the file server from which the partitioning process was conducted. This is called the Master replica. In addition and by default, the second and third file servers added to this partition of the NDS database (added to the replica ring) automatically receive Read/Write replicas of this partition.

When another partition is created, the file server on which it resides receives the Master replica, and a Read/Write and replica is placed on another file server in the replica ring. If a third partition is created, the file server on which it resides receives the Master replica, and a Read/Write copy of this replica is placed on another file server in the ring.

As the network administrator, you can control what happens to partition replicas. For example, you can view the current status of replicas for a partition or add replicas if you believe additional replicas should be added.

To view the current status of replicas for a partition, select the partition from the list of partitions displayed in the NetWare Administrator Partition Manager tool. Next, choose the Replicas page button to open the Partition Replicas window (see fig. 52.5).

To add a replica, select the partition from the list of partitions displayed in the NetWare Administrator Partition Manager tool. Next, choose the Replicas page button to open the Partition Replicas window, then choose the Add Replica button to open the Add Replica window.

Now, select the replica, then choose a replica type (Read/Write or Read/Only) and choose OK.

You can also delete a replica that is not the Master replica by selecting it from the list in the Partition Replicas window and choosing Delete Replica.

Note For more information on partitioning and replication, see Chapter 10, "Partitioning and Replicating NDS."

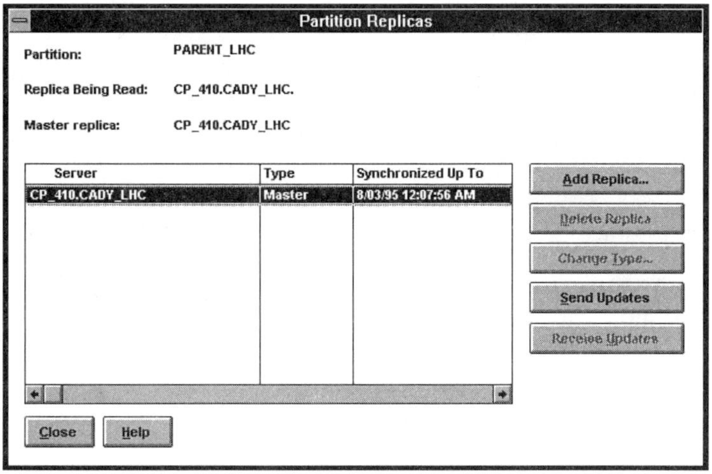

Figure 52.5
The Partition Replicas window.

Questions

1. The first partition created by default is ______.

   ○ A. [Root]

   ○ B. [Public]

   ○ C. named after the first container

   ○ D. dependent upon how many file servers exist in the NDS tree

2. The *two* types of replicas you can create after the first one is created are called ______ and ______.

   □ A. Read

   □ B. Read/Write

   □ C. Read Only

   □ D. Write Only

3. The second replica created automatically during the installation process is always a ______ replica.

   ○ A. Master

   ○ B. Read/Write

   ○ C. Read Only

   ○ D. Subordinate

4. A ______ is a copy of a portion of the NDS database.

   ○ A. Master copy

   ○ B. Replica

   ○ C. Partition

   ○ D. Read Only copy

5. The first replica created for any partition is the ______ replica.

   ○ A. Master

   ○ B. Read/Write

   ○ C. Read Only

   ○ D. Subordinate

6. When the partitioning process is complete, what color does NDS use to display a partition in the Partition Manager utility?

   ○ A. Black

   ○ B. Blue

   ○ C. Red

   ○ D. White

7. Of the following, which *three* are true statements?

   □ A. You cannot create additional partitions beyond those created when NetWare 4 file servers are installed.

   □ B. You can create additional partitions as long as you have at least one container in each partition.

   □ C. You can use the Partition Manager utility to create and delete partitions.

   □ D. You cannot delete a Master partition.

8. A ______ is displayed when you create a new partition.

 ○ A. confirmation of the replica dialog box

 ○ B. request to name the new partition dialog box

 ○ C. request to create a new partition dialog box

 ○ D. confirmation dialog box

9. The file servers on which replicas are stored is referred to as ______.

 ○ A. the replica master

 ○ B. the replica circle

 ○ C. the replica ring

 ○ D. the replica table

10. If you want to eliminate a replica, you must ______.

 ○ A. use the Delete Replica button on the Partition Replicas window

 ○ B. uninstall the NetWare 4 server holding the partition's Master replica

 ○ C. first change the Master replica to a Read/Write replica, then use the Delete Replica button on the Partition Replicas window

 ○ D. have only the delete right to the file server object on which the partition resides

Answers

1. A
2. B, C
3. B
4. B
5. A
6. C
7. B, C, D
8. D
9. C
10. A

PART PART PART PART PART PART PART PART

VII

NetWare 4.1 Design and Implementation

CHAPTER 53

Understanding the Design and Implementation Process

Implementing a WAN is much more complex than implementing a LAN. Whereas a LAN might consist of anywhere from two to a few hundred computers, WANs can consist of several hundred to several thousand. Planning (designing) a LAN is important, particularly if you expect it to grow in the future. Planning a WAN, however, is mandatory to its success. Although time and energy consuming, planning and implementing a WAN does not have to be a seat-of-the-pants effort. The process can be well-structured and methodical, particularly if some type of design and implementation guidelines are followed.

Novell's consulting group put together a suggested process for designing and implementing a NetWare 4 network that can be followed successfully for both LANs and WANs. The Novell *NetWare 4 Design and Implementation* course is based on this suggested process. In turn, this process is based on something with which many Information Systems (IS) personnel have long been familiar—the *System Design Life Cycle* (SDLC), also known as the information systems development method, the process model, and so on.

The SDLC can be approached from several different angles. These are the four most commonly known approaches:

- **Linear.** Process moves one step at a time from analysis to operation (bottom-up development)
- **Structured.** Process consists of performing multiple steps simultaneously where appropriate (top-down design)
- **Incremental.** Analysis and design to prototype stage, then continued design and development based on prototyping results
- **Spiral.** Development based on continually changing requirements where risk and cost are unstable

Novell's process is based primarily on the linear approach. Thus the *NetWare 4 Design and Implementation* course and this part of this book also are based on this approach.

This chapter discusses the NetWare 4 design and implementation process by breaking it down into the following three topics:

- Understanding the SDLC phases of design and implementation
- Understanding the design and implementation procedures
- Understanding Novell's phases of design and implementation

Understanding the SDLC Phases of Design and Implementation

Novell has defined four design and implementation phases you can follow to carry out the SDLC process of designing and implementing a NetWare 4 LAN or WAN:

- Analysis and specification
- Design
- Implementation
- Maintenance

These phases are relevant to any of the SDLC approaches listed earlier.

The following sections explain each of these design and implementation approaches.

Analysis and Specification

Before you begin any project, whether designing and installing a NetWare 4 WAN or adding a room to your home, you can benefit from initially analyzing the current condition of the object you're working with. Next, specify what changes you want to make, and then plan your approach to successfully completing the project.

As with all tasks, there are steps associated with the analysis and specification phase of designing and implementing a NetWare 4 network. The primary steps associated with this phase follow:

1. Identify and specify the need to be met.
2. Recognize the primary goals, restrictions, and requirements associated with the need.
3. Collect all relevant information.
4. Develop preparatory schedules for the project.
5. Obtain mutual agreement on the project's charter or scope.
6. Assign team members and delegate project responsibilities.

The primary purpose of the analysis and specification phase is to identify the need that must be met. Once identified, the need should be clearly defined, preferably in writing, for all to use as their center of focus in completing the other phases associated with this project.

Design

During the design phase, potential solutions for meeting the need are defined. From these potential solutions, a single solution (or a combination of solutions that ultimately constitute the single solution) is chosen. Then a design based on the chosen solution is created. The primary steps associated with this phase follow:

1. Propose potential solutions.
2. Evaluate various proposed solutions.
3. Design the best solution.

The design phase of designing and implementing a NetWare 4 network is given primary emphasis in this part of this book, as well as in the Novell *NetWare 4 Design and Implementation* course.

Implementation

The implementation phase involves the implementation of the pilot (for testing and revision) of the designed solution, until the pilot is adequately successful and can be put into place as the actual solution. Planning and scheduling are key steps in this phase, and as such, also are concentrated on in this section of this book as well as in Novell's *NetWare 4 Design and Implementation* course.

The primary steps associated with the implementation phase follow:

1. Determine which major goals or milestones must be met for the implementation to be a success
2. Develop, then test, the most likely potential (working) solution
3. Implement the pilot solution
4. Test the pilot solution and gain user acceptance
5. Implement the refined solution
6. Document the refined solution and train affected users
7. Test the final solution and again gain user acceptance

Maintenance

The final phase, maintenance, involves evaluating the success or failure of your solution, working out minor problems with your new system, and maintaining the new system. In addition, the maintenance phase is the starting point into the design phase of the next implementation of the System Design Life Cycle.

The primary steps associated with the maintenance phase follow:

1. Set up a method of continually checking and reporting on the implemented solution.
2. Perform associated maintenance tasks as long as the cost of maintaining the current solution does not exceed the cost incurred by replacing the current solution with an alternative.
3. Replace the current solution with an alternative solution (developed as the result of following the general SDLC) when maintenance costs begin to exceed replacement costs.

Although Novell's recommended design and implementation process is similar to the general SDLC just discussed, it does vary.

Understanding Novell's Phases of Design and Implementation

Novell also defines four phases of the design and implementation process, for example, but uses different names for two of them.

Table 53.1 compares the SDLC phases with those defined by Novell, and lists the procedures associated with each of the Novell-defined phases.

As shown in table 53.1, Novell's four phases include several procedures. Some of these procedures are not discussed in the Novell *NetWare 4 Design and Implementation* course; therefore, neither are they covered in this part of the book. The procedures discussed in this part are 1 through 7. Procedures 3 and 4, however, are discussed only briefly

Table 53.1
SDLC and Novell NetWare 4 Design and Implementation Phases

SDLC Phases	*Novell Phases*	*Procedures Associated with Novell Phases*
Analysis and Design	Project Approach	1. Determine the project approach
Design	Design	2. Design the directory tree 3. Determine a partition and replication strategy 4. Plan a time synchronization strategy 5. Create an accessibility plan
Implementation	Implementation	6. Develop the migration strategy 7. Create the implementation schedule 8. Implement NetWare 4
Maintenance	Manage and Monitor	9. Manage NetWare 4 10. Monitor NetWare 4

in this part and are covered in detail in Chapter 10, "Partitioning and Replicating NDS" and Chapter 55, "Designing NetWare 4.x Wide Area Networks," as well as in other Novell courses.

Understanding Novell's Design and Implementation Procedures

Each NetWare 4 design and implementation phase has associated with it several steps or procedures that can help ensure the successful design and implementation of a NetWare 4 network. Not all these procedures are required in every case, particularly when designing and implementing networks with only a few computers or file servers. Individuals responsible for designing and implementing a NetWare 4 network, however, should have a basic understanding of all these procedures.

Note Notice that the tasks associated with each of the Novell-defined project phases are similar to those associated with the SDLC phases.

Project Approach Procedure

The Project Approach phase of the NetWare 4 design and implementation process (step 1 of table 53.1) ultimately involves determining the parameters of the project. To accomplish this goal, you must complete several steps in a logical order:

1. Gather the project team.
2. Collect network design-related company information.
3. Train project team members.
4. Define the range of the project design process.
5. Prepare initial project schedules.

During the Project Approach phase, the team is expected to set realistic goals. Team members also are expected to develop an understanding of their own role as part of the team and in the planning, designing, and implementation of the project.

Design Procedures

Four primary procedures constitute the Design phase of the NetWare 4 design and implementation process (steps 2 through 5 in table 53.1). The main goal of these steps is to establish the basic framework into which the network can be placed. Depending on factors such as the number of objects in the network, its LAN and WAN topology, and so on, establishing this basic framework may require that you complete the following steps:

1. Design the NetWare Directory Tree.
2. Establish a strategy for partitioning the tree as well as creating and storing replicas of each partition.
3. Determine how to use and implement time synchronization throughout the directory tree.
4. Develop a plan for making network accessibility as simple as possible for users.

During the design phase, the team is expected to accomplish several goals. First is to set a framework for the network which allows NDS (NetWare Directory Services) to function as efficiently as possible. Next is to make the network as easy as possible to administer and to use. Third is to provide fault tolerance (protection against unforeseen hardware, software, and other problems).

Fourth is to ensure synchronization of time across all network servers. And finally, to provide as many of the services needed by network users as is feasible.

Implementation Procedures

Three primary procedures encompass the implementation phase of the NetWare 4 design and implementation process (steps 6 through 8 in table 53.1).

Note: The third of these steps (step 8—implement NetWare 4) is not discussed in Novell's *NetWare 4 Design and Implementation* course; thus, it is not discussed in this section of the book. It is assumed that individuals attending the CNE course, as well as those reading this book, already have experience with or exposure to installing NetWare 4.

The main goal of completing the implementation phase is to make the actual setup, upgrade, and migration process as smooth as possible. To accomplish this, complete the following steps:

1. Determine which Novell tools are most appropriate for accomplishing the task at hand (across-the-wire migration, in-place installation, and so on) and whether or not an in-house lab would be useful and appropriate.
2. List tasks to accomplish, determine their order and priority, set deadlines for completing those tasks, determine who is responsible for completing which tasks, and set a realistic implementation schedule.
3. Implement the schedule as defined.

During the design phase, the efforts put forth by the team should result in an implementation of the plan that is relatively painless, though not problem free. Efforts made in this phase as well as those made in previous phases can result in a logical and organized implementation.

Manage and Monitor Procedures

The Manage and Monitor phase of the NetWare 4 design and implementation process are referred to as steps 9 and 10. The goals of the Manage and Monitor procedures are to ensure the implemented process is functioning as intended, and to always be aware of flaws or problems that either must be corrected or may require that the entire process be updated or replaced. These are the main steps associated with the Manage and Monitor phase:

1. Establish and follow guidelines for managing the network and its resources.
2. Track and report on the results of the project.
3. Anticipate and troubleshoot network problems.
4. Implement procedures to recover from network problems.
5. Determine when it is appropriate to upgrade or replace the existing network.

Note: The Manage and Monitor process can be conducted by one or more individuals, but is most often carried out by network administrators. Therefore, including the company's network administrators in the project team is a logical choice if the team wants to ensure the final phase of the process is adequately conducted.

As previously noted, the Manage and Monitor phase is not discussed in any detail in the Novell

NetWare 4 Design and Implementation course because it covered in other Novell courses. (Nor is it covered in this part of the book.) Individuals attending the *NetWare 4 Design and Implementation* course are expected to be experienced NetWare 4 consultants, managers, or others with significant NetWare 4 experience or knowledge.

After you develop a basic understanding of the overall process involved in designing and implementing a NetWare 4 network, you can begin to incorporate the process in your own environment. Of course, a little practice might be helpful as well. The following four chapters explain each of the four phases of NetWare 4 design and implementation in greater depth and provide related examples to help you better prepare to implement these phases in your own or another business.

Questions

1. The SDLC can be approached from any of four angles. Which of the following is *not* one of those approaches?
   - ○ A. Linear
   - ○ B. Procedural
   - ○ C. Spiral
   - ○ D. Structured

2. The two terms used to describe the Incremental SDLC approach are ______.
   - ☐ A. Design
   - ☐ B. Top-down
   - ☐ C. Bottom-up
   - ☐ D. Analysis

3. The process suggested by Novell for designing and implementing a NetWare 4 network is similar to the ______ SDLC process.
   - ○ A. Linear
   - ○ B. Procedural
   - ○ C. Spiral
   - ○ D. Structured

4. The collecting of relevant (company) information is part of the SDLC ______ phase of design and implementation.
   - ○ A. Analysis and Specification
   - ○ B. Design
   - ○ C. Implementation
   - ○ D. Maintenance

5. Before trying a pilot solution, you must complete the phase that comes before this step. This is called the ______ phase.
   - ○ A. Analysis and specification
   - ○ B. Design
   - ○ C. Implementation
   - ○ D. Maintenance

6. When following Novell's NetWare 4 process, assigning team members and delegating project responsibilities is accomplished in the ______ phase.
   - ○ A. Project Approach
   - ○ B. Analysis and Specification
   - ○ C. Design
   - ○ D. Maintenance
   - ○ E. Manage and Monitor

7. Of the following, which two phases have the same name as part of both the SDLC process and the Novell-suggested process?
   - ☐ A. Analysis and Specification
   - ☐ B. Project Approach
   - ☐ C. Design
   - ☐ D. Implementation
   - ☐ D. Maintenance

8. Replacing the current solution with an alternative solution (developed as the result of following the general SDLC process) is part of the final NetWare 4 design and implementation phase, also known as the ______ phase.

- ○ A. Project Approach
- ○ B. Analysis and Specification
- ○ C. Design
- ○ D. Maintenance
- ○ E. Manage and Monitor

9. When following the NetWare 4 process, you should ______.

   - ○ A. determine the project approach; design the Directory tree; determine partition, replication, and synchronization strategies; and then create an accessibility plan
   - ○ B. determine the project approach; design the Directory tree; create an accessibility plan; and then determine partition, replication, and synchronization strategies
   - ○ C. design the Directory tree; determine the project approach; create an accessibility plan; and then determine partition, replication, and synchronization strategies
   - ○ D. determine the project approach; determine partition, replication, and synchronization strategies; design the Directory tree, and then create an accessibility plan

10. If you determine it is necessary to introduce additional partitions into your directory tree structure, you should establish your strategy for partitioning the tree during the NetWare 4 ______ phase.

   - ○ A. Project Approach
   - ○ B. Analysis and Specification
   - ○ C. Design
   - ○ D. Maintenance
   - ○ E. Manage and Monitor

Answers

1. B
2. A, D
3. A
4. A
5. B
6. A
7. C, D
8. E
9. A
10. C

CHAPTER 54

Determining the Design and Implementation Approach

Chapter 53, "Understanding the Design and Implementation Process," provides an overview of the approach to designing and implementing a NetWare 4 network. One of its primary topics is the design phase, and what actions should be completed during this phase. In the design phase, you define potential solutions for meeting the business need, choose a single solution (or a combination of solutions that ultimately constitute the single solution), and then create a design based on the chosen solution.

What Chapter 53 does not discuss, however, is the "who" of design and implementation. Before the design and implementation approach can be followed, someone needs to accept responsibility for designing and implementing the NetWare 4 network. In small- to medium-sized businesses, this might be only one or two people. In larger businesses, it is more likely a group of several people, each offering unique skills and knowledge.

After the person or persons responsible for the design and implementation of the network are determined, the process of determining the network design and how it will be implemented can go forward. This chapter discusses the responsibilities associated with determining the network's design and the implementation process under the following headings:

- Organizing the project team
- Determining the design of the network
- Planning the implementation of the network design

Organizing the Project Team

Whether the network is being designed and implemented by only one or two people or by a dozen, certain levels of skill and knowledge are needed. Such skills and knowledge can be broken into several job categories or project team roles. The following project team roles are defined in Novell's *NetWare 4 Design and Implementation* course:

- Information Systems (IS) Manager
- NetWare Directory Services (NDS) Expert
- Server Specialist
- Workstation Specialist
- Applications Specialist
- Printing Specialist
- Connectivity Specialist
- Testing Lab Coordinator
- Education and Training Coordinator

Each of these project team roles can be assumed by one or more team members. The assignment of responsibility should be based on each team member's knowledge. When there are fewer team members, each member may have to assume additional responsibilities. Sometimes this means each team member has to take time to learn the roles assigned to them. Table 54.1 lists these project team roles and describes the basic tasks for which the team member assigned to each role is responsible.

As table 54.1 also shows, in one way or another, each project team role must coordinate with one or more of the other project team roles for the network design and implementation to be fully successful. The Printing Specialist may need to carefully coordinate with the NDS Expert, the Server Specialist, the Testing Lab Coordinator, and the Workstation Specialist, for example, to ensure that printing is designed and then implemented to meet the needs of network users.

Table 54.1
Project Team Roles

Role Title	*Basic Responsibilities*	*Coordinates With*
IS Manager	Oversee design and implementation; Obtain funding and needed resources	All rolls, especially the NDS Expert
NDS Expert	Lead the project team; Design the tree and the network's security; Interface with other company personnel to determine network needs; Define partitioning, replication, and time synchronization approach	Connectivity, Server, and Printing Specialists
Server Specialist	Preserve current network performance levels; Plan pilot test; Implement upgrades, migrations, and time synchronization approach	NDS Expert; Workstation, Application, and Connectivity Specialists; and Testing Lab Coordinator
Workstation Specialist	Upgrade and automate workstations	Server, Applications, and Printing Specialists
Applications Specialist	Ensure NetWare 4 and applications are compatible; Transfer applications	Server and Workstation Specialists, Testing Lab Coordinator, and Education and Training Lab Coordinator
Printing Specialist	Upgrade printing software and drivers; Provide access to printers for users	NDS Expert, Server and Workstation Specialists, and Testing Lab Coordinator

continues

Table 54.1, Continued
Project Team Roles

Role Title	*Basic Responsibilities*	*Coordinates With*
Connectivity Specialist	Choose protocols to be used; Determine effect of routers, protocols, etc. on the WAN	NDS Expert, Server and Printing Specialists, and Testing Lab Coordinator
Testing Lab Coordinator	Establish performance benchmarks; Test software	NDS Expert; Server, Printing, and Workstation Specialists; and Education and Training Coordinator
Education and Training Coordinator	Train project team, administrators, and users; Determine implementation guidelines	Testing Lab Coordinator, and Application and Connectivity Specialists

After all project team members understand their roles and the interrelationship of theirs and other team members' responsibilities, the network design process can begin.

Determining the Design of the Network

The following are the four main steps associated with determining the design of a NetWare 4 network:

1. Gather all relevant information.
2. Define the scope of the design.
3. Establish the complexity of the project.
4. Develop a timeline for network design.

Gathering Relevant Information

The first step before designing the network is gathering and reviewing all relevant information. You must understand the company for whom the network is being created to achieve a successful design. Therefore you must gather, review, and analyze a great deal of company information.

Because gathering so much information can be a massive job, each project team member should be expected to gather information relevant to their responsibilities on the team. The IS Manager is responsible for obtaining funding and needed resources, for example. The IS Manager should, therefore, obtain such documents and information as an organizational chart for the company, a list of people responsible for administering the network, and a budget figure for the project.

Table 54.2 lists a sampling of the types of information each project team member can be expected to gather. Not all projects require that all the listed information be gathered, whereas some projects might require additional information.

After team members gather the needed information, sharing that information with each of the other team members is the second part of this first step toward designing a successful network. One way the sharing of information can be accomplished is by conducting one or more team meetings in which team members each take a turn presenting the information they have collected. Another approach may be to assign one team member the responsibility of collecting the information gathered by each individual team member, and then collating, printing, and distributing the resulting report for all team members to read and study.

Defining the Scope of the Design

After all team members have gathered, shared, and reviewed the relevant information, they can begin the second step in the design process—determining the scope of the design for the NetWare 4 network.

Table 54.2
Suggested Information to Be Gathered by Team Members

Team Member	*Information to be Gathered*
IS Manager	Organization chart; Budget; Resource list; Workflow information
NDS Expert	Current layout of offices, and other items that are part of or affected by the network's design; Hardware (network equipment) list
Server Specialist	Software (operating systems) list; Current/proposed location of servers
Workstation Specialist	Quantity and type of workstations to be connected to the network; Operating systems run on workstations
Application Specialist	Current applications; Proposed applications; Department/user future application needs

continues

Table 54.2, Continued
Suggested Information to Be Gathered by Team Members

Team Member	*Information to be Gathered*
Printing Specialist	Existing printers; Proposed printers; Other printing devices such as plotters; Department/user printing needs
Connectivity Specialist	Routers used on existing network; Topologies currently being used
Testing Lab Coordinator	Testing requirements; Testing equipment needs
Education and Training Coordinator	Names of administrators, users, and others who require training; Types of training required

The main factor that affects the scope of the project design is how complex the network currently is or will be after it is implemented. The project team should establish this first. Then the team can consider other factors such as how many people are available to help with the design and implementation, whether or not the entire company will be included in the implementation, how much time the implementation requires, and so on.

Establishing the Complexity of the Project

The major factor that influences complexity is directly related to the quantity and location of the network's equipment. If your network currently has fewer than 15 file servers containing replicas of partitions, for example, you can expect to spend approximately one day designing the partitioning and replication scheme. This would be considered a simple design. If, on the other hand, your network has more than 15 file servers containing replicas of partitions, you can expect to spend three to four days designing the partitioning and replication scheme. This would be considered a complex design. These other issues also affect the complexity of the network design:

- **Configuring time sources.** A simple design (fewer than 30 file servers) requires approximately one-half to one full day to configure time sources. A complex design (more than 30 file servers) requires approximately two to three days to configure time sources.
- **Determining partitioning, replication, and time synchronization.** A simple design (a single LAN or a few separate sites connected by a WAN) might require as little as one day to design. A more complex design might require up to four days.

- **Planning the Directory tree (or multiple trees to be merged at a later time).** A simple design such as a single tree for a small WAN can require as little as one-half day to design. A more complex design might require up to two days.
- **Planning for network growth.** A simple addition to the tree at the top of the structure (such as adding additional Organizational Units) or planning for the addition of partitions might require as little as one day or as many as three days of design time in a more complex network.

The complexity of designing a network also might be influenced by the experience, knowledge, and skills of the individuals participating in the design project.

Develop a Timeline for Network Design

After the team determines the degree of complexity of the network, it can use time guidelines to develop a network design timeline. Consider the following information when determining a timeline for creating the network:

- Information gathered about the company by each of the individual team members
- Expansion plans, corporate mergers or divestitures, and any other changes that might affect the ultimate design of the network
- How long the design process should take based on the complexity of the network
- Any other information that might influence the network

Any format deemed acceptable to your company can be used to present the timeline. Figure 54.1 shows a sample timeline for a simple network design. Note that it includes only the basic design procedures (discussed in more detail in later chapters of this part of the book):

- Design the Directory tree
- Design time synchronization
- Design partitioning/replication
- Design accessibility

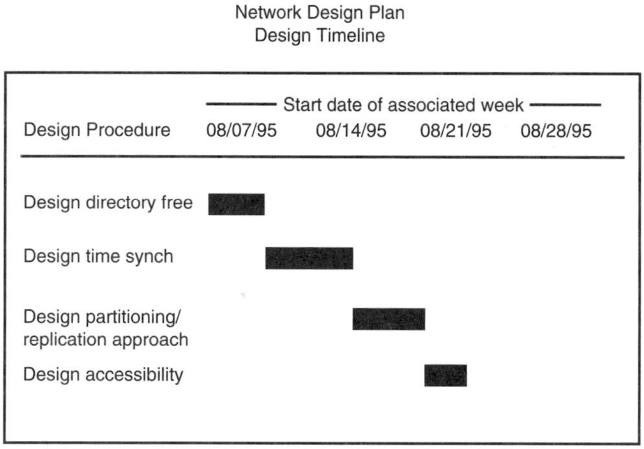

Figure 54.1
Sample design timeline.

Planning the Implementation of the Network Design

After the project team has created the network design, the next step is to figure out how to implement it. There is no right or wrong way to implement a network design. The goal is to plan an implementation that best suits the company's needs. To do that, the project team must consider many of the same factors that influenced their initial design decision. This also means the team must consider the information they gathered and, if necessary, update that information before planning the implementation.

Implementation can proceed one department at a time, one division at a time, one country at a time, all departments in a building at the same time, and so on. The following factors can affect that decision:

- Who is conducting the actual implementation
- How many experienced people are available to help with the implementation
- Whether routers and T1 links are part of the network
- Where the network is physically located
- Whether the network is small, medium, large, or extra large in size
- The budget allocated for the implementation
- Whether upgrades or only new installations are necessary
- The quantity and types of applications on the network
- How many users are on the network
- Whether there are any traveling users who require access to the network from offices other than their home office

This is only a sampling of the factors to consider when determining how and when to implement the network, as well as who will do the implementation. As the project team reviews the documents it gathers, many issues will become apparent, most if not all of which will have to be considered when determining how the implementation will take place, what time frame will be required, and who will be responsible for the implementation.

Questions

1. Of the following, which is *not* a responsibility generally assumed by the IS Manager role?
   - ○ A. Oversee design and implementation
   - ○ B. Obtain funding
   - ○ C. Lead the project team
   - ○ D. Obtain needed resources

2. The *two* responsibilities generally assumed by the Applications Specialist project team role are ______ and ______.
   - ☐ A. automating workstations to run applications
   - ☐ B. purchasing upgrade software
   - ☐ C. ensuring compatibility with NetWare 4
   - ☐ D. transferring applications to network

3. The Testing Lab Coordinator role might not need to coordinate with the ______ role because the network operating system software is likely to have already been tested before the network is installed.
   - ○ A. NDS Expert
   - ○ B. Server Specialist
   - ○ C. Application Specialist
   - ○ D. Education and Training Coordinator

4. A/an ______ Specialist is responsible for ensuring network users can access the network from their computers.
   - ○ A. Applications
   - ○ B. Connectivity
   - ○ C. Workstation
   - ○ D. Printing

5. The project team role whose occupant most likely has to work closely with all other project team members is the ______.
   - ○ A. IS Manager
   - ○ B. Server Specialist
   - ○ C. Application Specialist
   - ○ D. Education and Training Coordinator

6. When determining the design of the network, which of the following design-related steps must be performed before defining the scope of the design?
   - ○ A. Developing a timeline
   - ○ B. Determining the complexity of the project
   - ○ C. Obtaining a budget commitment
   - ○ D. Gathering relevant information

7. Of the following, which *three* are types of information likely to be gathered by the individual filling the IS Manager role?
   - ☐ A. Organizational chart
   - ☐ B. Budget
   - ☐ C. Operating systems being used
   - ☐ D. Workflow

8. The ______ of the project must be established before a timeline for the design can be determined.

   - A. number of WAN links
   - B. people responsible for administering the network
   - C. complexity of the project
   - D. design of the directory tree

9. Which of the following is not one of the issues that might influence the complexity of the network design?

   - A. Time sources
   - B. Partitioning
   - C. Directory tree design/plan
   - D. Number of existing administrators

10. Which one of the following statements is true?

   - A. After the project team creates the network design, the next step is to determine how to implement that design.
   - B. Networks with routers should be included on separate Directory trees, which can be merged into the main tree after the network is up and running.
   - C. Designing the Directory tree is one of the first steps in designing the network and is completed by the project team prior to developing a timeline for network design.
   - D. All of these statements are true.

Answers

1. C
2. C, D
3. A
4. C
5. A
6. D
7. A, B, D
8. C
9. D
10. B

CHAPTER 55

Designing NetWare 4.x Wide Area Networks

Up to this point, most of the work done by the project team has been in preparation for designing the NetWare 4 network. Regardless of whether that network is a small LAN or a large, global WAN, the steps leading to the actual design as well as the design process itself are basically the same. The main difference is that smaller LANs are generally less complex to design, mostly because you generally need only one Directory tree, minimal partitions and thus minimal replications, and so on. Designing WANs, however, might involve multiple Directory trees, possibly with the intent of merging them at a later date, a complex time synchronization scheme, multiple partitions and replications, and so on.

This chapter discusses the process of designing a NetWare 4 WAN. After you design a WAN, designing a LAN is simple. To explain the process of designing a NetWare 4 WAN, this chapter discusses the following:

- Designing the Directory tree
- Establishing a partition and replication approach
- Planning time synchronization
- Developing the accessibility plan

Designing the Directory Tree

The best approach to designing a Directory tree is to spend whatever time and resources necessary before implementing the tree to ensure that the tree meets your company's needs. A good design enables you to change the tree to meet future needs. You can design the main tree (when multiple trees are initially used) with an Organization container, for example, to simplify the process of merging other trees into one at a later date. Your network can benefit substantially from a correctly designed tree for these reasons:

- Partitioning and replication (copies of portions—partitions—of the NDS database) can be made as simple and successful as possible.
- Growth can be readily accommodated when planned for ahead of time.
- Additional network services such as gateways can easily be added to the network.
- User access can be reduced to the simplest process.
- Navigation of the tree can become relatively intuitive for the majority of network users.

To maximize the benefits of an effective Directory tree design, determine and implement basic naming standards before designing the tree. Naming standards should be applied to all objects in the tree including leaf and container objects.

Naming standards should take into consideration how users will navigate the network. If users are expected to navigate the network using mostly common names, for example, a naming standard for common names should be included.

Note The three types of names that can be used on a network are common names, distinguished names, and relative distinguished names:

- A *common name* (CN) is the name of a leaf object. DUSTAN, for example, is a common name for a User object.
- A *distinguished name* is the object's common name and its *context* (the object's location in the Directory tree). A distinguished name is identified with a beginning (leading) period, and all objects in a distinguished name are separated with a period. No two objects can have the same distinguished name. For example, .PS_PARENT.PARENT_LHC is a distinguished name for the Print Server object PS_PARENT in the PARENT_HLC container.
- A *relative distinguished name* lists the path to an object, does not contain a leading period, can contain an ending period, separates objects with a period, and uses the user's current context as a starting point. For example, in relation to the CADY_LHC

organization directly below [Root], a relative distinguished name for the PS_PARENT Print Server object in the PARENT_LHC organization (also directly below [Root]) would be PS_PARENT_LHC.CADY_LHC.

After establishing and documenting object-naming standards, you can establish and document IPX-number standards. Some questions you might need to answer to establish an IPX-numbering standard include the following:

- How many digits should the IPX external network number be? (Up to eight hexadecimal digits—0 through 9 and A through F—are allowed.)
- Do you want to code the IPX external number to help identify the cable segment to which it applies? The three cable segments that are part of the Canadian WAN may be numbered CA01, CA02, and CA03, for example.
- Should the internal IPX network numbers be assigned randomly by the installation software, or should they too follow some coding system to identify the source of network packets? All file servers on the first Canadian WAN segment might begin with the same four digits as the IPX external number (CA01), for example, and then any subsequent digits would provide more detail, such as the numbers 0001 to 0010 on a network with 10 nodes.

The next step in designing the network Directory tree is to draw the upper layers. This may include the tree from [Root] to the first layer of Organizational Unit objects, but can include additional levels of Organizational Unit objects. In addition, it may include a Country object, if you choose to use one.

The upper layer of the tree should be designed based on the company's topology, concentrating on the company's physical location. An upper layer resembling that shown in figure 55.1 would be suitable for the company PC International, with offices in Africa, Canada, Mexico, and the United States.

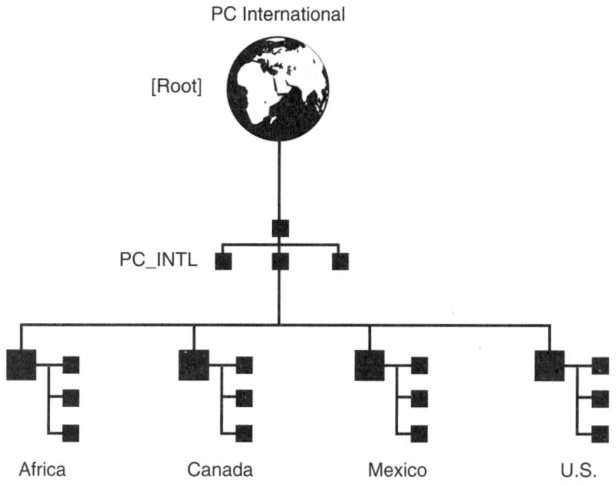

Figure 55.1
The top layer of PC International's Directory tree.

The top layer of the Directory tree should do the following:

- Reflect the structure of the company's WAN
- Be designed to reduce network traffic and the costs associated with it
- Simplify partitioning and replicating the tree
- Take into consideration what changes might be needed in the future to simplify those changes
- Help ensure the organization of the tree is logical and intuitive

When designing the upper layer of the Directory tree, keep in mind the following guidelines:

- The design, if drawn as a graphic, should represent a pyramid—narrow at the top, wider at the bottom.
- Include a single Organization object directly below the [Root] object.
- Create Organizational Unit objects for each separate physical location, a design that roughly follows the topology of the network.
- Further divide the structure to include regional Organizational Units (see fig. 55.2), particularly if the company is so geographically diverse that too many Organizational Units would be required directly beneath the Organization object, thus distorting the pyramid shape of the tree.

In some cases, you do not want to design the upper layers of your Directory tree using this suggested pyramid design:

- When location-based design is not important because the WAN links are high speed and very reliable
- When the entire network is physically located in one geographical area
- When costly dial-up lines are part of the network and can drastically increase network costs

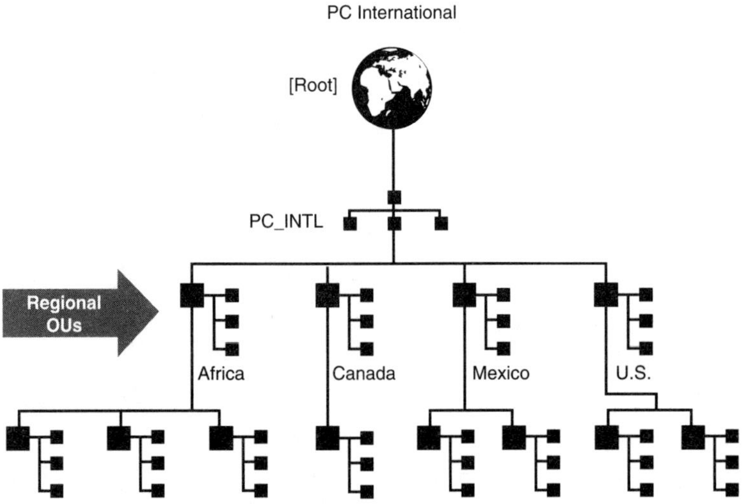

Figure 55.2
Directory tree design with regional Organizational Units.

After designing the upper layers of the Directory tree, move to the lower layers. Consider the following when designing the lower layers:

- Whether containers can be created to logically organize resources by the need for common access
- Location of resources (such as printers) in relation to users
- The type of network administration to be implemented—centralized or decentralized

> **Note** *Centralized administration* is the administration of the entire network from a single location or by a single group of people, such as the company's Information Systems department.
>
> *Decentralized administration* is the administration of each department's portion of the Directory tree by that department's administrator.

- Where partitions will be created—Each partition must have at least one Organization or Organizational Unit object at its top (except [Root], which can be either its own partition or part of a larger partition that includes other Organization or Organizational Units)
- Types of login scripts to be used (Container, User, and so on) as well as the login script users' needs to access such things as menus, applications, drive mappings, printers, and so on
- Whether bindery services will be provided, either on a temporary or a permanent basis

When designing the Directory tree, also consider how future changes might affect the tree's design. For example, consider this scenario. If the Directory tree was originally designed to be administered by the IS department, but for cost savings the IS department was substantially reduced forcing decentralized administration, could the current design handle decentralized administration? Or, what if the company started out as a small local company, but through rapid growth and expansion soon became an international company with offices around the globe. Could the Directory tree's current design accommodate such growth?

Establishing a Partition and Replication Approach

The next step after you design the Directory tree is to plan and design partitioning and replication. In general, consider the partitions of the Directory tree, along with which types of replications you need and how many. This information also must be considered in the design of the Directory tree itself.

When establishing a partition approach, consider the following partitioning guidelines:

- When first installed, only one partition is created by default. Other partitions must be deliberately planned and created.
- Do not create partitions that include container objects physically located across the WAN.
- Consider multiple partitions if the network includes more than 15 file servers (might help reduce synchronization traffic), has more than 5,000 objects (help avoid long delays in synchronization and thus reduce network traffic), or includes WAN links.
- Consider either not creating or eliminating partitions that contain 100 or fewer objects because the administrative overhead

associated with these partitions might not be worth the effort.

- When planning multiple partitions, keep all objects at a single location within the same partition. This makes it possible to keep all NetWare Directory Services (NDS) directory updates on local file servers.
- Where possible, group file servers connected through a single cable segment into the same partition.
- Whenever appropriate, design partitions for the upper layer of the Directory tree to center around the physical layout of the company. Design partitions for the lower layers of the Directory tree to center around the workflow or organizational divisions of the company.
- Avoid creating additional partitions if they would increase administrative overhead to a level greater than your company wants to support, if the complexity of the network would be excessive, if too much time would be required to navigate the network, if unacceptable (even if minor) increases in network wire traffic would occur, or if additional subordinate references for the child and parent partitions would be created.
- Follow the five main rules associated with partitioning when designing network partitions:
    1. Do not include information about the file system in a partition.
    2. Each NDS object can exist in only one partition.
    3. Store each partition on a NetWare 4 server.
    4. No partition's boundaries can overlap the boundaries of another partition.
    5. Each partition must contain a connected subtree.

Note: After installing the first NetWare 4 server and creating the Directory tree, use the NetWare Administrator or PARTMGR utility to create your network's partitions before you install subsequent network servers. This gives you control over where the servers are placed, as well as over the implementation of the Directory tree design.

The partitions you establish affect the replications that your network needs. When planning replicas and their placement, consider these points:

- Each partition should have a minimum of two Read/Write replicas (exact duplicates of the associated Master replica that can be updated and used for user login) in addition to the Master replica (the first replica of a partition containing all related object information) for fault tolerance.
- Each Read/Write replica should be positioned on a file server other than the file server that contains the Master replica for the partition. If both servers are located in the same geographic area, placing a Read/Write copy of a replica in another geographic location, although it may increase network traffic slightly, provides stronger fault tolerance than placing all replicas on file servers within the same geographic location.
- Adding an extra Read/Write replica might increase workstation performance, however, if it is placed close enough to the user to decrease the time required for login.

- Additional replicas use additional disk space: each object in a replica requires from 3 KB to 5 KB of storage space.
- *Tree walking*, accessing specific information in the Directory tree, can be reduced by placing replicas of NDS information that users frequently access on servers local to those users. This reduces the time it takes for NDS to *authenticate*, or resolve user names of, network users.
- Servers with bindery services enabled should contain a Read/Write copy of the affected partitions.
- If a file server contains a Master, Read/Write, or Read-Only replica that encompasses a child partition that exists only on one other file server, NDS automatically puts a Subordinate Reference replica (a pointer to the child partition) on that server.
- Placing replicas on the fastest file servers, and limiting the number of replicas (eight is a reasonable maximum) on any file server helps keep replica synchronization from proceeding too slowly.

When designing replica placement for your Directory tree, place them to accomplish three basic functions:

- **Ensure fault tolerance.** Use a Master and at least two Read/Write replicas placed in local and off-site file servers for disaster recovery.
- **Provide easy accessibility.** Locate replicas on file servers closest to the users who need to access them.
- **Simplify navigation.** Put replicas on servers located close to the resources and users they supply, taking WAN links into consideration.

If hardware problems cause a file server holding a Master or Read/Write replica to be inaccessible, the user whose login identification is part of that replica needs to be able to access the Master or Read/Write replica on the next closest file server. If no Read/Write copy of the replica is available elsewhere and the file server containing the Master is unavailable, the user will not be able to access the network.

A close Master or Read/Write copy of the replica containing a user's login-related information makes the entire login process quicker for the user. Even though a user might be able to gain access from a file server distant from their computer, the closer the file server containing a replica, the quicker the user can access the network.

Planning Time Synchronization

Every transaction that modifies the NDS database is given a time stamp. That time stamp specifies the date and time the modification took place. The time stamps on various NDS database transactions are then used to determine in what order to process transactions. To ensure transactions throughout the network are stamped with a time that is consistent across the network, time synchronization is used. *Time synchronization* is a process NetWare uses to compare and set time on file servers across the network.

Network services including the file system, electronic messaging, applications, and NDS all depend on network time synchronization. How you implement time synchronization on your network is based on the method most appropriate for your company. When determining time synchronization, consider whether you want it to occur locally or across the WAN. Time synchronization across the WAN is more time-consuming than local time synchronization.

To ensure that time is synchronized across NetWare servers, each NetWare server must be set up as one of four possible types of time servers. The four types of time servers are as follows:

- **Primary.** Polls other time sources to determine network time. It can poll Reference servers or other Primary time servers.
- **Reference.** Also polls other time sources to determine network time. Reference time servers require that at least one other server be a time provider.
- **Single.** The default time source. Only Secondary time servers can function with the Single time server. The Single time server obtains its time from either the computer's hardware clock or an external source. Provides time to Secondary servers as well as to network clients.
- **Secondary.** Remains synchronized with the time provided by a time source.

Synchronization can be accomplished using either the Service Advertising Protocol (SAP) method (the default configuration) or a custom configuration.

The SAP method is simpler to implement, efficient, and does not need to be reconfigured each time a new server is added to the network. This method is not as effective when WAN links are involved, however, because multiple Primary servers can increase network traffic. This is because Primary servers have to be contacted by all other time servers to receive the time and synchronize.

The custom configuration method gives you complete control of time synchronization so you can optimize network traffic and provide alternative time sources in the event of a failure. The custom configuration method requires more planning and maintenance than the default method, however, particularly when new servers are added to the network. The configuration files for some servers might require updating.

If you choose to establish a custom configuration, remember the following:

- Secondary servers should be synchronized to a time source that is not another secondary server.
- Limit the number of time sources to keep network traffic to a minimum.
- Create local time providers if the network configuration makes this possible.

Developing the Accessibility Plan

Accessing network resources and using the file system is simpler and more effective for users if you consider strategies for accessibility during the design phase. When developing guidelines for accessibility, consider the following possibilities:

- Different types of workstation clients such as OS/2, Macintosh, Unix, DOS, and MS Windows
- Different versions of the NetWare operating system being run on the network including NetWare 2, 3, and 4, and whether bindery services will be provided
- Network applications, printers, and other resources that require bindery-based access

- Which applications are provided on the network, whether access will be strictly local or across a WAN, and which users in specific containers need access to various applications and data files
- Hardware resources, which users are accessing them, and whether any hardware resources must be shared by different users in different containers
- Network administration concerns such as whether a common environment with shareable login scripts can be used, whether Profile objects will be included to simplify the sharing of resources by different users across the network, and whether Director Map objects can be used to ensure objects that are moved can still be accessed easily

You also can establish accessibility guidelines for any of the following objects and properties:

- Group
- Profile
- Organizational Role
- Directory Map
- Inherited Rights Filters (IRF)
- User Login Scripts
- Alias

You can specify security-related issues in the accessibility guidelines, defining such things as suggestions for creating and remembering passwords, security breaches to avoid, and warnings related to such issues as granting rights. The Supervisor NDS right for Server objects also grants file system rights, for example. Accessibility guidelines should specify when to use certain object types (such as Group and Profile objects), when not to use certain object types (such as Alias objects), and what standard network Application directories and drive mappings might be named or consist of.

In addition, a separate document specifying guidelines for mobile users might be necessary. This document can contain information such as where the user needs to access the network, and whether access to both local and distant resources is necessary. It also can include information about how long mobile users are gone during the course of an average trip. Other important points are whether computer equipment will be made available to the traveling user at the remote site, or whether the traveling user will be required to provide his or her own equipment. The mobile user's level of skill must therefore be considered when developing the accessibility plan.

With this information in hand, you can decide how to design the network to assist mobile users. Mobile users have varying degrees of network knowledge. For example, experienced mobile users who carry their own laptop computer may sometimes be expected (or may have to be trained) to understand the NetWare 4 login process, particularly how to specify their complete name and context. They may also need to be skilled at customizing their own login scripts, or may rely on a network administrator to set up those login scripts for them. Regardless of who performs the setup for mobile users, some level of skill and knowledge may be reasonably required of the mobile user.

After the project team has a detailed understanding of the needs of network users, and the Directory tree design, partition and replication approach, time synchronization strategy, and accessibility plan in hand, the design phase is complete. The next step is to implement the design the team has created.

Questions

1. Of the following, which is *not* an indication the tree was correctly designed?

   ○ A. Company growth is easily and painlessly accommodated.

   ○ B. New applications do not require much change to the file structure.

   ○ C. Two trees cannot be successfully merged because no Organization object exists at the top of the tree.

   ○ D. Most new employees seem to catch on quickly to using network resources.

2. The two standards that you should determine before designing the Directory tree are the ______ and ______ standards.

   ☐ A. IPX internal numbering

   ☐ B. IPX external numbering

   ☐ C. Hexadecimal numbering

   ☐ D. SPX maximum numbering

3. To maximize the benefits of an effective Directory tree design, what step should you accomplish before designing the tree?

   ○ A. Merge existing trees into one if more than one tree currently exists

   ○ B. Design and implement basic naming standards

   ○ C. Determine and create partitions

   ○ D. Designing the tree is the first step and no other step is required before it

4. A ______ is a combination of the object's CN and its context.

   ○ A. relative distinguished name

   ○ B. common name

   ○ C. distinguished name

   ○ D. naming standard

5. If corporation A uses relatively slow communication links to connect their New York, London, and Tokyo offices, the guideline to apply to designing the top layer of the Directory tree is ______.

   ○ A. design to keep network traffic to a minimum across the WAN

   ○ B. design to reflect the structure of each LAN

   ○ C. design to make all containers part of one partition

   ○ D. design to store a Read/Write replica in three servers in New York, if that is the home office, with Read-Only replicas on at least one file server in each of the other locations

6. The structure of the upper layer of the Directory tree should resemble ______.

   ○ A. the final output of a square box factory in Chicago

   ○ B. a baseball

   ○ C. the ancient pyramids of Egypt

   ○ D. a spinning top

7. Of the following, which *three* statements regarding partitioning are true?

   - ☐ A. When first installed, only one partition is created by default.
   - ☐ B. Crossing the WAN with partitions is not recommended.
   - ☐ C. If the network has more than 15 file servers or 5,000 objects consider using multiple partitions.
   - ☐ D. Provide fault tolerance by overlapping the boundaries of the most important partitions, such as [Root], with the partition boundaries of its nearest neighboring partition.

8. Each partition should have a minimum of ______ replicas, including the Master replica, to help ensure fault tolerance.

   - ○ A. 1
   - ○ B. 2
   - ○ C. 3
   - ○ D. 4

9. To help keep network time synchronization traffic to a minimum when using a custom configuration, the recommended approach is to ______.

   - ○ A. synchronize Secondary time sources with other Secondary time sources
   - ○ B. provide an external time source for the Primary time server
   - ○ C. limit the number of time sources on the network
   - ○ D. implement all three of the above approaches

10. When developing an accessibility plan, which among the following is the most important consideration?

   - ○ A. A single Directory tree regardless of the company's structure
   - ○ B. A single partition replicated across the WAN
   - ○ C. Applications, printers, and other network resources that require bindery-based access
   - ○ D. Local time providers for all file servers

Answers

1. C
2. A, B
3. B
4. C
5. A
6. C
7. A, B, C
8. C
9. C
10. C

CHAPTER 56

Implementing the NetWare 4.x WAN Plan

Depending on the size of your network and your company, it takes anywhere from a few days to several weeks to put together the NetWare 4 network design. After the project teams develops an effective design, the next step is to implement it. Implementing the plan involves two major processes:

- *Developing the migration strategy*
- *Creating an implementation schedule*

Developing the Migration Strategy

Migrating a company's existing NetWare network requires upgrading the network workstations and file servers. All network workstations must be upgraded to the version of the NetWare DOS Requester compatible with NetWare 4. The NetWare file servers must be upgraded from either their current NetWare 2 or 3 version to NetWare 4.

Part of the migration strategy involves determining whether to upgrade all file servers as soon as possible, or to run the existing version of some or all the NetWare 2 and 3 file servers for an extended period of time. If the latter is the case, your migration plan must include information about which file servers will continue to run, and thus about bindery services requirements as well.

A strategy for upgrading application programs to those compatible with NetWare 4 also should be developed during this stage, even if that plan means waiting to upgrade software not compatible with NetWare 4.

Before planning the migration of workstations, file servers, and application programs, you need the basic information listed in table 56.1.

The information in table 56.1 can help you successfully plan and implement the upgrade of applications, workstations, and file servers. Workstations that do not have the appropriate version of the NetWare DOS Requester installed must be upgraded, for example. The number of workstations to be upgraded can either place a heavy burden on the time frame for upgrading the network, or shorten the time depending on the approach you take. If you choose to have only a handful of individuals upgrade several hundred workstations, the time required is likely to be much greater than if you plan another approach such as holding a training session for users and then having each user upgrade his or her own workstation.

Table 56.1
Types of Information Needed for Planning Migration

Item Being Migrated	*Types of Information to Be Gathered*
Applications	Current applications and versions
	Which applications will run with NetWare 4
	Which applications require bindery services
	Which users need access to which applications
	Whether existing menus call applications
	What will be the new context for locating applications

Item Being Migrated	*Types of Information to Be Gathered*
File servers	What other versions of the NetWare operating system are currently being used
	Will other versions of NetWare be needed
	Will bindery services be necessary
	What hardware is currently being used for NetWare file servers
	Will additional hardware be included for NetWare 4 servers or will it be necessary to upgrade the existing hardware
	What other non-NetWare network operating systems are currently used on the network, and will they be replaced with NetWare 4
	Who will require training and how and where should it be accomplished
	What hardware and software testing should be done and will a testing lab be used
Workstations	If local applications exist, what are they and are they compatible with NetWare 4
	Do workstations have a NetWare 4 compatible version of the NetWare DOS Requester loaded on them
	Which protocols are used on workstations
	Who is responsible for solving workstation problems, and will additional support be needed during the transition to NetWare 4
	Will workstations be backed up using an SMS-compliant backup software, and if so, which workstations will be backed up
	What information will be sent between NetWare 4 file servers and the workstations, and should that information be encrypted for security purposes

Migrating Applications

Many new applications on your network might already be *NetWare-aware* (capable of running on a NetWare network), but not compatible with NetWare 4. You need to upgrade these applications to a more current version. When this is not possible, you can continue to use those applications in the new network environment, but access them using bindery services.

The strategy for migrating applications, while important, is not the main focus of migrating your existing network into a NetWare 4 network. Which applications can be migrated and which cannot, along with which applications can be eliminated, replaced, or updated must be considered when determining the migration strategy. The key point to remember is that, the network can successfully be upgraded, and existing network applications can still be used if bindery services are provided. When considering the upgrade of the network then, give some thought and planning to the time required to incorporate changes, upgrades, and replacements.

Migrating Workstations

When developing the strategy for migrating workstations to a NetWare 4 environment, follow the general process shown in figure 56.1 to ensure most if not all of the important aspects of workstation migration are considered.

The following list includes other information you need to know to successfully migrate network workstations:

- Protocols being used by workstations
- Whether network management tools, such as those based on the Simple Network Management Protocol (SNMP)
- If Large Internet Packet (LIP) or packet burst will be used at workstations

Migrating File Servers

Both file servers running non-NetWare operating systems and file servers running versions of the NetWare operating system earlier than NetWare 4.1 might have to be upgraded. Upgrading file servers helps ensure their successful migration into the NetWare 4.1 network.

You can use several methods to upgrade file servers currently running non-NetWare network operating systems, depending on the version of the network operating system you are currently running:

Figure 56.1
Workstation migration process.

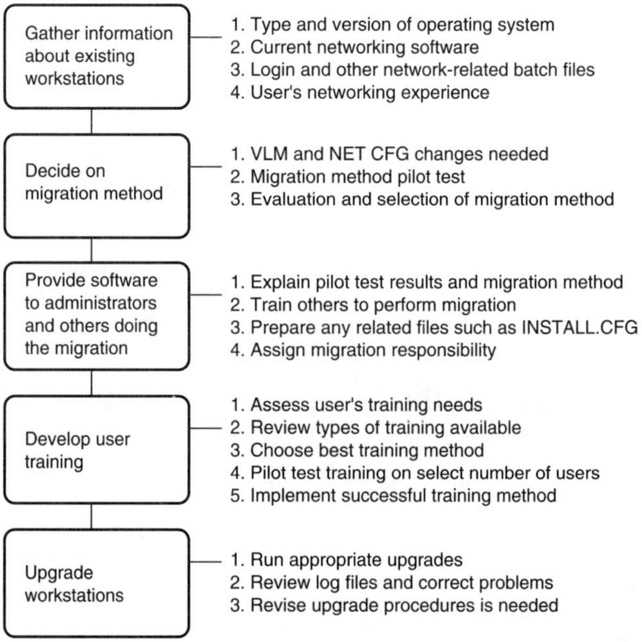

- **Across-the-wire.** Available for upgrading Banyan Vines, IBM PC LAN (PCLP) v1.3 Extended Services, IBM LAN Server v1.0 to v1.3, Microsoft LAN Manager v2.0, and NetWare versions 2.1*x*, 2.2, 3.1*x*, and 4.0*x*.
- **Same-server.** Available for upgrading Banyan Vines, IBM PC LAN (PCLP) v1.3 Extended Services, IBM LAN Server v1.0 to v1.3, Microsoft LAN Manager v2.0, and NetWare versions 2.1*x*, 2.2, 3.1*x*, and 4.0*x*.
- **In-place upgrade.** Available for upgrading NetWare 2.1*x* and NetWare 2.2.
- **NetWare 4.1 installation.** Available for upgrading NetWare 3.1*x* and 4.0*x* (using the Upgrade menu option).

The across-the-wire to another server method is considered the safest choice as it is actually performed on a different server, thus keeping the original server. If the upgrade is not completely successful, the original server still exists, and the process can be performed again.

The across-the-wire to the same server method requires only one server and one workstation, unlike the across-the-wire to a different server method. Across-the-wire to the same server is not as secure because the server is not online. In addition, this method does not enable you to change the disk allocation block size. Only 4 KB blocks are available on your NetWare 4 server.

The in-place upgrade is the least safe method because if the upgrade fails, you must restore the old file server from backups and try again. You cannot create a DOS partition while using this method either, in case the server uses an IDE disk and does not already have a DOS partition. Also, as with the across-the-wire to the same server method, only 4 KB blocks are available on your NetWare 4 server.

The NetWare 4 installation migration method enables you to simply install NetWare on an existing server, and does not require additional hardware.

Following the general process shown in figure 56.2 can help ensure that you consider the important aspects of file server migration.

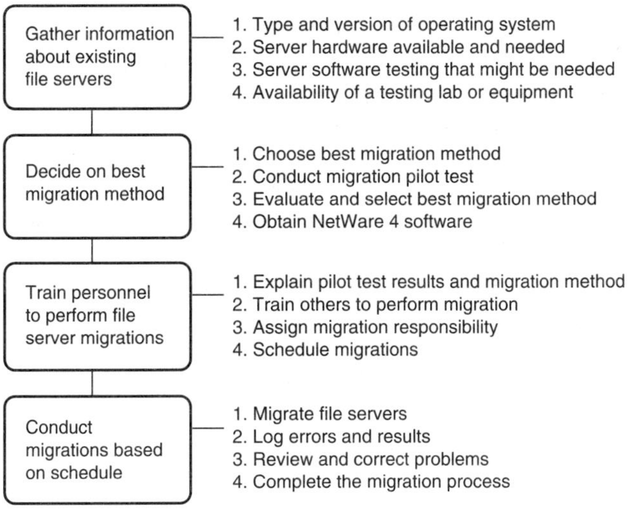

Figure 56.2
File server migration process.

After you gather all relevant application, file server, and workstation information, analyze that information, then decide what and how to migrate, the process of developing the migration strategy is complete. The next step is to create the implementation schedule.

Creating an Implementation Schedule

The process of creating an implementation schedule involves four basic steps:

1. Identify the tasks that need to be performed to implement the network plan.
2. Create a schedule to implement the network plan.
3. Conduct a pilot test.
4. Complete the implementation.

You also might have to include a fifth step in the implementation process—coordinating the schedule with schedules of other groups responsible for network upgrades. This step requires repetition until the final schedule is created.

The most difficult portion of the implementation process might be the very first step—identifying which tasks need to be performed to implement the network plan. The tasks, although likely similar from company to company, are not always the same. Each project team chooses for itself which tasks to include.

The following sample tasks could be included on an implementation schedule:

- Purchase NetWare software
- Purchase hardware for new installations or to upgrade existing hardware
- Assess workstation and file server upgrade requirements
- Set up a testing lab
- Conduct the pilot migration
- Review the results of the pilot migration and make needed changes
- Upgrade workstations
- Upgrade other file servers (by workgroup, geographic location, or another process appropriate for the company)
- Train administrators
- Train users
- Follow up after migration is complete

After you identify the tasks, list them in the order they need to be performed. Then assess the approximate length of time required to complete each task. Finally, prepare a timeline (with important milestones).

After the project team creates the implementation schedule, all that remains to be done is to follow it to the best of your ability. Then, the NetWare 4 network will be successfully planned and implemented.

You must follow up after implementing the NetWare 4 network to ensure it meets the needs originally defined. Review the successes and failures of the design and implementation, and monitor the network with an eye on future modifications and improvements.

Questions

1. The first step to take before planning the migration approach is to ______.

   ○ A. develop a timeline to follow

   ○ B. gather basic information about the items to be migrated

   ○ C. assign migration responsibilities to project team members

   ○ D. determine whether to upgrade all servers to NetWare 4, or only some of the servers

2. The *three* aspects of the network to consider when developing the migration strategy are ______, ______, and ______.

   □ A. applications

   □ B. workstations

   □ C. file servers

   □ D. network boards

3. Determining the protocol currently used is most important to which aspect of migration?

   ○ A. Applications

   ○ B. Workstations

   ○ C. File servers

   ○ D. Network boards

4. If Banyan Vines is used on the current network, determining whether to keep or replace it is important when analyzing the ______ aspect of migration.

   ○ A. applications

   ○ B. workstations

   ○ C. file servers

   ○ D. network boards

5. Determining what types of information the user needs and whether to encrypt it is part of analyzing the ______ aspect of network migration.

   ○ A. applications

   ○ B. workstations

   ○ C. file servers

   ○ D. network boards

6. The main focus of migrating the network is not ______.

   ○ A. applications

   ○ B. workstations

   ○ C. file servers

   ○ D. network boards

7. The NetWare 4 migrated network can include file servers running earlier versions of NetWare (2.*x* and 3.*x*) if ______ is (are) planned for when migration planning is conducted.

   ○ A. NetWare-compatible applications

   ○ B. Banyan Vines

   ○ C. bindery services

   ○ D. SMS-compliant backup software

8. Determining what VLM and NET.CFG changes are necessary is part of the ______ step in the workstation migration process.

   ○ A. gathering information

   ○ B. deciding the migration method

- C. providing software to migration personnel
- D. developing user training
- E. upgrading workstations

9. The migration method you can use to convert an existing PCLP file server to a NetWare 4 file server without requiring additional hardware is the ______ method.
   - A. across-the-wire
   - B. in-place
   - C. same-server
   - D. NetWare 4 installation

10. If you want make certain you can restore the previous version of NetWare if the migration process fails, use the ______ method, considered to be the safest upgrade choice.
    - A. across-the-wire
    - B. in-place
    - C. same-server
    - D. NetWare 4 installation

Answers

1. B
2. A, B, C
3. B
4. C
5. B
6. A
7. C
8. B
9. C
10. A

CHAPTER 57

Following Up after Implementation

The entire process of designing, planning, and implementing a NetWare 4 LAN or WAN can be brief, a matter of a few days on a small network (15 or fewer file servers), or quite lengthy, easily taking weeks or months. Regardless of whether the network is small, medium, large, or very large, the process is the same:

1. *Analyze the company.*
2. *Design the basic network.*
3. *Implement the network design.*
4. *Perform various maintenance tasks.*

The fourth step, performing maintenance tasks, is what most people perceive as following up after implementation. Indeed, maintenance does constitute the majority of the follow-up process. You also can apply follow-up to the first three steps of the network design process.

When performing the initial analysis of the company, the follow-up process can include verifying that all relevant company information has been collected. Other steps might include ensuring the information has been properly distributed and understood, and making certain each project team member is on track.

When designing the basic network, verifying the viability of the proposed accessibility design is part of a follow-up process.

When implementing the network design, following up after beginning to implement the design, as well as after the implementation of each portion of the design, can also be considered a follow-up process.

Performing Various Maintenance Tasks

Maintaining the new network can involve a wide variety of tasks. Network administrators are likely to perform the maintenance tasks related directly to their own areas of concern, such as adding users, printers, and other objects to the NDS database. In addition, they periodically review network security issues and new or upgraded applications. The project design team also has a variety of maintenance tasks to perform, most of which revolve around the efficiency and continued applicability of the network design. The following is a list of possible network design maintenance tasks:

- Comparing object naming standard documents created during the network's design against object names currently used on the network.
- Examining the top and lower levels of the directory tree to ensure their design is effective.
- Spot checking various network resources to verify they are located in the most logical place in the tree structure, based on how users access those resources.
- Reviewing network error logs to determine whether repetitive errors are the result of the network design, and what modifications can be made to correct any design problems.
- Analyzing network storage use to determine if actual user needs equal or exceed anticipated needs.
- Tracking the use of bindery services over a period of time to determine whether bindery services still are required, and if or when file servers running older versions of NetWare should be upgraded.
- Verifying time synchronization to ensure it is functioning as intended without generating an excessive amount of network traffic.
- Interviewing mobile users to determine if the network's design successfully meets their needs, as well as where changes in the network's design might make simplify network access.
- Checking the workload of network administrators to determine if the design of the network correctly balances the workload, or if it unfairly burdens one or more administrators over others.

- Reviewing the location and type of replicas available on the network to ensure sufficient replicas exist to provide fault tolerance without generating excessive network traffic or cost.
- Determining if partitions should be changed (split or merged) to accommodate users' needs for reduced access or increased access to network resources.
- Removing from or adding to the network NetWare file servers or volumes to reflect permanent network usage or company changes.
- Verifying communication across WAN links is still satisfactory.
- Monitoring the amount of space on the network's various file servers' SYS volumes to make sure the NDS database still has sufficient room to grow.
- Ensuring the current design adequately handles various security issues such as trustee assignments, object and property rights, inheritance, and effective rights.
- Determining the potential need for additional administrators to handle an expanding network directory tree (creating subtree administrators).
- Checking the usage and effectiveness of the design of special NDS objects such as Profile login scripts, Directory Map objects, Alias objects, and so on to improve user accessibility.
- Reviewing print queue and printer use to make certain these objects are properly located within the tree to simplify their access and use.
- Discussing concerns of a network auditor to determine if anything related to the network design can be added, removed, or corrected to make the network easier to use, more secure, and less congested.
- Verifying that workstation and file server backup and restoration is adequate and relatively easy, as a result of the design of the network.
- Deciding whether the current version of workstation networking software is adequate for users to access needed resources, or if spot or across-the-board upgrades should be implemented.
- Identifying current network protocols to determine if the network is adequately accounting for the variety of protocols currently in use and planned for the future.
- Reviewing whether various NetWare 4 features such as block suballocation, file compression, data migration, and internationalization meet the needs of network users and should be implemented.
- Checking on network optimization options such as packet burst and LIP to determine if additional network design changes could enhance network optimization.
- Monitoring usage statistics, particularly file server processor and memory usage, to determine whether file servers are placed in optimum locations within the directory tree structure, or whether modifications to partitions or container objects would improve usage.
- Reviewing the linear-based design and implementation process to determine if it was adequate, or if another approach—spiral, structured, or incremental—might be worth considering the next time around.

- Re-evaluating proposed solutions to the original network design and implementation to determine if the one implemented actually was the best solution for meeting the company's networking needs.
- Verifying overall user acceptance of the network design and implementation.

As Chapter 53, "Understanding the Design and Implementation Process," indicates, following up is part of the manage and monitor process defined by Novell. The goal of the manage and monitor process is to ensure the implementation is functioning as intended, and to ensure constant watchfulness and awareness of flaws and necessary updates and replacements.

The following are the main steps associated with the manage and monitor phase:

1. Establish guidelines for managing the network and its resources.
2. Verify that those guidelines are being followed.
3. Track and report the results of the project.
4. Anticipate and troubleshoot network problems.
5. Implement procedures to recover from network problems.

The last step is to determine when it is appropriate to upgrade or replace the existing process. If the review of network maintenance issues or network maintenance itself indicates the network design is no longer sufficient to meet the company's needs, or the cost of continued maintenance is greater than the company wants to spend, it is time to consider starting over. It is best to start over the design process with step one—analyzing the company's needs and current resources—and begin the design and implementation of the company's network in a manner similar to the original design and implementation process.

Regardless of how you look at network design and implementation, it is a process that turns full circle on itself (see fig. 57.1).

Ultimately, however, you will have the best possible network design in place. Of course, it likely will require change to accommodate the ever growing and improving nature of networking in general.

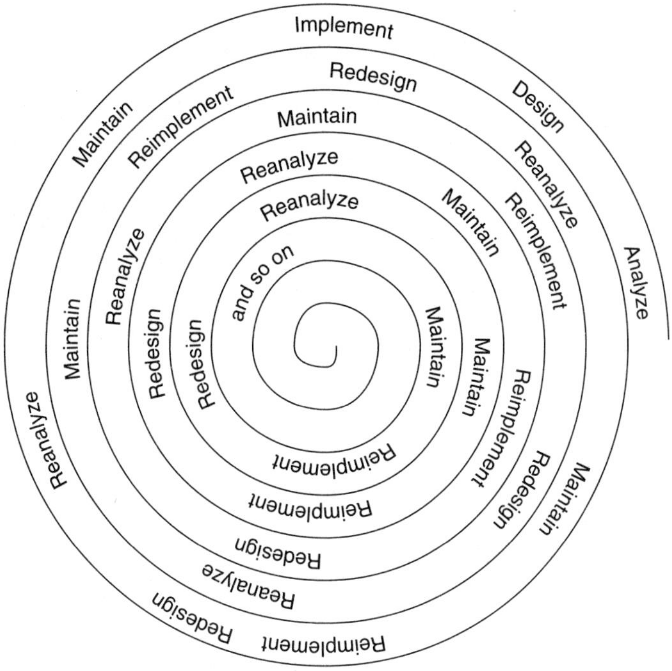

Figure 57.1
The spiral nature of the network design and implementation process.

Questions

1. The step *not* considered part of the general design and implementation process of a network is ______.
   - A. preparing corporate documents
   - B. analyzing company needs
   - C. designing the network
   - D. maintaining the network

2. Some follow-up can be done in all of the following areas of network design and implementation *except* ______.
   - A. preparing corporate documents
   - B. analyzing company needs
   - C. designing the network
   - D. maintaining the network

3. Spot checking various network resources to verify that they are located in the most logical place within the tree structure can be categorized as part of the ______ phase of network design and implementation.
   - A. analysis
   - B. design
   - C. implementation
   - D. maintenance

4. When conducting the initial design of the network, a step that could be considered part of a follow-up process is ______.
   - A. assigning research responsibilities to various project team members
   - B. analyzing recently gathered information about the network
   - C. verifying the viability of the proposed accessibility design
   - D. adding new users to the network

5. Tracking the use of bindery services over a period of time enables you to determine ______.
   - A. whether to add more file servers
   - B. when to upgrade non-NetWare 4 file servers
   - C. whether to create additional partitions
   - D. whether to add a WAN link

6. A lack of noted network security issues upon review by the network designer indicates that ______.
   - A. the network's design is adequate
   - B. security can be somewhat relaxed
   - C. the number of administrators is sufficient
   - D. network monitoring is no longer needed

7. Of the following, which *three* are network design maintenance tasks?
   - A. Deciding whether the current version of network workstation software is adequate.
   - B. Modifying IRFs to restrict user access to only their home containers.
   - C. Determining whether to split or merge any existing partitions.
   - D. Identifying current network protocols.

8. Which of the following is *not* a main step associated with the manage and monitor phase of network design and implementation?
   - A. Establishing guidelines for managing the network and its resources.
   - B. Determining the location of network partitions and their replications.
   - C. Anticipating and troubleshooting network problems.
   - D. Tracking and reporting on the results of the project.

9. The *last* step in the process of following up after implementation of the network design is ______.
   - A. deciding whether additional network administration is an issue
   - B. defining areas of the network where problems might ultimately occur
   - C. determining when it is appropriate to begin the design and implementation process again
   - D. encouraging acceptance of the network design as implemented by network users and administrators

10. ______ in nature, network design and implementation requires constant assessment, design, and maintenance.
    - A. Pyramidal
    - B. Spiral
    - C. Spherical
    - D. Cylindrical

Answers

1. A
2. A
3. D
4. C
5. B
6. A
7. A, C, D
8. B
9. C
10. B

INDEX

Symbols

A

B

fiber-optic cable, 253
high-power/single-frequency radio, 258
low-power/single-frequency radio, 257
point-to-point infrared transmissions, 264
satellite microwave transmissions, 263
spread spectrum radio, 259
STP (shielded twisted-pair) cable, 250
terrestrial microwave transmissions, 262
UTP (unshielded twisted-pair) cable, 251

C

D

E

F

G

H

I

J

L

M

N

O

P

Q

R

S

T

V

W

X-Y-Z

REGISTRATION CARD

CNE 4 Short Course

Name ______________________ Title ______________________

Company ______________________ Type of business ______________________

Address ______________________

City/State/ZIP ______________________

Have you used these types of books before? ☐ yes ☐ no

If yes, which ones? ______________________

____

How many computer books do you purchase each year? ☐ 1–5 ☐ 6 or more

How did you learn about this book? ______________________

Where did you purchase this book? ______________________

Which applications do you currently use? ______________________

____

Which computer magazines do you subscribe to? ______________________

____

What trade shows do you attend? ______________________

____

Comments: ______________________

____

____

Would you like to be placed on our preferred mailing list? ☐ yes ☐ no

☐ **I would like to see my name in print!** You may use my name and quote me in future New Riders products and promotions. My daytime phone number is: ______________________

New Riders Publishing 201 West 103rd Street ◆ Indianapolis, Indiana 46290 USA

Fax to **317-581-4670** Orders/Customer Service **1-800-653-6156** Source Code **NRP95**

Fold Here

NO POSTAGE
NECESSARY
IF MAILED
IN THE
UNITED STATES

BUSINESS REPLY MAIL

FIRST-CLASS MAIL PERMIT NO. 9918 INDIANAPOLIS IN

POSTAGE WILL BE PAID BY THE ADDRESSEE

NEW RIDERS PUBLISHING
201 W 103RD ST
INDIANAPOLIS IN 46290-9058